Women, Periodicals, and Print Culture in Britain, 1890s–1920s

The Edinburgh History of Women's Periodical Culture in Britain
Series Editor: Jackie Jones

Published Titles

Women's Periodicals and Print Culture in Britain, 1690–1820s: The Long Eighteenth Century
Edited by Jennie Batchelor and Manushag N. Powell

Women, Periodicals, and Print Culture in Britain, 1830s–1900s: The Victorian Period
Edited by Alexis Easley, Clare Gill, and Beth Rogers

Women, Periodicals, and Print Culture in Britain, 1890s–1920s: The Modernist Period
Edited by Faith Binckes and Carey Snyder

Women's Periodicals and Print Culture in Britain, 1918–1939: The Interwar Period
Edited by Catherine Clay, Maria DiCenzo, Barbara Green, and Fiona Hackney

Forthcoming Titles

Women's Periodicals and Print Culture in Britain, 1940s–2000s: The Contemporary Period

Visit The Edinburgh History of Women's Periodical Culture in Britain web page at www.edinburghuniversitypress.com/series/EHWPCB

THE EDINBURGH HISTORY OF WOMEN'S
PERIODICAL CULTURE IN BRITAIN

Women, Periodicals, and Print Culture in Britain, 1890s–1920s

The Modernist Period

Edited by Faith Binckes and
Carey Snyder

EDINBURGH
University Press

Edinburgh University Press is one of the leading university presses in the UK. We publish academic books and journals in our selected subject areas across the humanities and social sciences, combining cutting-edge scholarship with high editorial and production values to produce academic works of lasting importance. For more information visit our website: edinburghuniversitypress.com

© editorial matter and organisation Faith Binckes and Carey Snyder, 2019,2024
© the chapters their several authors, 2019

Edinburgh University Press Ltd
13 Infirmary Street, Edinburgh, EH1 1LT

Typeset in 10/12 Adobe Sabon by
IDSUK (DataConnection) Ltd

A CIP record for this book is available from the British Library

ISBN 978 1 4744 5064 5 (hardback)
ISBN 978 1 3995 4680 5 (paperback)
ISBN 978 1 4744 5065 2 (webready PDF)
ISBN 978 1 4744 5066 9 (epub)

The right of Faith Binckes and Carey Snyder to be identified as the editors of this work has been asserted in accordance with the Copyright, Designs and Patents Act 1988, and the Copyright and Related Rights Regulations 2003 (SI No. 2498).

Contents

List of Illustrations and Tables viii
Acknowledgements x

General Introduction: The Kaleidoscope, the Mirror, and the Magnifying
Glass – Reading Through the Lens of Periodical Culture 1
Faith Binckes and Carey Snyder

Part I: Locations
 Introduction 17
 Faith Binckes

 1. 'Watch this space:' Late Nineteenth-Century Women's Periodicals
    in Ireland 20
    Elizabeth Tilley

 2. Opening Doors: Women and Print Media in Scotland 33
    Margery Palmer McCulloch

 3. Marginal Places, Liminal Spaces: Welsh Women's Modernist Writing
    and the English 'Little Magazine' 48
    Claire Flay-Petty

 4. Home and Homeland: English National Identity in the Women's
    Magazines of Newnes and Pearson 60
    Chris Mourant and Natasha Periyan

Part II: The Sister Arts
 Introduction 75
 Faith Binckes

 5. 'A theme with many variations': Gertrude Hudson, Musical Criticism,
    and Turn-of-the-Century Periodical Culture 78
    Charlotte Purkis

6. Women, Drama, and Print Culture 1890–1929   92
   Elizabeth Wright

7. Dance, Modernism, and the Female Critic in the *New Age*, *Rhythm*,
   and the *Outlook*   106
   Susan Jones

8. Mixing the Brows in Print: Iris Barry's Film Criticism of the 1920s   120
   Miranda Dunham-Hickman

9. The Avant-Garde in the Drawing Room: Women, Writing, and
   Architectural Modernism in Britain   134
   Elizabeth Darling

10. The Dialogic Magazine: Advertisements and Femininity in the
    Lady's Realm   146
    Annie Paige

Part III: Key Literary Figures
Introduction   165
Carey Snyder

11. 'An Outpour of Ink': From the 'Young Rebecca' to 'the most important
    signature of these years,' Rebecca West 1911–1920   169
    Kathryn Laing

12. *Time and Tide* Waited for Her: Rebecca West's Journalism in
    the 1920s   183
    Margaret D. Stetz

13. Writing Revolution: Dorothy Richardson's Contributions to Early
    Twentieth-Century Periodicals   195
    Elizabeth Pritchett and Scott McCracken

14. Violet Hunt, Periodical Culture, and Emergent (Female)
    Modernisms   213
    Louise Kane

15. Dora Marsden and Anarchist Modernisms   226
    Henry Mead

16. Beatrice Hastings: Debating Suffrage in the *New Age* and *Votes
    for Women*   242
    Carey Snyder

17. 'A kind of *minute note-book*, to be published some day':
    Katherine Mansfield in the *Adelphi*, 1923–1924   258
    Faith Binckes

18. May Sinclair, Magazine Writer: Exploring Modernisms through
    Diverse Journals   274
    Laurel Forster

Part IV: Networks, Circles, and Margins

Introduction   291
Carey Snyder

19. On Poets and Publishing Networks: Charting the Careers of Charlotte Mew and Anna Wickham   294
Helen Southworth and Alina Oboza

20. Women's Poetry in the Modern British Magazines: A Case for Medium Reading   313
Bartholomew Brinkman

21. Wheelpolitik: The Moral and Aesthetic Project of Edith Sitwell's *Wheels*, 1916–1921   329
Melissa Bradshaw

22. *New Age* Women's Writing: Edith Nesbit, Florence Farr, and Nietzschean Socialist Modernism   342
Lee Garver

23. Horror in the Wax Museum: Edith Nesbit's 'The Power of Darkness' and the *Strand Magazine*   354
Anthony Camara

Part V: Social Movements

Introduction   371
Carey Snyder

24. Women, Periodicals, and Esotericism in Modernist-Era Print Culture   374
Mark S. Morrisson

25. Lysistrata on the Home Front: Locating Women's Reproductive Bodies in the Birth Strike Rhetoric of the *Malthusian* during the First World War   389
Layne Parish Craig

26. A Column of Our Own: Women's Columns in Socialist Newspapers   405
Elizabeth Carolyn Miller

27. Prayer Warriors: Denominational Feminism, the Vote, and the *Church League for Women's Suffrage Monthly Paper*   421
Krista Lysack

Appendix   436
Works Cited and Helpful Sources   458
Notes on Contributors   460
Index   466

List of Illustrations and Tables

Figures

1.1	Front cover of *To-Day's Woman: A Weekly Home and Fashion Journal*. September 1896.	23
2.1	Frances Macdonald, 'A Pond.' The *Magazine*. November 1894.	37
2.2	*Scottish Women and the Vote Scrapbook*, held at the Mitchell Library, Glasgow.	41
10.1	Advertisements from the *Lady's Realm*, January 1911, including the EWBANK SWEEPER.	155
10.2	Advertisement for Beecham's Pills. *Lady's Realm Supplement*. January 1911.	159
11.1	Extract from Rebecca West's 'Indissoluble Matrimony,' *BLAST* (1914).	175
13.1	Contents page of the *Little Review*. June 1919.	198
13.2	Front cover of the *Crank: An Unconventional Magazine*. January 1904.	200
13.3	Dorothy Richardson, 'The Responsibility of Dentistry.' The *Dental Record*. October 1913.	206
16.1	Correspondence columns, including replies to 'Woman As State Creditor.' *New Age*, June 1908.	246
16.2	Extract from Correspondence column, authored by 'Beatrice (Tina) Hastings.' *New Age*. May 1910.	253
17.1	Page spread from 'More Extracts from a Journal' by Katherine Mansfield. The *Adelphi*, January 1924.	268
18.1	Front cover of *Woman At Home*, showing May Sinclair's 'Woman's Sacrifices in the War.' February 1915.	284
18.2	Front cover of *Collier's: The National Weekly*, showing May Sinclair's 'Women's War Sacrifices.' November 1914.	286
20.1	Word clouds for 'suffrage,' 'sex,' and 'domestic' topics for the *Freewoman*, the *New Freewoman*, and the *Egoist*.	317
20.2	Distribution of 'women' and 'men' in the *Freewoman*, the *New Freewoman*, and the *Egoist*.	318
20.3	Distribution of topics in the *Freewoman*, the *New Freewoman*, and the *Egoist*.	319
20.4	Distribution of topics in the *English Review*.	320
20.5	Distribution of topics in the *New Age*.	321

20.6	Distribution of poetry topics in the *Freewoman*, the *New Freewoman*, and the *Egoist*.	322
21.1	Image from the first (1916) cycle of *Wheels*.	331
21.2	Image from the third (1918) cycle of *Wheels*.	331
25.1	Front cover of the *Malthusian*, produced during wartime. December 1916.	395
25.2	The 'Malthusian War Map' illustrating 'birth-rates of various countries.' November 1915.	396
26.1	Julia Dawson's column in the *Clarion* (August 1896).	413
26.2	Julia Dawson's column in the *Clarion* (September 1896).	415
26.3	Lily Bell's column in the *Labour Leader* (August 1894).	416

Tables

19.1	Timeline for UK and US publications by Charlotte Mew and Anna Wickham.	309
20.1	Term frequencies in the *Freewoman*, the *New Freewoman*, and the *Egoist*.	320

Acknowledgements

One of the many pleasures of working on women's periodical and print culture is that it is, entirely appropriately, such a cooperative and a capacious field of scholarship. This project has strengthened existing connections, and forged many new ones, and we would like to thank all our contributors for their hard work and commitment to the volume. Jackie Jones, at Edinburgh University Press, deserves much praise for supporting such a landmark series, and for her enthusiasm and encouragement throughout the process. Special mentions are also due to Catherine Clay, Barbara Green, and Faye Hammill, who provided valuable feedback at various points, and whose scholarship has informed the volume in so many ways. Andrew Thacker, Mark Gaipa, and Sean Latham also gave helpful input at different stages. Our anonymous readers at Edinburgh University Press made additional perceptive comments that enabled us to refine our aims at the proposal stage. Our editor Ersev Ersoy has graciously assisted us with contracts, production, and the submission of the manuscript. Saraya Abner, who ably copy-edited for us as part of a Research Apprenticeship through Ohio University's Honors Tutorial College, was a fantastic help in the closing stages. Christine Barton helped us to fine-tune our copy further still, while James Dale brought the final stages of production together.

In addition to the permissions outlined below, various libraries and archives must be acknowledged for their assistance. In particular, we would like to thank: the Women's Library at the London School of Economics; the Harry Ransom Research Centre at the University of Texas, Austin; the Beinecke Library, Yale University; the library of the Victoria and Albert Museum; the National Library of Scotland; the Schlesinger Library, Harvard University; the Glasgow School of Art; Brown University Library; the British Library; the Cambridge University Library, and the Bodleian Library, University of Oxford. Reading University (Special Collections) granted permission to use material from Dorothy Edwards's papers. Willa Muir's writing appears courtesy of the Muir literary estate, and the National Library of Scotland. While a resource such as the Modernist Journals Project (which we must also warmly thank) has altered the face of periodical scholarship for this period, the holdings of institutions such as these, and the expertise of their staff, remain absolutely crucial. The Dorothy Richardson Project generously supported the reproduction of certain images included here. Our respective institutions – Bath Spa University (UK) and Ohio University (US) – also facilitated our work, not least by approving periods of research leave.

Our cover image is reprinted with permission of the Modernist Journals Project and Brown University Library. Images from other magazines mounted on the MJP (the *Lady's Realm*, *Little Review*, the *New Age*, *BLAST*, and *Wheels*) are likewise reprinted here with their permission and the permission of Brown University Libraries.

The images included in Bartholomew Brinkman's chapter are copyright of the author, and should only be reproduced with permission. The timeline included in Helen Southworth and Alina Oboza's chapter is copyright Alina Oboza, and should only be reproduced with permission.

Images from the *Clarion* are reproduced with the permission of Cornell University Library.

Images from *To-Day's Woman*, *Woman At Home*, the *Dental Record*, and the *Crank* are reproduced with the permission of the British Library.

Images from the *Adelphi* appear with the permission of Cambridge University Library.

The image from *Collier's* magazine appears with the permission of Penn State University Library.

Images from the *Malthusian* appear with the permission of the University of Texas Libraries, the University of Texas at Austin.

Frances Macdonald's 'A Pond' is reproduced with the permission of Archives and Collections, the Glasgow School of Art. Images from the suffrage papers housed at the Glasgow Life Collection, appear with the permission of The Mitchell Library, Glasgow.

General Introduction: The Kaleidoscope, the Mirror, and the Magnifying Glass – Reading Through the Lens of Periodical Culture

Faith Binckes and Carey Snyder

Our cover image is taken from the January 1911 issue of the *Lady's Realm*. It features a flood of female figures, some of them carrying a flag bearing the just visible words 'We Demand Change.' The focal point of the image, however, is a banner emblazoned not with a demand but with a question: 'Quo Vadis?' This was not the first time that the magazine had pondered the directions open to women in a rapidly changing modern world. In 1902, during the hiatus between the death of Queen Victoria and the coronation of Edward VII, the *Lady's Realm* ran a series of speculative articles on 'The Future of Society.' The first of these asserted:

> It would require the most daring of prophets to predict what the new century might bring forth; but however wonderful its changes may be, it cannot produce so complete a social upheaval as that which has been brought about by the two great events which changed the whole conditions of Society – namely, the increased facility of communication, and the emancipation of woman. Nothing so subversive can await us in the future. (361)

Women, Periodicals, and Print Culture in Britain, 1890s–1920s: the Modernist Period brings together 'the two great events' of this statement. It considers a specific aspect of the 'increased facility of communication,' albeit one of the most conspicuous: the world of periodicals, and their associated print cultures. This includes periodicals aimed specifically at women – domestic magazines like the *Lady's Realm*, but also the feminist and suffrage press, and papers written by female students – along with the wider field of newspapers, literary and cultural reviews, specialist and general interest periodicals, and little magazines. It explores the multiplicity of ways in which 'the emancipation of woman' was demonstrated, figured, framed, and debated on their pages. By this, we mean not political emancipation alone, but the larger social movement through which women pushed toward greater visibility and influence, in decades remarkable for the cultural phenomena that they witnessed. In 1995, Rita Felski argued that the 'intersection of femininity and modernity plays itself out *differentially* across the specifics of sociohistorical context' (Felski 1995: 9) requiring both a method, and a medium, that attends to 'varied and competing representations' (7). Periodical culture offers exactly this, as we hope this volume will demonstrate. The rise of women's movements (frequently galvanised through the campaign for the vote), developments in literary and artistic 'modernism,' innovations in mass media and popular culture, shifting religious and political groupings, new scientific discoveries, debates surrounding national identity, empire, war, and peace – all of these intersected, clashed, and cross-pollinated in publications of equally various circulations and orientations. These dynamic combinations of topics, genres, images, and discourses presented contemporary readers with a kaleidoscopic modernity. At the same time, tied as they were both to the rhythms of the present moment and to existing print traditions, periodicals represented a form of stability, a connection to a recognisable world. Ann Heilmann and Margaret Beetham call this the '(periodical) looking glass' (2004: 49–50) through which readers could see their own reflections within a kind of continuity. Finally, as Heilmann and Beetham's metaphor also suggests, periodicals could be a transformative medium. They offered audiences the opportunity to shape the images they were presented with, not least as they made the line between reader and author unusually permeable. This was an important facility for many. For women, largely excluded from or marginalised within other public forums, it was crucial. As well as fleeting encounters in review and Correspondence columns, periodicals recorded women's detailed engagements with male figures and with one another – sometimes assenting, often dissenting – that could unfold over weeks and months. Whether they were polemical, analytical, humorous, or instructional, the levels of nuance that these forums generated applied a magnifying glass, or even a microscope, to innumerable issues. The same series of lenses are available to twenty-first century readers and scholars, as we look back at decades that 'The Future of Society' had attempted to imagine.

For the author of 'The Future of Society,' increased communication and female emancipation were 'great events' to be welcomed, on the whole. But they were also 'subversive,' not only positively creating a new order, but, more negatively, undermining the old. This choice of words is characteristic of the ambivalence that tends to accompany women's demands for 'change,' but it also echoes larger anxieties about the condition of modernity, as the heterogeneity noted above started to challenge hierarchies and classifications. Appropriately, this shifting of boundaries has been visible in scholarship too. This volume is placed across three very active, yet distinctive, fields: feminist periodical studies, modern periodical studies, and 'new modernist studies.'[1] While critics in each will be familiar with the specialisms of others – connected as they are by 'period' if nothing else – their perspectives and priorities are different. For instance, in special issues of *Literature Compass* and *Modern Fiction Studies* (2013), editors Jane Garrity and Anne Fernald independently came to the same conclusion: in spite of the innovative methodologies and expanded canon of the 'new modernist studies,' women writers continue to be marginalised. However, feminist periodical scholarship has produced a series of highly influential readings of the late nineteenth and early twentieth centuries. Some of these studies include discussions of modernism, others, very deliberately, do not. On top of this, modern periodical scholarship (and periodical scholarship more generally) has emphasised the fact that even flexible readings of key categories – of literary period, of cultural status, or of the unit of the writer herself – are problematic in a world refracted through the mobile forms of difference Felski identified. This volume, then, is driven by two main aims. First, it constitutes an extensive resource for new scholarship on women and periodicals, adhering to the idea that periodicals should figure as 'objects of study' in any analysis (Latham and Scholes 2006: 518). As such, it is concerned with women as agents in a range of projects, addressing a mixed economy of writers, readers, and editors. It also investigates the ways in which women were constructed by periodical culture, and their representations of it. Second, the volume demonstrates the frequent interpenetration and overlap between focal points separated by the parameters of academic specialisation. We explore the historical and scholarly background to these two contexts in a little more detail below.

The Northcliffe Revolution and the New Woman

The late nineteenth century witnessed an unprecedented rise in periodicals, in which women played a central role. Women pervaded the periodical press as writers, editors, subject matter, and increasingly sought-after readers. One sign of the times was the 1894 founding of the Society of Women Journalists, an event indicative that their numbers warranted a formal organisation. Frances Low's *Press Work for Women: a text book for the young female journalist* (1904) might have been published in the early twentieth century, but it was rooted in over a decade's journalistic experience. Revelatory of the trend to target an expanding female audience were the aggressive efforts of press magnate Alfred Harmsworth (later Lord Northcliffe). Harmsworth not only founded two women's magazines, *Forget me Not* (1891) and *Home Chat* (1895) – the latter referenced by Chris Mourant and Natasha Periyan in their contribution to this volume – he also incorporated a woman's column into the *Daily Mail* (1896). Harmsworth maintained that 'Movements in a woman's world – that is to say, changes in dress, toilet matters, cookery, and home matters generally – are as much entitled to receive attention as nine out of ten of the matters which are treated of in the ordinary daily paper' (*Daily Mail* 4 May 1896: 7). Though this narrow definition of 'a woman's world' is something that the feminist press would push back against, his trendsetting approach proved lucrative, contributing to a record-breaking circulation of one million. As Anne Varty's anthology *Eve's Century* (2000) demonstrated, between the years 1895 and 1918, the periodical press returned repeatedly to questions of modernity and gender. Varty closed her Introduction with a description of the frontispiece for the January 1901 number of *The Nineteenth Century (And After)*. Specially commissioned for that issue, it depicted 'the head of Janus from a Roman coin: the backward-looking face was that of a man, the forward-looking face was of a woman' (Varty 2000: 5).

Women's pages and women's magazines were two realms through which women territorialised the male-dominated journalistic field. As Adrian Bingham argues, this explicit gendering of periodical content was 'double edged': on the one hand, relegating purportedly feminine content to special columns risked reinforcing women's marginalisation; on the other, its inclusion ensured women 'both a greater visibility and opportunities to voice their concerns' (27). Women's pages and other gendered content – like fashion, advice, and gossip columns – formed part of the *fin de siècle*'s New Journalism, derided by Matthew Arnold in suggestively gendered terms as the 'featherbrained' counterpart to 'serious' news (*Nineteenth Century* May 1887: 638–9). The New Journalism was characterised by its chatty style; 'tit-bitty' form (pioneered by George Newnes's wildly popular *Tit-Bits*); human-interest features; and eye-catching visual elements. Alternately celebrated for its democratic possibilities and despised for 'impoverishing public discourse' (Collier 2006: 1), the New Journalism that fuelled the Northcliffe Revolution was closely associated with the New Woman – that *fin de siècle* icon who sought wider social, political, and professional opportunities and who was at once the New Journalism's 'subject and producer' (Beetham 2006: 234). Violet Hunt, Iris Barry, May Sinclair, Rebecca West, and other writers discussed in our collection, variously negotiated the legacy of the New Woman in the late nineteenth and early twentieth centuries.

Women were newly visible in modern periodicals not only in proliferating women's columns, in articles debating the merits of the New Woman and her descendants, and in the bylines of woman journalists; they also helped define modern magazines' new look. As the periodical press became increasingly reliant on advertising revenue, in turn enabled by innovations in print technology, periodicals were pervaded by large display advertisements featuring women's bodies, fashions, and domestic commodities. Magazines became 'texts embedded within the world of commerce' (Garvey 1996: 4). Indeed, mainstream periodicals aggressively courted the woman reader in large part because she was the period's primary consumer. Both Elizabeth Tilley (in Chapter 1) and Annie Paige (in Chapter 10) highlight the figure of the female reader-as-consumer, revealing the complex and sometimes contradictory representations of femininity that emerge in the interplay of advertisements and editorial content in women's magazines. In a 1913 proposal for a column entitled 'Women's Wider World,' Teresa Billington-Greig underscored the profitability of targeting an increasingly sophisticated female readership:

> The last ten years have made great changes in women's demands upon the Press and have increased enormously the number of women newspaper readers.
>
> Editors recognize the change and see that the old fashion column and domestic notes while still valuable are no longer sufficient for the modern woman whose interest in public affairs and the news of the world is becoming extensive and peculiar. [. . .] It will be seen at once that the possibilities of arousing discussion and correspondence are numerous, and furthermore women's articles in the modern spirit must attract those advertisers who seizing the present opportunity are catering more and more for the modern type of woman.[2]

The end-of-the-century boom in women's magazines correlates with this new partnership between periodicals and advertising, and – fashion columns and domestic notes notwithstanding – many of these aimed to interest 'the modern type of woman.' However, it was the feminist press that targeted readers with more extensive interest in public affairs and in women's changing experience in the 'wider world.'

Women's Magazines and the Feminist Press

Starting with pioneering studies by Margaret Beetham (1996) and Ellen Gruber Garvey (1996), a rich body of scholarship has explored the ways that femininity is constructed in women's magazines, often in relation to advertising and consumption. Highlighting the heteroglossia of the periodical form, these studies have worked to unsettle the assumption that women's magazines necessarily shore up conservative gender norms. Beetham, for example, rejects the premise that nineteenth- and early twentieth-century women's magazines functioned 'exclusively as instruments of a pervasive domestic ideology and a regime of sexual repression' (1996: 2), finding more subversive possibilities in the interplay of sometimes contradictory features. Judith Fetterley's concept of the 'resisting reader' has proven useful to others, who stress that actual readers (as opposed to the ones the magazine seems to intend) may read against the grain (see Fraser et al. 2003). Recently, scholars of the middlebrow and of fashion have contributed nuanced readings of the cultural work of modernist-era women's magazines.[3] Essays in our collection build on this scholarship, with particular attention to the intersection of gender identities with those of class and nationality.[4]

Along with the boom in women's magazines, a full-scale feminist press took shape. Beetham describes its growing power as 'a thin trickle which became a stream, if not a torrent, of words between 1900 and 1914' (Beetham 1996: 174). Feminist media scholars have demonstrated that periodicals were central to the formation of political and social movements as well as subjective identities. The suffrage press was particularly vital, with a multitude of publications that reflect the diversity of the movement. *Votes for Women* (1907–18), for instance, began as the organ of the militant Women's Social Political Union (WSPU), spurring the rival constitutional organisation, the National Union of Women's Suffrage Societies (NUWSS), to publish *Common Cause* in 1909; that same year, a group broke from the WSPU to found the Women's Freedom League (WFL) and launch their own journal, the *Vote*. Along with these better-known suffrage journals were myriad lesser-known ones, including the Church League for Women's Suffrage *Monthly Paper* (which Krista Lysack discusses in Chapter 27). In addition to these suffrage titles, the rapidly diversifying periodical marketplace included a wide range of other serious titles directed at women, such as the *Woman Worker*, the *Englishwoman*, the *Freewoman*, and *Time and Tide*, most of which are discussed in this collection.[5]

The feminist press did not spring out of a vacuum. Philippa Levine succinctly relates how in the last half of the nineteenth century, 'the principles of feminist journalism emerged as a challenge to and a means of circumventing reliance upon male-run papers,' furnishing women with 'an actively separate literary space' (1990: 299). Nineteenth-century forerunners include the *English Woman's Journal* (1858–64), published by the Langham Place group; *Woman's Signal* (1884–9); *Victoria Magazine* (1863–80); and *Shafts* (1892–1900) – all represented in the valuable recent collection of primary source material, *Feminism and the Periodical Press, 1900-1918* (2006), edited by Lucy Delap, Maria DiCenzo, and Leila Ryan.[6] As the editors affirm, 'The periodical press was the crucial vehicle through which women's movements debated and disseminated ideas, developed organizations and networks, and connected readers across social and geographic lines' (2006: xxvii). Part V of our collection demonstrates these propensities by exploring women's writing in a variety of social and political movement periodicals, including suffrage, socialism, esotericism, and birth control.

Women writers of the time affirmed the power of print culture to knit together social movements and forge collective identities. In her memoir *Up Hill to Holloway*, Mary Gawthorpe calls the socialist *Clarion* 'a sort of nationwide club on a non-dues paying basis which united readers everywhere in an atmosphere of camaraderie' (1962: 175).

Periodical scholars have found the concept of the counterpublic sphere useful in theorising the communities that accrete around counterhegemonic publications like the *Clarion*. Jürgen Habermas has influentially theorised the bourgeois public sphere that took shape in the eighteenth century as a discursive arena, comprised of print venues, clubs, coffee houses, and the like, where citizens could debate issues of common concern – a vital component of a functioning democracy. For Habermas, this ideally cohesive and consensus-driven public sphere became fragmented in the late nineteenth century under pressure from competing interest groups, including women and the working class. Challenging Habermas's characterisation of the public sphere as a once-unified and inclusive discursive arena, political scientist Nancy Fraser argues that it was always contentious and divided: 'Virtually from the beginning, counterpublics contested the exclusionary norms of the bourgeois public, elaborating alternative styles of political behavior and alternative norms of public speech' (1992: 61). Fraser goes on to define 'counterpublics,' as 'parallel discursive arenas where members of subordinated social groups invent and circulate counterdiscourses [. . .] to formulate oppositional interpretations of their identities, interests, and needs' (1992: 67). Rather than the ideal of a single public sphere, Fraser envisions a patchwork of counterpublics that correlate with the flourishing of social movement periodicals discussed in Part V.

While periodicals provide possibilities for affirming collective identities, they also provide forums for internal disagreement and debate. With second-wave feminist institutions as an example, Fraser characterises counterpublics as spaces for 'withdrawal and regroupment' and for strategising activism 'directed toward wider publics' (1992: 68). In this way, she conjures an image of an at least strategically unified counterculture contesting hegemonic ideas and practices. The suffrage press functioned in this way, discouraging public dissent in order to present a unified front in the battle for the vote. Yet this facade of consensus did not sit well with some suffragists. Helena Swanwick resigned from her position as editor of the *Common Cause* due to dissatisfaction with the policy of brushing disagreement under the rug. Similarly, after Teresa Billington-Greig broke with both the WSPU and the WFL, she rejoiced in having reclaimed the right of candid free speech, which she promptly exercised in penning a scathing critique of the militants in the *New Age* in 1911. As if in answer to her call, that same year Dora Marsden and Mary Gawthorpe founded the *Freewoman* to provide a 'free platform' for feminist debate, where a broad range of often-controversial issues could be discussed. The feminism that it espoused was not homogenous, but fractious and contentious, with boundaries and premises continually up for debate. These examples show that in periodicals, women writers sought forums as much for contestation as for community building. Examples from our collection – including Henry Mead's characterisation of Marsden as an 'anti-networker' and Snyder's discussion of Beatrice Hastings's combative exchanges in the *New Age* – provide further support that periodicals provided women writers with spaces for discord and dispute, as well as for fortifying collective identities and social movements.

Naturally, women's magazines and feminist periodicals were part of a much wider field of print culture, including women-run publishing houses like Harriet Shaw Weaver's Egoist Press and the WSPU's Women's Press; myriad print artefacts, such as the posters and postcards produced by the Suffrage Atelier; and Ruth Cavendish-Bentick's subscription library, which provided core materials for the present-day British Women's Library. Thus the writers, editors, and readers that are the subject of this collection were participants in a print culture which included, but was by no means restricted to, women's periodicals, presses, bookshops, and libraries. Rebecca West's neglected first novel *The Sentinel* depicts a suffrage activist surrounded by exactly the sort of texts noted above, as Kathryn Laing discusses in Chapter 11. Several other contributions also consider the intersection of periodical cultures with other forms of print. Helen Southworth and Alina Oboza's detailed reception history of poets Charlotte Mew and Anna Wickham draws attention to the role of anthologisation. Faith Binckes addresses the symbolic power of the unpublished writer's 'notebook' in the chapter on Murry's 'magazine edition' of Katherine Mansfield's papers in the *Adelphi*. Periodical studies provide a powerful means for exploring this terrain, just as their hybrid form encourages us to question traditional evaluative rubrics that discredit the popular, the mainstream, the non-literary. This freewheeling mix of material provides more opportunities for recovering women writers, as well as women editors and readers, but it also allows us to think about the disciplinary frameworks within which our own work is located.

Periodical Studies, Gender, Modernity, and Modernism

The most immediate context for this volume is the larger series of which it forms a part, but its wider critical location is worth analysing in more detail. This volume, like those that precede it in the series, profits from digital resources that have made a growing archive of magazines available to scholars around the world. This includes open-access resources connected to specific universities, such as the Modernist Journals Project (MJP), the Modernist Magazines Project and the Blue Mountain Project. There are plenty of other more (and less) stable online repositories, many of which are also freely accessible, in addition to numerous, overlapping, subscription services. The vagaries of copyright law have contributed to this tapestry, especially for the pre-1922 period, which is in the public domain in the United States. The volume also builds upon nearly two decades of pathbreaking critical work. Within modernist periodical studies we can think of major monographs or collections by Mark S. Morrisson (2001), Suzanne W. Churchill and Adam McKible (2007), Ann Ardis and Patrick Collier (2008), Robert Scholes and Clifford Wulfman (2010). Peter Brooker and Andrew Thacker's series of volumes *The Oxford Critical and Cultural History of Modernist Magazines* (2009–) provides invaluable readings of periodical texts in Great Britain, the United States, and Continental Europe, with further global perspectives in the pipeline. Sean Latham and Robert Scholes, drawing upon their experience on the MJP but gesturing beyond modernism, published their field-defining article 'The Rise of Periodical Studies' in 2006. Sharing this broader remit, the initiation of the *Journal of Modern Periodical Studies* in 2010 has provided a home for emerging scholarship on periodicals that appeared between 1880 and 1950s. Yet, although gender is a prominent feature in many of these projects, it does not play a defining role in their organisation.

In making gender a central concern here, then, we are drawing upon equally influential work in the field of feminist periodical studies. Some studies in this field – such as Jayne E. Marek's foundational monograph (1995) on women editors – are centrally invested in modernism. Others, such as Marysa Demoor in her study of female critics in the *Athenaeum*, or Margaret D. Stetz and Mark Samuels Lasner's study of the *Yellow Book*, explore the gender dynamics within specific periodicals (Demoor 2000;

Stetz and Samuels Lasner: 1994). However, more commonly, this scholarship considers modernist innovations through their connections to modern, female experience – including feminist activism. Broadly speaking, this describes much of Barbara Green's work – including her own state-of-the-field review essay of 2011 – and Lucy Delap's landmark study of the feminist avant-garde (2007). Other key works are not notably invested in modernism at all: for instance, Michelle Elizabeth Tusan's valuable readings of the women's advocacy press (2005); and Maria DiCenzo, Lucy Delap, and Leila Ryan's influential *Feminist Media History: Suffrage, Periodicals, and the Public Sphere* (2011). Scholars such as Margaret Beetham (1996) and Ellen Gruber Garvey (1996), noted above, focus on the construction of femininity in periodicals of this period, without investigating the category of modernism per se. Both these analyses, like that of Stetz and Samuels Lasner, and of Demoor, additionally traverse the boundary between the nineteenth and the early twentieth centuries, and are driven by the experiences of women as readers of periodicals within a commercially driven and highly gendered public sphere.

This brings us to perhaps the trickiest of our three foci: 'modernism' itself. Reappraisals of the unifying tenets of the discipline have given modernist scholarship new cultural capital, new energy, and new purpose. However, they have also prompted continuing questions about 'modernism' as a term of classification. This scholarly debate has generated a considerable literature of its own. In their introduction to the collection *Women's Experience of Modernity* (2003), Ann Ardis and Leslie W. Lewis outlined several pragmatic approaches: expanding the term 'modernism' to let in more cultural objects, defined by their shared response to modernity; pluralising it to allow for a variety of different modernisms; or, lastly, retaining the term to designate high modernist works, while rejecting the premise that these are the most worthy of study (4). Four years later, Ástráður Eysteinsson and Vivian Leska observed abiding tensions between this desire for expansion, and the risk that '"modernism" would dissolve into a random and arbitrary catchword' (Eysteinsson and Leska 2007: 7). Pamela Caughie's 2009 collection *Disciplining Modernism* reprinted Susan Stanford Friedman's 2001 article 'Definitional Excursions: the Meanings of Modern/Modernity/Modernism' next to Stephen Ross's 'Uncanny Modernism, or Analysis Interminable.' In a manoeuvre that will please periodical scholars, Ross took the opportunity not only to reflect on Friedman's piece, but to read it alongside Jennifer Wicke's article on modernism as a form of moribund 'brand,' which had appeared in the same inaugural number of *Modernism/modernity*. In *Modernism: the evolution of an idea* (2015), Sean Latham and Gayle Rogers made a sustained study of such shifting sites of definition and counter-definition, presenting the history of a concept at once 'ingrained yet somehow weightless' (Latham and Rogers 2015: 2). In *Modernism's Print Cultures* (2016) Faye Hammill and Mark Hussey reviewed aspects of this concept that carried undeniable weight, charting scholarship on the material manifestations of modernism. Nonetheless, this book confirmed that close attention to the conditions of publication, transmission, and textual form did not curtail debates around definition. Writing in the same year, in the conclusion to *Modern Print Artefacts*, Patrick Collier argued that the cultural capital attached to modernist studies was now such that scholars struggled to escape its gravitational force (234), and that even attempts to 'open' the modernist canon ended up 'reiterating the term's status as *the* rubric for the period' (234).

Collier's statement of 2016, polemically titled 'Postscript: Against Modernist Studies' is, like Wicke's, driven by the awareness that modernist scholarship itself is a form of cultural and material production. This can be connected to conclusions Collier drew in 2015, when he surveyed the contents of the *Journal of Modern Periodical Studies* in order to consider the question 'What Is Modern Periodical Studies?' at the end of a special number devoted to 'Magazines and/as Media' (*JMPS* 2015: 92–111).[7] Collier's decision to address *JMPS* itself as an 'object of study' follows in the footsteps of other scholars who, like Ross in 2009, have treated their own forms of publication as part of the analytic process. Twenty years before *Disciplining Modernism*, *Victorian Periodicals Review* (Fall 1989) produced a special number dedicated to 'Critical Theory.' Many of the paradigms that emerged in these critiques are still familiar from periodical studies today: the interest in dialogism, the periodical as a medium which is both 'open' and 'closed,' an exploration the line between 'text' and 'context,' the search for a theory that might help critics to tackle the complex patterns within and across the medium.[8] And, as this was a periodical, each of these critiques existed relative to, but separate from, the piece next to it, an aspect that played no small role in the theories under discussion. In a 1991 piece on the *English Review*, also published in the *Victorian Periodicals Review*, Laurel Brake reflected on the significance of medium by referencing not only the *English Review* itself, with its multiple contributors and discourses, but by self-consciously quoting a public lecture she had delivered on the same publication, under the rubric of 'Edwardian Literature' (Brake 1991: 163–70). By standing thus, 'both inside and outside the perimeter' of two different genres (public lecture and scholarly article) and several different disciplines (literature, history, bibliography) Brake brought her critical activity into contact with the eclectic process of meaning-making in the periodical itself. Editors of periodicals on periodical studies, even editors of a collection such as ours, might look with wry recognition at the statements made by the editors whose composite texts they study. These figures often had to present (or to resist) a particular vision of their magazine while dealing with the contingencies of production, the pressures of the marketplace, the unknown duration of their print run, the individual perspectives of their contributors, and the unknowably diverse interests of their readers. So, although adding 'women' and 'the modernist era' to 'periodical studies' helps us to focus our interests, this mercurial medium cannot be expected to settle any accounts definitively. Indeed, just as Collier celebrated, rather than mourned, the absence of a 'totalising theory of the periodical' (2015: 108), and Felski avoided the 'overarching feminist myth of the modern' (1995: 7) the risks generated by a collection comprised of multiple essays on composite texts are outweighed by the freedom they afford. Not least is the freedom to allow people to find their own patterns and pathways through the material, to make connections, to notice absences and to contest opinions. As Elizabeth Tilley observes in her chapter in this volume on Irish women's periodicals, this sort of freedom has significance for women, both as readers and as writers. We would suggest that this is as much the case in our own day as it was between 1890 and 1929.

These definitional challenges, and some of the questions generated by them, are visible across the collection. As editors, we are literary scholars by training but as readers will note, we have not tried to advocate a given methodology, and have gathered contributors from different disciplines and different areas of expertise. The category of 'modernism' is present not only because it continues to be an organising concept (and a less-than-moribund 'brand') but because it was an important touchstone for many of the women writers we examine. We did remove the term 'modernist periodicals' from the title, to indicate a firm intention to explore outside the boundaries of consecrated 'modernist' texts. This was not only due to the 'definitional excursions' surrounding modernism as a category, or the complexities that attend modernism and gender. It was also because a lot of excellent material, including work by canonical modernist women, was published in magazines that could never be convincingly described as 'modernist,' whatever definition was applied. Dorothy Richardson's contributions to the *Dental Record*, explored in this collection by Scott McCracken and Elizabeth Pritchett, are a case in point. Moreover, whether by necessity or by design, even those women engaged with more experimental forms of art do not seem to display anything like the 'outright hostility' to mainstream periodicals that Collier detected in 2016.[9] If anything, the opposite seems to have been true. As Miranda Dunham-Hickman shows in her discussion of Iris Barry's cinema criticism, this was particularly the case for women interested in the numerous modern mediums that crossed the line between 'highbrow' and 'popular,' 'art' and 'entertainment.' Thus, we hope that 'the modernist period' gives the impact of modernism its due, while accepting both its recognised diversity, and the fact that modernising impulses were frequently channelled through publications with entirely different agendas and expectations.

Our dates, as we are sure the reader will realise, are not an attempt to suggest that any 'era' can be said to officially conclude at a given point. A brief look at the next volume in the series will suggest otherwise, and some of the contributions included here (Louise Kane's study of Violet Hunt, Claire Flay-Petty's work on English-medium Welsh periodicals, and Elizabeth Darling's chapter on architectural writing) introduce the question of periodisation. The relationship between 'periodicals' and 'periodisation' addressed in these pieces reminds us that the 'nowness' and 'newness' of periodical texts will never produce a neat bow-wave of innovation, striking all shores more or less simultaneously. While particular historical and cultural factors may certainly be involved, this is also a question of publishing practice. Just as all periodicals can be located within long-standing print cultural traditions, so the battle for ownership of modernism and modernity was waged in magazines and newspapers through acts of recirculation and critical reappraisal, as much as it was through breakthrough moments of first publication. However, it is worth noting that twenty-first century scholarship on periodicals has presented a challenge to the notion that the watershed year for female modernists was on or around 1928 (Scott: 1996). Since those late twentieth-century feminist retrievals – most notably, Scott's own anthology *The Gender of Modernism* (1990) – it has been apparent that looking principally to book publication could not represent the scope, variety, or date-range of women's contribution. As Victorian periodical scholarship had already begun to reveal, not only did many women publish extensively in periodicals before securing a publisher for a book, others published prolifically in periodicals alone. Some of these crafted writing identities that altered substantially between different publications, or even within a single periodical outlet (see Carey Snyder on Beatrice Hastings and Anthony Camara on Edith Nesbit). The face of Janus mentioned by Varty is not only symbolic of the forward-looking modern woman of many twentieth-century magazines and newspapers. It also confirms the pluralistic figure of 'the author', a creature who could be as various as the venues in which she appeared.

We can suggest, then, that reading women's writing of this era through periodical texts allows for the possibility of all three intersecting perspectives – the kaleidoscope, the mirror, and the magnifying glass – to operate at the level of our own discipline, as well as in our approaches to primary texts. We can see a terrain that we already recognise, one that is familiar from Malcolm Bradbury's early readings, or from Cyril Connolly's attempt to classify the field in terms of 'dynamic' or 'eclectic' magazines, or from feminist scholarship of the 1960s and 1970s (Bradbury 1968; Connolly 1964). We can also see the refracted image of other, newer configurations, those that innovate around the parameters drawn up by the likes of Mao and Walkowitz, Latham and Scholes, Hammill, Delap, Collier, Ardis and Green. These are even more compelling, perhaps because it is our own reading and research that is causing the shifts to take place, before our very eyes. An important part of this is the ongoing discussion about the role that 'modernism' – however it is defined – should play in a scholarship as sensitive to definition, competition, and prestige as were the times and texts it studies. Finally, we can also see aspects of both pictures that have been invisible before: the revealing details of those who we think we already know, and the outlines of others who, for a whole series of reasons, are unlikely ever to have received more than passing critical attention. Jane Aaron has memorably alluded to 'the names of women [which] bob up and down like corks on the contents sheets' of magazines and anthologies, a metaphor that captures both the persistence and presence of women's writing, and its uncertain critical buoyancy (1994: xii) We hope that this collection will lift some of these authors and texts more securely to the surface, bringing with them new insights, new associations, and new agendas.

Notes

1. A key text here is Douglas Mao and Rebecca Walkowitz's 2008 *PMLA* position paper 'The New Modernist Studies.'
2. Teresa Billington-Greig Papers, Folder 7/TB-G2/G4/Box 404, Women's Library, London School of Economics.
3. On the middlebrow, women, and periodicals, see Catherine Keyser 2010; Alice Wood 2016; and Faye Hammill and Michelle Smith 2015. On fashion, women, and modern periodicals, there are several pertinent essays in Clay et al., *Women's Periodicals and Print Culture in Britain*, 2017.
4. See especially chapters by Tilley, McCulloch, and Mourant and Periyan, in Part I.
5. The *Woman Worker* is the only exception; for more on this title, see Green 2012. On suffrage journals, see Chapters 15 and 26; on the feminist press more broadly, see especially Chapters 11 and 14; and on women's columns in socialist newspapers, see Chapter 25.
6. For discussion of these magazines, see also *The Edinburgh History of Women's Periodical Culture in Britain, Volume 2: the Victorian Period*.
7. See Hammill, Hjartarson and McGregor 2015.
8. See Brake and Humphreys 1989, Hughes 1989, Pykett 1989, Beetham 1989.
9. 'Making matters worse in this case,' Collier noted, 'is the outright hostility of many prominent modernists and their supporters towards ordinary print culture: the world of popular periodicals, mainstream publishing houses, libraries, booksellers and other locations where a vast majority of the reading and writing in the period got done' (2016: 235).

Works Cited

Aaron, Jane. 1994. 'Introduction.' *Luminous and Forlorn: contemporary short stories by women from Wales*. Ed. Elin ap Hywel. Dinas Powys: Honno. x–xv.

Ardis, Ann and Patrick Collier, eds. 2008. *Transatlantic Print Culture, 1880–1940: Emerging Media, Emerging Modernisms*. London: Palgrave.

Ardis, Ann and Leslie W. Lewis. 2003. *Women's Experience of Modernity, 1875–1945*. Baltimore: Johns Hopkins University Press.

Beetham, Margaret. 1989. 'Open and Closed: The Periodical as a Publishing Genre.' *Victorian Periodicals Review* 22.3: 96–100.

—. 1996. *A Magazine of Her Own? Domesticity and Desire in the Woman's Magazine, 1800–1914*. London: Routledge.

—. 2006. 'Periodicals and the new media: Women and imagined communities.' *Women's Studies International Forum* 29: 231–40.

Billington-Greig, Teresa. 'Women's Wider World: Scheme for a Weekly Article,' Teresa Billington-Greig Papers, Folder 7/TB-G2/G4/Box 404, Women's Library, London School of Economics.

Bingham, Adrian. 2004. *Gender, Modernity, and the Popular Press in Interwar Britain*. Oxford: Clarendon Press.

Bradbury, Malcolm. 1968. '*Rhythm* and *The Blue Review*.' Special feature on 'The Little Magazines.' *Times Literary Supplement* 25 April 1968: 423–4.

Brake, Laurel. 1991. 'Production of Meaning in Periodical Studies: Versions of the *English Review*.' *Victorian Periodicals Review* 24.2: 163–70.

Brake, Laurel and Anne Humphreys. 1989. 'Critical Theory and Periodical Research.' *Victorian Periodicals Review* 22.3: 94–5.

Brooker, Peter and Andrew Thacker, eds. 2009. *The Oxford Critical and Cultural History of Modernist Magazines, Volume I: Britain and Ireland 1880–1955*. Oxford: Oxford University Press.

Churchill, Suzanne W. and Adam McKible, eds. 2007. *Little Magazines and Modernism: new approaches*. Aldershot: Ashgate.

Clay, Catherine, Maria DiCenzo, Barbara Green, and Fiona Hackney, eds. 2017. *Women's Periodicals and Print Culture in Britain, 1918–1939: The Interwar Period*. Edinburgh: Edinburgh University Press.

Collier, Patrick. 2006. *Modernism on Fleet Street*. Aldershot: Ashgate.

—. 2015. 'What is Modern Periodical Studies?' *Journal of Modern Periodical Studies* 6.2: 92–111.

—. 2016. *Modern Print Artefacts: Textual Materiality and Literary Value in British Print Culture, 1890–1930s*. Edinburgh: Edinburgh University Press.

Connolly, Cyril. 1964. 'Fifty Years of Little Magazines.' *Art and Literature* 1: 95–109.

Delap, Lucy. 2007. *The Feminist Avant-Garde: Transatlantic Encounters of the Early Twentieth Century*. Cambridge: Cambridge University Press.

Delap, Lucy, Maria DiCenzo, and Leila Ryan, eds. 2006. *Feminism and the Periodical Press, 1900–1918*. 3 vols. London: Routledge.

Demoor, Marysa. 2000. *Their Fair Share: Women, Power and Criticism in the Athenaeum, from Millicent Garrett Fawcett to Katherine Mansfield, 1870–1920*. Aldershot: Ashgate.

DiCenzo, Maria, Lucy Delap, and Leila Ryan. 2011. *Feminist Media History: Suffrage, Periodicals, and the Public Sphere*. Basingstoke: Palgrave Macmillan.

Eysteinsson, Ástráður and Vivian Leska, eds. 2007. *Modernism*. Amsterdam: John Benjamins.

Felski, Rita. 1995. *The Gender of Modernity*. Cambridge, MA: Harvard University Press.

Fernald, Anne E. 2013. 'Women's Fiction, New Modernist Studies, and Feminism.' *Modern Fiction Studies* 59.2: 229–40.

Fraser, Hilary, Stephanie Green, and Judith Johnston. 2003. *Gender and the Victorian Periodical.* Cambridge: Cambridge University Press.

Fraser, Nancy. 1992. 'Rethinking the Public Sphere: A Contribution to the Critique of Actually Existing Democracy.' *Habermas and the Public Sphere.* Ed. Craig Calhoun. Cambridge, MAb and London: MIT Press. 109–42.

Friedman, Susan Stanford. 2009. 'Definitional Excursions: the Meanings of Modern/Modernity/ Modernism.' *Disciplining Modernism.* Ed. Pamela Caughie. London: Palgrave Macmillan. 11–32.

Garrity, Jane. 2013. 'Modernist Women's Writing: Beyond the Threshold of Obsolescence.' *Literature Compass* 10:1: 15–30.

Garvey, Ellen Gruber. 1996. *The Adman in the Parlor. Magazines and the Gendering of Consumer Culture, 1880s to 1910s.* Oxford: Oxford University Press.

Gawthorpe, Mary. 1962. *Up Hill to Holloway.* Penobscot, ME: Traversity Press.

Green, Barbara. 2011. 'Around 1910: Periodical Culture, Women's Writing, and Modernity.' *Tulsa Studies in Women's Literature* 30.2: 429–39.

—. 2012. 'Complaints of Everyday Life: Feminist Periodical Culture and Correspondence Columns in *The Woman Worker*, *Women Folk*, and *The Freewoman*.' *Modernism/modernity* 19.3: 461–85.

Hammill, Faye, Paul Hjartarson, and Hannah McGregor. 2015. 'Magazines and/as Media: Periodical Studies and the Question of Disciplinarity.' Special number. *Journal of Modern Periodical Studies* 6.2.

Hammill, Faye and Michelle Smith. 2015. *Magazines, Travel, and Middlebrow Culture: Canadian Periodicals in English and French, 1925–1960.* Liverpool: Liverpool University Press.

Hammill, Faye and Mark Hussey. 2016. *Modernism's Print Cultures.* London: Bloomsbury.

Heilmann, Ann and Margaret Beetham, eds. 2004. *New Woman Hybridities: Femininity, Feminism and International Consumer Culture, 1880–1930.* London: Routledge.

Hughes, Linda. 1989. 'Turbulence in the "Golden Stream": Chaos Theory and the Study of Periodicals.' *Victorian Periodicals Review* 22.3: 117–25.

Keyser, Catherine. 2010. *Playing Smart: New York Women Writers and Modern Magazine Culture.* New Brunswick, NJ: Rutgers University Press.

Latham, Sean and Robert Scholes. 2006.'The Rise of Periodical Studies.' *PMLA* 121.2: 517–31.

Latham, Sean and Gayle Rogers. 2015. *Modernism: the evolution of an idea.* London: Bloomsbury.

Levine, Philippa. 1990. '"The Humanising Influences of Five O'Clock Tea": Victorian Feminist Periodicals.' *Victorian Studies* 33: 293–306.

Low, Frances H. 1904. *Press Work for Women: a text book for the young woman journalist.* London: L. Upcott Gill.

Mao, Douglas and Rebecca Walkowitz. 2008.'The New Modernist Studies.' *PMLA* 123.3: 737–48.

Marek, Jayne E. 1995. *Women Editing Modernism: "little" magazines and literary history.* Lexington: Kentucky University Press.

Morrisson, Mark. 2001. *The Public Face of Modernism: Little Magazines, Audiences, and Reception, 1905–1920.* Madison: University of Wisconsin Press.

Pykett, Lyn. 1989. 'Reading the Periodical Press: Text and Context.' *Victorian Periodicals Review* 22.3:100–8.

Ross, Stephen. 2009. 'Uncanny Modernism, or Analysis Interminable.' *Disciplining Modernism.* Ed. Pamela Caughie. London: Palgrave Macmillan: 33–52.

Scholes, Robert and Clifford Wulfman. 2010. *Modernism in the Magazines: an Introduction.* New Haven: Yale University Press.

Scott, Bonnie Kime. 1990. *The Gender of Modernism: a Critical Anthology.* Bloomington: Indiana University Press.

—. 1996. *Refiguring Modernism. Volume 1: The Women of 1928*. Bloomington: Indiana University Press.

Stetz, Margaret D. and Mark Samuels Lasner. 1994. The Yellow Book: *A Centenary Exhibition*. Cambridge, MA: Houghton Library, Harvard University.

Tusan, Michelle Elizabeth. 2005. *Women Making News: Gender and Journalism in Modern Britain*. Urbana and Chicago: University of Illinois Press.

Varty, Anne. 2000. *Eve's Century: a sourcebook of writings on women and journalism, 1895–1918*. London: Routledge.

Wicke, Jennifer. 2001. 'Appreciation, Depreciation: Modernism's Speculative Bubble.' *Modernism/modernity* 8.3: 389–403.

Wood, Alice. 2016. 'Modernism and the Middlebrow in British Women's Magazines, 1916–1930.' *Middlebrow and Gender, 1890–1945*. Ed. Christoph Ehland and Cornelia Wächter. Leiden: Brill Rodopi.

Part I
Locations

LOCATIONS: INTRODUCTION

Faith Binckes

THIS SECTION ADDRESSES women's engagement with the far from straightforward category of 'British' periodicals, in the years from the 1890s to the 1920s. Even discounting events unfolding in the further reaches of the empire, this was an era of dramatic social and political upheaval. To the First World War, the Easter Rising, and the foundation of the Irish Free State, we can add the depression that followed the war, the General Strike of 1926, and the sustained industrial unrest that had preceded it. While 1910 might be remembered as the year of the First Post-Impressionist Exhibition, the Russian Ballet, and of the spectacular Japan-British Exhibition, it was also the beginning of a series of union actions on the part of hard-pressed workers, particularly miners, railway workers, and female factory workers. Suffrage campaigns were organised across Ireland, Scotland, and Wales as well as within England, although positions varied on how to balance women's rights with the drive for self-government and improved working conditions. In higher education, a gradual increase in access to university degrees (rather than simply university-level teaching and examination) was replacing or transforming the network of women-only colleges established in the mid to late nineteenth century. Through visible activism, as well as through subtle and incremental shifts in attitude, women took up a range of positions with regard to questions of gender and nation, in periodicals of equal diversity. Their aesthetic and political agendas operated with a consciousness of the dominant, metropolitan, English publishing field and of the wider cultural scene outside the United Kingdom. They also functioned in combination and in tension with those of male writers, editors, and publishers. The texts and authors represented here, therefore, call attention to the importance of 'location' to British modernism and modernity in different yet related senses. These were women writing in or of a specific place (a publication, a nation), but also women in the process of placing themselves, locating a voice through which they could converse with the past and help to articulate the future. The four contributions examine women's participation in the periodical and print cultures of Ireland, Scotland, and Wales, and interrogate the way in which periodical media produced and marketed a certain sort of 'Englishness' for a female audience.

Margery Palmer McCulloch's discussion of several key Scottish publications, and female authors, pays particular attention to suffrage organisations, but also to the role played by higher education institutions as centres for women's artistic, literary, and political production. McCulloch introduces little-known texts from the Glasgow School of Art, and the Edinburgh University Women's Union. These were by, or for, female students, and have been confined mostly to university archives. All the same, McCulloch makes clear the significance of such small-scale ventures to women emerging into an overwhelmingly male professional sphere. McCulloch surveys these alongside Scottish women's engagements with larger literary magazines and publishing houses, considering the work and correspondence of women such as Catherine Carswell and

Willa Muir. Claire Flay-Petty's reading of Welsh women in periodical texts focuses on short fiction written in the 1920s and early 1930s. Like McCulloch, Flay-Petty indicates the importance of education and of networks forged at university, although educational opportunities for women also emerges as a theme within the work of her key figure, Dorothy Edwards. Flay-Petty notes Edwards's struggles to break into the London periodical scene, going on to explore the ways in which representations of gender and nation were privileged when she appeared in Edgell Rickword's *Calendar of Modern Letters*. These representations differed from the English-language Welsh fiction lionised by the dominant male figures in the Welsh canon, but also subverted the idealisations or misconceptions about Wales in circulation in England. The *Calendar* is known principally for its criticism (its series 'Scrutinies' was the inspiration for F. R. Leavis's *Scrutiny*), yet Edwards's writings – like the work of Mary Butts and Iris Barry, who also appeared – suggest that other interpretations are available, not least through the magazine's interest in myth, identity, and modernity. This could be glimpsed in the very first number of the *Calendar of Modern Letters*, in Robert Graves's poem 'A Letter from Wales.' Graves's startling meditation on memory, loss, and dislocation suggests a relationship with, as well as differences from, Edwards's short fiction about women and Wales. This was equally visible in the short fiction of Edwards's friend and fellow Classicist, Sarah Beryl Jones, a decade later.

Questions of identity and modernity outside the literary sphere drive Elizabeth Tilley's parallel study of two Irish women's periodicals: *To-day's Woman,* published from 1894 to 1896, and *Lady of the House and Domestic Economist*, which ran from 1890 to 1924. Rather than focusing on a single genre, Tilley reads across the 'periodical codes' (Brooker and Thacker 2009: 6) of these composite texts, examining the ways in which they negotiated changing images of Ireland, and of Irish women, while remaining marketable, aspirational, and family-friendly. One of these was the figure of 'Coming Woman' or the 'Higher Woman,' who existed to mediate the by then familiar 'New Woman.' Another was the investment in various forms of reader response, which allowed conflicting opinions to be aired and showed women to be articulate, analytical, and self-aware. Tilley explores the possibilities opened up by the miscellaneous format more generally, observing that it offered women readers 'an extraordinary degree of freedom in terms of the meaning they derived from the magazines' (p. 31) while allowing the smaller field of women's periodicals in Ireland to cater for an expanding range of topics.

Tilley's examination of a broad cross-section of periodical matter is similar to the approach taken by Chris Mourant and Natasha Periyan. Their essay addresses 'how tropes of empire, foreign travel, and racial otherness in Pearson's *Home Notes* and Newnes's *Woman's Life* helped to constitute ideas of "English" female identity' (p. 62). This analysis is bracketed by the writings of Stevie Smith, whose late-modernist novels satirised exactly these discourses, drawing upon Smith's experience of working for Pearson in the early 1920s. Reading the two aspects of this study generates an original perspective both on the magazines, and on Smith's novelistic writing. The edge of Smith's irony is keener for seeing examples, some of which would be hard for a parodist to improve, and others of which pose questions of tone in their own right. More significantly, Smith's double-edged narration helps Mourant and Periyan to access the tensions involved in locating 'home' both with, and against, an array of colonial experiences. The reader can consider the similarities between Tilley's Irish domestic magazines, with their appeals to readers in a diaspora, and *Home Life* and *Home Chat*'s features directed at 'English' women stationed across the globe. We can also make a connection with Kathryn Laing's essay (in Part III of this collection) on the early writings of Rebecca West, and consider women's representations *of* periodicals, as well as their representation *in* periodicals, as an important aspect of their negotiation of the field at this point.

Works Cited

Brooker, Peter and Andrew Thacker. 2009. 'General Introduction' to the *Oxford Critical and Cultural History of Modernist Magazines: Volume 1*. Oxford: Oxford University Press. 1–25.

1

'Watch this space': Late Nineteenth-Century Women's Periodicals in Ireland

Elizabeth Tilley

If a woman wants to be a journalist 'she will have to content herself with a kind of journalism, far enough removed from literature – with the chatty article, or the women's papers, with the *Forget-me-Nots*, the *Home Notes*, the *Nursery Chats* and the hundred-and-one scrappy periodicals which have so successfully hit off the taste of the rising generation, that they bid fair to reduce England once again to a condition of illiteracy.' (*Fortnightly Review* Dec 1897: 928)[1]

What is the particular gap which this strange-sounding new comer is destined to fill? Clearly, not to supply a long-felt want, – for that monster! the New Woman, is but the product of the end of this century.

Only a woman's paper! One with an ideal so elevated as to attempt to cater for woman in her higher development – to provide amusement and instruction for that many-sided individual contemptuously styled 'A Monster!' and anon 'New.' (*To-Day's Woman* 15 Dec 1894: 1)

WOMEN'S MAGAZINES PUBLISHED at the end of the nineteenth century present a rather baffling picture for those interested in trying to determine the intersections of gender and cultural change. The vast majority of these magazines continued to construct gender in traditional ways, but some productions of the 1890s do offer insight into alterations in and contradictory notions of female roles; certainly, the treatment of the New Woman in print has been examined as a barometer of public acceptance of these contradictions. Magazines employ a number of internal codes that establish their difference from other types of text: page layout, typeface, price, the presence of advertisements, a violation of reading conventions, etc. (Brooker and Thacker 2009: 1–23); in the 1890s this difference allowed for the insertion of new conceptualisations of Irish culture for women. Magazines are most often classified as miscellanies, and their periodicity is obviously of the utmost importance. External codes again confirm this difference: the presence of named (or unnamed) financial sponsors or owners, modes of distribution, a strong editorial presence – all of these factors have a bearing on the aesthetic and cultural meaning experienced by readers. As such, the magazine is an excellent vehicle through which a social group might establish its presence, and having done so, might consolidate its position through constant reiteration, with variations, of a central message. It is no accident then that political movements like that of the suffragettes adopted the periodical form as the central platform through which to promote and discuss issues surrounding the call for inclusion. Magazines are public documents in ways that standalone fiction is not, and the ideological shifts and reinventions that occur in the pages of a minority of titles from this period are revelatory. Irish versions of women's periodicals offered readers the virtual space in which their voices might be heard, in which their words would be published, in which they might express themselves as consumers of the 'new.' As domestic products of Ireland, the magazines also created a physical space in which county rivalries could be played out, in which a nationalism specifically aimed at women might be conveyed in an environment that insisted on the country being conceived of as a revitalised economic unit separate from England.

This essay offers readings of two Irish periodicals aimed at women: *To-Day's Woman*, published from 1894 to 1896, and the *Lady of the House and Domestic Economist*, which had a rather longer run, from 1890 to 1924 and later, incorporating various title changes along the way.[2] At first glance the two titles would seem to have a great deal in common. The *Lady of the House* was a commercial vehicle aimed at middle-class urban women and sponsored by Findlater's Stores in Dublin (Strachan and Nally 2012: 108–37). As its subtitle suggested, homemaking (including cooking, household management, gardening, fashion) formed the bulk of each issue, and articles were often tied to goods on offer from its main commercial sponsors. Though obviously geared toward a female audience and employing women writers, its editor was male.

The subtitle of *To-Day's Woman* in 1894 was *A Weekly, Literary, Artistic and Industrial Paper to Further Women's Pursuits* (Figure 1.1). By 1896 this subtitle had become *A Weekly Home and Fashion Journal*, to which the editors had managed to annex the *Ladies' Pioneer of Shopping*. Despite its rather forbidding first title, *To-Day's Woman*, like the *Lady of the House*, included advice on fashion, home management, employing servants, etc. for primarily urban readers. Titles are important, though, and a magazine aimed at women – despite changes in subtitle – is not the same as a magazine aimed at ladies (Beetham 1996). Around the edges of what seemed to present itself as a dominant narrative in *To-Day's Woman* were articles by and about women for whom the traditional had become either unstable or simply no longer applicable. Confusion around nomenclature creates an unclaimed theoretical space and offers the possibility of problematising gender through a symbolic reading of these periodicals.

The masthead of the *Lady of the House* neatly encapsulated its attempt to target the middle-class reader. Stylised palm fronds surrounded a banner that emphasised the figuration of women as 'Ladies,' whose sphere of influence remained firmly grounded in the domestic. As important as this coding was the declaration of the magazine that it was 'conducted,' or rather edited by Crawford Hartnell, a partner in the well-known advertising firm of Wilson, Hartnell & Co., established in Dublin in 1879. As would be expected, then, information on the circulation of the magazine ('guaranteed and vouched by sworn certificate more than double that of any journal in Ireland') was prominently displayed just under the masthead. As Stephanie Rains has pointed out, the *Lady of the House* as a whole gave the appearance of being an extended advertisement for Findlater's Grocers, and the information about circulation formed part of the discourse about coverage and quality that drove all aspects of the magazine, from layout to copy (Rains 2016). In fact, both magazines were encumbered by advertisements of all kinds; they ran along the foot of each page, interrupted columns of text, and occasionally created columns of their own.

The first issue of *To-Day's Woman* appeared just before Christmas 1894, cost one penny, and declared no editor, though it was clearly a Dublin product as its editorial offices were listed as being located at 33 Grafton Street in Dublin. The paper was owned and published by the firm of Sealy, Bryers & Walker,[3] the publishers responsible for the 'New Irish Library' series edited by Charles Gavan Duffy, John Redmond's *Historical and Political Addresses, 1883–1897*, and a host of other nationalist titles.

The dominant discourse in *To-Day's Woman* appeared more straightforward than that of *Lady of the House*; the paper's masthead declared that it would support the serious professionalisation of women's work and cultural endeavours, though very soon after the appearance of the first issues, advertising began to creep around the top of the title page, squeezing the title itself into a smaller space. Bracketing the masthead on three sides, and in a font that jarred with the still dominant free-form wood-engraved 'To-Day's Woman,' advertisements for umbrellas and hunting crops jostled for space with the announcement of a 'recommended servants registry' (that is, advertisements from servants looking for work who could produce recommendations from previous employers). By 1896 the masthead had altered again. The 'T' in the title of the magazine was now formed by a half-page wood engraving of a woman looking into a mirror (the 'O' of *To-Day's*), wearing a variation on an academic gown along with a mortarboard. There could be no better illustration of the attempt of the magazine to create a new public sphere than the imposition of this version of the New Woman on, and around, the confusion of other messages on the masthead.

It appears that *To-Day's Woman* was intended from the first to be a hybrid, as its opening address noted,

> by publishing the writings of eminent specialists, to show that the women of to-day are capable of filling many positions hitherto closed against them, by prejudice, in the fields of literature, art, and industrial pursuits. (15 Dec 1894: 1)

Advice 'to those who desire[d] improvement' but found themselves 'hindered by unfavourable surroundings' was to be an essential part of the mission of the paper (ibid.). All classes were to be catered for: there would be amusement for the young, with the inclusion of serial fiction 'by well-known writers' (ibid.); literary reviews would appeal to the educated young woman; the housekeeper would find much useful information about cookery and the elements of smooth domestic management; even the 'matron's helpers' would be 'stimulated to improvement' by a recommended registry, and prizes for continued service. *To-Day's Woman* would display the qualities of the 'Higher Woman,' the successor of that 'many-sided individual contemptuously styled "A Monster!" and anon "New."'

What seemed to be absent from this manifesto was any mention of the fact that the paper originated in Ireland and was most concerned with the welfare of Irish women; however, this apparent absence was belied by the presence everywhere of advertisements placed by Irish firms for local goods and news items that foregrounded Irish women within a continuingly reconfigured empire. There was a confidence expressed in the pages of the magazine, an understanding that Irish 'difference' was evident and need not be asserted, and that Ireland's own infrastructure and cultural resources would be sufficient to withstand the amount of printed matter flooding the country from England. To a certain extent the inclusion of social news from England and

Figure 1.1 Front cover of *To-Day's Woman: A Weekly Home and Fashion Journal*. September 1896.

Scotland in the pages of both *To-Day's Woman* and the *Lady of the House* made buying English papers superfluous, and news from abroad never overwhelmed the number of items about social goings-on in Ireland.

By the 1890s the idea of the New Woman had become common enough to be parodied, fictionalised, and visualised in the press, though the unsavoury aspects of the label made it risky for a mainstream periodical to declare allegiance to it; the result was the invention of new conceptualisations of women at the end of the century: the 'coming woman,' or the 'higher woman,' as she was called in these magazines, would have all the energy and drive of the New Woman, but none of her frightening aspects: none of the harridan, none of the uncertain sexual orientation. Even the demands for access to previously closed professions (such as medicine and law) to be made available to women were couched in terms of expansion of the fields concerned rather than active competition with men for the few places currently available. Excess energy was channelled into sport, into nationalism, and into the reimagining of women as having both a public and a domestic role, with the attendant demand that she excel at both.

The preferred reader of the *Lady of the House* enjoyed a healthy life, was bold and intelligent, and saw herself as the natural successor to the New Woman:

> We have buried the New Woman after wearing her threadbare – the rents revealing all the pitiful pretenses of her 'made to order' composition. We know her to be a thing of shreds and patches; we dread her no longer. Even on this side of the Channel ridicule kills! Victories, however, often cost us dear; and from the ashes of the New Woman comes forth the twentieth-century girl, the 'Coming Woman,' equipped as never were her sisters for the frantic struggle of increasing competition . . . (15 Mar 1895: 6)

The 'Coming Woman' was then described as often physically superior to man, though the comparison appeared less radical when the author of the article explained that his or her assertion was based on the ability of a woman to stand still for hours at a time for a dress fitting. Nevertheless, physical prowess was taken rather more seriously in the frequent conjunction of statements like these with their physical placement on the page; in this case wrapped around a large photograph of the new 'British Ladies' Football Club,' all shown wearing an approximation of a male football kit.

The transition from 'old' to 'new' was uneasy, as the pages of these magazines indicate (Liggins 2014: 613). The uncertainty regarding audience – or rather the allegiance of that audience – along with the debate over nomenclature was expressed as a certain crowding in layout, content, and advertising (both textual and visual), resulting in the cluttered look of the pages. However, it would be a mistake to expect a modernist aesthetic in what was essentially a nineteenth-century miscellany. The 'new' in both these magazines lay in the juxtaposition of the traditional with the experimental, and the populist with the radical. In comparison with English magazines, there were relatively few Irish titles for women, and consequently a clear necessity for Irish magazines to engage with a wide cross-section of notions about femininity, suffrage, desire, and the emerging consumerism of modern Ireland. The debate over new definitions of gender as a whole (the 'unmanly man' being as unwelcome as the 'unwomanly' woman) was played out in these magazines as a running discussion about the competing demands of consumerism and the place of art, music, and literature in the life of the individual.

Both papers adopted the techniques of the new journalism: a strong editorial presence (despite the anonymity maintained by the editor of *To-Day's Woman*), reader competitions, letters to the editor or to special beauty or homemaking consultants, news interspersed with interviews, along with the heavy use of illustration. The presence of readers was everywhere in these magazines and contrasts rather strangely with the absence of signed articles. In 1895 the *Lady of the House* ran, over a number of months, a feature entitled 'The Women's Parliament: for the Discussion of Debatable Subjects.' The feature was actually a competition, held once monthly, and it asked readers to produce essays of 200 words on such topics as 'Should Ladies make their own dresses,' or 'Is novel reading injurious,' or 'Should married women augment their husbands' incomes?' A selection of essays was reproduced in the month following the question, the number of entries often requiring two pages of miniscule type. The best essay won a prize, usually consumer goods like gloves, dress lengths, or linen; books do not appear to have been offered. As would be expected, Dublin suppliers of the prizes were prominently mentioned, and these firms often took out additional advertisements in the relevant issue of the magazine.

A very large proportion of writers signed their letters with initials, and with no indication of marital status, forcing the editors to record them as 'Miss (or Mrs.)—.' Occasionally aliases were used, and reproduced as such, without comment. The amount of space given over to these competitions reflected a desire to engage the public in discussions of great importance to their lives; the form of the debate as a competition for consumer goods placed that debate squarely within the culture of commerce, and acknowledging the omnipresence of the capitalist enterprise in any move toward modernity. It might be argued that the title of the recurring competition was ironic and the topics discussed trivial. However, there was certainly no parliamentary space for women in reality, and the questions asked by the magazine, and comments made by the participants themselves reveal a highly self-aware, articulate audience, perfectly capable of understanding – and accepting – the conflicting discourses present in the *Lady of the House*.

The Women's Parliament question for February 1895 was 'Is Chivalry Dead?' The familiar 'Dublin vs the rest of the country' debate was as active in the 1890s as it is now, and correspondents complained about the number of winning entries from Co. Dublin, amounting, they said, to clear favouritism. The conductor of the competition wrote indignantly that the majority of entries were from Co. Dublin, so it was hardly surprising that that county had more winners. The slowness of the post from the rest of the country was similarly discounted as the reason behind the low number of winners from outside Dublin, as it was pointed out that no envelopes were opened until the closing date for the competition. Some names appeared more than once as winners, no doubt fuelling the perception that Dublin had unfair access. Most correspondents assumed that the question referred to the 'rise' of the New Woman; Miss L. Holbrook from Celbridge wrote: 'Is chivalry dead? Not quite, though the "New Woman" is doing her utmost to kill it . . .' (15 Mar 1895: 22). Mrs B. Chastel de Boinville, writing from Fethard Rectory in Tipperary noted that 'Chivalry was never meant for "female" men; but must ever remain the gift of a manly man to a womanly woman . . .' (ibid.). Many more letters were received than could be reproduced in the issue, and those whose answers were not printed in full were listed by name instead, again the vast majority from Dublin.

April's question for the Women's Parliament was: 'Should highly-educated girls become domestic helps?' The debate attempted to come to terms with the problem of the 'finished' girl, 'half-way between the old system and the new . . .' (15 Apr 1895: 21) trying to find a way of combining domestic work with a career. The prize for the winning letter was a gold, silver, or ivory-handled umbrella or sunshade, to the value of £2 2s, from the best manufacturer of umbrellas in Ireland. The majority of letters published advocated the education of girls to the highest level, if the girl herself was so inclined, neatly relegating the performance of domestic duties to those whose lack of education, or disinclination for intellectual work, might make them best suited to such tasks.

Both the *Lady of the House* and *To-Day's Woman* engaged in investigative journalism, including sending correspondents to cover stories outside Dublin. In 1895 both magazines reported on the setting up of a woollen mill by the Sisters of Charity in Foxford, Co. Mayo, and the ways in which the enterprise was narrated reflected the central concerns of each. The *Lady of the House* published a two-part feature on the mill, entitled 'A Woman's Work in the Wild West,' in the 15 May 1895 issue. Presented as a special report, the article offered Dubliners a glimpse of a 'primitive' place, 'as shorn of the conventional decencies of civilisation almost as it must have been in the days of the Danes . . .,' a place where apparent apathy and superstition belied the forward-thrusting attitude of the magazine itself: '[I]f you really do wish to step back into bygone centuries . . . and see the most God-forsaken corner of Ireland, take a ticket on the Midland Great Western . . .' So advised, the writer from Dublin descended on Foxford and was introduced to 'Peggy,' recovering from a 'complicated and painful' illness of two and a half months and living in a hovel formed from the side of a hill. When the reporter asked why Peggy refused to take advantage of the relative comforts of the workhouse run by the Sisters of Mercy, she was assured that 'if a woman on the wrong side of eighty passed into the Swinford Union suffering, mind you, from only a "middlin dangerous" complaint, that the exception was when "she didn't lave it in her coffin"' (15 May 1895: 12). The condescension of the writer toward the subject of enquiry was clear; however, between the first and second parts of the report the tone of the piece altered. In the second part the Sisters of Charity were praised for recognising that the apathy of the people was due to the constant state of semi-starvation in which they existed rather than to a general disinclination for work. The article reported that, following the establishment of the mill, Protestant and Catholic worked together and could be found sharing newspapers of opposite political hues after the day's work was done. The high quality of the products turned out by the mill was commented on by English visitors and the writer ended by saying, 'In our industries SHODDY is unknown; every thread is of the purest wool. Let our people demand from the shopkeeper the produce of our factories, and refuse to purchase materials other than Irish goods' (15 June 1895: 11). So an article that began as a voyeuristic, anthropological study of a curious 'backward' community ended with praise for the industry both of the rectress of the community (nicknamed 'Bismarck' by the local priest) and that of her loyal employees, both male and female, as well as a strong call to readers to 'buy local,' thus rejecting the lure of English goods and services. The title of the article suggested that it was intended simply to showcase the efforts of the Sisters of Charity in their attempts to elevate the moral and physical well-being of inhabitants of the west of Ireland. But it is impossible to forget that the magazine was owned and published by Findlater's stores, putting its prime reason for existing squarely in the commercial realm. However, the change in tone of the piece, and the writer's emphasis on the native intelligence of the people of Mayo, indicate the presence of competing discourses within the *Lady of the House*, some of which militated against the relentless figuring of the female reader as consumer (Fraser et al. 2003: 174).

The work of the Sisters of Charity at Foxford was also covered by *To-Day's Woman* in an article entitled 'What a Woman can do' (29 Dec 1894: 9). As the title of the article indicates, the emphasis here was on the entrepreneurial spirit of Rev. Mother Morrogh Bernard (*not* called 'Bismarck' in this version of the story) and the journalist's visit to the factory was announced as arranged by the Irish Industries' Association. Hence the opportunities provided for women and girls to learn trades were highlighted, along with the advantages provided by the Sisters in the establishment of a school which was situated alongside the factory, and to which both boys and girls were invited to attend. There was no use of dialect, and no quaint stories about the peculiarities of the locality. The article was juxtaposed with a letter from a correspondent about a Manchester woollen warehouse, noteworthy due to its employment – and fair treatment of – its mainly female employees. Clearly, the emphasis in *To-Day's Woman* was on the industry of the workers; in the *Lady of the House* product and profit were stressed. But in both the ingenuity and tenacity of the Reverend Mother was praised, and in both the pride expressed in the development of such enterprise in Ireland was strong.

Information about trades unions was conspicuously absent from the pages of the *Lady of the House*. By contrast, *To-Day's Woman* noted with interest the development of women's trades unions in places like Aberdeen, where female carpet weavers had recently set up such an association: 'Already they speak among themselves of the advantages which their position has compared with the unprotected position of the girls in the other branches of the weaving industries' (5 Jan 1895: 5). Economic independence remained a prime concern for *To-Day's Woman*, with the recognition that emancipation would be impossible without it. An article on the workers' strike in Leicester in 1895 scathingly commented on the lack of a union for women affected by the actions of their male colleagues: 'The great Leicester strike inaugurated by the men flings many hundreds of girls out of employment. The strike fund will enable their male fellow workers to live, but the girls have no union. One employer has offered to advance them every week one half their usual wages, trusting to their honesty to repay it, but as they can barely live on full pay, the situation is a sad one' (30 Mar 1895: 16). Articles about the rise of professionalism in trades seen as traditionally female centred on the importance of the working environment; a piece on the opening of new laundries emphasised the benefits to women of working in an open, bright setting rather than in isolation at home. New opportunities for women as managers or overseers of such enterprises kept the focus on work rather than on class, in keeping with the holistic nature of the magazine. Indeed, *To-Day's Woman* seemed always to be aware of the class-based assumptions attaching to whether their readers were denominated 'women' or 'ladies.' 'Women' was an inclusive label; 'lady' was not. A long article on the task of organising workers and the fight for equal access to the universities (entitled 'What Yesterday's Women have done for To-Day's') began with this statement: 'The question of women workers was brought forcibly before us at the meeting of the National Association in Dublin in 1861. After due thought a society was formed for the training and employment of women (ladies they would be called in society) in suitable pursuits, and established as a branch of the London Society' (19 Jan 1895: 10). It was this generation of women the article praised – the ladies whose persuasive power enabled the next generation of women in their search for equality. In fact, the only 'Lady' whose title was offered as a bridge between the old and new was Tennessee Claflin, Lady Cook, the American suffragist whose articles were occasionally included in the pages of *To-Day's Woman*.

Professions for women: teaching, medicine, law, and the assumed affinity of women with managerial occupations, were discussed in both magazines, though *To-Day's Woman* offered more practical comment than did the *Lady of the House*. Nursing as a profession, and the training and reputation of Irish nurses in particular began to occupy a good deal of space in the pages of *To-Day's Woman* toward the end of 1895. The appointment of an Englishwoman to the post of Lady Superintendent in a hospital in Belfast raised strong objections from a number of readers, many of whom were themselves nurses. The slogans of the Home Rule movement were adapted for the occasion: 'Ireland for the Irish!! Home Rule in our hospitals!!' and the voice of a lone reader protesting that the 'best person' for the Belfast job had clearly been chosen was drowned out by letters from others who had felt themselves similarly discriminated against (8 June 1895: 9). The reference to Home Rule is not an accident. As Stephanie Rains has noted, women (and men) saw 'in the Home Rule movement a dramatic widening of their own opportunities for the exercise of power – political, economic, and social' (2014: 32). Emigration was also option; nurses from Scotland and America wrote in to praise the facilities and lifestyle of their adopted countries, recommending emigration for Irishwomen as a way to obtain personal freedom and prosperity. It was the by now familiar practices of the new journalism that facilitated this public debate, personalising both writers and readers and turning an issue about hiring practices into an argument about Ireland versus England and the rise of nationalism.

New journalism signalled the appearance (if not the reality) of a democratic space for women's voices. In an interesting reversal of expectation, admittance to the *To-Day's Woman*, rather than the *Lady of the House* circle of readers was figured as a commercial transaction, the implication being that engagement with issues worked best when combined with a modest financial investment. Potential correspondents were advised that letters would not be answered, nor would entries for competitions be accepted without the addition of a completed coupon from *To-Day's Woman*. This meant that, unlike the *Lady of the House*, *To-Day's Woman* would not accept anonymous contributions from readers, and proof of readership of the magazine itself was required. The result was the formation of at least two kinds of periodical communities: for the *Lady of the House*, this community was based primarily on consumerism, though as the years went on the original impetus for the magazine was masked by its increasing acceptance by a larger section of the female population. The periodical community formed around *To-Day's Woman* was perhaps more precarious, as the declared base audience of this magazine was smaller. However, advertising helped bridge the gap between these communities; that is between the lady and the woman, by appealing to both, and verbal clues helped the reader negotiate the difference between these two categories of reader. Even ostensibly serious articles on women's training and education, like the piece entitled 'Scientific Professions for Women' by Sir Charles A. Cameron,[4] were often accompanied by less than discreet advertisements for various consumer goods placed at the foot of the page. Cameron's lecture on the necessity for women to be admitted to medical schools, for instance, was juxtaposed with his own recommendation of Murray & Son's Pure Liquid Magnesia, an endorsement that was repeated in the same place at the bottom of each succeeding page of the issue, and that pointed to the inescapable character of the magazine as rather clumsily entwining consumerism and intellectual debate (Fraser et al. 2003: 191).

When the first issue of *To-Day's Woman* appeared on the shelves in 1894 it had been noticed by the *Irish Times*: 'This is the title of a new Woman's Paper, published in Dublin. It is a weekly review, literary, artistic, and industrial. It asserts the "rights" of women with marked ability and superiority of intellectual force and skill. Its contents are varied and abundant, and its editing is careful and spirited. It ought to have a rapid success' (14 Dec 1894: 5). The first anniversary issue of *To-Day's Woman* in December of 1895 repeated this praise, but removed the quotation marks around the word 'rights.' The editors also announced that *To-Day's Woman* had recently 'had the honour conferred upon us of becoming the medium of the Woman's Suffrage Movement for Ireland, so that we are catering for an ever-increasing number of classes of women' (14 Dec 1895: 1).[5] Letters from satisfied readers attested to the reach and comprehensive nature of the magazine; testimonials were published from Irish women in England, Scotland, and France, confirming that its Irish character was perceived as a distinctive selling point to the Irish abroad.

In its second year the anonymous editor of *To-Day's Woman* introduced a number of 'improvements' on the original format, noting 'To solve the momentous decision of where to shop and what to buy we are incorporating with *To-Day's Woman*, a Pioneer of Shopping, which will be a complete guide to all the leading shops in Ireland, with a short list of specialities' (ibid.). Though it might be argued that this supplement was akin to the thick Findlater's Directory included with issues of the *Lady of the House*, there does seem to have been an attempt to seriously evaluate the worth of the shops listed as more than one shop was frequently offered as a comparator, and it should be noted that all goods for sale (as in the *Lady of the House*) were of Irish manufacture. Issues published in 1896 followed the current craze for graphology and palmistry with the addition of a regular column on those subjects, and the editor assured readers that articles on fashion and on cookery would continue to join the highly popular 'personal' columns. Notes on temperance were relegated to the back pages of *To-Day's Woman*, but included more than warnings about the evils of drink. A reasoned argument around the shortage of appropriate accommodation for workers and the consequent temptation to take solace in the public house managed to combine calls for improvements in social housing with a rather toned-down version of the usual middle-class moralising found elsewhere.

The relentlessly practical cast of both these magazines meant that fiction, though frequently included, tended to be of rather pedestrian quality, and the foregrounding of Irish authors, or indeed of female authors, seems not to have been a priority for either paper. A cursory survey of issues of *To-Day's Woman* for the first quarter of 1895 reveals some sixteen serial stories, seven of them by women, but only two – Mrs Hungerford (Margaret Wolfe) and L. T. Meade – identifiably Irish. Short sensation fiction filled the pages of the *Lady of the House*: murderers, long-lost lovers, tales told in dialect, were staples. Neither magazine paid great attention to book reviews, though the portrayal in New Woman fiction of male characters as spineless did elicit some comment in *To-Day's Woman*: 'If things have been all wrong for women up to this, which we do not and cannot believe, they will not be set right by women belittling men, ignoring what heroism there is amongst them, or dragging them all down to a level of dull mediocrity' (29 Dec

1894: 14). In reality there was occasional slippage between fiction and advertisement; short tales (one half-page or so) seemed innocuous fillers, until it became clear to the reader that the solution to the problems posed in the narratives was often the application of a proprietary infant food, or the ingestion of Holloway's Pills.

Nevertheless, it is certain that the real 'work' of both magazines was not in such material but was conducted in the features about Ireland: on lady footballers, charity balls, musical evenings, as well as coverage of suffragette lectures and trades union meetings. Or perhaps the reality is that serial fiction was, by this time, being 'explicitly treated as a commercial entity . . . produced as commodities for the mass-market by newspaper proprietors' and was acknowledged as such (Hadjiafxendi and Plunkett 2009: 44). The last page of *To-Day's Woman* often contained personal advertisements, frequently ones offering books and periodicals for sale or exchange. Titles such as *Girls Own Paper*, *Quiver*, and *Ladies Home Journal* were sold in bulk by readers, recent years for 2s each (3s for *Ladies Home Journal*). As an afterthought, one advertisement also offered 'novels, cheap,' as part of the deal, suggesting that the titles of periodicals were a more important selling point than the titles of the novels on offer (12 Jan 1895:18).

Similarly, reviews of theatre performances included mention of the annoyances caused by crude representations of the New Woman on the stages of both Ireland and Scotland. *To-Day's Woman* wrote scathingly of plays on offer in Dublin in the spring of 1896:

> The theatres have given themselves over to farce this week. The 'New Woman' at the Royal; and the 'New Boy' at the Lyceum are causing much mirth to a people who are learning to laugh like their neighbours at the most shallow jokes and weakest of wit. Let us hope that the Scottish scare will re-assert itself ere long, and find something better to laugh at than the exhibition of a would-be new woman who becomes sick through smoking a cigarette! Evidently the real new woman is too complex a character for our present day comedians, who can find no exaggeration of her character more 'new' than a representation of a 'strongminded female' or a 'fast girl of the period.' Try again, Mr. Grundy, by taking a few hints from your mother who hates the new woman because she will no longer be coerced by Mrs. Grundy. Hate is a very good eye-opener; no one knows our good points so well as our enemy. (6 Apr 1895: 6)

Serial fiction was rarely illustrated in either *To-Day's Woman* or the *Lady of the House*; in fact, the visual element of both magazines was primarily reserved for photolithographs of notable professional women, or for local illustrations of women's hockey or tennis matches. The greatest variety of illustration could be found in the size and novelty of the obtrusive fonts used for advertisements, and in the repetition of those advertisements over a number of issues, so that they formed a running commentary on the articles they encircled, making it impossible to ignore the intrusion of the commercial into the cultural. As Brian Maidment has noted, illustrations (and here I am including advertisements as illustrative material) 'mirror and critique the culture that produces them' (2016: 107). Further, the graphic elements of these magazines contributed to what has been called the 'architecture of relationality' of the individual pages, each one establishing a 'pattern and shape' through the juxtaposition of text, white space, and illustration (Spuybroek 2011: 145). For instance, the placement of an advertisement that split a page in half, and whose large font competed for attention with the restrained appearance of the text on either side, forced a complexity of reading that made manifest the dual focus of such magazines: information or education, and consumerism. The meaning of the whole page was dependent on the juxtaposition of its visual characteristics and their informational relationship to each other (Kooistra 2016). In a fascinating appropriation of the space usually sold to advertisers, the editor of *To-Day's Woman* reserved a wide blank strip down the centre of a page in order to prepare readers for something exciting; what that something was was ultimately irrelevant. The space represented the infinite possibilities of the periodical form to create and control desire. Competing messages provided a way in which text and reader might interact, the text recognising and playing on multiple identities present in the woman reader.

It seems clear that toward the end of the century women's magazines became capable of harnessing the competing demands of a consumer culture, chiefly through their miscellaneous nature. Thus, there was no apparent contradiction in the pages of either *To-Day's Woman* or the *Lady of the House* in their construction of women as both producers and consumers of capital. Readers were offered an extraordinary degree of freedom in terms of the meaning they derived from the magazines. Those interested in the progress of the suffragette movement were catered for, as were those who looked for fiction aimed at women, or social news, or domestic help, or the prospect of professional opportunity, or just a good place to buy fabric. Though it is tempting to condemn the *Lady of the House* as conservative and blatantly commercial, and to laud *To-Day's Woman* as an experimental exponent of the new, neither pronouncement is ultimately useful; looking at materiality precludes such broad categorisations and demands a more nuanced understanding of the unclaimed spaces present in both magazines. Changes in composition and form, as well as alterations in content, are indicative of a transitional period in print culture that reflects an equally vibrant opening up of literature in the widest sense. Often visually complex and bewilderingly constructed, these magazines nevertheless form a graphic commentary on the exploding of codes: gender, social, discourse, and studying their materiality is crucial to an understanding of the formation of the modernist impulse. It should also be remembered that both titles were products of a domestic print industry that had, like Ireland's literature, been 'revived.' This too must be seen as part of a new confidence that made pronouncements on other types of 'newness' possible.

Notes

1. The title of this article, by Janet E. Hogarth, is 'The Monstrous Regiment of Women.'
2. See the *Waterloo Directory of Irish Newspapers and Periodicals: 1800–1900*. Available at <http://irish.victorianperiodicals.com/series3/> (last accessed 10 November 2016). Circulation of the *Lady of the House* is given as 20,000 copies per month; no circulation figures are available for *To-Day's Woman*.
3. The offices were located at 94, 95, and 96 Mid-Abbey Street and South Brown Street Dublin (in 1902).
4. Cameron (1830–1921) was a Fellow of the Royal College of Surgeons of Ireland and a public health officer in Dublin.
5. The announcement was not followed by any information about the movement in this issue.

Works Cited

Beetham, Margaret. 1996. *A Magazine of Her Own? Domesticity and Desire in the Women's Magazine, 1800–1914*. London and New York: Routledge.

Brooker, Peter and Andrew Thacker, eds. 2009. *The Oxford Critical and Cultural History of Modernist Magazines, Volume 1: Britain and Ireland, 1880–1955*. Oxford: Oxford University Press.

Fraser, Hilary, Stephanie Green, and Judith Johnston. 2003. *Gender and the Victorian Periodical*. Cambridge: Cambridge University Press.

Hadjiafxendi, Kyriaki and John Plunkett. 2009. 'The Pre-History of the "Little Magazine."' *The Oxford Critical and Cultural History of Modernist Magazines, Volume 1: Britain and Ireland, 1880–1955*. Ed. Peter Brooker and Andrew Thacker. Oxford: Oxford University Press. 33–50.

Kooistra, Lorraine Janzen. 2016. 'Charting Rocks in the Golden Stream: Or, Why Textual Ornaments Matter to Victorian Periodicals Studies.' *Victorian Periodicals Review* 49.3: 375–95.

Liggins, Emma. 2014. 'Not an Ordinary "Ladies' Paper": Work, Motherhood, and Temperance Rhetoric in *The Woman's Signal*, 1894–1899.' *Victorian Periodicals Review* 47.4: 613–30.

Maidment, Brian. 2016. 'Illustration.' *The Routledge Handbook to Nineteenth-Century British Periodicals and Newspapers*. Ed. Andrew King, Alexis Easley, and John Morton. London, New York: Routledge. 102–23.

Rains, Stephanie. 2016. 'Henry Crawford Hartnell.' *Irish Media History*, <http://irishmediahistory.com/tag/henry-crawford-hartnell/> (last accessed 16 November 2016).

Spuybroek, Lars. 2011. *The Sympathy of Things: Ruskin and the Ecology of Design*. Rotterdam: Lars Spuybroek and V2_Publishing.

Strachan, John and Claire Nally. 2012 *Advertising, Literature and Print Culture in Ireland, 1891–1922*. Basingstoke: Palgrave Macmillan.

2

Opening Doors: Women and Print Media in Scotland

Margery Palmer McCulloch

Introduction

INNOVATIVE MAGAZINES FOR a modern female readership and with female contributors were scarce in Scotland in the 1890s and early years of the twentieth century. On the other hand, there was no lack of Scottish women seeking to build lives for themselves in a way that differed from existing social expectations of a woman's role as principally that of wife and mother. This chapter will explore this changing situation and the print media in which it is reflected and which helped to further it first of all through a consideration of developments in the visual arts and the suffrage movement in Scotland in the early years of the century, followed by an exploration of literary contributions by women to print media in the post-1918 period with particular reference to Willa Muir's pamphlet essay *Women: An Inquiry* and *Atalanta's Garland*, a special issue magazine produced by Edinburgh University Women's Union.

The Pre-First World War Period

The visual arts had a strong presence in turn-of-the-century Scotland: in the capital city Edinburgh and especially in Glasgow where the Art School flourished under its Director Francis ('Fra') Newbery. A new School of Art building was designed by Charles Rennie Mackintosh, and built between 1897 and 1909, and Mackintosh himself and former female students such as Frances and Margaret Macdonald, Bessie McNicol, and Jessie M. King exhibited in Europe at the Vienna Secession exhibitions and in other Continental cities. Women as practitioners were therefore strongly represented in this modern Scottish art scene which provided a meeting place and support centre for the exchange of ideas and opportunities among these female artists. They were also contributors to new magazines with a visual arts presence. The *Scottish Art Review*, for example, was published in Glasgow monthly between June 1888 and May 1889, initially at the suggestion of the painters known as the 'Glasgow Boys,' who argued that a journal representing the new ideas would be valuable to them as well as to art lovers generally. However, under its editor James Mavor, the context of this magazine expanded to become a 'monthly illustrated journal of the fine arts, music and literature' (Cumming 2006: 8), and in this form it gave an increasing role to women contributors as creative artists and critics. Another new magazine featuring visual art and literature which gave good space to female contributors was Patrick Geddes' the *Evergreen*, published in

Edinburgh between 1895 and 1896, and reflecting Geddes' interests in the Arts and Crafts Movement and his belief in the possibility of a Celtic Renascence. Women were well represented in poetry and prose contributions, although female illustrators had to give way to the men in that their decorations were limited to headpieces and tailpieces while full-page illustrations were by male artists.

The visual arts magazine of this early period which speaks most strongly of women's aspirations in a changing modern world is titled simply *The Magazine*. Its self-styled 'editress' and its contributors were mostly female students at Glasgow School of Art during the directorship of Fra Newbery and were members of a group which called itself 'The Immortals.' These included the Macdonald sisters Margaret and Frances, together with Charles Rennie Mackintosh, his architectural partner John Keppie and his sister Jessie, his friend Herbert McNair, and students Janet Aitken, Katherine Cameron, and Agnes Raeburn, whose sister Lucy, although studying at the art school for a shorter period than the others, would become the organisational force behind the *Magazine*. 'The Immortals' met regularly at weekends in Dunure, close to the Keppie home in Prestwick, in two cottages rented for the female students by John Keppie and which gained the nickname of 'The Roaring Camp.' This may well have been the place where the idea for the *Magazine* took root.

The first issue appeared in November 1893, with its editorship clearly marked on a flysheet as 'Lucy Raeburn, Her Magazine'; and the ambition of the venture communicated by its description as an 'Artistic and Literary Magazine' (*The Magazine*). A sense of communal involvement and ironic camaraderie as well as her own awareness of editorial responsibility is conveyed by the 'Editress' – as Lucy calls herself – expressing her thanks to 'those who have lent their aid so far, more especially those who helped to pioneer the Literary Department' and her reminder to 'those who have not as yet contributed' to send 'original literary articles, poems, criticisms etc,' while 'reserving the right of selection' (Nov 1893: 3). In the 'artistic section' she calls for 'a front page for next issue, head and tail pieces, sketches, comical or otherwise' (ibid.). Fairy tales were popular publishing items in late nineteenth-century Britain and female artists were frequently employed as illustrators. This trend is displayed in the first issue of the *Magazine*. Lucy Raeburn's sister Agnes contributes 'A Briny Tale,' accompanied by a headpiece illustration and three main illustrations, which transfers a traditional fairy-tale pattern into a story of ocean characters such as Princess Froth, her virtuous suitor Prince Spray, and his rival, the wicked Prince East Wind. Jessie Keppie as author and Janet Aitken as tailpiece artist cooperate in another fairy story of the triumph of good over evil, this time involving more traditional figures such as evil witches, a high-born and beautiful heroine, and a gypsy girl. The editress's call for 'sketches, comical or otherwise' could be seen to be fulfilled by Katharine Cameron's 'From across the Atlantic' which tells an ironic story of technological progress and the wonders of the Far West where 'there is a machine for making sausages/The pigs run in at one end, and come out sausages at the other; but if you do not relish the flavour, just put them in again, and they go through the process within the machine, and come out pigs as they went in'(Nov 1893: 16). And the sketch ends with a tailpiece sketch of three pigs' heads.

This first issue of the *Magazine* communicates the lively experimental nature of the editress and her apprentice contributors, together with their youthful 'mateyness'; and this mood continues in Lucy Raeburn's own contribution 'Round the Studios, October 1893' where she reports on 'what will be forthcoming for the School of Art Show,' an important November item in the Art School Calendar (Nov 1893: 22). Lucy's characteristically provocative but friendly editorial irony is present in her responses to the items to be presented in the show. Her comments are retrospectively significant, however, in that a present-day curatorial comment in the online presentation of the *Magazine* gives the information that Lucy's 'Round the Studios' essay 'offers the only extant evidence of the work shown in the 1893 Glasgow School of Art Club exhibition, a year before the reviews in the Glasgow press of the 1894 show which saw the Glasgow Style first rise to public notice' (ibid.). Lucy's ironic commentary therefore provides evidence that Frances Macdonald in particular was already in the autumn of 1893 designing the 'spook-girl' figures and unusual colour schemes for which she became known, and which would outrage many critics from the mid-1890s onward. These elongated, even ghoulish or witch-like female figures were entirely different from the unthreatening representations of women familiar from Pre-Raphaelite paintings, for example; hence the derisive 'spook' designation given by the press and by many art critics (see also Burkhauser 1990: 85–9).

Both Macdonald sisters impressed Lucy, although her commentary is again wittily double-edged in the way she points to what the public might find troubling in this new work. She writes that 'the brilliant sisters Macdonald have some work which ravished my artistic "soule", by its originality of idea'; then adds: 'tho' perhaps in execution something is to be desired' (Nov 1893: 22). She continues: 'The younger's colour schemes made me ask myself tenderly, "is it possible your eye for harmony is out of tune?" I never could abide crude blues, they always made me think of the wash tub' (ibid.). She finds a stained-glass window design unsettling:

> A very much woe-stricken soul would no doubt feel it's [*sic*] grief embodied in her clever stain-glass window design, 'Despair', representing two figures whose sorrow has worn them to shadows, and whose tears have watered their eyelashes, & made them grow to rather an alarming extent. . . . while 'Reflections' – well on reflection I will not say anything about it; too original for me to get the hang of. (ibid.)

And she ends this review of her first day's visit with the comment: 'I had hoped to do two visits that same day, but "Tempus Fugited" me so quickly in the company of the "sweet girl artists with golden hair" as Tennyson has it, that the conclusion was – late for dinner again. I hope these remarks will be taken for what they are worth' (Nov 1893: 23).

November 1893 was to some extent a playful first attempt at a literary and artistic magazine by its editress and female contributors, although not all later readers would appear to have identified Lucy Raeburn's ironic approach, with Pamela Robertson of the Hunterian Museum and Art Gallery, for example, referring to her 'entertaining, if somewhat patronising' review of the Macdonald sisters in her 'Round the Studios' review (Burkhauser 1990: 109). The issues which followed in April and November 1894 and, with some reservations, Spring 1896 (there would appear to have been no issues in 1895) are more mature. The cover image for April 1894 by Agnes Raeburn features two female figures (classical in derivation as opposed to 'spook-girl'), identical in form but facing away from each other toward their respective cover edges, pouring water from their pitchers on the flowers and trees in the background, the green and yellow colours in the overall composition suggestive of spring. Raeburn also contributes a pen and ink drawing of Shakespeare's Ophelia to accompany Jane Keppie's essay 'Ophelia' which discusses Shakespeare's character not as a weak woman giving in to her unhappy fate, as she was frequently presented, for example in Pre-Raphaelite paintings, but as a woman 'overwhelmed' by the circumstances in which she found herself; and the author ponders what Ophelia might have done had circumstances favoured her (Apr 1894: 15). This issue also contains images of Frances Macdonald's design 'The Crucifixion and the Ascension' intended as a decoration for a church chancel; and of Margaret Macdonald's designs for stained glass 'The Path of Life' and 'Summer,' the latter featuring a male figure symbolising the sun and a female figure representing the growth of plant life, with swallows symbolising summer. As with Frances' 'Crucifixion' design, these designs by Margaret Macdonald, and their early showing in the *Magazine*, were among the works that brought the sisters to wider public attention.

The November 1894 issue reflects the continuing maturity of the contributors' artwork. Frances Macdonald's 'A Pond,' a pencil and watercolour drawing on grey paper, depicts two elongated female figures and strange tadpole-like creatures beneath the waters of a pond in a style that would become characteristic of what became known as the 'Glasgow Style' (Figure 2.1). Margaret Macdonald contributes a pencil and watercolour drawing 'The Fifth of November' with characteristic elongated and weeping female figures. In addition to the work of the Macdonald sisters, this November issue is overall a strong issue artistically with good illustrations by many contributors on a predominant theme of seasonal plant forms and female forms.

No issue of the *Magazine* was published during 1895, and its fourth and final issue appeared with a title-page heading of 'Spring 1896' and a cover design by an anonymous artist consisting of a pencil and watercolour drawing of a garland of spring flowers. Two frontispieces by Janet Aiken and Agnes Raeburn also feature colours and plant forms pointing to spring, with the words 'edited by L. Raeburn' on the first frontispiece (as opposed to the more usual 'Lucy Raeburn Her Magazine'). Lucy Raeburn herself ceased to be a student after 1895, and there is a sense of a loss of coherence in this final issue, despite its many strong design items. There are more male contributors who do not have a connection with the initial 'Immortals' group and who are photographers or caricaturists as opposed to designers. There are also more discursive essays, such as Janet Aitken's 'Is the modern stage elevating?' which argues that the theatre has an educational as well as entertainment role. There is a strong New Woman argument in her essay, especially in relation to the need for change in relation to contrary attitudes to female and male sexual infidelity. Similarly, there is a feminist approach in the anonymous essay 'Silly Ophelia' which returns to the analysis of presentations of the character of Shakespeare's Ophelia begun by Jane Keppie in the April 1894 issue. On the other hand, despite a sense that this final issue could have done with some stronger editing in order to retain the coherence of its established identity, it remains important for the public stage it continued to give to the students' visual art work, and especially to the work of emerging designers such as the Macdonald sisters who collaborate in the final issue with ambitious images for a 'Christmas Story' project.

As Elizabeth Cumming comments in her book on the Arts and Crafts Movement in Scotland, 'these exhibitions within and beyond the [Art] School's gates also gave women platforms for marketing their ideas and skills to manufacturers' (2006: 61). And one could add to 'these exhibitions,' the publicity given by the inclusion of their work in the *Magazine*. Cumming mentions the sisters Agnes and Lucy Raeburn 'who

Figure 2.1 Frances Macdonald, 'A Pond.' The *Magazine*. November 1894.

were key players in the publicity of School work,' and although Lucy herself did not continue with a career in art, her sister became 'a strongly creative graphic artist, producing fashionable, French-style designs for the Glasgow Lecture Association and other local societies' (ibid.). She mentions also that 'poster work was, of course, an obvious spin-off from *Magazine* graphics, and gave their designers a key entry into public art awareness' (ibid.). Margaret and Frances Macdonald, for example, designed posters such as the one for Joseph Wright's umbrella factory in Glasgow titled 'Drooka Umbrella Poster' which was then illustrated in the European Art magazine *Dekorative Kunst* in November 1898. As Cumming's comment about the interaction between *Magazine* graphics, poster work, and other public art work suggests, and as the exploration of other visual art magazines of the time such as the *Evergreen* and *Scottish Art Review* supports, there would appear to have been a subsequent undervaluing – or even an under-noticing – of the contributions by women to Scottish visual art periodicals at this time. This is not the only undervaluing in the Scottish visual art area, however. Fine women painters and designers who emerged from Glasgow School of Art at the turn of the century and the early years of the new century in addition to the Macdonald sisters – including Jessie M. King, Bessie MacNicol (who died in childbirth), Norah Neilson Gray (who painted soldiers and nursing staff when she went to work in the First World War at the Scottish Women's Hospital at the Abbaye de Royaumont in France) and many others – were almost entirely forgotten until Jude Burkhauser's '*Glasgow Girls': Women in Art and Design 1880–1920* (1990) was produced to accompany the Kelvingrove Art Galleries exhibition of the same name. And even then, the Director of the Art Galleries at that time did everything he could to stop the exhibition taking place, his reason being that it would be 'a flop': a surmise that the 20,000 visitors in its initial short run and the clamour for an extended run quickly disproved (*Glasgow Herald* 18 Oct 1990: 1).

Jessie Newbery, the wife of the Director of Glasgow School of Art in this important turn-of-the-century period, was not only a distinctive artist and teacher of embroidery but also a strong supporter of the campaign for female suffrage and an active member of the Women's Social and Political Union. Her encouragement of her students to design and make programme covers and banners for suffrage events therefore links two apparently very different examples of women in print media activities in these early years. Early research and publication on the suffrage movement in Britain focused principally on the movement in the south, and it was only with the publication of books such as Elspeth King's *The Scottish Women's Suffrage Movement,* published in 1978, Leah Leneman's *A Guid Cause: The Women's Suffrage Movement in Scotland* of 1991 and her complementary *The Scottish Suffragettes* of 2000, that the extent of the movement in Scotland was documented. Unfortunately, as King comments, with the exception of the collections in the Glasgow People's Palace (of which she was director at the time of the writing of her book), and the banners in the collections of the Fawcett society, 'few pieces of Scottish suffrage memorabilia survive, and records in archives and libraries are fewer still' (1978: 3). Scottish societies were mostly branches of societies established in the south, such as the Women's Social and Political Union (WSPU), led by the Pankhursts, or became local societies of the National Union of Women's Suffrage Societies (NUWSS), led by Millicent Garrett Fawcett. However, these Scottish societies and branches had considerable autonomy of action, and their activities were publicised and discussed in the various national suffrage publications such as *Common*

Cause (NUWSS) and *Votes for Women* (WSPU), as well as in the Scottish press and suffrage print media. The Women's Freedom League (WFL) was a breakaway movement from the WSPU, established in 1907. It had its own newspaper, the *Vote*, and had a particularly large membership in Scotland. The following discussion will focus on suffrage material by women in Scotland, and in the process hopefully expand awareness of Scottish women's contributions to suffrage periodicals.

An important aid in the publicising and discussion of women's suffrage affairs in Scotland was the establishment in Glasgow in 1906 of the weekly socialist journal *Forward* edited by Tom Johnston. Johnston was a long-time member of both the Fabians and the Independent Labour Party and the company he founded and which published his new socialist newspaper was supported by the Glasgow branch of the Fabian Society. He was also a strong supporter of women's suffrage, publishing himself on this topic as well as giving suffrage contributors good space to develop their arguments in the new *Forward* publication. He introduced a 'Women's Points of View' column in the paper to which suffrage campaigners regularly contributed. The first edition of 13 October 1906 included Teresa Billington's article 'Sex Bars and Prison Bars,' which offered a strong appeal for justice for women, followed in the next issue by an interview with Mrs Pankhurst, who was at that time on a visit to Glasgow. Mary Phillips, a Scottish member of the militant WSPU, wrote a regular column in *Forward*, and on 3 August 1907 contributed 'The Summer Suffragette,' which related to the summer crusades carried out by suffrage groups in Clyde coastal towns such as Rothesay on the Isle of Bute. The catchy title of Phillips's 'Summer Suffragette' was derived from the name given by the Glasgow *Evening Times* newspaper to the activities of Helen Fraser, a former Glasgow School of Art student now campaigning on the Clyde for the suffrage cause. Phillips wrote that the postcards of Miss Fraser and the Votes for Women buttons had sold out, 'whole families investing in them together. "Four buttons, please" was quite a common order' (3 Aug 1907: 7).[1] Other issues of *Forward* discussed the low wages of women homeworkers, with comments that meetings with such women were more a matter of 'gathering in the harvest' rather than 'making converts' (27 July 1907: 2). This readiness of women to join with an organisation founded to work for better rights and conditions for women is given fuller space some years later in the December 1913 issue of *Forward* in an article by Margaret Robertson, 'The South Lanark Struggle: A Rousing Story of a Great Fight.' Robertson talks of her meeting, while canvassing, with a woman who was 'struggling against the hopeless conditions of an insanitary one-roomed dwelling,' and quotes the woman's own words to her: 'We felt we'd nothing to live for. But when you came into the place it seemed all of a sudden different: it seemed as if there was somebody who was working for us' (6 Dec 1913: 1).

A journal whose specific purpose was the campaign for female suffrage was the *Vote*, the organ of The Women's Freedom League, which had been formed in 1907 when Scottish members of the WSPU joined some English colleagues in breaking away from the Pankhurst organisation. The Scottish breakaway movement was led by Eunice Murray who was also a Clydeside suffragette, speaking not only in coastal towns such as Rothesay but also to workers at Clydeside shipyards. Such speeches by women were then reported, often with excerpts, by women writers in the *Vote* and other suffrage journals. In addition to spreading news of the suffrage movement, and in many cases of the conditions working-class women had to suffer, these reports also testified to the capacities of women as speech-writers, public performers, and print-media reporters and essayists. Eunice Murray herself was the daughter of a prominent Glasgow lawyer, educated at St Leonard's School in St Andrews (which seemed to specialise, accidentally, in educating women for the suffrage movement, several leading Scottish activists also having been educated there). In addition to her speaking activities, Eunice Murray wrote regularly to the correspondence pages of the newspapers on suffrage matters. She also wrote a number of suffrage pamphlets with titles such as *The Illogical Sex*, *Prejudices Old and New*, and *Liberal Court*, all of which were published by the Scottish Council of the Women's Freedom League at the price of one penny.

Prejudices Old and New makes it clear from its opening words that 'it is prejudice, not reason, that has delayed the emancipation of women' (Murray 1914: 3). And its author spits out the forms of that prejudice which have prevented women from entering fully into society, including serious forms such as the exclusion of girls 'from good schools and universities' and the 'learned professions,' to the more nonsensical social prejudice 'that declared that a woman must not enter a hansom without a man to accompany her'; or go to a public swimming bath, or bathe in the sea (ibid.). Eunice Murray is certain that education is the critical step toward emancipation: 'Once a person can read and reason, liberty and freedom follow in due course, and the sex disqualification must give way before education' (1914: 5). Murray was writing in 1914, just before the outbreak of the First World War, and therefore had to experience yet another delay in the achievement of female suffrage. It is interesting to note that she was also writing so optimistically at least a decade before Virginia Woolf's lively but ironic feminist essays of the 1920s such as 'Professions for Women,' and 'A Room of One's Own'; essays that suggested that equality for women might still have some way to travel after the acquisition of political freedom.

The Women's Freedom League, to which Murray belonged, did not support the campaigns of violence which eventually developed in the suffrage movement and which were reported in the various suffrage journals as well as in the general press. In a scrapbook in Glasgow's Mitchell Library archives, an advertisement for *Forward* reports that 'on three occasions since the militant agitation began, the writer of the "Women's Point of View" in *Forward* has gone to prison for her principles' (*Scottish Women and the Vote Scrapbook*, 146), while in the *Suffragette* in 1914 Miss Arabella Scott, a regular offender, contributed an article describing her forcible feeding at Perth Prison. 'Holloway Jingles,' a collection of poems by those regularly imprisoned during the campaign of violence (which included many Scottish women) was published by the Glasgow Women's Social and Political Union in 1912 (Figure 2.2). While most suffrage groups, including the Pankhursts' WSPU, ceased their activities during the war, the Glasgow Women's Freedom League continued to campaign for women's suffrage, and Eunice Murray in particular was concerned with women's war work in munitions and factories, together with the danger of such women being expected to return to domestic service and other subservient positions when the men returned from the war. Her pamphlet *Woman – The New Discovery*, also published by the WFL, wrote about the achievements of women in the work they were doing during the war, and the praise they were receiving for this. Such campaigning material, journal articles, and pamphlet writing of women involved in the long struggle for female suffrage – war work of a different kind – made a significant contribution also to print media in this early twentieth-century period and, importantly, demonstrated women's capability for participation in such public roles.

Figure 2.2 *Scottish Women and the Vote Scrapbook*, held at the Mitchell Library, Glasgow.

Women and Print Media in the Post-1918 Period

Developments in Scottish print media in the 1920s were to a significant extent dominated by Hugh MacDiarmid's call for a Scottish literary revival and by the short-lived little magazines in which he argued his case for a new modernist poetry in Scots. Contributors to his magazines, especially of discursive material, were on the whole male supporters of the revival as well as the editor himself in various guises including that of the well-informed 'Isobel Guthrie': a choice of pseudonym that may have indicated his awareness of the comparative lack of female contributors to his magazines. On the other hand, the prominence of poetry in the 1920s as a result of MacDiarmid's own poetry writing and magazine editing did result in increasing publication possibilities for women poets even if they remained in the minority. For example, of the eleven poets in the first issue of the new poetry magazine *Northern Numbers* in 1920 only one was a woman – Violet Jacob, well-established with London publishers as a fiction and historical writer since the 1890s and with three collections of Scots-language poems published in London in 1915, 1918, and 1921. In contrast, by the third issue of *Northern Numbers* in 1922 nine of the twenty poets included were women, including Jacob and the little-known Marion Angus. Angus had recently published poems in the *Scots Pictorial* in July, October, and November 1921, which may have been her first appearance in print media as a poet, thus bringing her to the attention of MacDiarmid. She then appeared in August 1922 in the first issue of *Scottish Chapbook*, the flagship of the Scottish literary revival movement, with her Scots-language poem 'The Lilt.' Her poems were included in further issues of *Scottish Chapbook* in 1923, and from then onward in newspapers such as the *Glasgow Herald* and journals such as the *Scots Pictorial*, *The Scots Magazine*, and *The Scots Observer*. It has not been established when Marion Angus began writing poetry in Scots but the increasing prominence of her poetry in periodical publishing certainly began in the early 1920s when she was in her fifties, and it is as a result of that periodical publishing that she now has a significant place in Scottish literary history. A more traditional poet than MacDiarmid in relation to her use of the Scots language, her poetic scenarios are written from a female perspective while also exploring the tropes of time, memory, and other-worldly states of being found in the modernist period as well as in the enigmatic narratives of the ballad tradition. Angus's poetry also benefited from the establishment of a new publishing venture, The Porpoise Press, started by two Edinburgh University students in 1922. This supported the literary revival through its series of poetry broadsheets, its discursive pamphlets, and some larger works of fiction. Three collections of Angus's poems were published in the 1920s in the Porpoise pamphlet series.

While women prose writers were not absent from print media in the 1920s, their publishing medium was primarily the printed book, most often published in London and a medium which allowed them to explore the lives of women more fully in fictional form as opposed to journal or newspaper article. Women novelists of the 1920s who went on to contribute to print media both in books and other print forms in the 1930s include Dot Allan, whose city novel *Makeshift* (1928) tells the story of a girl from a country background who comes to work as a typist in the city; Nan Shepherd, whose *The Quarry Wood* (1928) is set in the north-east of Scotland, and explores the tensions between a clever farming girl's wish for higher education and her own love of her country environment (a narrative that may well have inspired Lewis Grassic Gibbon's *Sunset*

Song of 1932); and Catherine Carswell, whose Glasgow novels *Open the Door!* (1920) and *The Camomile* (1922) might be seen, in life-writing terms, as exploring in sequence the actual route her life had taken and, in contrast, the route it might have taken had she made different decisions along its road. Carswell also contributed in 1923 the essay 'Proust's Women' to a book of essays on Marcel Proust, while in the pre-1918 years she had acted as literary reviewer for the *Glasgow Herald* but was sacked from this post when she wrote a largely positive review of D. H. Lawrence's *The Rainbow* (1915), a book about to be banned because of its overtly sexual nature.

In relation to a consideration of women's contribution to non-fiction print media in the 1920s, there are two publications which in their different ways bring together themes which characterise the journey of women to self-determination during this historical period and which connect with the activities previously discussed in relation to women in the visual art area and the struggle for female suffrage. These are Willa Muir's extended essay *Women: An Inquiry* (1925) published in the Hogarth Press's pamphlet essay series, and *Atalanta's Garland*, a miscellany specially edited and published by Edinburgh University Women's Club in order to raise funds for the Club. Willa Muir was one of several 'New Women' in Scotland who achieved higher education in the early years of the twentieth century. She graduated from St Andrews University in 1911 with a first-class degree in Classics, followed by further English Literature studies at St Andrews and research in Psychology at Bedford College, London. In 1919 she married Edwin Muir, whose *We Moderns* had just been published in London after serialisation in Orage's *New Age*, and from 1921–4 they travelled in Europe, funded by Edwin's contract to write for the American *Freeman* magazine. *Women: An Inquiry* was Willa's first publication and readers who come to the essay after previously reading her later fine female *Bildungsroman* of 1931, *Imagined Corners*, are often puzzled, if not dismayed, by this essentialist and conservative text. Its inadequacies, on the other hand, bring into focus the debates about a woman's role in society that had been growing in scale since the mid-nineteenth century and were at the heart of the suffrage campaigns. Surprisingly, there is no mention of these campaigns in Muir's *Inquiry*, although its author is reputed to have been on the committee of a Suffrage Society while a student at St Andrews. Its more abstract proposal is 'to find a conception of womanhood as something essentially different from manhood'; and within that conception 'to discover if the division of the human race into men and women involves a division of spiritual as well as of sexual functions, so that the creative work of women is different in kind from the creative work of men' (Muir 1925: 2). From the outset of the investigation, therefore, the question of human individuality per se appears to have been set aside. Yet as Dora Marsden had argued in her *New Freewoman* magazine in the early years of the new century, what is important is human individuality, whether male or female, as opposed to human beings being considered as a class or a sex. And in Marsden's view, the problem women have to face, psychologically and socially, is that they are not seen by themselves or others as individuals, but as a sexual category.

One of the more problematic areas in Willa Muir's essay is the dominant place she gives to the sexual category of mothering as a marker of essential difference between men and women, together with her discussion of the energy resources reserved for childbearing purposes; resources apparently inherent in all women whether they become mothers or not. In *Gender in Scottish History Since 1700*, Eileen Janes Yeo's article 'Medicine, Science and the Body' refers to the biological research carried out by Patrick Geddes and J. Arthur Thomson into the differences between male and female evolutionary development, including this question of female energy reserved for a reproductive role, thus rendering women less able than men to direct energy toward a role in public life. For Geddes and Thomson in their *The Evolution of Sex* (1889), which built on the ideas of Herbert Spencer's *Principles of Biology* (1867), such gender differences in relation to energy are fixed, essentialist. While Muir does not refer to sources for the substantiation of her ideas, she may well have read Geddes and Thomson's theories during her psychology researches at Bedford College in their 1889 publication or in their small book *Sex*, published in 1914 in the Home University Library series. It is surprising, however, to find her subscribing so unquestioningly to them in 1925 and after the debates of the suffrage years in which she as a student took part.

Muir's correspondence of the time shows that her essay was originally presented to prospective publishers in book form before having to be edited down to meet the Hogarth Essay series pamphlet-size requirements. Such cutting may have contributed to the sense of muddled thinking which pervades the essay: the sudden switches to seemingly contrary developments of an argument, the connections left out. It is ironic that having started her enquiry apparently with a motivation to disprove the negative stereotyping of women in a patriarchal society, and to discover the ways in which women's artistic creativity differs from that of men (if it does), the essay ends by endorsing a female role not significantly different from the 'Angel in the House' proposed by John Ruskin in his *Sesame and Lilies* (1865): a woman's intellect not used for her own 'invention or creation, but for sweet ordering,' the making of a 'place of peace' (Ruskin 1986: 118–19); or as Muir expresses it: 'the tradition that woman's place is the home is possibly not entirely determined by the subordinate position of women, but may arise from a sound intuition about the nature of women and their functions. The home is a strategic centre for the creation of human beings' (1925: 24). Unlike Ruskin, Muir does allow women the opportunity to become creative artists but she appears to relegate them to more minor art forms or to performance forms. She writes:

> Certainly the greatest artists of the historical times have been men, and there is no reason to think that the domination of men is even partly responsible for the lack of great women artists. But if women are handicapped in those arts, such as literature, painting, and the composition of music, where the finished product takes a permanent form detached from the human personality of the artist, they should have an advantage in arts like dancing, singing and acting, where the actual personality is the medium of expression. (Muir 1925: 28)

She also suggests that women's weakness in 'form' renders them more successful 'in works of small compass and natural spontaneity, such as lyric poems, rather than in an epic or a long descriptive poem' (ibid.). Unlike Marsden's early 'Bondwomen' and 'Freewomen' arguments, and the arguments of the women campaigning for equality of education, female suffrage, and the possibility of taking up public roles in society, Muir in this essay seems imprisoned in an ideology belonging to a previous age. One possible explanation offers itself in a letter she wrote to a friend shortly after the publication of her essay, apologising for having been out of touch and telling her that she had had 'a bad miscarriage.' She wrote:

> I had no idea that I was pregnant (I thought I had got a chill & when I was sick I thought it was caused by lumbago) and then we were worried by a debt which suddenly cropped up – very worried – and then I had the miscarriage, to my own shock & surprise. No wonder I was brooding over the bearing of children.

And she ends by saying: 'My old essay has fallen very flat. . . . *The Nation* said it was as unexciting as boiled rice. *Time & Tide* has not reviewed it at all! I thought women's societies & associations would have been interested. However – I shall launch bombs next time!' (Muir 1926: n.p.). It is interesting that Muir's correspondence also shows that her miscarried pregnancy had been preceded by attempts to arrange an appointment with a gynaecologist to discover why she had not been able to become pregnant, and these attempts must have been taking place during the period of the writing of her essay in late 1924 to early 1925. While this explanation does to some extent explain her preoccupation with motherhood, it does not entirely excuse the miscarried nature of her essay's argument. In contrast, the liveliness of Willa Muir's correspondence generally, including the letter quoted above with its dramatic 'bombs' ending, together with the imaginative quality of the novels she published in the early 1930s, suggests that, despite her classical education, impersonal, intellectual argument was not her most fruitful medium of communication. Nevertheless, the issues her essay raises about the nature and contribution of women in a modern society were at the centre of social debates of her own time, and are still not irrelevant to ours, as we have seen recently in regard to comments made about the childlessness of the Prime Minister at Westminster and the First Minister of Scotland.

While Willa Muir's *Women: An Inquiry* reminds the reader of the distance still to be covered in these early years of the century in regard to female equality, *Atalanta's Garland*, published one year after Muir's essay, gives proof of the amount that had actually been achieved by women at that time. Published by Edinburgh University Women's Union to celebrate the twenty-first anniversary of its opening and to support the fund established for its extension and improvement, this miscellany of short stories, poems, articles, and reproductions of artworks gives evidence of the achievements of women in various areas of public life. Contributors are both Scottish and from beyond Scotland, and although the majority are women, their achievements and acceptance as equals in public life is reinforced by the support, through their contributions to the magazine, of several prominent male writers, including Hugh MacDiarmid and Edwin Muir. The prefatory note to the magazine, written jointly by its editorial committee, points to their choice of 'the bright, light name of ATALANTA' for their miscellany as paying tribute to 'the frank and fearless youth of this generation of University women' while also suggesting 'the swiftness with which the women graduates of the University, in the few years since full Academic status was accorded them, have won a place for themselves in every branch of the national life, both here and overseas' (1926: vi).

Throughout the magazine there are visual images by outstanding women artists. These include the frontispiece triptych by Phoebe Traquair of Edinburgh, 'Drawing of a Child' by Dorothy Johnstone from Aberdeen, the painting 'Under the Apple Tree' by Bessie MacNicol, considered the most outstanding painter in the group who studied at Glasgow School of Art at the turn of the century. Other Glasgow artists represented include Cecile Walton, Jessie M. King, and Katharine Cameron who had been one of the 'Immortals' contributing to Lucy Raeburn's *Magazine*. The photograph of a bust of Dr Elsie Inglis by the sculptor Ivan Meštrović reminds readers of the hospital staffed by women she established in Croatia during the First World War, as does the discursive article 'In the Path of the Pioneer Medical Woman' which celebrates the several women, including Inglis, who pioneered female entry to the medical profession. Creative writing by prominent women from outside Scotland includes Virginia Woolf's enigmatic prose piece 'A Woman's College from Outside' (uncollected until *Books and Portraits* in 1977), accompanied by a fine portrait photograph of Woolf in evening dress; and two unpublished and unfinished sketches of French children by Katherine Mansfield. These sketches, contributed to the magazine by Middleton Murry, were later published by him in *The Scrapbook of Katherine Mansfield* (1939) and corrected versions were recently republished in Volume 2 of the *Edinburgh Edition of the Collected Works of Katherine Mansfield* (2012). Their first appearance, however, as with Virginia Woolf's essay, was in the celebratory *Atalanta's Garland*. Contributions to the miscellany also included poems in Scots by Marion Angus and Violet Jacob, and one in English by Charlotte Mew, while the inclusion of short stories in French, German, Italian, Spanish, and English consciously pointed to increasing European relationships after the disaster of the First World War.

Atalanta's Garland, like the playful *Magazine* of the turn-of-the-century art students and the innovatory reporting activities of the Summer Suffragettes during the campaigns for female suffrage, is a fine example of print media's capacity to capture the adventurous spirit of a movement or a period in time. In contrast, that same print media can remind us of the distance that still has to be travelled as is found in Willa Muir's uncertainties in her *Women: An Inquiry* essay and the reminders of the hostile treatment of women protesters in the suffrage years. And in relation to the Scottish context of this present essay, it is hoped that the evidence uncovered in the print media of the past will assist in bringing to an end what has to a large extent been a hidden history of Scotland's women, allowing that history to interact with our present consciousness as we move into the future, thus becoming a motivating part of Scotland's story as a whole.

Note

1. Interested researchers can consult the *Scottish Women and the Vote Scrapbook*, at Mitchell Library, Glasgow, which contains many extracts from *Forward*, otherwise only available on microfiche.

Works Cited

Allan, Dot. 1928. *Makeshift*. London: Andrew Melrose.
Atalanta's Garland. 1926. Edinburgh: Edinburgh University Women's Union.
Burkhauser, Jude, ed. 1990. *'Glasgow Girls': Women in Art and Design 1880–1920*. Edinburgh: Canongate Publishing.

Carswell, Catherine. [1920] 1986. *Open the Door!* London: Virago.
—. [1922] 1987. *The Camomile.* London: Virago.
—. 1923. 'Proust's Women.' *Marcel Proust: An English Tribute.* Ed. C. K. Moncrieff. London: Chatto & Windus. 66–77.
Cumming, Elizabeth. 2006. *Hand, Heart and Soul: The Arts and Crafts Movement in Scotland.* Edinburgh: Birlinn.
Geddes, Patrick and J. Arthur Thomson. 1889. *The Evolution of Sex.* London: W. Scott.
—. 1914. *Sex.* London: Williams and Norgate.
Holloway Jingles. 1912. Glasgow: Glasgow Women's Social and Political Union.
King, Elspeth. [1978] 1980. *The Scottish Women's Suffrage Movement 1902–1933.* Wakefield: Microform Academic Publishers.
Leneman, Leah. 1991. *A Guid Cause: The Women's Suffrage Movement in Scotland.* Aberdeen: Aberdeen University Press.
—. 2000. *The Scottish Suffragettes.* Edinburgh: National Museums of Scotland.
The Magazine. Glasgow School of Art Collections and Archive, 2011, <http://gsathemagazine.net/> (last accessed 19 June 2018).
Muir, Willa. 1925. *Women: An Inquiry.* London: Hogarth Press.
—. [1926] Letter to Florence McNeill, 26 January. National Library of Scotland, Papers of Florence M. McNeill, Acc. 26194, 98.
Murray, Eunice G. 1914. *Prejudices Old and New.* Edinburgh and Glasgow: Scottish Council of the Women's Freedom League.
—. [n.d.] *Woman – The New Discovery.* Edinburgh and Glasgow: Scottish Council of the Women's Freedom League.
Ruskin, John. [1865] 1986. 'Sesame and Lilies.' *Culture and Society in Britain 1850–1890.* Ed. J. M. Golby. Oxford: Oxford University Press. 118–22.
Scottish Women and the Vote Scrapbook, Mitchell Library, Glasgow, f324.623094111/SCO.
Shepherd, Nan. [1928] 1987. *The Quarry Wood.* Edinburgh: Canongate Classics.
Yeo, Eileen Janes. 2006. 'Medicine, Science and the Body.' *Gender in Scottish History Since 1700.* Ed. Lynn Abrams, Eleanor Gordon, Deborah Simonton, and Eileen Janes Yeo. Edinburgh: Edinburgh University Press. 140–69.

3

Marginal Places, Liminal Spaces: Welsh Women's Modernist Writing and the English 'Little Magazine'

Claire Flay-Petty

In a letter to her university friend S. Beryl Jones, Welsh short-story writer Dorothy Edwards (1902–34) wrote: '*London Mercury, Criterion, Adelphi, Calendar*, I have had the honour to be rejected by all of them.'[1] Edwards's words here are characteristically self-deprecating: soon afterward, the *Calendar of Modern Letters* published three of her short stories, making her one of only a handful of women to grace its pages.[2] But Edwards's statement is also telling regarding the English-medium periodical culture of Wales in the early part of the twentieth century: though Welsh-medium publications were numerous and multifarious, and the English-medium liberal miscellany equally so, it was the 'little magazines' of London that offered a platform for experimental, English-medium writing from Wales (Ballin 2013).

Born in 1902 in Ogmore Vale, a small mining community in South Wales, Dorothy Edwards was a member of the generation that saw a significant decline in the percentage of Welsh speakers in Wales (Stephens 1998: 772). As well as the impact on the language of immigration from other areas of the United Kingdom into Wales during the Industrial Revolution, a deliberate anti-Welsh language education strategy saw Welsh-speaking parents refrain in increasing numbers from passing their native tongue on to their children. During the first quarter of the nineteenth century 80 per cent of the population was Welsh speaking; by 1901, this figure had dropped to 50 per cent (ibid.). As a non-Welsh speaker Edwards, like many of her contemporaries, was excluded from the vibrant Welsh-language magazine culture of the early twentieth century, where such publications as *Cymru* (1891–1927), *Baner ac Amserau Cymru* (1859–1992) and *Y Llenor* (1922–55) flourished.[3] Women played an active role in contributing to this thriving scene, where magazines such as *Y Gymraes* (literal translation: *The Welsh Woman*) (1896–1934) and *Y Frythones* (literal translation: *The British Woman*) (1879–91) were established and edited by women, for women, and focused on specifically Welsh issues including the temperance movement and the campaign for female suffrage in Wales (Stephens 1998: 255, 303).

English-medium publications at this time were also plentiful, but tended to be political and cultural, rather than literary, in nature. The complexities of industrial boom and bust, language politics, and the legacy of Wales's (now widely acknowledged) colonial relationship with England resulted in an English-language periodical culture dominated by political and cultural tensions as opposed to literary experimentalism. The *Welsh*

Outlook (1914–33), funded by industrialist David Davies, is a prime example of an English-medium Welsh journal that concerned itself with the politics, language, and culture of Wales in an international context (Stephens 1998: 775). Malcolm Ballin notes of *Wales: The National Magazine for the Welsh People* (1911–14), that:

> like its predecessors among Welsh periodicals in English, [it] only rarely gives a nod to the existence of an avant-garde. It concentrates on relaying traditional Welsh materials relating to well-established topics that it judges will be of interest – especially to a diasporic audience. (2013: 57)

It was not until the late 1930s, with the publication of *Wales* (1937) and the *Welsh Review* (1939) that English-medium writers from Wales had access to home-grown journals that provided a platform for literary experimentalism. Chris Hopkins notes that both magazines 'envisaged a mode of creative expression which gave them stylistic membership of an artistic metropolitan avant-garde' (2009: 715). But a class directive was intertwined in their literary purpose, and as a result the ideologies of both magazines privileged Welsh *industrial* fiction. In the first issue of *Wales* its editor Keidrych Rhys sets out a sort of manifesto for the magazine, stating: 'Welsh literature is carried on, not by a clique of moneyed dilettantes, but by the small shopkeepers, the blacksmiths, the non-conformist ministers, by the miners, quarrymen and the railwaymen' (Hopkins 2009: 720). Indeed, Tony Brown has suggested that there is something about the short story that makes it particularly suited to working-class writers in a manner akin to its appeal to women writers suggested by Nicole Ward Jouve: that is, both circumstantial and ideological.[4] Brown notes that most Welsh short-story writers of the 1930s wrote around full-time jobs and other commitments, and therefore the brevity of the form – what H. E. Bates termed the 'spare-time exponent,' was key (Brown 2001: 25–41; Bates 1941: 8). But in noting the privilege that was perceived to be characteristic of the English literary avant-garde in favour of a more authentic working-class Welsh experience in a way that aligns with gendered theories of the short story, Rhys's statement ironically still serves to prioritise the male. Women were of course merely the wives, daughters, and sisters of the shopkeepers, ministers, and miners to whom *Wales* sought to give a voice.

Though established to serve the working-class Welshman in a manner akin to *Wales*, the *Welsh Review* played a significant role in publishing work by women – though of course, having not been established until 1939, it falls outside the scope of this volume. Short stories from Margiad Evans, Sian Evans, Dorothy Morse Brown, Kate Roberts (in translation); words and woodcuts from Brenda Chamberlain; poetry from Lynette Roberts; essays by S. Beryl Jones and Winifred Kelly; numerous reviews from Alice Rees Jones: a reappraisal in the context of their original publication would add value to the role of magazines in publishing work from women in Wales in the 1930s and 1940s.[5]

Though, as Hopkins argues, the editorial statements featured in the *Welsh Review* were more restrained than those found amongst the pages of *Wales*, the editor and founder of the former, Gwyn Jones certainly shared Rhys's distaste for the 'moneyed dilettantes' of the English modernist literary scene. A contemporary of Edwards's who attended Cardiff University a few years after her, it is evident that Jones saw Edwards's more experimental approach as suspect, perhaps even as a betrayal of her industrial heritage. His summary description of her career, which appeared in his history of Cardiff University, stated that

> [she] published a volume of short stories [. . .] and a mildly experimental novel [. . .] which were sufficiently notable to gain her an *entrée* into off-Bloomsbury literary society. (Jones and Quinn 1983: 146)[6]

Although the title of Jones's study was *Fountains of Praise: University College, Cardiff 1883–1983*, 'faint praise' seems more appropriate in this particular case. What Jones fails to acknowledge is that, writing through the medium of English in 1920s Wales, Edwards faced a particular challenge in placing her work. In her Welsh-medium essay on Edwards and contemporary Welsh-language short-story writer Kate Roberts, Katie Gramich notes that, in this vacuum, such writers had little choice to publish their work in English literary magazines (1995: 83–4). Writing about his own attempts to publish his short stories in the early 1930s, another fellow Cardiff graduate Glyn Jones pointed out that '[t]here was no Anglo-Welsh magazine in existence then [i.e. prior to 1937]' (1968: 31). Instead, Jones published short stories in Seumas O'Sullivan's *Dublin Magazine* in 1931, and in H. E. Bates's *New Stories* in 1934–6 (ibid.). The London 'little magazine,' then, played a significant role in filling the gap left by the English-medium liberal miscellany and the Welsh-language literary periodical scene, as demonstrated by the literary career of Dorothy Edwards.

The first of Edwards's short stories to appear in Edgell Rickword's influential but short-lived periodical *Calendar of Modern Letters* was 'A Country House.' Published in Volume 1, no. 6 (Aug 1925) alongside work from Aldous Huxley, Bertram Higgins, and Rickword himself, Edwards is the only female contributor in this issue. This is reflective of the gender imbalance of this publication in general, although the *Calendar* published the work of some key women writers of the period, including Iris Barry, Stella Benson, Mary Butts, Kay Boyle, Laura Riding, and Beatrix Holms. Vernon Lee's essay 'Right Readers and Wrong Readers' appeared in July 1925, the year of her death. This critical neglect can partially be attributed to the fact that their work tended to be creative, while the *Calendar*'s reputation was built on, and was later consolidated by, its critical writing.[7] It is worth noting that Edwards participated in this genre too, although not in the magazine itself. In 1928, she contributed a short study of G. K. Chesterton to Rickword's edited essay collection *Scrutinies*, a series that emerged from the often-acerbic literary reviews that were published in the pages of the *Calendar* (Edwards 1928: 29–40). A modernist with an eye for talent, Rickword was quick to recognise Edwards's potential, and two further stories of hers, 'The Conquered' and 'Summer-time,' appeared in the *Calendar* soon afterwards.[8] Though her collection of short stories was published by Wishart in 1927, archival material shows that Edwards originally had a contract for this volume with The Calendar Press.[9] Her novel *Winter Sonata* appeared, along with her Chesterton piece, in 1928.

The *Calendar*, it seems, was especially suited to the experimental, almost ethereal quality of Edwards's work. David Ayers argues that the *Calendar*, like its contemporaries the *Criterion* and the *Adelphi*, 'were platforms from which the arts could test their purpose' (1999: 107). Indeed, Edwards did just that, producing short stories, as Gwyn Jones suggested above, that were not always recognisably Welsh in terms of setting, character, or focus. Instead, her work is carefully crafted to challenge and undermine the unequal power structures that underpinned contemporary discourses of gender, class, and nation.

Raised by socialist parents in industrial South Wales, Edwards won a scholarship to the independent Howell's School for Girls in Cardiff 1916, before taking her BA in Greek and Philosophy at Cardiff University (then the University College of South Wales and Monmouthshire) in 1920–4. It is worth noting here that Edwards's experience of higher education in Wales would have been quite different to that of her contemporaries in England: indeed, historians have long acknowledged Wales's egalitarian approach to higher education.[10] The University of Wales's 1884 Charter granted equality of admission to female students (and, incidentally, in terms of class); it opened its first university hostel for women in Cardiff in 1885 (and only the second in Britain), and appointed Britain's first female professor, Millicent Mackenzie, in 1904 (Beddoe 2001: 29). By the 1920s, this environment played host to a network of female students and academics with working-class backgrounds, many of whom were living outside the confines of convention both in their careers and in their personal lives. Archival evidence shows that Edwards and her contemporaries were actively engaged in college life both as students and as full academic staff members on a par with their male peers.[11]

Unsurprisingly then, the opportunities for and impact of education on girls is a recurrent, though understated, theme in her earliest stories. 'A Country House' is also the boldest in terms of its criticism of both class privilege and patriarchy. In his measured and polite address to an implied sympathetic reader, Edwards's male narrator reveals his tyrannical domination of his young wife as he describes the joy he takes in destroying anything that brings her pleasure. He relishes her 'cry of horror' on discovering that he has ordered her favourite, wild part of the garden to be cut back:

> A place must be tidy. There were bulrushes and water-lilies as it was. What more must she have? A lot of weeds dripping down into the water! There is a difference between garden flowers and weeds. If you want weeds, then do not have gardens. And I suppose I am insensible to beauty because I keep the place cut and trimmed. Nonsense! Suppose my wife took off her clothes and ran about the garden like a bacchante! Perhaps I should like it very much, but I should shut her up in her room all the same. (Edwards 2007: 34–5)

Edwards's use of myth here is significant: in highlighting the owner's perception of his wife as a wild, impetuous force akin to the followers of Bacchus, she also demonstrates her extensive knowledge of Greek myth gained while studying at Cardiff under classics lecturer Kathleen Freeman (1897–1959) (Deininger and Flay-Petty 2017: 42).[12] Freeman, herself a graduate of Cardiff and only five years older than Edwards, taught at Cardiff for almost thirty years. She began writing and publishing short stories around the same time as Edwards, which shifted the dynamic between the two from student/teacher to literary rivals.

But for the narrator's wife, it seems, marriage was the only option. A 'mere child' when they married, 'with black ringlets down her back and big blue eyes' (Edwards 2007: 32), the narrator overhears her confiding to houseguest Richardson, an electrician staying with the couple to oversee the installation of their new electrical generator. She says: 'Before I was married I stayed with my music master in London. He had two sons but no daughters. His wife was very fond of me. That was the happiest time of my life' (Edwards 2007: 47).

In 'The Conquered,' a story as interesting for its criticism of imperialism as of gender roles, Edwards comments on the limited opportunities available to women in a patriarchal, capitalist society. The young male narrator of the story, Frederick Trenier, has returned to the Welsh border country to visit his aunt and his two female cousins, Ruth and Jessica. Frederick makes it clear that there are far more important things that he would like to be doing: 'I must say I went there simply as a duty [. . .] I took plenty of books down so that it should not be a waste of time,' he says (Edwards 2007: 45). He considers himself to be an experienced and accomplished young man, culturally superior to his cousins, and he expects to find the place dull and restrictive: after doing his 'duty' he intends to move on quickly to his 'proper' holiday (ibid.). Frederick indicates his comparative worldliness in a naïvely arrogant manner, failing to acknowledge the fact that, as a young man, he has far more avenues of opportunity open to him than his female contemporaries: '[Ruth] remembered far more about what we used to do than I did; but I suppose that is only natural, since she had been there all the time in between, and I do not suppose anything very exciting had happened to her, whereas I have been nearly everywhere' (Edwards 2007: 46).

Similarly, in 'Summer-time,' the contrast between the plans of the two young people, Basil and Leonora, serves to emphasise the lack of opportunity, or choice, open to young women. Though ostensibly focused on the bumbling, middle-aged Mr Laurel's visit to the home of a family friend, it is the young host Leonora and her cousin Basil who are the focus of the narrative. Both are just out of school and are filled with an enchanting youthful exuberance that captivates Laurel. Basil has decided to be a dancer, but Leonora appears to have no particular ambition. Her mother, Mrs Chalen, asks Laurel's advice on Leonora's future:

> [Mrs Chalen] 'I don't know what to let her do.'
> 'Has she any particular talents?' he [Laurel] asked.
> 'None that I know anything about,' said her mother, looking at
> Leonora severely.
> [. . .] 'I think she should go to an art school,' he said to her mother.
> 'Do you really think so?' said she. 'Can you paint, dear?'
> 'I don't know,' said Leonora.
> 'Oh, that doesn't matter,' said Mr Laurel, smiling at her. 'Some artist will marry her because he wants to paint her hair, and they will live happily ever afterwards.'
> 'Yes,' said Leonora, with innocent approval.
> 'You really think so?' said her mother, smiling a little doubtfully.
> 'Undoubtedly,' said Mr Laurel.
> And thus her fate was decided, for sure enough she has gone to an art school.
> (Edwards 2007: 99)

The inappropriate and socially regressive nature of the comment is evident in the mouth of one of Edwards's archetypal pompous men. Laurel's humiliation at the end of the story on his sudden and fleeting realisation of the inappropriate nature of his behaviour toward the various women he has encountered is presented as just punishment. Basil's choice of a career that could potentially be considered to undermine his masculinity is all the more significant given that it goes unchallenged by those around him – while Basil is given the respect and autonomy to choose his own path, Leonora's must be carefully chosen for her in order to achieve the objective of her existence – marriage.

I have argued elsewhere that Edwards's use of the male narrative voice is unusual; indeed, when read in the broader context of modernist British women's writing, it is a technique that is as rare as it is powerful. In her essay 'Ventriloquising the Male: Two Portraits of the Artist as a Young Man by May Sinclair and Edith Wharton,' Diana Wallace argues that a woman writer using a male narrative voice 'exposes masculinity as constructed and contingent, thus undermining its traditionally universalised and normative status,' an act which 'destabilizes the primacy of the male voice as a norm, precisely because it reveals it not only as a construction but moreover as constructed by a woman' (2002: 327). The inclusion of these three stories in the *Calendar*, which presented itself in many ways as a robustly masculine mouthpiece, is significant. Indeed, a re-evaluation of all of the female-authored contributions to the *Calendar* listed above would be an illuminating exercise, particularly in the modernist context of the literary magazine.

Recent research carried out by me and Michelle Deininger on Edwards and her peers for our forthcoming volume *Scholarship and Sisterhood: Women, Writing and Higher Education*, however, has revealed that Edwards was not the only one of her Cardiff peer group of women writers to make use of a male narrative voice.[13] Indeed, Deininger has shown that Freeman was also writing and publishing short stories that featured a male narrative voice at the same time as Edwards, and to similar effect (2013: 121). More recently, I have also discovered that Edwards's close friend S. Beryl Jones published a short story with a first-person male narrator, entitled 'The Woman at the Well,' in H. E. Bates's literary magazine *New Stories* in 1935.[14]

Sarah Beryl Jones was born on 8 April 1900 in Pontypridd, and raised in Resolven, where her father was a mining engineer: like the Edwards family, the Joneses would have occupied a relatively middle-class position in an area where the majority of its inhabitants were manual labourers.[15] Jones, like Edwards, attended Howell's School for Girls, before gaining a BA in Latin and Philosophy and an MA in Philosophy at Cardiff University in the early 1920s, where she struck up a friendship with Edwards and Winifred Kelly. Dissatisfaction with the political climate (Jones was a communist) led her to abandon a DPhil at Oxford, before taking up a teaching post in Keighley, Yorkshire, in around 1926.[16] Kelly joined Jones in Keighley for a period in the late 1920s – they were, by this point, a couple – before going to Newnham College, Oxford,[17] and eventually taking up a lecturing post at Aberystwtyh. A former pupil of Jones's whom she taught in the 1940s, recalls that Jones 'liked to be controversial': it seems that Jones made no bones about either her sexual or political orientation.[18]

During this time, it seems that Jones's Yorkshire home provided a haven for Edwards to escape her increasingly strained home life, where she found it difficult to write. 'I should most certainly never have finished the novel – if I had not finished it there,' she wrote to Jones in 1927 of her novel *Winter Sonata* which is, appropriately, dedicated 'To S. B. J. and W. K.'[19] Edwards's suicide in 1934 undoubtedly had an impact on Jones, who had witnessed Edwards's ongoing struggle with her mental health since the mid-1920s. Jones defended Edwards's literary legacy for the rest of her life: she contributed a valuable essay, 'Dorothy Edwards as a writer of short stories,' to the *Welsh Review* in 1948, and even campaigned feminist press Virago to commission a new introduction to their 1986 editions of *Rhapsody* and *Winter Sonata*, for she felt strongly that Elaine Morgan's introductions to the volumes were misinformed and lacking in criticality.[20]

'The Woman at the Well' appeared in *New Stories* in 1935: true to my statement earlier that the English 'little magazines' were a key platform for Welsh writers, this edition also features a story from Jones's countryman Glyn Jones.[21] The story is narrated by Mr Fawcett, who is taking a holiday in a village bordering a coal mining community in Wales (presumably the south), where he lodges with a couple who have recently moved to the area from rural England. During a walk in the woodland surrounding his lodgings, Fawcett discovers the remains of an old well, and attempts to repair it. Like Edwards, Jones draws on her knowledge of classical myth in her allusion to the woodland-inhabiting nymphs, the dryads. Fawcett muses:

> Perhaps I should catch a dryad. They must have fled mourning from one wood after another as the landowners sold more and more timber with their taste for luxuries growing and coal not enough to pay for them, though it was being steadily drained from the deep black veins of the land. And these dry seams were the old forests buried and shrunk and hardened. Where had their nymphs gone? (Feb–Mar 1935: 70–1)

Fawcett's handiwork is met with outrage from two local women whose families had used the well as a healing-place for several generations. The older of the pair, Mrs Huws, who has struggled through the woods to bathe in its waters despite age and infirmity, chastises Fawcett:

> 'What are you doing then?' she asked in a soft Welsh voice, looking at my tools in consternation.
> Feeling somehow guilty, I said I was mending the walls.
> 'Ffynnon Gwala was all right with broken walls,' she answered, peering about her, curious and resentful under her ill-poised hat. Her companion had come up and was exclaiming and moaning as she walked round the walls and looked at the water flowing away to lose itself in the tangled grass.
> 'It's a bad bad thing you've been doing,' the woman went on. 'Haven't you any respect for tradition?'
> 'I'm sorry,' I said. 'I don't understand, I found this stonework falling to pieces and I've mended it. That's all. I don't see that I've anything wicked or disrespectful.'
> 'Nothing wicked or disrespectful indeed,' she said, drawing in her colourless lips with anger and outraged feeling. 'Don't you know what this place is indeed?'
> 'No,' I said. 'I don't.'
> 'And do you always go meddling with things you don't understand, I suppose? . . . here you come with your yellow hair and English ideas about tidying up the Welsh woods. But there's a dear lot you know nothing at all about, you and all these English people with your interfering ways.' (Feb–Mar 1935: 73–4)

Despite a growing storm, old Mrs Huws remains determined to bathe regardless of the weather or the company, and begins to remove her clothing. Fawcett, feeling rather awkward but able to recognise the woman's determination and faith, comes to her aid (Fawcett demonstrates a level of emotional awareness not found in Edwards's male narrators). Following her bath Mrs Huws falls ill, and Fawcett takes her to his lodgings (wheeling her, unceremoniously, in the trolley he had used to carry building materials to the well) and puts her in the care of his hostess, Mrs Jameson. Despite her lack of empathy for the local people and her scepticism for their superstitious ways, Mrs Jameson nurses Mrs Huws tenderly. She even goes so far as to bring the elderly lady water from her precious well to aid her recovery.

The impact of industrialisation is a key thread in the story, which aligns Jones's piece with her male Welsh short-story writers in a way that Edwards's work does not. Toward the end of his stay Fawcett describes his visit to a nearby coalmine:

> [T]he scene underground really seemed to come back as a barbaric offensive in the earth, with the picks and the shovels and the lights and the horse-drawn trams thundering behind like war chariots. Several times too I'd seen the colliers pouring home; first the boys headlong down precipitous short-cuts with a rattle of tin and tea-jack; then the young men in a thick irregular column pushing each other and singing, and last the few tired veterans each walking solitary with a bundle of stakes held firmly under his arm. It was no wonder after all that those with the country in their bones found it hard to understand these fire getters. (Feb–Mar 1935: 79)

Jones is undermining her narrator here: she would be well-aware that the 'fire-getters' would have originally flooded into the mining communities from the very country areas he describes, driven out by poverty and poor conditions on the promise of earning a living wage. Fawcett's empathy is superficial: it becomes clear that he lacks a deep understanding of the area, and this is underlined in the final scene of the story.

On the penultimate day of Fawcett's holiday he shares a picnic with Mrs Jameson and the much-improved Mrs Huws at Ffynnon Gwala. They talk about Mrs Huws's reaction to Fawcett's handiwork on Ffynnon Gwala on their first encounter:

> 'My word, you were angry with me that day, Mrs Huws!' . . .
> 'Yes,' she said slowly. 'I was angry, Mr Fawcett *bach*. But when I looked at you, I knew I'd seen you before somewhere.'
> 'Seen me before?' I said, surprised. 'But you hadn't, had you?'
> 'It was like this,' she said. 'I had a dream in which a man with fair hair and a fair beard like yours baptised me. So when I looked at you at last and saw you standing beside the water in that funny yellow light, I knew it was to be.' (Feb–Mar 1935: 80)

Fawcett's subsequent action seems all the more disrespectful in the light of the Mrs Huws's faith in the healing powers of the well and the acceptance that she has shown Fawcett despite his interference. He muses:

> 'I wondered what they would say if they knew that at that very moment possibly some of the water of this well was being analysed in the Birmingham laboratory to which I'd sent it. But all I said was:
> 'Look, there's a spectrum in the milk jug!'. . . (ibid.)

He reveals himself as the coloniser – the rational, scientifically minded man who basks in the respect of the forgiving old lady while simultaneously undermining her right to her faith, which is rooted in her heritage. He, like the colliers, has 'taken from the land,' but has done so surreptitiously and with intent to destabilise, rather than out of necessity.

Both Edwards and Jones, then, published short stories in English literary journals that made fascinating use of male narrative voices to undermine and criticise unequal distributions of power. Both were women who had benefited from a tradition of accessible higher education in their home country, where they could meet like-minded young women and, unlike many of their counterparts in wider Britain, benefit from a university education on a platform comparable with that of their male peers. Susan Leonardi, in her work on six women writers who attended Somerville College, Oxford, between 1912 and 1922, points out of her subjects: '[t]hey were not experimenters in form: for the most part they wrote novels which incorporate the romantic plot, that idealized the lives of women' (1989: 5). The same cannot be said of Dorothy Edwards, S. Beryl Jones, and their peers, whose writing was as unconventional as their lifestyle choices. That said, these women still ultimately had to function in a patriarchal, capitalist society and, while Beryl Jones reconciled herself to operating, albeit somewhat radically, within the fabric of society, Edwards's suicide at the age of thirty-one suggests that she could not.

At the time of her death in 1934, Edwards had been working on a newly commissioned volume of short stories: two of these, 'The Problem of Life' and 'Mutiny,' were published posthumously in *Life and Letters To-day*, another magazine that published a significant amount of work from Wales.[22] Indeed, *Life and Letters To-day* under the editorship of Robert Herring not only showcased the work of many new short-story writers from Wales in the 1930s, but even published regular St David's Day editions dedicated to Welsh writers.[23] But it was *after* Edwards's death that the short story truly began to flourish in Wales and, with the establishment of *Wales* and the *Welsh Review*, Welsh short-story writers finally had access to a home-grown platform for their work. As Gwyn Jones noted in his editorial to the first edition of the *Welsh Review*, the magazine owes its existence to 'the emergence during the 1930's [sic] of a considerable number of new writers of ability' (Hopkins 2009: 717). In his survey, H. E. Bates is quick to acknowledge the innovative nature of Welsh short-story writing: 'Towards Wales [. . .] the English short story may perhaps begin to look for a new influence,' he says (1941: 8). Indeed, his inclusion of S. Beryl Jones, Glyn Jones, and Dylan Thomas amongst the pages of his *New Stories* in the mid-1930s evidences this. Tony Brown, drawing on Clare Hanson's theories regarding the appeal of the form to marginalised writers, argues:

> Not only has Wales been for centuries geographically but (more importantly) politically and culturally away from the centers of power – especially London – but the Welsh writer in English is of course doubly marginalized. He or she is not English, not writing in the English literary tradition (though he or she will of course be very aware of that tradition, and writing within earshot of it). But the chances are that he or she will not be Welsh-speaking; aware of the rich and continuing cultural heritage in the Welsh language, he or she will be shut out from it. (2001: 26)

Perhaps it is more than a little ironic that it was the 'little magazines' of the cultural centre that gave voice to Welsh writers like Dorothy Edwards, S. Beryl Jones, and others, to articulate their specifically Welsh experiences through their literary experimentalism.

Notes

1. Dorothy Edwards, letter to S. Beryl Jones, n.d. [c. 1926]. Dorothy Edwards Collection, Reading University Library, MS 5085, packet 5, item 2. Hereafter referred to as 'Dorothy Edwards Collection.'
2. 'A Country House,' 'The Conquered,' and 'Summer-time' appeared in *The Calendar of Modern Letters* between 1925 and 1927. See Rickword and Garman 1966a: 436–48; and Rickword and Garman 1966b: 1–11, 216–25.
3. Edwards learned some Welsh as an adult. Dorothy Edwards, letter to S. Beryl Jones and Winifred Kelly, 2 December [c. 1928–33]. Dorothy Edwards Collection, packet 5, item 21.
4. '[G]enerally speaking, the time of the writing of the short story is easier to adjust to the time of living. If you are a busy woman (man, sometimes), continuously interrupted by household or career duties, then the shorter span of the story will accommodate that fragmentation better' (Ward Jouve 1989: 35–6).
5. *The Welsh Review* Feb–Nov 1939; Mar 1944–Dec 1948; Cardiff University, Special Collections.
6. The *Welsh Review* regularly published reviews and essays by S. Beryl Jones and Winifred Kelly during 1945–8, including Jones's appreciative literary essay on Edwards's work in 1948, some fourteen years after Edwards's death.
7. For instance, John Lucas did not discuss the *Calendar*'s creative content, or its female contributors, in Lucas 2009. Jason Harding's earlier chapter on the *Calendar*, also titled 'Standards of Criticism,' explores its position in relation to T. S. Eliot's *Criterion*. See Harding 2009.
8. In 1926 'A Country House' was included in Edward J. O'Brien's *The Best Short Stories*, alongside work by Aldous Huxley and D. H. Lawrence. See O'Brien 1926.
9. See the contract between Dorothy Edwards and The Calendar Press for a collection of ten stories, dated 20 December 1926. The contract is signed by E. E. Wishart, director of the Calendar Press. The collection, however, was eventually published by Wishart, London. Dorothy Edwards Collection, packet 12. Letters of the time suggest that Rickword played a role in securing Edwards's contract. Dorothy Edwards, letter to S. Beryl Jones, n.d. [c. 1926]. Dorothy Edwards Collection, packet 5, item 5.
10. See, for example, Beddoe 2001.
11. See *Cap & Gown: The Magazine of the University College of South Wales and Monmouthshire*. 1920–6. Cardiff University, Special Collections.
12. Alongside her academic career, Freeman sustained a successful career as a writer both under her own name, and of commercially successful detective fiction under the pseudonym Mary Fitt. See Stephens 1998: 254.
13. Michelle Deininger and Claire Flay-Petty, *Scholarship and Sisterhood: Women, Writing and Higher Education* (Cardiff: University of Wales Press, forthcoming).
14. Glyn Jones notes that *New Stories* (1934–6) was established by H. E. Bates to offer a platform to short-story writers (1968: 35). *New Stories* has disappeared into obscurity, so much so that it goes unmentioned in Peter Brooker and Andrew Thacker's comprehensive *The Oxford Critical and Cultural History of Modernist Magazines: Volume 1, Britain and Ireland 1880–1955* (2009).

15. Newspaper article on S. Beryl Jones, *Keighley News*, 6 Nov 1960. Courtesy of David Kirkley, Keighley Schools Heritage.
16. Dorothy Edwards, letter to S. Beryl Jones, n.d. [c. 1926]. Dorothy Edwards Collection, packet 5, item 5. I am grateful to Emrys Evans for this information.
17. I am grateful to Anna Teicher for this information.
18. Freda Matthews, email to Claire Flay-Petty, 12 April 2018.
19. Dorothy Edwards, letter to S. Beryl Jones, n.d. [c. 1927–8]. Dorothy Edwards Collection, packet 5, item 24.
20. S. Beryl Jones, letter to Virago, September 1986. Dorothy Edwards Collection, packet 11, item 1.
21. *New Stories* Feb–Mar 1935: 70–80. All further references will be in parentheses in the text.
22. Dorothy Edwards, 'The Problem of Life,' *Life and Letters To-day* 1934: 662–76, and 'Mutiny,' *Life and Letters To-day* 1934: 325–46.
23. Hopkins (2009) notes that *Life and Letters To-day* was advertised in almost every pre-war issue of *Wales* and the *Welsh Review*.

Works Cited

Ayers, David. 1999. *English Literature of the 1920s*. Edinburgh: Edinburgh University Press.
Ballin, Malcolm. 2013. *Welsh Periodicals in English 1882–2012*. Cardiff: University of Wales Press.
Bates, H. E. 1941. *The Modern Short Story: A Critical Survey*. London: Thomas Nelson.
Beddoe, Deirdre. 2001. *Out of the Shadows: A History of Women in Twentieth-century Wales*. Cardiff: University of Wales Press.
Brown, Tony. 2001. 'The Ex-centric Voice: The English-language Short Story in Wales.' *North American Journal of Welsh Studies* 1.1: 25–41.
Cap & Gown: The Magazine of the University College of South Wales and Monmouthshire. 1920–6. Cardiff University, Special Collections.
Deininger, Michelle. 'Short Fiction by Women from Wales: A Neglected Tradition.' Dissertation, Cardiff University, 2013.
Deininger, Michelle and Claire Flay-Petty. 2017. 'The Cash Box and the Specimen Tin: Women's Literary Networks.' *Planet* 226: 39–45.
Dorothy Edwards Collection, Reading University Library, MS 5085.
Edwards, Dorothy. [1927] 2007. *Rhapsody*. Cardigan: Parthian.
—. 1928. 'G. K. Chesterton.' *Scrutinies*. Ed. Edgell Rickword. London: Wishart. 29–40.
—. [1928] 1986. *Winter Sonata*. London: Virago.
Flay, Claire. 2011. *Dorothy Edwards*. Cardiff: University of Wales Press.
Gramich, Katie. 1995. 'Gorchfygwyr a Chwiorydd: Storiau Nyrion Dorothy Edwards a Kate Roberts yn y Dauddegau.' *Diffinio Dwy Lenyddiaeth Cymru*. Ed. M. Wynn Thomas. Cardiff: University of Wales Press. 80–95.
Harding, Jason. 2009. 'The Idea of a Literary Review: T. S. Eliot and *The Criterion*.' *The Oxford Critical and Cultural History of Modernist Magazines: Volume 1, Britain and Ireland 1880–1955*. Ed. Peter Brooker and Andrew Thacker. Oxford: Oxford University Press. 346–63.
Hopkins, Chris. 2009. '*Wales* (1937–9), *The Welsh Review* (1939–40).' *The Oxford Critical and Cultural History of Modernist Magazines: Volume 1, Britain and Ireland 1880–1955*. Ed. Peter Brooker and Andrew Thacker. Oxford: Oxford University Press. 714–34.
Jones, Glyn. 1968. *The Dragon Has Two Tongues*. London: Dent.
Jones, Gwyn and Michael Quinn, eds. 1983. *Fountains of Praise: University College, Cardiff 1883–1983*. Cardiff: University College Cardiff Press.

Leonardi, Susan J. 1989. *Dangerous by Degrees: Women at Oxford and the Somerville College Novelists*. New Brunswick, NJ: Rutgers University Press.

Lucas, John. 2009. 'Standards of Criticism: *The Calendar of Modern Letters* (1925–7).' *The Oxford Critical and Cultural History of Modernist Magazines: Volume 1, Britain and Ireland 1880–1955*. Ed. Peter Brooker and Andrew Thacker. Oxford: Oxford University Press. 389–404.

O'Brien, Edward J., ed. 1926. *The Best Short Stories of 1926*. London: Jonathan Cape.

Rickword, Edgell and Douglas Garman, eds. 1966a. *The Calendar of Modern Letters March 1925–July 1927, Volume I March 1925–August 1925*. London: Frank Cass.

—. 1966b. *The Calendar of Modern Letters March 1925–July 1927, Volumes 3 and 4 April 1926–July 1927*. London: Frank Cass.

Stephens, Meic. 1998. *The New Companion to the Literature of Wales*. Cardiff: University of Wales Press.

Wallace, Diana. 2002. 'Ventriloquising the Male: Two Portraits of the Artist as a Young Man by May Sinclair and Edith Wharton.' *Men and Masculinities* 4.4: 322–33.

Ward Jouve, Nicole. 1989. 'Too Short for a Book?' *Re-reading the Short Story*. Ed. Clare Hanson. London: Macmillan. 34–44.

4

Home and Homeland: English National Identity in the Women's Magazines of Newnes and Pearson

Chris Mourant and Natasha Periyan

THE LATE MODERNIST WRITER Stevie Smith's first book was shaped by her experience working from 1923 as a secretary to Sir Neville Pearson at the magazine publishers Newnes-Pearson. *Novel on Yellow Paper*, published in 1936, was supposedly written on the yellow paper provided at the firm. Together with its sequel, *Over the Frontier* (1938), the novel is narrated by Pompey Casmilus, who lives in a north London suburb and works as a private secretary to the magazine publisher Sir Phoebus Ullwater. Defying the conventions of chronological, linear plot, *Novel on Yellow Paper* is instead structured by the rhythmic repetitions of Pompey's roving consciousness. Toward the beginning of the book, Pompey issues this 'word of warning' to her reader: 'This is a foot-off-the-ground novel [. . .] And if you are a foot-on-the-ground person, this book will be for you a desert of weariness and exasperation. So put it down. Leave it alone' (Smith 1980: 39). The readership Smith expects for her novel is highlighted by contrast through Pompey's reflections upon 'our so-very-much-alike women's papers' that cater to a 'public which won't stand for highbrow nonsense,' 'the public on whom we rely to buy and read our twopenny weeklies' (1980: 192, 47, 114). Pompey clarifies:

> These are girls who believe everything our contributors tell them. They put a spot of scent behind the ear, they encourage their young men to talk about football, they are Good Listeners, they are Good Pals, they are Feminine, they Let him Know they Sew their own Frocks, they sometimes even go so far as to Pay Attention To Personal Hygiene. (Smith 1980: 115)

Smith here parodies the formulaic titles of articles in women's magazines giving advice to the reader about marriage and expected gender roles. Elsewhere, the novel incorporates the language used 'in our correspondence columns to all the girls who don't have young men' (Smith 1980: 111); describes the familiar 'Fiction for the Married Woman' published in these magazines (115), as well as 'the stories for unmarried girls, the ones that are so cleverly and coyly oh' (117); and satirises 'this advertisement-land full of easy rhymes' (156) and '*chic* balloon conversations' between women: 'My dear, how can we tell that nice Mrs Snooks? Why she still washes her face the old way. Won't anybody tell her she'll never get a partner while she talks about El Greco?' (88).

Smith's novel responds to the revolution in print pioneered by the publishing barons George Newnes, Arthur Pearson, and Alfred Harmsworth from the late nineteenth century. As Margaret Beetham has argued, the most significant journalistic development for women writers and readers in the 1890s was the publication of cheap 'penny domestic' magazines aimed at women (1996: 190). By the 1910s, women's magazines had become the leading market force, a dominance that continued throughout the rest of the twentieth century. Harmsworth was the first of the three publishers to realise the potential of mass-produced women's magazines, founding *Forget-Me-Not* in 1891 and then *Home Sweet Home* in 1893. The following year, in January 1894, Pearson released his own domestic women's magazine, *Home Notes*, the success of which in turn provoked competition from Harmsworth's *Home Chat* and Newnes's *Woman's Life*, both founded in 1895. Smith includes a veiled reference to *Home Chat* in her novel when Pompey describes a painting by Walter Sickert: 'Well perhaps it is called *Home Chat*, I forget' (1980: 113). While *Home Chat* has received sustained critical attention from scholars such as Beetham, however, the importance of *Home Notes* and *Woman's Life* in this period has often been overlooked, despite their evident popularity: figures cited by Richard Altick demonstrate that the circulation of *Woman's Life* was 200,000 in 1896, and in 1911 the magazine was still considered 'widely popular' (Altick 1963: 396; Friederichs 1911: 132). Newnes's mass-market publications provided a model of success for Pearson, who had begun his career as a journalist after he won a competition to work on Newnes's magazine *Tit-Bits* in 1884. In 1890, Pearson broke away from Newnes to establish his own company. These two rival publishing houses eventually merged in 1914, with *Woman's Life* and *Home Notes* enjoying astonishing longevity before each was incorporated into the magazine *Woman's Own* in 1934 and 1958 respectively.

This chapter examines how *Home Notes* and *Woman's Life* promoted ideals of domestic femininity in this period in tandem with notions of 'English' national identity. Smith's *Novel on Yellow Paper* prompts a consideration of this connection between Englishness and the gender politics of the 'home' in the women's magazines published by Newnes and Pearson. In satirising the plot of romance fictions published in such women's magazines, Pompey draws attention to the celebration of 'home' when ventriloquising a protagonist thinking about 'my lovely Home, my lovely Tommy, my lovely husband' (Smith 1980: 117). Elsewhere, she ironically imagines 'an average Englishman' declaring: 'We're just simple *English* folk, like you and me, fond of home and not a bit *clever*' (Smith 1980: 20). While Smith's book frustrates the 'foot-on-the-ground' person's want of an easily comprehensible, linear plot, *Novel on Yellow Paper* is nonetheless animated by the choice Pompey makes between her English fiancé Freddy and the German student Karl. Through her conversations with Karl, Pompey ruminates on what constitutes Englishness; and through her travels to Germany at a time when Nazism is on the rise, she also considers the connection between nationalism and the 'cruelty and viciousness' of racial prejudice (Smith 1980: 77). As we argue in this chapter, the women's magazines published by Newnes and Pearson consistently appealed to an imagined foreign or racial 'other' as a means of constituting ideals of English domestic femininity. In exploring this aspect of magazine culture, this chapter extends the work of critics such as Beetham, who has explored issues of race and imperialism as they were mediated through the 'agony aunt' columns of *Woman at Home*, another popular magazine of the period (1998: 223–33). We examine how tropes of empire, foreign travel, and racial otherness in Pearson's *Home Notes* and Newnes's *Woman's Life* helped to constitute ideas of 'English' female identity. The intimacy of the magazines' conversational discourses creates a register that blends the advisory, the exhortatory, and the inquisitive as editors and contributors counsel their women readers in how to negotiate aspects of English feminine identity through the lens of foreign cultures and traditions.

Neither *Home Notes* nor *Woman's Life* had a named editor, operating under the editorial anonymity that Kate Jackson has identified as a characteristic feature of the nineteenth-century periodical press (2001: 13). Readers of *Home Notes*, however, were familiar with the editor of the magazine as 'Isobel,' the pseudonym employed by K. Maud Bennett. In an article printed in *Pearson's Magazine* in 1896, titled 'Leading Lady Journalists,' we learn that Bennett was the sister-in-law of Arthur Pearson, who had 'recognised in her the qualities which make for success in the direction of a paper' (July 1896: 103). Noting that 'the good editor is born and not made,' the author of this article observes that Bennett's complete lack of 'journalistic experience' was compensated for by the fact that 'she thoroughly understood domestic economy, using the words in their fullest sense' (ibid.). Indeed, as suggested by its title, *Home Notes* was a magazine that focused almost exclusively on domesticity, providing practical advice on a range of issues relating to the home, including dressmaking, etiquette, cookery, and nursing, and often responding directly to enquiries sent to the editor by readers. The remarkable success of this 'charmingly bright little weekly' resulted in a wide-ranging series of other titles published by Pearson and edited by 'Isobel,' including *Home Cookery*, *Vegetarian Cookery*, *Household Hints*, *Dressmaking at Home*, and *Fashions for Children*, making Bennett 'one of the very busiest women on the London Press' (ibid.).

While almost always published in the metropolitan centre of London, as Beetham has observed, weekly and monthly women's magazines in the late nineteenth century often enjoyed an international distribution to colonies across the British Empire (1998: 224). In *Home Notes*, this wide-ranging readership is highlighted in an early campaign that ran in the magazine called the 'Fresh Air Fund,' which raised money to provide outings to the countryside for city children. In September 1895, Bennett reported to her readers of the support that the campaign had received from 'our compatriots scattered throughout the world. From India, China, South Africa, Australia, and I think I may safely say from every other country where there are English settlers and emigrants, we have received kind words of encouragement' (21 Sep 1895: 354). Indeed, in 1898, Bennett writes proudly that *Home Notes* 'may be found all the world over wherever the English tongue is spoken' (15 Jan 1898: 6). The magazine was addressed to this 'English' readership. At a time when it was common for those living in the colonies of the British Empire to speak of England as 'home,' *Home Notes* reiterated a link between the domestic space of the 'home' and the English nation, pointing to the role that women could play in both spheres. In an article titled 'How To Help Rural England,' for example, Bennett writes: 'I have spoken before of women's influence in the home, let me point out her influence in the home-land' (15 Jan 1898: 1). Moreover, the link between the domestic 'home' and the 'homeland' of empire was foregrounded in the cover image to every issue of *Home Notes* in its first years; invariably depicting a mother and child seated by a hearth, these illustrations were always accompanied by the motto: 'The hand that rocks the cradle rules the world.'

Woman's Life underscored the same link between a woman's role at 'home' and her position within the structures of empire. While not carrying 'home' in its title, early issues of *Woman's Life* had the subtitle 'An Illustrated Weekly for the Home' and the magazine explicitly grounded itself in discourses of domestic femininity. Indeed, during the First World War, the magazine appeared under the title *Woman's Life & Home Journal*. Like *Home Notes*, *Woman's Life* also occasionally made mention of readers who had written in from the colonies, as in one instance which reads: 'Amongst the letters in my post-bag this week is a delightful one from Mrs. M. S. W., who writes from Victoria, Australia' (14 Jan 1905: 44). In articles focusing on issues of domestic life, in particular, the editor of *Woman's Life* drew attention to colonial women as part of the magazine's implied readership. In the first issue of the magazine, for example, the column 'Dress Advice Bureau' suggested that 'Indian or Colonial outfits, &c., will also be given in this column if desired' (14 Dec 1895: 45). In later issues of *Woman's Life*, the cookery column also explicitly incorporated colonial perspectives. In an article printed in 1915, for example, a letter from a reader in New Zealand that enclosed 'some simple recipes' to be included in the magazine carried particular currency for the editors, they tell us, due to '[t]he amazing dash and courage of the New Zealand and Australian soldiers in the Dardenelles' which 'has filled those of us who live "at home" with unbounded admiration and given us a keen desire to know more of our kindred across the seas' (16 Oct 1915: 109). As in *Home Notes*, therefore, *Woman's Life* established England as 'home' to those women living across the British Empire. As is suggested by 'Recipes from A New Zealand Reader,' interest in the lives of colonial women became more acute in *Woman's Life* with the onset of the First World War. In 1915, the magazine circulated 'A New Badge of Patriotism' which was designed to 'commemorate the unity of the British Empire in the greatest war in history' and included 'emblematical figures representing Canada, Australia, India, South Africa, as well as the United Kingdom' (11 Sep 1915: 598). As such, through the 'patriotism' of empire, different national identities were aligned. In this context, *Woman's Life* emphasised unity and sameness, drawing attention to similarities in the domestic lives of women across the British Empire, at the same time as it focused on the inevitable national differences arising between those women living 'at home' and those abroad. In the article on 'Recipes from A New Zealand Reader,' for example, it is noted that 'the culinary methods of the wives and mothers of these brave men [in New Zealand and Australia] differ from our own very little, and serve to emphasise how thoroughly British they are in every way' (16 Oct 1915: 109). In an interesting slippage between 'British' and 'English' identity, the article goes on to note that only 'fish dishes [. . .] constitute the main difference between an English dinner and one in New Zealand' (ibid.). The New Zealand reader is both incorporated into 'British' identity, therefore, and implicitly excluded from 'our' English dinner table. This simultaneous sameness and difference is rendered in recipe titles that are both familiar and exotic to English tastes, such as 'Stafflin Pudding,' 'Tasmanian Pudding,' 'Pineapple Cake,' 'Melon Jam,' and 'Wagga Wagga Pudding' (ibid.).

Home Notes also emphasised how domestic life for 'English' women was the same all over the globe and suggested how women could adapt 'English' customs to new surroundings, yet it also revelled in celebrating Englishness against cultural difference and the foreign 'other.' In a series of articles printed in 1895 on 'Housekeeping in Many Lands,' for example, the magazine profiled domestic life in countries as various as Jamaica, China, Japan, France, Peru, and the Australian bush. In each case, life abroad is both familiar and strange. Elsewhere, short items of curiosity pivot on the difference between life 'at home' and abroad, such as one titled 'How the Arabs Make Tea': '[t]his is distinctly not a recipe that you will care to try at your next "At Home," but still, it will no doubt interest you to know how the fragrant beverage is used in an Arab's tent'; and another which informs the English reader 'How to Fight a Serpent': 'as lovers of *Home Notes* are to be found in all quarters of the globe, the information here given may be of practical use to many, while to others it will be interesting' (7 May 1898: 137, 150). This appetite for information from abroad was also satisfied by the regular publication of articles by tourists and interviews with travellers. In 1898, at the same time as *Home Notes* began a 'Special New Feature' titled 'Tourist Notes' that continued for several years, for instance, Bennett serialised interviews with 'Famous Lady Travellers.' In one interview, a woman describes how she went on 'fishing expeditions' in Africa wearing a 'serge skirt and a cotton blouse – the British woman's uniform!' and laments the fact that the African tribes were not 'affectionate domestically' (16 Apr 1898: 6). In another, Korea is described as 'a country still almost mediaeval in its aspirations and its mode of living. The people are childishly curious, almost unpleasantly so for strangers, and the women are so ugly' (23 Apr 1898: 51). In each case, travel serves to highlight the familiar and 'pleasant' attributes of English domestic femininity, with the foreign 'other' infantilised or depicted as uncultivated and backward by contrast.

The purpose of these interviews with 'Famous Lady Travellers' is suggested by an advertorial for a new Pearson's publication titled *The Rapid Review* that was printed in *Home Notes* in 1904. In this piece, a comparison is made between the publication space of the periodical and the social space of the 'women's club,' which affords 'such excellent opportunity for women to keep in touch with one another': 'The stay-at-home woman meets the woman who has travelled; the woman who is fond of reading meets the woman who writes, and so on. All of which is very desirable, but is not always possible' (4 Feb 1904: 232). Like the *Rapid Review*, *Home Notes* looked to fulfil this desire for socialisation between women. Not only did *Home Notes* print a series that profiled contemporary 'Lady Novelists,' such as Edna Lyall and Violet Hunt, for example, but its interviews with 'Famous Lady Travellers' also enabled the 'stay-at-home woman' to meet 'the woman who has travelled.' In this way, the magazine sought to put the woman 'at home' in contact with the rest of the world.

The 'Famous Lady Travellers' series in Pearson's *Home Notes* suggests a class-inflected distinction between the 'lady' and 'woman' traveller at this time, with travel often conceptualised as the preserve of the upper-middle classes. As Jackson has observed, Newnes also published periodicals that 'catered to various different reading communities' and the way in which foreign travel was negotiated in Newnes's *Ladies' Field* and *Woman's Life* demonstrates how each cultivated different, class-informed models of femininity (2001: 18). In *Ladies' Field*, with a regular Travel Bureau column in the magazine's 1905 issues, it was assumed that readers enjoyed the financial means to travel. By contrast, while early editions of *Woman's Life* carried a series of articles on 'How Women May Earn A Living' that contained occasional reference to the prospect of foreign travel, it was not until the 1920s that issues of the magazine alluded to the possibility of their reader travelling for leisure. A July 1925 issue of *Woman's Life* carried an article titled 'Holidays are Here,' which helped its reader to negotiate foreign climes and cultures, highlighting both similarities: '[w]hen taking rooms, fix the terms very clearly and definitely beforehand. Foreigners know just as much about extras as the seaside landlady!'; and differences: '[t]he Channel is cold, and the Continental trains much hotter than ours' (4 July 1925: 6). While the January 1925 issue of *Ladies' Field* carried an illustrated, double-page article suggesting holiday fashions for every occasion, including 'Riviera clothes,' a 'golfing suit,' and a dress '[f]or the Casino' (Jan 1925: 2–3), in the same year *Woman's Life* advocated a far simpler dress code, as befitting the more modest budgets of its readers, and advised: 'Wear clothes for travelling that don't soil easily' (4 July 1925: 6). *Ladies' Field* romanticised travel abroad as an act of individual self-discovery: 'there are many travellers always looking for something different than can be found nearer home. They yearn to sink their individuality in absolutely different surroundings, to study other folks and their mode of life' (Feb 1925: 40); but for the reader of *Woman's Life* travel was seen as a dirtier, messier, and more prosaic business: 'fuel burned in Continental engines produces an amazing amount of unbelievably dirty smuts and smoke [. . .] [t]ake your own soap' (4 July 1925: 6).

The reader of *Woman's Life*, therefore, had to be tutored on how to negotiate national and cultural difference, and the magazine policed English femininity overseas. Articles appeared on travel etiquette, reminding readers to be their 'very nicest self' when abroad (13 July 1929: 10). Language differences were regularly addressed in these articles, with an assortment of advice, such as: '[t]alk like a child, not bothering about correct grammar, but using signs and the essential words'; or, '[o]ften it is better to make a request *in English*, very slowly' (10 Aug 1929: 4; 13 July 1929: 10). The tone of these articles could be censorious, as when it is observed that '[m]any English people seem to think that much gesticulation will get them through. But our gestures mean as little to the officials as our language. [. . .] oh, *please* don't *shout*. It doesn't make you any more intelligible, though tourists invariably think so' (4 July 1925: 6). Not comfortable abroad, it seems, the reader of *Woman's Life* was a national, rather than international, creature, a 'tourist' who had to be tutored in being an Englishwoman abroad, rather than an experienced 'Lady Traveller.' Most articles on travel in the magazine specifically allude to English resorts. Ultimately, *Woman's Life* affirmed English national identity, as readers were encouraged not to forsake national and domestic ties in favour of the lure of the exotic, as suggested in the exhortatory tone of one article published in 1925: '[o]ur hearts may beat just as warmly for Linda in India, or darling Maudie who sends us postcards of the Niagara Falls, but have a heart and a hand for all the people "down our street," otherwise you will find yourself a lonely, friendless soul' (17 Jan 1925: 3). Unlike *Ladies' Field*, with its cultivation of the urbane upper-class traveller able to negotiate national difference with ease and style, *Woman's Life* references foreign cultures as objects of curiosity, with the construction of foreign peoples and climes providing a means for the reader to self-reflexively understand her own Englishness.

The way in which *Home Notes* envisaged its reader as a 'stay-at-home woman' desirous of information from 'the woman who has travelled' is clearly figured in a feature that regularly opened each issue of the magazine in its early years, titled 'Fireside Talks.' As Beetham has argued in her analysis of the late nineteenth-century magazines *Home Chat* and *Woman at Home*, penny weekly domestic magazines in this period sought to create a 'confidential tone' between editor and reader, most often through 'the creation of journalistic and editorial personae who addressed the reader as an intimate' (1996: 202). Like the persona 'Sister Rachel' in *Home Chat* or the distinctive editorial voice of the romantic novelist 'Annie S. Swan' who edited *Woman at Home*, the first-name persona of 'Isobel' in *Home Notes* was designed to cultivate an intimate relationship between the editor and her readers, who were often referred to as 'friends.' In an advert for the magazine printed in 1914, for example, the editor of *Home Notes* writes: 'my little paper is not content with being simply a woman's magazine, however good; it also tries to be a true friend to every reader' (3 Jan 1914: 48). This implied relationship was reiterated in the titles given to regular columns in *Home Notes* emphasising intimate conversation or 'chat,' such as 'Isobel's Weekly Chat' (which carried the subtitle 'From Friend to Friend'), or 'Chats with Women.' As Beetham has emphasised in her analysis of *Home Chat*, the general category of 'chat' across the periodicals market at this time is indicative of a shift in tone from an editorial voice that was commanding and authoritative to one that was conversational. In the illustrations that accompanied Swan's regular column 'Over the Teacups' in *Woman at Home*, for example, women are seen talking in an open and democratic fashion, with no central authority figure. Likewise, the 'Fireside Talks' in *Home Notes* emphasised the same comparison between the space of the magazine and the space of the home, with women able to conduct open, ritualised conversation with one another in both. In its form, too, the 'Fireside Talks' sought to figure anecdotal 'chat' by breaking the text up into snippets of disparate information, much in the tradition of Newnes's 'tit-bits,' with each item only a few lines long. Significantly, in the anecdotal snippets of the 'Fireside Talks' we can clearly see how Bennett sought to introduce the 'stay-at-home' woman reader of *Home Notes* to the traditions and customs of women from across the world.

Presenting a dizzying eclecticism of 'interest' or 'curiosity' items, the 'Fireside Talks' provide a kaleidoscopic vision of women from other nations. In one of these, published in January 1895, 'Isobel' informs her readers over a single page of print that '[o]ur Transatlantic cousins have formed numerous ladies' whist clubs'; that news has come from Paris that the use of red sealing-wax 'is henceforth to be reserved for the sealing of business letters' only; that '[t]he Queen of the Belgians has a little pet pony which is highly accomplished' and 'can do no less than fifty tricks'; and that '[i]n Greece women are awaking at last to the sense of their needs. They are now aroused to the fact that in their country as in all others, much of the advancement of the nation depends on the facilities provided for the education of women' (5 Jan 1895: 289). When it comes to marriage, these differing national customs are a recurring point of interest: for instance, the 'Fireside Talks' tell us that '[i]n many parts of Germany a bride wears a black dress instead of a white one at her marriage' (7 Sep 1895: 273); that 'AMONGST the Turks bath money always forms an item in every marriage settlement' (14 Sep 1895: 313); that 'in some parts of Belgium' the prevailing opinion is that women should be able to propose (3 Aug 1895: 73); that 'IN some countries a betrothal is regarded almost as sacred as marriage itself,' especially in Italy (21 Sep 1895: 353); and that 'BRIDAL veils, no doubt, are a remnant of the Oriental custom of holding a canopy over the heads of both bride and bridegroom' (12 Oct 1895: 498). This emphasis on relating a variety of national differences is forcefully captured in a single entry of the 'Fireside Talks':

The charms of women are very differently estimated in various parts of the world. A Chinese beauty must have deformed feet, eyes without lashes, and carefully blackened teeth. The fascinations of a fair Sandwich Islander are in proportion to her weight. The bride of an African prince must have her teeth filed like those of a saw, and the divinity of the masher of the South Sea Islands is tattooed sky-blue, and wears a ravishing nose-ring. (24 Aug 1895: 193)

Despite the fetishistic quality of much of this obsessive anthropological cataloguing of national and cultural differences in *Home Notes*, these observations were clearly intended to provoke the English woman reader to reflect back upon her own character and customs. One entry, for example, noting the 'great love of jewellery' exhibited by Hindu women, explicitly compares such cultural traditions to English marriage rites: 'married women have a superstitious fear of moving it [the gold nose-ring] from its place even for an instant, just as English women sometimes have about their wedding rings' (10 Aug 1895: 113). With its emphasis on the domestic space of home and hearth, the 'Fireside Talks' helped the 'stay-at-home' woman to position herself and her own national customs in relation to others from across the world.

Indeed, while *Home Notes* emphasised forms of 'English' looking, as in the 'Tourist Notes' section which repeatedly refers to 'our English eyes' and 'our island eyes,' for example, contributions to the magazine also admitted the possibility of everything appearing strange when seen from another perspective (31 Mar 1904: 640; 24 Mar 1904: 579). As one entry of the 'Fireside Talks' concedes (where it is made explicit that 'us' refers to 'English women'), '[t]o see ourselves as others see us, is no doubt sometimes a startling revelation' (31 Aug 1895: 233). Likewise, an article from 1898 is titled 'As Others See Us' and another 1904 article notes, 'there is an advantage in being able to see ourselves as others see us' (22 Jan 1898: 54; 11 Aug 1904: 244). Even on a page of the magazine where contributions revert to vile racial stereotypes, depicting a cartoon 'Nigger' and elephant alongside a pejorative rhyme titled 'The Hot Hottentot,' for example, another rhyme about the Chinese titled 'Who is the Queerest?' ends: 'So you see that while you're right / In this country, still you might / In China find they thought you somewhat queer' (11 Feb 1904: 266). Thus, although the magazine promoted the idea of English national and racial superiority, the eclecticism of its content about foreign cultures to some extent served to relativise 'English' characteristics and customs.

The refraction of Englishness through the lens of foreign cultures in *Home Notes* is also reflected in advertorial content in *Woman's Life*. Ros Ballaster, Margaret Beetham, Elizabeth Frazer, and Sandra Hebron comment that, with the increased integration of adverts into magazines after the abolition of the advertising tax in 1853, 'definitions of femininity became inextricably related to models of consumption' (Ballaster et al. 1991: 104). In particular the 'advertorial' with its 'confusion of adman and editor' naturalised consumerism as an integral part of domestic femininity (Beetham 1996: 193). These advertorials were absorbed into the rest of the magazine's editorial content through their adoption of the female penny weeklies' conversational codes and use of the anecdotal. The Mother Seigel series of advertorials which appeared in *Woman's Life* in 1905, to advertise their cure for indigestion, repeatedly triangulate the domestic, the pull of the exotic, and consumerism, as the interest of the magazine's reader was piqued by anecdotes of life abroad as a hook for the 'sell' of domestic products. One advertorial for this product appeared under the headline 'Japanese as Tea-drinkers' (28 Jan 1905: 135). This was naturalised within the discourses of the magazine, whose own editorial content frequently reflected upon how other traditions of drinking tea compared to those of the English.[1] Japanese models of femininity were also celebrated in the magazine; an article also published in 1905 and titled 'Why the Japanese Girl is Pretty' merged the anthropological with the exotic in its lingering physical descriptions of Japanese women: 'her hair is remarkable [. . .] scented and rolled off her white, wide forehead – a typical Japanese beauty' (8 Apr 1905: 78). Certain models of Japanese feminine conduct are also deemed desirable by the magazine. An article titled 'Husbands' Undesirable Friends,' accompanied by an illustration of a geisha girl, suggested a conciliatory approach when dealing with 'Husbands' Undesirable Friends': 'Never show your objection to your husband's undesirable bachelor friends – only use tact, TACT, TACT!!!' (21 Jan 1905: 118). However, the advertorial for the Mother Seigel indigestion cure jars with the magazine's adulatory stance toward Japanese culture by citing an Englishman's opinion on the Japanese from the 'last century': 'They are a stunted race' (28 Jan 1905: 135).

As well as associating the domestic with the foreign through its advertorial content, the magazine constructed this domestic sphere as capable of imaginative transformation. An article entitled 'Would you like "An afternoon in China?"' instructed the magazine's reader on how they could indulge their interest in the exotic in their own home, as the domestic sphere could be a space of cultural performance: '[t]he rooms should be decorated with Chinese carvings, hangings, ornaments, &c' and 'fitted up to simulate one of the picturesque restaurants' (18 Jan 1896: 238). The event would educate guests on Chinese culture: '[t]he programme might include the showing of photographs and curiosities, and a talk by a man or woman who had visited the East,' for example (ibid.). The hostess would adopt Chinese traditions in food and drink: '[t]he food may be tea, in shallow cups, without milk and very strong, and sipped with the aid of tiny porcelain spoons' (ibid.). Indeed, it is a recurring feature of these magazines that the tropes of oriental otherness provided a means for reconstituting or rethinking English domesticity.

More frequently, the domestic reader was imaginatively transported to more exotic locales through the magazine's short stories and serials. The popularity of Newnes's the *Wide World Magazine*, which was launched in 1898, for example, signalled reader interest in the exotic. In the women's magazines, this taste for adventure was satisfied in the regular publication of romance fiction. A prominent writer in this genre was Beatrice Grimshaw, who made her name in these magazines with serialised stories set in the South Seas. In particular, the trope of romance between an English protagonist and exotic native recurred across fiction published in the women's magazines in this period. In 1898, for instance, *Home Notes* ran a short story entitled 'Monckta or The Romance of an Indian Tea Garden.' The story features Monckta, a native 'quack doctor' possessed of a 'primitive' outlook (5 Feb 1898: 136, 138). Monckta falls in love with the typically Anglophile protagonist, the owner of a tea estate, Benjamin Hume, with 'honest, blue, English eyes,' whom she treats for '[f]ever' (5 Feb 1898: 137, 136). Monckta accepts the unattainable nature of her love: '"I want nothing but a grateful recognition of my services to you"' (5 Feb 1898: 137). However, Hume is unable to offer Monckta even this, distracted as he is by Hilda

Lowell, the sister of a neighbouring tea-estate manager, who is distinguished by her 'pale golden hair' (ibid.). The opening of the story orientates itself against the domestic English setting: '[i]t was towards four o'clock one March afternoon. In England, probably, we should be enjoying the first faint presage of summer sunshine [. . .] [b]ut out on the Akandy tea estate, a few hundred miles north of Calcutta, things were different' (5 Feb 1898: 136). While the topography is different, authorial interventions both assume the physical desirability of English 'fairness' and urge the reader to a humanitarian identification with the 'other':

> Monckta [. . .] had walked many miles to torture herself with the sight of Hilda's fairness and to find out for certain if her master were altogether lost to her.
> Perhaps you who read can scarcely be expected to pity a foolish dark woman on account of her hopeless love for a white man; but she suffered, remember, under her dusky skin, every bit as much as you would have done under yours of fair whiteness, for the heart beats and aches in the same way all the world over. (5 Feb 1898: 138)

Monckta goes on to treat Hilda and banishes herself from the estate: 'she will never work any more on the Akandy Tea Estate,' as the story ultimately affirms conservative social codes (5 Feb 1898: 139). More broadly, the exotic romance dominated Pearson's magazines in the early 1920s. H. de Vere Stacpoole contributed several series to *Pearson's Magazine* set in the Amazon jungle or the South Seas, such as 'Baited With Beautiful Eyes' and 'The Way of a Maid with a Man.' [2] Published in 1923, these stories were accompanied by illustrations of the travelling Englishman alongside bare-chested women. Such stories emphasised the foreign 'other' as the site of illicit, taboo desire, while travel, adventure, and exotic cultures provide the escapism from 'English' custom and convention that becomes a prerequisite of the romance genre. The plot of 'The Romance of an Indian Tea Garden,' with its focus on doomed native love for a white man, recurred in short stories in women's weeklies across this period. The short story 'Zazia: A Tale of the East,' which ran in *Woman's Life* in 1925, is set in the 'Soudan' and sees the story's eponymous heroine save the colonial Captain Anstruther from a deadly scorpion bite. Both stories play with the eroticism of the exotic romance, while ultimately maintaining conservative cultural codes in the sacrificial genuflection of the colonial subject on the altar of English man- and woman-hood.

Coda

Stevie Smith's *Novel on Yellow Paper* parodies the conservative parochialism of the women's magazines published by Newnes and Pearson, satirising the dominant ideologies of gender and nationhood. Laura Severin argues that Smith is in dialogue with the romance stories of periodicals, analysing stories from *Peg's Paper, Pearson's Magazine*, and *The Royal* to note that *Novel on Yellow Paper* 'would seem to be a rewriting of a story from a Pearson's publication, where the heroine eventually chooses the more steady male' (1997: 30). As Severin notes, Smith's resistance to conventional romance codes is suggestive of 'women's ability to recode their culture' (1997: 36). As we have argued, Smith's subversive act of recoding is also responsive to the intersection between gender and national identity in these magazines, and is evident also in Pompey's satiric relationship to the conversational codes of women's magazines, as Pompey ventriloquises the discourses of such magazines in order to ironise them. The novel's own eccentric discourse emerges as a marked contrast to the pedestrian conversational tone of such magazines, with lines such as 'How richly compostly loamishly sad were those Victorian days' reflecting Smith's self-consciously modernist style (Smith 1980: 4). In another instance, Smith parodies readers' letters to women's magazines in order to emphasise the confluence between tropes of 'romance' and 'domesticity' and nationalist, racist ideology:

> Should I Marry a Foreigner? . . . You do not say, dear, if he is a man of colour. Even if it is only a faint tea rose – *don't*. I know what it will mean to you to GIVE HIM UP but funny things happen with colour, it often slips over, and sometimes darkens from year to year and it is so difficult to match up. *White* always works well at weddings and will wash and wear and if you like to write to me again [. . .] I will give you the name of a special soap I always use it myself do not stretch or wring but hang to dry in a cool oven. My best wishes for your happiness, dear, I think it was very sweet of you to write. (1980: 36)

The conversational tone ('dear,' 'sweet of you') is overplayed to the point of condescension, and barely manages to suppress the aggressive impulse behind the journalist's advice: 'GIVE HIM UP.' This capitalisation allows Smith to capture variations in the dynamics of the journalistic voice and echoes the instructive force of 'tact, TACT, TACT!!!' in the 1905 issue of *Woman's Life* quoted earlier. In Pompey's narrative, the response to a letter on marriage transforms into advice on appropriate wedding attire, which bleeds into an instruction on how best to maintain 'whites' in the laundry. Apparently formulated in response to different letters on different topics, this concatenation of advice all pivots around the idealism of a pure 'white' race. The elision of the letters to which the journalist is responding suggests that seemingly benign advice can underscore a far more pernicious ideological outlook. In this light, 'Romance in an Indian Tea Garden' and 'Zazia' exhibit clear undertones of xenophobic nationalism, with both stories faltering on the edge of an unconsummated romance between a female colonial subject and English male. Such stories serve as points of comparison with Pompey's love affair with the German character Karl in *Novel on Yellow Paper*. In a period of heightening tensions between Britain and Germany, Pompey's relationship with Karl and her European travels serve to unsettle pretensions of both female propriety and national particularity.

Through parody and satire, Smith's subversive novel provides a window onto the dominant ideologies of both English nationalism and domestic femininity that permeated the women's magazines published by Newnes and Pearson from the 1890s to the mid-twentieth century. Exposing the racial prejudices behind the counselling tone of the popular women's press, Smith offers a creative reimagining of these magazines' perspectives on foreignness. As this chapter has examined, magazines such as *Home Notes* and *Woman's Life* promoted versions of female domestic identity as a means of reinforcing notions of English national and racial particularity. In these magazines, foreign travel and the lure of the exotic function as contrasts to the stability of 'home and homeland.' These magazines not only provide certainty to the reader of her place within both the family unit and the larger system of empire, but also underscore established class identities and relations. In this way, the presentation of racial and foreign 'otherness' in these magazines reaffirms dominant ideologies, positioning the woman reader as the gatekeeper of English custom and identity.

Notes

1. 'Queen's Tea,' *Woman's Life* 4 Jan 1896: 154; 'A London Girl's News and Views. Tea that is French,' *Woman's Life* 15 Apr 1905: 105.
2. H. De Vere Stacpoole, 'Baited with Beautiful Eyes,' *Pearson's Magazine* Mar 1923: 201–10; 'The Way of a Maid With a Man,' *Pearson's Magazine* May 1923: 395–404.

Works Cited

Altick, Richard D. 1963. *The English Common Reader: A Social History of the Mass Reading Public 1800–1900*. London: University of Chicago Press.
Ballaster, Ros, Margaret Beetham, Elizabeth Frazer, and Sandra Hebron. 1991. *Women's Worlds Ideology, Femininity and the Woman's Magazine*. Basingstoke: Macmillan.
Beetham, Margaret. 1996. *A Magazine of Her Own? Domesticity and Desire in the Woman's Magazine 1800–1914*. London: Routledge.
—. 1998. 'The Reinvention of the English Domestic Woman: Class and "Race" in the 1890s' Woman's Magazine.' *Women's Studies International Forum* 21.3: 223–33.
Friederichs, Hulda. 1911. *The Life of Sir George Newnes*. London: Hodder and Stoughton.
Jackson, Kate. 2001. *George Newnes and the New Journalism in Britain, 1880–1910: Culture and Profit*. Aldershot: Ashgate.
Severin, Laura. 1997. *Stevie Smith's Resistant Antics*. London: University of Wisconsin Press.
Smith, Stevie. [1936] 1980. *Novel on Yellow Paper*. London: Virago.

Part II
The Sister Arts

The Sister Arts: Introduction

Faith Binckes

However modernism and modernity have been critically constituted, there has been broad agreement that all the arts reflected, and shaped, them. During this period new forms, and new media, reconfigured the boundaries of traditional practice, while the increasing visibility and autonomy of women helped to build a newly diverse cultural marketplace. The role periodicals played in this emerging scene has been noted by scholars. As far back as 1994, Susan Cook and Judy Tsou's *Cecilia Reclaimed* contained a chapter on female composers in American magazines. Other studies placed periodicals front, middle, and centre, such as the anthology of material drawn from the film journal *Close-Up* that Laura Marcus produced with James Donald and Anne Friedberg. Others have illuminated the importance of print culture to architecture, an art form that saw only a small proportion of projects conceptualised on the page actually constructed (one of the most recent texts to address this is Hvattum and Hultzsch's *The Printed and the Built*). Elsewhere, scholars have explored print as a form of art, with honourable mention here to Johanna Drucker. The composite form of periodicals also encouraged dialogue between different audiences, disciplines, and projects, a hybridity that left its mark on the writing of women fighting their way into the male-dominated professions of critic or reviewer. However, this narrative of trans-disciplinary harmony only serves to indicate how much important work might still be done in this area, especially as so many periodical scholars are located in English, Cultural Studies, or History departments.

This section, then, can be considered as something of a tasting menu.[1] It comprises six essays: on dance, music, drama, cinema, architecture, and advertising.[2] These were fields in which women were active as practitioners and as theorists, with some performing both roles, or tracing their own experimental path across disciplines. The essays explore the central role played by periodical media in enabling women to fashion the art forms with which they were engaged, the languages of critique through which those forms were presented, and the audience to whom they were addressed. In this marketplace, the lines between avant-garde and popular publications – as between avant-garde and popular artistic practice – were increasingly uncertain, opening spaces in which women could draw out, but also interrogate, the existing relationship between women and the modern 'sister arts.'

Charlotte Purkis takes a single figure, music critic Gertrude Hudson, as her focal point. She explores Hudson's use of a Paterian, impressionistic aesthetic – and a male pseudonym – to mediate questions of voice and audience, and to navigate the shifting politics of place and gender. This notion of music as a medium active within the writing, rather than simply being described by it, allowed Hudson to break free from the conventional languages of critique, an experiment facilitated by the format of the periodicals in which she appeared (one of which, the *Acorn*, she edited). This curious periodical culture, Purkis suggests, enabled Hudson to operate as 'gossip and autoethnographer' whose 'reflections both witness the development of musical criticism as outsider and show us its reshaping as insider' (p. 78).

Elizabeth Wright uses a different methodology to examine the absence of women's drama from British periodicals of the same period. In its place, Wright's extensive survey presents a reception history of theatre criticism: of women as dramatists, as actor-managers, or as reviewers themselves. This account stretches from mainstream publications to specialist journals (such as Edward Gordon Craig's *Mask*), suffrage periodicals and modernist magazines, and intersects with Margaret D. Stetz's study of Rebecca West (Chapter 12 in this collection). Wright's essay moves thematically and chronologically through the period, uncovering a growing acceptance for women in the theatre and in drama criticism, which was nonetheless etched with long-established prejudices. While it was possible for a woman such as Edith Craig to 'dodge the "unwomanly woman" bullet' (p. 102) by 1920, Wright explores other obstacles to women attempting to advance 'the state of the drama.' These included divisions on the subject of realism versus experimentalism, and on the value of didactic drama, that connected theatre to wider debates within feminism and modernism.

Staying with performance and the role of the critic, Susan Jones looks at four female dance critics: Marcelle Azra Hincks (part of the *New Age* circle discussed by Lee Garver), the artist Anne Estelle Rice and fellow *Rhythm* contributor Dorothy 'Georges' Banks, and Rebecca West. While the role of theatre critic was well established, Jones reminds us that the situation for dance critics was the opposite. As dance modernised, creating a series of female superstars and drawing on diverse historical and international influences, so this already open field opened further still. The *New Age*, prescient as ever, stepped in early. Although Hincks's 1910 *New Age* article 'The Dance Critic' used a masculine pronoun when referring to her ideal figure, her list of desiderata demonstrated her own suitability for the role. Hincks's work reinforces the *New Age*'s modernistic preoccupation with 'the new,' and its interest in dance more generally, but also introduces a new element of comparison between the *New Age* and its younger rival, *Rhythm*. Considered together, these writings illustrate the importance of periodical texts as venues for the hybrid responses generated by modernist dance, placing women at the vanguard of critique, and illuminating some divergences between the theories of 'personality' espoused by Hincks and by West and ideas of 'impersonality' popular with male modernist critics.

Rather like dance, cinema was a form that combined avant-garde prestige with huge popularity, a fact that informs Miranda Dunham-Hickman's study of the 1920s cinema criticism of Iris Barry. Dunham-Hickman argues for a considered project on Barry's part, one which used a range of periodical venues to engage with 'the widely contested concept of "culture"' (p. 125). Dunham-Hickman explores the ways in which Barry, infused with a feminist awareness of both class and gender, used the dynamics of the texts in which she published – including the *Adelphi*, British *Vogue*, the *Spectator*, and the *Daily Mail* – to shape a critical canon. While figures such as I. A. Richards argued against cinema, Barry staked her own claim on Arnoldian ideas of 'culture' and 'the function of criticism,' reflecting on and defending the aesthetic and experiential value of film as a medium.

Elizabeth Darling addresses the relationship between women, modernism, and architectural design. While modernist buildings only appeared in Britain in the 1930s, Darling argues that by shifting our perspective we can locate an 'unexpected arena in which the ideas that we associate with modernist architecture and design, such as the demand for environments that represented the contemporary spirit and self, and the rationally planned interior and the use of modern materials' were already being circulated (p. 134). This arena can be found in an array of writings by women, and frequently for women, that appeared in magazines such as British *Vogue* and *Queen*. Darling untangles these varied discourses, in which aesthetic modernism (Omega and Vorticist-inflected interiors, for instance) ran parallel with a pragmatic material modernity (hot-water heaters, plywood), and with exhortations to a modern consciousness. In *Queen*, readers were introduced to figures like Le Corbusier, albeit with some emphasis on his innovative use of interior space. These periodical texts remind us 'that architectural modernism was a range of practices rather than one monolithic discourse and mode of being (the building)' (p. 136), and that the form of these female-orientated periodical texts (eclecticism, seriality) could reflect that range in breadth as well as in depth.

In the final essay of the section, Annie Paige explores a single 1911 issue of *Lady's Realm*, the magazine we quoted in the General Introduction, with a focus on its copious adverts. Paige outlines the methodological challenges that a study of periodical advertising represents, but argues for its value as a site where the binding structures of gender and class are not only articulated, but can be seen to flex and to fragment. Her reading points toward certain of the domestic ideologies explored in Part I. It can also be considered in the light of women-centred publications covered in the 'Social Movements' section.

Notes

1. For pertinent discussions of fashion and periodical texts, readers can look to the next volume in this series. For writings on women, textuality, feminism, and art criticism in this period, they can explore the writings of Lisa Tickner, Deborah Cherry, and Meaghan Clarke.
2. Those interested in the visual arts can also refer to Margery Palmer McCulloch's contribution to the 'Part I: Locations,' which discusses some of the women active in the Glasgow School of Art during this period.

Works Cited

Cook, Susan and Judy S. Tsou, eds. 2014. 'Ladies' Companion, Ladies' Canon?' Women Composers in American Magazines from *Godey's* to the *Ladies' Home Journal*' in *Cecilia Reclaimed: Feminist Perspectives on Gender and Music*. Urbana: University of Illinois Press. 156–82.

Hvattum, Mari and Anne Hultzsch, eds. 2018. *The Printed and the Built: Architecture, Print Culture and Public Debate in the Nineteenth Century*. London: Bloomsbury.

Marcus, Laura, James Donald and Anne Friedberg, eds. 1998.*Close-Up, 1927–1933: Cinema and Modernism*. London: Continuum.

5

'A THEME WITH MANY VARIATIONS': GERTRUDE HUDSON, MUSICAL CRITICISM, AND TURN-OF-THE-CENTURY PERIODICAL CULTURE

Charlotte Purkis

GERTRUDE HUDSON WAS a female writer and editor active from the mid-1890s to the late 1900s. Her colourful writings for multidisciplinary arts and general-interest magazines as well as for specialist music journals deployed intensely subjective, dialogic, even confrontational modes of writing to challenge established modes of music criticism. Hudson's writing explicitly connected music and the other arts exploring ways to enable readers to fine-tune connections between musical experiences, poetry, visual arts, and architecture, merging Walter Pater and Oscar Wilde's notions of aesthetic criticism with her own distinctive voice. Hudson's work is preoccupied with the nature of musical response by contemporary audiences and music's presence in global culture. Her essays range from portraits of performers, composers and performances of musical works, location pieces about audiences and music-making from London venues, and her travels and unusual commentaries on animals. All these topics show an enthusiasm for combining observations of her world with musical evocations in a range of sites and contexts. Hudson's writing offers unique subjective manifestations of topical debates, from the apparently passive position of a spectator and travelling consumer. Her reflections both witness the development of musical criticism as outsider and show us its reshaping as insider. As an observer specialising in celebrity culture in the 'classical' music world, she is both gossip and autoethnographer.

This chapter seeks to re-situate Hudson within literary and musical networks. In so doing, it continues the investigation from my earlier exploration of Hudson in *The Idea of Music in Victorian Fiction* (2004) looking now at her prose writing as critical theorisation and critical act. Examples of Hudson's well-informed witty rhetoric around musical preoccupations from the popular culture of her time demonstrate how the development of this unusually personal musical voice in conversation with other arts was stimulated initially by the journal format of the *Dome* for which she first produced essays. As Peter Brooker and Andrew Thacker comment in the introduction to *The Oxford Critical and Cultural History of Modernist Magazines*, such multidisciplinary formats encouraged 'tentative, exploratory, and dynamic' forms of writing which often challenged 'settled assumptions' (2009: 3). The *Dome* is best known as a literary magazine of the late 1890s, but articles on music were included reflecting its original subtitle: *A Quarterly Containing Examples of All the Arts*, and remained in its subsequent monthly subtitle: *An Illustrated Magazine and Review of Literature, Music, Architecture and the Graphic Arts*. Hudson's involvement with the *Artist*

(July 1902) and the *Musician* consolidated her involvement with the Arts and Crafts Movement. The *Acorn* (1905–6) deepened this interdisciplinarity in keeping with her enthusiasm for the Wagnerian ideal of the total-work-of-art and sustained an 'Arts and Crafts model of expressive creativity' into early modernism (Hart 2009: 129).

Musical Criticism and Periodical Culture

By the 1890s, the growing numbers of magazines, journals, and periodicals were able to support a diversification of critical response applied to music. 'Hundreds of articles and books on the theory and practice of musical criticism were published to regulate, reform and professionalize the industry and to lend musical criticism substance and authority,' according to Paul Watt (2018: 2). Musical criticism was welcomed not only in the daily press and the established specialist musical press, such as the *Monthly Musical Record*, the *Musical Standard*, the *Musician*, and the *Chord*, all of which Hudson wrote for, but also found an audience in other print media which covered arts and culture as a significant part of the growing leisure industry. There was an increase in educational literature supporting appreciation which encouraged writing on music beyond technical treatises, history, and biography traversing into territories concerned with meaning. Jeremy Dibble and Julian Horton consider the wide realm of intellectual thought underpinning developments far beyond reviewing in their new edited collection. The literary and art magazines Hudson wrote for, such as the *Dome* and the *Artist*, offered a sphere for experimentation in the relationships between opinion and fact, and the *Outlook: In Politics, Life, Letters and the Arts* welcomed her topical observations upon music in locations, which suited ephemeral weekly publication; they also extended the mindset of readers through armchair travel. Although her output was relatively small, Hudson was quite widely promoted as a writer of note. Reviews of, and references to, her writings appeared across the British and American press. Yet she now receives little recognition as a significant presence in turn-of-the-century culture.

The fact that Hudson has not yet found a place in the history of musical criticism is not helped by her denial of a critical role, the quixotic ways she expressed this, and her reputation for 'essays attacking critics generally' (*Daily Telegraph* 2 June 1899: 5). Hudson was not employed by any journal or newspaper in a critic's role, but commissioned to produce essays for enthusiasts. In her writing she clearly revels in being a 'virtuoso in passion,' an expression fitting both the performer she reports on and herself as writer witnessing impassioned performance and seeking to recreate it verbally (*Dome* Oct 1899: 227). Hudson enacted a caricature of a conventional male critic while constructing a different persona for herself as a creative-critical writer. In 'The Musical Critic (A Depreciation)' she confirms the 'weird fascination' she has always had for the critic, whom she yearns to be although typically critics are all similar: 'When you have read one of him you have read all of him . . . roughly speaking he is unanimous' (Hudson 1899: 228). Paradoxically, she then identifies him as 'also various': 'He is a theme with many variations.' Hudson goes on to suggest she can compose and play within the range 'from the most fantastic foolery and the dullest sense' (Hudson 1899: 229), noting that 'many of them are very charming essayists, and write us pretty little rhapsodies and reveries on Wagner' although 'sometimes they drown themselves in a sea of words' (Hudson 1899: 230). Furthermore, the 'hopelessly prosaic and incurably modern critic' 'really ought not to be permitted to criticise habitually'; when in need of rest 'for his overworked appreciative faculties' she 'should be delighted to take his place' being 'eminently suited for it, for I combine in one insufferable personality the savage brutality of the journalist and the cynical flippancy of the litterateur' (Hudson 1899: 232). This proposed role swap questions who is able to be a critic, who is not, as well as what sort of person would wish to be, confirming that there were different types of critics. In 'The Pianoforte Recital,' Hudson identified her 'extraordinarily supple genius' which she could 'but rarely restrain . . . from turning paradoxical somersaults' (Hudson 1899: 198). Stating that she does not wish to deploy this genius to explain music as a critic would, she confirms her ideal is to revel in the sound world, going beyond the fruitless task of the critic who 'burgeoning forth into passionate platitude' and sounding 'all the dictionary's deeps for the *mot juste*' . . . 'fail to find it' (Hudson 1899: 198). She prefers to criticise critics for what they leave out of consideration. It is creative people – performers, composers, and conductors – whom she depicts in moments of release from conceptual understandings underpinning criticism. This is the type of true interpreter she aspires to be: 'One day my soul, sharpest with academic vinegar, was fed with lovely sugary art' (*Dome* July 1899: 107). Such a responder becomes a vision of 'critic as humbug' – the standpoint expressed in her appreciation of Henry Wood (*Dome* Aug 1899: 76). The 'ideal humbug, the ideal critic' is able to see 'what isn't there' and is a 'charming feminine person who is ever under the influence of someone else': 'but it needs a fine, oh, a delicate! sympathy to apprehend the non-existent.' For example: 'Show him an October sunset dying redly behind a lattice of flaming, fantastic leaves, and he will see Tchaikowsky' (76).

It is not surprising that Hudson's pieces featured opinions on musical criticism, nor that this exploration coincided with her attempts to define herself. Discussions of various camps, arguments over the meaning of terms such as review, appreciation, impression, analysis, and, of course, how best to effect critical judgement, appeared regularly in periodical literature. The *Chord* magazine's reprinting of reviews as part of its self-marketing strategy in the back of Volume 2 (Sep 1899) summarises many key themes in the debate. From this lengthy and informative digest, it is interesting to extract what is praised, for example, 'very modern articles dealing with topics of the hour,' 'pages of vivacious musical criticism . . . far removed from the sober futilities of the outworn fashion,' and, 'no taste for reporting' (Sep 1899: 81–2). Hudson's impressionistic model of writing offered an alternative to the fact-based journalistic reporting assumed to be underpinned by educated judgement. Evidence that the position taken by the *Chord* was under attack can be found in Oldmeadow's defence 'As Others Don't See us' in Volume 3. Although he does recognise that Dr Charles Maclean is not being 'unfriendly,' the author of this unsigned article (presumably John F. Runciman, the editor), rejects the 'mainly aesthetic essayism' tag, the meaning of which 'we can only vaguely guess at,' saying: 'we make bold to tell Mr. Maclean that the public has shown a marked preference for the kind of writing that appears in THE CHORD . . . to the fatuous, unimaginative, inartistic kind of writing which he appears to like' (Dec 1899: 56–7).

'Each school of critics has its battle-cries,' declared E. A. Baughan, as he reflected on the possibility of 'perfect criticism' (*Monthly Musical Record* 1 Mar 1901: 363). And a few months later in the same journal he queried 'a certain clever essayist' criticising critics for being jaded and over-tired of music – something he had claimed (Aug 1899: 172), which was likely Israfel's source for depreciating the critic – and went on to complain that 'We live in days where subjectivity has gone mad' (Dec 1901: 266). In 1902 Baughan became vocal against 'poisonous appreciations' which he had located in some 'old magazines' (perhaps the *Dome*?) 'articles evidently meant for the musical amateur' (*Monthly Musical Record* May 1902: 84). He recounts himself sitting next to a comfortable matron listening to Tchaikowsky's Pathetic Symphony and then derides writers who hang 'decadent theories and invertebrate picturequesness of language' onto music, encouraging writing 'on a subject apart from music itself' (*Monthly Musical Record* May 1902: 85). A few years later J. H. G. Baughan, brother of Edward, attacked Miss A. E. Keeton, who published on music in the *Morning Post*, the *Musical Standard*, and the *Fortnightly Review* and this exposed how the literary nature of some writing on music continued to prompt its exclusion from the field of musical criticism proper: 'Musical people – we do not mean those literary people who have *acquired* a taste for music – are not interested in lengthy, padded-out criticism. What interests them is sound illuminating judgment conveyed in as few words as possible. They absolutely refuse to be humbugged by skilful language alone' (*Musical Standard* 22 Feb 1908: 115).

Hudson's Networks and Publishing Career

Hudson, who wrote under a pseudonym 'Israfel,' remains an elusive figure. However, she was embedded in a series of literary and publishing networks. In their exploration of *Modernism's Print Culture* Faye Hammill and Mark Hussey have commented how 'even small presses and magazines shared the vision of modernism as an international artistic community,' as did the groups frequenting literary salons (2016: 9). Hudson was a member of the literary circle of the Lyceum Club for women alongside Alice Meynell, and regular attender at her literary salons where she would have encountered Oscar Wilde through Ernest J. Oldmeadow (proprietor of 'At the Sign of the Unicorn' press, editor of the *Dome*, and musical critic of the *Outlook* 1900–4), and also Arthur Symons. Indeed, Hudson seems a potent example of the type of creative critic praised in the latter's *Dramatis Personae* (1925) which echoes in T. S. Eliot's referencing of Symons's attitude in 'The Perfect Critic' (*Athenaeum* 9 and 23 July 1920). Hudson was also connected to the Bedford Park set surrounding the Yeats family. She published alongside W. B. Yeats (*Dome* Apr 1899), referred to his evocation of music in poetry in 'Ysaye (An Impertinence)' (*Dome* May 1900), and as editor included him in the *Acorn* which she produced with artists George and Hesba Webb at the Caradoc Press, Priory Gardens. Symons and Oldmeadow both had musical interests, and as editor Oldmeadow brought in two other writers on music: Vernon Blackburn, another friend of the Meynells who became his subeditor on the weekly Catholic *Tablet*, wrote on music for the *Fortnightly Review* and was also music critic for the *Pall Mall Gazette*, and Runciman, music critic of the *Fortnightly Review* as well as editor of the *Chord*. As a frequenter of concerts and opera to inform her writing, Hudson would have had companions amongst audiences, and the Lyceum Club likely provided further contacts with other musical members. Ella D'Arcy of the *Yellow Book* coterie was also her advocate because correspondence exists with John Lane, in which she encourages him to support Hudson and 'to undertake the publication of *The Acorn*' (Windholz 1996: 129).

Intersecting with Hudson's journalistic career are seven books which navigate through established and niche companies. In 1897 the London firm H. Henry and Co. issued her first book: the short story collection *Impossibilities: Fantasias*. Holbrook Jackson notes in his survey *The Eighteen Nineties* (1913) that Henry was one of the publishers associated with the 'new literary movement' and what he considered the 'high journalism' of the decade (45). Then *Ivory Apes and Peacocks* (1899) appeared 'At The Sign of the Unicorn' in London, and simultaneously in a joint edition with M. P. Mansfield and A. Wessels in New York. This was at the same time as Hudson was most active at the *Dome*; two chapters were essentially reprints, and others were original. Oldmeadow also published *A Little Beast Book* (1902) of animal appreciations from the *Dome*. Hudson also published in the American *Monthly Musical Record and Review* and articles were reprinted alongside essays from the *Dome*, the *Chord*, and the *Artist* (music supplement) in *Musical Fantasies* (1903). That came out using identical typeface to the Unicorn press with Simpkin, Marshall, Hamilton, Kent and Co. Ltd, the largest wholesaler of books in England at mid-century which underwent further expansion in 1890–1. They also published *Travel Pictures* in 1904, a prose collection including essays from the *Outlook*. By 1908 she had moved to David Nutt, known for foreign bookselling, appropriate for *Lotus Leaves from Africa and Covent Garden*, a collection including essays from the *Acorn* and the *Musician*. The fact that many of Hudson's periodical essays were gathered into collections aids understanding now of her importance, because reviews of these books identify their contemporary appeal. And, as the *Outlook* commented, *Lotus Leaves* 'is another volume of collected pieces which may be said to deserve a more enduring form' (29 Feb 1908: 869). Parts of *Musical Fantasias* were also included in the Boston Symphony Orchestra's programme books for the season, for example, 'Dvorak' (1900) and 'Wagner: In a Liqueur Glass' (1901).

Israfel the Incredible: Performing Paradox

Hudson is not only significant as a writer on music, but notable for the content and style of her literary output. The 1903 collection – *Musical Fantasies* – was admired both for the 'remarkable . . . soundness' of its 'musical criticism' and as 'a marvel of words' and the reviewer expressed high praise for 'the incredible Israfel' for exposing 'critical truth' (*Outlook* 14 Nov 1903: 425–6). The *Yorkshire Post and Leeds Intelligencer* highlighted Hudson's self-declared 'verbal music' (1903: 25) and recognised the collection as proposing something new in criticism:

> One would not recommend it as a text book for a young ladies' boarding school, but it might have a refreshing effect upon the highly intellectual, non-emotional critic, who is too apt to regard a full score as he would a mathematical essay. (11 Nov 1903: 4)

Margaret D. Stetz has commented on Hudson's 'need to distance herself from the increasingly controversial and reviled figure of the New Woman' (2004: 174). The beginning of Hudson's literary career coincided with the vitriolic debates that followed the translation of Nordau's *Degeneration*, and with Wilde's trial and its repercussions. It is well known that the latter inflamed prejudices toward independent artistic women. Nordau's anti-Wagnerian views were also influential, and Hudson remained committed to Wagnerism through her writing career. Despite G. B. Shaw's promotion of an alternative perspective in *The Perfect Wagnerite* (1898), which defended the heroines as role models, the prevalent view was that 'Wagner's female supporters and protagonists were characterized both as New Women and as *femmes fatales*' fundamentally negatively (Sutton 2002: 96). Perhaps Hudson was inspired by G. B. Shaw's posing as a decadent in his music reviews of the 1880s and 1890s? Stetz's view, that Hudson's pseudonymous cloaking enabled her to 'appropriate a gentleman's freedom to be read and reviewed as a prose artist' (2004: 174), which builds on Talia Schaffer's search to determine the interrelationships between all *fin de siècle* women writers and artists and variously defined propagandist subgroups of 'female aesthetes' and 'new women' (2000: 11), supports Hudson's survival in publication through this difficult period.

Hudson's persona is an ambiguous construction. Assumed by most critics to be a man, due to 'several overt phrases' 'set forth as masculine,' what we are given is actually a masquerade (*Glasgow Herald* 22 Apr 1899: 9). Hudson's exploration of femininities and masculinities is contradictory and plays with her audience. In his discussion of Victorian sexual politics and their intersection with musical aesthetics Derek Scott argues that although a gendered vocabulary was consistently deployed to questions 'about the nature of music, its purpose, and whether it had a predominantly masculine or feminine character,' such terms were 'first used as metaphors in musical criticism, not as biological truths' (1994: 91, 95). Claims that 'Israfel' was a male voice, and publishers' decisions to quote these claims in advertisements, draws attention to the late Victorian perception that male subjects could best command verbal language to dominate the feminine language of music. This is consistent with Scott's analysis which draws upon evidence of musical meanings constructed as representing threats to effeminise men. Hudson often references gentlemen and ladies within narratives, for example in 'Music and Literature,' the essay concluding *Ivory Apes and Peacocks*, where women are referred to as 'them' foregrounding the masculine voice: 'Indeed, the whole entertainment breathes a gracious air of femininity, which is humanising and elevating to our masculine flippancy' (273). Here, Hudson is able to stress the positive nature of feminine characteristics and engagement, while playing with gendered designations.

In 'Chestnuts: A Study in Ivory,' Hudson discussed the Polish pianist Paderewski's appeal even when playing 'chestnuts' (a term for standard repertoire). Hudson literally waxes lyrical, comparing herself to the moon and finding an analogy between the pianist's touch and moonlight (*Dome* Mar 1899). This is an interesting allusion to Wilde's play *Salome* (1891) with its location of sexual desire in the moon. For Hudson: 'The moon is all temperament and personality, she puts her own ivory interpretation upon the world' (Mar 1899: 33). She connects the ivory keys played by the male performer to the 'silver sheen' of the moon who with 'her pale mystical glamour . . . in her own far-off divine way, is quite an egoist, and believes almost exclusively in subjective art' (32). Hudson becomes political in drawing comparison to the sun. It is the moon that 'transcends the sun'; the sun 'has no personality at all' (ibid.). The description begins to sound like her view of the musical critic: 'he is deplorably deficient in personal hypnotism, he conceives of an "object as in itself it really is"' (33). In this passage, she also proposes that a 'mere musician (pardon me!) cannot appreciate' 'the complex luxuries' of Paderewski's playing, but 'the romantic hedonist who has had a liaison more or less with each of the Arts . . . can better understand this lyric loveliness' (32).

Hudson's conscious feminisation of music and musician in several of her portraits of composers, such as in 'Grieg: A Study in Silver' follows this moon analogy through. She imagines the 'kittenish' male Norwegian composer as 'Pierette' 'charmingly dressed . . . in silver' with 'pale gold hair' whose 'dainty little pieces always suggest a witty woman' which on the surface seems merely satirical, but there is more going on (*Dome* Apr 1899: 54). It is in autobiographical moments that readers are presented with deliberately camp queering in Hudson's response to the music of favoured male composers, such as in the twist added to her *Musical Fantasies* reprint of 'Chopin' (*Dome* Oct 1899). While commenting on 'his feminine love for musical embroidery' she expostulates, 'For the life of me, I cannot cease to decorate Chopin with little verbal satin bows of a pleasing cherry tint' (1899: 230; 1903: 58, 64). Elsewhere, Hudson refers to her pen as female declaring it 'ravished' ('The Pianoforte Recital,' in Hudson 1899: 197), and then writing of 'Dvorak' in *Musical Fantasies* notes how the intoxicated nature of his music is 'so contradictory and unexpected' as to 'throw any well-broken hack-pen clean out of her stride' (94). This is either suggestive of a role reversal, making the man the muse and the woman the interpreter, or it is proposing a doubling of the pen and music itself and the controller/disguiser of the pen as male. Since Hudson is emphasising subjective impression as reality, following her reliance on Paterian aesthetics, the vision of the world she constructs seems to be a queered/feminised one, albeit written by a 'female' pen.

Whether this playful subtextuality enabled Hudson to bypass external definitions and achieve success because she offered a unique alternative to male music critics, other female aesthetes and New Women writers in the marketplace becomes obscured by the very features which attracted her supporters: satire and flamboyance. Some contemporary critics seemed dazzled by the style of her work, unable to assess where, if anywhere, new insights lay in her responses to music. Analysing examples of Hudson's 'brilliant impressionistic extravaganzas . . . coruscating with wit' (*Birmingham Post* cited in the *Acorn* 'Advertisement' section 1905) underlines that her writerly performativity is her way of confronting the dilemma at the heart of music's ineffability. This was expressed in aims such as that embedded in 'A Richard Strauss Festival' 'to bridge the yawning gulf between tone and speech with a rainbow arch of verbal music' (1903: 25). As an example, in 'The Pianoforte recital' she compares the 'verbal virtuosity' stemming from her 'ravished pen' to 'the pyrotechnical tone-journalese displayed at the end of a recital' (Hudson 1899: 197–8). As critical response in words follows a musical event, Hudson's own form of display can be seen as attempting equivalence.

Combining Amateurism and Cosmopolitanism into Critical Acts

The lack of appreciation of a multidisciplinary artistic perspective by the dominant voice of the male musical establishment led to literary critical approaches being undervalued as criticism professionalised and musicology developed as a discipline. In championing interpretation over judgement, Hudson's goal was to refine critical sensibility rather than master factual knowledge. A Hudson trait was to incite the reader/ordinary listener to find or make their own sense of 'critical truth.' Revisiting her comments on amateurs affords the opportunity to question how her creative-critical approach matched the needs and desires of her non-specialist but musically informed audience members and enthusiastic readers. Hudson shows her preference for the amateur over the critic, in her conclusion to *Musical Fantasies* (1903), based on a reprinted *Dome* essay 'The Amateur' (Mar 1899): 'The amateur ... can enjoy art quite simply ... he need not cast about in his mind to ... show how clever he is – as a critic must. ... he can really appreciate it. His mind is not blunted by Understanding or warped by Education' (*Dome* 1899: 258).

In reflecting upon the amateur essayist, Hudson suggests an insider perspective noting 'whole-hearted self-admiration': 'How he enjoys and insists on your enjoying his work!' (259). But is she genuinely self-deprecating, or merely playing with her readers, knowing that women were often allied with amateurs? Is she looking to something in what is regarded as amateur sensibility that she admires over so-called 'professional' established criticism? Commenting on Tchaikowsky, reprinted again in *Musical Fantasies*, initially published in the *Chord*, she pits the critic with 'a trained judgment and a clear knowledge of the music and of the fitness of things,' 'a gentle and conventional soul' 'all out of tune with Tchaikowsky's,' against a vision of a 'savage and superficial listener, unblinded by Education' (*Chord*: 1 May 1899: 43). This untrained, by implication amateur, enthusiast has a cosmopolitan outlook and is much more appreciative. By the end of the essay, Israfel is using 'us' and 'we' to explain Tchaikowsky's appeal based on how 'his intimate confession of his inner self ... moves us,' contrasting this unanimity with her assumed readers with her analysis of the complaints from critics refusing to deal with him (47).

Hudson is very explicit concerning those who were unable to appreciate the exotic dimension which saturated the contemporary music from Europe which was most popular. London was the key global centre hosting foreign performers and composers and the taste for novelties was very well developed by the turn of the century. The world of contemporary music took its listeners beyond the borders of England. Her fascination for the exotic fits with the sensory dimension of musical experience and in embracing 'escapist fantasy' in many of her essays she is opposing the actions of 'leading male figures' who were 'attempting to establish a national, masculine music' in the 'British Musical Renaissance' movement by 'upholding values of empire and eschewing associations linking music to ideas of the foreign and the feminine' (Fuller 2007: 7). The addition of cosmopolitanism as a literary characteristic connected to the theatricality embedded in her persona. Hudson did not inhabit international ideas and ideals of others, she rather absorbed impressions and reworked them in her own image. For example, Hudson desires to bring the world back to England, as in 'A Wagner Fantasy,' in the first volume of the *Acorn*. Imagining Tristan lying on his couch in the courtyard of his castle in Brittany, she declares: 'I would like to ship Dieppe castle over to the coast opposite' because the 'romantic loneliness of the Sussex downs' is 'entrancing'; the scenery of Normandy and Sussex is 'the kind of scenery that should frame Tristan's castle in Brittany' (1905: 151). Rebecca Walkowitz's argument that: 'In the early twentieth century, the term "cosmopolitan" was attributed to artists who seemed to invent identities rather than inhabit them and to work that dramatized this process of invention' provides a useful explanation for Hudson's approach (2006: 22).

Locating Hudson as a *Fin de siècle* Lady Journalist

Over the period this volume is concerned with 'the profession of the critic or writer was in the ascendant'; yet, the 'increasingly versatile critic,' 'both a generalist and a specialist . . . rarely a woman' (Watt 2018: 111). Women were expected to inhabit roles that responded to the association of music with the feminine. For example, it was natural to consider a performing woman reproductive. As the *Musical Standard* remarked in a column on 'Women and Originality': 'Very many question women's domain in music,' going on to advocate that the 'woman who chooses to inspire rather than write has chosen the better part' (15 May 1902: 171). Yet, the *Musical Standard* (June 1895), actually gendered music criticism as female in an editorial responding to Runciman's 'Women as Musical Critics' (*Monthly Musical Record* 1 Mar 1895) likely by its editor E. A. Baughan (also the musical reviewer of the *London Daily News*). In the context of the task of recovery of the female critical voice it is fascinating that such gendering occurs in contemporary debate about what was lacking. Current criticism – referred to as a 'cloud of dust that obscures the real weakness of musical criticism as she is wrote' – was not presented by Baughan as in a good state (Watt 2018: 118). Watt's view is that Runciman had been inconsistent in his attitudes, on the one hand praising women producing 'genuine musical criticism, that is, literature with music as its subject-matter,' for their 'crisp lightness and sparkling humour' suggesting that he often wished 'that ladies replaced some of the male critics,' but on the other hand complaining women were not showing they could discern music's qualities as well as men (1 Mar 1895: 49). Runciman was also reporting – on a lecture given to The Society of Women Journalists by Sidney Thomson, music critic of the *Star*, which had largely avoided discussing women even in a 'room full of ladies' – and observed simply 'whatever conclusions we may here reach' women will go in for musical criticism or not, as they, and not as I, will' (ibid.). Attempting to clarify what is necessary for women to succeed in theory, Runciman does allow the possibility for women to enter this domain in practice. He includes sensitivity to music and 'sanity of judgment' as necessary qualities, although he doubts women's capacity to discriminate is developed enough. He looks forward to their 'delightful, original and valuable literature about music' (1 Mar 1895: 50), but also warned: 'Lastly, and nearly but not quite chiefly, she must be mistress of her pen and "a style"' yet be careful not to build a style from 'affected tricks and mannerisms' (1 Mar 1895: 49). By 1904, however, writing on 'What is a Musical Critic?' Runciman falls back on the stereotype: 'What is wanted for a musical critic is, first, a thorough musician, a man who is educated, has read, can write, has enough imagination, and dares to say bluntly what he has experienced. The criticism of such men is worth reading; but as for the other stuff the less we have of it the better' (*Saturday Review of Politics, Literature, Science and Art* 2 Jan 1904: 11). Some women found a way around the limitations imposed by assumptions of male superiority. Fuller comments on the frequent use only of initials by women composers: 'Leaving one's gender ambiguous was a sensible move in a world where women's work was so automatically regarded as second-rate' (2002: 91). Stetz identifies anonymous and pseudonymous publishing as the key way women circumnavigated restrictions in the context of 'the burgeoning number of periodicals inspired by the aesthetic movement . . . eager to fill . . . issues' without worrying about identities (2004: 175).

This analysis is consistent with Hudson's work for the *Dome*: she did not publish in the five quarterly issues (1897–8), but once it was monthly her work featured regularly and additionally to those of the regular male writers.

Linda Peterson's comment, in her exploration of genres emerging in the burgeoning nineteenth-century periodicals marketplace, that writings in the forms used by Hudson – essays, reviews and travelogues – enabled both 'the modern woman of letters and her new self-constructions,' helps us to understand Hudson's position and manoeuvres in publishing culture (2009: 4). Hudson adopted a Poe-inspired nom de plume 'Israfel' for her late nineteenth-century periodical articles in the *Dome* and the *Chord* and her collections. But for the *Acorn* 'quarterly' of which two volumes only were produced, she made a change and published as 'G. H.' (on music) alongside 'Israfel' (travel pictures). Her twentieth-century travel writing for the *Outlook* appeared under the pseudonym; her music writing appears to then cease. Hudson initially adopted a full name 'Israfel Mondego' in 1897 for her first book. This surname surely echoes Israel Zangwill's character of that name who appeared as a singing celebrity in his satirical story *The Bachelor's Club* (1891). It cannot be that Zangwill is cross-referencing Hudson, since publications by her prior to 1891 have not been found. This borrowing is in keeping with Hudson's eclectic approach to contemporary culture, and also explains the masculine aura surrounding the androgynous first name. She briefly used a different surname 'Feist' for 'Jeypore' (*Dome* Dec 1898), identifying herself as one of the Maharajah's snappy little dogs. Her article 'Liszt: A Rhapsody' in the *Chord* (Mar 1900: 32–5) is published simply under 'I.'

In referencing Edgar Allen Poe's archangel of resurrection from his poem *Israfel* (1831), Hudson seems to propose retaining Romanticism in the aesthetic movement. In that poem, Poe expressed his ideal vision of the art of poetry through the image of an angel symbolising artistry. Israfel's singing bridges the real and the ideal by means of art, and thus the human artist aspires to the angel. Into Hudson's adoption of this spirit was bound huge admiration for Pater; her desire to mirror music in language references his terminology. For example, in 'Imaginary Portraits' she connects Pater's 'joys' 'ivory, apes and peacocks' to the name of the book collection the essay appears in and emulates his style as 'frozen music' (Hudson 1899: 264). She eulogises 'the music of Pater's thought,' his 'verbal symphonies' (Hudson 1899: 260), admiring his analysis of music's capacity for the 'absolute annihilation of fact, the infinity of expression' (Hudson 1899: 263). Hudson's 'ideal criticism' extended notions from Wilde and A. C. Swinburne in promoting literary approaches to all art forms and built on Pater's vision of music as a pre-condition of creativity. Furthermore, Hudson argues that because Pater's prose is at odds with journalism, hers is a literary as well as musical approach. In declaring Pater's diction 'a haven of rest from the fierce vitality of journalism,' she positions subjectivities against perceived objectivities, and herself resists definition as a 'lady journalist' (Hudson 1899: 253).

From her wide knowledge of women in music in this period, Sophie Fuller observes that 'Women were rarely part of the musical establishment and often stood far outside its boundaries' and also notes how this position supported women's capacity for innovation: 'They had less to risk in their exploration of what had previously been regarded as the province of dry scholars or dangerous aesthetes or decadents' (2007: 255). Interpreting 'Israfel' now, knowing hers to be a veiled female voice, maps Hudson onto

Fuller's thesis. But it is too simple to say that such gender concealment evades recognition of the woman's voice in the 'professional patterns and opportunities' of criticism and 'to undermine female authority,' as Meaghan Clarke discusses with respect to art critics (2005: 22). Potentially, it is rather Hudson's cross-dressing performativity that assists us reading her work so as to open up deeper explorations into emerging modernisms. Could it be Hudson's queer perspective rather than assumed masculine voicing that attracted those positive responses to her work which relished its challenges? One example is the praise for 'Irresponsibilities III: Henry Wood' (*Dome* Oct 1899) as the 'best thing' forthcoming in the magazines with quotation of her comments on the 'majestic impetus' Wood gives to music's 'splendid wave-like forces of hysteria' while noting provocatively his 'womanly' pathos and the 'dainty' touch of his art in responding to Tchaikowsky (*Outlook* 19 Aug 1899: 94).

Hudson was supported in her androgynous/queer critical persona by Oldmeadow. It can be assumed from the intersections between the two writers that he was promoting 'Israfel' through arranging or authoring favourable anonymous reviews. Perhaps Oldmeadow, who also wrote sometimes under a female pseudonym, was willing to risk betraying Hudson's disguise in referring to *Musical Fantasies* as a 'wanton volume,' using an adjective typically used of a woman (*Outlook* 14 Nov 1903: 426). Further evidence that this may be the case is enhanced by the lack of a personal pronoun. There is no 'he,' only 'Israfel' in inverted commas every time the name is used, and thus gender is avoided. Being taken usually for a gentleman helped Hudson avoid such extreme derision as had been directed against lady journalists at the start of her career. Paula Gillett has researched late Victorian attitudes exhaustively and concluded that 'discussions of women's creative deficiencies continued into the pre-World War One era' (2000: 26). Even just after the end of the war in a context responding to women's rising emancipation, and after Hudson had ceased publishing, patriarchal attitudes persisted. When J. Swinburne lectured to the Musical Association on 'Women and Music,' he informed his well-educated audience that 'musical women often tell stories well, and have generally other masculine traits, which goes to show that music is a male faculty' (*Proceedings of the Musical Association*, 46th Sess. 1919–20: 33).

Other Women Writers on Music

In the 1903 issue of the *Outlook*, referred to earlier, the favourable review of *Musical Fantasies* juxtaposes comment on two other examples of 'Music in Print' that are defined to have 'strutted or gambolled or minced from the press.' Israfel is praised as the gamboller. Commentary on the third book *About Music and What it is Made Of* by composer Oliveria Prescott serves to draw attention to the existence of other women writers on music. The reviewer derides Prescott's grasp of history and criticism as 'astonishing.' There is also disapproval that she mistakenly allows personal experience to dominate critical work, which is surprising in the light of Hudson's tendency to do this (14 Nov 1903: 426).

J. Swinburne's declaration, recorded in the *Proceedings of the Musical Association* that 'There has never been a woman critic' showed that he had not done his research adequately and was choosing to be unaware of the quite large number of women active in publication (28). Educational opportunities for women, changing attitudes from some editors, growing involvement in editing, and the founding of feminist journals, mark this out as a period of significant change. Fionnuala Dillane has researched Hulda Friedrichs's 1890s interviews with music-hall performers for the *Pall Mall Gazette* in *Women and Journalism at the Fin de siècle* (Grey 2009). Friedrichs was a member of the Lyceum Club for women founded by Constance Smedley who contributed 'In defence of modernity' on the British musical renaissance to Hudson's *Acorn*. The fulsome career of another Lyceum member, Rosa Newmarch, has been evaluated by Philip Ross Bullock in several publications and in my own research discussing her fostering of listening. Little is known about Emily Frances Holland who reviewed 'the literature of music' in European languages for *Musical Opinion and Musical Trade Review* (1896–1900). Christina Struthers, Edinburgh University music graduate, wrote for the *Monthly Musical Record* and was cross-referenced in the *Musical Standard*. Marie Harrison, editor of the society supplement of *Vogue* until 1910 also wrote regularly in the *English Review* on 'Current Musical Topics.' Annie T. Weston wrote for the *Music Student*; Emily R. Daymond, Marjorie Kennedy-Fraser, and Annie Patterson also worked actively as music writers. Mrs Franz (Louise) Liebich was commissioned by Newmarch for her 'Living Masters of Music' book series but her many articles for the *Musical Standard* are concealed through her husband's name.

Two women writing widely on the arts used male pseudonyms like Hudson. Vernon Lee (Violet Paget) wrote several articles and a book *Music and Its Lovers* (1920). Christopher St John (Christabel Marshall) wrote for the *Lady*, and her regular *Time and Tide* columns which included assessment of Ethel Smyth's operas are evaluated by Catherine Clay, and Amanda Harris deals with the dedicated promotion of women composers in that journal alongside new trends in European feminist criticism. Smyth wrote for the *Musical Standard* and the *English Review*, as well as for the *Contemporary Review*, *Country Life*, and the *New Statesman*. Another *Time and Tide* author, Velona Pilcher, who also contributed essays on performers to *Theatre Arts Monthly* and the *Island* (including on the cellist Suggia who also attracted Virginia Woolf) is contextualised in my work on the avant-garde between the wars. Emma Sutton and Adriana Varga consider Woolf's prose writings ranging from street music to Wagner.

Ursula Greville was the only female committee member of *Musical News and Herald*, contributor to the *Musical Quarterly* and the *Dominant* and edited the *Sackbut*, a magazine which promoted British contemporary music, from 1921 to 1934. Katharine Eggar wrote regularly on 'Women's Doings in Chamber Music' for the *Music Student* and co-founded with Marion Scott 'The Society of Women Musicians' (1911). Scott was a well-connected musician, active as a specialist writer into the 1930s on *Proceedings of the Musical Association*, the *Sackbut*, the British *Musical Times*, and the American daily *Christian Science Monitor*. In the 1920s Eva Mary Grew contributed her wide knowledge of historical topics to the *Sackbut*, The *Etude*, the *Contemporary Review*, British *Musician and Musical News*, and *The Musical Quarterly*, adding *Musical Mirror and Fanfare: Music, Radio and the Gramophone*, *The Musical Times*, *Music and Letters*, and the *Chesterian* from the 1930s to 1940s. The extensive critical work of so many women remains underacknowledged in spite of the recent surge of publication about music criticism. The fields of music history, periodical, and literary studies could all benefit from a wider range of past women's voices being heard.

Works Cited

Brooker, Peter and Thacker, Andrew, eds. 2009. *The Oxford Critical and Cultural History of Modernist Magazines, Vol. 1 Britain and Ireland 1880–1955*. Oxford: Oxford University Press.

Bullock, Philip Ross. 2010. '"Lessons in Sensibility": Rosa Newmarch, Music Appreciation and the Aesthetic Cultivation of the Self.' Ed. Stefano Evangelista and Catherine Maxwell. *The Arts in Victorian Literature: Yearbook of English Studies* 40: 295–318.

Clarke, Meaghan. 2005. *Critical Voices: Women and Art Criticism in Britain 1889–1905*. Aldershot: Ashgate.

Clay, Catherine. 2018. *Time and Tide: The Feminist and Cultural Politics of a Modern Magazine*. Edinburgh: Edinburgh University Press.

Dibble, Jeremy and Julian Horton. 2018. *British Musical Criticism and Intellectual Thought, 1850–1950*. Woodbridge: Boydell and Brewer.

Fuller, Sophie. 2002. '"Devoted Attention": Looking for Lesbian Musicians in Fin-de-siècle Britain.' *Queer Episodes in Music and Modern Identity*. Ed. Sophie Fuller and Lloyd Whitesell. Urbana and Chicago: University of Illinois Press. 79–104.

—. 2007. 'Creative Women and "exoticism" at the Last Fin-de-siècle.' *Music and Orientalism in the British Empire, 1780s–1940s: Portrayal of the East*. Ed. Bennett Zon and Martin Clayton. London and New York: Routledge. 237–55.

Gillett, Paula. 2000. *Musical Women in England, 1870–1914*. New York: St Martin's Press.

Grey, F. Elizabeth. 2009. *Women in Journalism at the Fin de Siècle: Making a Name for Herself*. Basingstoke: Palgrave Macmillan.

Hammill, Faye and Mark Hussey. 2016. *Modernism's Print Culture (New Modernisms)*. London: Bloomsbury.

Harris, Amanda. 2014. 'The Spectacle of Woman as Creator: Representation of Women Composers in the French, German and English Feminist Press 1880–1930.' *Women's History Review* 23.1: 18–42.

Hart, Imogen. 2009. '"The Arts and Crafts Movement": *The Century Guild Hobby Horse, The Evergreen*, and *The Acorn*.' *The Oxford Critical and Cultural History of Modernist Magazines vol. 1 Britain and Ireland 1880–1955*. Ed. Peter Brooker and Andrew Thacker. Oxford: Oxford University Press. 120–43.

Hudson, Gertrude ['Israfel']. 1899. *Ivory, Apes, and Peacocks*. London: At the Sign of the Unicorn.

—. 1903. *Musical Fantasies*. London: Simpkin, Marshall, Hamilton, Kent and Co. Ltd.

Jackson, Holbrook. [1913] 1922. *The Eighteen-Nineties: A Review of Art and Ideas at the Close of the Nineteenth Century*. London: Grant Richards.

Peterson, Linda H. 2009. *Becoming a Woman of Letters: Myths of Authorship and Facts of he Victorian Market*. Princeton: Princeton University Press.

Purkis, Charlotte. 2003. '"Leader of Fashion in Musical Thought": The Importance of Rosa Newmarch in the Context of Turn-of-the-Century British Music Appreciation.' *Nineteenth-Century British Music Studies*. Ed. Peter Horton and Bennett Zon. Vol. 3, Aldershot: Ashgate. 3–19.

—. 2004. '"You Might Have Called it Beauty or Poetry or Passion just as well as Music": Gertrude Hudson's Fictional Fantasies as Explorations of the "Impossibilities" Within Fin-de-siècle Musical Experience.' *The Idea of Music in Victorian Fiction*. Ed. Sophie Fuller and Nicky Losseff. Aldershot: Ashgate. 197–223.

—. 2016. 'Velona Pilcher's Promotion of an Intercontinental Theatrical Avant-garde.' *Intercontinental Crosscurrents: Women's Networks Across Europe and the Americas*. Ed. Julia Nitz, Sandra H. Petrulionis, and Theresa Schön. Heidelberg: Winter Verlag. 71–90.

Schaffer, Talia. 2000. *The Forgotten Female Aesthetes: Literary Culture in Late-Victorian England*. Charlottesville: University of Virginia Press.

Scott, Derek. 1994. 'The Sexual Politics of Victorian Musical Aesthetics.' *Journal of the Royal Musical Association* 119.1: 91–114.

Stetz, Margaret D. 2004. 'Pre-Raphaelitism's Farewell Tour: "Israfel" [Gertrude Hudson] Goes to India.' *Worldwide Pre-Raphaelitism*. Ed. Thomas J. Tobin. New York: State University of New York Press. 171–84.

Sutton, Emma. 2002. *Aubrey Beardsley and British Wagnerism in the 1890s*. Oxford: Oxford University Press.

—. 2013. *Virginia Woolf and Classical Music: Politics, Aesthetics, Form*. Edinburgh: Edinburgh University Press.

Swinburne, J. 'Women and Music.' *Proceedings of the Musical Association*. 46th Session, 1919-20: 21–42.

Varga, Adriana L., ed. 2014. *Virginia Woolf and Music*. Bloomington: Indiana University Press.

Walkowitz, R. L. 2006. *Cosmopolitan Style: Modernism Beyond the Nation*. New York: Columbia University Press.

Watt, Paul. 2018. 'The Rise of the Professional Music Critic in Nineteenth-Century England.' *The Music Profession in Britain, 1780–1920: New Perspectives on Status and Identity*. Ed. Rosemary Golding. London and New York: Routledge. 110–27.

Windholz, Anne M. 1996. 'The Woman Who Would Be Editor: Ella D'Arcy and "The Yellow Book."' *Victorian Periodicals Review* 29.2: 116–30.

6

WOMEN, DRAMA, AND PRINT CULTURE 1890–1929

Elizabeth Wright

WHEN IT CAME TO 'the drama,' British newspapers and magazines of this period were interested in two central issues: the poor quality of it and whether a national theatre or the demise of censorship might cure it. Two full sections of the *English Illustrated Magazine* entitled 'State of the Drama: An International Symposium' in 1904 were devoted to a discussion of these concerns by a range of largely male playwrights, theatre managers, actors, and other creative professionals. In his introduction to the series of responses, Tiburce Beaugeard made clear that 'since Goldsmith and Sheridan, the Drama has contributed nothing to English literature' (July 1904: 331). Elsewhere, Dora Marsden writing for the *New Freewoman* speculated: 'Just now it appears that it is the dramatists that are missing' (1 Nov 1913: 182), while Richard Aldington in the *Egoist* assessed the contemporary drama as 'hardly noticeable' and observed that it is merely used as a means to 'escape doing something which requires thought' (15 Apr 1914: 146). These laments were mirrored across almost every type of print media that engaged with the topic, from the popular press to the modernist little magazine. As a very public form of art which was accessible to all who could pay the entrance fee, periodicals and newspapers seemed to provide the best, because most immediate, platform from which to offer judgements on and posit solutions to the 'state of the drama.'

At this time, women's dramas were largely realist in mode, written in prose, and followed the dominant stage fashion of the times for **problem plays, thesis plays, or** *pièce bien faites*. Therefore, they did not offer a solution to the 'state of the drama' demanded by the British press, and as a consequence their work contributed to 'the problem' bemoaned by both mainstream and modernist publications. Not only were their scripts less likely to be published as standalone texts, they are almost completely absent from modernist little magazines (which willingly printed the literary poetic plays of male contributors),[1] and they were not considered by reviewers to offer any meaningful solution to the artistic void in British theatres, though their plays certainly grappled with modern themes. Nevertheless, for women playwrights, realism presented a number of possibilities. It arguably gave the woman dramatist her first chance to write women as they actually were, not as male writers or society saw them or wanted them to be, nor as modernist avant-garde abstractions. This was the chance that Elizabeth Robins saw in her speech to the Women's Suffrage League at the Criterion Theatre on 23 May 1911 in which she called for women to write 'the Real Girl' (1913: 250). Given realism's affordances, perhaps a women's formally avant-garde stage was inappropriate at this theatrical juncture. Their stage was modern in thought if not experimentally modernist in form, a view of the late nineteenth- and early twentieth-century stage for which Toril Moi argues more generally (2004 and 2006). Maggie B. Gale suggests that 'there appears to have been a direct correlation between the authors' choice of subject and theme and their position as women within their culture' (1996: 9), and by extension there is a direct correlation between the author's choice of style (realism) and their gender as well. In an article for the *Woman's Signal*, Jerusha D. Richardson (Mrs Aubrey Richardson) suggested that it was from drama that 'the historian of the future will learn more perhaps of the real nature of the social disturbances and perplexities that trouble us to-day than he will from the perusal of many blue-books and whole files of daily papers' (9 Aug 1894: 88). Yet, the daily papers and other forms of print media that engaged in a dialogue about women's writing for the theatre give a sense of how these plays were received – an important element in piecing together the public reaction to women's play-writing and indeed the many other contributions that women made toward the theatre from critic to actress, from manager to director.[2] It is also particularly interesting to see the reaction to women's theatre pieces that reveal the 'disturbances and perplexities' of the times in connection with contemporary sociopolitical issues specific to women.

This chapter examines how women playwrights and their plays were received in newspapers and periodicals in light of both the widespread concern for the quality of drama and the changes in women's sociopolitical situation taking place over these decades. It will also tackle the associated issues surrounding the public perception, partly cultivated and partly reflected by British print media, of those women who earned their livings in associated professions as actresses and those working in what were seen to be the 'preserves' of men such as critics, directors, and managers. Finally, this chapter will suggest the changes in how women writers and producers of drama and theatre between 1890 and 1929 were spoken about in these fora.

In *Innocent Flowers: Women in the Edwardian Theatre*, Julie Holledge estimates that there were 400 female playwrights active in the UK in the early twentieth century, a number also used by Naomi Paxton in her introduction to *The Methuen Drama Book of Suffrage Plays* (Holledge 1981: 2; Paxton 2013: vii).[3] In *The Years Between: Plays by Women on the London Stage 1900–1950*, Fidelis Morgan hopes to locate a 'lost masterpiece' (1994: xv) and is disappointed to find no such thing, but as Maggie B. Gale and Tracey C. Davis point out, 'Morgan falls into the trap of censoring' (Gale 1996: 2) by expecting to find this female magnum opus rather than performing the task of 'validat[ing] the experience' and 'connect[ing] the woman with the work and the work with the world at large' (Davis qtd in Gale 1996: 2). Contemporary magazines and newspapers are one of the best ways to connect their work with 'the world at large.' Gale (amongst others) explores the critical silence, both then and now, surrounding women playwrights of this period and argues that 'they were largely middle-class, writing for a commercially oriented theatre and so the assumption is that their work does not warrant serious examination' (2000: 23).[4] For this reason Gale argues that 'most productions [and I might add published scripts] were largely ignored by the press' (2000: 24). For example, in his review entitled 'Printed Plays' for *Poetry and Drama*, a list of which included several by women playwrights, Ashley Dukes only examines those written by male authors (Dec 1914: 420–3). When plays by women (either as script or production) *are* considered in newspapers and magazines they are often coloured by gendered language and many by essentialist judgements. This is illustrated in John Francis Hope's 1921 review of Clemence Dane's *Will Shakespeare: An Invention in Four Acts* for the *New Age* in which he argues that her poetry 'may be anything one likes, except poetry' and observes sarcastically that this is 'the product of the higher education of women' (29 Dec 1921: 104). He goes on to argue that 'she does not understand men,' snidely remarking that 'so far as a feminist can be a woman, Miss Clemence Dane is a woman; and it is on the women that she lavishes her "invention"' (ibid.). But it is 'the love of a housewife and shrew invented by a feminist' that produces Anne Hathaway and he concludes, dismissing her completely: she 'has no value outside of a modern High School for Girls' (ibid.). Elsewhere, John Wightman notes in the *Playgoer and Society Illustrated* that 'A Sense of Humour' by Beryl Faber and her husband Cosmo Hamilton contains 'real live feminine characters' which 'unmistakably reveal the touch of a woman's hand' (Nov 1910: 67). The unsigned review of Jess Dorynne's 'The Surprise of His Life' in the *Academy and Literature* claims that 'full reparation was made to the feminists, for here two exceedingly despicable males were thoroughly vanquished' (27 Apr 1912: 532). Indeed, in an attempt to have her play judged without this gender-bias Cicely Hamilton initially billed herself as C. Hamilton for the production of her 'Diana of Dobson's' at the Kingsway Theatre in 1908. American *Vogue*'s claim in 1915 that Katherine Githa Sowerby, Edith Craig, Lady Gregory, Cicely Hamilton, and Mabel Dearmar represent '[f]ive dramatists to prove that England grants success with no distinction against women' is thus not tenable (1 Aug 1915: 61). Tracey C. Davis and Ellen Donkin remind us that such reviews could have a negative impact on the 'professional momentum' of the female playwright and has led to a skewed writing of their place in the history of the stage by subsequent historians who 'do not trouble to balance the evidence of the reviews against the length of the run' (1999: 6). The female dramatist, according to many of the male-authored reviews in the print media of the time, was a women first, a professional second, and an artist hardly at all.

This essentialist attitude toward women playwrights intensified when reviewers critiqued the agitprop dramas sympathetic to women's fight for the vote or indeed any play that attempted to highlight gender double standards. 'The Cause,' more than any other sociopolitical issue of the age, encouraged women (and some men) to take up their pens in order to promote women's rights. Several strident suffrage plays were produced in the first decade of the twentieth century including: Elizabeth Robins's 'Votes for Women!' (1907), Beatrice Harraden's 'Lady Geraldine's Speech' (1909), and Cicely Hamilton and Christopher St John's 'How The Vote Was Won' (1909). The *London Illustrated News* ignores, as far as my searches have shown, Harraden, Hamilton, and St John's plays, but includes an unsigned review and photographs of Robins's play. As in many reviews of 'Votes for Women!' the crowd scene is admired for its realism, after which the reviewer discusses the characters as 'type[s]' and 'kind[s] of Suffragette' and concludes by finding that the 'play proper is not so interesting' and 'its melodramatic story . . . is dragged out too long and becomes far too thin' (13 Apr 1907: 546). Though a mixture of praise and blame, the review is *not* laden with anti-suffragist vitriol, though the suggestion that suffragettes can be divided into types is troubling, and the reviewer emphasises his (presumably his) issues with the structure and technicalities of the plot and staging using neutral ungendered language. However, other reviewers were more biased – of Robin's heroine the *Times* critic comments that 'the cause would make much more headway than it does if all its advocates were as fair to look upon, as agreeable to hear and as beautifully dressed as Miss Wynne Mathison' (qtd in Farfan 2004: 28–9). In his flattery of Miss Wynne Mathison the reviewer promotes the stereotype of the ugly and dowdy suffragette by contrasting her with the attractive actress; and equating beauty with female success, plainness with female failure – on and off the stage.[5]

Nevertheless, suffrage and feminist theatre at this time whether art or propaganda, whether penned by man or woman, was a force to be reckoned with and mainstream print media tried to tackle it in a variety of different ways from exclamations of outrage to supercilious dismissals, from rational engagements with the plays' arguments to simply ignoring them. Only 'The Pageant of Great Women' written by Cicely Hamilton and Edith Craig performed on 13 November 1909 seemed to transcend the virulent or simply absent criticism of suffrage pieces published in the Edwardian and Georgian press, partly because, Roberta Gandolfi argues, it was more experimental in form than the usual realist agitprop offerings (1997). Suffrage papers such as the *Vote*, *Votes for Women*, and *Suffragette* occasionally reviewed these performances; if they did they responded positively, but not uncritically, and saw them partly as ways to attract new recruits while simultaneously unpicking the opposition's arguments. The recruitment of women playwrights and actresses to the fight for women's suffrage, Maria DiCenzo argues, 'accounts in part for the increased attention paid to theatre work in the pages of these periodicals' (2008: 44). However, reviews of, or simply a general engagement with, these productions remained largely absent from the more modernist journals for creative reasons and from mainstream print media for political reasons. It was left to the feminist and suffrage press to engage with these productions directly and in doing so they revealed how useful drama was for getting the message to wider audiences who would not attend a meeting but might attend a play.

Journals, magazines, and newspapers which actually printed play-scripts or parts of plays, rather than simply reviewing productions, were few and far between; most preferred to print poetry, short stories, sections of novels, and visual artwork which fitted into the number of requisite pages. *Fin de siècle* journals such as *Pageant* (1896–7) edited by J. W. Gleeson White and the *Yellow Book* (1894–7) edited by Henry Harland rarely printed play scripts. The *Yellow Book* printed only three plays or parts of plays in its thirteen issues, one of which was a dialogue, while the *Pageant* also printed three in its two annual issues – all were by male writers.[6] Later little magazines rarely or simply did not publish plays by women. *Poetry and Drama* edited by Harold Monro, published plays by Lascelles Abercrombie, Lord Dunsany, and Edward Storer; *New Numbers* published plays by Wilfred Wilson Gibson, Lascelles Abercrombie, and John Drinkwater; 'Two Dialogues of Lucian' and 'Dialogues of the Dead' by Richard Aldington appeared in the *Egoist* (2 Mar 1914 and 1 Apr 1914); Frederick Fenn and Richard Pryce published 'The Love Child' in the *English Review* (15 Feb 1910); the *Open Window* contained plays by Keith Henderson, Geoffrey Whitworth, Hugh de Sélincourt, and Gilbert Cannan; *Owl* published 'The Sun' by John Galsworthy and 'The Interchange of Selves: (An Indian Actionless Drama for three actors and a Moving Background)' by B. K. Mallik (May 1919 and Nov 1923); the *Dome* published J. E. Woodmeald's dramas; and Wyndham Lewis printed his virtually unstageable 'Enemy of the Stars' in the first number of *BLAST*. Of such modernist little magazines one of the few to have printed original or translated drama by women was the *Green Sheaf* edited by Pamela Colman Smith which ran for only one year between May 1903 and May 1904. The *Green Sheaf* published work by Christopher St John (Christabel Gertrude Marshall) and Mary Brown.[7] The *Freewoman* also published one drama entitled 'The First Line of Defence' by Helen Hamilton (30 May 1912: 34–6; 6 June 1912: 51–3). Plays by women did appear in some of the suffrage print media, such as the WSPU newspaper *Votes for Women* which was the first to publish 'Lady Geraldine's Speech' by Beatrice Harraden (2 Apr 1909: 494–8) and in feminist periodicals such as the *Englishwoman* which advertised one of its key elements in February 1909 as 'Short stories, poems, scientific articles, and short plays' and published Cicely Hamilton's 'Mrs Vance' in its first issue. However, even in print media directed at women their scripts very rarely appeared, either in part or in full.[8] If we agree that there were fewer women writing drama than men, that full-length drama was too long for publication in print media, and that when it came to little magazines women's dramas were too conventional in form or too overtly political in subject to catch their interest, the absence is perhaps more explicable.

Drama was clearly something to be reviewed or discussed rather than published in these mediums, but female theatre critics were few and far between. Indeed, in his book, *Our Stage and Its Critics* based on his articles for the *Westminster Gazette*, E. F. S. refers entirely to male theatre critics, though many reviewers were anonymous, and so it is difficult to establish their gender at all. Female reviewers seem to have appraised books about drama or drama scripts rather than performances, though again even this was a male-dominated realm. *Poetry and Drama* does not contain a single essay by a woman about drama, and it is difficult to tell in the March 1912 issue of *Poetry Review*, dedicated to poetic plays, whether any of the reviews or articles are written by women because many are signed with initials. The reasons why women drama and theatre critics were largely absent from the columns of the print media in these years are varied. Gay Gibson Cima highlights the nocturnal nature of theatre reviewing and that certain theatres were not suitable for middle-class women to attend unescorted (1999). Kerry Powell notes that even at the end of the nineteenth century it was unusual to see women attending theatres alone and 'at venues where unescorted women were regularly admitted – as at the Alhambra music hall – "you may be sure," as a policeman put it, that most were "women of the town"' (1997: 33). Women were not welcome to theatrical journalism partly because drama is such a public art form and the drama critic, like the actress, such a public figure. Cima notes that the critic, unlike the novelist, 'was not toiling behind the scenes, submitting copy, but rather was visibly public, dressed as other women, but actually engaged in a process of "manly" judgment and even caricature' (1999: 43–4).[9] As women, they were not considered to be in a position to voice an opinion which guided the general public's artistic and theatrical tastes, nor were they considered by many to be capable of writing criticism well, see for example Arnold Bennett's comments on the perception of women journalists (1898: 6–7). 'RITA' (Mrs Desmond Humphreys) writing in the *Freewoman* describes female theatre critics, with a degree of truth, as insignificant scribblers writing for minor periodicals and unable to throw off their interest in fashion when reflecting on a production:

> The lady journalist appends to her dramatic opinions interesting details as to who looked 'smart,' and why. One always catches the 'frou-frou' of the leading actress's skirts throughout the maudlin inefficiency of feminine criticism. It is essentially feminine, and that says – all.

> The lady journalist who does dramatic criticism for minor periodicals is not of such importance as her male prototype who does them for major journals, such as the *Times* and the *Daily Mail*. She is put aside in a corner of the dress circle, or upper boxes, or given a chair at a back angle of the stalls.

She adds that, '[w]hen women get the vote all this will, of course, be altered' (22 Aug 1912: 273). However, it was most likely that the visibility of women in the workplace during the war, combined with The Sex Disqualification Removal Act 1919 making it a legal right for women to earn money on the same basis as men, played a part in the slight rise in the number of female theatre critics after 1920 and a small part in their male-colleagues' increasing, if reluctant, respect. DiCenzo argues that it was journalists writing for the feminist press who admired and defended female playwrights and encouraged women to critique performances in order to 'provide more detailed accounts of the reception of specific playwrights and tendencies from critical voices conscious of their positions on the margins of mainstream culture' (2008: 52). The feminist press produced critics who were interested in righting the imbalances introduced by the interpretations of the largely male reviewers of the general press and were responsible for promoting some of the more free-thinking women theatre critics in this period.

Some of the women writing intelligently and critically about drama included Dorothy Neville Lees, Virginia Woolf, Storm Jameson, Rebecca West, and Marjorie Strachey. The *Mask* contains some articles (not production reviews) by Dorothy Neville Lees, but she often wrote, like Craig, under various, often male, pseudonyms.[10] Virginia Woolf reviewed printed dramas and theatrical memoirs for *Nation and Athenaeum*, *Cornhill*, *Guardian*, *New Statesman and Nation* and the *Times Literary Supplement*, but rarely and reluctantly reviewed performances most of which appeared in the *New Statesman*.[11] Interestingly four out of five of Woolf's theatre reviews were published in or after 1920, perhaps signalling a new confidence and the growing respectability of the profession. Storm Jameson, a frequent writer of theatrical reviews, vented her spleen in the *Egoist* at the insipid copies of Ibsen's problem plays that she saw on the British stage and used her experience as a theatre critic to write *Modern Drama in Europe* (1920) in which she 'state[d] a case: the case against mediocrity and imitative drama' (1920: x). Marjorie Strachey added a further voice to this criticism of contemporary drama in the *Englishwoman* in her article 'Women and the Modern Drama': 'The theatre, it is universally recognised, is always among the most conservative of institutions' (May 1911: 186). When Rebecca West tackled the subject she was an able and unflinching critic. Her dislike of propagandist feminist drama was poured forth passionately and articulately in her article entitled 'A Modern Crusader' for the *Freewoman* in which she responded to Florence Edgar Hobson's play and critiqued the ideas for Home Schools which are contained within it. West levelled her invective at 'The Pioneer Players and the Actresses' Franchise League' which she considered to be 'the most shameless offenders in the way of producing degradations of the drama written by propagandists, whom nothing but the fire of Prometheus could make into artists.' She worried that 'these impertinences towards Art' were a symptom of the degradation in 'public taste' which 'has already been so perverted that dislocated Suffrage speeches, such as Miss Cicely Hamilton's plays, stand the chance of wide popularity' (23 May 1912: 8). West, alongside Jameson, Strachey, and Woolf were some of the few women who offered shrewd, cogent, and energetic judgements on the stage of the time and in doing so began to move the female theatre critic away from being the polite, apologetic, unintelligent figure described by 'RITA' and toward an assured and influential critic able to offer balanced judgements and engage with the tricky ethical and aesthetic issues with which plays of this time were concerned.

The woman theatre critic had to battle against assumptions that women should not be engaged in public work unchaperoned and that women's intellectual abilities undermined the credibility of their work – criticism also faced by the actresses of the time. Unlike the female critic who could be silenced by editors, the actress was a conspicuous figure, needed in a way that female critics were not, unless one concurs with Edward Gordon Craig who argued for women to be banned from the stage altogether. Edward Gordon Craig's journal the *Mask*, mostly written by him and partly by his assistant Dorothy Neville Lees, both writing under various pseudonyms, was one of the only, if not *the* only, British journal that properly tackled the stage intellectually in every branch of its art.[12] However, Craig's editorship was manifestly egoist and chauvinist. He repeatedly called for women to be banned from performing, was overtly anti-suffrage and even refused to allow his female readership to respond to questions posed by the publication. In 1909 he asked six questions of his readers in the guise of John Semar, the 'editor' of the *Mask*, but with the following caveat:

> We respectfully request that ladies shall refrain from replying to these questions for the reason that we are loath to put any strain whatever upon them, . . . and then we are sure they would not know what they were writing about, or why; also because we know that they are too well occupied to trouble their beautiful heads about such trifles. (July 1909: 45)

Craig spends a great deal of time refusing the female voice in general as well as her presence on the stage in particular which he calls a 'great calamity' (Jan 1911: 143), a 'colossal blunder,' and a 'danger' (July 1911: 62, 71), and instead asks for a masculine theatre. 'The advantage' of banning women from the stage, he claims, 'is two-fold.' Firstly, women are:

> saved, even against their will, from making this public display of their persons and their emotions which serves to foster all their latent folly and conceit [. . .] Secondly, it is an incalculable gain to the art in that it replaces a personality by a symbol. For men, when they act female roles, do not parody womankind as do women themselves when they let loose their silliness and vanity on the stage as representative of the beauty of the female sex. (July 1911: 41)

Indeed, he thanked the suffragettes for 'opening hundreds of other doors through which the women will enter, and, in entering these, will leave the stage' (Apr 1910: 171). Only then, he repeatedly stated, will the theatre be 'reform[ed]' (Jan 1911: 143), 'saved' (July 1911: 64), and 'revive[d]' (July 1912: 82). Some of his claims may well have been professional jealousy and most of his calls to ban the actress were ignored by other publications at the time, but the figure of the actress in British print media in these decades was certainly contentious and some of Craig's antipathy can be found in the general consensus that actresses were vain and fame-hungry at best, prostitutes at worst.

Barbara Green and Kerry Powell notice how journalists used 'male-configured language' (Powell 1997: 3) to speak about the actress who represented a woman able to compete with and even control men in a public space and who had obtained their independence through commercial exchange. Green argues that in writing about the actress they:

> reconstructed the performing woman as more than actress – as a renegade female, one fundamentally different from normative wives and mothers, marginally 'feminine' if feminine at all, quite possibly inhuman. In thus rhetorically dividing her from other women, their own wives and daughters, Victorian men could permit the actress a limited freedom and a certain power. They could do so, in large part, because of a tactical rhetoric that underwrote and even guaranteed the unequal distribution of power by gender across society as a whole, and in their own personal relations. (Green 1997: 3–4; See also Powell 1997: 13–63)

Indeed, newspapers and journals over the course of the nineteenth century encouraged this impression by using the terms actress and prostitute interchangeably. Both Kerry Powell and Martha Vicinus highlight the unsigned 'Actress and "Actress"' article published in *Theatre* on 28 August 1896 as an example of the confusion in terms, and E. F. S writing for the *Westminster Gazette* stated: 'women of the oldest profession open to the sex miscall themselves actresses when in trouble – the term actress being like the word "charity"' (Spence 1910: 220). Clement Scott warned women against attempting a career on stage in an interview with Raymond Blathwayt for *Great Thoughts* in 1898: 'I should be terrified for her future [. . .]. It is nearly impossible for a woman to remain pure who adopts the stage as a profession' the life 'render[s] it impossible for a lady to remain a lady. But what is infinitely more to be deplored is that a woman who endeavours to keep her purity is almost of necessity foredoomed to failure in her career' (1 Jan 1898: 228). Scott's interview, though ostensibly discussing both male and female actors, assigned the worst of the profession's characteristics to women who he argued are vain, unable to take criticism and sexually corrupted by the stage. Fictional representations of the actress in the print media of the time reinforced these prejudices, see for example Frank Price's January 1891 short story 'Mashing an Actress' for *Era Almanack* in which his hapless hero unsuccessfully tries to woo the actress who lives next door. The assumption the 'hero' makes is that due to her profession she is more sexually available than other women. To be an actress in the 1890s, according to largely male-authored British print media, was to walk a fine line between the public and the private and therefore the seemly and the unseemly. Even into the twentieth century the actress Beatrice Carr exposed herself to the accusation of being an 'unnatural' woman for seeking public recognition for her work rather than fulfilling the 'usual' roles of wife and mother: 'the knowledge that domesticity, nurseries, and fireside virtues, have no charm for Beatrice Carr is common property, and being an unusual – some say unnatural – attribute, naturally enhances her value as a subject for public interest and curiosity' (*Era Almanack* Jan 1907: 34).

The British press distanced the actress from the respectable woman partly through the language they selected to speak about them as Powell and Green suggest, but also in their cartoons and caricatures that are at best disparaging. One such cartoon by George Morrow entitled 'Miss – , the Versatile and Charming Actress, in Some of her Favourite Rôles' (*Punch* 20 Nov 1907: 368), portrays the numerous roles of an actress who poses in each image with exactly the same expression, another by Charles Harrison entitled 'Scale of Importance in the Production of a Modern Revue' (*Punch* 28 Jan 1914: 65) demonstrates the order of importance of the contributors to a production: the leading lady and her costumier come first, while the playwrights are put at the bottom of the pecking order. Well into the 1920s *Punch* ran a cartoon by Arthur Watts entitled 'A celebrated actress, not averse from publicity, conceives the idea of attending a fashionable night club with her own husband' (28 Oct 1925: 467). *Punch*'s satirical cartoons exemplify in visual form the general impression in the public consciousness of actresses' follies and foibles: their pursuit of fame, fashion, and beauty in lieu of actual talent and their morally questionable private life – the latter, interestingly transformed in both words and images from a cause of scandal in the early decades of this period to a subject of ridicule in the more permissive 1920s.

Nevertheless, it is in these decades from 1890 to 1929, particularly following the First World War and enfranchisement, when actresses slowly became more respectable and acceptable to society with mainstream periodicals rejoicing in their celebrity status and in doing so leading public opinion away from visions of prostitution and disreputability toward a shaky respectability. *Playgoer and Society Illustrated* revelled in the glamour and gossip that actresses attracted, running interviews alongside polished publicity shots – not dissimilar to those we see today. In their conversations with actresses the interviewers were often careful to stress the femininity and respectability of the interviewee, presumably to counteract both her independent income earned from the public world and the old impression of acting as another version of prostitution. In the *Playgoer and Society Illustrated*, Miss Winifred Emery is suitably deferential to her husband on matters of theatre censorship (Nov 1909: 76), while in his interview with Miss Lily Brayton, John Wightman notes that her home is characterised as having 'a strikingly gracious femininity': 'You enter, the subtle atmosphere is there – a book, a photo, a song on the piano, they are "she" the Lady of the House – the most powerful power on earth, vote or no vote' (Oct 1910: 25). Both of these actresses, thanks to the language used to describe them, their opinions and their environments epitomise the 'womanly virtues' expected at the time.

Flattering and fashionable images (photographs, drawings, and paintings) of actresses were frequently reproduced in periodicals, while specialist publications carried more artistic images such as Aubrey Beardsley's 'Portrait of Mrs. Patrick Campbell' for the *Yellow Book* in April 1894 or costume designs by E. W. Godwin for Ellen Terry in the *Mask* in October 1910, January 1912, October 1913, and April 1913. Mainstream illustrated periodicals such as the *Playgoer and Society Illustrated* appealed to their readership by giving them a peek into the glamorous fashions worn by the leading ladies of the time and fostered the image of actresses as trendsetters. Indeed, the majority of its issues had a photograph of a leading actress on their cover either in costume or in the latest dress design. E. F. S. writing for the *Westminster Gazette* notes with disgust what he calls 'the puff system':

> Nowadays there are from thirty to forty photographs a week in the illustrated papers of actresses – using the term in its widest sense. Many young ladies, who twenty years ago could not by any decent means have got their likenesses exhibited to the public except in shop-window photographs, now simper at us fifty-two times

a year, or more, and are sometimes described as 'the celebrated actress,' though a few of them never get beyond the dignity of a single silly line in the book of a musical hodge-podge. (Spence 1910: 220–1)

Indeed, George Morrow drawing for *Punch* ridicules the publicity hungry actress in the same year in a cartoon entitled: 'Improbable Scenes IV: Photographers being refused admittance to the house of a musical comedy actress' (26 Oct 1910: 306). In many ways this engagement with the unobtainable and aspirational sex appeal of the actress was the beginnings of the pin-up culture noted by Maria Elena Buszek (2006). While Catherine Hindson proves that print media and businesses at this time also realised the marketing power of the beautiful pin-up actress whose celebrity endorsement in advertisements could help to sell more products (2008).

As contemporary print media became more tolerant of the actress, so too did it become less bitter in its attacks on the actress-manager and female director of which there were several in the period 1890–1929. Those who managed theatres included: Marie Bancroft (née Wilton), Mrs John Wood (née Matilda Charlotte Vining), Madge Kendal, Janette Steer, Kate Santley, Sara Lane, Lena Ashwell, and Annie Horniman. They turned to this form of work partly due to the poor range of roles open to women, as well as the potential earnings that successful theatre management offered; while other actresses such as Elizabeth Robins chose to produce or direct plays that suited their talents without the risk of running theatres. Those who dared to take on these 'masculine roles' whether manager or director, were spoken of in the press in terms which, like those used about actresses and women critics, deliberately un-womaned them, see for example A. B. Walkley's review of 'Warp and Woof' (1904) produced by Mrs Patrick Campbell and analysed by Kerry Powell (1997: 71–2). Annie Horniman was described by Edward Gordon Craig (writing as John Semar) in the *Mask* as 'an ideal of womanhood' when he thought she was a self-sacrificing, silent lady 'doing much' for the theatre by donating money to the cause, but when she took on the management of the Manchester Gaiety and professed feminist opinions in *The Referee* he attacked her for daring to speak about the stage and presuming to 'rule' it:

> If she wishes to rule let Miss Horniman emulate our loved queen, Victoria, that true Englishwoman; and let her learn that woman is nothing but selfish accident drifting aimlessly or to the bad without the guiding influence of a man. (Oct 1910: 84)

Without a man to lead her as a theatre manager Horniman became, according to Craig, an unwomanly, even unpatriotic, woman incapable of artistic endeavour. Though Craig's chauvinism was more strident than many views found in British newspapers and periodicals, he did reflect the general consensus that women in positions of power in the theatre, whether playwright, critic, actress, director, or manager necessarily sacrifice their femininity, respectability, and nationality.

However, Edith Craig, Edward Gordon Craig's sister no less and one of the founders of The Pioneer Players, is referred to in various publications and seems to be less of a slave to gender-criticism, partly perhaps because she was the daughter of the celebrated Ellen Terry who, for Dora Marsden in the *Freewoman*, was a 'Freewoman who has become a sufficiently national figure to make her mention impersonal' (23 Nov 1911: 1). Early Pioneer productions were offered by Craig's own admission in 'place of tracts' for the feminist cause and suffered negative criticism from many quarters of the press as a consequence (Craig qtd in Cockin 2001: 46). An unsigned review in *Academy and Literature* called these plays 'typical of the "Women's Movement"' and 'purely biased' (13 May 1911: 587), while an anonymous reviewer in the *Observer* felt that as 'a mere male critic' he was 'at a disadvantage in discussing the diatribes . . . in which the pretty Pioneers indulged' (14 May 1911: 9). However, this resistance was as much to do with the combination of art and propaganda as it was to do with the feminist messages contained within these particular productions. For example, the anonymous reviewer in the *Academy* concludes his critique with the hope that 'they will not over step the mark and kill the interest of a play (for those who value good artistry) by forcing the propaganda side of their scheme' (13 May 1911: 587); in the *Observer* the critic opens with the comment that the plays 'are nothing if not propagandist' (14 May 1911: 9); while *The Times* reviewer suggests that the 'programme' should 'have been printed in mauve and green on a white background' (9 May 1911: 13) – the colours of the suffrage movement.

As the Pioneer productions became less propagandist and more experimental, so the reviews became less defensive and essentialist in their language. In the *Academy* three years later, Egan Mew stated that the latest Pioneer production managed by Miss Edith Craig is 'another way of saying that it is excellently carried out and that each of the three plays is well worth seeing' (27 June 1914: 831).[13] Her sex was not mentioned in this review and the plays (an adaptation of Guy de Maupassant's 'The Duel' by Harcourt Williams, 'The Level Crossing' by Mrs Herbert Cohen, and 'Idle Women' by Magdalen Ponsonby) offered, according to Cockin, no 'sex antagonism' (2001: 47). By 1920 Edith Craig was well respected as a theatre practitioner such that a review of three Chekhov plays produced by the Pioneer Players under the direction of Craig provoked the hope from M. Lykiardopoulos that 'what I had heard of the work of the Pioneers and Miss Edith Craig's name on the programme as producer roused faint hopes. I am glad to confess that these hopes were justified beyond my expectations' (*New Statesman* 31 Jan 1920: 496). J. T. Grein heaped praise upon her in his article for the *Illustrated London News*: '[f]or years she has stood at the head of affairs: she built the ship; she manned it; she stood firm at the tiller in fair weather and in storm' and he worried about 'the great loss that our theatre will suffer if The Pioneers cease to exist' before enumerating Craig's gifts: her ability to cast well, to create a scenic picture, to 'mould' actors and calls her 'the doughtiest champion' of women playwrights (10 July 1920: 64). Craig seems to have dodged the 'unwomanly woman' bullet in the print media of this time partly by being the daughter of Terry, but mostly by simply being good at her job and by being willing to experiment formally with the stage as an art form. Katherine Cockin notices that productions by Craig and The Pioneers 'involved the prioritisation of form over the significance of the sex of the writer' (2001: 192) and it is partly this that allowed Craig to be taken seriously by the largely male critical community. She was one of the women working in theatre who were contributing to a solution for the 'state of the drama.' However, we might also attribute the improvement in the tone of reviews of her work to when The Pioneers shifted focus from overtly feminist propaganda plays. Craig was certainly one of the female pioneers carving a path for women wishing to make their careers on the stage or behind the scenes. Her increasingly positive representation in the print media of the time is a fitting example of the shifts in attitude taking place in print and in society at large.

Women like Edith Craig were certainly fighting for a place in theatre history at this time and are only now beginning to be recognised by modern historians thanks in part to digital databases which have made searching for contemporary reviews and essays in print media much easier. Magazines, newspapers, and other periodicals are one of the ways by which we can chart the contribution of women to 'the state of the drama' from 1890 to 1929. Not only do they sketch ephemeral productions in words and images enabling researchers to piece together the performances of plays by women, but they also contain the responses of the critic, editor, and ultimately the readership to women's playwriting, their productions and women's roles on and behind the stage more generally. However, as primary resources they are not always reliable, often coloured by the gender, class, or personal tastes of the journalist and editor and tainted by the social status, political affiliation, and gender of the readers.

The late nineteenth- and early twentieth-century theatre and print-media industries undeniably 'presented a misogynist obstacle course' to women who dared to write for the stage, venture on stage or work behind the scenes (Newey 2005: 1). 'Victorian gender ideology . . . theorized the public nature of the playwright's task [and by extension all women working in the theatres] to be unfeminine' (ibid.), and as such women 'had no real power in what was a theatre system in transition but largely owned and run by men' (Gale 2000: 32). On top of which they then had to contend with the pride and prejudice of male critics and editors in newspapers, journals, and little magazines. However, these decades do demonstrate a shift in the response of print media and by extension their readership to women playwrights, critics, actors, managers, and directors, who were taking advantage of the increasing respectability of the stage in order to gain a firmer footing in the various professions that it offered. The rise of feminist and suffrage presses supported this sea change. Women's transference from private angel to public professional during the First World War, enfranchisement, and The Sex Disqualification Removal Act 1919 helped to deconstruct the idea that women working in these public arenas were unsexed by their choice of career, or inferior artists. Thus women surged forward in spite of both male-dominated industries (the stage and journalism) – printing their own plays on their own presses, cultivating a more respectable and respected image for themselves as actresses, unapologetically offering their judgements and entering centre stage as players on both page and stage.

Notes

1. See for example the poetic plays of Lascelles Abercrombie, Wilfrid Wilson Gibson, and John Drinkwater in *New Numbers*: Lascelles Abercrombie, 'The Olympians,' Feb 1914: 31–54; Wilfrid Wilson Gibson, 'Bloodybush Edge,' Feb 1914: 5–27; Lascelles Abercrombie, 'The End of the World,' Apr 1914: 61–96; John Drinkwater, 'The Storm,' Aug 1914: 119–31; Wilfrid Wilson Gibson, 'Hoops,' Aug 1914: 135–46; Lascelles Abercrombie, 'The Staircase,' Dec 1914: 170–91. Or the March 1912 issue of *The Poetry Review* edited by Harold Monro which was dedicated to poetic drama.
2. Although the term actor is now preferred for both men and women, I will be using the term actress here because it was the word used by all at this time to describe women actors.

3. For an extensive, though not exhaustive, list of women playwrights and their work see Newey 2005: 190–237.
4. See also Davis and Donkin 1999: 1–12.
5. See the suffragette rejection of such reductive representations in 'The Outlook: The Anti-Suffragist' *Votes for Women* 17 Oct 1907: 13.
6. The plays in the *Yellow Book* are: John Oliver Hobbes and George Moore, 'The Fool's Hour: The First Act of a Comedy,' Apr 1894: 253–72; Fred M. Simpson, 'The Dedication,' Apr 1894: 159–84; Walter Raleigh 'Poet and Historian,' Jan 1896: 349–65. The *Pageant* contains: Maurice Maeterlinck, 'The Death of Tintagiles,' Alfred Sutro (trans.), 1896: 47–71; Michael Field, 'Equal Love,' 1896: 189–228; Maurice Maeterlinck, 'The Seven Princesses,' Alfred Sutro (trans.), 1896: 163–84.
7. Christopher St John, 'How Master Constans Went to the North,' in the *Green Sheaf* (May 1903 and June 1903); Mary Brown, 'The Lament of the Lyceum Rat,' in the *Green Sheaf* (Sep 1903); H. Heijermans, 'Cobus on Death,' Christopher St John's (trans.) in the *Green Sheaf* (Oct 1903). The *English Review* also published *Edge o' the Dark* by Gwen John in November 1912.
8. Establishment-affirming plays might occasionally appear in ordinary women's magazines such as *The Gentlewoman*, see for example, 'An Inconvenient Sentiment' in which an author called Peggy seeks fame, but is unable to achieve it without writing something 'New' and shocking. When she succeeds in writing such a novel she sacrifices her 'self-respect': 'Peggy. (*sadly, but with conviction*). "I shall never get it [her self-respect] back, Hilda. Perhaps in time I may learn to do without it"' (11 Apr 1896: 484).
9. See also Clarke 2005 and Latta 2006.
10. Dorothy Neville Lees was one of the first to translate works about the Commedia dell'Arte into English, though Craig took much of the praise for it.
11. Woolf reviewed 'Lysistrata' in the *Englishwoman* (Nov 1910), The Pioneer Players' *The Higher Court* (*New Statesman* 17 Apr 1920), *The Cherry Orchard* (*New Statesman* 24 July 1920), *Love for Love* (*New Statesman* 2 Apr 1921), and *Twelfth Night* (*New Statesman* 30 Sep 1933).
12. I have chosen to include the *Mask* as a British journal because, though printed in Italy, the contributors were almost exclusively English and, as Olga Taxidou points out, Craig in his European isolation became increasingly nationalistic (1998).
13. Mew's earlier review on 17 January 1914 of 'Paphnutius' by Hroswitha is similarly positive and ungendered (88–9).

Works Cited

Bennett, Arnold. 1898. *Journalism for Women: A Practical Guide*. London: John Lane.
Buszek, Maria Elena. 2006. *Pin-Up Grrrls: Feminism, Sexuality, Popular Culture*. Durham, NC: Duke University Press.
Cima, Gay Gibson. 1999. '"To Be Public as a Genius and Private as a Woman": The Critical Framing of 19th Century Women Playwrights.' *Women and Playwriting in 19th Century Britain*. Ed. Tracy C. Davis and Ellen Donkin. Cambridge: Cambridge University Press. 35–53.
Clarke, Meaghan. 2005. *Critical Voices: Women and Art Criticism in Britain 1880–1905*. Burlington: Ashgate.
Cockin, Katharine. 2001. *Women and Theatre in the Age of Suffrage: The Pioneer Players 1911–1925*. London: Palgrave Macmillan.
Davis, Tracy C. and Ellen Donkin, eds. 1999. 'Introduction.' *Women and Playwriting in 19th Century Britain*. Cambridge: Cambridge University Press. 1–12.

DiCenzo, Maria. 2008. 'Feminism, Theatre Criticism, and the Modern Drama.' *South Central Review: Staging Modernism* 25.1: 36–55.
Farfan, Penny. 2004. *Women, Modernism and Performance*. Cambridge: Cambridge University Press.
Gale, Maggie B. 1996. *West End Women: Women and the London Stage 1918–1962*. London: Routledge.
—. 2000. 'Women Playwrights of the 1920s and 1930s.' *Cambridge Companion to Modern British Women Playwrights*. Ed. Elaine Aston and Janelle Reinelt. Cambridge: Cambridge University Press. 23–37.
Gandolfi, Roberta. 1997. 'Edy Craig and Suffrage Theatre.' *The Open Page: Theatre Women Politics* 3: 54–9.
Green, Barbara. 1997. *Spectacular Confessions: Autobiography, Performative Activism and the Sites of Suffrage, 1905–1938*. New York: St Martin's Press.
Hindson, Catherine. 2008. *Female Performance Practice on the Fin-de-siècle Popular Stages of London and Paris: Experiment and Advertisement*. Manchester: Manchester University Press.
Holledge, Julie. 1981. *Innocent Flowers: Women in the Edwardian Theatre*. London: Virago.
Jameson, Storm. 1920. *Modern Drama in Europe*. London: W. Collins and Sons & Co. Ltd.
Latta, Carolyn. 2006. 'The Lady is a Critic.' *Women in American Theatre*. Ed. Helen K. Chinoy and Linda W. Jenkins. New York: Theatre Communications Group.
Moi, Toril. 2004. 'Ibsen, Theatre, and Ideology of Modernism.' *Theatre Survey* 45.2: 247–52.
—. 2006. *Ibsen and the Birth of Modernism*. Oxford: Oxford University Press.
Morgan, Fidelis. 1994. *The Years Between: Plays by Women on the London Stage 1900–1950*. London: Virago.
Newey, Katherine. 2005. *Women's Theatre Writing in Victorian Britain*. London: Palgrave Macmillan.
Paxton, Naomi. 2013. *The Methuen Drama Book of Suffrage Plays*. London: Methuen.
Powell, Kerry. 1997. *Women and Victorian Theatre*. Cambridge: Cambridge University Press.
Robins, Elizabeth. 1913. *Way Stations*. New York: Dodd and Mead.
Spence, Edward Fordham. 1910. *Our Stage and Its Critics*. London: Methuen and Co.
Taxidou, Olga. 1998. *The Mask: A Periodical Performance by Edward Gordon Craig*. London: Routledge.
Woolf, Virginia. [1920] 1988. '*The Cherry Orchard, New Statesman*, 24 July 1920.' *The Essays of Virginia Woolf: 1919–1924*. Ed. Andrew McNeillie. Vol. 3, San Diego, New York, and London: Harcourt, Brace, Jovanovich. 246–9.
—. [1921] 1988. 'Congreve, *New Statesman*, 2 April 1921.' *The Essays of Virginia Woolf: 1919–1924*. Ed. Andrew McNeillie. Vol. 3, San Diego, New York, and London: Harcourt, Brace, Jovanovich. 295–7.
—. [1929] 2015. *A Room of One's Own and Three Guineas*. Oxford: Oxford University Press.
—. [1933] 2011. '*Twelfth Night* at The Old Vic, *New Statesman*, 30 September 1933.' *The Essays of Virginia Woolf: 1933–1941*. Ed. Stuart N. Clarke. Vol. 6. London: Hogarth. 4–8.

7

Dance, Modernism, and the Female Critic in the *New Age*, *Rhythm*, and the *Outlook*

Susan Jones

WHEN SERGEI DIAGHILEV, the great Russian impresario, directed the Ballets Russes season at its opening in London in 1911, he repeated his company's spectacular 1909 Parisian success. The Russians' performances in Britain generated an unprecedented flurry of favourable reviews in the arts columns of contemporary journals such as the *Bystander*, *New Statesman*, and the *Athenaeum*, written by a range of columnists who adapted their experience to the field of dance criticism. The extraordinary impact of the Ballets Russes on the periodical press has in part resulted in that company's acquiring a special status as *the* influence of dance on modernism in the period. Reviews tended to be written by men – frequently well-known literary figures or specialists in music and the visual arts, including Lytton Strachey, his brother James (an expert in psychoanalysis), Clive Bell, Roger Fry, and the music critics Francis Toye and Edward J. Dent, who used their knowledge of other artistic fields to interpret the new theatrical aesthetic taking London by storm. Their interest in the Ballets Russes frequently turned on their perception of the company's modernism, and often drew closely on ideas developed principally from literary modernism and the contemporary visual and musical arts. Bell pronounced in the *New Republic* that 'The New Ballet' registered an aesthetic shift relating to experiments in other art forms. Writing of Léonide Massine, Diaghilev's chief choreographer in 1919, Bell declared: 'M. Massine's achievement' puts '[ballet] on a level with literature, music, and the graphic arts' (30 July 1919: 415).[1]

Yet it was a female critic, Marcelle Azra Hincks, who was among the first to consider dance as a pursuit worthy of particular critical attention, long before the Ballets Russes hit London and before that company's productions were appropriated by the literati as the watchword for the new aesthetic.[2] Before the arrival of the Russian Ballet in Britain Hincks had already written an important article in A. R. Orage and Holbrook Jackson's *New Age*. On 4 August 1910 she wrote on 'The Dance Critic,' in which she lobbied for 'a special and intelligent criticism of the dance' (328). It is true that a good deal of lively dance criticism was generated in the pre-war and postwar years of the Ballets Russes, but the idea of a dance critic, and especially one who was female, dedicated to specialised reviews of the art form in non-specialist newspapers and journals remained relatively elusive.

In fact, specialised dance criticism *did* exist in the early twentieth century. The Royal Academy of Dance (RAD), which started life in 1920 as the Association of

Teachers of Operatic Dancing of Great Britain, had been born out of an association with the *Dancing Times* (established 1894 as the house magazine of the Cavendish Rooms, London, a ballroom dancing establishment). The RAD thus originally came into being at a meeting led by Philip Richardson, the editor of the *Dancing Times*. Women wrote for this journal, but Richardson had controlled the dissemination of specialised dance criticism as editor of the periodical from 1910. It was not until 1963 that Mary Clarke became the first female editor of the *Dancing Times*. Before and after the First World War, dance criticism in print media continued to be written principally by male literati, and Hincks's advocacy of a specialised dance critic that would appear in non-specialist newspapers and periodicals remained unfulfilled for many years.

Nevertheless, there are a few female writers who bring a distinctive voice to the genre during this period. Like their male counterparts, they were writing from the perspective of expertise in other art forms, such the painters Dorothy (Georges) Banks and Anne Estelle Rice in *Rhythm*, or the writer Rebecca West in the *Outlook*. These women's sensitive handling of their observations differs in tone and style from their male counterparts and produces some of the most illuminating dance criticism of the period.

Marcelle Azra Hincks in the *New Age*

Hincks (who sometimes used the nom de plume, Countess Morphy; or for her later writing Marcelle Azra Forbes) was something of an innovator in the field of dance writing in contemporary journals of the period. She wrote initially on Greek dance in the *Nineteenth Century* in 1906 and *Revue Archéologique* in 1909, and in 1910 she published a book on *The Japanese Dance*, possibly to coincide with the Japan-British Exhibition at London's White City. She later turned to cookery writing, but before this she was taken up by the *New Age* to write regular columns on performances and scholarly discussions of dance. Her work deserves particular attention for a number of reasons. She not only displayed a knowledge of, and interest in the history of dance in all its forms in pre-Ballets Russes criticism, but she also provides evidence for the often-forgotten fact that an audience for performance dance had already been generated in London before the Ballets Russes arrived. As Jane Pritchard has observed, Arthur Symons, the poet, critic, and friend of W. B. Yeats, excelled in the criticism of dance in the music halls from 1891 (Pritchard 2003: 36–89). This audience had encountered and had been further educated in the aesthetics of Greek dance, contemporary innovations choreographed by Maud Allan, Margaret Morris, Isadora Duncan, and the work of Russian soloists such as Anna Pavlova and Mikhail Mordkin.

Hincks found her voice in the *New Age*, which was certainly in the vanguard of this burgeoning cultural interest in dance and which covered the art in a variety of genres up to 1920. The range of discussion in the *New Age*, often to be found in the context of columns on drama or music, is exemplified by articles including those by L. Haden Guest, G. R. S. Taylor, and Huntly Carter. Haden Guest muses on whether dance should be included in drama: 'No play without a dance would be perhaps too hard a saying. It would be difficult, for instance, to fit one conveniently in "Ghosts," or in Shaw's "Man and Superman." But many plays would be humanised by a dance' (9 May 1907: 28). G. R. S. Taylor continues the debate in 'The Legitimate Drama' (18 Jan 1908: 229), by examining the role of dance in a discussion of contemporary pantomime as the popular form of the *Gesamtkunstwerk*, as well as the place of dance in drama (as in Ibsen's use of the tarantella in *A Doll's House*). Haden Guest turned to dance as an art form in itself when he reviewed the soloist dancer Maud Allan appearing at the Palace Theatre in London (11 Apr 1908: 476). Allan was renowned for her 'Salome' dance and Herbert Hughes had already reviewed Richard Strauss's opera in the 7 December 1907 issue (118). In an article on Isadora Duncan in 1908, W. R. Titterton promoted a place for understanding the 'semiotics' of dance: 'Just as music, sculpture, painting, literature have their conventional languages, dancing is to have its language. Every movement of the limbs is to have its meaning, every primitive emotion its conventional sign; the leit motif transformed into gesture, in fact' (18 July 1908: 226). Huntly Carter wrote on drama, dance, and frequently responded to the aesthetic principles of the rival journal, John Middleton Murry's *Rhythm*. Carter appears to have 'spotted' Hincks – he wrote a favourable notice of Hincks's book on Japanese dance in the *New Age* (7 July 1910: 235). In the same notice he references an article in the *Mask* (Apr 1910) on Francis Douce's 1807 book on Ancient English Morris dancing.

The *New Age* even published occasional poems on dance, such as 'Four Poems on Pavlova' by A. Cull (25 Jan 1912: 302–4); and 'The Dancer' by 'Vectis' (2 Apr 1914: 695), which satirically compares the movement of the dancer to that of film in contemporary cinema. And the *New Age* was swift to cover Émile Jaques-Dalcroze's (1865–1950) influential invention of Eurythmics, an innovative dance and music system practiced at Hellerau, a garden suburb of Dresden, Germany, where Dalcroze had received a grant to build a centre and develop his experimental arts project. In the anonymous 'Letters from Abroad' section of 10 August 1911, one of several subsequent discussions of Dalcrozian Eurythmics appeared: 'We should be made conscious of the rhythmical expansion of the soul of the one into the soul of the other by means of speech, song, dance, music or decoration as the case may be' (346). The Ballets Russes was covered mainly by male columnists – Herbert Hughes would later elaborate on various dance topics, including the Russian Ballet, Maud Allan and Isadora Duncan, Anna Pavlova and other Russian soloists, in his music review (10 Aug 1911: 356); and in 1919, after the war, Ezra Pound joined the regular commentators of dance in his reviews of the Ballets Russes as William Atheling and B. H. Dias.

Dance quickly became an important preoccupation for aesthetic modernism in the early twentieth century, and in this respect is aligned with the *New Age*'s general emphasis on 'the new.' In many ways it was Hincks who gave foundation to the *New Age*'s contemporary focus on dance. When the Ballets Russes arrived in London there was already, as Hincks's 1910 *New Age* essay 'The Dance Critic' shows, an appetite for the serious treatment of dance in all its forms that accorded with the interests of literary writers like Woolf, Mansfield, Eliot, and Lawrence. Hincks uses the masculine pronoun inclusively in her essay, presumably imagining herself in the role of dance critic, but she is clear on the range of treatment she envisages: 'every manifestation of dancing should receive his consideration, that the whole range of the Dance from the crude jumpings and gesticulations of the savage to the formal and rigid ballet, should be within the reach of his understanding and the scope of his emotional sympathy' (4 Aug 1910: 328). Moreover, she gestured to her historical knowledge by invoking the classical precedent of the Greek satirist, Lucian, as the ideal model for the range of scholarship that should be brought to bear on the subject of writing about dance.

Hincks already participates at this point in an explicitly modernist discourse about the relationship of history to the contemporary; and about the relationship between corporeal movements in space and time. Her early writing on Greek dance emphasises the art form's connection to literature, art, and philosophy, all of which were influences on Isadora Duncan and the Greek dance movement. Most importantly for the dissemination of modernist aesthetics, Hincks wrote in 1906 in the *Nineteenth Century* of the way in which Greek 'sculpture and painting can tell us how the Greeks danced in *space*; their poems, if sufficiently analyzed, how they danced in *time*' (Mar 1906: 449–50). To some extent Hincks is alluding to correspondences between poetry and movement, rooted in ideas of rhythm, established by Stéphane Mallarmé, W. B. Yeats, Arthur Symons, and her own book on Japanese dance. But here Hincks is in tune with classical precedents for modernist preoccupations with the body's interaction with the coordinates of space and time (as in, for example, Plato's *Timaeus*). Interestingly, she anticipates Henri Bergson's contemporary philosophical enquiries (1910) in his identification of gestural grace as it relates to the physical distension of the mind and its perception of present and future states of being and action: 'As those movements are easy which prepare the way for others, we are led to find a superior ease in the movements which can be foreseen, in the present attitudes in which future attitudes are pointed out and, as it were, prefigured' (1971: 11–12). Bergson makes the connection with our perception of time: 'thus the perception of ease in motion passes over into the pleasure of mastering the flow of time and of holding the future in the present' (1971: 12). Hincks, however, also engages with a late nineteenth-century preoccupation with 'the primitive' which would become a foundation of modernism. In the same essay (and in subsequent pieces), Hincks goes on to explore anthropological perspectives on dance, gesturing to the influence of Friedrich Nietzsche (borrowing from his perspective on the Dionysiac and Apolline in *The Birth of Tragedy* (1872)) as well as to proto-modernist impulses that turned to primitivism and to new configurations of movement and the body. Hincks's writing suggests a new 'modernist' turn in attitudes to dance. In part she is picking up on the emphasis on the corporeality of all texts, encouraged by writers such as Mallarmé, who indicated that dance is far from a peripheral or decorative art form but a 'thing in itself,' constitutive of a creative practice close to poetics that gave rise to and inspired a range of aesthetic innovations during this period.[3]

Hincks's discussion of the dances of antiquity informs her approach to future criticism, including her reading of the work of individual contemporary Russian dancers (i.e. soloists who appeared in London in concert performance before, and apart from Diaghilev's Ballets Russes). In a *New Age* article on Anna Pavlova, entitled 'Personality in Dancing' (28 July 1910: 303), Hincks establishes a formalist discussion of the work of the Russian ballerina who introduced theatregoers at the Palace Theatre, London, to her country's individual dance virtuosity. Emphasising the renowned expressivism of Russian style, Hincks first claims the 'emotional significance' of the ballerina's performance as having revived 'that "expressive" dancing of antiquity which the Greek and Roman poets praise beyond measure' (ibid.). But she goes on to assert that the Russians had not renounced tradition but had 'infused new life' into 'conventional technique' in such a way as to 'show that "form" may reveal, and not extinguish or hide, those emotions and feelings which alone give some artistic value to dancing' (ibid.). She continued to lobby for a new kind of dance criticism – one that recognised such attributes as 'self-realisation' and 'expression of temperament' and suggested that these qualities were illustrated by Pavlova. The crucial distinction of Pavlova's dancing came from a Russian style that favoured personality in the performance – a quality that Hincks conflates somewhat with a notion of 'individuality' and which she claimed was unfamiliar to English audiences: 'Individuality in dancing has been hitherto very little considered either by dancers themselves or by the public' (ibid.) and, she observes, only exhibited in modern dance by such exceptional figures as Isadora Duncan and Ruth St Denis. Otherwise, she continues, within the present limitations of modern dance and ballet, 'it is almost inevitable that the individuality of the dancer shall be absorbed in the ensemble, which levels all dancers to the rank of unthinking and unfeeling puppets' (ibid.).

What is striking about this position in the light of later formalist discussions of dance by Strachey, T. S. Eliot, and Ezra Pound, is its favouring of 'personality' as a positive and innovative phenomenon – very different to the aesthetics of 'impersonality' (considered by these writers as a corollary of literary impersonality) demonstrated by Léonide Massine, Lydia Lopokova, and other Russian exponents of the Ballets Russes' 1919 season's repertoire. Furthermore, Hincks establishes here a need for a new kind of critic who is capable of identifying this ephemeral quality of individuality. Thus Hincks effectively initiates a ten-year discussion in the periodical press of what constitutes 'modern' in the art of dance – with a position that would much later be supported by Rebecca West in *her* review of the Ballets Russes in 1919. These women's promotion of self-expression and the personality of the performer lies in contrast to the male literary modernists' preference for the performer's subsumption of subjective feeling in a cult of 'impersonality,' which, as T. S. Eliot would write of Massine's dancing, does not *express* emotion, but rather 'symbolises' it (*Criterion* Apr 1923: 305–6). Of course, Eliot was not advocating that the dancer should have no personality (Massine's presence on stage and on film was famously riveting), but, drawing on his musings on the role of the poet in 'Tradition and the Individual Talent' (1919), that the dancer should provide a vehicle for the delivery of choreographic form, rather than an emotional expression of the self.

Another distinctive feature of Hincks's approach is that she does not limit her discussion to Pavlova. In spite of the Russian dancer's celebrity status, she gives equal column inches in the previous issue of the *New Age* (21 July 1910) to Pavlova's partner, Mikhail Mordkin. This in itself is a striking move – we normally think of the Ballets Russes soloist, Vaslav Nijinsky, as the great artist who provoked discussion of the new status of the male dancer in the twentieth century, but Hincks demonstrates an unacknowledged precedent in Mordkin, whom she considered to be the first male dancer she had seen display exceptionally expressive qualities beyond his role as 'support' of the ballerina.[4] Mordkin, she wrote, 'alone of all dancers is worthy of that high praise which to the modern mind seems so exaggerated when it is bestowed on a thing which has no parallel at the present day' (21 July 1910: 278). Hincks bemoans the current state of dance as having been reduced to empty 'form' and claims that Mordkin, like Pavlova, contributed that essential ingredient of 'personality' and expressiveness that elevated dance to something more meaningful to be taken seriously as an art in itself. Again, she takes her position from views she initiated in previous articles in which she privileged the dance of ancient Greek culture, proposed initially by critics such as Lucian as the model for aesthetic excellence.

However much Hincks praised the ballet dancers Pavlova and Mordkin, she found very specific inspiration in the individuality of what she considered to be 'ethnic dance.' Spanish dance, and particularly flamenco, held great interest for Hincks, as it did for many followers of dance in this period – encouraged and promoted to some degree by Ballets Russes choreographers' bona fide research into folk and ethnic dance to inform their work. Michel Fokine had travelled through Russia to find the folk-dance vocabulary for his Polovtsian Dances from *Prince Igor* (1909), and a decade later Léonide Massine's studies of flamenco for his 1919 ballet *Le Tricorne* sustained his choreographic methodology. On 22 September 1910 in the *New Age* Hincks published her own perspective on 'Spanish' dance (she is really referring to the Andalusian form, flamenco, already popular beyond its original territory in southern Spain). In 'A Letter from Spain: A Spanish Dancer,' Hincks recounts her witnessing of the great, dramatic flamenco dancer La Pepita, whom she encountered at a café performance in 'Gerona' (the Catalonian city Girona). Pepita is of interest to literary modernists in that she was the grandmother of Vita Sackville-West, who wrote a biography of the dancer in 1937.[5] Hincks focuses on the notion of primitivism in describing Pepita's performance of flamenco form, her Dionysiac abandon unleashing erotic energy:

> Then gradually the dance became more animated, the rhythm quickened, and Pepita wakened; her eyes ... flashed fiery glances at the audience ... her figure swayed and bent, she bounded from one side of the stage to the other. She whirled around madly, like a frenzied Maenad, with her head thrown back, as if in an ecstasy; the long fringes of her shawl seemed to fly around her as she twisted rapidly; at times she would give a jerking forward movement, and bend backwards till her head almost touched the ground. There was something barbarous and savage in her dancing, and almost brutal in its excess; and as the singer's voice rose, and as the guitar became louder and harsher, Pepita grew more and more excited, and danced with a passion and mad delight such as I have never seen before. (22 Sep 1910: 493)

The punchline to Hincks's story, however, lies in the gory outcome of the performance, as two male audience members vie for Pepita's attention. When the dancer, 'callous and indifferent, laughing and flirting,' throws a rose on the table between the two men, one stabs the other's hand as the first reaches to grab the flower. Despite the sensationalism of Hincks's story, in which she presents Pepita's action through the conventional lens of the femme fatale, Hincks closes with a return to her admiration for the dancer's extraordinary artistic ability, observing that 'I felt that one had but to see Pepita to forgive her for any crime!' (ibid.).

However, Hincks sustains a more weighty exploration of unfamiliar ethnic forms elsewhere in the *New Age*, commencing with her article on 'Dancing and Anthropology' (25 Aug 1910). Although Hincks uses the terms 'tribal' and 'savage' in abundance, it is interesting to note that a distinction so often made between 'civilized' and 'savage' rituals by her contemporaries in discourses on dance (when alluding on the one hand to classical Greek and on the other to all other atavistic forms) is never really addressed, and often Hincks uses arguments from her perspective on the recovery of Greek dance in her assessment of other kinds of ethnic forms. In part her researches derive from the work she did for an important essay in the *Revue*

Archéologique in 1909 in which she undertook a comparative study of classical Greek and other 'primitive' tribal dances. Drawing on studies in the British Museum and the work of classical and anthropological scholars such as Emmanuel Loewy, H. Ling Roth, Maurice Emmanuel, and with reference to Carlo Blassis' 1820 dance manual, the *Traité élémentaire, théorique, et pratique de l'art de la danse* ('Elementary, Theoretical, and Practical Treatise on the Art of the Dance'), she proposes both a universalist and structuralist perspective on all dance forms. She employs several visual references and suggestions of how consciousness works through the function of memory to reconstruct an image of dance on objects such as vases and paintings. She uses these visual aids to accompany Blassis' 'balletic' vocabulary in order to advance her comparative argument, where she shows the commonality of certain dance forms across time: so that the *plié* in second position of Blassis' treatise can also be found in the drawings of the Aryballos figure of vase painting from Cumae; or in a representation of the Australian *corrobboree*; and the balletic *jeté* appears elsewhere as the dance of a Maenad from a fragment of a situla, found in Daphnae in 1888 (July–Dec 1909: 355–6). Thus Hincks proposes reconstruction of atavistic forms of dance with reference to visual art and nineteenth-century balletic discourse. But, of course, she has no way of ascertaining the accuracy of a comparative study, where subtle variations occur between forms. The distribution of weight of the figures, the connective gestures between poses, the kinaesthetic quality is often hard to interpret with such limited information, in that the nuanced rhythms and force of execution of dances differ radically according to context. The effect or implied meaning shifts even when what appears to be an identical representation or description of a 'pose' or movement is considered comparatively.

Nevertheless, Hincks's later 1910 essay in the *New Age* constitutes a serious critique of the way in which dance had been marginalised in the scholarship of ethnic customs and rituals, and Hincks begins with the difficulties she experienced while attempting to pursue the topic as an object of study. She writes that after

> reading innumerable books on savage life and wading through volumes of anthropological and ethnological journals published in England and abroad, I found that the information which I obtained therefrom was practically useless for my purpose. There were few precise and accurate descriptions of savage dances, and still fewer attempts to interpret their postures and movements, whilst the scientific methods of investigation and comparative study which have been applied so successfully to other branches of anthropology were never applied to the study of dancing. (25 Aug 1910: 400)

Yet, as Hincks goes on to remark, the 'importance of dancing as one of the principal factors of social and religious life is not disputed by anthropologists' (ibid.), whether associated with expressions of eroticism, social/religious ritual, or war. She imagines that issues of delicacy and prudery have had their effect on limiting the presentation of information, but still cannot credit that this could have impeded scholars such as James Frazer, who, she writes, brings nuance and lyrical description to other aspects of anthropological study. In order to rectify the situation, she advocates 'comparative methods' taken from 'the sphere of religion, and art, and to substitute for the uncritical and disconnected work which has hitherto been done with regard to dancing a scientific examination into its origins and sources' (25 Aug 1910: 401). She thus suggests the method that should be used: 'dances of existing savages should be studied; we should know amongst which tribes dancing is extensively used as a means of expression; we should find what are the feelings which incite to dancing; and dances should be classified and grouped according to their meaning and purpose' (ibid.). Moreover, she insists that anthropologists undertaking such enquiries should be trained for research in dance and become experts in the subject. Effectively she is proposing a stronger place for dance specialism in broader anthropological fields – a discussion already emerging to some extent in Classical Studies in the context of the work of figures like Jane Harrison, Gilbert Murray, Francis Cornford, and the Cambridge Ritualists. In the 1920s and 1930s Ruby Ginner would analyse Greek dance in much the same way that Hincks had suggested in her 1910 article on the dance of the ancient Greeks.[6] By the twenties this kind of evaluation is forthcoming in the US in *Theatre Arts Monthly*, from D. H. Lawrence in essays such as the 'Hopi Snake Dance' (Dec 1924: 836–60), or from the critic Florence Gilliam, who compared Lydia Sokolova's interpretation of the Chosen One in Massine's version of the *Rite of Spring* to 'the fantastic ecstasy of the dervish' (*Theatre Arts Monthly* Mar 1924: 192–3). But at this earlier moment, Hincks presented a lone voice with an innovative position, as the specialist field of dance anthropology was undertaken in the late twentieth century by scholars such as Georgina Gore (and embraced by scholars such as Mariana Torgovnik), did not really take hold until Katherine Dunham's work on Haitian dance in the 1930s.

Hincks developed her theories in two further articles of August and September 1912, on 'Primitive Dancing,' which sought to give greater emphasis to forms not just associated with Greek and Roman history, but rather to include all tribal and ritual dance activities of peoples universally. The argument is of considerable importance in that she has presumably now seen the Ballets Russes and is implying that there has been a shift toward non-mimetic contemporary forms of ballet and modern dance in which these arts move into the period of modernist abstraction. But in the field of anthropology she emphasises particularly the need to rediscover and understand the importance and mimetic nature of gesture, arguing effectively for a recovery of gestural language that has lost its semiotic significance:

> The fact that dancing was originally both pantomimic and religious is one of the greatest stumbling-blocks to the student who is seeking to grasp the full import and significance of the dance of primitive peoples, or of ancient times, for our own dancing entirely overlooks the original purpose of the art, and consists mainly of stereotyped and meaningless evolutions of the lower limbs, the arms and hands being called in merely as an aid to equilibrium. (*New Age* 29 Aug 1912: 427)

By contrast, Hincks feels that in order to ascertain the correct 'significance' of ancient and tribal dances the anthropologist should study the rhythmic structures, formations, and plans of even the most 'wild and unregulated' or 'rough and primitive' dance in relation to social purpose and function, as in the example of 'the "corroborees" (dance rituals) of the Australians,' whose dances 'are much in the nature of plays, wherein are given dramatic representations of the habits and movements of animals, or of hunting, fighting, love-making, and all the important incidents of daily life' (*New Age* 5 Sep 1912: 450). Moreover, these dances integrate ancient traditional forms with the expression of new events accompanying colonisation – such as the first time aboriginal peoples witnessed the white man's capture of whales:

> The most striking and characteristic features of the incident were reduced to rhythmic form, and having made an effigy of the whale, they danced around it, driving their spears into the figure, and with ape-like ability giving a pantomimic display of the scene which they had witnessed. In these corroborees there is frequently a leader of the dance, who, by means of a bunch of feathers, guides the movements of the others. (ibid.)

Later in the article Hincks likewise describes the practical function of dance for the Mandan Indians, who 'depend on the buffaloes for their food,' and 'have a dance which they perform when the hunt has been unsuccessful' (5 Sep 1912: 451). She discusses how distinctions should also be made between those dances that retain their function as conduits of social activity or spirituality, those initiated by religious beliefs, but surviving only in form and becoming over time empty of religious fervour; or again, a different sort of 'pantomimic dance,' celebrating the natural habitat, such as the Emu dance performed by the Tasmanians (5 Sep 1912: 450).

As we have seen, a characteristic of Hincks's method is the citation of Lucian as a model and ancient precedent for anthropological study of dance, but she refers to other more closely contemporary figures such Sir James Frazer (who published the highly influential comparative study of mythology and religion, *The Golden Bough* in 1890) and also specifies the work of nineteenth-century French ethnographer, Élie Reclus, on the 'Inoits.' When it comes to Hincks's own voice in her comparison of 'tribal' and 'civilised' dance forms, we hear a familiar, somewhat patronising, Eurocentric tone (to be heard, for example in Richard Burton's description of the *pas de deux* of Dahomean dancers (1864: 10)) and again, as in the *Revue Archéologie* article, a comparison with the technical specificity of ballet, or *danse d'école*. This tone creeps into the comparison of 'primitive' and 'Western' dances in which Hincks borrows from Reclus the description of one Inoit dance, 'The Happy Hunter' as 'a kind of ballet' and another that 'resembles a minuet' where the 'rhythm is very precise, the music grave and measured, slow and monotonous' (5 Sep 1912: 450) and where 'the women wear a clinging garment of white deer-skin, very similar to the tights of a ballerina, and over this a tunic of the most fairy-like material, brilliant and light, transparent and silver-streaked' (ibid.). Nevertheless, Hincks concludes with a strong critique of the current state of the art, declaring that study of 'primitive' dance shows that 'from a purely artistic standpoint' the expressiveness of the 'savage dance' is 'immeasurably superior to that mechanical and inexpressive substitute for it which we see to-day in our great centres of civilisation' (5 Sep 1912: 451).

The Ballets Russes in *Rhythm* and the *Outlook*

Hincks does not write directly about the Ballets Russes. However, the 'mechanical and inexpressive substitute' she talks of in her observations on primitive dancing had already generated acclaim from critics who saw the company in 1909 in Paris, and after 1919 the postwar seasons in London were drawing high praise in the *New Age* from the intellectual milieu. Even a rigorous critic such as William Atheling, or B. H.

Dias (aka Ezra Pound, writing in the *New Age* under these two different pseudonyms), who had not thought highly of Massine's choreography for the Ballets Russes production of *Tricorne* in 1919, welcomed the Craigian principles of the 'super-marionette' as a 'justification' for 'modern aesthetic ideas,' delivered in dance by Massine in *La Boutique Fantasque* (23 Oct 1919: 427).

Yet two female critics, Dorothy (Georges) Banks and Anne Estelle Rice, had elsewhere already suggested the modernist turn in choreographic design in the ballets presented by the Ballets Russes in London in their initial seasons of 1911 and 1912, and one of them, Dorothy Banks, was ahead of Pound in her identification of the Craigian theme in the new ballets. Turning back to the publication of the journal *Rhythm* during these years, these women stand out for their incisive characterisation of Diaghilev's avant-garde aesthetic. In fact, they may have helped to further the dialogue between this journal and the *New Age*, since their writing on the Ballets Russes complements Hincks's contributions on Greek dance and anthropology in a modernist context. The title *Rhythm* suggests how dance might have had an important impact on the editors' conception of the avant-garde aesthetics actively debated in the 'little magazine' culture of British and American modernism.[7] Established in 1911 by John Middleton Murry and Michael Sadler (later Katherine Mansfield replaced Sadler as editor), *Rhythm*'s manifesto was in part driven by Bergsonian philosophical accounts of time and subjectivity, which, according to Middleton Murry, 'conquers the crude opposition between subject and object' (June 1911: 9). In 1912, Murry and Mansfield wrote of *Rhythm* facilitating the 'expression' of the 'symbol of the idea' as a basis for modern aesthetics (June 1912: 19). As part of a preference for economy of form in the arts, the journal's critical assessment of choreographic innovation may be identified as an important aspect of their overall evaluation of the Ballets Russes' relationship to modernism in other art forms. Banks and Rice both provided reviews of the Russian Ballet accompanied by their own illustrations.

As we have seen, a common theme of male commentators such as Clive Bell in the *New Republic* and Pound as B. H. Dias in the *New Age* was to praise the expression of the dramaturg Edward Gordon Craig's ideas as they were manifested in choreography. But they were actually pre-empted by Banks in 1912, echoing what she had valued in *Petrouchka* (first performed in 1911) as 'one of the most complete achievements in stagecraft in the modern theatre,' proclaiming it to be a fulfilment of the 'idea of the Über-marionette' and offering an important statement about the relationship of musical and visual form as the essence of the choreographer Michel Fokine's dramaturgy: '"Music" becomes "*visual*"' in form, as the Charlatan's (puppet master's) gift of life to Petrouchka is realised through the puppet's 'embodiment in the very music itself.' Furthermore, Banks perceives the way in which the viewer's understanding of choreographic structure in the ballet evolves from the close connection between music and visual art: 'As we reconstruct the tableaux from mental images, notes return which bring with them the necessary action and movement for each' (Jul 1912: 58). Banks thus insightfully anticipates late twentieth- and twenty-first-century studies of 'affect' and what would develop into neuro-scientific explorations of the physiological responses of audiences to sight, sound, and movement in dance performance (Reynolds 2007).

Rice evokes an even more striking correspondence between experimentation in ballet and in the other arts at this time. As a visual artist she was sympathetic to

Fauvism, which Sadler had identified in painting with 'the desire for rhythm,' and 'the use of strong, flowing line, of strong massed colour, of continuity' in the composition (*Rhythm* June 1911: 17), and her own work drew her to the visual aspects of the Ballets Russes productions. She found much to praise in the designs of Leon Bakst and Nicholas Roerich, with their 'daring juxtapositions' creating 'life and movement in masses of colour, where costumes, drapery and decorations reverberate to sound, action, and light' (*Rhythm* Aug 1912: 107). Like Banks, her perspective as painter does not detract from her sense of the ballet's construction as *Gesamtkunstwerk*, driven by a unifying principle binding together all the art forms. Rice's allusions to the formal patterning of the dance elements emerge from her understanding of line in painting, but she gives equal weight to design, music, poetry, and choreography as constituent parts of innovative dramaturgical production, anticipating to some extent Yeats's experiments with form in his *Plays for Dancers* (1921):

> The genial and dominant idea of the Russian Ballets is based upon *line*. They have given a practical and artistic realization of what can be done with a fusion of theatrical elements, most successfully where the scenic decorator, costumier, musician, 'maître de ballet' and poet, by their harmonizing qualities, have created a scheme of one palette. (ibid.)

Rice's most individual contribution to dance criticism, however, appears in her observations about lighting – a topic rarely covered in contemporary reviews of the Ballets Russes. She emphasised the importance of lighting design in the delivery of narrative as well as visual enhancement. When comparing three separate Ballets Russes pieces from the 1912 summer season she observed how lighting 'can utterly destroy a representation when all the other elements are of equal strength' (Aug 1912: 109). Writing first of *Thamar* (1912) she commented that 'the extreme perplexity of cross lighting' led to the loss of 'essential effect' and that 'the eye is tired by the very evident multitude of details,' whereas the lighting of *Le Dieu bleu* (1912) and *Petrouchka* (1911) adds 'a strong decorative value, following the main lines, without destroying the literary interpretation' (ibid.). Lighting could either interfere with the action or shape its narrative flow.

Rice's sensitivity to geometric pattern and design gave her assessment of the Ballets Russes the flavour of a contemporary modernist aesthetic, in which at times she even anticipates the correspondence between structures of choreography in these ballets and those of the modern novel. Somewhat in the manner of Woolf's representation of character in *To The Lighthouse* (1927), when the artist Lily Briscoe paints a 'triangular purple shape' to indicate mother and child, Rice observed how 'Scheherazade obviously expresses a circle, the sensuous note . . . voluptuous fullness, where designs, drapery, arms, legs, bodies, groups have a circular movement' (Aug 1912: 108). Most convincingly Rice reveals the modernism of the choreographic design of Nijinsky's *L'Après-midi d'un faune* (1912): 'Nijinsky has given to choreography a new value which corresponds to certain modern tendencies in other forms of expression, by introducing into each movement a definite design, arbitrary in relation to the preceding one, but complete in itself, and harmonious with the whole' (Aug 1912: 110). Interestingly Rice's comment anticipates an often mystical perspective on the nature of geometry circulating in the work of dance innovations of the period, such as the

French dancer and theorist Valentine de Saint-Point's claim in 1917 that 'Everything is geometric; . . . I see life as figures, as – designs, as squares, as triangles . . .' (qtd in Barnes 1985: 233); or even later, emerging from traditions of Ausdruckstanz (expressionism), Rudolf Laban's interest in Plato's *Timaeus* as the basis for understanding bodily motion in space through the imagined construction of geometric solids surrounding the centred body.

Nevertheless, female critics of the period still focused on the fundamental expressiveness of the dancer's body, in the manner of Hincks's review of Pavlova. As late as 1919, at the beginning of the postwar Ballets Russes season, when Bell and Eliot were extolling the virtues of 'impersonality' revealed to them in the two new Massine creations, *La Boutique fantasque* and *The Good-Humoured Ladies*, one of the most compelling reviews, offering quite contrary observations of that season, was written by Rebecca West in the *Outlook*, when she was acting as temporary drama critic for that journal. Initially one might detect a similar reverence for the ritualistic aspect of the corps de ballet, but West's framing of her review, opening with a poetic image of her view from the deck of a steamer moored in the Thames in the early morning, initiates a very different feeling from that of Eliot's focus on Massine's work as an example of 'symbolising' emotion. West describes how she looked up from her position on the steamer and saw that 'men and women were streaming over London Bridge on their way to work' (7 June 1919: 568). She watched 'this mob of clerks and typists on their way to the City,' and was captivated by the distinctiveness of the moving image, which drew her attention to the purpose of the choreographic art, where 'beauty lay in the movement of the marching crowd, in the obedience of all these figures . . . to the common rhythm' (ibid.). In fact, Eliot himself echoed this very image in *The Waste Land* (1922), suggesting he may have read the review. But he reverses West's sentiments. His lines on the 'Unreal City' from 'The Burial of the Dead' section of the poem describe the mechanical monotony of a faceless population in the modern metropolis: 'Unreal City / Under the brown fog of a winter dawn, / A crowd flowed over London bridge, so many / I had not thought death had undone so many' (Eliot 1980: 39). Eliot's direct allusion to Dante and Baudelaire gives the vision of moving hordes a diabolical colouring, whereas West delivers an uplifting scene: 'From where I stood their silhouettes, velvet black against the clear acid grey of the cold spring sky . . . made a continuous ribbon of life that unrolled itself perpetually from bank to bank of the river . . . the rhythmically moving frieze was a spectacle of the supremest beauty' (7 June 1919: 568).

West's vision led her to reflect on the 'enormous aesthetic importance of the Russian Ballet' in solving 'the problem of the representation of rhythmic movement' (ibid.). She shows how dance as an art form transforms the 'evanescence' of such sights, 'making them immortal by using them as material' for the movement of the corps de ballet (ibid.). Yet her praise does not emphasise the desire, present in so many other critics of the period, to utilise the ballet as an aesthetic model for practice in other art forms. Instead she declares that because ballet can now be recognised as a medium of sufficient technical difficulty to represent such phenomena, 'writers, painters, and musicians need no longer waste their time trying to express these things' (ibid.). In fact, she closes on a note of regret for what she considers the impossibility of achieving in literary language the effect of communication beyond words identified with the ballet. She furthermore shows her preference for those dancers who do not appeal to the 'intellectual.' Unlike Bell and others, who particularly praised Lopokova's performing 'intelligence,' West singled out Lubov Tchernicheva, in whose performance of *Les Sylphides* she detected abandonment to the music of Chopin, 'her pale face destitute of all those emotions that are the material of literature and yet full of passion, full of the delight of her own movement' (7 June 1919: 569). West's sensitivity to Tchernicheva's passionate self-expression echoes a little of Hincks's delight in the originality of Pavlova's extraordinary lyricism, adding to the nuance and suggestiveness of the female perspective on dance innovations at this time. In her final statement, West offers Tchernicheva's dancing as a 'symbol,' but not of the kind preferred by those critics who often used dance to think through the problems of literary aesthetics. West claimed that Tchernicheva 'may stand as a symbol of how much there is that an over-intellectual art, that concerns itself too much with wit and the written word, leaves out' (ibid.).

While we often hear the bravura and the voice of confidence in reviews of dance written by men in this period (whether or not they were experts in the field), the less well-known but sensitive accounts by these female critics often go unremarked. Yet Hincks, Banks, Rice, and West are unique in opening up and extending our understanding of the burgeoning dissemination of dance in print media at the beginning of the twentieth century. Not only do these women contribute to the wider debates about modernist aesthetics that were hotly contested in both *Rhythm* and the *New Age*, they frequently add a distinctive alternative to dominant comparisons of dance and literary aesthetics. Banks and Rice showed great originality in their treatment of the visual aesthetics of the Ballets Russes and the way in which elements of design and lighting had developed a new relationship between choreography and the other arts. But in some ways, Hincks turns out to be the most radical. She forcefully advocates for the place of a specialist dance critic, one who treats the art as a form in its own right. By basing her argument on classical precedent and furthering the role of the specialist ethnographer of dance she anticipates many future discussions that lead to the establishment of dance scholarship in the later twentieth century. In addition, both Hincks, and more skilfully, perhaps, Rebecca West, bring to their reviews of individual dancers of the period a rare insight into the expressivism of the Russian style. Through their writing we get a chance to re-encounter that initial shock when the effect of a startlingly new and nuanced artistry was communicated through dance to London audiences.

Notes

1. For a history of the Ballets Russes, see Garafola 1989.
2. For a more detailed discussion of female critics in the *New Age* in this period, a context with particular relevance to Hincks, see Lee Garver's excellent chapter in this collection, and his scholarship more generally.
3. See Jones 2013: 13–43.
4. American dance critic and historian George Dorris wrote in an email of 16 May 2018, 'Mordkin was very much a Bolshoi (Moscow) rather than a Mariinsky (St Petersburg) dancer, big and muscular. Of course he was a sensation and considered very sexy, although that was more implied than stated. He has been overlooked in all the Nijinsky mania, as has Adolf Bolm, who I suspect was a more interesting dancer than Mordkin. Both of them had an important role in American ballet, with Mordkin as the forerunner of Ballet Theatre and Bolm in Chicago, Los Angeles, and San Francisco. Interesting as they were, though, neither had the dramatic life that Nijinsky had, one that would seem overly melodramatic if it had

appeared in fiction.' See also Djuna Barnes on Adolf Bolm, 'Philosopher Among Russian Dancers,' *Bruno's Weekly* 29 Jan 1916: 408–9 (later collected in Barnes 1985).
5. Vita's mother, raised in a Parisian convent, was the illegitimate daughter of Lionel Sackville-West, second Baron Sackville, and a Spanish dancer, Josefa de Oliva (née Durán y Ortega), known as Pepita.
6. See Ginner 1933: 1960.
7. For the full history and intellectual discussions of *Rhythm* in the context of the avant-garde see Binckes 2010.

Works Cited

Barnes, Djuna. 1985. *Interviews*. Ed. Alyce Barry. Los Angeles: Sun and Moon Press.
Bergson, Henri. [1910] 1971. *Time and Free Will: An Essay on the Immediate Data of Consciousness*. Trans. F. L. Pogson. London: Allen & Unwin.
Binckes, Faith. 2010. *Modernism, Magazines, and the British Avant-garde: Reading Rhythm, 1910–1914*. Oxford: Oxford University Press.
Burton, Richard F. 1864. *A Mission to Gelele, King of Dahome*. Vol. 1, London: Tinsley Brothers.
Eliot, T. S. 1980. *The Complete Poems and Plays 1900–1950*. New York: Harcourt Brace.
Garafola, Lynn. 1989. *Diaghilev's Ballets Russes*. New York: Oxford University Press.
Ginner, Ruby. 1933. *The Revived Greek Dance: Its Art and Technique*. London: Methuen.
—. 1960. *Gateway to the Dance*. London: Newman Neame.
Jones, Susan. 2013. *Literature, Modernism, and Dance*. Oxford: Oxford University Press.
Pritchard, Jane. 2003. '"More Natural than Nature, More Artificial than Art": The Dance Criticism of Arthur Symons.' *Dance Research: The Journal of the Society for Dance Research* 21.2: 36–89.
Reynolds, Dee. 2007. *Rhythmic Subjects: Uses of Energy in the Dances of Mary Wigman, Martha Graham and Merce Cunningham*. Alton: Dance Books.

8

MIXING THE BROWS IN PRINT: IRIS BARRY'S FILM CRITICISM OF THE 1920S

Miranda Dunham-Hickman

SHORTLY AFTER BEING named first curator for the new Film Library at New York's Museum of Modern Art, Iris Barry was remembered in a 1936 *Pall Mall* article on the 'Newspaper Woman.' The piece pays tribute to an earlier stage of Barry's career, when Barry was based in England rather than the US. After moving in the 'rarified and highbrow atmosphere' of the literary modernists, Barry secured a post at the *Spectator* in 1923, becoming one of the first 'serious' film critics during a decade when 'people started treating the film seriously in Britain' (Low 1971: 20):

> The *Spectator* at that time (first of the weeklies to do so) was considering carrying a regular column of film notes, and Iris Barry . . . was offered the job. She did it for some years, the film notes expanding at the touch of her vigorous enthusiasm into long weekly articles, and a large section of the film-going public began to look for the initials 'I. B.' every week in *The Spectator*. So much so that in 1925 the editor of the *Daily Mail*, firmly of the opinion that 'I. B.' was a man, sent . . . with the intention of making 'him' *Daily Mail* film critic . . . The years that followed were . . . busy, crowded . . . [Barry] wrote endless articles, film criticisms, poems, stories and gossip paragraphs under an endless variety of names. (Aug 1936: 105)

In breezy phrases, *Pall Mall* highlights Barry's pathfinding profile, prolific *oeuvre*, and wide readership. With the category of 'Newspaper Woman,' it also emphasises the important link between Barry's film criticism and periodicals[1] – her work would appear regularly in both newspapers and various magazines – as well as the crucial role of gender in the development of her film criticism.

With typical wit, Barry recounts how she began writing for the *Spectator* (to which she would contribute more than forty articles 1924–7) through the influence of editor John St. Loe Strachey:

> Mr Strachey with his customary dash and foresight felt that 'something should be done' by his *Spectator* to call attention to the currently sad state of the English film and the deplorable consequences . . . in England. Articles or even editorials should be written. His son, recently graduated from Oxford and now a member of the *Spectator* staff, said in his inimitable drawl: 'there is a woman whom I have met who *seems* to know quite a little about the subject. I think we might try her.' No sooner said than done. The woman was myself. (Hankins 2004: 490)

As this indicates, a major impetus for Barry's hire was the widespread sense that British films needed improvement – and that a knowledgeable film critic in a widely circulated, authoritative journal could contribute importantly to ameliorating the 'British Film situation.'[2] Barry herself would resist writing in service of this British nationalist effort, but its momentum would help to propel her into film criticism. Her work became an integral part of the new 'surge of writing about cinema in Britain' in the 1920s (Marcus 2007: 238). Along with C. A. Lejeune – another 'newspaper woman' noted in *Pall Mall* – Barry achieved status as both one of the era's most prominent women film critics (women who, as Laura Marcus notes, 'played a substantial role in the early years of film criticism' (2007: 236)) and major pioneering film critic more generally.

Behind Barry in 1923 was a decade of ties to figures in London modernist circles such as Ezra Pound, Harriet Shaw Weaver, and Wyndham Lewis. Moving among such artists and intellectuals in the 1910s, Barry had been an outsider from Birmingham, from a country family, educated for a few years in a Belgian convent, able to pass entrance examinations for Oxford but ultimately unable to attend because the advent of the First World War compromised her family's ability to pay for her education; instead, she went to work. During the war, having sent poetry to little magazines such as *Poetry*, attracting the notice of fabled tastemaker Ezra Pound, Barry relocated to London to seek her fortune. As of 1916, she corresponded with Pound about training as a poet; then formed a partnership with artist Wyndham Lewis, by whom she had two children. By 1921, Barry had separated from Lewis, placed her children with others, and was navigating independently in non-modernist contexts.

With her foray into film criticism, Barry changed domains and moved into a new cultural role. During the 1920s, Barry wrote not only for the influential weekly the *Spectator* and the *Daily Mail* – the latter was the largest-circulation mass periodical in England (Wasson 2006: 157, 161) – but also for the upscale British *Vogue* and John Middleton Murry's *Adelphi*. Accordingly, by the time Barry largely left film criticism in 1930, not only had she become one of the era's most productive and recognised film critics – as Haidee Wasson notes, 'hers was the most widely circulated film writing of its day' (2006: 157) – but also a figure who vitally shaped emerging film culture as it evolved. 'Culture' is one of this essay's keywords: at a moment when, as Hankins observes, movies were often 'scorned by the largely male highbrow culture industry' (2007: 813), through her contributions to periodicals, Barry fostered, theorised, and mobilised 'film culture' so as to change perceptions of the cultural roles of both film and film-going. Countering a prevalent cultural trend of the time, whereby 'critics and connoisseurs demonstrate[d] their deep sense by damning films in every key' (Barry 1926: viii), Barry sought to legitimate film by emphasising its value as art, entertainment, and above all, source of cultural literacy for a wide public.

More specifically, through her film criticism in periodicals, Barry offered contributions to the 'battle of the brows' of the interwar years (the 'culture wars' of this moment) that were shaped by her gender and class positioning. Among these were film-going strategies aimed to surmount social and ideological restrictions for both women of her time and others comparably shut out through socio-economic factors from the gates of 'Culture.' In fact, Barry's criticism, often addressing film's impact on spectators and its contributions to the wider culture, bears many surprising affinities to criticism of this time focused in a post-Arnoldian spirit on 'culture,' from high-profile literary-cultural critics such as I. A. Richards, F. R. Leavis, and Q. D. Leavis.

In 1924, the same year Barry's film criticism began appearing in periodicals, Richards published his landmark *Principles of Literary Criticism*, whose commentary was inspired both by efforts to renew postwar culture and by the work of T. S. Eliot. Austerely, Richards turned toward poetry and away from film: his position exemplified how those aligned with the emergent 'modernism' of this moment often stood with respect to cinema. Fearing a 'collapse of values' in the culture, 'by which popular taste replaces trained discrimination,' Richards comments, '[W]e have not yet fathomed the more sinister potentialities of the cinema' (2001: 31). He groups film with 'best-sellers' and magazine verse – phenomena which debase the taste and erode 'discrimination' (ibid.).

Richards's ideas would resound in the work of fellow Cantabrigians F. R. and Q. D. Leavis, both of whom, as Chris Baldick suggests, followed Richards in the latter-day Arnoldian 'social mission' of redressing what they read as the dire state of culture in England of this moment (Baldick 1983); as F. R. Leavis would note in *Mass Civilization and Minority Culture*: 'It is a common-place to-day that culture is at a crisis' (1930: 5). Like Arnold, Richards and the Leavises regarded culture not only as a body of texts carrying the 'best that is known and thought in the world' (Arnold 1949b: 248), but also as an endeavour toward personal and social improvement, carried out in a spirit of 'free play' of the mind and what Arnold famously called 'curiosity' (1949a: 471–2).

Barry pursued a comparable post-Arnoldian effort to enrich the culture of her time, yet through 'the cinema.' In her book on film, she even offers a mischievous Arnoldian touch: 'I suppose if the religious habit had not a good deal died out, the cinema might not have succeeded as it has done' (Barry 1926: 6). If positioned contra Richards and the Leavises in the 'culture wars' of this time – committed to cinema as they cast suspicion on its effects on minds and culture – Barry nonetheless significantly shared 'values' with them, seeking ways to improve culture not for the 'minority,' but for the many, through film. For her, cinema could benefit the surrounding culture by kindling and satisfying viewers' 'curiosity' about places, experiences, and ideas remote from their ordinary lives (Barry 1926: 7). In 'The Scope of the Cinema,' she notes:

> [The] moving picture ... besides entertaining in the good old way ... puts one *au courant* with places, eras, customs and types of mind foreign, but infinitely interesting because of their strangeness. It is no longer true that one half of the world does not know how the other half lives; travel films make that impossible ... [It] is obvious that the cinema would not have established itself as it has but for the fact that it does in some way solve the complexes of our age. (British *Vogue* Aug 1924: 65)

In another article in British *Vogue*, she remarks on cinema's ability to 'bring to every individual an intensification of life, all kinds of vicarious experience denied by the ever-narrowing grooves in which a mechanical civilization fixes us' (Feb 1925: 78). In Barry's reading, film could afford access to what counted for Barry as 'Culture' to audiences of diverse socio-economic and cultural positions and levels. As Wasson notes, 'For Barry, the cinema provided a privileged form of knowledge ... transcendent of not only geographic space but also historical time and national psychology' (2002: 327).

Barry's own sense of 'social mission' in this regard was legibly shaped by both gender and class positioning – and the intersection of the two. The impact of gender is more evident: as Hankins notes, 'Barry was . . . a New Woman writ large: outspoken, bohemian, and intelligent' (2004: 490). Barry herself identified as a 'New Woman,' as language in her biography of Mary Wollstonecraft (1927) suggests.[3] Invoking this figure, Wasson raises the possibility of gendering not just Barry herself, but also Barry's journalism, as 'new-womanly' (2006: 161). Yet Barry's New Womanhood was not characterised by a legible middle-class positioning generally associated with the New Woman,[4] and her approach to criticism bears the imprint of this difference.

Cued by this and a Bourdieu-inflected sense of feminist periodical studies, I construe Barry's work as 'New Woman criticism' to frame the question guiding this essay: how Barry's notably brow-crossing film criticism was structured by her habitus as emancipated woman and class outsider. Here I respond to Barbara Green's challenge to contemporary periodical studies to approach newly the issue of the 'woman writer' (2013); I do so by turning to an adjacent topic, the 'New Woman critic.' With an intersectional feminist approach to periodical studies, this essay considers how Barry's 'New Woman criticism' was carried out through periodicals. The periodical venues in which she made her name allowed her film criticism to effect certain forms of cultural work; considering their specifics helps to plot the cultural coordinates of Barry's interwar work on the problem of culture – and note how gender and class positioning show up in that work. The case study featured below is Barry's writing for British *Vogue* (particularly her essay, 'The Scope of the Cinema'), since this magazine's 'contextual code' casts into especially sharp relief the vectors of Barry's critical project.

Barry's 'catholicity of taste'

Barry's influential book on film, *Let's Go to the Pictures*, appeared in 1926, much of it developed from her commentary in the *Spectator*. In her introduction, she emphasises the work of criticism, calling for 'critics' to 'arise,' 'invent terms,' and 'lay down canons' (Barry 1926: ix). Through her own emergent work, Barry modelled practice for the nascent discourse of film criticism. Publishing essays in periodicals enabled Barry to 'invent' not only such 'terms' and 'canons,' but also an adaptable persona and modus operandi as a film critic, in ways that publishing in book form did not allow. A 1926 review of *Let's Go* notes that 'Miss Barry is no dilettante intellectual' (*Spectator* 13 Nov 1926: 864). Important to what allowed Barry to establish herself not as 'dilettante' but as authoritative 'professional cinema critic' (ibid.), even 'public intellectual' (Hankins 2004: 490), was publishing in a diverse array of periodicals during the 1920s, in articles of various lengths, genres, and styles that demonstrated versatility and reached audiences great in number and range.[5]

'The Scope of the Cinema' immediately shows Barry's characteristic ability to assess new films knowledgeably in the context of the medium's history:

> The cinema, from the penny-in-the-slot affair it was twenty-five years ago, has become not only the regular entertainment of millions of people, but a subtle and very catholic influence, a sort of waking dream into which everyone can dissolve while retaining as much consciousness as he chooses. (British *Vogue* Aug 1924: 65)

The way 'catholic' is deployed here – suggesting 'comprehensive' or 'broad' in 'sympathies, tastes, and interests' – signals the values shaping Barry's criticism in ongoing ways over time. Used in this sense, the term would often be applied to Barry's approach to tastemaking. In 1925, together with Ivor Montagu and Sidney Bernstein, Barry became co-founder of the London Film Society, whose considerable influence grew rapidly. The deliberately 'eclectic mix' (Hankins 2007: 814) of the Society's programmes, featuring a high 'aesthetic standard' in a range of genres from various countries (as Marcus notes, 'France, India, America, Belgium, Sweden and Japan') rhymed with the marked diversity of films Barry would typically recognise and celebrate.[6] Accordingly, Hankins also calls Barry 'catholic' in taste, reflecting a lexical emphasis in commentary on Barry (2004: 502). In a 1970 tribute to Barry, for instance, Ivor Montagu twice uses variants of 'catholic' to describe Barry's critical taste: he credits her with 'literary catholicity,' signalling wide awareness and 'encyclopedic knowledge' (1970: 107). Moreover, addressing Barry's positioning as outsider to both ordinary middle-class lives and the Oxbridge elite so influential on 1920s culture,[7] Montagu identifies such 'catholicism of taste' as part of Barry's equipment for social navigation and survival (1970: 106). This chapter intertwines these two ideas associated with such 'catholicity' (i.e. Barry's position as outsider and role as tastemaker) – to read Barry's contributions to film criticism when, in Britain, cinema was significantly imbricated in the 'culture wars' of the interwar moment.

Barry's renowned 'catholicity' entailed a critical eye open to celebrating a remarkable diversity of genres: avant-garde landmarks like the German expressionist *Cabinet of Dr Caligari* (1920) and René Clair's Dadaist *Entr'acte* (1924); witty satirical romance-plot films such as Ernst Lubitsch's *The Marriage Circle* (1924); historical dramas such as *Abraham Lincoln* (1924); extravagant epics such as Fritz Lang's *The Niebelungen* (1924); and popular Hollywood films such as *Stella Dallas* (1925), 'melodrama pure and simple' (British *Vogue* Feb 1926: 53). Barry championed Charlie Chaplin, whose films, like her criticism, straddled the brows – and lauded with equal praise films framed as art and those intended primarily as history, record, and entertainment. Moreover, when nationalist loyalties in Britain often guided allegiances, Barry refused to privilege films of any one nation. This had a cost: Lord Rothermere fired Barry from the *Daily Mail* for reviewing a British film harshly during committed efforts to boost the 'ailing British film industry' (Sitton 2014: 145).

Also enabling the 'catholic' reach of her work was that as of the mid-1920s, Barry wrote simultaneously for several periodicals of markedly different scale, cultural positioning, and readership. In March 1924, she began publishing in the *Adelphi*; its profile resembled that of periodicals in which she had published poetry, such as the *Little Review* and the *Egoist* (Hankins 2004: 490), although its circulation was impressively high for such a little magazine, often remaining above 10,000 (Mellown 1983).[8] Just before this, in February 1924, Barry had begun publishing in the highbrow weekly the *Spectator*, whose numbers at the time were about 13,500 (Courtauld 1999: xiii): as a venerable British institution, the *Spectator* carried considerably greater cultural weight. In August of that year, partly on basis of the *Spectator* work, Barry also began writing for the bi-weekly British *Vogue*, targeting upper-class women, with a circulation of about 140,000 (Garrity 1999: 33). In late 1925, Barry also began at the *Daily Mail*, the largest mass-circulation daily in England, with a circulation of approximately 2 million (Wasson 2006: 157).

Thus not only did Barry *display* 'catholicity of taste' in the pages of these periodicals; publishing on film in such a disparate group of periodicals, often concurrently, also enabled her to *establish* such 'catholicity' in other ways, by reaching many different audiences and, through connections with different venues, traversing what were increasingly read as different cultural 'brows.' This pattern of periodical publication thus significantly shaped Barry's cultural role – what she could achieve through her film writing – configuring her criticism's scope, wide and diverse influence, and forms of authority. Her *Vogue* work showcases especially clearly the lineaments of her film criticism: its criteria for selection, guiding project, and the classed, gendered standpoint from which these emerged.

Recognising the nature of this 'catholicity of taste' – its formative commitments and entailments – can counter misrepresentations of Barry's taste as merely 'inclusive' (Hankins 2004: 510) on the basis of enthusiasm for the new medium's potential. For instance, Barry's biographer Robert Sitton suggests that Barry displayed a 'curatorial' taste, appropriate to her later role at MoMA: '[Barry's] early writings presage the wide-ranging curatorial aesthetic of Barry's later career. Throughout her life, she remained so genuinely devoted to a variety of filmic achievements that she never developed a rigid sense of what a good film must be' (2014: 126). The comment suggests praise for Barry's openness; just after this, Sitton attributes 'eclecticism' and 'curiosity' to Barry in an affirmative tone (ibid.). Yet the aggregate impression left by his comment suggests an approach which is unsettled, inchoate: Barry's 'aesthetic' comes across as the inclusivity of a collector and historian rather than the discernment of a tastemaker. This rhymes with a critical comment from Robert Herring, known for film writing of the 1920s, who in 1927 quipped about Barry's apparently rudderless criticism, 'She should make up her mind as to which public she is writing for and not, in trying to place her experience at the service of too many, fall foul of the vulgar without touching the highbrows' (Hankins 2004: 510). Such an assessment does not credit Barry sufficiently for coherence of approach, nor for the intentional taste-work of ranging with agility from 'highbrow' to 'vulgar' – and many places in between.

In her work for culture, Barry 'made up her mind' to appeal deliberately to a wide range of audiences, as part of a coherent critical project. She attended to what cinema could do *for* and *in* culture – by providing 'layers of experience' and 'resources' for the 'future' to a diversity of cinema-goers (British *Vogue* Aug 1924: 65). And importantly, her project, shaped by a specific set of cultural commitments, was made possible both by featuring for critical assessment a marked diversity of films, from avant-garde to popular; as well as by publishing in a range of different periodical contexts – and thus, in her criticism, varying notably in scope and pitch from case to case.[9] This multiplex strategy, dependent for impact on the range of periodicals in which she published, allowed Barry to enter the public sphere as versatile public intellectual appealing to, and seeking cultural access for, the many. Accordingly, it allowed Barry to contribute to the interwar 'battle of the brows' with a legible, if complex, position about the widely contested concept of 'culture.'[10] To adapt Lawrence Rainey's theoretical position on the understanding of modernism at this time, Barry's criticism was 'configured' by a specific 'dynamics of transmission,' achieved through the gamut of periodical venues in which she published (Rainey 1998: 78).

Barry on the Interwar Culture Wars

Barry's early film criticism emphasised the benefits of film to a wide variety of film-goers. Unlike British *Vogue*, she was not interested in appealing only to an upper-crust, elite audience. One of the sharpest captures of what matters for Barry about film appears in one of her first articles, this one for the *Adelphi* in 1924:

> I often consider, when I am in the cinema, how much each unique individual sitting in the darkness there, watching the representation of other interacting individuals on screen, resembles the solitary creatures who sit at home behind a veil of window-curtains, peeping out at passers-by. There is the same isolation, . . . there is something of the same need. But how little the curiosity of the watchers behind curtains is satisfied . . . I think the curiosity is to know how life is lived: its resources. At least the watchers in the cinema get more satisfaction; for there, besides the spectacle of moving creatures they are constantly drawn out of themselves by a vicarious participation in the action . . . and they are sometimes drawn into themselves to comment and reflect upon the causes and effects of the action. (1 Mar 1924: 926–7)

Barry's early film criticism continued to emphasise how film can, importantly, 'satisfy' such 'curiosity' and 'need,' drawing individual viewers beyond the ambit of their ordinary perspectives – as well as how it could provide film-goers with 'resources' for living. Again, in the 'The Scope of the Cinema' Barry offers an analogous passage:

> [The] moving picture is really extraordinary in that besides entertaining in the good old way . . . it puts one *au courant* with places, eras, customs and types of mind foreign, but infinitely interesting because of their strangeness. It is no longer true that one half of the world does not know how the other half lives; travel films make that impossible . . . (British *Vogue* Aug 1924: 65)

For Barry, not only travel films, but films more generally allowed for imaginative 'travel' to worlds familiar to cinema-goers: through its 'scope' – its wide range of offerings – film provided audiences with perspectival 'scope': geographical, historical, and intellectual.

> The immense scope of the film-play proper, both in manner and in matter, cannot sufficiently be realized. It is a long cry from the pageantry of *Robin Hood*, *Scaramouche* and *The Fall of an Empress*, with their vast swirling crowds and their historical atmosphere, from the cold visual beauty of *The Niebelungs*, that dignified screen-epic of the Dragon era of Europe's past, to the riotous farces of Buster Keaton. Every mentality is catered for between those two extremes, in the melodramas . . . in the social satires, the sex dramas, the Wild West films with their exciting tempos (rushing express trains, avalanches, motor-dashes, aeroplane flights . . .), in the witty comedies of Constance Talmadge, the fantasy of *Felix the Cat*, and the very intellectual films of Charles Chaplin. (Aug 1924: 65, 76)

In Barry's view, her developing canon *needed* to cover such a wide cultural distance and appeal to many different 'mentalities' (which parlance of the time read as 'brows').

Why? This brings into focus Barry's reading of the 'function' of 'criticism,' as reflected in her canon-making. In part this was because she was interested in how diverse genres of film could, through different forms of virtuosity, all rise to a high 'level' (Barry 1926: 17), even if Buster Keaton comedies, Felix the Cat cartoons, or *Stella Dallas*. But beyond this, such marked 'scope' afforded a 'gradual broadening process' (Barry 1926: 15) to diverse audiences. By making such cultural and intellectual excursions affordable for a wide audience, many of whom normally would not have access to the experiences depicted, film allowed audiences to move imaginatively and empathically across boundaries generally separating groups and classes:

> City men slip away (you can see them in the West End cinemas any afternoon) to follow the allure of a roguish Mae Murray or drop an easy tear for a white-haired mother. Typists wallow in the supposed goings on of the very smart, and the very smart safely court danger in the squalor of a Bowery crook's life. (Aug 1924: 76)

Given this, how best to characterise the tones and targeted audiences of Barry's criticism? Adapting Marcus's term, Cuny offers 'demotic' (2016: n.p.), and Hankins suggests that Barry wrote for 'the people.' In an even more sensitive capture of Barry's intentionally mercurial positioning, Wasson notes that 'Barry's persona' in criticism 'might best be described as internationalist, opinionated, argumentative, sometimes populist, sometimes highbrow' (2006: 159). British *Vogue's* project at this time, taken as 'ground,' illuminates especially effectively the 'figure' of Barry's hard-to-read combination of 'populist' and 'highbrow' – her hybrid, mobile, boundary-crosser, elastic positionality as critic. Barry indeed wrote for 'the people,' in that she was interested in how film especially, as a medium equally open to all, could allow access to those traditionally kept out of the halls of high culture; yet also in that she used her criticism to interrogate the privileging of the kind of culture available in such 'high' echelons as the only culture that counted.

If Arnold famously imagines the 'function' of 'Culture' as a nourishing, educative 'current' (1949b: 249), Barry was likewise interested in what she calls in *Let's Go* the 'educative' powers of film (1926: 16). When Barry was young, her mother took her to the cinema every Monday for 'education'; Barry later called this 'ritual' the 'only instruction' she had received in 'the facts of life' (Sitton 2014: 14). In *Let's Go*, Barry notes how 'experience afforded by motion pictures' (1926: 15) can turn a 'stay-at-home citizen' into a 'man of the world' (1926: 13). Like the Leavises, whose lower-middle-class origins shaped their cultural 'mission,' Barry as class outsider worked for access to transformative culture for those who, by virtue of socio-economic and educational positioning, had not traditionally enjoyed such access. In so doing, she entered much the same arena as the Leavises, who famously valued forms of mental acuity, by likewise celebrating such and suggesting that the 'habit of watching films develops a special kind of alertness' (ibid.). And if Q. D. Leavis lamented the 'stratification' of the 'reading public' of this time (1932: 33) into different levels or 'brows,' Barry's position reckoned with much the same problem from a similar value-position, though with an entirely different reading of cinema. While Leavis famously dismissed film as merely 'passive and social amusement' (1932: 55), for Barry film could bring people of different classes and standpoints together in the space of the cinema and through cultural literacy achieved by film-going.

Commenting on film in the 1920s, Barry wrote in a climate increasingly emphasising the 'battle of the brows,' involving a nexus of questions on levels of taste: to which 'brows' – cultural levels of taste in a hierarchy – did specific works belong, which levels were appropriate and valuable for specific audiences, and which could contribute to cultural health and strength? If reluctantly, Q. D. Leavis's *Fiction and the Reading Public* (1932) separates cultural materials and standards of taste into 'highbrow,' 'middlebrow,' and 'popular,' reflective of preoccupations of the moment. The same year that Leavis's book appeared, Woolf penned her now famous essay, 'Middlebrow,' at the time an unsent letter to the editor, yet it registered debates of the day, also involving figures such as J. B. Priestley and Harold Nicolson. As Priestley wrote an essay on 'brows' entitled 'High, Low, Broad' (1926), flagging the era's growing concern with cultural levels, Barry offered her reading through film criticism on the question of which 'brows' of culture, and film culture in particular, would benefit the wider culture.

Since Barry pledges allegiance neither to the 'highbrow' nor sheerly popular and entertaining, it is tempting to read Barry's implied cultural position as 'middlebrow,' mediating between the two. Yet historicist care is needed in the use of 'middlebrow,' as, during the 1920s and 1930s, the idea came to mean many different things to different people:[11] often it was a term of distaste, as for Woolf, who deplored 'middlebrow' standards she called 'betwixt and between,' neither genuinely 'highbrow' nor honestly 'lowbrow' (1966: 198). Even when used affirmatively for film in particular, the 'brow' associated with Barry's preferences in film was not, for instance, the 'middlebrow' register associated with the British nationalist project of making better British films – which justified film, as Jamie Sexton notes, as an extension of 'middlebrow' theatre and literature – nor that linked with the films Lawrence Napper highlights as forming part of a British interwar effort to create an accessible 'national culture' (2002: 291; 2009: 1–10). Barry's chosen 'brow' should even be distinguished from that of Priestley, who advocated a 'broad-brow' position, encompassing diverse levels of taste (*Saturday Review* 20 Feb 1926: 222). Barry's 'brow' corresponds more exactly to what Elizabeth Gregory, addressing the array of cultural materials featured in the poetry of Marianne Moore, calls a 'mixed brow' position (2005: 208), in that Barry strategically favoured a canon consistently markedly mixed in genre, mode, and register, a conglomerate of notably distinct and disparate elements.

Thus Barry's mixed-brow position, as cultural strategy, offered a pointed rejoinder to typical modernist valorisations of this time of avant-garde experimental work ('high-brow' work) – in film, literature, and other domains of culture; and it provided equipment for redressing the cultural stratification deplored by Q. D. Leavis. In Barry's reading, film-goers, as they improved their cultural awareness through film, could surmount the barriers of such stratification. And it was publishing in a notable variety of periodicals of the time that allowed Barry to take such a position (on standards of taste and the work of culture) as public intellectual *on* culture.

The New Woman Critic

Barry's work as 'New Woman Critic' in the context of British *Vogue* brings into especially sharp focus how Barry credits film, particularly if viewed for its scope and variety, with power to provide a 'way out' and new mobility, through filmic/cultural literacy, for shut-ins of class and gender. Barry signals especial concern for women without cultural access: her image of 'solitary creatures who sit at home behind a veil of window-curtains' (especially given the use of 'veil') is strongly gendered (*Adelphi* 1 Mar 1924: 926).[12]

In general, at times the imprint of a New Woman's position on the 'habitus' of Barry's critical work appeared overtly in the topics and claims her writing – in a line of argument about women as cinema-goers, for example – as Barry maintained, cinema 'exists for the purpose of pleasing women. Three out of every four of all cinema audiences are women' (1926: 59) – or in another that advocates that women be the makers of cinema (1926: 176–7). Moreover, Barry sometimes looked explicitly to film to help disrupt the usual cultural narratives for women: at one point she deplored American and English films for their emphasis on romance, noting irritably that 'it is not the whole function of woman to get herself married' (1926: 61). She applauded a number of French and German films for transcending this hackneyed narrative, and thus freeing women by removing 'the love stuff': 'I suppose we have liked Jane Austen for ridiculing this 'getting married' business. But women in those days really had some excuse for feeling so urgent about matrimony. It was the only career open to them. To-day, thank heaven, we're crawling out of that bog!' (Barry 1926: 64). This emphatic comment surfaces Barry's interest in directing film criticism toward liberating women from the cultural 'bog' of inherited cultural scripts for women.

Yet elsewhere, Barry's position as New Woman leaves subtler traces in suggestions about how to navigate the brow battles of this time. Here the placement of her articles in British *Vogue* highlights the classed, gendered positionality of her New Woman criticism and the arguments issuing therefrom. That Barry was very much *not* a woman of the stylish upper crust associated with British *Vogue*'s 'elite female audience' (Garrity 1999: 2) contributed crucially to her specific form of New Womanhood as habitus, and accordingly, imprints the projects of her film criticism. Barry's status as both New Woman and class outsider to the crowd that read British *Vogue* structured the brow-crossing, 'catholic' tastes guiding her cultural work. Moreover, Barry's signature emphasis on 'scope,' diversity, and 'range' in her criticism was also in part importantly directed into *producing* a kind of New Womanhood markedly different from the forms suggested in the 'glossy pages' of *Vogue* (ibid.).

The female audience Barry's criticism often invokes, I would suggest, is composed of those who were precisely not entitled as was the 'cultivated upper-class readership' courted by *Vogue*. Accordingly, the project she carves out in *Vogue* differs markedly from what *Vogue* itself signals – through both its advertisements, which as Cynthia White notes, 'appealed to those with extravagant tastes and ample resources' (Garrity 1999: 35), and through its articles on culture.

Thus rather than feed into the project of *Vogue* – that of creating the appropriate body image and repertoire of cultural awareness, toolkit of cultural capital, for the savvy modern woman – the project of Barry's articles pulls against the grain of the kind of 'modern womanhood' *Vogue*'s cues generally aimed to foster. And it often does so in the name of producing another kind of New Womanhood, in tandem with another kind of modern sensibility that eludes the class-bound, upper-crust savvy chic represented by the magazine. The magazine's culture-vectors generally work in the service of cultivating the 'in-the-know' upper-crust woman of 'charm' with a 'lovely' figure: as Garrity suggests, 'Although *Vogue* at times celebrates the modern woman's greater possibilities' (for instance, publishing an anonymous editorial on 'Women and Education'), 'the magazine more often invokes antiquated models of femininity' (1999: 36) – those increasingly prevalent as backlash against the earlier generation's militant feminisms, as well as against sheer 1920s flapperdom. In this context, Barry's articles smuggle into the magazine a kind of ulterior project, offering 'resources' for interrogating and transcending the limitations of this 'lovely,' putatively modern womanhood by breaking past its classed frame of reference.

Material from what Sean Latham and Robert Scholes term the 'hole in the archive' (2006: 520) – the rich bibliographic detail, including advertisements, that frame the magazine's written contributions – highlights through juxtaposition this contrast between Barry's and *Vogue*'s projects. That Barry's 'The Scope of the Cinema' features fantasy images from Fritz Lang's *Die Niebelungen* in an article neighboured by *Vogue*'s prevalent ads for Elizabeth Arden ('The modern science of Elizabeth Arden brings sure and natural beauty to every woman'), beauty treatments from 'Jeunesse Salons' and 'Phyllis Earle, Ltd.', and 'Condor Hats' highlights the contrast, and in fact *contest*, between two models of 'New Womanhood': *Vogue*'s devoted to chic, Barry's to cultural awareness in service of knowledge rather than style; one devoted to the production of 'cultural elitism' (Garrity 1999: 1), the other to access to a wide gamut of cultural spaces for those positioned by culture outside the 'elite.'

Moreover, if *Vogue* editor Dorothy Todd seeks to make such 'elite culture' part of the affluent modern woman's equipment, Barry underscores how film can open the horizons of a wide diversity of spectators: film is accessible, itself diverse, capable of helping those closed in by barriers of culture (such as women and those whose class positions don't allow them access to culture) to 'travel' beyond the boundaries and frames of reference usually shutting them in. If Barry's comments sometimes indicate how film allows viewers fleeting 'class-mobility' in fantasy, I'd add here that Barry, in an Arnoldian mode, suggests that film literacy can foster valuable moments of cross-class connection. She hints at this through 'praise' for *Stella Dallas*, one of her touchstone films, in 'The Cinema':

> One scene in particular calls for praise: Stella Dallas, painstaking arrayed in her gaudy best, goes to her former husband's new wife to beg her to take the little girl into her house. The wealthier woman with her exquisite simplicity and self-assurance is a little startled by the arrival of the befeathered, slightly defiant and talkative Stella. Emotions varied and evanescent as clouds pass across the two women's faces: then for a moment the social bar is lowered while decency and generosity recognize each other . . . There is something rare and lovely in the film at this moment. (British *Vogue* Feb 1926: 53)

Appropriately, a photo of Charlie Chaplin, that film icon and maker of films pleasing a diversity of audiences, hovers impressively on the other side of the page from this article (Hankins 2004: 506). The *Vogue* readership is implicitly aligned with the 'exquisite simplicity and self-assurance' of the wealthier woman; Barry signals interest in how, through film, figures such as Stella Dallas, the working-class girl who marries up, can cross into worlds other than those they have known. The film's scenario does not indicate conditions for social change, and in fact underscores painfully the barriers facing Stella. Yet this scene tropes Barry's interest in meeting points, empathy across boundaries of social station, and forms of mobility.

'Chaplin' here, with its associations of crossing brows and levels, thus serves as metonym for film as Barry argues for it. She emphasises film's potential to help people fashion themselves not as members of a particular class (as does *Vogue*), but rather as agile brow- and boundary-crossers. As critic, she herself demonstrated such flexible cultural 'scope' through her range of periodicals, films, and voices, and implicitly encouraged readers and film-goers to do the same. Barry – by 'laying down canons,' writing in heterogeneous mix of periodicals – deliberately mixed the brows, so as to model a way of 'going to the pictures' that could empower a diverse audience, composed of both women and others similarly culturally disadvantaged in her time, to widen their experience beyond what was allowed by the usual 'social bars.'

Notes

Warm thanks to Lisa Banks, Mitchell Brown, Michael Jaeggle, Suvij Sudershan, and Rory Williamson for research toward this article.

1. See Wasson 2006 on dimensions of the 'the intimate relationship' during the 1910s and 1920s 'between cinema and newspapers': newspapers served as a vital channel for information about developments in film, and the two media often influenced each other and depended on each other. For instance, newspapers could augment their sales by addressing film, and publicity in newspapers could increase film box office. Operating at this nexus, Barry's criticism, in both newspapers and magazines, contributed to creating a film culture – as Wasson puts it, 'forming expectations, framing debates, defining interests before and after people attended movie theatres' (2006: 156).
2. See Sitton, where a notebook entry from Barry registers the 'near-demise of the British film industry' perceived as detrimental to the 'health of the nation' (2014: 84); see also *Spectator* 9 Jan 1926: 43. Marcus (2007: 236–7, 239) notes that 'the perceived need to improve the quality of British films was at the heart of much of the writing on cinema in the 1920s.'
3. The discursive construct of the 'New Woman,' dynamic and evolving from the late decades of the nineteenth century to the mid-twentieth, has seen so much play in cultural criticism as to have lost specificity and lustre: here it denotes an array of life strategies pursued by early twentieth-century females to transcend the limits culture of this time placed on women – especially to overcome the enclosures of women's domestic roles as interwar backlash discourse urged women, as Deidre Beddoe (1989) puts it, 'back to home and duty.' See Laura Severin (1997) on this resurgence of the domestic ideology, in which women's magazines played a significant role. The New Woman of this period swam against this current, like Barry venturing actively into personal and economic independence and professional authority.
4. See Montagu 1970: 107; Sitton 2014: 182–4; and Hankins 2004: 507, on Barry's sense of social and class outsiderdom.
5. Hankins comments that Barry's 'review-essays' are 703 and 1048 words each; her *Spectator* articles range from 600 to 1,500 words; the *Vogue* essays hover just above 1,000 words, and the *Daily Mail* columns were 300–500 (2004: 512).
6. Marcus 2007: 261–74; 'aesthetic standard' appears in the informational leaflet for the Society (qtd on page 263).
7. See Hankins 2004: 507, on the influence of the 'Oxbridge elite' on the 'culture industry' of this time.
8. As Garrity notes, 'Circulation figures for most such comparable little magazines ranged from few hundred to a couple of thousand' (1999: 33).
9. See note 5, and see Hankins (2004: 508), who captures the different emphases of Barry's varying rhetoric for different audiences through the trope of different 'voices.' Comparing her commentary on Douglas Fairbanks, for instance, in the *Daily Mail* (19 Mar 1926: 8)

and the *Spectator* (20 Mar 1926: 525) reveals that for the *Daily Mail* column, Barry lauds Fairbanks's ability to present a 'keen mind' and 'fit body' and the film's 'swift, refreshing action' (such 'swift' action can 'purify the mind' and appeal to the 'finer emotions'); whereas in the *Spectator*, likewise addressing Fairbanks's latest films, she stresses the 'good' that a well-made film, like *The Black Pirate*, can do for 'cinema as a whole,' and for an audience so poor as not to be able to afford any other entertainment but the pub. An essay on Fairbanks from two years earlier, in British *Vogue* (Oct 1924: 104), accents 'romance.' Thanks to Suvij Sudershan for this astute comparison.
10. See Magnanaro 2002 on the 'culture concept' of this time.
11. See Brown and Grover 2011.
12. Dorothy Todd, highbrow editor of British *Vogue* 1922–6 who brought Barry in, sought to remake *Vogue* as more than just a magazine for fashion, aiming to foster wide cultural awareness among its upscale female readers. As Hankins suggests, 'The magazine fashioned film as another modernist must-have for the intelligent, chic modern woman' (2004: 500).

Works Cited

Arnold, Matthew. 1949a. 'Culture and Anarchy.' *The Portable Matthew Arnold*. Ed. Lionel Trilling. New York: Viking Press. 469–573.
Arnold, Matthew. 1949b. 'The Function of Criticism at the Present Time.' *The Portable Matthew Arnold*. Ed. Lionel Trilling. New York: Viking Press. 234–67.
Baldick, Chris. 1983. *The Social Mission of English Criticism*. Oxford: Clarendon Press.
Barry, Iris. 1926. *Let's Go to the Pictures*. London: Chatto & Windus.
Beddoe, Deirdre. 1989. *Back to Home and Duty: Women Between the Wars, 1918–1939*. London: Pandora.
Bourdieu, Pierre. 1984. *Distinction: A Social Critique of the Judgement of Taste*. Trans. Richard Nice. Cambridge, MA: Harvard University Press.
Brown, Erica and Mary Grover, eds. 2011. 'Introduction: Middlebrow Matters.' *Middlebrow Literary Cultures: The Battle of the Brows, 1920–1960*. London: Palgrave Macmillan. 1–24.
Courtauld, Simon. 1999. *To Convey Intelligence: The Spectator, 1928–1998*. London: Profile Books, Ltd.
Cuny, Noëlle. 2016. 'Gender, the Demotic and the Cinema in the Early *Adelphi* (1923–1924): The Iris Barry Moment.' *Revue de la Societe d'Etudes Anglaises Contemporaines* 50: n.p. <http://ebc.revues.org/3080> (last accessed 3 July 2018).
Garrity, Jane. 1999. 'Selling Culture to the "Civilized."' *Modernism/ modernity* 6.2: 29–58.
Green, Barbara. 2013. 'Recovering Feminist Criticism: Modern Women Writers and Feminist Periodical Studies.' *Literature Compass* 10.1: 53–60.
Gregory, Elizabeth. 2005. '"Combat Cultural": Marianne Moore and the Mixed Brow.' *Critics and Poets on Marianne Moore*. Ed. Linda Leavell, Cristanne Miller, and Robin G. Schulze. Lewisburg, PA: Bucknell University Press. 208–21.
Hankins, Leslie Kathleen. 2004. 'Iris Barry, Writer and Cinéaste, Forming Film Culture in London, 1924–26: *The Adelphi,* the *Spectator,* and the *British Vogue.*' *Modernism/ modernity* 11.3: 488–515.
—. 2007. 'Cineastes and Modernists: Writing on Film in 1920s London.' *Gender in Modernism*. Ed. Bonnie Kime Scott. Urbana-Champaign: University of Illinois Press. 809–24.
Latham, Sean and Robert Scholes. 2006. 'The Rise of Periodical Studies.' *PMLA* 121.2: 517–31.
Leavis, F. R. 1930. *Mass Civilization and Minority Culture*. Cambridge: The Minority Press.
Leavis, Q. D. 1932. *Fiction and the Reading Public*. London: Chatto & Windus.
Low, Rachael. 1971. *History of the British Film, 1918–1929, Vol. 4*. London: Allen & Unwin.

Manganaro, Marc. 2002. *Culture, 1922: The Emergence of a Concept*. Princeton: Princeton University Press.
Marcus, Laura. 2007. *The Tenth Muse: Writing About Cinema in the Modernist Period*. Oxford: Oxford University Press.
Mellown, Elgin. 1983. 'The Adelphi.' *British Literary Magazines, Vol. 4: The Modern Age, 1914–1984*. Ed. Alvin Sullivan. Westport, CT: Greenwood Press. 9–18.
Montagu, Ivor. 1970. 'Birmingham Sparrow: In Memoriam, Iris Barry.' *Sight and Sound* 39.2: 106–8.
Napper, Lawrence. 2009. 'Introduction.' *British Cinema and the Middlebrow Culture in the Interwar Years*. Exeter: University of Exeter Press. 1–15.
Rainey, Lawrence. 1998. *Institutions of Modernism: Literary Elites and Public Culture*. New Haven, CT: Yale University Press.
Richards, I. A. [1924] 2001. *Principles of Literary Criticism*. London: Routledge Classics.
Severin, Laura. 1997. 'Introduction.' *Stevie Smith's Resistant Antics*. Madison: University of Wisconsin Press. 1–23.
Sexton, Jamie. 2002. 'The Film Society and the Creation of an Alternative Film Culture in Britain in the 1920s.' *Young and Innocent?: The Cinema in Britain 1896–1930*. Exeter: University of Exeter Press. 291–305.
Sitton, Robert. 2014. *Lady in the Dark*. New York: Columbia University Press.
Wasson, Haidee. 2002. 'Writing the Cinema into Daily Life: Iris Barry and the Emergence of British Film Criticism in the 1920s.' *Young and Innocent?: The Cinema in Britain 1896–1930*. Exeter: University of Exeter Press. 321–37.
—. 2007. 'The Woman Film Critic: Newspapers, Cinema, and Iris Barry.' *Film History: An International Journal* 18.2: 154–62.
Woolf, Virginia. 1966. 'Middlebrow.' *Collected Essays, Vol. 2*. London: Hogarth Press. 196–203.

9

The Avant-Garde in the Drawing Room: Women, Writing, and Architectural Modernism in Britain

Elizabeth Darling

In seeking to engage with the nexus – women, architectural modernism, print culture – this chapter proceeds from the acknowledgment that of all the forms of aesthetic modernism, architectural modernism was most dependent on the written word (and the illustration) for its material existence. As Hyungmin Pai notes, in the modern period 'architecture was established as an institution through the agency of an array of texts and images' (2002: 13), while John Summerson dated the emergence of modernism in Britain to the publication of a book, an English translation of Le Corbusier's influential *Vers une Architecture* (originally 1923). He further noted how, for the subsequent six years, 'the modern movement in England was mostly talk: talk, travel and illustration,' before concluding: 'Nothing of substantial importance in the new spirit was built here before 1933' (Summerson 1959: 12). That is to say that modernism's vanguard nature, combined with the expense of building, required an extended period of production by print (and other non-spatial discourses) before it reached full expression. And while Summerson's definition of what constituted 'substantial' will be challenged, it is certainly the case that writing about modernism in interwar Britain far outweighed the number of modernist buildings, interiors, and other artefacts that were designed and made.

Most studies of this phenomenon have focused on male writers, editors, and audiences, the publications of the Architectural Press, especially the *Architectural Review*, and on the 1930s, but this is to relate an incomplete story (Higgott 2007). Yet, if we accept the notion that modernism existed primarily in mediated rather than built form, and turn our attention to the 1920s and a print culture aimed at women, a rather different account of modernist architectural culture in Britain emerges. There we find a perhaps unexpected arena in which the ideas that we associate with modernist architecture and design such as the demand for environments that represented the contemporary spirit and self, the rationally planned interior and the use of modern materials, were thoughtfully and systematically promulgated.

Featuring only rarely, and latterly, in professional architectural journals, women's writing on modernist architecture and design appeared in sites that ranged from society magazines such as *Vogue* and the *Queen* to the more middle-class *Good Housekeeping*. The authors were as diverse as the types of publication. Some were architects or designers, such as Doris Lewis (writing as Mrs Howard Robertson) and Miriam Wornum, but far more often they were journalists like Nora Shackleton Heald and

Alice Baines. The work of editors, especially Dorothy Todd at *Vogue*, also created important early environments for the presentation of modernist design practices. The resulting articles, written by and for women, demonstrate a sensibility which, whether discussing a Bloomsbury interior, a villa by Le Corbusier or new technologies and materials, was active in the establishment of a discourse of 'the modern' in architecture. This would become more widely disseminated as the 1920s wore on, linked to modernising impulses in other arenas (such as the professional architectural press), and anticipated or constructed a reader who was keen to be as modern as the subjects of the articles she read. Ultimately it coalesced into an expectation, and a demand, among women of all classes about the form that modern environments should take; one which reached fruition in the architectural and design landscape of the British Welfare State.

To navigate the relationship between women, architectural modernism, print and periodical culture, is, therefore, to substantially revise our understanding of the formation of architectural modernism in Britain. It focuses attention on debates about the modernisation of architecture beyond the discourse of professional practice, and shows how a demand for new forms of spatial and material culture emerged. Equally, the sort of writing discussed here shows that *a* British modernism (whether in the concepts used by authors or in projects referred to) was extant in the early 1920s, when many historians have argued that this was not the case: Summerson's starting point was, after all 1927, and as far as he was concerned, confined to words not buildings.

It is in the British edition of *Vogue*, especially under the editorship of Dorothy Todd (1922–6), that we see this early articulation of a modernist architectural culture. *Vogue* is now well understood as a significant site from which, as Elgin Mellown writes, the avant-garde was presented to 'a wealthy and socially superior audience' (Mellown 1996: 229). His focus, like many who have written on Todd's regime, has been on her patronage of literary modernism. However, as Christopher Reed has noted, although his primary interest was not in a discussion of print culture, she also consistently commissioned articles that discussed contemporary design, especially as it related to the domestic interior (Reed 2004 and 2006). Their importance to her vision of the magazine is evident in the fact that they were allotted a separate section called 'Decoration,' (the table of contents for the 'Winter Fashions' issue of late October 1924 (64:8), for example, lists it alongside 'Special Features,' 'Fashion,' 'Society,' and 'Regular Features,' although the articles themselves were interwoven across the magazine) and took two main forms. The first comprised features that related to recently designed interiors, which at once offered a guided tour of their up-to-date design and played up the exclusivity of this glimpse into the life of an elite individual or couple. Thus the article on the Cambridge rooms of Maynard Keynes, which appeared in early March 1925 (65:5) under the title 'The Economist and Modern Art,' noted that *Vogue* was the first to reproduce images of the interior. In a similar vein were articles such as 'The Work of Some Modern Decorative Artists' (Aug 1926: 27–31). These referenced the work of numerous designers and interiors or artefacts they had designed, and often discussed more broadly the nature of modern design. These features were invariably positioned toward the centre of the magazine, close to the society pages, and were thus relatively prominent. They were complemented, usually further into the magazine where the pages became more domestically oriented, by one or two more general articles about furnishing and decoration. So while Keynes's interiors occupied pages 46 to 47 (after 'The Hon Mrs Baring' on page 42, and 'Snapshots' on pages 44 to 45), an article on 'Bureaux of To-day and Yesterday,' was placed on pages 74 to 75 followed by 'Smart Frocks at Moderate Prices' and the *Vogue* Pattern Service.

The feature articles are notable for their almost singular devotion to the work of the designer-painters of the Bloomsbury Group, Vanessa Bell and Duncan Grant. This is not surprising given Todd's fondness for their literary counterparts, but it is a coming together of modernism and mass culture (albeit in a fairly rarified form) that has been largely ignored by architectural historians. This is because, as Christopher Reed has shown, they document a strand of modernism that has been largely written out of histories of British modernism (Reed 2004: 251–77; Reed 2006 *passim*). In what he calls the Amusing Style, designers blended eclectic historical references in one interior (a Chippendale chair, a painting by Wyndham Lewis, a screen by Vanessa Bell) as a signifier of a modern subjectivity. Decorative, 'painterly' and colourful, and mainly expressed through interiors, it was in sharp contrast to the more ascetic, homogenous, materials derived and spatially experimental, forms that modernism would begin to take from the later 1920s onward. It is that modernism – Summerson's idea of a more substantial expression of the new spirit – designed by architects such as Wells Coates, Raymond McGrath, and Tecton, which has come to dominate the historical record; its qualities of seriousness and, as Reed notes (2006: 383), 'timeless or eternal values' (for which read 'masculine') eliding the 'transient' and individualist (ergo 'feminine') values of the Amusing Style, and rendering it modernism's Other.

Yet, the suggestion here is that a consideration of how the Amusing Style was discussed and presented in the pages of *Vogue* reminds us that architectural modernism was a range of practices rather than one monolithic discourse and mode of being (the building), something more recent architectural histories have sought to argue (Darling 2007; Goldhagen 2005). As a set of responses to the condition of modernity, modernisms were both stylistically diverse and, as this chapter's premise signals, existed in media as diverse as the interior, the building, the text, the photograph, inter alia, and none more important than another. The very phrases and points of reference the anonymous authors (conceivably Todd herself) of these articles use would not be out of place in the writings of 'orthodox' modernists some ten or more years later.[1] There is, for example, a very firm insistence on the necessity of design for the 'now,' attended by an incredulity at nostalgia, as the early 1924 text, 'The Contemporary Style of Decoration' (Jan 1924: 51, 74) shows:

> Those who enjoy living in the present, and who are sensitive to its character, will be able to surround themselves, as people of taste have always done, with work not imitated from the fashions of their ancestry. A Georgian connoisseur who furnished his house with Elizabethan objects would have rightly been considered very eccentric for not employing Chippendale. We all like modern books, modern clothes, and modern music, while recognising the great achievements of the past. What we need is that the library in which we place these books, the drawing room in which we wear these clothes, and the music rooms in which we listen to the music should be marked with the same imprint. (74)

Likewise, later the same year, we find an author reflecting on the fact that 'for some time period rooms have been the fashion' but problematising this situation by continuing 'is there any reason we should not consider our own day as a "period," the only period for us which is not in some sense artificial – and set aside at any rate one room in our own house which shall be truly representative of the best in it' (Nov 1924: 43). Compare this with the words of the modernist Wells Coates, writing eight years later of 'the horror of embalming ... the characteristics of an architecture once noble, grand, all-powerful, but incapable of life amid the new social and material characteristics of the twentieth century' (*Architectural Review* Nov 1932: 167).

The emphasis on the 'now' is complemented by a frequent assertion of the momentousness of that 'now.' The same article declares 'there is at present in this country an artistic activity which is producing work more interesting and more vital than anything that has made its appearance during the past hundred years,' while the article on Keynes positions his patronage of modern art and interiors as having restored a tradition 'that been lost to our Universities since the Renaissance' (Mar 1925: 47). A year later, we find similar invocations. In 'The Work of Some Modern Decorative Artists' (Aug 1926: 27–31), the author declares 'the twentieth century has the vitality of the Renaissance' having characterised the late nineteenth century as a 'feeble age' when 'one had to choose between old things and ugly ones' (27). The idea of the Victorian age as a particular nadir for culture would, as it was for literary modernists, become a favoured trope of modernist architectural rhetoric in the 1930s. Speaking in 1932, the architect Amyas Connell would reference the 'unfortunate break' that the 1830s had inaugurated, and argue that the modernism he practised was a restoration of the civilised, rational, and ordered tradition of eighteenth-century architecture (*Listener* 28 Nov 1934: 886–9; Darling 2016).

The promotion and promulgation of Bloomsbury Group artists' design as well as literary modernism by *Vogue* under Todd fits with her broader project to make the magazine more than just a fashion paper, and to construct a mode of 'au courant femininity' through its pages (Mahood 2002). So at the same time that these articles allowed a privileged glimpse into interiors usually accessible only to an avant-garde elite, their reader is addressed, flatteringly, as though she is familiar with the practitioners and ideas which are referenced (or, equally, given a clear steer on those she needs to know about). A modern woman should, it is implied, know, or aspire to know, about the very latest in culture in order to *be* modern. Furthermore, in keeping with the Amusing Style's connection between a modern selfhood and its expression through interior design, *Vogue* also sought to enable its reader to project herself similarly. The Winter Fashion number of late October 1924 offers an interesting case study of this process (53–5, 92). It devoted four pages (text and image) to the Chelsea town house of Osbert and Sacheverell Sitwell, in which, it reported, 'ancient and modern jostle each other strangely' (Oct 1924: 54). On their 'tour,' visitors (real and vicarious) were, for example, led from a hallway in which eighteenth-century paintings were hung alongside Vorticist work 'in its extreme form' (a Gino Severini, 'the violent Italian,' flanked by canvases by 'his English comrades,' Wyndham Lewis and William Roberts) into a dining room where a plain table was surrounded by chairs 'of an Italian rococo beyond dreams' (Oct 1924: 55, 92). Such jostling, the author concluded, while it 'makes the imagination boggle,' after a while assumed a logic: 'a unity emerges from the diversity' and 'we perceive they are bound together by a mental tie, which is the intellectual experience of those who have collected them' (Oct 1924: 92). It is the modernity of the Sitwells' sensibility which binds work from two centuries apart and refracts it through the lens of their self-fashioning.

Ostensibly, the article is an exemplar of *Vogue*'s blend of celebrity peeking with more philosophical musings on design. Read against the magazine as a whole, however, the idea of the interior as self-expression takes on an additional implication, a means to enable the reader to perform another act of contemporary modernity, to be a discerning consumer. This multi-purposing of meaning was set up in the brief editorial text that accompanied the issue's table of contents:

> Being a noted explorer of houses, *Vogue* is pleased to add to its record of exploration a portfolio of photographs of the Chelsea House of Mr Osbert and Sacheverell Sitwell, and goes on to describe some original ideas for beautiful beds and the decoration of bedrooms. (Oct 1924: 78–9)

The syntax here is important. Although these articles (and, indeed, a third, on the 'Style Directoire') were distributed across the magazine, that conceptually they occupied a common ground is evidenced in their inclusion in one sentence. The Sitwell article offered a particular notion of modern selfhood and a model to be imitated; the articles that followed showed the reader where to go and what to buy in order to do this herself. If more subtly inscribed into the Sitwell article, this additional function of these features was more evident in texts such as 'The Work of Some Modern Decorative Artists' (Aug 1926: 27–31). This surveyed the work of a number of practitioners, not just Grant and Bell, but also emerging designers such as Marion Dorn and Allan Walton and, crucially, noted where their designs could be bought.

Vogue continued to commission articles on design after Todd's acrimonious departure in 1926, although their skilful admixture of the avant-garde, the discursive, and a subtle consumerism gave way to more prosaic and descriptive texts. The eye for the progressive, nevertheless, remained. Todd's successor, Alison Settle, may have been a less controversial figure but she was a quiet modern who, in the 1930s, served on the government's modernist-inclined design advisory body, the Council for Art and Industry, and after the war on the thoroughly modernist Council of Industrial Design. The 11 December 1929 issue of *Vogue*, for example, had a two-page article on what was arguably the most innovative British modernist interior of the day, Finella. This was designed by Raymond McGrath for the Cambridge don, Mansfield Forbes who wanted a setting for the modernist salon through which he sought to reorient cultural life both in Cambridge and beyond; among his guests were Paul Nash, Henry Moore, and Jacob Epstein (11 Dec 1929: 60–1). He was subsequently instrumental in one of the first attempts to formally organise British modernist architects through the founding of the Twentieth Century Group in 1930 (Darling 2012). Very much a response to the same sort of debates outlined in the articles that have been discussed above, the use of modern synthetic materials such as plywood, hardened glass, and metal leafs throughout the interior, however, represented a rather different aesthetic sensibility from that of the Amusing Style (see Darling 2011). But *Vogue*'s article makes no mention of the ideas that underpinned its designer's work, preferring instead to describe the interior in a tone that is more one of reportage than philosophy ('the architect uses metal and glass with new effect') with none of the delicacy or delight in phrase that characterised the descriptions by Todd (11 Dec 1929: 60). Nevertheless, despite the shift in tone, this choice of content meant that the *Vogue* reader was able to maintain her modern womanhood through her up-to-date knowledge of cultural matters.

That such content was not unique to *Vogue* is increasingly acknowledged, although the referent is invariably literary modernism (Mahood 2002; Wood 2016). Todd and her authors may have applied modernist ideas in their analyses, and featured modernist architectural designs consistently and earlier, but the editors of a number of other women's magazines did the same. Their vision of an 'au courant femininity' was not dissimilar to Todd's but in the *Queen* and *Good Housekeeping*, for example, the intersection between modernist ideas and a modern selfhood was framed not just as a matter of personal self realisation but also, as the right to vote was extended first in 1918 and then fully in 1928, as part of a process of creating a woman who was an informed and useful citizen. Their reader, as Judy Giles has argued (although she does not link this to architectural modernist principles), was thus constructed as '[a] "modern" woman, unlike her Victorian counterpart, [who] should take up the opportunities, conferred by education and labour-saving efficiency, to look up from her household tasks and outwards to the public sphere of rational discourse, politics and work' (2004: 123–4). In both magazines, we find architectural modernism discussed and done so in multiple terms of reference: for its immediate newsworthiness (especially in the *Queen*, which came out fortnightly and was more news-oriented), as a vehicle for selling something, and as something important to know about and understand because it related to a pressing issue of the day, which, in the 1920s, meant housing. Across the classes, the state of the nation's housing stock was a matter of grave concern: there was a housing shortage while the housing (whether mansion or slum) which existed was perceived as out of date and unfit for purpose. There was much debate about the form new housing should take and, in the interim, in techniques through which current homes could be improved. It was in this context that the theory of Scientific Management in the home, which Christine Frederick had developed in the US, grasped the collective imagination (Henderson 1996). Through the application of Taylorist principles of time management to household tasks, the rationalisation of space, and the use of dust-resistant materials, the mistress could offer servants a better working environment at a time when other and better forms of employment for working-class women were emerging or, a bit further down the social scale, as a 'modern housewife' work more efficiently herself. Taken up enthusiastically across Europe, it had many English advocates, not least Mrs C. S. Peel, a long-time contributor to the *Queen* (Watkins 1985: 193–5; Darling 2007: 96–7). Architectural modernism, which owed not a little to such ideas, as Susan Henderson has shown, was seen to offer an exemplary way forward in domestic design for many editors and writers, as an item in the 2 November 1927 issue of the *Queen* demonstrates.

It is a small feature – a photograph plus caption – placed in the centre of the 'Letters from Home' page (12) and shows the pair of houses that Le Corbusier had designed that year as his contribution to the *Weissenhof Siedlung* exhibition in Stuttgart. This was an estate of experimental houses designed by the leading modernists of Continental Europe; a project usually understood to have been of interest only to the most progressive of British architects. Yet, here it is in a woman's magazine, nestled on a page otherwise devoted to a column on French cuisine and its author's problem with a cook who is reluctant to wake before 7:15 a.m. to light the furnace. The tone of the caption is chatty – 'An interesting double house designed by the Swiss architect Le Corbusier' – and thus has the immediacy of a news item (the exhibition opened in July 1927 and was intended as a permanent addition to Stuttgart's housing stock, so readers could continue to visit the site) (*Queen* 2 Nov 1927: 12). Short though the caption is, it quickly gets to a larger point, linking the feature to the broader and common discourse (German and British) of which the *Siedlung* formed part: the modernisation of the domestic sphere. Disregarding the appearance of the houses, it tells us that Corbusier's were designed 'in keeping with present day materials and needs' and with a particular concern to provide 'full access to sun and air' (ibid.). Furthermore, in order that the reader can become more fully informed (if they cannot quite stretch to a trip to Stuttgart), the caption finishes by directing them to a source of information: the German (and rather esoteric) journal *Deutsche Kunst and Dekoration* which costs 2.5 marks.

Arguably, the decision to emphasise the planning of Corbusier's houses (rather than their stark flat-roofed forms) and the way they created a healthy environment was a means to 'domesticate' or 'middlebrow' an avant-garde discourse (Hammill 2007). The suggestion here, however is that the slippage between architectural modernism and the principles of Scientific Management (efficiency, rationalisation, an embrace of technology, and so forth), made it immediately recognisable to readers, even if its forms were rather unfamiliar. That it needed no 'translation' is reinforced by a consideration of the page in which the short article is placed. At first glimpse we might see one as the antithesis of the other – domestic musings versus high modernism – but each, in different ways, feeds into the same narrative of how to make the home modern. The end to the story of reluctant cook is not for her employer to sack her but to improve and update her working environment by buying a 'Bastian' hot water heater which does not require lighting daily: an exemplary modernist act of using technology to resolve a problem (just as Corbusier used reinforced concrete to create a healthy modern environment). At the same time, each article allows an act of consumption to take place, thus fulfilling the commercial aims of the magazine.

The interrelationship between these two features is a reminder of the broader interconnectedness across each issue of a magazine, and from one issue to the next. Editors and writers could anticipate their reader would pick up on themes because they were constantly reiterated and reinforced across the year; thus the feature on the *Weissenhof Siedlung* houses is referred to in an article published later the same month, which again focused on the work of Le Corbusier. Indeed, in a way not dissimilar from Todd's focus on Bloomsbury designers, the *Queen*'s editor, Nora Shackleton Heald, seems to have had a particular fondness for his modernism, commissioning, and herself writing, a number of articles about him. The source of this predilection is unclear. A rather elusive figure, she joined the magazine having previously worked as a music and drama critic and then as the editor of the women's pages of the *Daily Herald*. On leaving the *Queen* in 1930 she became editor of the *Lady* (Souhami 1988: 214). As an independent, unmarried, professional woman journalist we might understand her as inherently modern; likewise the journalists she employed.

In some respects, Heald's *Queen* did not stray so very far from that of her predecessors. Founded in 1861 as a weekly paper aimed at ladies of the upper classes, for much of its history at the same time as it printed society news and serial fiction, and published book and concert reviews, it had sought to address (and construct) an intelligent woman reader who was engaged politically (if not party politically) with significant current and foreign affairs of the day, especially as they pertained to women's emancipation and the improvement of her life (Watkins 1985). It also had a tradition of publishing articles on the design of the home, both those of well-known people and in terms of advice to readers (it had a section on 'Domestic Economy'). Two of the later nineteenth-century's most significant – and progressive – writers on decoration, Charles Eastlake and Mrs M. E. Haweis, wrote regularly for the magazine on home furnishing, and went on to publish these articles as books (Eastlake 1868; Haweis 1881).

Heald continued the emphasis on decoration: an article of 14 September 1927 was a sermon on the virtues of plywood in modernising the home written in the clear expectation that the reader herself might be undertaking such work (27–8). Plywood, it should be noted, was a quintessentially modern material. No older than the century, it was a manufactured product (its production much refined thanks to its use in aeroplane construction during the war), cheap and multipurpose. It was much loved by modernist architects, in various permutations it was used throughout Finella, for instance. Of more interest and importance to Heald, it seems likely, were long feature articles on modernism. Generally, these were placed toward the centre of the magazine across two pages with perhaps a further column on the subsequent page, and followed sections of society photographs and news, fashion, letters, and gardening. And while *Vogue* had sometimes had fun with the layout of its Decoration section – favouring blocks of text mixed with photographs, often placed askew on the page to create the effect of a scrapbook, a confection that echoed the Amusing Style they discussed – presentation in the *Queen* was uniform throughout with columns of text around or alongside photographs.

In tone the pieces are serious. Heald's November 1927 article 'Towards a New Architecture: When Engineer and Architect Work Together' is a thorough and rigorous discussion of Corbusier's *Vers une Architecture* (she used the English title) (23 Nov 1927: 17–20). It also records her visit to Paris to see modern houses by his contemporary, Robert Mallet Stevens. Throughout, their ideas are related to the British context and British debates, not least in suggesting how his urban plans could help prevent 'the spoliation of the countryside' which the first proper wave of speculative house building was by then causing. She also laments the fact that such houses were 'out of date at the moment of their building' with Corbusier's house prototypes, and Mallet Stevens's actual houses posited as the way forward (23 Nov 1927: 17). As with the texts in *Vogue*, her rhetoric could be taken for that written ten years later in the key modernist paean to new urban dwelling forms *The Modern Flat*.[2] 'If we are to have efficient houses we must gain a new conception of building. We discard our old clothes, our old tools, we design new implements to take their place. Yet still we go on building, by old methods, houses which do not fit the life we want to lead' (23 Nov 1927: 18). Her overall point is clear, as is her expectation of action by her reader. 'It is to be hoped' she writes 'that this book will be widely read in England . . . [it] might provoke a wholesome revolution in modern house building and that merely by reminding us what we need and suggesting simply what we might have did we but insist on having it' (23 Nov 1927: 19).

Heald went on to write at least one further article on Corbusier's second major book, *Urbanisme* (translated as *The City of Tomorrow*, and published in 1929). This was published on 24 July 1929 and was followed in the next issue by an article on his Villa Stein de Monzie, which had been completed the previous year. The author this time was not Heald but Mrs Howard Robertson, who represents another type of woman writer in the contemporary print culture: the professional expert. Robertson, whose byline always included the ARIBA (Associate of the Royal Institute of British Architects) which signalled her professional status, was among the first women to qualify as an architect in Britain. The Australian-born Doris Lewis trained in London at the most progressive school in the country, the Architectural Association (which had first admitted women in 1917), graduating in 1925 (Willis and Hanna 2001: 24). Her marriage to the director of the school saw her choose to take his name professionally, and focus her practice primarily on interior design and on writing (a decision which also reflected the difficulties women architects faced in finding full-time work once qualified). She enjoyed a considerable career as a journalist, writing for a number of women's magazines (but not for the architectural press) for whom she represented both an exemplar of a modern career woman who successfully combined work and marriage, and whose writing, because it was born of professional training, was especially trustworthy and could help readers themselves become experts.

In tone, Robertson's article on the Villa Stein is not so very different from Heald's (*Queen* 7 Aug 1929: 8–9). It assumes an intelligent reader, 'trained' in the preoccupations of the magazine and who will refer back to previous articles about him. There is, for example, no attempt to explain who Le Corbusier is. Her subject is somewhat different, since it is an actual house, rather than one of his books, but the discussion is presented very much as interpreting the design for what it might offer in terms of a precedent. So while she acknowledges that to 'English eyes' the 'stimulating' house might be 'strange and even shocking,' she stresses that it has 'many unusual aspects and possibilities' (7 Aug 1929: 8). As might be expected from an architect, Robertson has an eye for detail and the reader's attention is drawn to features and devices which might improve their homes. On entering the hall, for example, she notes how it is aglow with light because of its 'great horizontal window' (7 Aug 1929: 9). 'Why,' she asks, 'do we never light our floors? The effect is enchanting and fine rugs take on a new and unsuspected brilliance' (ibid.). The reader is walked through the rest of the house before Robertson concludes her tour with the kitchen, which is 'as charming as it is workmanlike' (ibid.). She approves of its labour-saving design, which, adhering to the principles of Scientific Management featured 'a continuous shelf on which takes place in sequence the ritual of cooking' (ibid.). It is, she declares in homage to Corbusier's famous aphorism, 'a machine to cook in' and 'a joy to the eye and [which] must be a joy to cook in' (ibid.).

In the *Queen*, we find architectural modernism written about by women, and presented to a female readership as something both newsworthy and very much in keeping with their interests. Armed with her knowledge and understanding of its principles, these articles put women in a position to be the intelligent clients and consumers who might instigate that wholesome revolution in housing that Heald had written about in 1927. If the readership of *Good Housekeeping* were not quite affluent enough to commission a new house, the presence of architectural modernism in that magazine's pages was used similarly to inform and to inculcate a sense of the necessity for, and right to, a modern domestic environment, something that women should themselves be able to shape (if not physically then through demand). In particular, as widely noted, *Good Housekeeping*, through its focus on a middle- and lower-middle-class readership, was at the forefront of constructing the housewife as a professional homemaker, something that did not preclude, indeed required, as noted above, a turning of these interests outward. So, as with the articles in the *Queen*, *Good Housekeeping*'s treatment of architectural modernism invariably entails a mixture of newsworthiness, advice, and intellectual weight.

Two articles may serve here as typical. In May 1929, Alice Baines contributed the article 'The Scandal of English Flats' to the magazine. This was a substantial piece of writing, beginning as a double spread across pages 36 to 37, and then concluding, far deeper into the magazine, across pages 99, 100, and 102. A lament for decently designed and well-situated accommodation for the urban middle classes, Baines, like Heald, makes frequent reference to contemporary concerns about suburban sprawl, the poor design of existing accommodation – 'thousands of city-dwellers, especially in London, are slaves to the tyranny of super-rented, inconvenient, pygmy "homes"' – and the need for homes designed on labour-saving principles (May 1929: 36). And again like Heald, the argument is made through the accompanying images; the preference here for Germanic modernism. Among the good examples shown is one of the blocks of social housing constructed under the socialist regime in 1920s Vienna, which, Baines comments have 'excellent design' and are rented 'very cheaply' (ibid.). She also includes a photograph of the *Weissenhof Siedlung*. The caption notes 'The use of steel and concrete and glass have evolved a new architectural style . . . They have no dark passages and corners' (May 1929: 37). The article as a whole concludes 'Why cannot London do something like this for people who do not happen to be millionaires?' (May 1929: 102)

Less argumentative is an article published later the same year, this time focusing on an example of native modernism and one which, as discussed above, featured in *Vogue* (and also the April 1930 issue of *Ideal Home*): Finella. Written by N. L. Gall for the 'Furnishing and Decoration' section of the magazine, as part news item part house visit, the text again demonstrates how the discourses of the modernisation of the home and the modernisation of architecture overlapped. The focus of the article is on the extensive use of glass in the house, which, Gall notes, is a material 'increasingly used as a decorative unit' but, as she continues, this was not the only aspect which made the house of interest to readers: 'in addition the fullest possible use has been made of all other modern materials and apparatus, and the saving of domestic labour has been made a special feature' (*Good Housekeeping* Nov 1930: 24–5, 150). There follows a careful tour of the interior, more detailed than that in *Vogue*; a specification of sorts for the reader to emulate.

By the late 1920s, a variety of women's magazines were featuring in some depth examples of British and Continental European architectural modernism, a subject hitherto understood to have been largely in the purview of the professional architectural press and addressed to a predominantly male audience. Only very rarely, perhaps uniquely, is there an example of a woman writing on this topic for an architectural journal: a 1928 article by Miriam Wornum on Le Corbusier's villa designs written for the *Architect and Building News*, a rather conservative weekly magazine. Wornum was an interior designer and, like Robertson, her husband was an architect with whom she sometimes collaborated. Unlike Robertson, who was able to see beyond the 'strange and shocking' language of his architecture to the benefits it embodied for the improvement of a woman's domestic environment, Wornum's comments remain critical and disapproving. Referring to an illustration of the double-height main salon in the Villa La Roche in Paris, she asks 'can you imagine a woman feeling at home in a room like this,' while her analysis of the same house's hall adds '[it is] wonderfully light and airy, but obviously needing more touches to make it a real home' (*Architect and Building News* 29 July 1928: 73–4). Quite why or how Wornum came to write this article is unclear, and she does not seem to have made any further contributions to this or any other journal. More typical seems to have been a transfer of expertise in the opposite direction: the woman architect to the woman's magazine.

Wherever it was located, and whoever was its author, this chapter has shown how, by nuancing understandings of what constituted architectural modernism, and looking elsewhere than the architectural press, during the 1920s a vibrant discourse evolved that brought together architecture, print culture, and women as writers, audience, and editors. That this created a popular audience sympathetic to modernist principles such as the use of technologies in the home, rational planning of interior space, and labour-saving designs was made evident in wartime when countless surveys asked women about the homes they wanted once hostilities ceased. The *Daily Mail Book of Post-war Homes*, published in 1944, and based 'on the ideas and opinions of the Women of Britain' (Pleydell-Bouverie 1944: n.p.), is typical in its emphasis on better standards, listing the 'six essentials' needed in the labour-saving home (Pleydell-Bouverie 1944: 82), and noting 'the national importance of good housing – every citizen's responsibility' (Pleydell-Bouverie 1944: 10). While more work remains to be done to uncover further instances of women writing modernism in 1920s print culture, and how they came upon this new architecture, what is clear is that architectural modernism in Britain was not some alien discourse latterly imposed, as so often and lazily argued, but something generated from a set of genuine and native and, above all, gendered concerns.

Notes

1. It is probable that Dorothy Todd was the principal author given that in 1929 she co-wrote *The New Interior Decoration* (London: Batsford) with Raymond Mortimer, which made extensive use of plates from *Vogue*.
2. See Yorke and Gibberd 1937. This was compiled from articles on flats that had featured in the monthly *Architectural Review*, with the addition of a polemical introduction that stressed the necessity of the flat if the city were to become modern. It went into multiple editions.

Works Cited

Darling, Elizabeth. 2007. *Re-forming Britain: Narratives of Modernity before Reconstruction*. London: Routledge.
—. 2011. 'Finella, Mansfield Forbes, Raymond McGrath, and Modernist Architecture in Britain.' *Journal of British Studies* 50: 125–55.
—. 2012. 'Institutionalizing English Modernism 1924–1933: From the Vers Group to MARS.' *Architectural History: Journal of the Society of Architectural Historians of Great Britain* 55: 299–320.

—. 2016. 'A Live, Universal Language: The Georgian as Motif in Inter-war English Architecture.' *Neo-Georgian Architecture 1880–1979: A Reappraisal*. Ed. Julian Holder and Elizabeth McKellar. Swindon: Historic England. 167–78.

Eastlake, Charles. 1868. *Hints on Household Taste, in Furniture, Upholstery and other Details*. London: Longmans, Green.

Giles, Judy. 2004. *The Parlour and the Suburb: Domestic Identities, Class, Femininity and Modernity*. Oxford: Berg.

Goldhagen, Sarah Williams. 2005. 'Something to Talk About: Modernism, Discourse, Style.' *Journal of the Society of Architectural Historians* 64.2: 144–67.

Hammill, Faye. 2007. *Women, Celebrity, and Literary Culture between the Wars*. Austin: University of Texas Press.

Haweis, M. E. 1881. *The Art of Decoration*. London: Chatto & Windus.

Henderson, Susan. 1996. 'A Revolution in the Woman's Sphere: Grete Lihotzky and the Frankfurt Kitchen.' *Architecture and Feminism*. Ed. Debra Coleman, Elizabeth Danze, and Carol Henderson. New York: Princeton Architectural Press. 221–47.

Higgott, Andrew. 2007. *Mediating Modernism: Architectural Cultures in Britain*. London: Routledge.

Mahood, Aurelia. 2002. 'Fashioning Readers: The Avant Garde and British *Vogue*, 1920–9.' *Women: A Cultural Review* 13.1: 37–47.

Mellown, Elgin W. 1996. 'An Annotated Checklist of Contributions by Bloomsbury and other British Avant Garde Writers (and of Articles Relating to Them) in *Vogue* Magazine During the Editorship of Dorothy Todd, 1923–27.' *Bulletin of Bibliography* 53.3: 227–34.

Pai, Hyungmin. 2002. *The Portfolio and the Diagram: Architecture, Discourse and Modernity in America*. Cambridge, MA: MIT Press.

Pleydell-Bouverie, M. 1944. *Daily Mail Book of Post-war Homes*. London: Daily Mail Ideal Home Exhibition Department.

Reed, Christopher. 2004. *Bloomsbury Rooms: Modernism, Subculture and Domesticity*. New Haven and London: Yale University Press.

—. 2006. 'Design for (Queer) Living: Sexual Identity, Performance and Décor in British *Vogue*, 1922–26.' *GLQ: A Journal of Gay and Lesbian Studies* 12.3: 377–403.

Souhami, Diana. 1988. *Gluck, 1895–1978: Her Biography*. London: Pandora.

Summerson, John. 1959. Introduction. *Modern Architecture in Britain*, by Trevor Dannatt. London: Batsford. 11–28.

Watkins, Charlotte C. 1985. 'Editing a "Class Journal": Four Decades of the Queen.' *Innovators and Preachers: The Role of the Editor in Victorian England*. Ed. Joel Wiener. London: Greenwood Press. 185–200.

Willis, June and Bronwyn Hanna. 2001. *Women Architects in Australia 1900-1950*. Red Hill: The Royal Australian Institute of Architects.

Wood, Alice. 2016. 'Modernism and the Middlebrow in British Women's Magazines.' *Middlebrow and Gender, 1890–1945*. Ed. Christoph Ehland and Cornelia Wachter. Leiden and Boston: Brill, Rodopi. 39–59.

Yorke, F. R. S. and Frederick Gibberd. 1937. *The Modern Flat*. London: The Architectural Press.

10

THE DIALOGIC MAGAZINE: ADVERTISEMENTS AND FEMININITY IN THE *LADY'S REALM*

Annie Paige

Introduction

THE WIDE-RANGING contents of this collection confirm that periodical and print culture expanded in impressive and innovative ways at the turn of the twentieth century. In addition to the prevalence of periodicals in general, women's magazines in particular enjoyed an explosion starting in the 1880s and continuing through the 1940s and beyond (White 1970: 58). Many of these – ranging from the penny papers to the lady monthlies – were aimed at a popular audience and made their money through advertising, an industry that also became increasingly active due to tax reform in the mid-nineteenth century (White 1970: 63). Despite the growth of the woman's magazine, few popular female-oriented mass magazines have become canonical in the same way that modernist little magazines like the *Little Review* and feminist publications like the *New Freewoman* have. One such little-remembered women's magazine is the *Lady's Realm*, a periodical that ran from 1896 until 1914 and appears to have been intended for upper- and middle-class audiences. As the title suggests, the magazine encouraged its readers to engage with the broader public sphere outside of their own home and catered to a certain type of cultured and educated audience. While the magazine's editorial content is politically engaged, the advertisements in the *Lady's Realm* tell a different story, and suggest a less clearly defined readership.

Any magazine's advertisements involve a certain degree of instructional material, as the overt messaging invites readers to pursue an ideal, offering a woman the ability to take control of her own life through her purse. James Joyce's Gerty of the 'Nausicaa' episode of *Ulysses* is one of modernist literature's most enduring examples of a young woman influenced by these instructional texts.[1] Joyce imagines her to only be capable of understanding her world through the language provided for her in women's magazines. For example: 'It was Madame Vera Verity, directress of the Woman Beautiful Page of the Princess Novelette, who had first advised her to try eyebrowleine' (Joyce 1986: 286). She dreams of following the romantic models presented to her in these magazines (examples such as 'Gander and Goose,' a story from the January 1911 issue of the *Lady's Realm*, in which a country squire falls in love with an elegant young woman), all the while venerating the beauty cues she learns from the magazines' advertisements. All the same, Gerty's interactions with Bloom do suggest that women were able to subvert the models they consumed.

As a colonised subject, Gerty exists in a more powerful position than the imagined *Lady's Realm* reader. But while the *Lady's Realm* targeted the upper-class woman, the social position of that figure was unstable. To what extent was the 'lady's realm' in the home and private sphere, as it had been predominantly in the past century, or was it in the novel opportunities opened up by the era's New Woman? The abundance of advertisements suggests that expanding consumer culture allows women to craft their own identities and enact their own vision of femininity. However, the expected and accepted nature of that femininity is shaped by competing, sometimes contradictory, and often restrictive gendered scripts.

Discussing the history of the feminist press, Maria DiCenzo argues that feminist media histories 'invariably begin by noting the absences, silences, gaps' in current scholarship (DiCenzo et al. 2011: 1). While feminist readings of late twentieth-century ads are fairly prevalent,[2] comparable scholarship regarding early twentieth-century advertisements is surprisingly scarce, in spite of important work by scholars like Faye Hammill, Catherine Keyser, and Laurel Brake. Similarly, work on popular women's magazines of the time is also slim when compared to the mountain of primary research left to be explored, a mountain that is growing as digitisation efforts persist. Yet advertisements exist in a paradoxical position. Overall, the magazine archive is enormous, yet it is relatively unusual for a publication to have survived with its advertising matter intact. Because advertisements were considered ephemeral, it was common practice to cut out a magazine's ad pages and to discard them, binding only the editorial content. This practice has resulted in what Robert Scholes and Clifford Wulfman term a 'hole in the archive' (2010: 169). Mass magazines were financed by advertisements and yet few archived issues of mass periodicals contain their original ad content. Therefore, studying ads from a complete number of the *Lady's Realm* presents an opportunity to examine this understudied aspect of 'advertising-driven' (Scholes and Wulfman 2010: 60) mass magazines by embracing a different scope and methodology than that of previous studies. A renewed perspective on historical advertisements affords an opportunity to problematise and to more clearly understand the complex aspirations of the imagined twentieth-century female reader, while getting closer to her historical lived reality.

This essay will first examine the *Lady's Realm* as an exemplary though long-neglected magazine, and then attempt to position it more broadly within the history of mass magazines. It will briefly address the challenges posed by scholars interested in the period's advertising. It will examine the ads from one single issue of the magazine, volume 29, issue no. 171 from January 1911. Narrowing the scope of study to one issue allows more in-depth study of the dialogic interaction between individual texts within the magazine. Doing so reveals that the magazine presents a fluctuating representation of femininity that juxtaposes advertisements presenting a womanhood built on selfless domesticity with one focused on physical appearance, all the while concentrating its editorial content on the potential of the *Lady's Realm* beyond that of the private domestic sphere. Because of the dialogic nature of its form, the *Lady's Realm* presents a vacillating femininity that is simultaneously in the home, in beauty, and in politics. Ultimately, the odd jumble of editorial and advertising content within the *Lady's Realm* presents a consumerist model of femininity that is fragile, fragmented, and in flux. The dialogic nature of the magazine reinforces the mutability of not only the magazine medium, but also the historical moment and its shifting definitions of womanhood.

The Archival Gap

The *Lady's Realm* presents an interesting and befuddling case study as relatively little about the magazine is known. In fact, even its publishers neglected to keep any kind of comprehensive records (Huddleston). This archival gap frustrates an attempt to historicise by examining biographical information on its editors and publishers, while simultaneously forcing a more thorough textual analysis because issues of the magazine exist as its key source of evidence. This essay proposes that a close textual analysis of the *Lady's Realm* works around the issue of archival inadequacy particularly with regard to advertisements, while demonstrating how the magazine as a dialogic medium presents fluctuating images of femininity.

In *Modernism in the Magazines*, Scholes and Wulfman outline a methodology for studying early twentieth-century magazines that begins with discovering the basic facts of each magazine: the editor's biography, circulation information, dates of publication, and other key facts as a starting point for scholarship (2010: 54, 146–8). Yet even some of these most basic facts are difficult to determine, or must be inferred, in the case of the *Lady's Realm*. In the *Victorian Research Guide*, Joan Huddleston indexes the fiction found in the *Lady's Realm* and provides an introductory essay in which she explores what little is known about the magazine. Marketed as an 'illustrated monthly magazine,' the *Lady's Realm* published thirty-six volumes between 1896 and 1914. The end date of the magazine's run remains in dispute, as records suggest that the magazine continued to be published into 1915. This is the date given in the *Dictionary of Nineteenth Century Journalism*, for example (Brake and Demoor 2008: 342). Despite this, no known libraries contain the missing 1915 issues. Huddleston explains that the 'whereabouts of Volume 37, November 1914 to April 1915, remain a mystery. These issues may never have been published, or if published, they may never have been bound' (Huddleston). This singular mystery demonstrates how the *Lady's Realm* – and other magazines like it – present both a unique conundrum and an exhilarating opportunity for scholars.

Despite the mysteries regarding the *Lady's Realm*, some basic facts are known. It was originally published by Hutchinson's and Co. before transferring ownership to Stanley Paul in 1909 and then Amalgamated Magazine Company in 1910. The first issue to be published under Amalgamated Magazine Company is volume 29, number 171 published in January 1911, which has been digitised with its advertisements in place – a significant accomplishment considering the lack of advertisements that have been archived from this period. Records kept by Hutchinson's were partially destroyed in the Blitz, and no known records from the magazine's last two publishers can be found. Circulation figures for the magazine are not known (Huddleston); however, the January 1911 edition contains more than twenty pages of advertisements, suggesting a fairly high readership base.

In writing about the magazine, Huddleston suggests that the *Lady's Realm* is aimed at 'an upper class or aspiring middle class audience' (Huddleston). The magazine was produced on nice quality, glossy paper and – according to its covers – included over 500 illustrations in every issue. Each issue was approximately 120 pages long and included sketches and illustrations by notable artists, such as Mabel Lucie Attwell. The magazine's features included all of the elements of a quality lady's magazine and sold at the relatively high price of sixpence. For example, *The Weekly Tale-Teller* sold for a penny, while the more high-class *The Review of Reviews* also sold for sixpence

(Modernist Journals Project). In tracing the history of the woman's magazine as a genre, Ros Ballaster et al. note a distinction between types of magazines: the glossy lady's magazine, the middle-tier housewife's periodical, and the cheap penny papers (1991: 94). Based on this monetary distinction, the *Lady's Realm* again confirms itself as a ladies' paper, intended predominantly for the servant-keeping classes – or those who aspired to join them.

For the first six years of its existence, the magazine was edited by William Henry Wilkins. A novelist and journalist, he wrote on sociopolitical issues of the day and boasted social connections to Lady Isabel Burton (wife of Sir Richard Burton the explorer), as well as to Lord Dunraven (then Under Secretary for the Colonies). While his editorship is recorded, little else is known about what he actually did while serving as editor. During his time at the helm, no editorial comments appear in the journal and it is not until after he retired as editor that editorial notes begin to appear. In fact, it is not even clear who succeeded Wilkins as editor. It is likely that the new editor was a man, but little else is known about him. As Huddleston notes, relatively little about the magazine changed, even as its editors and publishers shifted: 'On the whole the journal's format remained very constant and there is no evidence that changes in publisher or editor caused any alteration to the formula' (Huddleston). The methodology Scholes and Wulfman outline is difficult to employ when studying magazines that have been all but forgotten. However, as so many publications suffer from one form of 'hole in the archive' or another, the mission to examine such periodical texts is especially important.

Women's Magazines, Advertisements, and Previous Scholarship

The *Lady's Realm* is not a unique magazine in terms of the challenges it presents to the archival researcher, or in terms of the complexity of its ideological message. Clearly, scholarship on other magazines can help us position this periodical and its advertisements. This section will explore the history of advertising in women's magazines and how previous critics have studied both advertising and women's magazines from a feminist perspective.

Cynthia White, a sociologist, wrote the earliest comprehensive study of the history of women's magazines and their effect (1970), while David Reed produced a similar encyclopedic landscape of popular magazines in the United States and Britain (1997). Building on the early work of White in particular, Ballaster et al.'s *Women's World: Ideology, Femininity and the Woman's Magazine* (1991) focuses on the question of why women read magazines and what ideology and view of femininity those magazines enforce. Tracing magazines from the eighteenth century to their contemporary moment, the authors try to establish some sense of continuity between the woman's magazine of the past and of the present. The authors explain that they strive to challenge the either/or criticism, the current mode of reading women's magazines either as 'a source of pleasure (to be celebrated)' or 'as a purveyor of a pernicious ideology (to be condemned)' (Ballaster et al. 1991: 4). One way to challenge such binary criticism is to understand the magazine as a dialogic medium and to study the way individual texts within a magazine interact.

Margaret Beetham tracks the development of the woman's magazine as a broad genre, paying particular attention to the distinction between upper-class lady's magazines and penny papers aimed at the middle and lower class. In tracing the history of women's magazines, Beetham notes that the depiction of ideal womanhood is not consistent from one type of magazine to another. In the middle-class periodicals and penny papers, ideal femininity is presented as selfless domesticity, while the lady's magazines alternatively suggest that a focus on beauty, dress, and physical appearance produces the perfect woman. Yet within the magazines of each class, Beetham traces a fragmentation of the ideal femininity they present. In reference to the consistent motif of splintered femininity, Beetham argues: 'the fragmentation of the woman reader into different target groups was echoed in the cheap, as in the expensive journals, by the representations of the feminine self as fragmented' (Beetham 1996: 191). As each magazine structures its editorial content in order to align with its precise intended audience, each also paradoxically incorporates disjointed and oddly juxtaposed advertisement content.

As Ballaster et al. acknowledge, criticism regarding women's magazines needs to go beyond dichotic thinking regarding the ideology that magazines promote (1991: 4). Looking within specific women's magazines, such as the *Lady's Realm*, it becomes clear that these magazines do not present one coherent ideological message as they remain fragmented in form and content. Beetham, in fact, reminds us that magazines lack a powerful author ensuring a consistent messaging: 'For the periodical is also marked by a radical heterogeneity. It refused, and still refuses, a single authorial voice . . . All this suggests a fractured rather than a rigidly coherent form' (Beetham 1996: 12). While periodicals do have editors who often serve as a consolidating ideological force,[3] as already noted, the editorial voice is not particularly powerful or invasive in the *Lady's Realm*. Ballaster et al. similarly argue that the magazine is a medium uniquely capable of addressing the contradictions of femininity precisely because of its formal fragmentation: 'the form of the magazine – open-ended, heterogenous, fragmented – seems particularly appropriate to those whose object is the representation of femininity. Femininity is itself contradictory' (Ballaster et al. 1991: 7). This 'contradictory' nature is clearly seen in the abundant and diverse visions of femininity encouraged by both the magazine's editorial content as well as its advertisements. However, since magazines do have editors who approve and theoretically align content, they are not texts existing at random in a void. While Mikhail Bakhtin applies the terms dialogism and heteroglossia to the novel (1981: 259–75), it is appropriate to think of the magazine as further building on the dialogic impulses of the novel, with different aspects of the text shaping, reinforcing, and even contradicting one another.

Despite its often inconsistent representations of femininity, the woman's magazine nevertheless tends to take on an instructional role, teaching women how to dress, how to act – even how to keep their hands soft, as in the lengthy article 'How to Procure Manual Beauty' (*Lady's Realm* Supplement: 14). Not only does the magazine provide instructions for enacting an idealised or aspirational vision of sophisticated femininity in its editorial content, but its advertisements often employ an instructional tone in advising what products to purchase and how to use them. The pedagogical nature of women's magazines reveals an important unspoken distinction: while the *Lady's Realm* claims through its editorial content to exist for those who already possess social capital, its advertisements reveal that it also seeks to appeal to those wishing to pursue social capital by purchasing the right products.[4] The puzzling nature of the magazine is suggested in this paradox – a magazine attempts to be coherently instructional and present a consistent message of femininity, while nevertheless maintaining an inherently fragmented form. However, it is not only the periodical as a medium that encourages fragmentation; gender as a performance likewise hinges on just this kind of variety. In fact, the women's magazine is a unique medium for exploring gender, as it can encourage a femininity of multiplicity: 'The model of femininity extended by the magazine to the reader is severely contradictory, or rather, fragmentary. Perhaps instead of talking of contradiction, we should talk of multiplicity' (Ballaster et al. 1991: 12). While the contradictions of a magazine's representation of gender suggest a disintegration of coherent gender presentation, thinking in terms of multiplicity instead allows for a problematising of current understandings of early twentieth-century ideas of femininity. As DiCenzo argues, feminist media history allows for a revision of 'entrenched' historical narratives (DiCenzo et al. 2011: 8) and examining the woman's magazine in terms of a femininity of multiplicity provides such revision.

While it is not wise to generalise about all women's magazines, we can begin to separate them into broad categories based largely on their implied audiences. As Beetham and White make clear, the difference between women's magazines based on the class of their intended audience makes a great deal of difference (Beetham 1996: 191; White 1970: 74–8, 82). When women's magazines first developed in the late 1700s and early 1800s, they were predominantly enjoyed by an upper-class audience – in part due to literacy rates at the time. However, in the mid to late 1800s, new publications began to 'to look beyond the servant-keeping classes for new readers' (White 1970: 70). White argues that by 1910, women's magazines coherently arranged themselves by class rank, and each type of magazine had settled into a recognisable form in which magazines for the upper class focused on society events (White 1970: 78) and more 'serious-minded' content (82) while middle-class magazines focused on domesticity (78). In the interwar period, there is a 'reorientation of women's journalism away from the servant-keeping leisured classes, and towards the middle ranks' (96). Despite the rather clear lines of demarcation White describes, which are mostly based on and consistent in editorial content, women's advertisements display more fluid lines between upper- and middle-class magazines. Prior to the First World War, the ads in the *Lady's Realm*, for example, had already started to move 'towards the middle ranks' even while its editorial content remains outwardly focused (on politics and social issues, as opposed to housework). The middle-class audience implied by its ads reflects the aspirational quality of the *Lady's Realm* as hopeful readers try to gain cultural capital not only by purchasing the right products, but also possessing the correct opinions.[5]

Due to taxes on paper, periodicals, and advertisements in the early nineteenth century, the growth of periodical culture in Britain the first half of the century was slow. When these so-called knowledge taxes were abolished in the 1850s, both magazines and advertisements proliferated (Nevett 1982: 67). In the mid to late nineteenth century, advertisements became critical to the periodical industry. Marjorie Ferguson explains how advertisements shaped the explosion of the women's press in particular: 'During the last two decades of the nineteenth century, advertisement revenue emerged as the critical factor in the profitability of the women's periodical press' (Ferguson 1983: 16). In *The Adman in the Parlor*, Ellen Gruber Garvey traces the development of advertising in relation to the magazine market and notes the same expansion in ads and women's magazines in America as Ferguson notes in Britain: 'In the new press of the 1880s and 1890s both the material and symbolic importance of advertising grew. This was especially true in the women's press where consumption and control of spending were inseparable from the ideological project of defining the female reader' (Garvey 1996: 142). As Garvey notes, the idea of consumption was becoming connected to, and associated with, the idea of femininity. As consumer culture began to develop, shopping, purchasing, and choosing household goods was defined as the woman's task. While the husband theoretically provided the family's purse, the wife wielded it. As women were quickly becoming associated with developing consumer culture, women's magazines became a highly profitable target for the burgeoning advertising industry. As Garvey notes, not only was this important in the material development of the women's press, but it was symbolically important as well. Advertisements began to take up more physical space and affected the editorial development of magazines as women's magazines became more visual and consumer-focused. The effects of this visual development can be seen in the *Lady's Realm*'s literally boasting of its abundant illustrations.[6]

Advertising is not only associated with the imagined female reader, but it is also aligned with modernity as consumerism promotes a mechanism for a new type of agency (Garvey 1996: 13). The modernity of advertising is clear in its visual appeal, its mechanics, and – potentially most significantly – its capitalist perspective. In exploring the history of advertising in magazines, Ballaster et al. acknowledge how a new-found focus on advertising allowed for magazines to 'sell the same space twice – once to the reader and again to the advertiser' (Ballaster et al. 1991: 79). As more products began to be purchased rather than made in the home, advertising developed by appealing to markets who would be interested in specific products and the publishing industry began to make note of the importance of market groups: 'Publishing in the nineteenth century, developed in the context of capitalist industrialisation, depended on identifying and or creating markets in order to make a profit' (Ballaster et al. 1991: 77). In order to appeal itself to the most potential consumers, it is likely that the magazines presented a fragmented femininity in order to cater to the broadest possible market. If the imagined female reader of a particular magazine was both envisioned as a physical beauty and as a domestic goddess, the magazine could make itself appear more attractive to two different groups of potential advertisers, such as the dress and jewellery companies interested in appealing to women's physical beauty and the household goods companies interested in catering to women's domesticity.

Advertisements, Editorial Content, and the *Lady's Realm*

As should be clear by this point, the methodological difficulties involved in finding, contextualising, and interpreting advertising in early twentieth-century women's magazines are acute.[7] Scholars like Reed and White have attempted to sample representative issues at regular intervals, while others, like Beetham, have built their analyses around specific case studies. For this study, rather than looking for breadth and scope in women's advertisements, I have chosen to focus on depth and closely read the advertisements from a single, intact issue of one largely forgotten magazine – albeit one that can be taken as a successful exemplar of its type. This choice is in part practical, since advertisements from this period were rarely collected and saved. The *Lady's Realm*, for example, is archived and digitised almost in its entirety at HathiTrust; however, these copies of the *Lady's Realm* contain only the magazine's editorial content, not its advertisements. There is only one edition of the magazine readily digitally available that contains the entire magazine, ads and all, found in the Modernist Journals Project's 1910 Collection. Studying this single issue from January 1911 reveals that the magazine is fundamentally dialogic as it makes a space for several, often contradictory, voices to speak at once.

The decision to take so narrow a cut also permits us to step back from broad historical patterns and instead use the time-tested literary skill of the close reading to imagine what it might have been like to navigate the contradictions and challenges presented by this difficult modernist text. While the New Critics developed this technique in the early twentieth century, it has since become a key critical and pedagogical technique in literary studies. The advertisements in the *Lady's Realm* do not contain the potentially 'confusing' rhetoric of modernist stream of consciousness or free indirect discourse, but the ads are small, historically removed from us, and contain easily overlooked details in a way that makes them similar to a high modernist text. This close-reading methodology has its own scholarly legacy. In *Modernism in the Magazines*, Scholes and Wulfman employed a similar technique as one potential starting point for periodical studies, deciding to look at the advertisements from one single issue of a magazine in order 'to see what pleasures it may hold and what we may learn from taking advertising seriously' (128).

In order to understand a magazine as a whole, it is beneficial to treat it as its original readers would have by looking at both its advertisements and editorial content because 'any insistence on an editorial/advertising split distorts the experience of actual magazine readers, who took the magazine as a whole' (Garvey 1996: 4). Most of the ads in the *Lady's Realm* promote a femininity that is focused on perfected domesticity performed, purchasable beauty, and the interplay of the two. The fractured nature of how femininity is presented in the advertisements is further complicated by the magazine's editorial content, which typically invokes or imagines a female reader who is politically engaged and concerned with the public sphere. The disjointed nature of the editorial content and advertisements reinforce the notion of a femininity that is imagined to be invested in the broader public sphere, but in reality is caught up in the culture of capitalism and the possibility of improving social status through consumption. As is to be expected from the heterogeneous medium of the magazine, the editorial content often includes contradictions and oppositional opinions as well – with this issue including pro-suffrage and anti-suffrage opinion pieces placed one after the other. Examining the politically engaged editorial content allows for a more nuanced understanding of how the advertisements, articles, and short fiction interact to promote a dialogic reading of femininity.

The January 1911 issue includes a series of articles titled 'Quo Vadis?' (235) – 'where are you going?' – in which three women from England, Germany, and France attempt to address the woman question in her own country. These three articles report positively on the burgeoning feminist movement, with writers discussing the hope and fervour women are beginning to feel. The English writer notes that 'Englishwoman are stirred by a vague unrest. They are asking themselves the question, Are the lights in New Year's sky of 1911 a false dawn, or do they presage the coming of a new and better day?' (237) while the German one conveys that 'Women of the new and old way of thinking lift their voice in public strife' (264). In this article, the three female journalists note feelings of feminist hope in their home countries; importantly, as the German writer notes, these feelings are not just felt by the New Woman type, but rather are felt by women 'of the new and old way of thinking.' In addressing the situation of women, the three writers attempt to bridge the gap from the older generation to the new; in doing so, they suggest the possibility for a feminist vision that extends beyond binary groupings. 'Quo Vadis?' presents a nuanced and complex perspective on the woman question, which suggests that the readers of the *Lady's Realm* likewise contain sophisticated viewpoints on feminist issues.

Considering that suffrage magazines themselves contained ads for consumer products (Lysack 2008: 142), it is not too surprising to find pro-suffrage content in a magazine consisting of an abundance of advertisements for beauty and domestic goods.

However, following this feminist proclamation, the *Lady's Realm* editor includes a copy of an article reprinted from the *Ladies' Home Journal*, which he includes as 'a statement of facts and not as an expression of opinion' (255). In the accompanying article, 'What Women have Actually Done where they Vote,' Richard Barry examines the political records and results of American states in which women have achieved the vote. Barry clearly comes from a reactionary perspective and seeks to point out the lack of change in states where women have the vote. He looks at issues that he sees as connected to female concerns, such as reform in child-labour laws and improved marriage laws. However, he finds that the states in which suffrage has been granted to women do not show better policies in these areas of concern. Based on these findings, he blames the women who have the vote for not improving their own conditions; by doing so, he seeks to discredit the suffrage movement in its entirety.

The *Lady's Realm* includes conflicting positions on issues such as suffrage – though the editorial content does posit a potential reader who is engaged with political debates. Likewise, within the January 1911 edition of the *Lady's Realm*, advertisements reflect dialogic definitions of femininity – incorporating sometimes conflicting or contradictory images that remain, because of their container, in conversation with one another. As White suggests, women's magazines at the time often proposed differing pictures of ideal womanhood based on the class of their intended audience. There is, she argues, a distinction between ads promoting two different types of femininity: the lady's magazine endorsing one that is focused on the ideal woman as a symbol of physical beauty, and the middle-class magazine connecting the feminine with the selfless and domestic housewife (White 1970: 82). Despite White's arguments for the distinction between these two types of content based on the class of magazine they are found in, the *Lady's Realm* instead displays a surprising intermingling of these two factions of ads within the same pages. The mixing of differing depictions of femininity suggests a complex dialogism rather than a monolithic ideology. By including ads for both elegant gloves and for insect repellant, the *Lady's Realm* suggests that its intended audience is broad enough to be interested in both products, and potentially allows that one reader could need both.

The focus on purchasable products within the magazines position femininity itself as a construction or performance. As Lisa Shapiro Sanders argues in 'Making the Modern Girl: Fantasy, Consumption, and Desire in Romance Weeklies of the 1920s,' advertisements in young women's weeklies specifically 'reflected the period's emphasis on self-display, in framing women as performers of their own beauty, and indeed, in unmasking beauty as itself a performance' (2017: 92). Various ads within vol. 29, no. 171 of the *Lady's Realm* encourage a similar understanding of self-display and beauty as manufactured performance. Ads that direct attention to the constructed nature of beauty include those for 'Tensfeldt electrolysis' hair removal for 'superfluous hair' (14), 'Mrs. Dora Mole's Hair Tonic' for 'bright, glossy, and silky' hair (14), and 'Oatine Cream' to cleanse pores (6). Most of these advertisements are, of course, accompanied by illustrations of pretty women with clear faces and perfect hair.

The use of markers of physical beauty is not isolated to beauty-focused content, however. The ad for the Ewbank Sweeper (9) appeals to ideas of femininity as domesticity, but does so by using the ideal of physical attractiveness (Figure 10.1). The ad

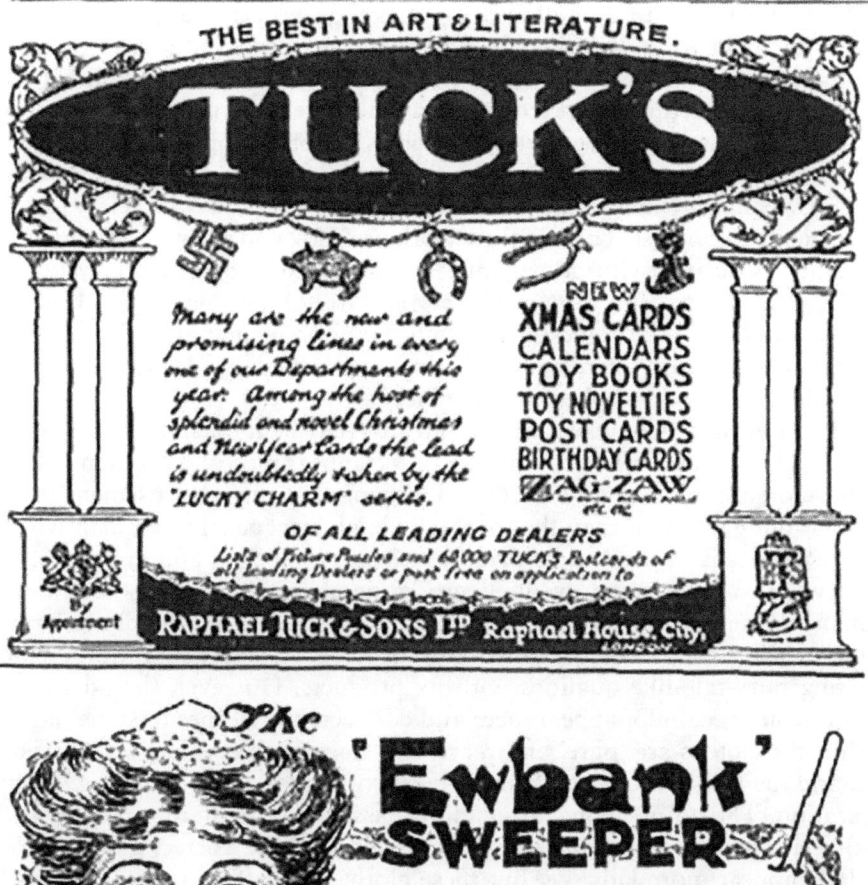

Figure 10.1 Advertisements from the *Lady's Realm*, January 1911, including the EWBANK SWEEPER.

associates the sweeper with the woman's emotions (it will 'gladden her heart'), reduced work for women, and a tidy house; it suggests the sweeper is a gift for the woman, as well as the man – it will reduce the housewife's work, but also ensure a well-kept house and happy wife for the husband to enjoy. Appealing to the woman's emotion while displaying a picture of a pretty woman's face, the Ewbank sweeper associates its power with a woman's inner emotions as well as her outer appearance. The variety of the ad's messages continues as it connects the sweeper to British nationalism as well as bicycles: 'Ewbanks are all British, and run as smoothly as a new bicycle – last as only British machinery can last. They do their work perfectly and silently.' The ad promotes a femininity associated with domesticity, selflessness, and quiet work, yet also connected to a modernity defined by machinery and freedom of movement. Demonstrating that the trinkets of the domestic housewife do not remain in the private sphere, the ad reaches outward into the realm of physical beauty and self-display, as well as into the masculine and modern sphere of machinery.

The London Glove Company displays an advertisement for shoes, evening dresses, and gloves that focuses explicitly on the outer appearance of a woman. The clothing is promoted 'for evening wear' (12), implying that the advertisement's intended audience is quite different than that of the Ewbank Sweeper. The woman who might buy these clothes is in the middle or upper classes of society and in need of a dress she can wear to an evening event. Considering that the company also boasts its 'Unequaled Variety' it is likely that this imagined woman is in need of more than one evening garment. The clothing is positioned as 'stylish,' 'fancy,' and 'Cinderella'-like, associating fairy-tale-like qualities with its products. However, the ad also moves beyond the outer realm of appearances and connects the clothes to some more internal value: the clothes are 'pure' and represent 'Remarkable Value.' The 'Cinderella' gloves, and the mention of good 'value,' both conceal and reveal the raw economics of aspiration. The ad promotes a femininity associated with appearance, and suggests that a woman can doubly improve herself with the correct clothes; not only can a lady appear more ladylike, but these clothes can affect a woman's inner self. The logic of this ad works in the opposite direction of that for the Ewbank Sweeper, as it promotes an outside-in mentality; women can improve their inner self by first improving their outer self. The ads suggest a two-way traffic between subjective and objective worlds. The result is a sort of cycle in which each rebounds on the other in an endless cycle of acquisition and transformation.

Returning again to domestic products, the advertisement for Adam's Furniture Polish holds the prominent spot of the inner cover. In marketing itself in the *Lady's Realm*, Adam's Furniture Polish employs an intertextual technique by including a review from another magazine, the *Queen*, which states: 'Having made a fresh trial of its virtues after considerable experience with other compounds of the same nature, we feel no hesitation in recommending its use to all housewives.' The ad works under the assumption that housewives will be interested in the product and that they will also be well enough immersed in women's periodical culture to make note of this review from another publication, which was itself focused on British high society and the lives of aristocracy and socialites. By doing so, it associates the world of domesticity with the larger realm of periodical culture, while also reaching out to the wider public sphere beyond the home of the housewife. The polish is 'the oldest and the best.' Boasting of its quality and legacy, the ad promotes a femininity that is associated with inner qualities, such as value and tradition, and also focused on the work of a housewife; the ad reasserts the significance of domestic work. The way in which this ad celebrates domesticity suggests that some members of the magazine's intended audience are likely to be involved in domestic work, or else Adam's Furniture Polish has wasted their money. Likewise, the ad maintains a linear connection between domesticity, nationalism, and global importance. Just as the Ewbank Sweeper reached out to the world beyond the domestic, Adam's Furniture Polish is 'Made at Sheffield and Sold all over the World.' The ad connects its product to Yorkshire, England, while also reinforcing its importance on the global level. The housewife labouring alone in rural England can enjoy the importance of her work, while imagining herself transported to another part of the world.

The *Lady's Realm* also employs a technique still used in magazines today: formatting advertisements to look like editorial content and thus blurring the distinction between the two. Even though the two types of content were bound separately, there was clearly an exchange of ideas and formal technique between the two. This section, named 'Practical Hints and Necessities,' offers advice on practical matters, and then produces a particular product that can solve the problems discussed. For example, Whitlock pearl reproduction promises a string of pearls that looks genuine, for a reduced cost: 'the celebrated Whitlock daylight pearls cannot possibly be distinguished from the genuine pearl of the ocean, being identical in shape, colour, and radiance' (18). The ad reveals the constructed nature of ladylike femininity by replacing a status symbol and marker of class with a replicated, artificial lookalike. In comparison to the ad for the London Glove Company (12), which boasts a true elegance, Whitlock Pearls reinforces the performative nature of gender. The same housewife who is interested in the ads for the Ewbank Sweeper and Adam's Furniture Polish is likely to be the intended audience for this ad as well, since she can now perform a domestic femininity while also maintaining her physical beauty. The ad demonstrates the possibility of a purchasable femininity in which a woman is able to look like a lady for half the cost. However, this is not to suggest that the Whitlock ad intentionally unmasks femininity as a lie or hoax. Instead, the playful nature of Whitlock Pearls suggests the pliability and fluidity of both gender and class.

The magazine's format itself welcomes these connected readings. When pages that are next to each other are compared, the fragmented nature of the magazine's readership becomes increasingly visible – as does the instability of the boundaries surrounding 'the *Lady's Realm*.' As a dialogic medium, with many voices operating at once, the ads interact in surprising and disruptive ways that emerge without deliberate editorial control. For example, a full page cognac ad on one side of the page (7) is placed next to a page of small one-eighth and one-sixteenth ads on the other side (6). The cognac described as 'The brandy of Napoleon' suggests high-class femininity, while the ads on the other side of the page suggest the opposite. The smaller ads address middle-class or crude concerns, including those for Keating's flea powder, two fortune tellers, and Widow Welch's Female Pills – a pharmaceutical remedy that is believed to have been abortifacient (Pelt 2010: 42; Knight 1977: 61) and is mentioned by Gerty in Joyce's 'Nausicaa' episode. Not only does the content of an advertisement suggest differing levels of class, but the size of the ads themselves reveal the economic situation behind the advertising companies. The juxtaposition of a full-page ad and many smaller ads suggests an uncertainty about the magazine's audience – it might be readers looking for expensive cognac or those who have a flea problem. A broad diversity of advertising creates a dialogism that creates intersectional readings between gender and class. The grandiose nature of the cognac message is diminished by its surroundings. The fabricated nature of the magazine's title and audience is revealed in this juxtaposition: the cognac-serving lady exists in the same textual space as the flea powder-using housewife or the pregnant woman in need of Widow Welch's Pills.

According to T. R. Nevett, medicinal companies were particularly active advertisers; for example, he notes an increase in money spent by Beecham's Pills in the last two decades of the nineteenth century (1982: 71). The economic investment in Beecham's Pills is made clear by its full-page ad in the *Lady's Realm* (Supplement 20). These laxatives that were often advertised as a 'cure all' for women are sold with a full-page ad featuring an elegantly done-up woman coyly looking over her shoulder (Figure 10.2). Here a bowel-focused medicinal product is marketed as something high class that is associated with feminine beauty. With regard to medicinal pills and female readers, Beetham argues that advertisers often employed rhetoric of 'female pathology' or the 'unsound female constitution' (1996: 150). However, the logic of unsound female constitution is absent from this ad. Instead, Beecham's Pills are associated with physical beauty and elegance.

When read closely and in active dialogue with one another, the ads in the *Lady's Realm* reveal the fluctuating nature of femininity and class. Based on analysis of its advertisements, the magazine attempts to simultaneously cater to both a middle-class audience and an upper-class audience. Looking at the ads intended toward the middle class specifically, the magazine promotes attainable as well as aspirational products, advertising realistically necessary furniture polish as well as playful fake pearls. A close reading of the ads makes clear the aspirational quality of the magazine in a way that studying its editorial content alone would not reveal. Yet studying the advertisements and the editorial content together reinforces the continued mobility afforded its readers by the dialogic magazine.

Conclusion

The articles in the magazine try to promote a view of femininity that is outward looking; according to the magazine's editorial content, the realm for women does and should include politics and the public sphere – even if the political discussion is not consistently pro-suffrage, it is still publicly concerned. The ads, however, do not address the same political and public-oriented concerns, and continue to suggest instead that the proper 'lady's realm' remains the home, defined here by family, decoration, and personal beauty. The juxtaposition of these two spheres of concern reveal the contradictory nature of the magazine as a dialogic medium. The middle-class woman is able to purchase and perform ladylike femininity; however, the social capital she can gain through consumption is potentially meaningless in her economically constrained position. The advertisements only allow women to enter a few spheres of femininity, such as domesticity and physical beauty, while the magazine teases the realms of politics and suffrage, without providing any instructional material for how to involve oneself in these progressive realms. That the interplay of the advertisements promotes readers to travel between two arenas of womanhood – domesticity and beauty – suggests that

Figure 10.2 Advertisement for Beecham's Pills. *Lady's Realm Supplement*. January 1911.

monolithic visions of femininity were already beginning to shift, but there remained a great deal of work to be done to evolve the definition of ideal femininity in womens' magazines.

Ultimately, an analysis of the *Lady's Realm* no. 171 reveals neither consistently feminist nor consistently oppressive messaging. Instead, the advertisements and editorial content suggest a nuanced understanding of an imagined Edwardian reader and the woman's magazine as a textual category that goes beyond binary thinking (Ballaster et al. 1991: 4). The dialogic possibilities of the magazine format allow for a chance to 'look beyond the general accounts' and 'see the complexities' (DiCenzo et al. 2011: 13) of mass-magazine history and women's periodical culture. Studying the advertisements from this singular issue in relation to its editorial content does not only reveal insights about the nature of gender and femininity in 1911, but it also reaffirms why the magazine itself is a unique form, with its various voices, opinions, and texts interacting in a dialogic mode that continues long past its historical moment of publication.

Notes

1. For more on the influence of advertising on Gerty, see Pelt 2010.
2. For example, Jean Kilbourne's lecture series and the documentary series based on her work ('Killing us Softly') explore the objectification of women in mid-century American advertisements.
3. For example, see Philpotts (2012) and Scholes and Wulfman (2010) on the role of Ezra Pound as a periodical editor.
4. For more on the complicated relationship between middle-tier magazines and their aspirational quality, see Faye Hammill (2010: 154–5).
5. For further scholarship on early twentieth-century women's magazines, see Catherine Keyser's *Playing Smart*, Adrian Bingham's *Gender, Modernity, and the Popular Press in Interwar Britain*, as well as the adjacent volume *Women's Periodicals, and Print Culture in Britain, 1918–1939: The Interwar Period* (Clay et al. 2017).
6. For a thorough history of photomechanical reproduction, see Gerry Beegan's *The Mass Image* (2008), in which he discusses the technological developments that led to periodical illustrations.
7. For a lengthy discussion of methodology and periodicals – albeit nineteenth-century periodicals – see Easley et al., *Researching the Nineteenth-Century Periodical Press* (2018).

Works Cited

Bakhtin, Mikhail. 1981. *The Dialogic Imagination*. Austin: The University of Texas Press.
Ballaster, Ros, Margaret Beetham, Elizabeth Frazer, and Sandra Hebron. 1991. *Women's World: Ideology, Femininity, and Women's Magazine*. New York: New York University Press.
Beegan, Gerry. 2008. *The Mass Image: A Social History of Photomechanical Reproduction in Victorian London*. Basingstoke: Palgrave Macmillan.
Beetham, Margaret. 1996. *A Magazine of Her Own?: Domesticity and Desire in the Women's Magazine, 1800–1914*. London: Routledge.
Bingham, Adrian. 2004. *Gender, Modernity, and the Popular Press in Interwar Britain*. Oxford: Oxford University Press.
Brake, Laurel and Marysa Denmoor, eds. 2008. 'The *Lady's Realm*.' *Dictionary of Nineteenth Century Journalism*. The Nineteenth Century Index.

Clay, Catherine, Maria DiCenzo, Barbara Greene, and Fiona Hackney, eds. 2017. *Women's Periodicals and Print Culture in Britain, 1918–1939: The Interwar Period*. Edinburgh: Edinburgh University Press.
DiCenzo, Maria, with Lucy Delap, and Leila Ryan. 2011. *Feminist Media History: Suffrage, Periodicals and the Public Sphere*. Basingstoke: Palgrave.
Easley, Alexis, Andrew King, and John Morton. 2018. *Researching the Nineteenth-Century Periodical Press: Case Studies*. Abingdon: Routledge.
Ferguson, Marjorie. 1983. *Forever Feminine: Women's Magazines and the Cult of Femininity*. London: Heinemann.
Garvey, Ellen Gruber. 1996. *The Adman in the Parlor: Magazines and the Gendering of Consumer Culture, 1880s to 1910s*. Oxford: Oxford University Press.
Hammill, Faye. 2010. *Sophistication: A Literary and Cultural History*. Liverpool: Liverpool University Press.
Huddleston, Joan. 'The *Lady's Realm* – Indexes to Fiction.' In *Index to Fiction in The Lady's Realm. Victorian Research Guides: 5*, by Margaret Versteeg, Sue Thomas, and Joan Huddleston. Available at *Victorian Research Guides* <https://victorianfictionresearchguides.org/the-ladys-realm-indexes-to-fiction/> (last accessed 30 November 2018).
Joyce, James. [1922] 1986. *Ulysses*. New York: Vintage Books.
Keyser, Catherine. 2011. *Playing Smart: Women Writers and Modern Magazine Culture*. New Brunswick, NJ: Rutgers University Press.
Knight, Patricia. 1977. 'Women and Abortion in Victorian and Edwardian England.' *History Workshop* 4: 57–68.
Lysack, Krista. 2008. *Come Buy, Come Buy: Shopping and the Culture of Consumption in Victorian Women's Writing*. Athens: Ohio University Press.
Modernist Journals Project. 'The 1910 Collection.'
Nevett, T. R. 1982. *Advertising in Britain: A History*. London: Heinemann.
Pelt, April. 2010. 'Advertising Agency: Print Culture and Female Sexuality in "Nausicaa."' *James Joyce Quarterly* 48.1: 41–53.
Philpotts, Matthew. 2012. 'The Role of the Periodical Editor: Literary Journals and Editorial Habitus.' *The Modern Language Review* 171.1: 39–64.
Reed, David. 1997. *The Popular Magazine in Britain and the United States of America, 1880-1960*. Toronto: University of Toronto Press.
Sanders, Lisa Shapiro. 2017. 'Making the Modern Girl: Fantasy, Consumption, and Desire in Romance Weeklies of the 1920s.' *Women's Periodicals and Print Culture in Britain, 1918–1939: The Interwar Period*. Ed. Catherine Clay, Maria DiCenzo, Barbara Greene, and Fiona Hackney. Edinburgh: Edinburgh University Press. 87–102.
Scholes, Robert and Clifford Wulfman. 2010. *Modernism in the Magazines: An Introduction*. New Haven: Yale University Press.
White, Cynthia. 1970. *Women's Magazines, 1693–1968*. London: Joseph.

Part III

Key Literary Figures

KEY LITERARY FIGURES: INTRODUCTION

Carey Snyder

IF 'MODERNISM BEGAN in the magazines,'[1] our collection shows that women were a vital part of that inception. The writers showcased here are familiar figures in modernist studies, though some are known more by reputation than by their writing. Violet Hunt, for example, is remembered more for her role as salon hostess or mistress to male modernists than for her copious literary output, and Beatrice Hastings, whose love life once similarly eclipsed her literary talent, is only now beginning to get the recognition she deserves.[2] Alongside essays on these known yet understudied figures, others offer fresh scholarly angles on noted modernists with established links to periodical culture, including Dora Marsden, Katherine Mansfield, and Rebecca West, whose formidable output is addressed in two chronological chapters. Still other essays investigate the largely unexplored periodical contributions of acclaimed modernists Dorothy Richardson and May Sinclair. While by no means exhaustive, this list highlights women's wide-ranging contributions to modernist-era magazines, as editors, journalists, and fiction writers.

The present section contributes to recent scholarship that documents how women writers forged their careers through periodicals. The writers featured here and elsewhere in this collection emerge as often savvy professionals who navigate increasingly expansive and eclectic periodical networks that include radical weeklies, avant-garde littles, mass-circulation dailies, professional journals, movement organs, and middle-brow magazines. Most writers span the cultural spectrum, negotiating relationships with a wide range of publishers, editors, and publics. This free-wheeling participation in an eclectic mix of print venues serves as a reminder that cultural hierarchies were less rigid than critics might imagine: that pioneer of stream-of-consciousness writing Dorothy Richardson was as much at home in the *Dental Record* as in the *Little Review*. May Sinclair's periodical writing was similarly wide-ranging. In her chapter on Sinclair, Laurel Forster emphasises how instrumental the author's diverse periodical publications were in shaping her career and allowing her to engage with a range of modernisms and modernities. These contributions include not only short and serialised fiction, but also reviews of the work of prominent writers, like T. S. Eliot, which provided opportunities for networking, and a series of unconventional essays entitled 'Women's Sacrifices for the War,' published in the popular magazine, *Woman at Home*. The essay also pays particular attention to Sinclair's contributions to the *Author*, demonstrating her awareness of the shifting dynamics of the profession.

Writers discussed in this section traverse not only distinctions of genre and 'brow,' but the lines of periodisation, with careers in some cases spanning the Victorian and modern periods. Indeed, our collection dates – the 1890s to the 1920s – invite scrutiny of any line sharply demarcating these periods. For instance, according to Louise Kane, Violet Hunt troubles period binaries by not simply 'evolving' from a Victorian realist into an experimental modernist, but switching back and forth between different styles and periodical venues. Hunt's eclectic and copious output is worthy of attention in its own right, Kane shows, and it reveals not just the heterogeneity of the periodical field, but that periodicals themselves are 'capacious, heterogeneous, variegated repositories' (p. 223).

At the dawn of the twentieth century, as now, a single magazine often combined incongruous styles and voices, resisting easy categorisation. In an influential essay theorising a 1913 exchange between Ezra Pound and Beatrice Hastings in the *New Age*, Ann Ardis conceptualises this dynamic interplay of different voices and viewpoints as the 'dialogics of modernism(s)' (2007b). We see this dialogism within single issues of a magazine like the *New Age*, among sets of magazines that address one another, and even, in the case of a multivocal writer like Hastings, among a single writer's different voices. Lucy Delap has termed groups of magazines that engage in dialogical exchange 'periodical communities': as Delap elaborates, such communities 'identify each other as important players, promote debate and controversy between each other, exchange material, share contributors, and generally inhabit the same intellectual milieu' (2005: 388, note 48). Most writers discussed in this collection seek out a multitude of print venues, but even those rare exceptions – like Dora Marsden, in her role as editor of the *Freewoman* and its successors, and Hastings, with her nearly exclusive affiliation with the *New Age* – still exemplify the interconnectedness of early twentieth-century periodical culture by provoking exchanges with other magazines in their periodical communities. While contextualising these writers' careers within a variety of periodicals, our contributors also trace the threads that bind those periodicals to one another in a larger community or network. For example, my chapter places Hastings's *New Age* writings in dialogue with *Votes for Women*, highlighting the importance of tracking suffrage debates between as well as within modern periodicals. I contribute to scholarship on Hastings's experiments in modernist voice by demonstrating how Hastings used pseudonyms and Correspondence sections to provoke intellectual debate and to try out different points of view.

The essays in this section also track how magazines shaped the form and content of modernist women's writing. Elizabeth Pritchett and Scott McCracken make a strong case for a direct relationship between periodical context and the creative process, arguing that Dorothy Richardson's 'revolutionary prose style' was heavily informed and shaped by the 'open and democratic form of little magazines such as the *Crank* and the *Freewoman*.' Countering ingrained readings of Richardson's style as elitist and apolitical, Pritchett and McCracken argue that her lesser-known contributions to these radical magazines reveal an author whose aesthetic is 'democratic' – both in its inclusivity and in the way it invites 'debate and dissent.' In a similar vein, Kathryn Laing argues that Rebecca West's early writings in the suffrage and feminist press (1911–20) served as a vital part of her 'literary and political apprenticeship.' Laing homes in on West's self-reflexive writings on femininity, feminism, and the woman writer, including her unpublished novel, *The Sentinel*, whose protagonist sells *Votes for Woman* on the street – underscoring the crucial role that periodical culture played in social movements (as explored in greater detail in Part V: Social Movements).

Pushing discussion of West's career and Laing's analysis of West as 'the most important signature of those years' (p. 179) into the following decade, Margaret D. Stetz reveals how Lady Rhondda's *Time and Tide* capitalised on West's growing stature as a feminist icon – associated with youth, rebelliousness, and modernity. Stetz focuses on

West's unorthodox theatre criticism, noting how unusual it was for women to review drama at this time (something Elizabeth Wright explores at length in Chapter 6). She argues that West's theatre criticism, like her other writing, was distinguished by its willingness to topple male idols like J. M. Barrie and to take up issues of social justice.

In addition to tracking the professional and creative development of women writers within periodical networks, two essays in this section and one in the next highlight the work of editors. Jayne Marek (1995) was the first scholar to elaborate the vital, behind-the-scenes work of female editors, like Margaret Anderson and Jane Heap, in curating and shaping the modernist canon. Although Marsden does not figure centrally in Marek's study, she has been the subject of several recent articles, and has been of perennial interest over the past two decades to scholars of feminist and modernist print culture. Building on this scholarship, Henry Mead challenges the critical commonplace that after spearheading the feminist *Freewoman* and its successor the *New Freewoman*, Marsden ceded control to male modernists in the *Egoist*; instead, Mead argues that Marsden's philosophical ideas and aesthetic sensibility left their marks on all three magazines. Specifically, Mead traces the anarchist and radical feminist roots of Marsden's thought, positioning her journals in relation to others in these periodical communities, including A. R. Orage's *New Age* (a magazine discussed in detail in chapters by Snyder and Garver) and Emma Goldman's *Mother Earth*. He presents a complex portrait of Marsden as at once a 'networker and an anti-networker,' urging 'her contemporaries to support her venture and her ideas, only then to sabotage and destroy potential alliances' (p. 223). Faith Binckes shifts the focus to a male editor, the *Adelphi*'s John Middleton Murry, who has been criticised for creating a sentimental image of Katherine Mansfield through his role as her literary executor and editor. By using editorial theory to analyse Murry's selection and framing of Mansfield's previously unpublished writing in the *Adelphi*, Binckes complicates this received view. Given that Mansfield's 'journal' was a hybrid combination of assorted loose papers, exercise books, and bound notebooks, any publication of this material would necessarily involve editorial intervention. Binckes argues that the ramifications of Murry's editorial choices were complex, simultaneously positioning Mansfield in line with, and at odds with, other modernist competitors. (In Part IV, Melissa Bradshaw extends this discussion of the gendered dynamics of editing by examining Edith Sitwell's critically neglected *Wheels*, which she describes as a 'woman-headed magazine whose focus was decidedly not on women's issues or on supporting or fostering a community of woman-writers.')

By positioning these key literary figures in new periodical contexts, our contributors challenge established readings and recover a richer understanding of these writers, the periodicals they frequented, and the competing modernisms they helped form. The new perspectives offered here on (mostly) canonical writers complement the recovery of neglected figures undertaken in the 'Networks, Circles, and Margins' and 'Locations' section.

Notes

1. The phrase is from Scholes and Wulfman 2010.
2. Delap (2005) and Ardis (2007a) pioneered the recovery of Hastings's complex pseudonymous writings; the first book-length study, edited by Benjamin Johnson and Erika Jo Brown, was published in 2016 by Pleiades Press: *Beatrice Hastings: On the Life and Work of a Lost Master*.

Works Cited

Ardis, Ann. 2007a. 'Debating Feminism, Modernism, and Socialism: Beatrice Hastings's Voices in *The New Age.*' *Gender in Modernism: New Geographies, Complex Intersections.* Ed. Bonnie Kime Scott. Champagne: University of Illinois Press. 160–71.

—. 2007b. 'The Dialogics of Modernism(s) in the *New Age.*' *Modernism/modernity* 14.3: 407–34.

Delap, Lucy. 2005. 'Feminist and Anti-feminist Encounters in Edwardian Britain.' *Historical Research* 78.201: 377–99.

Johnson, Benjamin and Erika Jo Brown. 2016. *Beatrice Hastings: On the Life and Work of a Lost Master.* Warrensburg, MO: Pleiades Press.

Marek, Jane. 1995. *Women editing modernism: 'little' magazines & literary history.* Lexington: The University Press of Kentucky.

Scholes, Robert and Clifford Wulfman. 2010. *Modernism in the Magazines: An Introduction.* New Haven: Yale University Press.

11

'An Outpour of Ink': From the 'Young Rebecca' to 'the most important signature of these years,' Rebecca West 1911–1920

Kathryn Laing

The lean arms that curved above the girl's head were informed by a strange blue shade. In the middle of the plumpness below the armpit there was a diffused blackish stain, something like an outpour of ink on blotting paper. (West 2002: 168)

And I – I was a black-browed thing scowling down on the inkstain that I saw reflected across the bodice of my evening dress. I was immeasurably distressed by this by-product of literary life. (*New Republic* 8 Jan 1916: 243–4)

These two quotations, the first from Rebecca West's early and unfinished suffragette novel, *The Sentinel*, and the second published in the American magazine, the *New Republic* in 1916, offer a framework for this essay and a prevailing trope. The suffragette-inspired image of bruising as spilled ink, foregrounding the body as text and thus writing as a 'by-product' of women's suffrage, recurs in various guises and transformations in these early writings. Embedded in this trope is the conundrum of the figure of the woman writer, also central to debate carried out 'in book reviews, biographical sketches, interviews, notes and paratextual materials such as advertisements' (Green 2013: 54). As Barbara Green goes on to highlight:

Careful study of modern periodicals reveals the ways in which efforts to think through the relation of gender and writing were inflected with this twinning of women writers and modernity, as well as revealing how considerations of the 'woman writer' were entangled with emerging discourses concerning the literatures of modernity (experimental, middlebrow, socialist and more). (2013: 56)

Attention to Rebecca West's early journalism within periodicals, including specialist and more commercial newspapers, has proven rich terrain for such scholarship. It is a territory that requires further excavation and examination. The broad focus of this essay is a selection of published and unpublished short fiction, journalism, and review essays that are often a hybrid form of both, published during the war and up to but not including the 1920s. The aims of this piece are twofold. First, to pay special attention to continuities and transitions in West's suffrage-inspired rhetoric and hybrid writing. Second, to trace in more detail the trajectory of her self-conscious construction of herself as a 'modern woman of letters' through her meditations on the nature of art, of fiction and journalism, and of feminism. I conclude by considering in brief the significance of some of the ways in which the name 'Rebecca West' and its associations became a valuable literary, cultural, and feminist by-product or currency, circulating among both 'highbrow' modernist magazines and the popular press during this era.

As Jane Marcus points out: 'In her early years (1911–17) as a journalist, it sometimes seemed as if there was hardly a left-wing paper in England or America to which Rebecca West did not contribute' (1982: 351). The range of her publications was even more extensive up to 1920. An outline of these recovered publications will give a flavour of the considerable body of her writing in newspaper archives that remains unlisted, uncollected, and largely unexamined. This extension of Marcus's 1911–17 framework enriches and complicates existing scholarship on West and feminist periodical culture. I begin then by situating West's early writing up to 1920 in the burgeoning field of modern periodical and print culture studies. Consideration of her earliest preoccupations with representations of feminism, women and writing, and the press in her unfinished novel, *The Sentinel*, follows, establishing a foundational context for this essay. West had been schooled in suffragette activism and rhetoric, and in the recognition by the WSPU and other suffrage movements of the power of the word, on the body or in print, as well as in their expert exploitation of emerging feminist print culture practices. The second part of the essay shifts to the relatively neglected post-1914 publications, especially in the American *New Republic* and *Atlantic Monthly* magazines (1916–18). By this time, the young Rebecca had already made an international name for herself as outspoken feminist, socialist, and literary critic.

Marcus's project reinvigorated scholarship on West's early journalism and its relevance, beginning the challenge to her canonical exclusion.[1] Observing the extent to which West was still marginalised from histories of modernism despite this groundbreaking work, Lyn Pykett argued for the need to read her early journalistic writing, not only 'as a form of intervention in the public sphere' but also as distinctive kind of literary work 'by means of which a particular writer self-consciously constructed herself as a modern woman of letters' (2000: 172). While she did not specifically consider West's early writing in the context of modern periodical cultures and broader print media, Pykett's reading highlighted the relevance of West's work to necessary conceptual shifts advocated in the later work of newspaper and periodical scholars.[2] Over the last two decades critical reconsiderations of West's early work has flourished in these new contexts. Feminist scholars and specialists in periodical and print culture have redirected attention back to West's short story, 'Indissoluble Matrimony' published in Wyndham Lewis's *BLAST* for example, initiating altered approaches to the story and *BLAST* itself.[3] Within the field of modern feminist periodical studies Barbara Green has demonstrated how West's political and cultural commentary offers 'an excellent example for studying the formation of this emerging feminist periodical culture' (2003: 222).[4] Identifying certain periodicals of this era as 'the sites in which "feminism" was most commonly enunciated and observed,' Lucy Delap gives fulsome attention to Marsden's *Freewoman* magazine, its transatlantic networks and West's writing within these contexts (2007: 4). The multiple enunciations of feminism in the *Freewoman/ New Freewoman* have received detailed readings in a raft of publications that feature

West's contributions in diverse ways. The *Freewoman* Correspondence section offered West, for example, 'the space to debate with her responders, and became especially necessary when the conversation featured an identity category – like "spinster" – with which she identified' (McMahon 2015: 71).[5] Murphy and Gaipa's network analysis illustrates the dominance of West as a reviewer: she was 'single-handedly responsible for three-fourths of the books reviewed in the magazine' (2014: 37). This extensive reviewing practice continued in a variety of publications up to the 1920s and well beyond, and awaits the detailed critical attention now paid to the *Freewoman*, its later permutations, and to a lesser extent the *Clarion* and the *Daily News*.[6]

West contributed to what are now iconic 'little magazines' as well as an array of publications that cross the cultural divides from high to middlebrow to popular. For example, as well as publishing in the more left-leaning *Daily News*, the *Daily Herald*, and the *Daily Chronicle*, her writing featured in more conservative and popular Sunday papers too: the *Sunday Pictorial* and the *Illustrated Sunday Herald*.[7] She also started writing for less commercial print enterprises such as the London *Bookman*, a 'resolutely middlebrow' monthly magazine, and expanded her American readership through contributions to the *Atlantic Monthly* and the *New Republic*.[8] Neither of these latter two were classic modernist or 'little magazines' but their contributor networks and interests intersected in surprising ways with modernist and indeed feminist discourses of the period. This cross-section was the result of significant literary and publishing networks established through West's earliest feminist affiliations, her early publications, serendipity, and economic necessity. The range and sheer volume of this body of writing and the diverse print culture through which her writing was disseminated, even within the relatively short ten-year period chosen, make it impossible to negotiate at one sitting.[9] Paying particular attention to the trope of the bruised body as text and to West's later ironic and self-reflexive reflections on feminism, femininity, and the writing life during the war years serves then to sharpen the focus on this *oeuvre*.[10] In this way, aspects of West's literary and political apprenticeship and her canny observations about and contributions to the developing feminist public sphere or 'counterpublic sphere' can be foregrounded.

Suffrage, Writing, and Periodical Culture

The considerable and growing body of work on suffrage writing has illustrated very persuasively how women's suffrage, and the militant turn in particular, gave birth not only to suffragette papers such as *Votes for Women*, 'but also set the scene for a flood of women's writing in other pro-suffrage periodicals, newspapers, magazines and pamphlets.'[11] Lady Rhondda, militant suffragette and later successful proprietor and editor of the feminist paper, *Time and Tide*, drew attention to this 'by-product' of political activism in her memoir, *This Was My World*, noting that 'the militant movement did more than force me to educate myself and to learn to speak; it also made me take to writing' (1933: 130). Like Lady Rhondda, 'West's entry into writing was through her feminism' (Pykett 2000: 176), and even more specifically, it was through her brief involvement as a teenager with the WSPU (Women's Social and Political Union) before joining dissenting members, Dora Marsden and Mary Gawthorpe, in their rebel enterprise, the *Freewoman* magazine. The most vivid and visceral example of this birth into writing (though not print) is her early, unfinished novel, *The Sentinel*. The novel, started while West was a teenage member of the WSPU and possibly not abandoned until after she began writing for the *Freewoman* (in 1911), is a collage of personal experience, retrieved evidence from existing suffragette memoirs, newspaper reportage, stories told at first or second hand, and imaginative engagement with the aims and activities of 'the cause.'

The most obvious intersection between the unfinished novel and the *Freewoman* magazine is that its editors, Dora Marsden and Mary Gawthorpe, were partial models for the suffragettes Psyche Charteris and Mary Gerald respectively. Significantly, while the portraits of both characters offer examples of 'classic' heroic suffragette fiction – self-sacrificing, courageous in the face of extreme danger while retaining their faery-like femininity – there are glimpses of deviations too. The often conservative ideologies in relation to sex and suffrage promoted by the WSPU are challenged by Mary Gerald's dismissal of Adela's (the heroine's) apparently fallen state (the novel begins with the story of her seduction by an older man when still a schoolgirl), and a preoccupation with sexual desire, particularly female heterosexual desire while same-sex love is hinted at. While West did not finish her novel, the magazine Marsden and Gawthorpe launched introduced a forum in which these and other taboo topics could be discussed.

For the purposes and focus of this essay, I want to return to three scenes in the novel that foreground the imbrication of women's suffrage, the body, and print culture. The first opens the second part of the novel, where Adela, the young schoolmistress, meets with Mary Gerald, prominent figure in the suffragette movement. Of particular interest here is Adela's impression of the 'space' Mary Gerald inhabits. It is overwhelmingly cluttered with printed matter, vividly evoking a feminist environment embedded in and constituted by a vigorous print culture:

> Adela stood by the window between the green rep curtains, looking out into the rain. She would have liked to sit down, as she had just come from school, but every chair in the room – not excepting the opulent emerald plush armchairs – was white with the snow of letters and papers that was lying in even greater depth on the table and whatnot. The whole room was very untidy: even that indiscreetly loyal chromolithograph 'Queen Alexandra's Courtship' was edged with visiting cards and printed slips, and the fire screen was festooned with purple, white and green ribbon. Against a mountain of literature leant the top of a banana crate which someone had been adorning with a flaming poster: hammers and nails lay on the sideboard. A roll of news bills lay curled up in the fireplace.
>
> To Adela this disorder gave a pleasing impression of an exciting press of affairs. [. . .] At last the door opened and a little woman, gay with red cheeks and dancing hazel eyes, came in with a stir of green linen skirts and mauve petticoats. She held her ruffled brown head on one side, her eyes far away in the abstraction of the busy organiser, and hugged an armful of letters to her bosom. (West 2002: 25)

The news bills, visiting cards, and posters are not the only form of print culture that Adela is exposed to by joining the movement. In contrast to the suffrage paper, *Votes for Women* that Adela both reads and sells, daily newspapers and literary weeklies with specifically anti-feminist perspectives attract her attention. The *Times* is full of 'polysyllabic hysteria' on the subject of 'the cause,' its 'sneering reference' to prominent suffragettes is 'couched in the massive Mid-Victorian form of bad taste peculiar to the sheet' (West 2002: 120). 'A Liberal weekly with an ancient name and reputation' offers 'an entertaining leader in which the editor raised a peppery invocation to the Deity to flay and bottle in boiling oil these viragoes' and 'a literary weekly which she had bought for its famous name altho' she knew it had fallen on evil days, contained an article on Woman's Suffrage which she would not have believed possible to find in any English periodical' (ibid.). Such observations illuminate West's already savvy understanding of the formats and political functions of the press and of how central a diverse print culture was to feminist and anti-feminist discourses and the drives for women's suffrage.[12] It is this understanding that underpins the recurring trope of bruising/ink/print and develops into sometimes satirical and self-satirising metanarrative in her later journalism. The final image in the above passage of the 'armful of letters,' writing literally 'pressed' on the sexualised female body illustrates this further: it accentuates the sustained attention to contemporary and often contradictory discourses around 'woman,' 'femininity,' and 'feminism.'

In the light of later scenes in the novel depicting Adela's growing involvement in 'the cause' and her increasing exposure to physical violence, the image evokes a profound and troubling connection between violence, the act of writing as a woman, and the forging of a new feminist identity. This is especially evident through Adela's increasingly intimate friendship with prominent suffragette, Psyche, witnessing on one occasion that:

> The lean arms that curved above the girl's head were informed by a strange blue shade. In the middle of the plumpness below the armpit there was a diffused blackish stain, something like an outpour of ink on blotting paper. From a distance the shade had the appearance of a bloom as on fruit. On continued inspection it assumed a terrifying aspect – livid, menacing, loathsome. She stepped forward and pointed to the girl's arms.
> 'Oh, that!' said Psyche, looking down: – 'Bruises. I've been like that ever since we founded the Liberty Union. I'm like that all over. Old bruises.' She slipped the green gown over her head and looked with her unmoved face into the mirror. (West 2002: 168)

Barbara Green has written extensively about the ways in which suffragettes exploited the intersections between specularity, publicity, and print culture. Of particular relevance here is the attention drawn in suffragette literature to the female body in pain, to what Green describes as 'spectacular confessions' (1997: 7), where as 'bodies became texts that carried the traces of violation and recorded the histories of rebellion, suffragettes contemplated the project of writing the body – indeed, the project of writing itself' (1997: 98). *The Sentinel* embodies and extends this point. In keeping with contemporary suffragette narrative, Adela is inspired by these bruises to fight even more fiercely for the cause, but the detailed attention drawn to Psyche's anatomy, the bruising on the female breast, imaged as both a fruit and blotting paper (recall the letters pressed to Mary Gerald's bosom), conflates in even more unsettling terms discourses of female sexuality and motherhood with textual production.[13] The initial impression of the shadow Adela glimpses as something natural, 'a bloom as on fruit' is revealed to be unnatural on two counts. Firstly, it becomes clear that the bruising on the arms and, it is implied, on the breast ('In the middle of the plumpness below the armpit'), is the result of violent assault that is also sexualised (West 2002: 168). Second, and even more radically, the conventional associations invoked through the analogy of the breast as fruit and the initial correlation of the word 'outpour,' in the context, with milk and thus suggestive of maternity, is replaced by a quite different act of reproduction. The bruising glimpsed as 'something like an outpour of ink on blotting paper' visualises not just the project of writing contemplated by suffragettes but the transmutation through violence against the female body into writing (ibid.). The trope of the bruised breast is reconfigured in another scene where Adela along with fellow suffragettes has been attacked by a group of liberal stewards. Her physical wounding is conflated here with femininity, thwarted sexual desire (Adela has refused a lover in favour of the cause), and again writing: 'Then at the new stinging of the hurt on her bosom, she sat up and unbuttoned her blouse. The sight of the purplish blot spilt over her breasts made her cry in self-pity. Already it was livid' (West 2002: 206).

That this palimpsestic image of blood, milk, and ink, signalling the coexistence of female sexuality and maternity with writing or speaking was perceived as a dangerous combination, is satirised in 'Indissoluble Matrimony.' Published in the first issue of Wyndham Lewis's short-lived but seminal avant-garde magazine *BLAST*, this story was more than likely written during the same period as *The Sentinel*. West's earliest suffragette figures in her unpublished writing are clearly distinguishable in the portrayal of the sensuous and politically engaged Evadne Silverton. In this story, however, the trope of the bruised and violated female body is replaced with the depiction of a desiring and energetic female body.[14] Attention paid to writing, different kinds of journalism, and print cultures in *The Sentinel* is evident in 'Indissoluble Matrimony' too, resonating with the flagrant and self-conscious staging of these themes in contemporary 'little magazines,' particularly in *BLAST*. Evadne's writing for the socialist press and popularity as a public speaker enrage and terrify her ridiculous and emasculated husband, George:

> His eyes blazed on her and found the depraved, over-sexed creature, looking milder than a gazelle, holding out a hand-bill to him.
> 'They've taken it for granted!' He saw her name – his name –
> MRS. EVADNE SILVERTON.
> It was at first the blaze of stout scarlet letters on the dazzling white ground that made him blink. Then he was convulsed with rage. (20 June 1914: 103)

In response to Evadne's protestations about the innocence of her relationship with the socialist candidate, George's lips stick 'together like blotting-paper' as he stutters:

> 'he's not the sort of man my wife should – should – '
> With movements which terrified him by their rough energy, she folded up the bills and put them back in the envelope. (ibid.)

This exchange between Evadne and George and the reproduction in print format of the capitalised and emblazoned name centred on the printed handbill is worth dwelling on (Figure 11.1). The 'stout scarlet letters on the dazzling white ground'

He saw her name—his name—

MRS. EVADNE SILVERTON.

It was at first the blaze of stout scarlet letters on the dazzling white ground that made him blink. Then he was convulsed with rage.

" Georgie dear! "

She stepped forward and caught his weak body to her bosom. He wrenched himself away. Spiritual nausea made him determined to be a better man than her.

" A pair of you ! You and Longton — ! " he snarled scornfully. Then, seeing her startled face, he controlled himself.

" I thought it would please you," said Evadne, a little waspishly.

" You mustn't have anything to do with Longton," he stormed.

Figure 11.1 Extract from Rebecca West's 'Indissoluble Matrimony,' *BLAST* (1914).

conjure several allusions, the first being a literary one to Hawthorne's famous novel and the association between the sexual women, adultery, and writing (George perceives Evadne as over-sexed and accuses her of being a woman off the streets). The second, more speculatively, is to recent events in suffragette activism and Lady Constance Lytton's literal writing in scarlet/blood through her attempt to carve 'Votes for Women' across her chest while imprisoned in 1909. She described the attempt in some detail:

> I had decided to write the words 'Votes for Women' on my body, scratching it in my skin with a needle, beginning over the heart and ending it on my face.... I succeeded in producing a very fine V just over my heart. This was the work of fully twenty minutes, and in my zeal I made a deeper impression than I had intended. The scratch bled to a certain extent. (Lytton 1914: 164–5)

The bruising on Psyche's body, subcutaneous bleeding resembling an outpour of ink on blotting paper, and Constance Lytton's self-wounding as protest writing has, in the short story, been transfigured into stout scarlet letters on a white handbill. The passive body as text has become the active woman speaker and writer whose identity, forged through violence, is flagrantly enunciated in the large red poster print. The typesetting of this section of the story is striking for its imitation not only of the poster formats typical of suffragette advertising in papers including *Votes for Women* but also because, at this juncture, it mimics the very manifesto form that dominates Lewis's *BLAST*.[15] In addition, George's chagrin at seeing Evadne's name emblazoned on a poster and recognising its hybridity – Evadne's name combined with his own – anticipates the satire that is played out on notions of 'indissoluble matrimony.'

What is particularly pertinent in the attention West pays to the print features of the advertising bill in 'Indissoluble Matrimony' is her understanding of the power of print in all its materiality to shock and subvert: the spectacle of print itself. It is a power that Lewis arguably learned from suffragette advertising and publishing and that he exploits and experiments with to the full in the *BLAST* volume in which the story appears.[16] The imbrication of suffrage writing and iconography in, and indeed contribution to, newly evolving avant-garde periodical culture is evident here. George's outrage at the sight of Evadne's name on a poster highlights the social and cultural ambivalences surrounding the feminist modern woman writer whose renegotiated identity is clearly entangled with new forms of print culture, art and literature, and their dissemination. The subversive potential of this new identity is evident by the conclusion to the story. George cannot kill Evadne, despite his intentions, and by implication cannot suppress her will to speak, her will to write, or her will to take her place as a public figure, inscribed in print. Rebecca West was equally resilient. Her fiction and journalism published after 'Indissoluble Matrimony' are marked by both continuity – in theme – and a development in new directions and toward new publishing outlets.

'This By-Product of Literary Life'

By 1916 'Rebecca West' was a recognisable name in feminist, socialist, and avant-garde circles in Britain and in the United States too, although that signature encompassed a plurality of writing identities. She was former suffragette, *Freewoman* contributor and editor, short-story writer, literary critic (her short book of criticism on Henry James was published in 1916), prolific journalist, and commentator for a range of papers and periodicals. Yet the trope of the bruised breast, a metaphor for the troubled and conflicted birth of women's writing through feminist activism, was still visible. In her essay, 'The World's Worst Failure' it was transformed into a literal ink stain on the breast/bodice. This piece was the first in a series of five devoted to an analysis of 'femininity' as a debilitating form of false consciousness, published between January and March in the New York based magazine the *New Republic*.[17]

West was one of the first contributors to this newly inaugurated publication which was to provide her with a platform to write on diverse topics, from reviews of Dostoevsky and Shaw, theorising war and aesthetics, to critiques of prominent feminists and discourses on feminism and femininity.[18] The *New Republic* was established as a 'literary and current affairs periodical' where feminism was highly topical and debate about art and literature encouraged (Delap 2007: 89). Prospective subscribers to the magazine were assured that '"the New Republic will respect no taboos; it will play no favorites; it will be confined to no set creed and tied to no political party. Its philosophy will be a faith rather than a dogma. Its editorial attitude will be good-natured, open-minded, eager to find and accept facts"' (Levy 1985: 201) – a credo that shared some of the ambitions of Marsden's *Freewoman*. And it was through the *Freewoman*, 'a self-declared Anglo-American space' (Delap 2007: 78) particularly welcomed in feminist avant-garde circles in America, that West would have had her earliest 'transatlantic exposure,' laying the groundwork for a periodical network there.[19] Randolphe

Bourne, another contributor to the *New Republic* was an admirer of West's feminist writing and it is possible that through his connections as a contributor to the *Atlantic Monthly* that Ellery Sedgwick, the editor, approached her for work in 1915.[20]

West's 'World Worst Failure' series published in the *New Republic* continued transatlantically, then a conversation began about feminism, femininity, the act of writing, and print culture itself in *The Sentinel*.[21] Two book reviews published in the *Daily News* between 1915 and 1916 dwell on the predicament for feminism and the woman writer, offering a taste of West's already distinctive satirical style from which no subject or person was exempt:[22]

> Miss B. L. Hutchins has conspicuously escaped from the Fabian tradition of conscientious bad writing. *Women in Modern Industry* is written in a straight and sexless manner which is always pleasant and a little unexpected in works that are even indirectly a part of the feminist movement. (Marcus 1982: 307)

And:

> The ordinary suffragist was a woman too enraged by contempt to think calmly on a philosophic level. And so there were very few books on feminism which kindled more than a passing admiration for their properly fierce spirit and gained a permanent dwelling in the readers' mind by their idea or the craft of their writing. (Marcus 1982: 327)

In her 1916 essay the female activist has become a writer, but the conflicts and contradictions that shaped feminist identity in the suffrage era are still evident in West's eviscerating tale of two women she encounters at a hotel in Maidenhead. Her critique of the Frenchwoman, who insists that women must strike 'the feminine note' as her life's work, and of the Chicago woman who 'lived and worked that she might be worshipful' is followed by her accusing self-portrait (*New Republic* 8 Jan 1916: 243). Continuing with her lament about the ink-stained evening dress, she declares with self-conscious irony:

> It was a new evening dress, it was becoming, it was expensive. Already I was upsetting the balance of my nerves by silent rage; I knew I would wake up in the night and magnify it with an excited mind till it stained the world; that in the end I would probably write some article I did not in the least want to write in order to pay for a new one. (8 Jan 1916: 244)

The craft of writing compromised by the 'fierce spirit' of feminism that West identified in her earlier feminist journalism is now compromised by notions of femininity itself, 'the ideals of elegance and propriety that cursed women of all classes,' outlined in the series (Delap 2007: 317).

The 'World's Worst Failure' series and this article in particular are significant for two reasons. First, it is part of a conversation about feminism and the woman writer constructed out of contradictions and conundrums West had voiced across a range of different publishing contexts.[23] The 'types' of 'failures' for feminism exhibited in her

New Republic series are counterbalanced, for example, by a different and much more positive 'typology' outlined in a book review published in the same year.[24]

> Turning over its pages is to look into the suffrage world as it was before August 1914. One sees passing before one the goloshes-and velour-hat type of suffragist who was very well up in facts and figures, but a little unsympathetic about changes in the marriage laws; the amber-cigarette-holder type of suffragette who called stridently across the Soho restaurant for the wine-list, and whose trump card was her speech on unmarried mothers; the stoutish type who affected purple djibbahs and spoke in a rich, almost greasy, contralto about the Mother Soul; the white-faced type whose courage in gaol was one of the few intimations of how we would meet our enemies. (Marcus 1982: 330)

West's critique of feminine consumption in the name of elegance in the 'World's Worst Failure' article offers an alternative approach but is not at odds with the multiple endorsements of female appetite, leisure, pleasure in her writing, across the political and cultural spectrum of papers and magazines to which she contributed up to 1920.[25] Janet Lyon makes a related point that underlines the significance of West's highly self-conscious dialectic or performance of differing feminisms, noting that her reviews of anti-suffragist books in the *Clarion* are not only 'hilarious but astutely demonstrate that one can be both avant-garde and pro-suffrage when the situation warrants' (2010: 245).

Second, encoded in West's ironic allusion to the article she does not wish to write is a teasing challenge to the cultural status of her *New Republic* work and therefore its readers. It is also more than likely a nod to her forays into the more popular tabloid press during this period. For West's redeployment and revision of her suffragette trope in her 'World's Worst Failure' article not only complicates connections between the 'literary' and the 'political,' it also demonstrates 'the permeability and fluidity of the range of print media available to journalists/writers at the time' and her willingness to exploit these fluidities (Delap and DiCenzo 2008: 51). Already her name and her command of feminist discourses of the day, especially in relation to women and war, were clearly highly marketable for these papers. She is described as the 'vigorous feminist writer' and listed alongside other prominent contributors including Jerome K. Jerome and Will Crooks, 'the able Labour Leader' in an advertisement in the *Sheffield Daily Independent* for the *Illustrated Sunday Herald* (3 Apr 1915: 7). In a *Daily Mirror* advertisement for its Sunday edition in 1917, the *Sunday Pictorial*, she is labelled 'the brilliant feminist writer' who 'discusses the question – Should women be warriors' (18 Aug 1917: 2).

It was not only popular Sunday papers that were promoted and marketed by advertising and publishing assessments of the high-profile feminist thinker and writer Rebecca West during this period. Post-1914 avant-garde publications both in Britain and in America circulated news of her work through supportive advertising and reviews, even though her publishing venues had shifted by this time. Margaret Anderson's avant-garde *Little Review*, keen to assert its feminist credentials in various ways, promoted her 'World's Worst Failure' series: 'Read Rebecca West's brilliant articles in the *New Republic* (Jan–Feb 1916: 20).[26] Her first book of criticism, *Henry James* (1916), was advertised as 'A brilliant study by the brilliant young Englishwoman' in Max Eastman's *Masses* (Feb 1917: 40) and in his review essay, 'Rebecca West,' he ranked her among other 'revolutionists' he names and notes that 'If radical wit and poetry and full-blooded brilliancy of scorn could arrive there, she would have no competitor' (Feb 1917: 30).[27] West's name is equally traceable in some British 'little magazines.' By the time the *Freewoman* had evolved into the *Egoist*, West had distanced herself from Marsden and Ezra Pound, with whom she had worked briefly on the *New Freewoman*, her own involvement with the magazine ceasing in 1913. She features in the *Egoist*, however, in advertisements for and reviews of *BLAST*, and in a long and quirky review essay, 'The Work of Miss Rebecca West' by Dora Marsden, in the October 1918 issue. Sandwiched between contributions by T. S. Eliot and Ezra Pound (May Sinclair, Herbert Read, and Richard Aldington also feature), Marsden's not uncritical assessment of West's recently published novel, *The Return of the Soldier*, dominates this particular issue.[28] 'It is certain Rebecca West possesses gifts,' Marsden concludes:

> the world has acknowledged them; and we think it probable she possesses others of an even more solid worth. There exists, therefore, every hope that when she emerges from the groping twilight of the process of finding herself and her true form, she will be able to combine indisputable high gifts with the high, but necessary moral forces of courage, independence, and unashamed truth. (*Egoist* Oct 1918: 119)

Finally, Douglas Goldring's semi-ironic homage in *Coterie*, 'a classic "little magazine" of the period after the First World War' (Thacker 2009: 464), sums up Rebecca West's early iconic status that in fact crossed the 'great divide' from transnational cosmopolitan coterie periodicals to Sunday tabloids:[29]

> I had been well brought up: I liked the best.
> My prose was modelled on Rebecca West, (4 Apr 1920: 50)

Published in 1920, Goldring's comic couplet recognised the cultural and feminist capital West had accrued early on in her career. Partially inspired into writing through feminist activism and the literal and metaphorical bruising of women's bodies and lives that she had witnessed as a teenager and young woman, West had already acknowledged with irony the complexities of feminism and the growing reputation of her work and name in 'The World's Worst Failure' in 1916. The bruised body of her earliest forays into fiction is replaced by the ink-stained bodice, the by-product of a writing life that now pays. By the 1920s Lady Rhondda, editor of *Time and Tide*, was quick to capitalise on the value of her name to promote the magazine. As Catherine Clay has outlined: 'it was guaranteed to increase the paper's value; West's high cultural stature made her name highly marketable,' it was quite simply 'the most important female signature in these years' (2010: 77).

Notes

1. Marcus 1982; Scott 1990; Pykett 2000.
2. See for example Ardis and Collier 2008.
3. See also Hertz 2016 and Laing 2017.
4. West's journalism and short story also feature in Green 2017.
5. See also Green 2012, where West is alluded to briefly and a comprehensive list of publications on Marsden and the *Freewoman* is given (484).

6. West's contributions to *Time and Tide* are an exception. Margaret D. Stetz's essay that follows this chapter continues renewed interest in the magazine and its contributors initiated by Catherine Clay in a variety of publications. West's transatlantic networks and contributions to the *New Republic* are touched on in Delap 2007 and Collier 2006 but the significance of and continuities between her writing for British periodicals and this weekly as well as the *Atlantic Monthly* remain under-examined.
7. These Sunday paper publications have not been noted or included in existing bibliographies of West's journalism.
8. See Sutherland 2013: 72.
9. Another hindrance to approaching and understanding West's work more fully within periodical and broader print culture contexts is precisely the fragmented nature of these bibliographies and, apart from Jane Marcus's collection, the practice of listing or compiling as collections her essays and articles alphabetically rather than by magazine or newspaper publication. This is a future project.
10. West's writing about the war and particularly women and war across diverse publications deserves further attention.
11. See Park and Laing 2018.
12. West's first foray into print on feminist matters was on the letters page of the *Scotsman* when she was aged fourteen (16 Oct 1907). This letter is reproduced in Scott 2000: 5. Her early interest in and sophisticated understanding of the press came from her father, as Victoria Glendinning outlines: 'he brought the world of newspapers and current events home with him, talking to the children as equals and insisting they be literate and articulate' (1988: 18). Her feminist insights came initially from her older sisters who were both involved in women's suffrage movements.
13. See the discussion of bruising in West 2002: xxvii.
14. In this story, as Green has outlined, 'Reading and writing, speaking, eating, and sexuality are permeated by unruly feminine appetite' (2003: 233).
15. In the manuscript notebook in which West wrote a version, probably the first version, of 'Indissoluble Matrimony,' Evadne Silverton's name is capitalised and centralised on the page but the distinctive spacing of the text in *Blast* is not suggested here (Rebecca West Collection). Without seeing the version Lewis used it is not possible to say categorically that he introduced this feature to replicate the manifesto format, although it is likely.
16. See Reynolds 2000 and Morrisson 2000, for example.
17. See works cited for the full list and references.
18. All of West's contributions to this magazine are available through the *New Republic* Online Archive.
19. Delap has traced in detail the 'extensive, frequently transatlantic, interaction between individuals and groups' that constituted an intellectual formation and a highly influential feminist network during this period (2007: 3–4).
20. See Delap on Bourne (2007: 74). Carl Rollyson in his biography of Rebecca West suggests H. G. Wells was responsible for her *New Republic* connections (1995: 39). News and commentary about the war was also highly sought after in American publications and West contributed several pieces responding to the impact of the war, particularly on women's lives. See *New Republic* 27 Feb 1915: 98–100 and *Atlantic Monthly* 16 Jan 1916: 1–11.
21. More specifically, it can be read as an extension of her focus and development on the 'parasitic woman' in numerous early pieces. West was more than likely indebted to Olive Schreiner's definition of this figure: 'In place of the active labouring woman, upholding society by her toil, has come the effete wife, concubine or prostitute, clad in fine raiment, the work of others' fingers' (1988: 81).
22. Jane Marcus includes many but not all her *Daily News* contributions and notes that, 'Though Women, art and labour continued to be the loudest notes on her trumpet, she also attacked anti-semitism, irresponsible pacifism and the cult of the Earth Mother' (1982: 294).

23. That some of the readers of her 'World's Worst Failure' pieces were not as familiar with West's feminist dialectic as she expected them to be is comically revealed in the letters columns of the *New Republic* where indignant schoolmistresses in particular protested at her critical portrayal of their profession.
24. See Delap 2007: 317 on feminist 'type thinking' of the period.
25. See Green 2003.
26. 'Anderson conceived the *Little Review* as a feminist magazine,' (Francis 2002: 55). The magazine promoted other *New Republic* articles by West too.
27. West also received attention for her first novel, *The Return of the Soldier*, in the *Dial* (28 Mar 1918: 299) and her work featured in several reviews published in the more middlebrow monthly *Current Opinion*.
28. In addition to mischievously or absent-mindedly misremembering her real name, Marsden traced, with some irony, West's literary and journalistic success since joining the *Freewoman*: 'Her literary contributions [to *The Freewoman*] could scarcely have run to a dozen weeks before the American publisher [. . .] was hot on the trail' (*Egoist* Oct 1918: 115).
29. West was never a contributor but she had shared copy with many of those who were (Wyndham Lewis and Richard Aldington, for example). No feminist magazine, *Coterie* nonetheless shared some of the features of these publications. As Andrew Thacker has pointed out, 'in its attention [. . .] to the uneasy alliance between the political and the cultural [it] echoes prewar magazines such as *The New Freewoman* or *The New Age*' (2009: 478).

Works Cited

Ardis, Ann and Patrick Collier, eds. 2008. *Transatlantic Print Culture: Emerging Media, Emerging Modernisms*. Basingstoke: Palgrave Macmillan.

Clay, Catherine. 2010. 'Winifred Holtby, Journalist: Rehabilitating Journalism in the Modernist Ferment.' *A Woman in Her Time: Winifred Holtby*. Ed. Lisa Regan. Cambridge: Cambridge Scholars Press. 65–88.

Collier, Patrick. 2006. *Modernism on Fleet Street*. Aldershot and Burlington, VT: Ashgate.

Delap, Lucy. 2007. *The Feminist Avant-Garde: Transatlantic Encounters of the Early Twentieth Century*. Cambridge: Cambridge University Press.

Delap, Lucy and Maria DiCenzo. 2008. 'Transatlantic Print Culture: The Anglo-American Feminist Press and Emerging "Modernities."' *Transatlantic Print Culture: Emerging Media, Emerging Modernisms*. Ed. Ann Ardis and Patrick Collier. Basingstoke: Palgrave Macmillan. 48–65.

Francis, Elizabeth. 2002. *The Secret Treachery of Words: Feminism and Modernism in America*. Minneapolis: University of Minneapolis Press.

Glendinning, Victoria. 1988. *Rebecca West: A Life*. London: Papermac.

Green, Barbara. 1997. *Spectacular Confessions: Autobiography, Performative Activism, and the Sites of Suffrage 1905–1938*. London: Macmillan.

—. 2003. 'The New Woman's Appetite for "Riotous Living": Rebecca West, Modernist Feminism, and the Everyday.' *Women's Experience of Modernity, 1875–1945*. Ed. Leslie W. Lewis, Ann L. Ardis. Baltimore: Johns Hopkins University Press. 221–36.

—. 2012. 'Complaints of Everyday Life: Feminist Periodical Culture and Correspondence Columns in *The Woman Worker, Women Folk*, and *The Freewoman*.' *Modernism/Modernity* 19.3: 464–5.

—. 2013. 'Recovering Feminist Criticism: Modern Women Writers and Feminist Periodical Studies.' *Literature Compass* 10.1: 53–60.

—. 2017. *Feminist Periodicals and Daily Life: Women and Modernity in British Culture* (Cham, Switzerland: Springer International Publishing, Palgrave Macmillan).

Hertz, Erich. 2016. 'The Gender of Form and British Modernism: Rebecca West's Vorticism and Blast.' *Women's Studies: An Inter-Disciplinary Journal* 45.4: 356–69. <http://www.tandfonline.com/doi/full/10.1080/00497878.2016.1160751> (last accessed 11 July 2018).

Laing, Kathryn. 2017. '"Am I a Vorticist?": Re-Reading Rebecca West's "Indissoluble Matrimony."' *Blast at 100: A Modernist Magazine Reconsidered*. Ed. Philip Coleman, Kathryn Milligan, and Nathan O'Donnell. Leiden: Brill. 44–61.

Levy, David W. 1985. *Herbert Croly of the New Republic: The Life and Thought of an American*. Princeton: Princeton University Press.

Lyon, Janet. 2010. 'Review.' *The Journal of Modern Periodical Studies* 1.2: 241–6.

Lytton, Constance. 1914. *Prisons and Prisoners: Some Personal Experiences*. New York: George Doran.

McMahon, Shannon. 2015. 'Freespinsters and Bondspinsters: Negotiating Identity Categories in the *Freewoman*.' *The Journal of Modern Periodical Studies* 6.1: 60–79.

Marcus, Jane, ed. 1982. *The Young Rebecca: Writings of Rebecca West 1911–1917*. London: Macmillan.

Morrisson, Mark S. 2000. *The Public Face of Modernism: Little Magazines, Audiences, and Reception, 1905–1920*. Wisconsin: University of Wisconsin Press.

Murphy, Stephen J. and Mark Gaipa. 2014. 'You Might Also Like . . . : Magazine Networks and Modernist Tastemaking in the Dora Marsden Magazines.' *The Journal of Modern Periodical Studies* 5.1: 27–68.

Park, Sowon S. and Kathryn Laing. 2018. 'Writing the Vote: Suffrage, Gender, and Politics.' *Futility and Anarchy? British Literature in Transition 1920–1940*. Ed. Charles Ferrall and Dougal McNeill. Vol. 2. Cambridge: Cambridge University Press.

Pykett, Lyn. 2000. 'The Making of a Modern Writer: Rebecca West's Journalism, 1911–1930.' *Journalism, Literature and Modernity: From Hazlitt to Modernism*. Ed. Kate Campbell. Edinburgh: Edinburgh University Press. 170–90.

Rebecca West Collection, MS, Box 99, F. 5, Department of Special Collections and University Archive, McFarlin Library, The University of Tulsa.

Reynolds, Paige. 2000. '"Chaos Invading Concept": Blast as a Native Theory of Promotional Culture.' *Twentieth Century Literature* 46.2: 238–68.

Rhondda, Lady/Margaret Haig. 1933. *This Was My World*. London: Macmillan.

Rollyson, Carl. 1995. *Rebecca West: A Saga of the Century*. London: Hodder & Stoughton.

Schreiner, Olive. [1911] 1988. *Woman and Labour*. London: Virago.

Scott, Bonnie Kime. 1990. *The Gender of Modernism: A Critical Anthology*. Bloomington: Indiana University Press.

—, ed. 2000. *Selected Letters of Rebecca West*. New Haven: Yale University Press.

Sutherland, John. 2013. *The Longman Companion to Victorian Fiction*. London and New York: Routledge.

Thacker, Andrew. 2009. 'Aftermath of War: *Coterie* (1919–21), *New Coterie* (1925–7), Robert Graves and *The Owl* (1919–23).' *The Oxford Critical and Cultural History of Modernist Magazines: Vol. 1, Britain and Ireland 1880–1955*. Ed. Peter Brooker and Andrew Thacker. Oxford: Oxford University Press. 464–84.

West, Rebecca. 2002. *The Sentinel: An Incomplete Early Novel*. Ed. Kathryn Laing. Oxford: Legenda.

12

TIME AND TIDE WAITED FOR HER: REBECCA WEST'S JOURNALISM IN THE 1920S

Margaret D. Stetz

The twenties were, as decades go, a good decade; gay, decorative, intelligent, extravagant, cultured. There were booms in photography, Sunday film and theatre clubs, surrealism, steel furniture, faintly obscure poetry, Proust, James Joyce, dancing, rink skating, large paintings on walls of rooms. (Macaulay 1942: 46)

WHEN REBECCA WEST (1892–1983) married Henry Maxwell Andrews on 1 November 1930, one of the guests whom she invited to the wedding was Margaret Haig Thomas, Viscountess Rhondda (1883–1958) (Glendinning 1987: 135). The presence of *Time and Tide* editor Lady Rhondda was an indication of how significant she was to West not merely as a friend, but also as an employer. Throughout the 1920s, West earned her living as a journalist, while simultaneously raising her illegitimate son by the writer H. G. Wells (1866–1946) and writing novels such as *The Judge* (1922) and *Harriet Hume* (1929), along with short stories for the Philadelphia-based magazine *Saturday Evening Post*. Meanwhile, she appeared regularly as a book reviewer in the *New Statesman* (with her 'Notes on Novels' column); taking commissions from American periodicals such as *Harper's Magazine*, *Hearst's International Cosmopolitan Magazine*, and the *New York Herald Tribune* newspaper; and producing a column titled first 'A London Letter' and then 'A Letter from Abroad' for the New York-based *Bookman*. 'Journalistic assignments . . . paid her way and "kept the wolf from the door," as she told Eric Pinker, her agent' (Rollyson 1998: 30).

No periodical was more central to West's career in the 1920s than Lady Rhondda's *Time and Tide*, which provided her with a reliable source of income. Between 1920 and 1929, she contributed more than forty articles to it. Although she was never the sole drama critic for the paper – in its first year of publication, it included reviews of productions in London by I. A. R. (Ida Alexa Ross) Wylie, W. R. (William Richard) Titterton, and J. M. Harvey, before Christopher St John (Christabel Marshall), who was writing about musical performances, also took charge of writing about plays – nearly thirty of West's articles were focused on various sorts of theatre, from West End plays to music hall entertainments, and even cinema. Through these reviews, West demonstrated her range as a commentator on the arts in general, while also consolidating her reputation as an idiosyncratic critic, who combined self-consciously modern viewpoints with an appreciation of the past. Paradoxically, what was most reliable about her journalistic pronouncements was their unpredictability; thus, she offered readers of criticism what they might ordinarily receive from fiction: the thrills of surprise and an element of suspense. Looking back at the 1920s from the year 1942, Rose Macaulay (1881–1958) would define the decade through its 'extravagant' character and its jarring contrasts in register, which juxtaposed the popularity of 'obscure poetry' with that of 'rink skating' (1942: 46). For *Time and Tide*, Rebecca West served as a one-woman encapsulation of this heterogeneous spirit. Deliberately daring and provocative, she brought greater public attention to this feminist venture, even as she ensured its cultural relevance through her eclectic choice of subjects and equally unorthodox expressions of opinion on them.

If Lady Rhondda's *Time and Tide* mattered greatly to Rebecca West – like a number of the frequent contributors, she was a member of the paper's Board of Directors and would remain so until it ceased publication in 1958 (Gibb 2013: 214) – West was also of enormous importance to the early years of *Time and Tide*. She helped to set its tone, to secure its reputation, and to determine the sort of readership it would attract. As Catherine Clay has said, 'Launched on 14 May 1920 *Time and Tide* began as an overtly feminist review of politics and the arts, directed and staffed entirely by women, and later evolved into a less woman focused, more general audience journal, establishing a position among the leading political weeklies in Britain' (2011: 60). Although West had initiated her career in journalism before the First World War by writing for pro-suffrage papers that appealed chiefly to women readers, her own contributions even then were rarely addressed to a single-sex audience. Making her a conspicuous part of *Time and Tide* from the first number onward sent an unmistakable signal that the new periodical's ambitions were, from the outset, to be 'a newspaper which would not only give prominence to women's demands and activities,' but would generate a broader mainstream interest in these and 'exert some pressure on the other publications to do likewise' (Spender 1984: 4).

Bringing Rebecca West into the project was, nonetheless, a controversial move, which embroiled Lady Rhondda herself in personal and professional conflicts. She was good friends simultaneously with West and with Elizabeth Robins (1862–1952) – playwright, novelist, and long-time suffrage activist – and admired the literary judgments of both the young feminist and the older pioneer. The esteem in which she held Robins may be gauged by the appearance, in the very first number of the weekly, of an article by Lady (Florence) Bell, titled 'Elizabeth Robins: An Appreciation,' that praised this writer for 'flinging down the gauntlet of defiance to the conventional playgoer' in her dramatic works (14 May 1920: 8). Robins, however, was adamantly opposed to West's participation in *Time and Tide*, as Angela V. John reports: 'Although Margaret wrote enthusiastically to Robins about Rebecca West's contributions to the paper in the autumn of 1921, Robins disliked West, largely because of her relationship with H. G. Wells' (2013: 301). So far as Robins was concerned, Wells was a scoundrel, who 'had used . . . the suffrage movement' opportunistically and selfishly, 'to promote his own sexual freedom' (Gates 1994: 194). In Robins's eyes, West was tainted by association with him, and she balked at serving alongside her on any board of directors. Lady Rhondda, therefore, regretfully accepted Robins's resignation, as she refused to encourage West to leave instead.

Was Rebecca West worth keeping? Certainly there is ample evidence that Lady Rhondda considered her a valuable property, whose presence in the first decade of the paper she fruitfully highlighted and even exploited in a variety of ways. Perhaps the most unexpected instance of such exploitation occurred in the 9 February 1923 number of *Time and Tide*. Despite the seriousness of this journalistic enterprise, with its determination not merely to comment upon, but to influence, weighty and pressing political concerns, this was the column that readers encountered midway through the issue:

> COMPETITION
> 1st Prize – An original pen and ink portrait of Miss Rebecca West.
> 2nd Prize – One Guinea.
> 3rd Prize – Any Book (Value not exceeding 10s. 6d.) mentioned in this week's issue of 'Time and Tide.'
> We offer the above prizes for
> An Original Limerick
> on the subject of one of the articles in this week's Personalities and Powers, – i.e., Miss Rebecca West, – the material for the verse to be derived from the article referred to ... (9 Feb 1923: 168)

As Rose Macaulay would later remind readers in *Life Among the English*, the 1920s had been a 'gay' decade (1942: 46). Playfulness was undoubtedly one of the prized qualities of the period, and Rebecca West's own contributions to *Time and Tide* were often playful in the extreme. Lyn Pykett has rightly praised this quality in West's journalism, speaking of her 'lively, witty, iconoclastic body of writing ... [as] itself a significant contribution to the literature of the early twentieth century' (2000: 187). To invite readers to compete for prizes had long been, moreover, a standard feature of mainstream magazines and newspapers aimed at a general audience, as well as of papers intended either for women or the young in particular. Nevertheless, this particular contest and the tone used to speak of it introduced a jocular note that was quite jarring. The anonymous writer of copy for the 'Competition' stated archly, 'It is assumed that everybody knows that [sic] a "Limerick" is, but anyone in doubt will find a surviving specimen of this prehistoric monster further down this column,' and then spoke derisively of those who had sent entries on a previous occasion: 'had all competitors indeed been on trial for their reputation, the majority would have gone to prison' (9 Feb 1923: 168). In the context of an issue that included Rebecca West's fire-breathing polemic titled 'Equal Pay for Men and Women Teachers,' where she asserted that 'It is ... [a] savage form of sex antagonism which makes people desire that women teachers should be paid less highly than men who are performing the same work,' and that this injustice demonstrated the continuing 'need for a sex-conscious and rebellious army of women' (9 Feb 1923: 142), to level ridicule at anyone merely for producing weak limericks seemed puzzling and ill-advised.

Such a 'Competition' was problematic for other reasons. For one thing, it encouraged readers to focus on Rebecca West's appearance and to enter the contest with the hope of winning a portrait of her – thus of possessing her. The image in question was a sketch of the young writer's head by 'Capt. J. W. Ginsburg' that represented her as glamorous, spiritual yet intellectual (looking far off in the distance, as though rapt in thought), and also as vulnerable, with lips parted in a way that signaled erotic possibilities. In writing her theatre criticism for *Time and Tide*, West herself had not hesitated to pay close attention to the faces and bodies of other women. While, for example, reviewing a revival of *La Tosca*, she had appreciatively described Sarah Bernhardt in an earlier era as having looked 'slit-eyed and tawny-coloured, liker a lean lioness than one would have thought a woman could be; she seemed to emit an actual radiance, tawny-coloured like herself' (8 Oct 1920: 448). West had also spoken of a contemporary actress in the play *Cherry* as 'beautiful in the large English way, so well built that one feels that she is beautiful even down to her skeleton' (6 Aug 1920: 267), while writing somewhat mockingly of a particular film star as 'a young woman composed solely of concave curves beside whom an Aubrey Beardsley lady would seem a nice motherly body' (27 Aug 1920: 328). Her close attention to the physical aspects of public figures had extended even to men; in 'The Other Wisdom,' a meditation on the appearance of 'one of the lesser known French boxers,' she meticulously catalogued his 'immense sea-blue eyes, sunk deeply in exquisitely vaulted sockets . . . his long-lashed lids . . . [his] sleek golden hair . . . [and his] lips, which . . . were in the form of a perfect Cupid's bow' (13 May 1921: 455). Nevertheless, it was an audacious decision on the part of *Time and Tide* to dangle as the prize in this competition an image of West. It was an act that risked reducing a woman writer to a body – one to be imagined, below the attractive head, and possibly desired – and it commodified her in a way inconsistent with feminist principles.

Encouraging readers to focus on this sketch of West's unlined face, with a coronet of dark hair framing it, also meant highlighting her youth, a move that might seem to have undercut West's authority as a serious commentator elsewhere in the same issue of the paper. But this emphasis on her status as a girlish rather than as a mature and sober figure was, in fact, deliberate, and it echoed the textual representation of her in the journalistic profile on which the 'Competition' centred. The anonymous author of 'Personalities and Powers: Miss Rebecca West' had underlined the issue of her youth and her precociousness – 'She is now twenty-seven years of age, and the reading public has been aware of her for eight years' (9 Feb 1923: 149) – while simultaneously insisting that she often seemed old beyond her chronological age, calling to mind women of a much earlier generation, who were similarly 'stiff of back' and 'stiff of temper' (9 Feb 1923: 150): 'although she is young in years and . . . almost a schoolgirl in spirit, those of us who are old are reminded by her of those who are even older than ourselves' (ibid.). What would have struck those who had subscribed to *Time and Tide* since its inception was the inaccuracy of the author's computation. Indeed, in 1923 West, who was born in 1892, was no longer twenty-seven years old. Readers would have known this, because they had encountered precisely the same profile three years earlier, in the 16 July 1920 issue of the paper; they would have seen at the time the identical calculation of her age (along with the identical pen-and-ink portrait sketch of her).

Why did *Time and Tide* reprint this article about West with its accompanying drawing only three years after its original publication and, when doing so, leave this important detail about her age unchanged? Clearly, West was more than merely one among a number of *Time and Tide*'s 'regulars'; she was iconic, and part of her iconicity had to do with her youth. Lady Rhonda used West literally as the 'face' of this paper in its early years. When, for instance, *Time and Tide* published work that was not part of West's ordinary theatre column, such as the essay 'On Nagging' in the 31 October 1924 number – a defence of so-called women's magazines, with their inevitable advice about cooking, as equal in value to specialised publications that were geared to men and filled with financial tips – it was accompanied by Capt. Ginsburg's sketch of her, slightly reduced in size. The black-and-white line drawing of that girlish, ardent countenance was again present to remind readers both of the youth of the author and, it would appear, of the youth of this paper, as well as of *Time and Tide*'s wish to associate itself with new and fresh perspectives.

When it came to offering such perspectives, West never disappointed. After all, smashing idols was how she first had secured her fame as a journalist. As Susan Hertog reminds us, 'Within her first year at *The Freewoman*, Rebecca, not yet twenty, had earned a reputation as a savage critic eager to attack the eminent literary figures of the day. After denouncing George Bernard Shaw and Arnold Bennett as superficial . . . she set her sights on dethroning Wells' (Hertog 2011: 37). (It was, of course, her 'savage' review of H. G. Wells's novel *Marriage*, in the 19 September 1912 issue of the *Freewoman*, that had excited his desire to meet her and had led to their long love affair.) Laura Heffernan has attributed the hostility that West aroused not only in Old Guard figures of an earlier generation, but in the 'male modernists' who were her contemporaries, to her boldness in intruding upon their territory, labelling this as the 'vitriol that greets the close imitator or rival' (2008: 319). Although this was undoubtedly the case, it was also true that, as a journalist, West courted controversy and invited outraged responses from male literary targets in particular, by judging their work mercilessly and by couching her objections in phrases that were at once beautifully crafted and derisive.

With her initial review for the new 'The Theatre' column, in the inaugural number of *Time and Tide*, West immediately established herself as a drama critic who could be counted upon to take down giants. The subject was J. M. Barrie's *Mary Rose*, and West's comments upon it were inflammatory. She did more than merely denigrate the work itself, as well as the London production of it, calling it 'a bad play, atrociously produced, and inappropriately acted'; she went after the playwright, then at the zenith of his eminence, by insisting that he was weakest precisely in the area where readers would have assumed him to be unassailable (14 May 1920: 10). Her attack on the creator of the internationally beloved fantasy *Peter Pan; or, the Boy Who Wouldn't Grow Up* (1904) centred on his alleged inability to deal with the realm of the magical and the imaginary: 'But whenever he touches the supernatural in this play he displays a casualness which shows that he does not believe in faeryland' (14 May 1920: 11). The unhappy result, she insisted, was that 'Sir James Barrie profanes faeryland, and passes off as a magic casement what is really a piece of frosted glass' (14 May 1920: 10).

This was not, however, the end of her assault on Barrie's reputation. Knowing that he was famed, as well, for plays such as *What Every Woman Knows* (1908) that had put women characters front and centre and presented them in an admiring light, West also lambasted *Mary Rose* for its 'extraordinary obtuseness' regarding gendered 'psychological knowledge': 'It is amazing that Sir James Barrie, with his desire to be sensitive about women's nature, does not see' that the chief situation in the drama 'disturbs and troubles all the women in his audience' with its lack of understanding of what a mother would feel under the circumstances (14 May 1920: 11). As might have been expected, she ended her first foray in theatre criticism for the new feminist journal by asserting her own superior knowledge on the subject of women's thoughts and emotions.

Perhaps more surprisingly, she also concluded by claiming a deeper comprehension of the fantastic and of 'faeryland' as a 'real place':

> Anyone who has rowed on a calm sea with the sun on their right and the moon on their left and has felt the disposition to turn the nose of the boat away from the shore, anyone who has walked on a moor and has felt the secret pricking to take the wrong path though the darkness is falling, has been at the frontiers of faeryland. It is the place where those dwell who find contentment in places rather than people [and] who will cut themselves off from human society that they may have a more solitary view of the sunrise. (14 May 1920: 11)

Here, she not only democratised access to the 'faery' world – the sphere that Barrie supposedly had mapped so authoritatively in *Peter Pan* – and thus empowered readers (including women) to recognise their own expertise on the subject, but elevated her review from journalism into poetry. In the process, she challenged Barrie from the position both of a critic and of a writer capable of working in the same lyrical and mystical register that he was known for having brought to the stage. (West would, of course, soon explore this 'supernatural' realm herself in her 1929 novel, *Harriet Hume: A London Fantasy*.)

With these first statements in the role of theatre reviewer for *Time and Tide*, West proved her mettle, while demonstrating her worth in drawing the public's eye and, presumably, in helping to sell copies of the new journal. What Victoria Glendinning has described as the keynote of her later criticism – 'Her strength was that she was both well-informed and . . . funny at the expense of received wisdom, at the expense of the great and good of the establishment' – was already on view in this early journalism (1987: 41). Rebecca West justified, therefore, what can only be described as a leap of faith on the part of Lady Rhondda, when assigning her to the paper's 'The Theatre' column, for her qualifications as a drama critic were somewhat questionable. At the time of taking on this role in 1920, West had never so much as written a play, let alone had one produced. The sole dramatisation of one of her novels, *The Return of the Soldier* (1918), would not be undertaken for another eight years, and this work would be adapted and brought to the stage by a writer (John Van Druten) other than West herself. When West later proved unavailable, by the mid-1920s, to continue turning out weekly columns and became a more occasional reviewer, Lady Rhondda filled her place with a rotating group of critics, each of whom was also a playwright: Christabel Marshall (1871–1960), who wrote under the pen name of 'Christopher St John'; Monica Ewer (1889–1969); and Velona Pilcher (1894–1952). The only exception was 'Anne Doubleday' – the pseudonym of Lady Rhondda herself, who pitched in with reviews and kept the column on schedule, though she had no claim to being a dramatist.

On the other hand, West did have some early experience with the theatrical world, although there is controversy and disagreement among biographers on the nature of that involvement. As J. R. Hammond points out, 'Since childhood she had been fascinated and enthralled by the stage,' and her initial career ambition was to be an actress (1991: 61). She trained at the Academy of Dramatic Art in London for nearly a year, from 1910 to 1911: 'While still at the Academy her first piece of paid journalism had been published: a review of Gorky's *Lower Depths* in the *London Evening Standard*. This had whetted her appetite for more but the attempts to follow up this beginning with further drama criticism came to nothing' (ibid.). A year after leaving the Academy, moreover, she gave up the name with which she had been born, Cicely Fairfield, to become 'Rebecca West' in 1912, borrowing this new appellation from Ibsen's play, *Rosmersholm*, and thus affiliating her future identity as a writer directly with the sphere of High Art drama.

Yet her efforts to make a splash (and a living) in the theatre were by no means a success. Carl Rollyson, another chronicler of West's life, tells of her year-long training at the Academy of Dramatic Art as a story of frustration on her part and of rejection by the school's officials, who considered her both undisciplined and less than promising: 'She made herself even more unpopular by asking the teachers why they did plays that were such rubbish. She persisted for three terms, hoping that the fourth and final term, which included a public performance, might yield a good role, but she was not promoted' (1995: 16). The upshot was, for West, a lifelong sense of disappointment and grievance associated with her attempts to enter the theatre: 'To biographer Lovat Dickinson, she confided that even "decades afterwards" she would pass the RADA building (it had become the Royal Academy of Dramatic Art) in tears' (ibid.).

There was more, of course, to comprehension and appreciation of stagecraft than a gift (or a lack of talent) for acting on the part of a critic. But even the issue of whether or not West had the true instincts of a performer has been subject to dispute. Although West's acting teachers may have been unpersuaded, her son, Anthony West – with whom she quarrelled fiercely after the publication in 1955 of his *roman-à-clef* about his childhood, titled *Heritage* – insisted that his mother was a compulsively self-dramatising figure, who innately understood theatricality as a practice and as a way of life. Indeed, when creating a protagonist based on his mother, he turned her into a professional actress who only comes alive and is herself on stage: 'Beyond the orchestra pit in that rich blaze of light behind the proscenium arch, she existed fully and completely, she was there' (West 1955: 26). Away from the public's gaze and without an audience to respond to her, 'at home she was not a real person at all,' but instead 'in the state of a victrola that was not playing, a radio that was not switched on, a toy shut up in a box or drawer' (West 1955: 25). West might or might not have deserved this harsh appraisal by someone close to her. There is, however, no question that she believed herself to be a shrewd judge of stage performance, and she weighed in freely, throughout her reviews for *Time and Tide*, on the question of how well actors and actresses not only played their roles, but created their personae, while writing on this subject in ways that were unflaggingly entertaining, as in her review titled '"Daddalums" and "The 'Ruined' Lady"':

> There is another occasion for rejoicing in the acting of Miss Eva Moore. It must be the most delightful thing in the world to be Miss Moore; to be quite the prettiest and most lovable woman on the stage for [a] quarter of a century and to know that at seventy, one will still be the prettiest and most lovable woman on the stage, because one has a physical and mental charm indestructible by middle age or age. She is at once the type and the idealisation of the English bourgeoisie. She speaks the clipped English that they speak in Surbiton, every vowel a little fake; she never makes a gesture that the hostess does not make behind the strawberries and cream at the tennis party; and yet this personal genius of hers makes the whole entrancing and delicious, a figure of real and tender beauty. (9 July 1920: 186)

When writing about the theatre for *Time and Tide*, however, she never treated the stage as a space apart from the larger issues of labour, politics, and gender. In this sense, she was wholly unlike most conventional drama critics, especially those who were men. As someone who was both cognisant of and who shared the larger aims espoused by Lady Rhondda – a figure 'actively committed to the promotion of women in professional life' (Clay 2013: 210) – West used her reviews to invite the audience behind the curtain and to raise awareness of matters such as the abysmal, substandard living conditions of actresses as workers. The same 9 July 1920 review that extolled the 'charm' of Eva Moore and praised her for evoking onstage a privileged, leisured suburban milieu through her accurate performance of a class-specific type also reminded readers why this was such a marvellous accomplishment: it stood in stark contrast to the reality of how actresses lived and what they actually had to suffer, in order to pursue their chosen profession. Far from reflecting the domestic ease and sheltered conditions of the characters she portrayed, Moore's own experiences offstage, according to West, would have been those of many other female labourers, struggling within a system that put women at a grave disadvantage:

> The reason that we have so few vital and attractive actresses is that when a girl goes on the stage she is sent out on a life that for discomfort is second to none except that of an Arctic explorer's. From week to week she cannot be sure of lodgings free from vermin or a landlady who can cook eatable food; every Sunday she must spend in travelling, which is in these days an even more serious business than it used to be, because as three syndicates have now the first choice of booking dates at the provincial theatres, other companies have to take what dates are left, regardless of their own convenience and consequently have to make lengthy journeys from end to end of the country almost every week. It is a life that weeds many out of the profession who are probably the very people who would make the most sensitive artists, and it takes the edge off almost every woman who endures it for any length of time. (9 July 1920: 186)

West's journalistic work for *Time and Tide* as a whole functioned as an invaluable reminder to readers that this was a paper in which the production and reception of the arts would never be examined in isolation from broader questions of social justice and injustice. Her early criticism for *Time and Tide*'s weekly feature titled 'The Theatre' thus aligned perfectly with the free-standing articles that she submitted throughout the 1920s, including her 1923 'Equal Pay for Men and Women Teachers,' as well as with later contributions, such as her 1929 review of Anna Seghers's novel, *The Revolt of the Fisherman*, for the column 'Books: A Commentary on Books and Things.' In the latter, she turned from purely literary concerns to protest how 'middle-class writers, treating of the poor, often indulge in falsification. They adopt that pretence, which got its impetus in the Dark Ages when Europe was poor and had to find consolations for her poverty, that there is something ennobling in not having enough material goods' (1 Nov 1929: 1810). If frequent visual and textual allusions to West's youth were deployed strategically, as a means of branding *Time and Tide* and announcing its commitment to new perspectives, new ideas, and new voices, so her approach to culture as integrally linked to questions about the working and living conditions of both women and men – including those in the arts – helped to broadcast the paper's sociopolitical philosophy and to define its feminism.

It is worth remembering that even in the year 1920, when Rebecca West assumed the post of drama critic for *Time and Tide*, women were still something of a rarity in such a role. The presence of her name, therefore, at the top of the first page of each number of the paper, next to the words 'The Theatre,' was an attention-getting device in itself. As Gay Gibson Cima has explained, the traditional exclusion of women from the position of theatre critic had to do with gender-specific notions of respectability that dominated nineteenth-century thinking and remained in place for much of the twentieth: 'Women who nightly traversed this market-driven landscape' of the theatre world, in order to write their reviews of performances, 'risked the possibility that they would be perceived as prostitutes,' as indeed actresses long had been; 'As late as 1952, the journalist and novelist Philip Hamilton Gibbs still sustained this myth in his description of Fleet Street' (Cima 1999: 44). But there were other reasons why, despite widespread professional success in the late nineteenth and early twentieth century as book reviewers, British women found it difficult to be accepted as drama critics. Again, Cima proves helpful in elucidating the issues:

> The critic was required not only to send her writing out into the public domain, but also routinely to appear, herself, as a woman-worker in public. She was not toiling behind the scenes, submitting copy, but rather was visibly public, dressed as other women in the theatre auditorium and masquerading as a woman, but actually engaged in a process of 'manly' judgment and even caricature. (1999: 42)

Into this gender minefield, West strode briskly and without hesitation, offering up both judgements and caricatures. The prose caricatures, of course, were what drew readers to her column, as Lady Rhondda must have hoped they would. Despite West's professed dislike of Oscar Wilde – whose wit she compared unfavourably to that of the young Noël Coward – and her scorn for Wilde's 'convulsive phrases known as epigrams' (30 July 1920: 246), her own pronouncements often took epigrammatic form. West's review of one unfortunate playwright's work opened, for instance, with this bon mot: 'Mr. Edward Knoblock's "Cherry," which is being played at the Apollo, is certainly preferable to his "Tiger, Tiger!" but only as an ache is preferable to a pain' (6 Aug 1920: 266). Even more characteristic of her comic style, though, was her use of unexpected metaphors to deflate the subject at hand. While ridiculing not merely the play adapted from Robert Hichens's novel, *The Garden of Allah*, but also the 'elaborate and ineffective scenery' of its London production, she resorted to this rhetorical technique, decrying 'such perverse and expensive ingenuities as the sandstorm, which is of no value at all except to add to our stock of knowledge by showing us how life must seem to a cockroach who has inadvertently vanished inside a vacuum cleaner' (23 July 1920: 227). Hichens, of course, had first established his literary reputation as author of *The Green Carnation* (1894), a satire aimed at Oscar Wilde for which he had created his own collection of imitation Wildean witticisms; thus, there was perhaps an element of competitiveness in West's mode of attack, as well as sheer revelling in her own linguistic bravura through comic metaphors. Likewise, her review of a 1921 Ballets Russes production of *Chout* spun out, through the whole of the first paragraph, an extended image of Sergei Diaghilev's company as having 'acquired something more than a travelled appearance. It now looks as if it had at one time or another lost its luggage in every European country' (1 July 1921: 627). This allowed her to attribute the production's misguided use of Futurist scenery to the kind of 'fatigued state of credulity towards the pretensions of any work of art that declared itself modern' that 'worn-out travellers' display, when they 'say of even the worst hotel, "Oh, this will do"' (1 July 1921: 627). Through her linguistic agility, West landed blows at two targets: at the ballet company's lapse in artistic taste when turning to a variety of modernism that she found visually unappealing, and at Futurism itself, which she dismissed as a local phenomenon best suited to Italy, where it originated with Filippo Marinetti, and as a site-specific reaction to places such as Florence, 'that strange city which gives one the impression that a museum has eloped with a tramway system' (ibid.).

That she was able to produce these outrageously amusing turns of phrase to order for her *Time and Tide* column on a weekly basis suggests that West had found a way to channel her love of performance, which was frustrated by her unhappy experience at drama school, into a kind of literary performance art that went beyond conventional journalism. Indeed, Laura Cowan suggests as much in her discussion of West's early essays (2015: 15). Praising West for the 'exuberance' of her 'vivid metaphors,' Cowan invites us to see this as more than tour-de-force writing for its own sake, but instead as an attempt to 'transport the reader into an imaginative space ... where logic and imagination encounter each other to foster the transformative potential of art' (ibid.). The resulting 'hybridity' served to move her critical pronouncements 'beyond normal polemic into an "uncharted" realm/genre' that was 'subversive'; 'Extravagance and irrelevance are precisely the point,' Cowan asserts, as West carried her readers into new literary territory (2015: 14–15).

What this pursuit of 'hybridity' on West's part also demonstrated, however, was the increasing capaciousness of the category of mass-market journalism. By the 1920s, it had absorbed the experimental qualities formerly associated with the sort of self-consciously artistic prose found in 'little' or avant-garde magazines, whether the *Savoy* of the 1890s or *BLAST* of the First World War period. Thus, in branding itself through the prominent and frequent display of West's 'subversive' forms, *Time and Tide* could feel assured simultaneously of being positioned at the cutting edge of literary taste while still appealing to a large readership. Alice Wood has claimed that, in the 1920s, West deliberately sought to write for popular 'women's magazines,' because she 'embraced the opportunity' that they in particular 'offered to experiment with journalistic forms' (2016: 58). West's theatre criticism for *Time and Tide*, however, proved that there were just as many avenues open for experimentation in more highbrow, general-interest periodicals geared toward politically minded women and also to men, and that West took full advantage of these possibilities.

In 'Miss Rebecca West,' the profile that appeared in the 16 July 1920 issue of Lady Rhondda's journal and was reprinted three years later, the anonymous writer of it claimed that West

> suffers from an unusually acute personal diffidence, which makes her an astonishingly bad public speaker, and there is indeed no evidence that she attaches the slightest importance to her own opinions. All she feels is an absolute necessity to express them. And the world, accustomed to opinions that are qualified and trimmed to suit the interests of those who give them forth, listens in amazement and delight, and feels that it is in contact with some crude, primitive form of energy, and accordingly feels refreshed. (205)

Coming as it did less than two months after West began writing a regular column for *Time and Tide*, as well as less than two months after the first number of the magazine was issued, this statement represented an unusually blatant attempt to anticipate and to shape the reception both of West's reviews and of the periodical as a whole. It told readers unambiguously that the writing they would find in *Time and Tide* would break with the norms of journalistic etiquette; that its novelty would stem from a sincere impulse to speak from the heart, rather than from a desire either to shock or to call attention to its author; that readers were to put aside conventional expectations and respond with 'amazement and delight' to such work; and that the experience of engaging with direct and uncensored 'opinion' would leave them 'refreshed.' It assured them, moreover, that the modernist desire for contact with 'energy' and interest in the 'primitive' could be satisfied by the work of a middle-class Englishwoman – a young one at that, who still bore the title of 'Miss.' For a periodical determined to establish itself as an outlet for frank expressions of opinions by and about women – though not exclusively *for* women – the message could not have been more plain.

When she eventually moved on from her role as a weekly columnist and became a less frequent contributor, West left not only the proverbial large shoes to fill, but a problem. What broader function would 'The Theatre' serve, beyond reviewing individual productions? In the absence of West's distinctive voice, would this column continue to brand *Time and Tide* in the same way? By the mid-1920s, having found no single suitable replacement, Lady Rhondda turned to a stable of critics. Chief among them was 'Christopher St John' (Christabel Marshall), who often did double duty, supplying drama criticism alongside reviews of performances of classical music. Like West, she was prickly and sometimes caustic, and her barbs were amusing in themselves. She was, however, less given to leaping from the spectacle at hand to more universal political issues or to raising questions about labour conditions for actresses. This more narrow focus and concentration on the specifics of the plays and the performances also marked the reviews of Velona Pilcher and Monica Ewer, who alternated with her in surveying the London theatre scene. In the guise, however, of 'Anne Doubleday,' Lady Rhondda proved the most conventional of the periodical's regular drama critics and, surprisingly, the one least likely to rattle theatrical hierarchies. If West had deliberately drawn attention, both to herself and to *Time and Tide*, through her dedication to idol-smashing, Lady Rhondda's inclination was the opposite. Reviewing plays in the 1920s by J. M. Barrie, John Galsworthy, and especially by G. B. Shaw, among other (mostly male) notables, 'Anne Doubleday' usually chose to affirm, rather than to cast doubt on, their mastery as artists. Perhaps this was a strategic decision, linked to Lady Rhondda's wish either to secure or to keep such prominent figures as contributors, as well as to offer an occasional sop to their legions of fans, who numbered among the readers of *Time and Tide*. It may, however, have been a sign instead of how well Rebecca West had done her work at the outset, making it less crucial to include displays of such aggressive iconoclasm in every subsequent issue of the paper.

Rebecca West epitomised and embodied in many senses the New Journalism of the 1920s and the heterodox character of the decade itself that Rose Macaulay, another contributor to Lady Rhondda's enterprise, later identified. In its early years, West would be the magazine's standard bearer, and *Time and Tide* had waited for her.

Works Cited

Cima, Gay Gibson. 1999. '"To be Public as a Genius and Private as a Woman": The Critical Framing of Nineteenth-Century British Playwrights.' *Women and Playwriting in Nineteenth-Century Britain*. Ed. Tracy C. Davis and Ellen Donkin. Cambridge: Cambridge University Press. 35–53.

Clay, Catherine. 2011. '"What We Might Expect – If the Highbrow Weeklies Advertised Like the Patent Foods": *Time and Tide*, Advertising, and the "Battle of the Brows."' *Modernist Cultures* 6:1: 60–95.

—. 2013. 'The Woman Journalist, 1920–1945.' *The History of British Women's Writing, 1920–1945*. Ed. Maroula Joannou. Basingstoke: Palgrave Macmillan. 199–214.

Cowan, Laura. 2015. *Rebecca West's Subversive Use of Hybrid Genres, 1911–41*. London: Bloomsbury.

Gates, Joanne E. 1994. *Elizabeth Robins, 1862–1952: Actress, Novelist, Feminist*. Tuscaloosa: University of Alabama.

Gibb, Lorna. 2013. *West's World: The Extraordinary Life of Dame Rebecca West*. London: Macmillan.

Glendinning, Victoria. 1987. *Rebecca West: A Life*. London: Weidenfeld & Nicolson.

Hammond, J. R. 1991. *H. G. Wells and Rebecca West*. Hemel Hempstead: Harvester Wheatsheaf / Simon & Schuster.

Heffernan, Laura. 2008. 'Reading Modernism's Cultural Field: Rebecca West's The Strange Necessity and the Aesthetic "System of Relations."' *Tulsa Studies in Women's Literature* 27.2: 309–25.

Hertog, Susan. 2011. *Dangerous Ambition: Rebecca West and Dorothy Thompson, New Women in Search of Love and Power*. New York: Ballantine.

John, Angela V. 2013. *Turning the Tide: The Life of Lady Rhondda*. Cardigan: Parthian.

Macaulay, Rose. 1942. *Life Among the English*. London: William Collins.

Pykett, Lyn. 2000. 'The Making of a Modern Woman Writer: Rebecca West's Journalism, 1911–1930.' *Journalism, Literature, and Modernity: from Hazlitt to Modernism*. Ed. Kate Campbell. Edinburgh: Edinburgh University Press. 180–90.

Rollyson, Carl. 1995. *Rebecca West: A Saga of the Century*. London: Sceptre / Hodder & Stoughton.

—. 1998. *The Literary Legacy of Rebecca West*. Bethesda, MD: International Scholars Publications.

Spender, Dale. 1984. *Time and Tide Wait for No Man*. London: Pandora.

West, Anthony. 1955. *Heritage*. New York: Random House.

Wood, Alice. 2016. 'Modernism and the Middlebrow in British Women's Magazines, 1916–1930.' *Middlebrow and Gender, 1890–1945*. Ed. Christoph Ehland and Cornelia Wächter. Leiden: Brill Rodopi. 39–59.

13

Writing Revolution: Dorothy Richardson's Contributions to Early Twentieth-Century Periodicals

Elizabeth Pritchett and Scott McCracken

Introduction

Dorothy Richardson's pioneering long modernist novel, *Pilgrimage*, was the work of a lifetime: its first volume, *Pointed Roofs*, was published in 1915, followed by a collected edition of twelve volumes in 1938, and the posthumous addition of a thirteenth, unfinished volume in 1967. Over the course of its long history, *Pilgrimage* has become synonymous with the birth of stream of consciousness. Though Richardson objected to May Sinclair's designation,[1] the category has proven at once defining and a locus of critique. Anne Fernihough maintains that *Pilgrimage*'s method of adhering only to protagonist Miriam Henderson's mind at work 'enacts, at the level of form [. . .] a rejection of democracy and a contempt for the masses' (2013: 96). In this chapter, we maintain that, on the contrary, Richardson's writing evinces an enduring, though subtle, aesthetic engagement with emergent forms of British democracy and that nowhere is this clearer than in her contributions to early twentieth-century British periodicals.

Living on the margins of Bloomsbury and Parisian modernist coteries, Richardson was eclectic in her politics and wary of any firm commitments, once even claiming that any 'wood-louse' could see that *Pilgrimage*'s Miriam was not a feminist (1995a: 299). Such wariness prompts readings of Richardson's aesthetic as one opposed to the emergence of radical mass politics at the dawn of a new century. It also explains why Fernihough (though she convincingly unsettles other ingrained misconceptions about the divide between Edwardian and modernist periods) misreads *Pilgrimage*'s defining stream of consciousness as anti-democratic. Such deliberations on Richardson's relationship to the emergence of modern mass democracy have precedent. Even the author's friend and patron, Bryher (Annie Winifred Ellerman), was not wholly convinced that Richardson was a political revolutionary. In 1942, Bryher maintained that 'Richardson's novels about the little lives of obscure men and women contain more true communism than some study of a strike done with enthusiasm' (*Life and Letters To-day* Apr 1942: 33, 57), but after Richardson's death she dismissed the author as 'Victorian.'[2] One aim of this chapter, therefore, is to complicate catch-all depictions of Richardson and politics by placing her contributions to early twentieth-century British periodicals at a nexus between late Victorian and Edwardian radicalisms and the modern rise of mass democracy. Our other related aim is to propose a new critical framework with which to consider the relationship between modern forms of democracy and the parallel rise of modernist literary aesthetics more broadly.

Richardson's earliest writing for British periodicals attests to the fact that the author's Victorian and modernist identities are not mutually exclusive. Between 1901 and 1926, Richardson wrote for an eclectic mix of radical, mainstream, and professional magazines and journals. Much of her material had to do with her political and cultural interests, as she attended Tolstoyan and Fabian meetings and was intimately involved with both Russian revolutionaries and suffragists.[3] This catholicity of political, philosophical, and intellectual interest and thought, Richardson described as 'a kind of archipelago' amidst which she explored 'various islands' (*London Magazine* June 1959: 18), many of which were, of course, rooted in late Victorian radicalisms: the feminism of Olive Schreiner and Charlotte Perkins Gilman, utopian and state socialism, and the anarchism of Charles Daniel and Florence Worland.[4] Rather than a break from the past, therefore, we might think of Richardson's modernism not so much as '*new* work,' but as Marx described in his letter to Arnold Ruge 'the completion of its old work' (1975: 209).[5] Neither a remnant of a residual Victorianism nor an enunciation of an emergent and wholly new modernism, Richardson's modernism created a space in which both the residual and emergent interact to produce new cultural and political formations that challenge the dominant culture.[6] If, as Perry Anderson contends, the chief revolutionary aspect of European modernism is that it 'flowered in the space between a still usable classical past, a still indeterminate technical present, and a still unpredictable political future,' then Richardson's modernism is indeed revolutionary (1984: 105). But, democratic?

In defining Richardson's aesthetic as democratic, we mean two things: first, that it is inclusive and expansive, and second, that it subjects itself to the terms of its own contestation by inviting debate and dissent. While the basis for our theory of a democratic aesthetic is rooted in Bakhtinian theory of the dialogic, we go beyond Bakhtin to consider the active role that aesthetics play in the development and maintenance of democracy (see Bakhtin 1981). For Jacques Rancière, aesthetics and democracy are inextricable in that both seek to produce discursive openings: spaces where society's marginalised and silenced voices might expand and modify the bounds of public discourse and representation, confines that Rancière refers to as society's 'distribution of the sensible which defines the common of a community' (2014: 8). Aesthetics, as Rancière maintains, poses a critical and continual challenge to this distribution, by expanding the formal and epistemic conditions of representation. In this way, aesthetics is central to providing cultural conditions for political change: the creation of space for previously invisible and muted identities and ideologies to assume public expression and shape.[7]

Our second basis for defining Richardson's aesthetic as democratic is made with regard to theories of democracy that emphasise the epistemic value of incompletion and uncertainty, principles that modernists famously embraced. Rancière, for instance, defines democracy in terms of dissensus: 'not a definite set of institutions, nor [. . .] the power of a specific group' but instead a 'power that at once legitimizes and de-legitimizes every set of institutions or the power of any one set of people' (2009: 52). Rancière's understanding of democracy as an institution built on the terms of its own contestation echoes Claude Lefort's earlier description of democracy as an 'open space' that disincorporates power from a single figurehead to relocate it to a more amorphous and constantly shifting body public (Lefort 1988 and 1986). Similarly, Stuart Hall describes a Marxist democratic ideal as an '*open horizon* of marxist theorizing – determinacy without guaranteed closures' that, therefore, counters the 'illusion of theoretical *certainty* . . . [which] stimulates orthodoxy' (1996: 44, original emphasis). Theories that posit democracy as a process of countering authoritarian regimes by forming new spaces of dialogue and debate, we maintain, are fundamental to understanding Richardson's unique aesthetic as it develops from her earliest writing ventures in British periodicals.

In her self-styled 'First literary effort,'[8] 'The Russian and His Book' (1902), Richardson satirises how a small-town Russian library uses literature and reading to maintain a social hierarchy and an intellectual elite. The speaker divides the patrons of this fictive library into two groups: those who read 'simply "books"' and those who read only '"intellectual books" [. . . and] wear only a pince-nez' (*Outlook* 4 Oct 1902: 268). A pince-nez wearer herself, Richardson is self-reflexive here, subjecting herself to the satire as she exposes her blind spots and biases to readers. The notion of reading itself as a gauge of society's democratic commitments is elaborated on more cogently in Richardson's later essays such as 'About Punctuation' (1924), 'Adventure for Readers' (1939), and 'Novels' (1948). In these essays, Richardson frames the reading of modernist texts in particular as participatory and democratic. The text itself becomes a space of dialogic exchange with the reader, who embarks on an adventure (see Richardson 1990b) as 'the text *speaks* itself' and is afforded human-like agency as both 'a tour guide and a tourist . . . engaged in a collaboration' with the willing reader (Richardson 1990a: 415; 1990c: 435).

This chapter's interests are in Richardson's lesser known contributions to a variety of periodicals: primarily her interventions in Charles Daniel's *Crank* and Dora Marsden and Harriet Shaw Weaver's *Freewoman*, but also her articles for the professional journal the *Dental Record* and, more cursorily, her experimental non-fiction for the *Saturday Review*. Given the breadth and eclecticism of Richardson's periodical writing (which addressed everything from the benefits of proper mastication to the advent of the talkie film), there are many accounts we might offer of this body of work. In this chapter, we discuss articles in which Richardson explicitly engages with the radical and democratic politics of her day, particularly socialism and feminism, to develop what we call a democratic aesthetic that expands the 'distribution of the sensible' by creating spaces of dialogism and dissensus on the page.

The pieces we have chosen are representative though not comprehensive.[9] Richardson was a prolific contributor to many other periodicals, from mainstream magazines and newspapers such as *Vanity Fair*, the *Daily Herald*, and the *Daily Mail* to journals for the arts such as Ford Madox Ford's *transatlantic review* and Bryher's film monthly, *Close-Up*. The fifth chapter-volume of *Pilgrimage*, *Interim*, was serialised alongside *Ulysses* in the *Little Review*,[10] and several of Richardson's poems were published in *Poetry* (Figure 13.1). Additionally, Richardson wrote for John Middleton Murry's *Adelphi*, both under her own name and under a male pseudonym, R. Theobald. She later published articles in *Life and Letters To-day*, including 'Novels' and 'The Poet of Bloomsbury,' a retrospective of the two years she lived across from W. B. Yeats.[11] Throughout, Richardson's central concerns

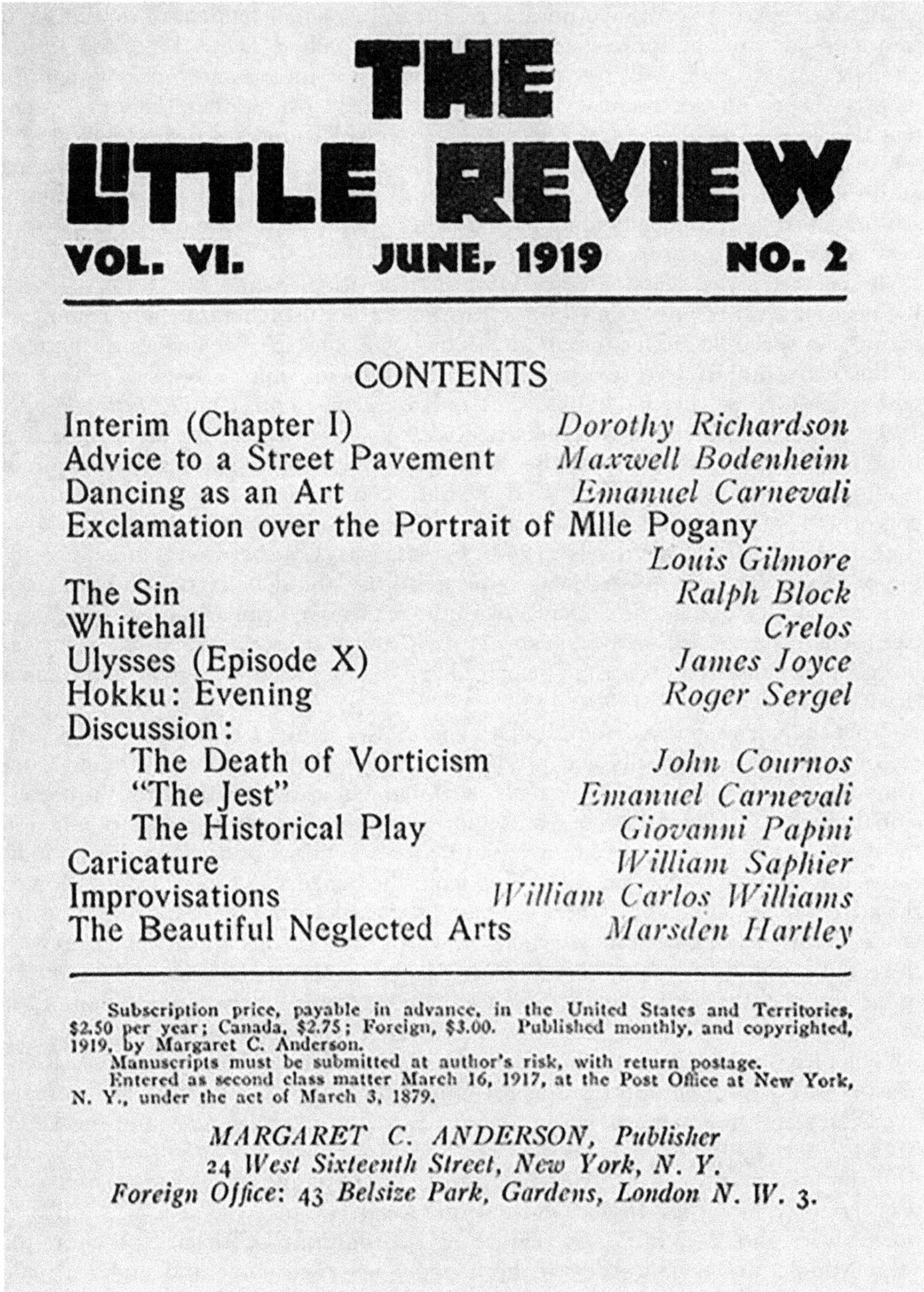

THE LITTLE REVIEW

VOL. VI.   **JUNE, 1919**   **NO. 2**

CONTENTS

Interim (Chapter I)	*Dorothy Richardson*
Advice to a Street Pavement	*Maxwell Bodenheim*
Dancing as an Art	*Emanuel Carnevali*
Exclamation over the Portrait of Mlle Pogany	
	Louis Gilmore
The Sin	*Ralph Block*
Whitehall	*Crelos*
Ulysses (Episode X)	*James Joyce*
Hokku: Evening	*Roger Sergel*
Discussion:	
The Death of Vorticism	*John Cournos*
"The Jest"	*Emanuel Carnevali*
The Historical Play	*Giovanni Papini*
Caricature	*William Saphier*
Improvisations	*William Carlos Williams*
The Beautiful Neglected Arts	*Marsden Hartley*

Subscription price, payable in advance, in the United States and Territories, $2.50 per year; Canada, $2.75; Foreign, $3.00. Published monthly, and copyrighted, 1919, by Margaret C. Anderson.
Manuscripts must be submitted at author's risk, with return postage.
Entered as second class matter March 16, 1917, at the Post Office at New York, N. Y., under the act of March 3, 1879.

MARGARET C. ANDERSON, Publisher
24 West Sixteenth Street, New York, N. Y.
Foreign Office: 43 Belsize Park, Gardens, London N. W. 3.

Figure 13.1 Contents page of the *Little Review*. June 1919.

emerge: an interest in the relationship between culture and sociopolitical change, an abiding feminism if not expressly under that banner, and an understanding of reading as a potentially democratic practice. Placing Richardson's contributions to early twentieth-century periodicals in conversation with each other allows us not only to correct misconceptions of her work as hermetic and undemocratic but also to understand the early twentieth century's coinciding surges of print culture, modernism, and democratic mass politics as part of an interrelated network of processes all invested in making the modern and remaking the new.

The *Crank*: Richardson and the Odd Man

The *Crank*, which began life as the *Tolstoyan* (1902–3), was so christened in 1904 by one of its chief contributors, the mathematician and progressive educator, Mary Everest Boole, because, as the first cover asserts, '[a] crank is a little thing that makes revolutions' (Figure 13.2). In contrast to 'little modernist magazines' which were funded and circulated by wealthy patrons,[12] the *Crank* was a small magazine whose editor-in-chief and founder, Charles Daniel was also a radical printer, Tolstoyan, and Christian anarchist.

In this respect, the *Crank* stemmed from a tradition of radical printers who did not, as Nicolas Walter observes, 'follow any powerful person or join any powerful party' (2011: 225). A pacifist group that met between December 1900 and November 1901, Daniel's Tolstoyan Society was typical of the publisher's bespoke and eccentric approach, belonging 'to the shadowy world between progressive religion and progressive politics' (2011: 226). Richardson first met Daniel and his wife, Florence Worland, while lecturing at these Tolstoyan meetings. Eventually, she became so close with the couple that she raised money to help Daniel avoid imprisonment for his 1918 publication of *Despised and Rejected*.[13] Publishing in his later cranky periodicals, *Focus* and *Purpose*, throughout the late 1920s, Richardson maintained her friendship with Daniel, paying homage to him and his wife by dedicating *Revolving Lights* (1923) to Florence Worland Daniel and, in this same volume, introducing them as characters, George and Dora Taylor.

An outgrowth of late Victorian radicalism, Daniel's *Crank* nevertheless prefigures later more definitively modernist magazines such as A. R. Orage's, *The New Age*, whose hallmark was, according to Ann Ardis, its 'refusal to separate the aesthetic from the political sphere' (2002: 144). Likewise, Richardson's aesthetic interests developed alongside her participation in a distinctly pluralist, politically radical culture established in the previous century but flexible enough to accommodate modern re-imaginings. In Richardson's writing for the *Crank*, therefore, a certain genealogy can be traced to residual Victorian and Edwardian culture, such as Tolstoyanism as well as Edward Carpenter's simple life and socialist movements.

But Richardson's articles and letters also evince a yearning to become part of an emergent, modern revolution: the Fabians via her relationship with H. G. Wells, pacifist anarchism through Daniel and Worland, and radical Christianity, which will later transform into an interest in the Socialist Quaker Society.[14] Though Richardson's friendship with Worland and Daniel lasted a lifetime, she wrote for their monthly for just two years (1906–7), initially contributing book reviews and later a debate on socialism, published

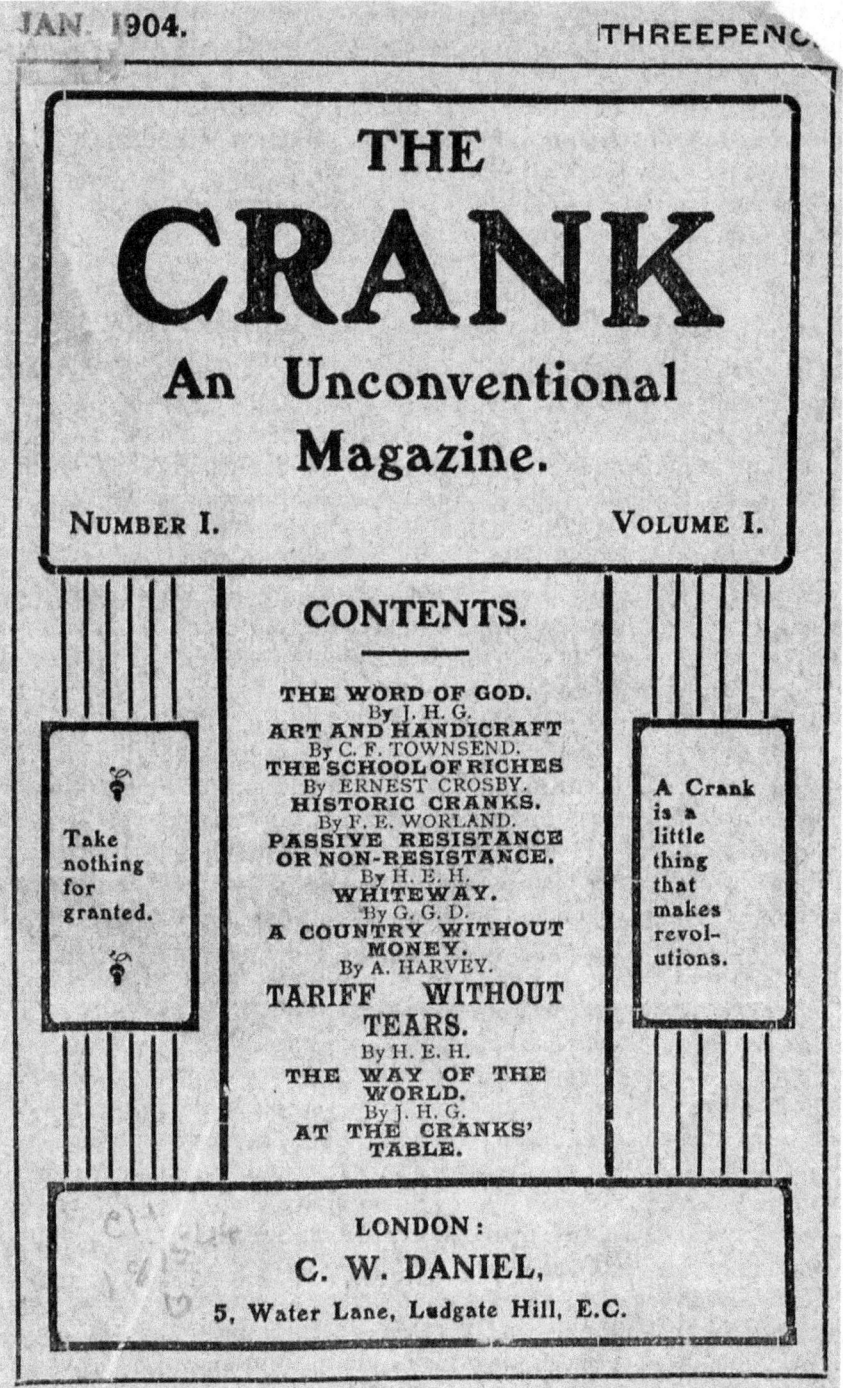

Figure 13.2 Front cover of the *Crank: An Unconventional Magazine*. January 1904.

between January and May 1907. In the latter, a series of open letters between Daniel and Richardson, the content and aesthetic is democratically dialogic and dissensual. While their debate focuses on socialism, Daniel and Richardson also explore various related topics such as feminism, vegetarianism, pacifism, and anarchism throughout their eight-letter exchange. Even at this early stage in her career, well before her stream-of-consciousness breakthrough, Richardson is already experimenting with democratic forms of writing.

Richardson initiates the debate in the January 1907 issue with 'The Odd Man's Remarks on Socialism,' a response to Daniel's anarchist critique of socialism as outlined in the *Crank*'s November and December 1906 issues. To Daniel's critique that socialism will simply create a new class system, with socialist bureaucrats on top, Richardson replies that a new ruling class will be an impossibility under socialism because both the 'individualistic enterprise' of capitalism and, thus, a proletariat class will cease to exist (Jan 1907: 31). In response to Daniel's pointed critique of a Fabian brand of 'municipal socialism' that advocated state-owned and controlled public services, Richardson, not yet a Fabian, argues, first, that municipal socialism cannot be taken as an example of socialism proper because it currently functions within actually existing capitalism and, second, that progress consists in mitigating, limiting, and regulating competition. In response to Daniel's final analysis that socialism represents a form of pseudo-cooperation where in fact 'the employers of to-day will become the overpaid officials of to-morrow' and that socialism is 'soulless' (Nov 1906: 364),[15] Richardson vaguely counters that the socialist ideal is testimony to the 'indomitable spirituality of humanity,' concluding that 'the "Odd Man," has, clearly, entered so very little into modern Socialistic thought that one feels that this unsupported assertion [of 'soullessness'] is hardly worth consideration' (Jan 1907: 33).

Although Richardson suggests that Daniel's anarchism is the opposite of 'modern Socialistic thought,' in fact both are engaged in two different currents of early twentieth-century radical politics whose ideals were established in the nineteenth century by activists and artists such as Carpenter but also Henry Hyndman, William Morris, and American economist and land-tax reformer, Henry George (Apr 1907: 181). Maintaining in the April 1907 issue that 'the main business of Socialism is to propagate the Socialist state of mind' rather than to propose specific policy agendas, Richardson explains that the socialist 'state of mind' is one that regards 'wealth as that which satisfies desire, and not the piling up of incomes' (ibid.). Richardson's idea of socialism as an everyday habit of thought is strikingly echoed forty years later in her description of post-Second World War democracy as a 'state of mind' (1995b: 423). Though partially a concession to the *Crank*'s overall anarchic individualism,[16] the idea of one's mindset as the locus of political reform also anticipates a late twentieth-century shift away from late capitalist models of democracy to conceptions of radical democracy where conflict, dissensus rather than consensus, is fundamental to extending margins of public debate and enlarging the body politic.[17]

While Richardson and Daniel's exchange represents two different strands of radical politics that gesture toward later radical democracy, a clearer difference between Richardson and the Odd Man is her feminism. Richardson's most powerful critique of Daniel's interpretation of socialism is that he views it as a 'sublimated policeman swooping down on the newly born infant, tearing it from its mother's arms, labelling it and forthwith dropping it into an automatic rearing machine' (Mar 1907: 147).

Far from oppressive, Richardson views this form of government as a positive step toward women's independence. As she reasons, a socialist government would recognise motherhood as a 'civil service' and pay mothers accordingly so that they may be 'independent of the accidents which may befall her man' (ibid.), a clear nod to Charlotte Perkins Gilman's *Women and Economics*, a book about which Richardson once enthused 'brought me the greatest happiness that has come into my life' (Richardson letter [c. 1900]). Like Gilman, Richardson argues that socialised childcare and women's economic independence will result in widespread social improvement. For Richardson this is because women will then be able to 'make of the whole world a home – for the art of life, the social art, the arts of arts is woman's art' (Mar 1907: 148). The idea of women's art as the art of making atmospheres is later fully laid out in *Pilgrimage* in a discussion between Miriam and Hypo Wilson, H. G. Wells's fictional counterpart.[18] But its earlier iteration in the *Crank* – the idea of socialism as a state of mind that enables women's art – highlights Richardson's intuitive understanding of the inextricable relationship between politics and aesthetics. Throughout their dialogue, Daniel and Richardson establish a form of social art made visible on the page whereby each author's tone, mode of address, and even genre of argument (the letter) creates a space of ideological and textual dissensus.

Quite apart from their content, these letters testify to both Daniel and Richardson's desire to forge, test, and debate democracy in print culture. At the heart of their debate is a civility that invites further political discourse and, thus, the ongoing testing of ideas and doctrine '[t]hrough all differences' as Richardson puts it in her closing to one letter (Mar 1907: 149). Likewise, Daniel refers to Richardson in this same issue as 'my opponent and friend,' a paradox to whose truth their enduring friendship attests (Mar 1907: 150). In Richardson's last letter in the series, she highlights not the political ideologies that informed their debate but rather an intersubjectivity and its concomitant capacity for epistemic transformation that their exchange has effected: 'We have [. . .] for the first time become aware of each other, have interchanged greetings and goods, have quarreled and fought, and learned to respect each other' (May 1907: 237–8). Richardson's summation importantly outlines the conditions of a democratic 'state of mind': aware and open to change as well as rigorously and respectfully dissenting. By lending this democratic state of mind public form, Richardson's letters to the Odd Man define and model a democracy that is based on 'not merely the free expression of beliefs or commitments,' as Ken Hirschkop has it, but rather 'the question of the very form those beliefs and commitments assume' (1999: 202–3). In this way, Daniel's *Crank* and Richardson's contributions to it model the terms of a dialogic and dissensual democratic aesthetic for a rapidly shifting early twentieth-century British print culture.

Richardson and the *Freewoman*

If Richardson's writing for the *Crank* evinces both her interest in socialism and the foundations of her democratic aesthetic, her writing for the *Freewoman* provides strong evidence of Richardson's feminism. This feminism is still a contested point because her fictional alter ego in *Pilgrimage* often shows marked antipathy toward conventional forms of middle-class femininity. Yet, if any 'wood-louse' can see that Miriam is no feminist, Richardson clearly is. Some of Richardson's most canonical and explicitly feminist essays, including 'The Reality of Feminism' (1917), 'Women and the Future' (1924), and 'Women in the Arts' (1925), were published concurrent to the writing of *Pilgrimage*. Richardson was also a regular reader of the *Freewoman*, the paper that, under Rebecca West's literary editorship, drew articles from Henri Bergson, Ezra Pound, and William Carlos Williams and, in its later life as the *Egoist*, published May Sinclair's canonical review of *Pilgrimage*.[19] The history of the *Freewoman* and its founding by radical feminist, Dora Mardsen, and more mainstream suffragette, Mary Gawthorpe, is better known than that of Daniel's *Crank*. But like the *Crank*, the *Freewoman* was more than a publication; there was also a vibrant 'Freewoman Discussion Circle' that informed its content. Richardson contributed two pieces to the *Freewoman*, 'The Disabilities of Women' and a short letter to the editor titled 'The Original Impulse,' pieces that speak to the periodical's concern with women's role in a modern Britain.

While Richardson's first piece, 'The Disabilities of Women' (1912), hearkens back to the Daniels' brand of Tolstoyan clean-living, it advances a distinctly feminist agenda. Richardson begins by lamenting how '[t]he Feminist movement has been accompanied at every stage of its progress by an undertow of commentary from the medical profession' (15 Aug 1912: 254). In particular, she maintains that a 'chorus of triumphant finality' from male gynaecologists has caused women either to accept the doctors' findings believing that they 'appl[y] only to pathological women' or to claim 'freedom in the name of these differences' by embracing their supposed gendered 'disabilities' and thereby rejecting 'masculine schemes of value' (ibid.). Carving out a middle ground between philosophical absolutes, Richardson argues that a 'third possibility' might be to consider that scientists are not always right (ibid.), something she says is evident in the '"scrapping" of the deductions of orthodox medical science [. . .] taking place under our eyes to-day with regard to "feminine ailments"' (15 Aug 1912: 255).

As Richardson explains, precedent for a more modern view of women's health comes from Dr Trömner, author of *Diseases of Women* (a book reviewed in the previous month's issue of the *Dental Record* for which Richardson also wrote) in which a traditional neurologist outlines the success of Andrea Rabagliati in using a raw food and a fruitarian diet to help ease women's labour pains and postnatal recovery. If women's supposed disabilities can be alleviated through a 'rational diet,' Richardson reasons that this information is 'worth a very great deal to the Feminist movement, and should effectually arm even those who are at present pathological against orthodoxy's list of "inherent disabilities"' (ibid.). Marshalling both alternative medicine and simple-lifer philosophy, Richardson critiques and modifies masculinist scientific discourses, campaigning for a feminist gynaecology as well as a less-pathologising approach to medicine generally. The argument also proposes a distinctly modernist epistemology that challenges the nature of truth itself to deconstruct the sociopolitical processes through which knowledge is constructed and ratified and, in so doing, to reconfigure 'the distribution of the sensible' where women's bodies and public identities are concerned.

Richardson's many and intersecting commitments to the progressive politics of her day are further evident in that the footnote of Rabagliati's pamphlet, 'Conversations with Women,' lists Daniel as the publisher and Amen Corner, the small bookshop he opened in 1908 in Ludgate Hill, its place of publication. The 'Disabilities' article engages other voices too – not just the feminist readership of the *Freewoman* or the radical audience of Daniel's readers but also the more conventional, middle-class, and largely male readership of the *Dental Record*. This intersection between the diverse 'islands' or societies within the larger 'archipelago' of movements and societies around which Richardson navigated in the early 1900s speaks to her desire to unify without homogenising as she places diverse voices and discourses in dialogic encounter within the pages of early twentieth-century periodicals.

That Richardson viewed the 'little' magazine as a hospitable forum for diverse and often conflicting voices to interact is evident in 'The Original Impulse,' her second and much shorter intervention in the *Freewoman*. Here Richardson writes in response to Marsden's earlier editorial 'On Machines' in which Marsden argues that syndicalism, rather than socialism or capitalism, will prevent individuals from becoming slaves to machines and from making machines of humans to further their material interests. At the end of the editorial, Marsden maintains that '[m]achine-labour rests on an expropriated class' and reproaches those 'fine freewomen whose freedom requires the existence of a slave-class to keep it pink' (12 Sep 1912: 324). Though sympathetic to the simple life and anti-mechanisation movements, here Richardson's response to Marsden smacks more of a strategic essentialism. She opens the letter by rejecting Marsden's advocacy of free-land reform on the grounds that 'the mechanistic tendency . . . [is] the dominant characteristic of the human male' and concludes with the pragmatic suggestion that whether men are 'temporarily maimed by or inherently limited to mechanistic conceptions' is irrelevant as 'men are not likely in the near future to cease trying to live by them' (26 Sep 1912: 372).

At the same time, Richardson's is not a wholly essentialist logic. She resists Marsden's suggestions of 'calling women to the rescue' in returning society to a pre-mechanised and natural order: 'the original impulse' to which the title of the letter refers. Here the seeming incongruence of Richardson's proof attests, first, to the inherent incompletion of the epistolary form, whose meaning is contingent on the prior and absent dialogue to which it responds and, second, as with her interventions in the *Crank*, to Richardson's interest in the periodical as a means of intervening in and expanding realms of political discourse. As a fragment of a larger and ongoing public deliberation, Richardson's letter suggests that the author viewed the format and serialisation of the 'little' magazine as solid ground on which to lay new foundations for democratic debate amongst an ever-widening intersection of communities, discourses, and voices.

A 'shifting and provisional tool': Richardson's Epistemology in the *Saturday Review* and the *Dental Review*

Between 1908 and 1914, Richardson wrote twenty impressionistic sketches of rural life ('middles' as she called them) for the *Saturday Review*, a journal of politics, arts, and culture edited by Harold Hodge from the 1890s until 1913. In many ways studies for *Pilgrimage*, the *Saturday* middles defy absolute generic categorisation as they oscillate between representing the immediacy of initial experience and disinterested contemplation: 'not the scene itself,' as Rebecca Bowler has it, 'but the scene as perceived by someone with a rich, mediating consciousness' (2016: 200). At the same time, the middles are a cohesive body that, as Isobel Maddison observes of *Pilgrimage*, 'draws together the various strands of humanitarian reform central to the early twentieth-century Fabian agenda' and thus blurs 'simplistic generic distinctions like "political history" and "experimental literature"' (2010: 53). They also enjoy an afterlife in *Pilgrimage* as

Richardson incorporates descriptions, scenes, and characters, then dramatises Miriam's writing of them.[20] If *Pilgrimage* represents the culmination of Richardson's efforts to give 'contemplated reality [. . .] its own say,' the *Saturday* middles represent Richardson's earliest experiments toward this end (1979a: 9).

While not explicitly political, the experimentalism that informs Richardson's middles is itself a revolutionary attempt to reconfigure not only the terms of writing and narrative itself but also to uncover the subjective processes through which an individual's knowledge of her world is constructed. In 'The Wind' (1909), for instance, a modernist self-reflexivity is coupled with a subversive strain of sexuality and gender ambiguity that challenges fixed conceptions of gender. While 'A Sussex Auction' (1908) and 'A Sussex Carrier' (1909), Richardson's first two middles, adhere solely to third-person reportage, the use of second-person, personification, as well as present and future tenses in 'The Wind' breaks down textual priority and authority to highlight the reader's role in shaping meaning. The piece opens with a description of a quiet November afternoon bleeding into a night 'when the wind is still, when there is no rain to mitigate the sound of the ceaseless going to and fro, and sleep stands far off' and which she further describes as a 'full moment between memory and promise . . .' (4 Dec 1909: 691). Here the use of ellipses marks a transition as the subject (the 'you,' hence reader) enters into an intermediate state between memory and promise. But it also anticipates *Pilgrimage*'s signature use of ellipses to mark not only Miriam's contemplation but also to build in time for the reader to contemplate Miriam's own contemplation. In this way, as Anna Lindskog explains, ellipses are 'used to indicate passages in [*Pilgrimage*] where there is content below the surface of the words, a content that the reader must retrieve through contemplation' (2013–14: 8). Like Richardson's open letters in the *Crank*, the form of these *Saturday* middles calls attention to knowledge as provisional, in process, and intersubjectively constructed over time. While much more could be said about the epistemic implications of these middles, they provide clear evidence of the way in which, despite Richardson's transition from writing about society to writing about consciousness around 1908, her developing literary aesthetic continually seeks to create spaces of textual dissensus available for the 'reader's collaboration' (Kunitz 1933: 562).

Like the middles, Richardson's contributions to the *Dental Record*, a professional journal for which she penned over forty mainly anonymous articles between 1915 and 1922, also represent a curious body of work. As a dental assistant for a Harley Street practice from 1896 until 1908 when she began to write for the *Saturday*, Richardson had first-hand knowledge of the field.[21] 'Diet and Teeth,' the article to which Richardson alludes in 'The Disabilities of Women,' was one of only two such *Dental Record* articles to appear under her byline; the other was 'The Responsibility of Dentistry' (1913) (Figure 13.3). In this latter one, Richardson takes aim at a masculinist discourse of medicine 'whose prestige' she says 'was established in the days [late 1880s] before the characteristic limitations of the expert had been discovered' and has for her 'achieved a kind of tyranny' (1 Oct 1913: 635). For Richardson, dentistry must reject such Victorian discourse to embrace a modern epistemology whereby scientific '"[k]nowledge"' can be seen as 'a shifting and provisional tool' (ibid.). As Richardson reasons, because dentists know they cannot prevent teeth from decaying altogether, theirs is a field that, unlike 'medicine in its headlong career "stamping out" diseases,' could use that uncertainty to impel further investigation into the true causes of tooth decay (ibid.).

THE DENTAL RECORD.

Vol. XXXIII. October 1st, 1913. No. 10.

Original Communications.

THE RESPONSIBILITY OF DENTISTRY.

By Dorothy Richardson.

Twenty years ago the thing known as the "unanimous consensus of expert opinion" threatened to rule our daily life. It daunted even the toughest minds. It was the thing with which any sane enemy could be silenced. It was humanity's newest tool. To many very earnest and discriminating people it was the hope of the world. There had been, it is true, experts of sorts in the dim world of an earlier day; experts in vague questionable things—philosophy, theology, "art." But they rarely emerged from their fastnesses to challenge everyday humanity. They always seemed, as it were, a little askew from life. They did not offer a rational explanation of anything in particular. They made dogmatic statements which "the man in the street" could take or leave according to his temperament. One body of them, it is true, the theological, achieved a period of authority, practised coercion to the death and was, inevitably, overthrown.

"Science," the new learning, using the "common sense" of humanity—its faculties of observation and analysis—arose as it were over against these large dim things challenging and dissecting them, re-reading the data of consciousness and of authority and giving us a new world. Its genius, untrammelled by persecution, ranged free, threw out, like tentacles, hypothesis after hypothesis, enclosed and classified more and more facts, inspired group after group of experts, described, more and more minutely, the furniture of the universe.

Humanity began to wait upon its words. The world grew very dark. Life was overshadowed by something far worse than the threatenings of the theologians. The state of affairs is typified in that moment when an eminent scientist announced in the people's *vade mecum** that daily life would come to have to wait upon and be guided by the dictates of experts.

---

* Professor Karl Pearson in the Encycl. Brit.

Figure 13.3 Dorothy Richardson, 'The Responsibility of Dentistry.' The *Dental Record*. October 1913.

Richardson's distrust of 'expert' scientific knowledge is founded in a fear that scientific certainty would stunt medical advancements and future discoveries. Throughout her anonymous column, 'Comments by a Layman,' Richardson offers a 'lay' (though by no means untutored) perspective on diverse and notably contemporary issues: the relationships between medical access and social change, diet and mental health, and health care and identity politics. Given their sheer volume, these articles merit their own in-depth study, but our present interest is in the way they insert the voice of the non-specialist, the Lay(wo)man, into discourses otherwise reserved for the 'tyrannical' medical expert.

Just as the middles' experimentalism prioritises the individual's subjective encounters with the everyday, so do the 'Layman' articles prioritise the quotidian, inexpert encounters with modernity over the scientific, professional, and expert view. Though largely unsigned and therefore not attributed to a female author, the 'lay' voice is nonetheless counterposed to the masculinist voice of the expert, as if it is the laywoman's job to reinterpret details of modern medicine and place them in a larger context for ordinary men and women.[22] In this sense, the 'Layman' articles are more like editorials, disrupting the specialist professional journal with commentary of more general interest: the benefits of a fruitarian diet,[23] the dangers of seeing marriage's function as solely procreative, the importance of rhythmic movement ('the flow of vital energy') in increasing workers' productivity,[24] the need to train more female doctors in London's universities and hospitals,[25] and the social benefits of understanding the 'delinquent child' not as a criminal but as a figure deserving of social and material support.[26] Though there are sporadic attempts throughout the 'Layman' articles to address dentists' particular interests, the preponderance of these articles concerns the overall physical, social, and mental health of the diverse population that early twentieth-century dentists were likely to encounter.

Throughout, 'Comments by a Layman' insists on the value of the non-specialist's opinion, contributing to Richardson's development of an everyday democratic aesthetic, one that finds its apotheosis in *Pilgrimage* but is firmly rooted in Richardson's earliest periodical non-fiction. In the early 1900s, according to the British Dental Association (BDA), the number of Britons in need of dental care dramatically outstripped supply and the poor relied on home-care remedies, many of which only exacerbated the problem.[27] With the onset of the First World War, the issue of dental care again raised public interest as members of the armed forces were denied free access to care. But even access did not ensure dental health. Dentists did not have to officially register with the state until 1921, so treatments and protocols were far from uniform. Indeed, the stark class and social disparities that Britons' oral health highlighted in the early twentieth century might have been what prompted Richardson's preposterously apt claim that 'civilization is based upon the stability of molars' (1 Aug 1918: 38). If tongue-in-cheek, this assertion also clearly argues for the importance of the ordinary citizen understanding and engaging in a debate otherwise reserved for the medical expert.

By the close of 1919, Richardson had published five volumes of *Pilgrimage* and her work for the *Dental Record* was still going strong. In the first two paragraphs of her June 1919 column, written just seven months post-war, Richardson is war-weary. The first suggests that by sending a navy seaman to see a dentist the 'world seems to be a sort of conspiracy to make a chap suffer,' and the second item mocks the dubious and myopically optimistic logic of the suggestion 'at the opening of the Church Army of Limbless Men' that amputation would benefit the heart by making it work less (1 June 1919: 215). Richardson's gallows humour nods to the grim realities of post-war Britain: the need for soldiers to take advantage of long overdue state-sponsored dental care and for veterans to be reintegrated in civilian life. In the column's third and final item, Richardson launches a full-frontal attack on the male authoritarianism she believes has led to the post-war disarray of Europe.

The fervour of Richardson's argument in this section, 'A Dying World!', clearly explains the editors' prefatory note: 'We do not necessarily endorse these views' (1 June 1919: 214). Arguing against the exclusion of women as chief hospital administrators, Richardson rejects the injunction's founding premise that 'women display genius only in certain emotional spheres, not in action' (ibid.). Just as she argues for a revaluation of women's so-called disabilities in the *Freewoman*, here too Richardson turns falsely dichotomising logic on its head to observe that the assumption of women's ineffectuality is a product of the very male-driven misconceptions that led to the First World War and, now, the League of Nations (or, as she calls it, 'the world-wide league of policemen'). Calling this 'very general male assumption' evidence that '"authority" is a doomed weapon,' Richardson counters that '[f]orce is not power' (ibid.). Instead, she offers a different definition of power, not as an exercise of authority but as the capacity to empathise and engage with diverse others: 'Women might be defined as emotion active, perhaps. Emotion active is the principle of social life, the moving on, by the power of imaginative sympathy from self towards other selves. The desire for the welfare of the other selves' (ibid.). By looking to Richardson's eclectic contributions to equally eclectic early twentieth-century periodicals a picture begins to emerge, not only of a writer inventing new ways of representing lived experience but also of a writer viewing writing as itself a kind of life or society – an encapsulation of 'emotion active,' a 'moving on [. . .] from self to other selves.'

Writing itself as a means of 'moving on' – revolutionising the dominant and even residual cultures without leaving them entirely behind – is evident when we consider how Richardson's writing for these periodicals creates formal spaces for ever-widening spheres of modern gender identities, interlocutors, readers, and philosophies to emerge alongside modernist aesthetics that challenge the divide between the political and literary, the masses and the elite. Of course, it is possible to read Richardson's magnum opus, *Pilgrimage*, and her dogged desire to render individual consciousness in literary form as apolitical and elitist. Yet when placing Richardson's later modernist aesthetic alongside her earlier interventions in a variety of British periodicals, we can more accurately understand Richardson as a writer interested in finding forms and forums for democratic representation as democracy took shape in early twentieth-century Britain. In particular, we might think of her articles in the *Crank*, the *Freewoman*, the *Saturday Review*, and the *Dental Record* as attempts to engage aesthetically with the political question of women's status in a developing democracy. This repositioning will importantly allow us to challenge ingrained understandings of Richardson's modernist aesthetic as hermetic, elitist, and anti-democratic.

That the seeds of Richardson's revolutionary modernist aesthetic were germinated in little early twentieth-century periodicals is no mistake. After all, the very format of a periodical attests to the gaps, excisions, and contradictions inherent in any written work. Indeed, Richardson's work for early twentieth-century periodicals as well as modernist magazines attests to Peter Brooker and Andrew Thacker's contention that 'the relation of [modernist] magazines to a hegemonic mainstream [is] an active and changing set of relationships' (2012: 17).[28] Designed not to proselytise but rather to explore an active and changing set of relationships between the individual and political systems of representation, Richardson's writing for early twentieth-century periodicals was a revolution of aesthetic form in arenas where democracy was contested and defined. Further, this body of articles, editorials, and published letters is revolutionary in that it seeks alternative – namely, aesthetic – means through which to expand extant political distributions of the sensible by finding alternative systems of representation through which to explore the individual's experience in her rapidly changing world. Finally, Richardson's interventions in early twentieth-century periodicals develop a dialogic aesthetic whereby the written work is not conclusive but is instead dissensual: open to the reader's collaborative consciousness and thereby subject to modification. At stake in Richardson's experimental, modernist aesthetic is the idea of democracy not as a static institution or set of governmental regimes but rather as 'a state of mind' shaped by and accessible to any citizen willing to engage in the everyday art of creating, preserving, and broadening spaces of public dialogue and debate.

Notes

1. Sinclair first applied 'stream of consciousness' to literature in her review of *Pilgrimage*: 'In this series there is no drama, no situation, no set scene. Nothing happens. It is just life going on and on. It is Miriam Henderson's stream of consciousness going on and on' (*Egoist* Apr 1918: 58). Richardson rejected Sinclair's coinage, referring to it in derisory terms throughout her life.
2. Bryher, Letter to John Lehmann, 30 May 1959, Harry Ransom Center, University of Texas at Austin (Texas).
3. Many of these relationships are fictionalised in *Pilgrimage*: Richardson's affairs with Russian revolutionary, Benjamin Grad (Michael Shatov), and suffragette, Veronica Leslie-Jones (Amabel), as well as her friendship with Olga Sokoloff (Olga Feodorova), a Russian revolutionary she met while living in St John's Wood.
4. For more on Richardson's late nineteenth-century political and cultural influences, see McCracken 2007, especially Chapters 9 and 10.
5. (Translation slightly altered). Benjamin cites the letter at the beginning of Convolute N of *The Arcades Project*. Original emphasis.
6. Raymond Williams distinguishes the archaic 'which has been wholly or largely incorporated into the dominant culture' from the residual that 'is still active in the cultural process and, therefore, may have an alternative or even oppositional relation to the dominant culture' (1977: 122). For Williams, the emergent 'depends crucially on finding new forms or adaptations of form' (1977: 126).
7. For an earlier version of a similar argument see McCracken and Pritchett 2013–14.
8. This note is written in DMR's hand, across the top of a newspaper clipping of the article that belonged to its author ('The Russian and His Book'). The *Outlook* was the successor of W. E. Henley's *New Review*, and was a conservative and imperialist weekly in which Joseph Conrad, E. M. Forster, and Henry James were also published.
9. We have attempted to select work that has not been discussed extensively elsewhere. For a full discussion of Richardson's work for the *Dental Record*, for instance, see

the chapter, 'Dietetics and aesthetics' in McCracken 2007. For a critical anthology of Richardson's 'Continuous Performance' column for the film magazine, *Close Up*, see Donald et al. 1998.
10. Recently discovered letters from Richardson to the *Little Review* have shed further critical light on Richardson's unconventional and inconsistent use of punctuation. See Guy 2017.
11. On 15 May 2015, a blue plaque was unveiled on Woburn Walk in Bloomsbury at the site where Richardson lived opposite Yeats from 1905–6.
12. For an excellent account of more established modernist magazines in Britain, Ireland, and America, see Brooker and Thacker 2012.
13. *Despised and Rejected* by A. T. Fitzroy, the pseudonym of Rose Allatini (1890 – c. 1980), sympathetically depicted homosexuality and pacifism. Daniel disavowed any knowledge of homosexuality in the novel. It was republished in 1988 as part of the Gay Man's Press.
14. The SQS was later affiliated with *The Ploughshare* for which Richardson wrote one of her best known essays, 'The Reality of Feminism,' in 1917.
15. Daniel's description of modern socialism as 'soulless' is almost certainly a rejection of Oscar Wilde's aesthetic defence of socialism in 'The Soul of Man under Socialism' (1891).
16. Fernihough describes Richardson's prose style, along with D. H. Lawrence's, as marked by an 'anarchic individualism' that she reads as characteristic of Edwardian individualistic radicalism more generally (2013: 122).
17. See Laclau and Mouffe 1985.
18. See Richardson 1979b: 257.
19. For a critical history of this periodical, see Rabaté 2012.
20. Amongst those middles intratextually incorporated in *Pilgrimage* are: 'A Sussex Auction,' 'A Sussex Carrier,' 'Haven,' and 'The Wind.'
21. See Chapter 3 of Richardson 1979c, in which Richardson depicts Miriam's entire working day at the dental surgery.
22. For an earlier iteration of this argument, see McCracken 2007: 77.
23. See 'Diet and Teeth,' 1 August 1912. 553–6.
24. 'Comments by a Layman, 1 July 1916. 357–8, 358.
25. 'Comments by a Layman, 1 August 1916. 427–8, 428.
26. 'Comments by a Layman, 2 October 1916. 541–4, 544.
27. According to the BDA, in the first years of the 1900s, there was only one dentist per 8,500 people.
28. General Introduction to Brooker and Thacker 2012: 1–26 (17).

Works Cited

Anderson, Perry. 1984. 'Modernity and Revolution.' *The New Left Review* 144: 96–113.
Ardis, Ann L. 2002. '"Life is Not Composed of Watertight Compartments": *The New Age*'s Critique of Modernist Literary Specialization.' *Modernism and Cultural Conflict 1880–1922*. Cambridge: Cambridge University Press. 143–72.
Bakhtin, M. M. 1981. *The Dialogic Imagination: Four Essays*. Ed. Michael Holquist. Trans. Caryl Emerson and Michael Holquist. Austin: University of Texas Press.
Bowler, Rebecca. 2016. *Literary Impressionism: Vision and Memory in Dorothy Richardson, Ford Madox Ford, H.D. and May Sinclair*. London: Bloomsbury.
Brooker, Peter and Andrew Thacker, eds. 2012. *The Oxford Critical and Cultural History of Modernist Magazines*. 3 vols. Oxford: Oxford University Press.

Bryher, Letter to John Lehmann, 30 May 1959, Harry Ransom Center, University of Texas at Austin (Texas).
Donald, James, Anne Friedberg and Laura Marcus, eds. 1998. *Close Up: 1927–1933 Cinema and Modernism*. Princeton: Princeton University Press.
Fernihough, Anne. 2013. *Freewomen and Supermen: Edwardian Radicals and Literary Modernism*. Oxford: Oxford University Press.
Guy, Adam. 'Richardson and the *Little Review*.' Dorothy Richardson Website (Blog), 22 February 2017, <https://dorothyrichardsonblog.wordpress.com/2017/02/22/richardson-and-the-little-review/> (last accessed 20 June 2017).
Hall, Stuart. 1996. 'The Problem of Ideology: Marxism Without Guarantees.' *Critical Dialogues in Cultural Studies*. Ed. David Morley and Kuan-Hsing Chen. London: Routledge. 24–45.
Hirschkop, Ken. 1999. *Mikhail Bakhtin: An Aesthetic for Democracy*. Oxford: Oxford University Press.
Kunitz, Stanley, ed. 1933. 'Dorothy M. Richardson.' *Authors Today and Yesterday*. New York: H. W. Wilson.
Laclau, Ernesto and Chantal Mouffe. 1985. *Hegemony and Socialist Strategy: Towards a Radical Democratic Politics*. London: Verso.
Lefort, Claude. 1986. *Political Forms of Modern Society: Bureaucracy, Democracy, Totalitarianism*. Ed. and trans. John B. Thompson. Cambridge: Polity Press.
—. 1988. *Democracy and Political Theory*. Trans. David Macey. Cambridge: Polity Press.
Lindskog, Annika J. 2013–14. 'Dorothy Richardson and the Grammar of the Mind.' *Pilgrimages: A Journal of Dorothy Richardson Studies* 6: 6–24.
McCracken, Scott. 2007. *Masculinities, Modernist Fiction and the Urban Public Sphere*. Manchester: Manchester University Press.
McCracken, Scott and Elizabeth Pritchett. 2013–14. 'Plato's Tank: Aestheticism, Dorothy Richardson and the Idea of Democracy.' *Pilgrimages: A Journal of Dorothy Richardson Studies* 6: 84–106.
Maddison, Isobel. 2010. '"Trespassers will be Prosecuted": Dorothy Richardson Among the Fabians.' *Literature and History* 19.2: 52–68.
Marx, Karl. 1975. 'Letter to Arnold Ruge, Sep 1843.' *Early Writings*. Harmondsworth: Penguin. 209.
Rabaté, Jean-Michel. 2012. 'Gender and Modernism: *The Freewoman* (1911–12), *The New Freewoman* (1913), and *The Egoist* (1914–19).' *The Oxford Critical and Cultural History of Modernist Magazines*. 3 vols. Ed. Peter Brooker and Andrew Thacker. Oxford: Oxford University Press.
Rancière, Jacques. 2009. *Dissensus: On Politics and Aesthetics*. Trans. Steven Corcoran. London: Continuum.
—. 2014. *The Politics of Aesthetics*. Ed. and trans. Gabriel Rockhill. London: Bloomsbury Academic.
Richardson, Dorothy. [c. 1900.] Dorothy Richardson to Charlotte Perkins Gilman. Gilman Papers, Schlesinger Library, Radcliffe Institute for Advanced Study, Harvard University.
—. 1979a. 'Foreword.' *Pilgrimage*. 4 vols. London: Virago Press. 9–12.
—. 1979b. *Revolving Lights* (*Pilgrimage*, Volume III). London: Virago Press.
—. 1979c. *The Tunnel* (*Pilgrimage*, Volume II). London: Virago Press.
—. 1990a. 'About Punctuation.' *The Gender of Modernism: A Critical Anthology*. Ed. Bonnie Kime Scott. Bloomington and Indianapolis: Indiana University Press. 414–18.
—. 1990b. 'Adventure for Readers.' *The Gender of Modernism: A Critical Anthology*. Ed. Bonnie Kime Scott. Bloomington and Indianapolis: Indiana University Press. 425–9.
—. 1990c. 'Novels.' *The Gender of Modernism: A Critical Anthology*. Ed. Bonnie Kime Scott. Bloomington and Indianapolis: Indiana University Press. 432–5.

—. 1995a. 'Letter to Koteliansky, 1 Nov 1935.' *Windows on Modernism: Selected Letters of Dorothy Richardson*. Ed. Gloria G. Fromm. Athens: University of Georgia Press. 299.
—. 1995b. 'Letter to Peggy Kirkaldy, 28 July 1948.' *Windows on Modernism: Selected Letters of Dorothy Richardson*. Ed. Gloria G. Fromm. Athens: University of Georgia Press. 423–4.
'The Russian and His Book,' [unsigned], Article clipping from the *Outlook*, 10 (3 Oct 1902), 267–8, Box 10, Folder 267, Dorothy Richardson Collection, General Collection, Beinecke Rare Book and Manuscript Library, Yale University (New Haven).
Walter, Nicolas. 2011. *Damned Fools in Utopia: And Other Writings on Anarchism and War Resistance*. Ed. David Goodway. Oakland, CA: PM Press.
Williams, Raymond. 1977. *Marxism and Literature*. Oxford: Oxford University Press.

14

Violet Hunt, Periodical Culture, and Emergent (Female) Modernisms

Louise Kane

Introduction

As the author of twenty novels, three story collections, and over seventy contributions to periodicals, Violet Hunt (1862–1942) was a prolific and highly productive writer. After her first publication in 1879 – a poem in *Scribner's Monthly* – Hunt produced several non-fiction works, including *The Story of Westminster Abbey* (1902), while also carving out a name for herself as the author of female-centred 'New Woman' novels, including *The Maiden's Progress* (1894), *A Hard Woman* (1895), *The Workaday Woman* (1906), *White Rose of Withered Leaf* (1908), and *The Wife of Altamont* (1910). Through the 1910s and 1920s, Hunt continued to produce novels. She also published a supernatural short-story collection, *Tales of the Uneasy* (1911) along with several pieces of poetry, short stories, letters, and reviews in periodicals including the *English Review*, *Poetry*, *Outlook*, the *Fortnightly Review*, and the *Nation and Athenaeum*. Her final publication, *The Wife of Rossetti: Her Life and Death* (1932), a biography of Elizabeth Siddall, espoused her lifelong interests in art history and the Pre-Raphaelite movement. The Hogarth Press declined to publish it, although Hunt's papers contain a letter from Virginia Woolf praising the study for its wealth of information ('Letter' 7 Oct 1932).

Despite her considerable *oeuvre*, however, Hunt's literary achievements and her leverage of the periodical as a medium through which she published a diverse array of work – frequently politicised and focused on female experience – have remained critically neglected and overshadowed by her personal life. Her status as the hostess of the 'South Lodge' literary salons and her affairs with several married lovers, including Ford Madox Ford and Oswald Crawfurd, have received particular attention, but few attempts have been made to recover Hunt in her own right. As Bonnie Kime Scott has recognised, 'Violet Hunt has survived chiefly in personal anecdotes, while her reading of modernism and the merits of her own writing have been largely ignored' (1996: 56). Many of Hunt's contemporaries were also quick to assess her personally instead of professionally. She was 'at one time [. . .] a bright star in the London Bohemian literary world,' Marie Belloc claimed, 'but never, in any way, what was ordinarily called 'Society'' (Lowndes Marques 2007: 96). Belloc's was one of the more generous criticisms. Aware of Hunt's status as the daughter of Alfred Hunt, the Pre-Raphaelite painter who counted Wilde and Ruskin as regular visitors, several of Hunt's peers questioned the validity of her own literary connections and society pedigree. The painter W. Graham

Robertson ungraciously dismissed Hunt as an 'awful pig . . . among that circle [the Pre-Raphaelite Brotherhood] though never of it . . . and she *does* know a good many things with which the public has no concern' (Robertson 1953: 107). Joan Hardwick's attempt at 'bringing Violet Hunt once more to the forefront' began to redress the critical legacy that has 'woefully underestimated' Hunt's works (1990: xiii), but most recent scholarship continues to be framed by the figure of Ford Madox Ford.[1]

Rather than using an approach centred primarily on biographical detail, this chapter proposes a re-evaluation of Violet Hunt's literary work through a framework that takes into account intersections and overlaps between new modernist studies, modernist periodical studies, feminist media history, and feminist periodical studies. A decade ago, Latham and Scholes argued that the 'the rapid expansion of new media technologies' evidenced in the proliferation of new electronic archives, projects like the Modernist Journals Project (MJP), and the wider digital humanities, would inevitably necessitate scholars to view periodicals 'as texts requiring new methodologies and new types of collaborative investigation' (2006: 517). The publication of several recent studies focusing on the intersections between women, print culture, feminist criticism, and periodicals illustrates this collaborative investigation. Lucy Delap and Maria DiCenzo, Ann Ardis, and Catherine Clay have conducted important studies into the ways magazines like the *Freewoman*, the *New Age*, and *Time and Tide* stimulated and supported the development of uniquely female 'periodical communities' (Delap 2000: 270) and 'friendship networks' (Delap and DiCenzo 2008: 56) that operated behind and between their pages.[2]

The result of these studies is a sense of reclamation, a reminder of the fact that before and alongside the 'Men of 1914' – the generation of male writers whose work has become enshrined as part of modernism's canon – many women writers were already working hard to produce, procure publication of, and receive good payment for their own literary works, striking deals with publishing houses and negotiating fees and payments for their skills in writing, editing, and translation. This is no more apparent than in the pages of periodicals, a medium uniquely geared toward providing women writers not only with the prestige of publication, but with the ability to showcase and convey literary innovation in an immediate fashion. For some women writers, periodicals represented the opportunity to pioneer and document modernism's evolving experimental aesthetic. In the early 1910s, Katherine Mansfield worked hard to rejuvenate and internationalise John Middleton Murry's magazine *Rhythm*; Harriet Monroe established *Poetry: A Magazine of Verse* and Margaret Anderson founded the *Little Review*. For others, periodicals were political tools. The increasing momentum of the suffrage movement in the early twentieth century saw several female editors and writers exploit the periodical as a medium with a unique ability to stir debate and discussion, with publications like Teresa Billington-Greig's *Hour and the Woman* producing a sort of feminist periodical counterculture that chimed against the prevalent anti-suffrage ethos of popular periodicals like the *New Age*.

This chapter explores how Hunt used periodicals to develop her literary reputation and engage in writerly experimentation that saw her work evolve from unsure juvenilia to confident, highly stylised examples of prose fiction and poetry. Firstly, I argue that although Hunt's earliest periodical publications were largely conservative in the Victorian sense, the 1890s saw Hunt begin to experiment with forward-looking, progressive themes and formal experiments that were proto-feminist and proto-modernist.[3] Secondly, I assert that the 1910s marked Hunt's movement into a new network of periodicals, her publications reflecting distinctly modern tendencies in their formal experimentation and engagement with the suffrage movement, ongoing war, and other political concerns. Underpinning these lines of inquiry is the argument that Hunt was increasingly conscious of the power of her chosen medium. Faye Hammill has emphasised the need for scholars and contemporary readers to continue 'theorizing magazines as media' (2015: 7), but it is important to remember that early twentieth-century writers like Hunt were amongst the first readers to view periodicals in this way. Indeed, Hunt's later discussion of how Ford consciously designed the *English Review* as a form of alternate media, a magazine that aimed to use 'distinction of individuality or force of conviction' to undercut the 'glitter of a popular statement,' (Hunt 1926: 26–7) suggests that she possessed an acute awareness of the periodical as a medium uniquely able to communicate frequently politicised ideas and arguments to receptive, sometimes reactive, audiences.

With this in mind, I explore how Hunt published in certain periodicals as part of a conscious, targeted agenda. Far from acting as passive vessels through which she happened to grasp at publication, Hunt capitalised on the unique opportunities afforded to her by an increasingly heterogeneous print culture, choosing to publish in certain magazines due to their ability to frame and ensure the impact of select ideas or concerns. This approach is twofold: primarily, it allows us to view Hunt as a literary figure in her own right, a brilliant but often sidelined writer who was more than capable of directing and controlling her own career; additionally, it reasserts the now familiar dictum of modern periodical studies that periodicals, too, must be viewed in their own right as 'autonomous objects of study' (Latham and Scholes 2006: 519).

Inevitably, the fact that she wrote across the nineteenth and twentieth centuries means that this chapter raises questions about how we periodise the work of writers like Hunt. Despite their temporal positioning at the metaphorical 'book ends' of the late Victorian and late modernist periods (her first publication appeared in 1879, her last in 1932), Hunt's periodical publications possess threads of aesthetic and stylistic continuity that challenge the critical parcelling of literary tendencies and genres, and indeed periodicals, into neatly labelled groupings indicated by the terms 'Victorian' and 'modernist.' Another debate that this chapter references is the apparent 'modernism/ mass culture' binary. While Hunt sought publication in quintessentially modernist magazines like the *English Review*, she also wrote for large circulation periodicals, complicating the familiar paradigm of the modernist writer's apparent anxiety about mass culture and popular discourse.

Beginnings: Early Experiments

After gaining her first publication with 'An Invitation,' a twenty-line poem published in *Scribner's Monthly* when she was a seventeen-year-old pupil at South Kensington Art School, throughout the 1880s, Hunt published poetry in several magazines, including *Belgravia*, *Longman's Magazine*, and *Chambers's Journal of Popular Literature, Science and Arts*. Much of her early poetry was heavily influenced by Oscar Wilde and exhibited a strong use of classical myth and adapted fairy tale.[4] While this poetic style remained largely unchanged during this period, her engagement with periodicals was strikingly diverse, reflecting at least an emerging self-awareness of the need to market her work to different readerships. The periodicals Hunt sent her work to connoted divergent audiences and literary interests. *Scribner's* was a New York-based 'Illustrated Magazine for the People'; with a circulation of 127,000 monthly readers, its editor, Josiah Gilbert Holland, promoted the periodical as a purveyor of 'popular magazine literature' for 'a public not only in America, but in Great Britain and nearly all the British colonies' (Dec 1874: 248). In contrast to *Scribner's*, *Longman's* was a British periodical noticeably more 'literary' in its outlook, with contributors including Thomas Hardy, Margaret Oliphant, and Henry James. *Belgravia*, edited by the sensation novelist Mary Elizabeth Braddon, was a popular London illustrated magazine with a strong female readership, and *Chambers's Journal* was an accessible one-penny weekly best known for its serialised fiction.

Although there is little evidence suggesting Hunt shaped her early work to 'fit' different readerships, her strategic pursuit of publication across different periodical networks demonstrates how Hunt capitalised on the expanding breadth of a capacious periodical market that saw exponential growth in the late 1800s. As her 1892 diary entry reflects, Hunt now conceived of herself as a writer 'steadily building a career in journalism and fiction' (Hughes 2005: 155); publication across divergent periodicals allowed Hunt to forge a career independent of her family's legacy and to establish herself amongst as wide an audience as possible.

Recent attempts to recover the work of neglected female writers through modernist periodicals have demonstrated the increasing self-awareness women possessed as they embarked on careers as writers and journalists. As Barbara Green has noted, '[t]he archive of early twentieth-century periodicals offers new ways of understanding the figure of the author, the category of the woman writer' (2013: 58). The development of online archives like the Hathi Trust that provide instant accessibility and 'flipbook' viewing of magazines has also enabled a greater understanding of the ways women writers utilised the periodical and 'encourages us to recover not the single woman writer, but the network, the dialogue, the conversation' (ibid.). In the modernist period women writers developed strong networks of mutual publication. Dora Marsden gave Rebecca West her first publication in the *Freewoman*; May Sinclair published a highly favourable review of Dorothy Richardson's *Pilgrimage* in the *Egoist* at a point when Richardson desperately needed more promotion for the multi-volume novel, which led to Margaret Anderson personally soliciting the fifth installment, *Interim*, for serialisation in the *Little Review* (Joyce et al. 2015: 407). Hunt was 'instrumental' in securing the publication of West's 'Indissoluble Matrimony' in Wyndham Lewis's *BLAST* (Scott 1996: 57). Yet it is important to note that at the early stages of Hunt's career, prior to this mutual female networking, Hunt was networking independently, her publications in various periodicals evidencing her singular determination to advance her own literary career, rather than the careers of other women writers.

The 1890s: Early Experiments: The Short Story and Serialisation

Hunt's new-found determination can be seen in her emergence in 1892 from a five year 'gap' during which she failed to publish. A poet until this point, she now began to experiment with prose fiction. She published the short stories 'Old Scores' (1892) and 'A Sin Against Love' (1893) in the illustrated monthly *Black and White*, began drafting her first novels, *The Maiden's Progress* (1894) and *A Hard Woman* (1895), and simultaneously branched into other literary genres. In keeping with the 'dialogue' format of *The Maiden's Progress*, in September 1894 she published 'The Tenth Wave,' a short, melodramatic play depicting two lovers caught in a shipwreck, in the *English Illustrated Magazine*. In March 1895 she contributed 'Reminiscences of a Portrait Painter,' a review of the German-English portrait artist Rudolph Lehmann's *Artist's Reminiscences*, to *Current Literature*. In April 1895 she published a short story, 'The Encore,' in the *English Illustrated Magazine*.

'The Encore' exemplifies Hunt's use of the short story genre as a means of engaging with the themes of womanhood, society, and female experience that became hotly debated as the 'New Woman' movement gained momentum. The story's protagonist, a young concert singer named Emily Quick, exemplifies the proto-feminist spirit of Hunt's prose fiction. Emily Quick 'had no lover.' She is independent, having 'gained her living' entirely through her own musical talent, even if that means living in 'one dingy room in a flat' (Apr 1895: 91). Yet Emily's feminism is lost to the world. When she falls ill the male doctor in the hospital sees only a 'poor girl' who needs to be 'looked after' (Apr 1895: 94). Emily dies, seemingly out of choice: 'Oh, why must I go on living? . . . The song's done. I did my best . . . It's all over . . .' (ibid.). The death of the female proto-feminist protagonist here is symbolic; female independence is still perceived through a mistaken public perception of pathos and pity: with Emily's death dies the dream of enduring female equality. By publishing this piece in the *English Illustrated Magazine* – a popular London-based monthly with a fairly high circulation – Hunt reached a readership featuring 'adults of different kinds of reading sophistication' (Sillars 2004: 78) while simultaneously publicising her feminist characters to the more intellectual, literary readership of *Cosmopolis*, the multilingual, upmarket monthly literary review in which she published another proto-feminist story, 'The Truth, the Whole Truth,' in 1896.

At this point, Hunt's poetry also becomes increasingly vocal in its assertion of female independence. While her early poems were somewhat naïve, her 1890s poems are characterised by strong female speakers and fleeting, disappointing love affairs in which men are incapable of understanding female emotion. 'Faith Unfaithful,' published in the *Speaker: the liberal review*, concludes with the female speaker offering a scathing statement of resignation: 'Let's have an end of memory, Forget that you were ever mine . . . I never loved you, nor you me' (Oct 1892: 172). Hunt revisits her emotionally cool, disillusioned female speaker more fully in another *Speaker* poem, 'Livre D'amour,' offering a similarly matter-of-fact conclusion: 'The story's told of you and me. Why add a sequel to it?' (Mar 1897: 350). A magazine whose contributors included Joseph Conrad and Arthur Conan Doyle, the *Speaker* was a distinctly left-wing publication, its liberal politics espoused in the magazine's refusal to support the Second Anglo-Boer War and promotion of Free Trade. Arguably, Hunt may have viewed the liberal, forward-thinking agenda of the *Speaker* as more suited to her pro-female poetry, but it is also likely that, like any emerging writer, she desired publication in an established magazine well known for its high quality contributions and intellectually refined audience.

As her early short stories and increasingly outspoken poetry reflect, the 1890s saw Hunt capitalise on the development of an increasingly feminised periodical press that accompanied *fin de siècle* constructions of the New Woman and contemporary debates about the 'Woman Question.' Whereas the early Victorian periodical press was 'dominated' by 'polite and scholarly' (Brake and Demoor 2009: 538) reviews, with *Blackwood's* and the *Quarterly* catering primarily to the tastes of educated, conservative male readers, by the 1880s a new subset of magazines was reshaping the periodical scene: the woman's magazine, its rise bolstering female writers' confidence in exploring proto-feminist narratives and simultaneously legitimatising the idea of women working professionally as journalists and editors.[5] Magazines like the *Lady's Realm*, established in 1886, amassed a growing readership of upper-class women and celebrated the fact that 'on almost all the various departments of the papers women are at work' as 'interviewers, reporters, paragraphists, essayists, critics, and descriptive writers' (May–Oct 1897: 467). *Woman's World*, edited by Oscar Wilde from 1887–9, only employed female journalists whose works he solicited personally. *Woman* appeared in 1890, followed by *Woman at Home* in 1893, and many periodicals began incorporating special 'women's pages' specifically geared toward nurturing and retaining female readerships.[6] This revolution in the periodical press offered writers like Hunt the opportunity to pursue careers in writing with greater conviction. As Margaret Beetham has recognised:

> For women, the new press seemed to offer much. Firstly, it identified women as important targets for its marketing and as central to its readership. Secondly, women began to move into journalism and authorship as paid professionals in increasing numbers. In addition to these more evident and even quantifiable changes . . . [d]ebates about gender and sexuality, and particularly about women's social and political roles became the subject of much journalistic interest. (2006: 234)

For Hunt, the newly feminised press offered another benefit: literary serialisation. Since Chapman and Hall's serialisation of Dickens's *The Pickwick Papers* in pamphlet form between 1836 and 1837, Victorian authors were conscious of the opportunities serialisation offered, including a regular income, widespread promotion, and a vastly enlarged potential readership. Hunt was careful to secure serialisation at an early point in her career. Her first novel, *The Maiden's Progress* (1894), was serialised across *Black and White*, the *Pall Mall Gazette* and *Sketch*. Again, the different nature of these periodicals shows how Hunt aimed for a wide-ranging readership for her novels. Winnie Chan describes *Black and White* as a popular illustrated magazine 'conceived to court both sides of a growing divide between high art and mass culture,' (2007: 103) and Hunt's recollection of the periodical as a 'frankly commercial' magazine 'on which I spent the best blood of my girlhood' (1926: 26) fits this characterisation. In contrast, *Sketch* was a more highbrow illustrated weekly society magazine that pinpointed high society and aristocracy as its key interests.

That Hunt could publish a New Woman novel like *The Maiden's Progress* in a predominantly conservative magazine like the *Sketch* attests to her ability to network with and successfully market herself to magazine editors. Hunt's networking was at once deliberate and opportunistic: she sought out opportunities to see her name in print, and alongside the more traditional method of sending work for consideration, Hunt gained publicity by sending various reactive 'letters to the Editor' to well-known publications like the *Spectator* and the *Nation*. In one such letter – 'The Censorship of

Plays' – Hunt responded to the Lord Chamberlain's Office's controversial shutdown of Edward Garnett's *The Breaking Point* by arguing that 'the censorship of plays should be reformed,' the Office replaced instead with an independent committee of assessors (*Nation* 23 Nov 1907: 274). Her presence in the *Nation* – a political magazine whose contributors debated socialism, suffrage, and 'The Future of Unionism' in the regular 'Politics and Affairs' column – marks her adoption of a new style of public, politicised writing, one which manifested most fervently in the 1910s as Hunt became increasingly involved with the 'Votes for Women' movement.

The 1910s: Becoming Modern(ist)

By 1909 Hunt, now aged forty-seven, had been writing for periodicals for some thirty years and was 'one of the leading women writers of her time' (Goldring 1943: 42). She was also now 'writing as a Suffragette' (Hunt 1926: 209). Having joined the Women Writers' Suffrage League in 1908, Hunt was committed to 'the cause,' raising collection money from passers-by at Kensington High Street Station and working with contemporaries like May Sinclair to fight 'injustices against women' (Hunt 1926: 129). Her engagement with the *Nation* and the *New Age* would have fuelled her renewed commitment to attaining the vote. In an issue of the *Nation* published just three weeks prior to Hunt's letter about censorship, an anonymous female writer wrote an impassioned letter outlining the case for 'a limited bill for women's suffrage' that would 'enfranchise a large proportion of working women, both professional and wage earning,' and protect them from 'the disability of marriage' (*Nation* 2 Nov 1907: 129).

Hunt's early twentieth-century periodical contributions dovetail with this rallying cry. Since the publication of *The Maiden's Progress*, Hunt's novels had developed an increasing degree of candidness and daring in their depictions of women. For some critics Hunt had gone too far. *The Celebrity at Home*, for example, attracted clamorous disdain:

> the heroine, or the chief character . . . whatever you like to call her, is one of these child-woman-devils. Almost at the very beginning she says that it is nice to do what you like even if it isn't good for you. And she acts up . . . She *does* do exactly as she likes, and gets everyone into all sorts of scrapes and taxes. (*Egoist* 1 Jan 1914: 17–18)

By the 1910s Hunt began to use the novelty of the modernist periodical, with its catalysis of increasingly radical ideas, politics, and literary techniques, to her advantage. The publication of 'The Coach' in the March 1909 issue of Ford Madox Ford's (then Hueffer) *English Review* reflects Hunt's framing of pro-female, or pro-feminist ideas through modernist textual experimentation. Established in December 1908, the *English Review* was quintessentially 'new.' Aiming 'to start a Movement and . . . to found a 'school'' (Goldring 1935: 25) and championing of relatively new writers like Pound, Lawrence, and Mansfield, characterised it as a magazine whose originality derived largely from its gradual supplementing of older, comfortable values with new modes of radical modernist literary experiment. This comfortable convergence of 'old' and 'new' is embodied in 'The Coach.' In a scene reminiscent of the train journey Woolf would imagine in 'Mr. Bennett and Mrs. Brown,' Hunt begins by describing her subject, a young woman who shocks the carriage by sharing that she earns her living by 'baby-farming,'[7] in the externalised 'Edwardian' manner Woolf decried:

> The woman opposite her belonged as unmistakably to the people. She was hard-featured, worn with a life of sordid toil and calculation, but withal stout and motherly, a figure to inspire the fullest confidence. She wore a black bonnet with strings and black silk gloves heavily darned. (Mar 1909: 667)

However, Hunt soon probes the psyche of the baby-farmer via an unspoken internalised monologue detailing her innermost thoughts: her doubts about her profession, status within society, and sense of injustice that men are relieved of the task of looking after children. The story concludes with a strange, supernatural vision that erodes any sense of textual realism. In an example of how the materiality of publication affects its meaning, Hunt's tale was placed immediately before Conrad's 'Some Reminiscences,' creating an effect in which her prose seems to echo Conrad's use of impressionistic narration and confused temporality. This placement is also a neat emblem of Hunt's increasing networking with defiantly modernist writers: as her affair with Hueffer began shortly after the publication of 'The Coach,' she was soon able to count Hueffer, Pound, Lawrence, West, and Conrad himself as regular visitors who literally 'sat alongside her' (Goldring 1943: 82) during her now thriving literary salons at South Lodge.

Between 1913 and 1915, Hunt's affiliation with a new journal – the *Outlook* – marked the beginning of her engagement in a new form of discourse: the manifesto. At this point, the manifesto had already become synonymous with the little magazines: owing to the immediate nature of its periodicity, the magazine was a medium perfectly placed to showcase the urgency, and sometimes controversial nature, of its editor's beliefs. Wyndham Lewis's *BLAST* remains the best-known example of this use of the manifesto-magazine hybrid, the bright puce-coloured, oversized periodical asserting its infamous 'blasts' and 'blessings' through its now equally infamous bold typeface. Yet an earlier example of this hybrid magazine form exists in Douglas Goldring's the *Tramp*. Published from March 1910 to March 1911, the *Tramp* asserted itself as a new publication combining 'the literary distinction of the *English Review* . . . with the commercial success of *Country Life*' (Goldring 1935: 105), its title deriving from the distinct type of outdoor rambling or 'tramping' that W. H. Davies had made famous through his *Autobiography of a Super-Tramp* (1908). The *Tramp*'s declaration of its curious combination of literary refinement and comfortable Edwardian 'little England' values appeared almost as a manifesto in itself, the heralding of a new type of heterogeneous magazine that pitted experimental contents like Wyndham Lewis's 'Breton Innkeeper' against advertisements for camping gear, luxury hotels like 'The Savoy,' and the gentleman's 'Masta Pipe.' Yet it was Goldring's publication of Marinetti's Futurist Manifesto in August 1910 – the same issue as Lewis's short story – that captured the magazine's irreverent sense of militant experimentation and showcased the modernist manifesto in a manner that *BLAST* later repeated.

Initially, Hunt's publication of a quaint story, 'The Little Spark of Blue Bonnet,' in the March 1910 issue of the *Tramp* seems surprising. Set in the Yorkshire moors, the story depicts a well-heeled tourist party stumbling across the manor house of the

Daunet family who participated in the Jacobite Rebellion of 1715. Yet in 1910, as nascent modernism became less a new term and more an increasingly universal movement, Hunt's decision to publish in a magazine like the *Tramp* shows two things. Firstly, Hunt was now attempting to gain publication in a magazine whose contributors were defiantly modern. For example, the *Tramp*'s publication of the Futurist manifesto and Wyndham Lewis confirmed its commitment to a newly experimental, defiantly modernist aesthetic. Secondly, she was actively using her connections to gain publication in these new modernist magazines: Goldring had originally served as subeditor of Hueffer's *English Review*.

In a move that confirms this awareness of her changing style, Hunt's new association with another periodical, the *Outlook*, documented her own negotiations with the emerging modernist aesthetic of the early 1910s. Her first *Outlook* publication, 'Victorian Swan Song,' explores her tension between the realms of the Victorian and the modern: 'I seem . . . to be sitting disconsolate in a world of toppling standards, of wrecked ideals, of neglected literary conventions – conventions which in my saner modern moods I realise were meant to be disregarded' (11 Oct 1913: 498). Torn between the formula of a 'beginning, a middle, and an end,' and the need to listen to her internalised 'more modern mentor,' she surrenders herself to the 'regenerative influence' of 'modern literature' (ibid.). The consciousness of Hunt's tone is reminiscent of the manifesto form; aware of the fact that she was on the cusp of something new, Hunt debates her own place within the older and emergent modern traditions.

Throughout the mid to late 1910s, Hunt continued to alter not only her prose, but also her poetic style. In 'A Call in Hell,' published in Harriet Monroe's new magazine *Poetry: a Magazine of Verse*, Hunt advances a modernist poetics that anticipates the Imagist movement that would soon explode through the pages of *Poetry* and the *Egoist*:

> The door opens on Chinoiseries.
> The mild white maid with many frills
> Stands expectant.
> There are curtains at her back
> Hot and red – no grey.
> It is the East in Cromwell Road,
> The East where man is polygamous
> And without reproach. (Feb 1915: 219–20)

The poem is the embodiment of the signature Imagist experience of being paradoxically 'out of time' and yet visually anchored to one's surroundings, a throwback to Pound's 'In a Station of the Metro' that had appeared in the magazine some two years previously. 'What the Civilian Saw' (*Poetry,* Mar 1917) continued in this new modernist-Imagist vein, appearing in the same issue as poems by Amy Lowell herself. It seemed that Hunt's periodical community had changed. No longer the front cover 'draw' of illustrated magazines, her output was now characterised by a sense of economy, quiet contemplation, and political agenda, as evidenced in publications like 'Germans in Joyous Gard' (*Outlook*, Apr 1915), 'Why the Workman Enlists' (*Nation*, Sep 1915), and 'Is it Worthwhile' (*Poetry*, Apr 1918).

Conclusions: Late Periodical Contributions and Challenges

Yet the narrative of Hunt's movement from 'Victorian' to 'modernist' periodicals is problematic. Firstly, along with publishing in modernist magazines like *Poetry* and the *Egoist*, Hunt was simultaneously publishing in popular reviews and magazines. In 1910 she contributed to the *Tramp*, but she also published 'The Witness' in the *Fortnightly Review*, a somewhat whimsical, sensationalistic story that depicting a murderous love affair. The *Fortnightly*, a long-standing, Victorian-established periodical, featured some modernist contributors but was by no means overtly experimental. Secondly, the uncomfortable possibility arises that Hunt may simply have been engaging with modernist periodicals out of a desire to stay topical or to follow Hueffer's more modernist endeavours. It was, after all, through her connection to Hueffer that she published in the *Tramp* and the *Outlook* (Ford's multi-issue 'Literary Portraits' series began publication in the *Outlook* just one issue prior to the issue in which Hunt's 'Victorian Swan-Song' appeared).

As the 1920s dawned and modernism's energy began to diffuse, Hunt returned to more conventional publications and prose styles. 'The Death of Hudson' and 'The Bull Ring for Rabbits' both appeared in the *English Review* in 1923 and 1924 respectively, but neither story was particularly modernist. The publication of 'Read, Mark,' another sensational short story, in the *Saturday Review* in early 1922 signified the beginning of Hunt's association with the magazine, but this association saw Hunt publish anecdotal, memoir-style articles, such as the five-part 'The Beginning of the Pre-Raphaelites' series that the magazine published weekly throughout August 1931. 'Mr. Swift MacNeill and Mr. Ruskin,' published in the *Nation and Athenaeum* in June 1925 was also an anecdotal article, along with her last periodical publication, 'Arnold Bennett in Paris,' which appeared in the *Bookman* in August 1932.

However, rather than seeing Hunt's contradictory engagements with modernism as a sign that she was a sort of turncoat modernist – a woman writer who dabbled in modernism whimsically, perhaps to 'keep up' with her peers, before returning to conventional forms – I would like to suggest that the problem with how we view writers like Hunt lies in the way we view and study periodicals themselves. As Latham and Scholes pointed out, the 'still-emergent' nature of modernist periodical studies means we do not yet know how to really theorise periodicals (2006: 517). There is 'a lack of communication across fields' that has led to 'the divide between all things "Victorian" or "traditional" and all things "modern" or "modernist" ... between high and low culture; and the divide between art (or modernist high seriousness, more particularly) and everyday life' (Hammill 2015: 4–5).

Instead of functioning as divided spaces, periodicals were heterogeneous print cultures which unified these divides. A magazine like the *Outlook* may have contained some modernist stories, but its *raison d'être* was to engage with debates about current, everyday life against which modernism is so often assumed to be opposed. This unification is evident in another publication in which Hunt published: the *Century*. The Victorian publication site of Hunt's highly stylised early poetry some thirty years earlier, the magazine was still in existence until the 1930s. It thus 'bridged' the Victorian and modernist periods, but is hardly considered a modernist magazine, even though it serialised quintessentially modern fiction like H. G. Wells's *The World Set Free*. As

Serres and Latour's work suggests, periodicals like the *Century* are multi-temporal in their long lifespans: they 'reveal a time that is gathered together, with multiple pleats' (1995: 60). The point is that many of the periodicals Hunt began to publish in later in her career – especially those like the *Tramp* – were capacious, heterogeneous, and variegated repositories, but our focus on defining them as 'modernist' or 'Victorian' obscures this temporal gathering. As Delap and DiCenzo have argued, in some ways 'modernism' is 'too selective and distorting a framework' through which to explore periodicals; a useful 'point of reference,' but a 'problematic' framework 'for the analysis of press and periodical history' (2008: 49). Of course, some periodicals were set up to pioneer a distinctly 'new' modernist form and aggressively rallied against older conventions, but, in an era in which the term was barely present either in writing or in speech, the periodical's function was to provide space for experimentation, not to define its writers forevermore. In this light, we might consider writers like Hunt as engaging in forms of experiment that were not always consciously fashioned in line with a particular 'school' or movement, but fashioned in such a way that reflected the periodical's natural 'openness': the magazine was a place where writers like Hunt could experiment with what it meant to be 'modern' in publications which were negotiating the very same question. Publishing in a Victorian periodical does not necessarily make a writer a lifelong conventionalist and publishing in a modernist magazine like *Poetry* does not necessarily make a writer like Hunt irreversibly 'modernist.'

This blurs the distinction between what it means to be 'Victorian' or 'modernist.' The wide range of publications Hunt published in, including periodicals with high circulations, mass readerships, elite literary audiences, and magazines with just a few thousand subscribers shows that Hunt networked across the perceived 'great divides' between mass and modernist and between Victorian and modern print cultures (Ardis 2012: vi). Her works, although evolving in their style and concerns, were nonetheless knitted together by an overarching thread of self-awareness, a narrative style that framed provocative questions with scenes and situations utilising traditional, conservative themes like love and marriage, 'truth,' and characters who often embodied 'olde worlde' values or chivalrous ideal, that, like the interconnected 'pleats' of the *Century*, draws the periodicals in which she published into a close, yet paradoxically distant, grouping.

Her publications also challenge what it means to be a networking woman writer. Unlike many female writers, Hunt's networking was most frequently self-serving, undertaken not to generate networks of feminist counterculture through periodicals, but to achieve the publication of her literature and its wider aims and messages. In keeping with this, Hunt's engagement with periodicals was not borne out of a conscious desire to become a modernist per se, but to capitalise on and explore, like many other women writers included in this volume, the experimental space offered by modernist magazines, to enter into new communities and cultures of literary production that were exciting and innovative. Like Miss Varney in Hunt's story 'His Widows,' who 'read all the modern magazines, and kept herself up to date,' (*Cornhill Magazine* Aug 1899: 220), so too did Hunt. After her death in 1942, amongst her possessions were found various copies of magazines: *Rhythm*, the *Tramp*, two issues of the modern poetry magazine the *Thrush*, one *Smart Set*, the *Fortnightly Review*, one *Hour and the Woman* on suffrage tactics, a *Revue pour Les Jeune Filles*, a copy of *Scribner's* from 1880, and issues of the *Cornhill*, the *Anglo-American Magazine*,

Pearson's Magazine, and *Macmillan's* were just some of the periodicals Hunt had read and treasured ('List of Magazines,' n.d.). In many ways, these magazines are representative of Hunt and her writing: ambitious and eclectic, resisting easy categorisation and definition in their mixture of aesthetic experiments and more conservative writing styles, and in possession of the ability to appeal to different readerships and tastes depending on the messages they wished to share.

Notes

1. Wiesenfarth's study takes this approach, describing Hunt in the context of her personal relationships with Ford and status as 'a New Woman who lived her life as such, refusing offers to marry to pursue a series of affairs with older men who, in the end, preferred their wives' (2005: 7). Belford (1990) explores Hunt's relationships with male writers but also discusses the merits of Hunt's own writing.
2. See Clay 2006; Ardis 2007.
3. I use the term 'feminist' with caution; the term, after all, was 'anachronistic' in the late 1800s, only being first recorded in 1894 (Rendall 1985: 1).
4. In 1881, Hunt wrote to Wilde: 'I cannot help writing to you just to tell you how much I admire your poems, which I have just read. I think they are beautiful . . . I particularly like "Panthea" "Requiescat" "Theocritus" & the "New Helen" & "Apologia"' (Hunt 1881).
5. By the 1890s, '[t]he female journalist was frequently upheld as a positive role model in journals aimed at young educated middle-class girls who may have been contemplating a writing or journalistic career. Persuasive periodical accounts of women journalists emphasised both the rigors and attractions of the profession, often casting the female journalist as a heroic New Woman figure adaptable to modern and challenging work environments' (Shelley 2009: n.p.).
6. See, for example, 'Tea-Time Talk' in Jerome K. Jerome's *To-Day*, or 'Five-o-clock Tea Talk' in *T. P.'s Weekly*.
7. 'Baby-farming' referred to a practice in which individuals raised the children of (often wealthy) families for money or other rewards. Unlike official forms of fostering or adoption, baby-farming involved little genuine care and instead was often undertaken purely for financial gain.

Works Cited

Ardis, Ann. 2007. 'The Dialogics of Modernism(s) in the *New Age*.' *Modernism/ modernity* 14.3: 407–34.
—. 2012. 'Editor's Introduction.' *Modernism/modernity: Special issue: Mediamorphosis: Print Culture and Transatlantic/Transnational Public Sphere(s)* 19.3: v–vii.
Beetham, Margaret. 2006. 'Periodicals and the New Media: Women and Imagined Communities.' *Women's Studies International Forum: Special Issue: 'Feminisms and Print Culture, 1830–1930s, in the Digital Age'* 29.3: 231–40.
Belford, Barbara. 1990. *Violet: The Story of the Irrepressible Violet Hunt and Her Circle of Lovers and Friends – Ford Madox Ford, H. G. Wells, Somerset Maugham, and Henry James*. London: Simon & Schuster.
Brake, Laurel and Marysa Demoor. 2009. *Dictionary of Nineteenth-Century Journalism in Great Britain and Ireland*. Gent: Academia Press.
Chan, Winnie. 2007. *The Economy of the Short Story in British Periodicals of the 1890s*. London: Routledge.
Clay, Catherine. 2006. *British Women Writers 1914–1945: Professional Work and Friendship*. London: Routledge.

Delap, Lucy. 2000. 'The Freewoman, Periodical Communities, and the Feminist Reading Public.' *Princeton University Library Chronicle* 61.2: 233–76.

Delap, Lucy and Maria DiCenzo. 2008. 'Transatlantic Print Culture: The Anglo-American Feminist Press and Emerging Modernities.' *Transatlantic Print Culture, 1880–1940: Emerging Media, Emerging Modernisms*. Ed. Ann Ardis and Patrick Collier. Basingstoke: Palgrave Macmillan. 48–65.

Goldring, Douglas. 1935. *Odd Man Out: The Autobiography of a 'Propaganda Novelist.'* London: Chapman and Hall.

—. 1943. *South Lodge: Reminiscences of Violet Hunt, Ford Madox Ford and the English Review Circle*. London: Constable.

Green, Barbara. 2013. 'Recovering Feminist Criticism: Modern Women Writers and Feminist Periodical Studies.' *Literature Compass* 10.1: 53–60.

Hammill, Faye. 2015. 'Introduction.' *English Studies in Canada: Special Issue: 'Introducing Magazines and/as Media: The Aesthetics and Politics of Serial Form'* 41.1: 1–17. <https://ejournals.library.ualberta.ca/index.php/ESC/article/viewFile/27509/20254> (last accessed 27 February 2016).

Hardwick, Joan. 1990. *An Immodest Violet: The Life of Violet Hunt*. London: Deutsch.

Hughes, Linda. 2005. *Graham R.: Rosamund Marriott Watson, Woman of Letters*. Athens: Ohio University Press.

Hunt, Violet. 'Letter to Oscar Wilde.' July 1881. Box 3, Folder 1. MS 81699: 1876–1891. Violet Hunt Papers, British Library, London.

—. 1926. *The Flurried Years: An Autobiography*. London: Hurst and Blackett.

—. 'List of Magazines.' [n.d.] Box 3, Folder 1. MS 57752. Violet Hunt Papers, British Library, London.

Joyce, James. 2015. *The Little Review 'Ulysses.'* Ed. Mark Gaipa, Sean Latham, and Robert Scholes. New Haven: Yale University Press.

Lowndes Marques, Susan. 2007. 'Marie Belloc Lowdes on Ford and Violet Hunt.' *Ford Madox Ford's Literary Contacts*. Ed. Paul Skinner. Amsterdam: Rodopi. 95–7.

Rendall, Jane. 1985. *The Origins of Modern Feminism: Women in Britain, France, and the United States, 1780–1860*. Basingstoke: Macmillan.

Latham, Sean and Robert Scholes. 2006. 'The Changing Profession: The Rise of Periodical Studies.' *PMLA* 121.2: 517–31.

Robertson, W. Graham. 1953. 'Letter to Kerrison Preston.' May 1923. *Letters from W. Graham Robertson*. Ed. Kerrison Preston. London: Hamish Hamilton.

Scott, Bonnie Kime. 1996. *Re-figuring Modernism Volume 1: Women of 1928*. Bloomington: Indiana University Press.

Serres, Michael and Bruno Latour. 1995. *Conversations on Science, Culture, and Time*. Trans. Roxanne Lapidus. Ann Arbor: University of Michigan Press.

Shelley, Lorna. 2009. 'Female Journalists and Journalism in *Fin-de-siècle* Magazine Stories.' *Nineteenth-century Gender Studies* 5.2: n.p. <https://www.ijpc.org/uploads/files/Female%20Journalists%20Lorna%20Shelley.pdf> (last accessed 20 May 2016).

Sillars, Stuart. 2004. 'The Illustrated Short Story.' *The Art of Brevity: Excursions in Short Fiction Theory and Analysis*. Ed. Per Winther, Jakob Lothe, and Hans H. Skei. Columbia: University of South Carolina Press. 70–80.

Wiesenfarth, Joseph. 2005. *Ford Madox Ford and the Regiment of Women*. Wisconsin: Wisconsin University Press.

Woolf, Virginia. 'Letter to Violet Hunt.' 7 October 1923. Folder 3. RP 4566/2. Violet Hunt Papers, British Library, London.

15

Dora Marsden and Anarchist Modernisms

Henry Mead

Introduction

WHEN DORA MARSDEN famously interrupted a speech by Winston Churchill at the Southport Empire Hall in 1910, the trajectory of her politics was already evident (Garner 1990: 3–40; Fernihough 2013: 9–11).[1] Churchill was making the case for the 1910 'People's Budget,' the first step toward a welfare state in Britain. As he took to the stage, arguing that the bill had the support of the people as represented by the House of Commons, Marsden, who had hidden behind a window high above the hall, called down: 'But it does not represent the women, Mr Churchill' (Garner 1990: 39). Usually seen in the context of suffragette protests of the period, Marsden's question already indicates her path away from her WSPU peers and their concern for legal and political equality. The collective, 'the people,' is indicted as an abstraction, an irrelevance distracting from the rights of 'the women.' In fact, Marsden's logic would soon take her well past calls for legal and political rights of any kind. By degrees her call for attention to 'women' would soon be redirected to 'individuals,' and direct action would be replaced by an indifference to political process. Her hostility to the 'People's Budget' would be accompanied by an increasing disdain for democratic participation. She thus aligned herself with an anti-statist view of welfare provision as a sop, and parliamentary democracy a device to undermine the profounder sovereignty of the individual. Her attack on Churchill is consistent with her status among the individualists and demophobes who formulated and advanced the case against an encroaching state authority pandering to the perceived 'general will' of the masses.

Accounts of Marsden's career as a suffragette and periodical editor can perhaps be treated in distinct groupings: for example, scholarship that focuses on her contribution to modernist studies, whether peripheral or central; and that which treats her as a radical feminist writer. In more recent work, these lines of approach have been informed by the rise of periodical studies, including both reconstructions of early cultural modernism, and political-historical studies that seek new insights into the Edwardian feminist press.[2] She has been a key figure in the project of recovering overlooked women writers in the overlapping fields of modernist studies, histories of feminism, and histories of print (Green 2013). It is interesting to note that she has been a problematic figure for each of these arenas. Modernist scholars have disputed her significance, a debate won with some certainty by those who demonstrate her influence on 'canonical' writers as well as her significance in her own right[3] (Clarke 1996; Hallberg 1995; Kadlec 2001; Rabaté 2009). For historians of feminism, she has been problematic in that she seemingly rejected the feminist cause: changing the subtitle of the *New Freewoman*, 'A Weekly Feminist Review' to 'A Weekly Humanist Review,' and eventually the main title to the *Egoist* were symbolic departures from the suffragette and feminist project. Rachel DuPlessis has notably presented this as a betrayal of the early feminist cause (1990: 45). Conversely, one could see her project as a militant demand for androgyny – not for 'personhood' in the abstract liberal sense, but for the status of the self as the sole arbiter of value: perhaps a variant of a radicalised feminism, at odds with 'difference feminism' in its disdain for gender, but also posing a revolutionary challenge to liberal egalitarian feminism. Jean-Michel Rabaté connects her work to that of Ayn Rand in its individualism; conversely, Marsden's vision of the 'freewoman,' attainable, like the similar concept of the 'superman,' through a kind of 'self-evolution,' seems to anticipate themes in post-humanism[4] (Fernihough 2013: 30–1; Clarke 1996: 1–46; Wallace 2017: 47–8). Meanwhile, for scholars of periodical culture, another complexity arises in Marsden's apparent separation from the journal which she nominally edited; particularly after her departure for Southport, her speculative front-page articles increasingly reflect an intellectual and geographic estrangement from the network she had created. Stylistically, her work presents challenges, its complex, curlicued prose resisting interpretation – a seemingly avant-garde performance in itself.

This chapter draws on all these approaches, with a focus on the Marsden magazines' place among a field of small anarchist journals, well known to each other and to their shared readers, published in Britain, the US, and in Europe. The field of anarchist studies has significantly overlapped with modernist studies in work by David Kadlec and Allan Antliff among others (Kadlec 2001: 54–89; Antliff 2001: 75–81). This chapter connects her work to shades of radical political opinion, also touching on her relations with the socialist rhetoric of the *New Age* and to show how her radical individualism put her at odds with modernism's apparent shift from its early 'individualist' phase to its high 'conservative' phase, as described influentially by Michael Levenson (1984: 79). Indeed, Marsden's actions might be treated as those of both a networker and an anti-networker, as she both implored her contemporaries to support her venture and her ideals, only then to sabotage and destroy potential alliances. Like Stirner, her model, she wrote to persuade but also seemingly to alienate. Just as Stirner would have cast scorn on there being such a thing as a 'Stirnerian,' an abstract category itself, so Marsden's work precludes the emergence of a 'Marsdenian': she asked much of her followers in terms of practical support for her work, but at the same time reviled any form of enslavement, and her style seemed to exclude as much as communicate.

This leads us to a consideration of Marsden's thought in relation to other anarchists, and to place her at the far reaches of radical individualism in contrast with her contemporaries – for example, Emma Goldman and Benjamin Tucker, and with A. R. Orage, her *New Age* counterpart. Notably, these contemporaries sought liberation from an abstracting liberal statism through a similar 'intensification' of the self but presented this egoism as a stage of growth toward the renewal of social bonds, underpinned by shared values. Marsden stood alone in both modernist, feminist, and periodical networks – paradoxically, given her energetic entry into these spheres as means to a seemingly political end.

The Political Background

Marsden's individualism was expressed against the backdrop of an expanding democracy and an expanding Liberal state. The Reform Acts of 1832 and 1867, and the 1884 Representation of the People Act, had granted the vote to ever wider numbers of the male population, removing property qualifications and other limitations. Meanwhile a reaction against Liberal welfarism was exemplified by Hilaire Belloc's famous polemic, *The Servile State* (1912). Belloc made the case that the proposed measure of national insurance only tinkered with the existing capitalist system. These changes in fact had worse consequences in dividing society into two classes, one free, the other 'constrained by positive law to work for the advantage of the other' (Belloc 1912: 16).[5] New Liberal reforms concealed a path toward compulsory participation in a collectivist system, cementing the lowly status of the working class. One alternative, taking various forms in discussion, was a community organised around small property owners living independently of any state intervention. Fears over the tyranny of the majority were nothing new, but as several critics have shown, an anti-populist rhetoric coincided with the emerging modern movement in the arts (Potter 2006: 1–11; Fernihough 2013: 37–9). It was this rhetoric that informed Marsden's departure from the suffrage campaign and her establishment of the *Freewoman* journal in 1911.

After gaining attention for her arrest and for her interruption of Churchill's speech, Marsden had become an unpredictable element within the suffrage movement. She increasingly acted without consulting the Pankhurst leadership, and left the WSPU in 1911 after a final quarrel (Garner 1990: 43–6).[6] A brief involvement with the Women's Freedom League ended with another falling out and parting of ways (Garner 1990: 51–2). From 1911 she turned her attention to journalism, both as a medium for her activism and for her growing interest in philosophy. Writing to Charlotte Wilson in May 1911, she made clear her impatience with the WSPU and her interest in profounder matters of economic and political organisation. She urged the formation of a 'Society for the Promotion of the Economic Independence of Women.'

> What is really needed is a popular demand. Neither Mr Asquith or any other can withstand a really popular agitation and the Women's Suffrage agitation is not popular because the women have not been taught the connection between abstract political rights and concrete matters such as work and wages. To make it a natural movement the philosophy of the women's movement will have to be worked out in terms of everyday life . . . The Suffrage Societies are trying the short cut to Women's freedom and there are no short cuts. (qtd in Garner 1990: 55)

It was clear that her divergence from the Suffrage movement had an intellectual impetus: she wanted, as Rebecca West put it, to 'stand aside and ponder the profounder aspects of feminism' (1989: 5) Yet her appetite for philosophical depths was held in tension with this interest in 'concrete matters of work and wages' (ibid.). Indeed, there would always be a vagueness about how her economic and philosophic radicalism might connect.

Pursuing these by no means reconcilable goals, Marsden moved to London to begin her new project. In an interview with the *Evening Standard and St James Gazette* in October 1911 Marsden made explicit her aims with the new journal.

Acknowledging problems surrounding the word 'feminism,' which for Marsden was still associated, incorrectly, with the fight for suffrage, she argued that her new venture would 'give [the word] new significance . . . the great change which the Feminist movement seeks to bring about is not merely a matter of political readjustment.' Rather, 'it would accomplish a vast revolution in the entire field of human affairs, intellectual, sexual, domestic, economic, legal and political.' Marsden clearly had in her mind already the kernel of her new line of argument, seeing the force of individual sentience as outweighing any gender distinction. She argued that 'woman is a distinct entity . . . she must be taught that she is not an adjunct to man' (25 Oct 1911; qtd in Garner 1990: 57).

Anarchist Touchstones

In doing so, Marsden drew on a radical literature distinct from the liberal touchstones of the suffragette mainstream. In arriving at the format and style of her new venture she was entering an avant-garde discourse with its own literary landmarks. As is well documented, the radical peripheries of the feminist movement were attentive to a Continental literature of liberation, following the lead of early mediators like Shaw and Ibsen (Fernihough 2013: 1–46; Jackson 1913: 126–31). By the 1890s Nietzsche's writing was gaining recognition across Europe, as were the rediscovered works of Max Stirner, whose *The Ego and His Own* (1844) was written in response, and opposition, to Ludwig Feuerbach's *Essence of Christianity* (1841). The most radical of the Young Hegelian group active in 1840s Germany, Stirner was condemned by his contemporary Karl Marx for his adaptation of Hegel's dialectic to justify an extreme individualism, rejecting all social structures and obligations. His work, fallen into obscurity, was rediscovered by the Scottish-German intellectual John Henry Mackay in 1898, and a 1907 English translation extended his influence among radical circles in Britain and America (Stirner 1995: xi–xxiii). Inspired by Feuerbach's reworking of religion as a projection of unrealised human self-idealisation, Stirner presented a very similar philosophy in terms of its rejection of abstraction in favour of solidly felt, localised, particular experience. He argued that the apparently liberating celebration of humanity is really just another kind of idealism, albeit internalised.

> I am owner of my might, and I am so when I know myself as *unique*. In the *unique one* the owner himself returns into his creative nothing, of which he is born. Every higher essence above me, be it God, be it man, weakens the feeling of my uniqueness, and pales only before the sun of this consciousness. If I concern myself with myself, the unique one, then my concern rests on its transitory, mortal creator, who consumes himself, and I may say: All things are nothing to me. (Stirner 1995: 324)

These ideas inspired forms of *fin de siècle* anarchism with close links to the literary and artistic avant-garde. Early modernist writing has often been associated with the Stirnerian premise that 'society,' its rules and codes are an abstraction, and the only reality lies in the individual's sensibility and desires. The utopian notion of reconciling individual freedom and communal unity was in fact a motif across a swathe of British Romantic writing, reflecting the impact of German Idealism, as does a persistent analogy between social and aesthetic harmony. The modernist aesthetic inherited such a utopianism – as Terry Eagleton puts it, 'a dream of reconciliation – of individuals woven into intimate unity with no detriment to their specificity, of an abstract totality suffused with all the flesh-and-blood reality of the individual being' (1990: 25). For Marsden, however, this dream was decidedly one-sided, its focus lying on that specificity, resisting being woven into any other being or entity. In this, like Stirner, she emphasised one side of a dialectic over its opposite number, the individual over the collective.

The Anarchist Spectrum

Early British readers of Nietzsche and Stirner used their ideas to support a spectrum of anti-statist thought. Readers of advanced literature tended toward radical progressive ideology, and it was natural that Stirner, along with Nietzsche, should be received first by the left.[7] Some of those inspired by Stirner and Nietzsche called themselves socialists, others anarchists. George Woodcock has provided a useful taxonomy of the range of anarchist thought at this time, ranging from the exponents of cooperative networks of the sort proposed by Peter Kropotkin and Mikhail Bakunin (1963: 17–19). In the reception of these ideas, many were synthesised, sometimes awkwardly, to support variously evolutionary, revolutionary, communist, or mutualist thinking. For example, an important venue for Stirner's reception was the London-based journal *Eagle and Serpent*. Edited by John Erwin McCall and Malfew Seklew, this minor but influential magazine ran from 1898 to 1902.[8] Its coverage of *The Ego and His Own* together with various of Stirner's contemporaries is typical of the way anarchist ideas were received in combination with others, lumped together with a rhetorical facility that disguised deep differences. Bakunin, Nietzsche, Stirner, and Kropotkin were quite different thinkers, their political recommendations varying significantly, yet for the anarchist groups that used their names as rallying cries, they formed ironically an abstract collective and an unsystematised attitude.[9] The composite portrait that emerged borrowed from Stirner's pronouncements selectively, including his words among lists of quotations by Emerson, Nietzsche, and Thoreau. Seeking to present a practicable politics, many anarchist publishing venues ultimately homed in a cooperative social structure at odds with Stirner's determined egoism.

Thus Nietzsche, Marx, Emerson, Whitman, and Edward Carpenter could be read together as prophets of 'egoism' but also champions of a reformed social structure that allowed individual freedom but maintained social bonds of cooperation and culture.[10] In Britain, the Romantic tradition of Ruskin had one legacy in the militant politics of William Morris, a leading member of the anarchistic Socialist League and proponent of small self-sufficient communities. The influential works of Carpenter exemplify the diffuse field of anti-statist socialisms informed by a sense of spiritual progress, both echoed Hegelianism but also Eastern religions and American transcendentalism (Rowbotham 2008: 71, 144; Mead 2015: 65–77).

The *New Age* and Orage

This field of speculation is exemplified by the *New Age*, which would have an important relationship with Marsden's journals as both a model and a disputatious rival. Its editor, A. R. Orage drew on a spiritual and political influences including Carpenter,

Plato, the *Bhagavad Gita*, various Theosophical and occult texts, Ruskin, Morris, and Nietzsche. *The Ego and His Own* was reviewed in the *New Age*:

> Man [. . .] is not a particular man, but a being from whom all particularities have vanished through sublimation. In place of the concepts of myriads of individuals as they are, and myriads of individuals as they actually might be, we abstract from both, and make Man as he is, and Man as we think he ought to be [. . .] But this sacrifice of real individuals to the non-existent and impossible Perfect Man is exactly similar to sacrifices made to any other abstract Mumbo-Jumbo. (15 Aug 1907: 251)

These ideas informed the *New Age*'s pursuit of the Servile State argument and its anti-democratic stance; as its reviewer goes on to ask, 'Except for the change of regime is there any difference between serving a majority of one's fellow citizens and serving a feudal baron?' (ibid.).

Such questions set a precedent for the Marsden journals' position from 1911 onward. Marsden first read Stirner in 1912, a fact she recorded in her *New Freewoman* leaders of that time. However, her writing prior to this piece suggests that she had already absorbed, perhaps indirectly, roughly similar ideas emanating from anarchist circles. The first leader of the *Freewoman* has a Stirnerian ring, also echoing the Servile State principle, but in significantly gendered terms:

> Bondwomen are distinguished from Freewomen by a spiritual distinction. Bondwomen are the women who are not separate spiritual entities who are not individuals. They are complements merely. By habit of thought, by form of activity, and largely by preference, they round off the personality of some other individual, rather than create or cultivate their own. Most women, as far back as we have any record, have fitted into this conception, and it has borne itself out in instinctive working practice. (23 Nov 1911: 1)

In the *New Freewoman* of 8 August 1912, a direct encounter with Stirner's text was first apparent, as documented in an editorial entitled 'The Growing Ego' (221–2). Marsden reported, using the editorial pronoun: 'We have just laid aside one of the profoundest of human documents, Max Stirner's "The Ego and his Own"' (8 Aug 1912: 221). The work clearly chimed with her temperamental iconoclasm: 'Morality, religion, God, and man are all brought low. They no longer rule as external powers influencing the Ego. [. . .] The Ego is supreme and reigns in his lonely kingdom. His joy lies in self-enjoyment, he reigns over himself; his business is to "use himself up"' (8 Aug 1912: 222).

Among the Suffragettes

Understandably, the *Freewoman* was immediately controversial among suffragette readers, not least because of Marsden's deliberate pursuit and provocation of that audience. Marsden was both appealing to her former colleagues and alienating them. As Lucy Delap has shown, Marsden deliberately broke from the format of publications such as *Common Cause* and *Votes for Women*. Pankhurst wrote to Marsden in 1909, recommending that she cover acts of resistance by suffrage campaigners as a way of 'arousing interest and sympathy' (Delap 2000: 254). Marsden did no such thing. Instead, the *Freewoman* took aim at these saintly figures, attacking the Pankhursts' direct action in a strategy that was in turn seen as an act of violence against the cause. For example, Hertha Ayrton wrote:

> Miss Gawthorpe, Your vile attack on Miss Pankhurst in *The Freewoman* fills me with amazement and disquiet too deep for expression . . . You, who have worked and suffered for the cause, are now betraying it, just when it is about to triumph, out of some petty personal spite. (ibid.)

The Marsden journals also alienated the suffrage press by their accommodation of hostile views, cultivating what Ann Ardis has called the 'dialogic of modernism' central to periodical writing (2007). The journals were 'open' on principle, but, as Marsden wrote: 'We do not mean "open" in the sense that we have no point of view, but "open" in the sense that we are prepared not only to accept but to welcome opposing points of view' (23 Nov 1911: 31). Last but not least, Marsden's editorial tenor was rhetorically distinctive. The *Freewoman* opened with a leader column that asserted:

> The chief event of the week is our own appearance. The publication of *The Freewoman* marks an epoch. It marks the point at which feminism in England ceases to be impulsive and unaware of its own features and becomes definitely self-conscious and introspective. For the first-time feminists themselves make the attempt to reflect the 'feminist movement in the mirror of thought.' (ibid.)

The contrast with the suffrage press is conspicuous immediately. The manner is provocative, self-regarding, even hubristic.

Marsden's play upon the norms of suffrage periodical texts, and her position relative to 'open' periodical debate, were complex, and hard to measure without a sense of other networks operating simultaneously. A key part was played by the woman at whom Hertha Ayrton directed her outrage: Mary Gawthorpe. Gawthorpe, a fascinating figure in her own right, acted as an interstice or axis between two dominant figures in the periodical-political network of the period: Orage and Marsden. She had formed a close relationship with Orage years earlier when she first encountered him as a leader of the Leeds Art Club, a network that merged anti-statist socialist, Theosophical and pro-suffrage debate from 1902 onward. Orage and Holbrook Jackson had been its leading lights before their move to London in 1907 (Steele 1990).

Gawthorpe thus served not only as a link to the suffragette world, but also to a regional avant-garde (Thacker 2013: 22–43). Marsden too was a product of provincial networks; a graduate of Victoria University in Manchester, where she was classmates with Gawthorpe, Christabel Pankhurst, and other WSPU luminaries, she lived in London for less than two years (Garner 1990: 14–49). What she shared with the Leeds network was an abhorrence of individuals being artificially marshalled, to their detriment, into abstract communities and states. Later, the *New Age* would hark back to the Leeds Art Club's efforts to formulate a new kind of socialism that intensified man's spiritual life while overthrowing capitalism and the alienating effects of industrial modernity. Gawthorpe recalled 'I have sometimes pondered that the Club, founded by Orage and Jackson, had the germ of a new future' (Gawthorpe 1962: 197; Thacker 2013: 28).

It was Gawthorpe who, in letters through late 1911, advised Marsden not only to consider the *New Age* circle as a source of contributors but to treat the journal itself as a template (Delap 2000: 262–3). At a time when Marsden's antagonism toward the WSPU was at a peak, the *New Age* was suggested by Gawthorpe as a model of independent but neutral discussion. She advised Marsden in a long letter to 'see the moral of the N. A. [*New Age*]. It can only do what it does by being independent of every movement' (qtd in Delap 2000: 32).[11] Through Gawthorpe's friendship with Orage, Marsden was able to use the *New Age* circle as a source for contributors and as a radical model for her new magazine, distinguishing it further from the suffragette papers. The largely male writers of the *New Age* circle included many such as J. M. Kennedy, C. H. Norman, E. H. Visiak, C. E. Bechhofer, Huntly Carter, and Allen Upward, who were destined to become contributors to the *Freewoman* and the *New Freewoman*. The individualist tone of the paper was then partly a refraction of debates in the *New Age*. The leader column cited above has something in common with the *New Age*; and its code words 'self-conscious,' 'introspective,' the desire to see oneself in 'the mirror of thought' all evoke the language of 'advanced' literature, the register of the self-proclaimed intellectual, familiar from the *New Age*'s tone of address, assuring their readers of their intellectual status, however far-flung in provincial, working-class environs they might be. To read or even carry these journals was an act of self-identification and empowerment; modelling itself on the *New Age*, the *Freewoman* was providing a gendered version of this self-affirming strategy. Marsden's early rhetoric can be viewed as part of this project. Its declared aim accepted no limits: it would define a new state of being, 'what women may become.' This meant clarifying the new category declared by the journal's title – the *Freewoman*, and 'her psychology, philosophy, morality and achievements' (23 Nov 1911: 3). The useful term 'Bondwomen' referred to the conventional position of women as a subordinate participant in the domestic sphere, 'a kind of human poultice,' protecting men from the outside world. This dynamic, a product, Marsden speculated, of the process of child-rearing, was however a matter of choice, not necessity.

> Nothing but one thing – the sense of quality, the sense that a woman has gifts, the sense that she is a superior – a master – can give her the strength to slip the comfort and protection and to be content to seize the 'love' in passing, to suffer the long strain of effort and to bear the agony of producing creative work. (ibid.)

Preceding second-wave feminist conclusions by several decades, Marsden proposed that women had a choice. Consequently, there would need to be 'vast changes in housing, nursing, kindergarten, education, cooking, cleaning, in the industrial world and in the professions' (ibid.). The mission to draw these distinctions and identify means for change led Marsden over time to open the pages of the journal to a heady mix of ideas, permitting discussions of spiritualism, heterodox economics, Eastern religions, Continental literature in translation, art, poetry, and drama.

The *New Age*'s approach to gender politics was also variable. Earlier volumes included contributions by suffragettes and radical feminist writers. Orage often identified his own politics with that of a sexual revolution, for example writing in his 'Notes of the Week' column, 'we have already hinted that the mystical idea of the emancipation of women is not unlike the mystical idea of the transfiguration of man into superman' (22 Aug 1912: 389). Indeed, he was close to, and politically supportive of suffragettes at Leeds and in his early days in London; he had been the only man arrested at the large suffrage march on Parliament in March 1907 (Mairet 1936: 52). The *New Age* published articles by Teresa Billington-Grieg and Florence Farr; Lee Garver's piece in this volume gives a fuller account of its feminist contributors. However, when Gawthorpe and Marsden asked for help with the production of their journal in September 1911, Orage declined; his attitude was hardening against the suffrage cause as his disillusion with democracy grew (Delap 2000: 262). By 1914, he was actively hostile toward the journal Marsden had now renamed the *Egoist*, on the grounds that it described a stage of individualism subsumed, to his mind, by a higher level of social union, reminiscent of Carpenter's cooperative vision, or more pertinently, by the Guild idea which from 1912 he had refined as a new form of socialism:

> egoism is necessary and inevitable in the early phases of intellect, it is neither necessary nor desirable in the later. One can tell, in fact, the stage of intellectuality at which any individual has arrived by noting the curve of his egoism. If it is ascending, his intellect is still in its green youth. If it is descending, his intellect is becoming ripe. [. . .] because intellect in its early phases is necessarily egoistic; and since women, as we say, are just beginning, it follows that their egoism is very pronounced. (*New Age* 30 July 1914: 300)

Emma Goldman

As the *Freewoman* became the *New Freewoman*, and later the *Egoist*, it became clear that Marsden's anarchism was *sui generis*, appropriately. Yet she remains one of a field of thinkers, and her contribution is worth seeing alongside her contemporaries, notably two prominent figures in the United States, Emma Goldman (1869–1940) and Benjamin Tucker (1854–1939).

Goldman grew up in the Russian Empire and came under the influence of nihilist literature before she immigrated to America in 1885. Her interest in radical ideas developed during a period of labour in sweatshops in Rochester, New York before, in 1889 she moved to New York City and became known as an anarchist speaker. Here she was first powerfully affected by the writings of Nietzsche and Stirner. In 1906 she had founded *Mother Earth*, which ran from 1907 to 1915. In format, the journal comprised long, serious articles with few illustrations, aside from a few picture covers and political cartoons. The first number opened with a capsule history of humanity, from the first waking of consciousness to the discovery of America, noting a pattern of worship of abstract values and the neglect of genuine individual freedom. The tone, clearly informed by Nietzsche's and Stirner's similar genealogies, was earnest, intellectual, and intensely committed to the cause of freedom. Later in the journal Goldman, writing with M. Basinski, looked to the future of the women's movement:

Salvation lies in an energetic march onward towards a brighter and clearer future. We are in need of unhampered growth out of old traditions and habits. The movement for woman's emancipation has so far made but the first step in that direction. It is to be hoped that it will gather strength to make another. The right to vote, equal civil rights, are all very good demands, but true emancipation begins neither at the polls nor in courts. It begins in woman's soul. (Mar 1906: 9)

Although its direction was less narrowly individualist than Marsden's papers, *Mother Earth* took aim at the same abstract political and moral values. Goldman's opening statement declared that it would be a forum for anarchist debate on every subject, without 'sectarian favouritism,' taking on education, free love, prison reform, education, and the labour movement (ibid.). Contributors included many of the most prominent radicals of the time, including Americans like Floyd Dell, Margaret Sanger, C. L. R. James, and Max Nettlau, and Europeans including Kropotkin, Tolstoy, and Gorski. Producing the magazine from her apartment in New York, a hub of anarchist activity, Goldman paid for many costs herself, gathering funds through her lecture tours. The journal only came to a halt in 1917 owing to a post office ban (Gornick 2011: 62).

As Allan Antliff has argued, Goldman belonged to the anarchist-communist tradition descending from Bakunin, who had attacked Marx's advocacy of state control at the Second International. Instead, Bakunin argued, the workers should rise up and attack the state apparatus and replace it with small self-governing guilds (Antliff 2001: 5). Like the *Freewoman*, Goldman's journal took little heed of the campaign for the vote. 'Red Emma,' as she became known, was more concerned with the individual's freedom, and focused in many instances on women's rights and birth control, subjects on which she lectured to thousands. Just as the *New Age* and the *Freewoman* harnessed Continental anarchism to sexual politics, so Goldman invoked Nietzsche in support of a new free love. She proposed to establish 'a transvaluation society' in Mayville, Wisconsin: a kind of free-love commune (Fernihough 2013: 40).

There are remarkable echoes of Marsden's rejection of democracy and Goldman's attitudes in *Mother Earth*. In her dismissal of the vote, Goldman's words could be Marsden's as she argues that 'true emancipation . . . begins in woman's soul' (Mar 1906: 17). However, Marsden accepted the need for property rights, while Goldman like many anarchists identified this as an evil. Goldman had an interest in the cooperative model of society, based on Bakunin's logic, which Marsden ruled out. This would bring her into direct conflict with anarchists otherwise closely aligned to her position. Many, though deeply committed to individual freedom, combined this with a belief in community. Other American magazines, for example the *Forum* and the *New Review*, were less concerned with suffrage than a deeper definition for 'feminism,' a flourishing of 'free personality.'

Benjamin Tucker

Similarly, Benjamin Tucker also combined his interest in Stirner with a belief in cooperation. His anarchism took an evolutionary form, envisioning the natural emergence of small social groupings as an alternative to large-scale liberal democracy. An important influence here was Pierre-Joseph Proudhon, who believed such an economic system, comprising autonomous farming and artisan communities, would naturally supplant hierarchical forms of social organisation (Woodcock 1963: 21). A key mediator of transatlantic anarchisms, Tucker established a publishing house and bookshop in New York which brought European radicalism to a US readership. In 1907 he published the first English edition of *The Ego and His Own*, translated by his collaborator Steven Byington, as was Paul Elzbacher's key study *Anarchism* (1900; trans. 1908), which included chapters on Stirner, Bakunin, Kropotkin, and Tucker himself. The journal *Liberty* was edited and published by Tucker from August 1881 to April 1908. Issued at first from Boston and after 1892 from New York, *Liberty*, like the *Eagle and Serpent*, combined readings of a variety of texts from Thoreau and Emerson through William Morris and Oscar Wilde to Bakunin, Kropotkin, Stirner, Nietzsche, and Proudhon: it became a key venue for the discussion and synthesis of their ideas (McElroy 2003). In 1899 Tucker's New York printing press and anarchist bookshop were destroyed in a fire and he moved to France. Here he became aware of Marsden's work and began to make regular contributions to the *New Freewoman*. Tucker, who proposed that Stirner's philosophy should be read alongside forms of cooperative anarchism, was taken aback when Marsden attacked his position in several commentary pieces. In his view, Stirner's egoism would have to be moderated and adapted to fit with a theory of social union. As had the *Eagle and Serpent*, *Liberty* placed Stirner's work within a larger library of anarchist writings; his name formed part of a bigger mosaic of thought. When Marsden insisted on pure egoism, Tucker wrote to remonstrate, seeing this reading as reductive and impracticable. At this time, he had hoped the *Egoist* would provide him with a new organ to promote his beliefs in Europe after the closure of *Liberty*. Unfortunately, the editor was unwilling to adopt his latitude of interpretation, and engaged him in a fierce debate, which tells us much about Marsden's positioning within the anarchist field.

The debate began with an article of 1 October 1913, entitled 'Proudhon and Royalism,' in which Tucker attacked the French radical right group the Cercle Proudhon, which brought together the neo-royalist rhetoric of the Action Française group together with a Proudhonian ethic (Parker 1987: 149–57). George Valois's new bi-monthly Parisian journal *Cahiers du Cercle Proudhon* promoted this outgrowth of Maurassian royalism toward a kind of syndicalism represented by Georges Sorel. The mechanism they proposed was for a simultaneous cooperative ethic at local level, harnessed to a radical nationalism and a renewed fidelity to the French crown. The combination seemed to promise empowerment to the individual worker via their commitment to the objective order represented by the monarchy; in fact, it prefigured a kind of fascism in many ways (Douglas 1992: 28–33; Weber 1962: 73–82). Tucker objected strongly and launched an attack on the journal *L'Action Française* in which the neo-royalist aspects of the argument had been formulated. The debate reflected an emerging fault line in British modernist ideology. The *New Age* had recently been paying attention to same French network of ideas, as Orage began to refine his Guild Socialism's moral underpinning, seeking what he called a 'conservative ethic': a code of objective values upon which to structure his community of self-governing guilds (Mead 2017). This brought him into a dialogue with two *New Age* contributors, Ramiro de Maeztu and T. E. Hulme who from 1913 were exploring the same interfusion of Charles Maurras's royalism with Sorel's syndicalism (Mead 2015: 204–17).

Tucker's reading of anarchist texts is in line with the hopeful anarchist synthesis that marked *Liberty* and other anarchist journals. Quoting at length from Proudhon, he argued that his statement of of society 'would have been acceptable even to Max Stirner as a charter for his 'Union of the Free' (*New Freewoman* 1 Oct 1913: 156–7). This was surely wishful thinking given how little allowance Stirner made for cooperation between individuals. His austere doctrine merely described temporary collaborations based on mutual benefit in what otherwise was a war of all against all. Marsden's response helps place her anarchism not only in relation to Tucker's, but also to her London contemporaries. She had remained silent during Tucker's earlier articles, but intervened now to comment. According to Marsden, Proudhon's 'outlined Social Contract' was yet another construction of abstract terms: 'if we outlined a scheme for building a block of flats as high as St Paul's, with lily-stalks for materials, and carefully went into the joys of living therein, and assessed the penalty for occupants who damaged the joinery, may we say, we should consider we were doing very similar to that which Proudhon does in outlining the social contract' (15 Oct 1913: 165). Always a demoniser of abstractions, Marsden attacked Proudhon's style:

> we should put a pencil through half of [his writing] as bombast and fustian. The half left would consist of adjectives and prepositions. It is the kind of thing that overpowers our mental digestion. (ibid.)

She continued in the same vein a month later:

> We frankly do not understand why Mr Tucker, an egoist, and Stirner's English publisher, does not see the necessity of cleansing current language of padding as a preliminary of egoistic investigation. It is a task which pioneers of a new branch of science are always faced with. Stirner himself worked like a navvy on the job. (15 Nov 1913: 204–5)

Ironically, Marsden at each step displays her own stylistic quirks and convoluted metaphors intended to provoke which, in this case, had the desired effect. Her piece prompted a confrontational personal letter from Tucker asking 'for an explanation of the sub-title: "An Individualist Review"? . . . if in truth, *The New Freewoman* is not, or is no longer, a co-ordinated effort toward a definite end, but has become, instead, a mere dumping-ground for miscellaneous wits, then . . . my interest will diminish materially and speedily' (15 Dec 1913: 245).

Marsden was unapologetic. Writing in the newly retitled *Egoist*, she noted that Tucker's refusal to continue the argument 'until we have explained why it is a sign of insanity for people to "associate for mutual protection, on the basis of a contract defining the protective sphere"' (15 Jan 1914: 25). Marsden attacked again 'the theatricality of Proudhon's style with its faked matter and pompous manner rendered it impossible' (ibid.). Defensively she elucidated her own figures of speech, 'As for the lily-stalks . . . they were intended to refer to M. Proudhon's assumptions regarding human nature. We meant that the kind of people he describes never walked on earth: figures with no genuine insides, stuffed out with tracts from the Church of Humanity and the Ethical Society' (ibid.). Proudhon's hope for cooperative understanding returns us to the humanist realm of 'spooks,' scarecrow figures padded with abstract, moralising treatises, far from the flesh-and-blood reality of individual existence. The crux of the conflict between a cooperative and a radically individualist ideology can be seen spelt out as Marsden distinguished between two attitudes, both claiming the name Anarchism. The first, pure form 'fixes upon the absence of a State establishment' (2 Mar 1914: 84). The second shares this but in addition admits 'the *presence* of . . . order which obtains when each member of a community *agrees to want only* the kind of order which will not interfere with the kind of order *likely to be wanted* by individuals who compose the rest of the community' (ibid.). The contorted style tells us much about Marsden's thinking: in essence, the contrast is between a rejection of all authority, and mutual consent to a code of values by a community. This second principle can be seen in Proudhon's mutualism. Marsden draws a clear distinction and rejects the second thesis: 'We should call it rather a sort of Clerico-libertarian-Anarchism . . . Compared with the [state's] power of egoistic repression . . . the shape of conscience is infinitely more repressive and searching' (ibid.). Marsden is resolute in rejecting any shared code of values: these, she argues are even worse forms of tyranny,

> more subtle, more tyrannical power of repression than any the world has yet known, its only distinction being that the Policeman, Judge and Executioner are ever on the spot, a Trinity of Repression that has a Spy to boot, i.e., 'Conscience,' the 'Sense of Duty.' By contrast, the Archism [of] the Armies, Courts, Gowns and Wigs, Jailers, Hangmen . . . is but light and superficial as compared with our Clerico-libertarian friends. (ibid.)

Tucker ceased writing for the *Egoist* shortly afterward, having restated his serious objections; his hope of finding a venue in Europe to continue his New York project was clearly disappointed. What is interesting about this exchange is how it chimed with another debate going on between radical periodicals in London. At the *New Age*, Orage, Hulme, and Maeztu through 1915 explored the possibilities of a moral, possibly religious code that would bind individuals together while preserving their individuality. It is perhaps this ideological logic that Levenson detected in his account of how an 'anarchist' early modernism transformed into a conservative 'high' form (Levenson 1984: 79). In contrast, Marsden insisted on her Stirnerian principles, ignoring this *rappel à l'ordre*.

Conclusion

Much has been written on the development of specifically female periodical communities.[12] In Marsden's case a close but possibly exploitative relationship with Gawthorpe evidences how a network of female friendship co-existed with a strategy of manipulation to achieve Marsden's apparent goal: to acquire the readership and sponsorship of the suffrage network, in order to expose them, however painfully or provocatively, to even more radical new ideas. Marsden wrote to ask Gawthorpe for help with the *Freewoman*, explaining 'What we wanted was the use of your name to give [the *Freewoman*] a preliminary and quite artificial kick-off' (qtd in Delap 2000: 236). Gawthorpe, who wrote affectionately to Marsden as they planned the journal together, agreed to the use of her name, despite her ill-health that precluded great involvement in editorial duties. The strategy worked. Gawthorpe did attract initial support, for example from Hertha Ayrton: 'your name is enough to ensure [my readership])' (ibid.). As we know, Gawthorpe was also named in the ensuing controversy. This clearly distressed her, and over the course of the *Freewoman*'s publication her relations with Marsden deteriorated rapidly. (Garner 1990: 51–9). This wilful irritation of her former suffragette colleagues, using a rare remaining ally in that world as bait, says much about Marsden's intentions. Was she always actively seeking a more select network of her own, distilled from the larger feminist counterpublic? She was in many ways an anti-networker, self-exiled, fragmenting her public sphere systematically, a process accelerated by her avowal of Stirnerian individualism.

Marsden's ruthlessness in networking was followed notably by her removal from the centre to the periphery. Just as Orage cultivated the Leeds Art Club and then the Fabian Arts Group when he arrived in London, so, as Marsden's journal developed, it generated a similar network, the Freewoman Discussion Group (Delap 2000: 271–3). However, her place in this community was to some extent virtual following the collapse of the *Freewoman* and her departure from London. Through the lifespan of the *New Freewoman* and the *Egoist*, she participated in the London network from a far remove in Southport. Her interventions were made through postal correspondence (more frequent, of course, in the early twentieth century, permitting conversations to unfold within hours), occasional visits, and the representation of her wishes by certain key allies. Despite her seclusion, her cast of mind framed the periodical communities that subsequently flourished under the watchful eye of her allies in London, West and Weaver. This absence surely represents Marsden's unusual attitude; both soliciting and spurning allies and supporters, company, intimacy. Having striven to free herself of slave morality, she required others to support her cause. It was through West that the cultural modernist addition to the *New Freewoman* and the *Egoist* would take form, eventually displacing West, and inserting into the periodical network around the *New Freewoman* an unarguably largely male network of writers and artists. That said, Harriet Shaw Weaver would remain as the coordinator and patron of Joyce's key contributions years after Eliot, Pound, and Aldington had moved on to very different venues (Lidderdale and Nicholson 1970).

Marsden's withdrawal from these groups also presages the way her ideas seem to shape her practice as a thinker and participant in intellectual circles. Interestingly, Woodcock notes how both Proudhon and Stirner were given to removing themselves from networks. He describes the famous sketch of Stirner among the Young Hegelians in Berlin: 'a lonely figure . . . look[ing] on ironically' (1963: 90). There is something almost Zarathustran in the way Marsden took herself out of the scene, having declared the death of God, leaving her lieutenants and representatives the task of voicing her ideas.

Notes

1. See Garner 1990 for the fullest account of Marsden's life and career.
2. For examples, see Clarke 1996; Delap 2000; Brooker and Thacker 2009.
3. See Clarke 1996; Hallberg 1995; Kadlec 2001; Rabaté 2009 for studies of Marsden as a radical individualist.
4. See Fernihough 2013: 50–60; Clarke 1996; 1–46; Wallace 2017: 47–8 for readings of Marsden in this light.
5. See Villis 2005: 64–6 for an account of this widespread antipathy to the 'Servile State.'
6. National organisers were troubled by her plans for a bazaar complete with a shooting range that encouraged attendees to fire upon effigies of leading politicians.

7. The latter's 'transvaluation' of ethics brought out the elitism of the intellectual left and would soon be appropriated to support a new radical right.
8. A belated last issue appeared in 1927.
9. See Forth 2001 for a good account of this blurring of very different writers in *fin de siècle* Paris.
10. Carpenter's developmental thesis can be seen in *Civilisation: Its Cause and Cure* (1889). See Rowbotham 2008 for accounts of Carpenter's thinking and Mead 2015: 65–77 for its influence on the *New Age*.
11. Gawthorpe recorded her first acquaintance with him in her memoir, *Up Hill to Holloway*, in which she describes the Leeds Art Club milieu in which she, like many other women, fell for Orage's 'seductive' personality. See Gawthorpe 1962: 199.
12. See Delap 2000; Hanscombe and Smyers 1987; Winning 2000.

Works Cited

Antliff, Allan. 2001. *Anarchist Modernism: Art, Politics, and the First American Avant-Garde*. Chicago: University of Chicago Press.
Ardis, Anne. 2007. 'The Dialogics of Modernism(s) in the New Age.' *Modernism/modernity* 14.3: 407–34.
Belloc, Hilaire. 1912. *The Servile State*. London and Edinburgh: T. N. Foulis.
Brooker, Peter and Andrew Thacker. 2009. *The Oxford Critical and Cultural History of Modernist Magazines*. Vol. 1. Oxford: Oxford University Press.
Carpenter, Edward. 1889. *Civilisation: Its Cause and Cure*. London: Sonnenschein.
Clarke, Bruce. 1996. *Dora Marsden and Early Modernism: Gender, Individualism, Science*. Ann Arbor: University of Michigan Press.
Delap, Lucy. 2000. 'The *Freewoman*, Periodical Communities and the Feminist Reading Public.' *Princeton University Library Chronicle* 61.2: 233–76.
Douglas, Allen. 1992. *From Fascism to Libertarian Communism: George Valois Against the Third Republic*. Berkeley: University of California Press.
DuPlessis, Rachel Blau. 1990. *The Pink Guitar: Writing as Feminist Practice*. London: Routledge.
Eagleton, Terry. 1990. *The Ideology of the Aesthetic*. Oxford: Blackwell.
Fernihough, Anne. 2013. *Freewoman and Supermen: Edwardian Radicals and Literary Modernism*. Oxford: Oxford University Press.
Forth, Christopher. 2001. *Zarathustra in Paris: The Nietzsche Vogue in Paris 1891–1918*. De Kalb: Northern Illinois University Press.
Garner, Les. 1990. *A Brave and Beautiful Spirit: Dora Marsden, 1882–1960*. Aldershot: Avebury/Gower.
Gawthorpe, Mary. 1962. *Up Hill to Holloway*. Penobscot, ME: Traversity Press.
Gornick, Vivian. 2011. *Emma Goldman: Revolution as a Way of Life*. New Haven and London: Yale University Press.
Green, Barbara. 2013. 'Recovering Feminist Criticism: Modern Women Writers and Feminist Periodical Studies.' *Literature Compass* 10.1: 53–60.
Hallberg, Robert van. 1995. 'Libertarian Imagism.' *Modernism/modernity* 2.2: 63–79.
Hanscombe, Gillian and Virginia Smyers. 1987. *Writing for Their Lives: The Modernist Women, 1910–1940*. London: The Women's Press.
Jackson, Holbrook. 1913. *The Eighteen-Nineties*. London: Grant Richards.
Kadlec, David. 2001. *Mosaic Modernism: Anarchism, Pragmatism, Culture*. Baltimore: Johns Hopkins University Press.
Levenson, Michael. 1984. *A Genealogy of Modernism: English Literary Doctrine 1908–22*. Cambridge: Cambridge University Press.

Lidderdale, Jane and Mary Nicholson. 1970. *Dear Miss Weaver: Harriet Shaw Weaver 1876–1961*. London: Faber & Faber.

McElroy, Wendy. 2003. *The Debates of Liberty: An Overview of Individualist Anarchism, 1881-1908*. Lanham, MD: Lexington Books.

Mairet, Philip. 1936. *A. R. Orage: A Memoir*. London: J. M. Dent.

Mead, Henry. 2015. *T.E. Hulme and the Ideological Politics of Early Modernism*. London: Bloomsbury.

—. 2017. 'A Conservative Ethic: T. E. Hulme and A. R. Orage,' in *Edwardian Cultures: Beyond the Garden Party*. Ed. Naomi Carle, Samuel Shaw, Sarah Shaw. London: Palgrave. 236–60.

Parker, Sidney. 1987. 'The New Freewoman: Dora Marsden & Benjamin R. Tucker,' in *Benjamin R. Tucker and the Champions of Liberty: A Centenary Anthology*. Ed. Charles Hamilton, Mark Sullivan and Michael Coughlin. St Paul: Coughlin & Sullivan. 149–57.

Potter, Rachel. 2006. *Modernism and Democracy: Literary Culture, 1900–1930*. Oxford: Oxford University Press.

Rabaté, Jean-Michel. 2009. 'Gender and Modernism: *The Freewoman* (1911–12), *The New Freewoman* (1913), and *The Egoist* (1914–19).' *The Oxford Critical and Cultural History of Modernist Magazines: Volume 1, Britain and Ireland 1880–1955*. Ed. Peter Brooker and Andrew Thacker. Oxford: Oxford University Press. 269–89.

Rowbotham, Sheila. 2008. *Edward Carpenter: A Life of Liberty and Love*. London: Verso.

Steele, Tom. 1990. *Alfred Orage and the Leeds Art Club*. Aldershot: Scolar Press.

Stirner, Max. [1844] 1995. *The Ego and His Own*. Ed. David Leopold. Cambridge: Cambridge University Press.

Thacker, Andrew. 2013. '"That Trouble": Regional Modernism and "Little Magazines."' *Regional Modernisms*. Ed. Neal Alexander. Edinburgh: Edinburgh University Press. 22–43.

Villis, Tom. 2005. *Reaction and the Avant-Garde: The Revolt Against Liberal Democracy in Early Twentieth-Century Britain*. London: I. B. Tauris.

Wallace, Jeff. 2017. 'Modern.' *The Cambridge Companion to Literature and the Posthuman*. Ed. Bruce Clarke and Manuela Rossini. Cambridge: Cambridge University Press. 41–53.

Weber, Eugen. 1962. *Action Française: Royalism and Reaction in Twentieth-Century France*. Stanford: Stanford University Press.

West, Rebecca. 1989. *The Young Rebecca: The Writings of Rebecca West 1911–1917*. Ed. Jane Marcus. Bloomington: Indiana University Press.

Winning, Joanne. 2000. *The Pilgrimage of Dorothy Richardson*. Madison: University of Wisconsin Press.

Woodcock, George. 1963. *Anarchism: A History of Libertarian Ideas and Movements*. London: Penguin.

16

Beatrice Hastings: Debating Suffrage in the *New Age* and *Votes for Women*

Carey Snyder

In the last decade, Beatrice Hastings (1879–1943), the self-proclaimed 'subeditor' of A. R. Orage's radical weekly, the *New Age*, has begun to garner attention for her modernist experiments in voice; her withering and witty satire; and her controversial views on maternity, women's suffrage, and feminism. Hastings's relationship to feminism is particularly vexed because she seems to swing from endorsing women's political, economic, and sexual freedom to virulently attacking women and professing their unfitness for public life. Not only did Hastings's views apparently shift as they unfolded in the ephemeral medium of journalism (as well as in her poetry, fiction, and satire), but she employed over a dozen pseudonyms to try on different perspectives such that her own perspective is difficult, if not impossible, to pin down. What is certain is that she prized fierce intellectual debate, and utilised periodical conventions – especially pseudonyms and the Correspondence section – to generate it. Hastings's myriad voices and her polemical exchanges, sometimes carried on in the margins of the paper, at once make her a challenge to recover, and a figure worthy of more sustained attention.

One of the central debates that engaged Hastings in her first years at the *New Age* was that over women's suffrage. With the rise of militant methods and mass demonstrations from about 1905 on, suffrage was becoming front page news in the dailies and producing a burgeoning press of its own. Hastings entered the ring in June 1908 with her first major pseudonym, the firebrand Beatrice Tina, to spar with the infamous anti-suffragist Belfort Bax. While trumpeting the militant policies of the Women's Social and Political Union (or WSPU) and echoing the rhetorical modes of its organ, *Votes for Women*, this persona riled readers by controversially repudiating motherhood. In January 1910, Hastings deployed a new persona, the pro-suffrage, anti-militant D. Triformis, to attack WSPU leaders and their paper, which she assiduously read and cited. Through Triformis, Hastings expressed increasing frustration that *Votes for Women* refused to answer her attacks, noting in one essay that since the suffrage paper was obviously aware of the *New Age*, its contributors must regard Triformis herself as 'too insignificant to notice' (17 Mar 1910: 462). By April 1911, Hastings largely abandoned the suffrage debate to pursue other political and literary topics, veering into the terrain of anti-feminism.[1]

One might conclude that Hastings was driven from the topic by a lack of interlocutors, but this is not the case: although *Votes for Women* never directly responded to Hastings's pseudonymous attacks, Hastings nevertheless succeeded in engaging both prominent and rank-and-file members of the WSPU in a series of exchanges that took place largely within the Correspondence section of the *New Age*. Indeed, I will argue that in spite of its reputation as an 'anti-feminist' magazine, the *New Age* actually served as an important forum for the women's suffrage debate from 1907 through July 1911, through its strategic interplay of feature articles and Correspondence, in which Hastings played a major role. This forum was all the more valuable because it was a space foreclosed by *Votes for Women* – a periodical that, as Maria DiCenzo has observed, minimised dissent (2011: 77).

Votes for Women can be seen as part of an expanding feminist press, dedicated to helping see women as political actors in a modern public sphere (Kelly 2004). Founded in October 1907, after several monthly issues, it became a weekly with the highest circulation of any suffrage paper, reaching 30,000 in 1909 (Tusan 2005: 155). The paper was edited by Emmeline and Frederick Pethick-Lawrence and served as the WSPU organ until September 1912, when leaders Emmeline Pankhurst and her daughter Christabel expelled the Pethick-Lawrences for criticising the escalation of violence in the campaign. *Votes for Women* was designed to correct the distortions and omissions of the mainstream press and to serve as propaganda – defending militancy, advertising WSPU demonstrations and meetings, and covering parliamentary politics and developments in the movement, while also including fiction, poetry, and columns on fashion and culture, along with numerous advertisements.

In its propagandistic focus on the WSPU brand of militancy as the best route to achieve the vote, *Votes for Women* paved over the heterogeneity of a movement riven not only by divisions between the militants (or *suffragettes*) and the constitutional *suffragists*,[2] but also by dissent within the WSPU itself. The expulsion of the Pethick-Lawrences, along with the proliferation of breakaway suffrage organisations like the Women's Freedom League (WFL), founded in 1907 by Teresa Billington-Greig among others, and the East London Federation of Suffragettes (ELF), founded in 1913 by Emmeline Pankhurst's daughter Sylvia, attests to disagreements about policy and priorities among professed militants. The desire to suppress dissent is evident in the limited real estate the paper devoted to readers' letters: DiCenzo notes that 'the occasional correspondence sections . . . featured, almost exclusively, supportive letters, in contrast to the other suffrage organs' (2011: 102), and the few critical letters that were included were thoroughly rebuked, becoming object lessons in the supposed weakness of anti-militant arguments. While *Votes for Women* did see itself as engaging in debate with the mainstream media – by republishing and responding to its coverage of militancy and the movement – that debate did not advertise dissent within the movement.[3]

In contrast, fomenting dissent was central to Orage's mission as editor of the *New Age* (1907–22). Hastings and Orage were romantically involved from 1907 to 1914, and partners in orchestrating political and aesthetic debate. The magazine started out with ties to the Fabian Society, though it was never a political organ, but rather an independent review of politics, literature, and art, with an average circulation of about 3,500, rising to 22,000 in 1908, as Hastings helped promote controversy with Beatrice Tina. When one reader accused the journal of being 'run in the interests of [. . .] the Liberal Government,' Hastings (as Triformis) retorted, 'readers [. . .] support the NEW AGE mainly because the contras as well as the pros of any argument may be found therein,' a policy she explicitly contrasted with the partisanship of suffrage papers like *Votes for Women* (28 Apr 1910: 620). The hefty Correspondence section played a central role in promoting this ethos of open debate, in keeping with the historical role of the genre outlined by journalist Rasmus Kleis Nielsen. Nielsen argues that Correspondence enables readers to 'intervene and contribute – [historically] something of an anomaly in predominately one-way mass media' – thus anticipating 'the newer and potentially more interactive technologies' of today (2010: 22). While *Votes for Women* limited the genre's potential to allow reader engagement, the *New Age* exploited it to the full, and in this it resembled two other journals familiar to modernist scholars: Dora Marsden's *Freewoman* (1911–12) (discussed in Henry Mead's chapter in this volume) and Margaret Anderson and Jane Heap's *The Little Review* (1914–29). Barbara Green has characterised the *Freewoman* as unusually committed to 'staging debate through mechanisms of audience participation' (2012: 464), and, similarly, Jayne Marek writes that the *Little Review* 'created its legacy through inviting and enacting opinionated debate about the nature and value of art, between the two editors as well as between the magazine and its readers and contributors' (1995: 75). Like these periodical peers, the *New Age* choreographed lively debates among contributors and readers, which would sometimes continue for several weeks or even months. The high status of Correspondence is evident in the magazine's intermittent practice, starting in 1909, of listing the names of letter-writers in the Table of Contents, thus elevating letters on a par with the status of articles and other features. The premium the *New Age* placed on spirited debate extended to the ethically dubious practice of fabricating letters. As John Carswell notes, in the *New Age* letters were 'often made up to quota by members of the staff writing under their own or assumed names to keep controversies on the boil' (1978: 50). In her professional memoir, *The Old 'New Age,' Orage and Others* (1936), Hastings recalled watching Correspondence 'as the pulse of the paper, darting in under some name to stimulate it by picking up a dropped point' (1936: 26).

The *New Age* was unusual among socialist papers in its extensive coverage of women's suffrage and in its highlighting of 'points of conflict' within this debate (Ardis 2007: 162). Even before Hastings unleashed Beatrice Tina, the *New Age* provided a platform for pro-suffrage writers like Billington-Greig, who, as one of the first to be arrested for the cause, wrote a series of *New Age* articles on women's suffrage from May to July 1907; actress Florence Farr, who wrote a feminist column from May 1907 to January 1908 (and whose writings are discussed in Lee Garver's chapter in this volume); and WSPU speaker, Mary Gawthorpe, who regularly intervened in Correspondence on behalf of the WSPU (1908–11). Christabel Pankhurst herself sent in a letter to an early issue of the *New Age*, scolding the prime minister for failing to prioritise the enfranchisement of women over the reform of the House of the Lords (27 June 1907: 143). Published a few months before *Votes for Women* was founded, the letter highlights the WSPU leadership's sense that the *New Age* would furnish a receptive audience for the cause, and that Correspondence could serve as a virtual political arena, since British prime ministers repeatedly refused to meet in person with women's suffrage delegates.[4] At the same time, the *New Age* gave a platform to prominent anti-suffragists such as Belfort Bax and C. H. Norman, orchestrating debate by inviting pro-suffrage writers to respond and publishing reader responses to both articles and letters. From 1907 to 1911, women's suffrage was also discussed in Orage's leader-column (often sympathetically); both celebrated and mocked in other features;[5] and, on 2 February 1911, comprised the subject of a fifteen-page special supplement, to which Emmeline Pethick-Lawrence responded favourably in a column the following week (*New Age* 9 Feb 1911, 344).⁶ Along with this coverage, the high number of WSPU members and *Votes for Women* contributors that wrote letters to the *New Age* during this period, as detailed below, confirm that these two magazines were part of the same 'periodical community,'⁷ with the *New Age* serving as an auxiliary space to host a multifaceted debate on women's suffrage that could find no place within the WSPU organ.

In the 27 June 1908 issue, Hastings launched Tina full force into a debate already under way with the provocative article, 'Woman as State Creditor.' The well-known barrister and socialist Belfort Bax had recently published a pair of articles called 'Feminism and Female Suffrage,' followed by two reply articles by Fabian feminist Millicent Murby. The exchange, advertised in advance, was one of what Carswell calls Orage's 'staged controversies' (1978: 36) – debates between well-known individuals on contentious, topical issues. Describing suffragists as a 'clamouring,' 'shrieking,' 'ranting sisterhood' bent on 'anti-man legislation,' Bax polemically argued that women were a legally 'privileged class,' seeking suffrage 'as a weapon wherewith to carry on a sex-war' (30 May 1908: 88). In response, Murby highlighted the economic imbalance that necessitated these so-called legal 'privileges,' pointing out that women earned one-third their male counterparts' salaries and were not recompensed for domestic labour (6 June 1908: 108–10). Hastings enlisted Tina to ramp up the argument, countering that the dubious legal privileges Bax lists are 'insulting and contemptuous' repayment to women for the 'torture of child-birth' and the 'odious' degradation of maternity (27 June 1908: 169). Aligning herself with the militants, Tina concludes with an impassioned call for women's emancipation: 'the fiercer the opposition, the more certain we become of the extent of men's addiction to tyranny ... The militant suffragettes have saved us from the last ignominy of the slave – the obligation to give thanks for enfranchisement' (ibid.). Hastings thus employed Tina as an uncompromising pro-militant voice, one that appealed to pathos and deliberately courted controversy, not just among 'antis' like Bax, but among women within the movement. The article hit its mark, eliciting a storm of reader response (Figure 16.1). This included a letter from children's author, Edith Nesbit, who labelled Tina's views of motherhood 'unholy' and 'unnatural,' and another that objected, 'The exaggerated Feminism of Beatrice Tina is far more damaging to the Suffragist cause than the anti-Feminism of Belfort Bax' (4 July 1908: 197–8). The following week Tina replied to her readers, comparing herself to 'Miss Pankhurst [. . .] who fights the political battle for other women': in 'articulating the sufferings' of women who abhor childbirth and motherhood, but haven't the courage or the freedom to demand reform, Tina insists, 'I repudiate the suggestion that I am not a good Suffragette' (11 July 1908: 217).

Hastings's contention that Tina can denigrate motherhood and still be a 'good Suffragette' is deliberately provocative – indeed, her characterisation of childbirth and mothering would still be controversial today. But within the context of suffrage debate, Hastings was deliberately attacking a sacred cow: as media historian Michelle Tusan explains, many in the movement 'appropriated the ideology of motherhood ... in order to advance women's status as legitimate political subjects' (2005: 163). The *Common Cause* reinforced this message, proclaiming, 'every Suffragist worth her salt ... *wants the vote for the sake of the baby*' (12 Sep 1913: 389). The image of the maternal suffragette or suffragist countered the threatening stereotype of women in revolt, while at the same time insisting on women's special expertise in matters currently being save your case by saying that it is the "highly developed imaginative" woman who finds ignominy in the fulfilment of her natural function, who is afraid to pay the price of pain that she may gain the greatest joy and triumph possible to woman—a child born of her body. The highly developed imaginative woman knows better.

* * *

"The enormous disability . . . . the law of maternity." This, Beatrice Tina thinks, makes it impossible for women to compete with men.

Well—it does. And what then?

"No pregnant woman shall be left to the mercy of her ignorant husband."

If Beatrice Tina tries to take the pregnant woman away from the husband she loves, Beatrice Tina will find her work cut out.

"Husbands and their consequences."!!!

My dear Beatrice Tina, how can you be so silly? Is it really possible that you don't know that the passion for the lover and the child is the strongest passion in the world? Why scream and kick and bite and scratch and make faces at the Life-force? It won't take any notice of you. And it will be wise.
E. NESBIT.

* * *

"WOMAN AS STATE CREDITOR."
To THE EDITOR OF "THE NEW AGE."

May I express thanks to Beatrice Tina for rendering articulate the cry of the "highly-developed, imaginative woman"? We no longer believe in self-sacrifice—The Race: c'est moi!

From the first moment a thinking girl realises what sex means to her, darkness falls on her horizon. Why perpetuate such suffering? Let all women who think the price of a child too dear, refuse to pay it. Men must love, either way.
D. C. A. M.

* * *

To THE EDITOR OF "THE NEW AGE."

The exaggerated Feminism of Beatrice Tina is far more damaging to the Suffragist cause than the anti-Feminism of Belfort Bax.

If service rendered to the State constitute a claim to the franchise, then undoubtedly the child-bearing sex has as strong a case as the fighting sex. There is no need to descend to the undignified course of haggling about the relative risk and pain of the mother's lot as compared with the soldier's. What we women desire is to persuade men that we are intellectually and morally capable of fulfilling the responsibilities of voters. We shall never do that if we allow our cause to be pleaded by a woman who has so little want of generalising that she can say, "Maternity is neither adventurous, stimulating, nor enjoyable"—a statement which is true only for that small minority of women who take no delight in babies. "Not adventurous"—to surrender oneself to hours of anguish for the hope of a new little life! "Not stimulating"—to spend months in loving preparation, always with the wonder—a boy or a girl? "Not enjoyable"—to take a baby into one's arms!

In agitating for the vote we can only do ourselves harm by attempting to stir up sex-hostility. Even if it were otherwise, if we could win by a policy of taunts and invectives, the result would be disastrous to progress. The future will not lie with haters, whether they hate men, women, or children, but with those who love the race.
MARGARET M. MACK.

* * *

ENGLISH FOREIGN POLICY.
To THE EDITOR OF "THE NEW AGE."

I would willingly do what I can to assist you in the most necessary protest which you, almost single-handed, are making against the unconstitutional methods by which our English foreign policy is being directed—not by a Minister responsible to Parliament, but by the King, without even consulting it—the obvious endeavour being to hedge round and threaten the German nation by a league of hostile States. I was in Hamburg last week, during the Kaiser's visit to that town, and some information which I have on good authority—that of an officer of the Reserves attached to the staff of his Army Corps on mobilisation—may be of service.

In the first place, he and his fellows have within the last three weeks been officially warned not to leave Germany; this has not happened before within his experience—he is a man of thirty-six—and is highly significant. In the second place, the German nation bitterly resents the policy of isolation: I gather that it is in no small degree attributed to a personal enmity between our King and the Kaiser, and the latter is, in some German circles, highly unpopular because he has hitherto persisted in keeping the peace; in this regard it seems not altogether impossible that such recent successes as the Socialists can boast may be due less to discontent with the direction of their social, than with that of their foreign politics—the desire to give to the German people an unrestricted power to protect its interests and freedom as, and when, it may think necessary.

As I am informed the German nation has calmly faced the possibility of a war—an early war—with England: it is prepared to lose its colonies, which it values very low, and its fleet—it believes its naval bases to be quite safe from our attack by sea and of course laughs at the idea of an invasion by our army.

The policy is to invade, crush, and hold France as a hostage; to crush her, as Bismarck and Möltke wished to crush her in the seventies—beyond hope of recovery—stripping away whole provinces and restricting her army to a mere 50,000 men as a sort of extra police. The vast loans by France to Russia, which cannot be repaid in our time, would render her speedily bankrupt in case of war, and only some knowledge of her imminent danger could have driven her to an alliance with us who, until we have conscription, can give only moral support. It is this alliance, and that with Russia which follows from it, which our King takes such credit to have arranged: it has brought us perilously near to war, what gain does it promise us? It may be the wisest policy, now that matters have been allowed, since the Algeciras Conference, to drift to their present state, but I understand you to contend for the right of the English people to have the facts set before them and to decide the policy to be followed through their Parliament and elected Ministers, and not by the King, behind the screen of a sycophant Ministry, who mistake subservience to the throne for loyalty to the nation. It is in this spirit that I write and urge you to renewed and persistent endeavour.
HOWARD INCE.

* * *

To THE EDITOR OF "THE NEW AGE."

I trust you will vigorously continue your protests against the attempt which the King is evidently making, with the connivance of the Liberal Government, to unduly increase his influence in the political affairs of this country in the interests of despotism. His Majesty's snub to Mr. Arthur Ponsonby, Mr. Keir Hardie, and others for their action over the Reval visit by not sending them an invitation to his

Figure 16.1 Correspondence columns, including replies to 'Woman As State Creditor.' *New Age*, June 1908.

legislated by men (Tickner 1988). By having Tina disparage motherhood, Hastings positioned this persona as an outlier in the movement, even among the militants with whom she aligned herself.

Hastings's Tina continued to serve as a bold militant voice in 'Suffragettes in the Making' (3 Dec 1908), an exposé of prison conditions by one who has not yet been 'initiated.' The essay opens with a protest against assigning suffragettes to the 'second division' among ordinary criminals, rather than awarding them the 'first division' status reserved for political prisoners – a topical issue since Emmeline and Christabel Pankhurst had been sentenced to three months in the second division in October 1908.[8] *Votes for Women* regularly reported on suffrage imprisonments, including, along with the leaders' 'Speeches from the Docks' and prison correspondence, testimonials from ordinary women in the movement, such as Maud Joachim's 'My Life in Holloway Gaol' (1 Oct 1908), which Tina's piece echoes in describing the unsavoury prison fare, uncomfortable prison garments, and general demoralisation of prison life.

Tina questions the biases of the ruling elite by asking if Prime Minister Asquith's and Home Secretary Gladstone's wives would, 'with the Suffragettes, be set among the convicts? Would they be given skilly [e.g. gruel] to eat and cocoa with lumps of meat floating in it to drink? Would they have nothing but a charwoman's rag to wash with?' (*New Age*, 3 Dec 1908, 169). Tina combines the graphic details found in prisoner testimonials (such as Joachim's) with a sensationalising register that is part of this persona's modus operandi: 'silence about the filthy tortures practiced on the political (and other) prisoners in Holloway is not possible,' she declares (ibid.). The first hunger strike would not occur until July 1909, so the 'tortures' Tina has in mind don't include force-feeding, but rather the habitual 'torture' inflicted on ordinary prisoners:

> They [the suffragettes] have felt how the horrid prison system dehumanises. They have lain down, stark awake, on the plank bed, numb as all prisoners are numb, from the whole day's long horror. They recognise victims, whom a hundred Governments of men have failed to redeem, hunted back to a death in life. (ibid.)

As Barbara Green notes, the WSPU also 'took up the rhetoric of prison reform' (1997: 58), arguing, as Tina does, that enfranchisement would enable women to 'demand a change in the brutal, senseless, mocking laws' that unjustly incarcerate and inhumanely punish (ibid.).

Advocating unambiguously for militancy, detailing the indignities and discomforts of prison life, and using rousing language to glorify prisoners as martyrs, 'Suffragettes in the Making' echoes key conventions of *Votes for Women* prison reporting. Edwardian militants lionised suffrage prisoners with banquets, parades, and military badges, and lauded them in *Votes for Women*, for, as Emmeline Pethick-Lawrence commented, 'every prisoner means a harvest of converts' (qtd in Rosen 1974: 109). When Christabel and Emmeline were serving their terms in Holloway, Pethick-Lawrence commended their sacrifice with characteristically effusive language: 'For where the dauntless founders and leaders of our movement are, there the forces of will-power, enthusiasm, and self-immolating love that move through this agitation are focused' (19 Nov 1908: 128). Hastings, a master of pastiche, has Tina channel Pethick-Lawrence's overblown style in describing the appeal of this rite of passage: 'I, also, want to learn what it is that a woman brings in her soul out of that hell. For certain is this – that she comes forth endowed to conquer, solemn and illustrious!' (*New Age,* 3 Dec 1908, 109). Significantly, though, even at her most militant, Hastings's Tina still stood outside the movement, exalting a sisterhood that she had not fully joined.

The following week, Hastings incited further controversy with Tina's 'On Guard,' a call to arms alleging that Liberal stewards had sexually assaulted suffragettes at political meetings. Denouncing the stereotypically feminine virtue of polite reticence as inexcusable under the circumstances, Tina insists that every bystander is duty-bound 'to communicate the whole truth of the atrocities to which her comrades were subjected': 'Modesty must not prevent you from publishing throughout your ranks the abominable villainy practiced at the Albert Hall' (10 Dec 1908: 179). The reference is to a meeting in which Lloyd George addressed the Women's Liberal Federation, from which historian Andrew Rosen reports a large number of WSPU hecklers were 'ejected roughly,' with 'cuts, bruises, and torn clothing' (1974: 113). Among them was Helen Ogston, who gained notoriety by using a dog-whip to defend herself, a decision she justified in a letter to *Votes for Women* on the grounds that she had previously been 'subjected to very serious violence' and even 'disgracefully mauled by stewards' (10 Dec 1908: 179). Ogden's expression is notably sexually suggestive, but not explicit, whereas Tina leaves no room for ambiguity: 'Rape is irrevocable. Any means taken to prevent it are justified' (ibid.). The 'modesty' Hastings references may well have kept women from speaking out. Elizabeth Robins's suffrage novel, *The Convert* (1907), alludes to the silencing effect of sexual shame, as the suffragette, Miss Ernestine Blunt, blushingly tells the soon-to-be-converted protagonist, Vida Levering, that the stewards at political meetings 'punish us in ways the public don't know . . . They punish us by underhand maltreatment – of the kind most intolerable to a decent woman.' When Vida demands, 'How *dare* they!', Ernestine replies simply, 'They know we dare not complain' (Robins 1980: 158). In any case, given its explicit reference to rape, 'On Guard' was bound to create controversy. Its success in doing so was confirmed the following week, when Tina alludes to the copious response the article has elicited: 'It is impossible for me to reply personally to the correspondence, confirmatory, incredulous, and abusive' (17 Dec 1908: 171). While this correspondence was not printed, the reference to it functioned as a barometer of the topic's importance.

In July 1909, Hastings bundled an abridged version of 'Woman as State Creditor' with six new Tina articles to form *Woman's Worst Enemy, Woman*, the title underscoring the book's polemic intent. In keeping with Tina's reputation as a provocateur, the book not only criticised compulsory marriage and motherhood, but also controversially advocated for birth control and sex outside of marriage, as well as for political enfranchisement. Hastings envisioned *Votes for Women* readers as part of her audience, later complaining that the paper had not even acknowledged receipt of the book (19 May 1910: 69). Not only was the subject matter controversial, the style was openly confrontational, with Tina declaring in the second paragraph, 'This book is written for the pleasure of denouncing the sort of female whose modesty howls for silence on such important matters as sex and maternity' (1909: 2). Tina's open advocacy of free sexual unions would be anathema to those who wanted to shore up a respectable, middle-class image for the suffrage cause.

Hastings's desire to foreground the contentiousness of her ideas is evident in an unusual feature of *Woman's Worst Enemy, Woman*: its inclusion, along with the 'reprint . . . of the much-discussed article "Woman as State Creditor,"' of 'Answers to [twenty-four] Correspondents on the same,' amounting to a whopping twelve out of sixty-seven pages.⁹ Hastings thus incorporated an element of periodical form into the book – the prized give and take between readers and contributors. Here, Hastings breaks with the *New Age* norm of respecting the integrity of the individual letter, taking the liberty of actively excerpting letters to suit her argumentative purposes. For instance, to a male reader's remark, 'These suffragettes are undoubtedly man-haters. [. . .] Let all true women march with us to our mutual emancipation, and then we shall be able to show our chivalry and true love,' Tina replies, 'We don't want your chivalry. It has meant that we have been deluded into being amenable to the laws laid down by men' (1909: 60–1). To be sure, editors always shape Correspondence through the selection and arrangement, if not the excerpting or outright falsifying of letters; as Nielsen argues, 'letters must be seen as a co-production between editors and letter writers' (2010: 24). Because there is no archive of the letters themselves, there is no way of knowing whether Hastings has justly excerpted them, or instead misrepresented (even fabricated) letters to her own ends. Even if contrived, however, this exchange highlights how for Hastings, Correspondence was a forum for polyphonic and pugilistic debate.

One of Tina's final appearances in the *New Age* is an October 1909 exchange with WFL member and New Woman novelist Mona Caird. In a letter responding to escalation of violence within the movement, Caird expresses ambivalence, 'bitterly' regretting recent violent tactics, 'terrible as the provocation has been,' yet simultaneously urging respect for the 'heroic' hunger-striking militants (14 Oct 1909: 448). The following week, Tina chides Caird for 'wavering':

> Are women to wait for the vote until men have lost their belligerent instincts, or are they to fight for the vote immediately? . . . There are only two dignified positions possible to women who are not actually facing the physical sufferings of the campaign: to speak uncompromisingly for or against the suffragettes. (21 Oct 1909: 466)

There is much irony in the staunchly militant Tina criticising Caird for fence-sitting, given that Hastings was on the cusp of changing her pseudonym to change her point of view. Having spoken 'uncompromisingly for' militant tactics as the impassioned Tina, in January 1910, Hastings took Tina out of circulation, creating the more coolly rational suffragist D. Triformis to attack the WSPU and the 'overdeclamatory pieces' in *Votes for Women* (Grey 2004: 209). Unlike Tina, who Hastings would eventually own as her persona in the pages of the *New Age*, Triformis was an effective disguise, not associated with the author herself until Hastings's 1936 memoir. This stealth persona enabled Hastings/Tina to change her mind without seeming to be inconsistent, and to try out a blunter mode of attack on an organisation she had previously condoned.

In 'The Failure of Militancy' (20 Jan 1910), Hastings used Triformis to respond to a recent *Votes for Women* article, 'Powder and Shot for the Campaign' (14 Jan 1910), in which Christabel Pankhurst comments sarcastically that it is 'edifying' to note 'how quick' politicians are to justify the use of violence in Northern Ireland, when these same politicians condemn the militant tactics of the WSPU (14 Jan 1910: 249). In a complete reversal of Tina's stance, Hastings's new persona Triformis deplores the use of violence: 'there can be nothing really edifying, that is, spiritually strengthening, comforting, improving, in the spectacle of men, who in their calmer mood deprecate violence, being carried in a moment of temptation beyond sanity and the ways of peace' (20 Jan 1910: 273). She opposes WSPU militancy on both pragmatic and principled grounds, arguing that women are unlikely to use sufficient force to win by that means, and that employing violence for political ends is 'barbaric.' Lastly, she criticises WSPU leaders for 'egging [their] followers on' while they remain exempt from the 'tortures' these followers suffer (ibid.). Pankhurst did not take the bait, but one of her foot soldiers, Eleanor Jacobs, did. In a letter the following week, Jacobs offers familiar defences of militancy – that rebellion is necessary when peaceful means have failed, that it is an effective way of rousing support, and that militancy and constitutional methods are not mutually exclusive (27 Jan 1910: 310). In reply, Triformis diplomatically highlighted her commonality with Jacobs – 'All of us, who are suffragists, believe the vote to be the symbol of our needs' – then takes Jacobs to task for dodging her complaint that 'none of the leaders have suffered so badly as those they have goaded' (3 Feb 1910: 333). As the voice of moderation and reason, Triformis functioned to flout the fanaticism of *Votes for Women* authors, a role Hastings's Tina would have been ill-suited for, given that her rhetoric was equally impassioned.

Hastings next employed Triformis to respond to a series of *Votes for Women* articles by the famous actress Elizabeth Robins, a prominent member of the WSPU since authoring in 1907 both the popular play *Votes for Women* and the aforementioned novel, *The Convert*, based on it. In a nine-instalment series called 'Why?' running from 3 December 1909 to 4 February 1910, Robins set out to justify WSPU methods and their demand for the vote, presented as the key to a host of other social reforms. In 'The Whys of the WSPU' (*New Age* 10 Feb 1910), Triformis attacks Robins's series for being ill-reasoned – full of unsubstantiated claims, anecdotal evidence, and redundant points. Triformis claims that Robins glosses over weaknesses in her argument with colourful anecdotes, such as a lurid story about a daughter wrongfully admitted to a mental institute after her mother dies: 'Bad as it is,' Triformis comments, 'we fear that a very wicked man might find one quite as bad to prove that some woman once horribly treated her own child; from which the conclusion would be that women should not be allowed to appoint guardians!' (10 Feb 1910: 346). Triformis further disputes Robins's argument that the vote will give working women equal wages, or improve the conditions of married women. She concludes that many of the problems that Robins raises cannot be answered by the vote, but rather through women's economic independence and a broader 'sex revolt.'[10]

Hastings follows up with the Triformis article 'Why Not?', demanding why *Votes for Women* has not replied to Triformis's 'just attack' (17 Mar 1910: 462). Here, Triformis becomes less diplomatic, dismissing the whole programme of the militants as 'stupidity': 'violence is evidence of mental stupidity'; 'misrepresentation of facts to married women and factory hands is stupidity'; and Robins's articles 'will do much to confirm the opinion . . . that this is not a movement of ideas, but of wild whims' (ibid.). Triformis further attacks the inflated style of the paper, specifically the 'dithyrambic hymns of Mrs. Pethick Lawrence,' whom she quotes mockingly: '"Feel the pulse of life that throbs at the heart of the union" . . . That is, in plain English, rant.'[11] At stake for Hastings is the principle that any important issue should be subject to strenuous debate, not mere partisan promotion.

A recent *Votes for Women* letter to the editor becomes a case in point of the paper's refusal to fairly engage in debate:

'we were astounded to read an adverse criticism in the organ itself,' Triformis remarks, 'but our bewilderment cleared up when we saw the editors' reply. It is well to be a reader of "Votes for Women." The editors incur the danger of thinking for oneself, and one need not risk it at all.' (17 Mar 1910: 462)

The letter, criticising militant methods, was penned by the father-in-law of suffragette Lillian Mary Dove Willcox, who had recently published an account of her imprisonment and hunger strike in *Votes for Women* (13 Aug 1909: 1056). Mr Dove Willcox began by diplomatically praising the paper's 'vivid' reporting, before criticising the WSPU tactic of hunger-striking as 'unlikely to help forward the cause' and lamenting the leaders' glamorising of its members' 'totally unnecessary sufferings' (11 Mar 1910: 368). The letter is not allowed to stand on its own, but is preceded by the editors' refutation of it in the *Outlook*: 'From it,' the editors write, 'our readers will gather how weak is the case on the other side, even when clearly and logically expressed' (11 Mar 1910: 366). The editorial goes on to offer a point-by-point rebuttal to Mr Dove Willcox's argument before the readers even encounter it. As Triformis notes, 'if left to themselves, the readers might have thought [the letter] convincing'; however, 'the editors stepped in' (ibid.). This rare instance of criticism-and-rebuttal in *Votes for Women* differs from Orage's 'staged controversies,' which it superficially resembles, in that the editor throws her authoritative weight against the scantly represented opposition. *Votes for Women* existed to promote and justify the WSPU, whereas the *New Age*, Hastings insisted, 'existed for free discussion' (14 Apr 1910: 573). We have seen that Hastings's practice does not always live up to this ideal: she too 'steps in' to pointedly rebuke readers' letters in *Woman's Worst Enemy, Woman*. However, her goal is markedly different: rather than refuting the opposition to win converts to a cause, Hastings seeks to proliferate dissent, even changing her own position within a combative, multivocal exchange.

Hastings continued to use Triformis to goad the WSPU leaders, next attacking Emmeline Pethick-Lawrence for soliciting donations in *Votes for Women* for a massive WSPU procession, at a price tag of one thousand pounds ('The price of freedom is heavy,' Pethick-Lawrence admits, 'but the bonds of subjection are heavier' (29 Apr 1910: 499)). In her article 'Women and Freedom,' Triformis likens the planned procession to a Roman gladiator show, objecting at once to its crass commercialism and to the herd mentality that pageantry promotes. Reiterating that women 'are not bodily slaves' whose freedom can be 'bought' as Pethick-Lawrence's rhetoric implies, Triformis urges women to seek freedom within: 'with mental freedom . . . we could scarcely fail to convince our fathers and brothers of our right to the vote' (12 May 1910: 29). In Triformis's voice, Hastings thus shifts the responsibility for achieving emancipation onto the individual, and away from a women's collective movement.

Hastings next took an extraordinary step to provoke controversy – pitting Triformis not only against Pethick-Lawrence, who was sure to ignore her, but also against her own alias, Tina, manufacturing the feisty exchange that had eluded her. Triformis declares, 'When Miss Beatrice Tina wrote [in the June 1908 article quoted above]: "The militant suffragettes have saved us from the last ignominy of the slave – the obligation to give thanks for enfranchisement," she penned, though in a spirited style, one of the most foolish fancies of the average thoughtless woman' (ibid.). This extraordinary periodical moment – where one persona calls another a fool – highlights not only Hastings's playfulness, but also how her view has shifted. It reminds the historical reader that Tina was equally guilty of the rhetorical excesses that Triformis has ridiculed in Pethick-Lawrence's writing: clearly Hastings once saw the effusive, passionate mode as a useful rhetorical stance, one that she availed herself of with Tina, and discarded when she took up Triformis. While her frequent shifting of personae and penchant for sarcasm and satire suggest that Hastings valued argument for argument's sake, there is also evidence that she genuinely changed her mind on this issue, becoming disenchanted with the WSPU, and with the women's movement more broadly, as we shall see.

The following week, Hastings replied to Triformis in a letter signed 'Beatrice (Tina) Hastings' – a signature that seems to unmask Tina as an alias, while preserving the fiction of Triformis as a separate individual (Figure 16.2). However, unlike 'Triformis' and many other pseudonyms that Hastings used as effective disguises, Tina never fully shielded the author's identity, but rather, as I've argued elsewhere, was closely linked to the woman known as Beatrice Hastings, a name that was also a pseudonym (Snyder 2016: 178–80, 186). 'Beatrice Tina' can be seen as Hastings's militant alter ego – an alter ego that she spectacularly 'kills off' (Hasting's word) to dramatise her break with the movement (19 May 1910: 69). Hastings vowed to have 'learned a good deal from D. Triformis,' while also to be smarting from her criticism: 'she need not have thrust me out as merely a foolish woman' (ibid.). Her real quarrel, of course, is with the 'advanced movement,' whom she's accused of ignoring her 'just attacks' and boycotting her book. By May 1910, Tina had lost her utility for Hastings, as Hastings began to lose interest in the suffrage debate.

Hastings employed Triformis just a few more times, notably in an exchange with the aforementioned Billington-Greig, erstwhile defender of suffrage militancy. When the Pankhursts suspended the WSPU constitution in October 1907, Billington-Greig broke with the organisation, becoming a founding member of the Women's Freedom League (WFL). Subsequently breaking with the WFL in 1910, Billington-Greig went on in January 1911 to publish a scathing critique of both militant organisations in the *New Age*, in a three-article series entitled 'Emancipation in a Hurry.' Significantly, in the first instalment, she rejoices to 'have won back [. . .] that right of frank and free speech which membership and official position have denied me' (12 Jan 1911: 246) – implicitly identifying the *New Age* as a forum permitting free speech. Her criticisms echo those of Triformis: she faults the WSPU's autocracy as well as its narrow focus on the vote, arguing that other avenues of feminist activism have become 'hostages to hurry,' sacrificed to the expediency of pursuing 'votes [for women] on a limited basis' (12 Jan 1911: 247). She also faults its fanaticism ('noise and show have come to be the accepted substitutes for argument' [19 Jan 1911: 270]) and its 'misuse of militancy as a medium of advertisement.' Like Triformis, Billington-Greig suggests that the movement has become a spectacle catering to public lust for blood, drama, and thrills.

Having herself endured the WSPU's 'conspiracy of silence,' Hastings revives Triformis to express her annoyance that the organisation 'would not dare to answer Mrs. Billington Greig.' In 'To Your Posts, Feminists!' (16 Feb 1911: 368), this observation becomes a springboard for Triformis to renew her withering attack on *Votes for Women*, charging that she can find in it 'no single intelligible word' apart from 'news of caucuses, amounts of money received, cheerings-on to glory and abuse of opponents. Not a humane, lettered or truly political sentiment is expressed from cover

CORRESPONDENCE.

WOMEN AND FREEDOM.

TO THE EDITOR OF "THE NEW AGE."

I certainly do not wish to be named with those who creep away from a public criticism; but the fact is I have no defence to make for my unlucky epigram. I admit that it is not true as it stands, and that the idea (unexpressed) in my mind at the time was certainly of "mental" freedom, and then I am bound to agree with D. Triformis that mental freedom must be gained by thought. I have learned a good deal from D. Triformis and I hope I may learn more; but some things I have *not* to learn. I have long since protested against several of the undesirable aspects of the suffrage movement. In a reply to Mr. G. K. Chesterton I wrote: "The real question of women's suffrage is whether it will lead to progressive or to reactionary legislation." Later I objected to the way certain notoriously narrow-minded suffragists used the name of Mary Wollstonecraft and distorted her ideals; and further, I complained of the growing mercenary spirit among so-called advanced women. I have not complained publicly, hitherto, about the official boycott of my book, partly because it sold all the same; but I am a living example for D. Triformis of the "prohibitive and censorial preferences" she notices among the leaders of the various sections. For all these reasons she need not have thrust me out as merely a foolish woman. One is not altogether foolish who has been killed for speaking the truth. It is also a distinction to be the only woman in England who does not want a family. No, I am not altogether silly. I should feel more of a laughing stock for the immortals if I had given sons to a State which might hang my son for some sudden act due to his inheriting my own and my father's temper. I resent the lies about marriage which I was allowed to grow up believing, and my ignorant and unwilling maternity I regard as an outrage. For saying these things I was cast out by advanced women. "Votes for Women" would not even mention that it had received a copy of my book. At a Fabian soirée I was cut by at least a dozen women, and I resigned my membership, not wishing to contaminate these noble creatures who of course have, all of them, forty children each.

Well, it is the fate of martyrs to be subsequently canonised. Meanwhile, D. Triformis may well spare me from her gallery. I have been killed out of the "advanced" movement. I now devote myself in the shades to art and humanitarianism. *De mortuis nil nisi bonum.*

BEATRICE (TINA) HASTINGS.

* * *

Figure 16.2 Extract from Correspondence column, authored by 'Beatrice (Tina) Hastings.' *New Age.* May 1910.

to cover of this journal. Its make-up proves that it circulates among the uninformed. Who could care about it?' (ibid.). The question is ironic, since obviously Hastings has cared enough to spill a great deal of ink attacking the journal in Triformis's name, though this is her next-to-last onslaught. To remedy the lack of genuine debate within the WSPU, Triformis invites Billington-Greig to organise her own feminist league. Her fellow dissenter replies to Correspondence the following month, reporting that she has been showered with letters echoing Triformis's suggestion, but declining on the grounds that she is too 'generally execrated' to serve as a leader of the movement; instead, she urges women to start their own 'discussions and debates on a free platform': a 'movement of action would naturally follow' (30 Mar 1911: 525). Other suffrage magazines were more open to dissenting views – for instance *Common Cause* defended 'intelligent criticism' as 'the very salt of life and the condition of progress'[12] – and after its founding in November 1911, Dora Marsden's *Freewoman* would provide just such an open forum.[13] In its early years under Orage, largely thanks to Hastings's interventions, the *New Age* served as another such platform, though by the end of 1911, with Hastings's withdrawal from this arena, the opportunities for feminist debate in the *New Age* were significantly narrowed.

By August 1912, the *New Age* no longer could be said to offer a 'free and open forum' for debating women's issues. That month, Orage published a pair of anti-suffrage editorials which decisively tipped the bias of the paper in an anti-feminist direction, such that it became, in Dora Marsden's phrase, 'a paper written by men, and for men' (*Freewoman* 29 Aug 1912: 281). Orage denounced the Women's Movement as a failure, asserting (with Triformis) that not only was it impossible to win the vote by force, but also that WSPU tactics had lowered the public's estimation of women. Blaming the women's movement for dismantling the family unit, Orage alleges that women 'naturally' desire to remain economically dependent on men (22 Aug 1912: 389), and that they have been misled by 'the dangerous doctrines of Ibsen' (29 Aug 1912: 411). Though he abandoned his formerly objective stance on the issue by publishing these polemics, Orage still proved willing to devote considerable space to readers' responses to his editorial – four out of twenty-four double-columned pages. Among the letters was one by WSPU speaker Mary Gawthorpe, who, ironically, had four years earlier satirised anti-suffrage leader-writers in a feature article in the *New Age*. The earlier piece depicted the patriarchal leader-writer as revelling in his 'slashing attack' against female 'invaders of the stronghold of tradition' (31 Dec 1908: 204), as indeed Orage in 1912 seems to revel in his twenty-two column attack of the movement. In her letter, Gawthorpe observes how Orage now used editorial prerogative to tip the balance against the suffragettes: 'What a powerful ally is your editorial "we." By its means your phrases become charged with all the force of impersonal sanction; and natural strength and authority meet us with intensified appeal. To this redoubtable "we" I must oppose, compare and contrast the conclusions of the single "me"' (12 Sep 1912: 479). Among the other readers who objected to the paper's new reactionary stance on women's suffrage was Reginald Pott, who identified himself as 'one of the earliest readers of your plucky paper': given that Orage's 'attacks on the women's movement contain a large amount of such masculine arrogance, coupled with a great deal of prejudice and misstatement,' Pott planned to cancel his membership (12 Sep 1912: 477).

Even before Orage apparently shut the suffrage debate down, Hastings turned her back on it, after having played such a key role in promoting this debate during the journal's early years. The nagging question of *why* remains for those who yearn to glimpse the woman behind her many pseudonymous masks. I can offer some speculations. First, like other former WSPU supporters, Hastings increasingly lost patience with suffragettes who apparently sidelined other social and political issues in their narrow pursuit of the vote. One of her last remarks on the subject comes in an exchange in *New Age* Correspondence with Lady Constance Lytton, famous for her daring experiment of enduring force-feeding disguised as a London seamstress to expose class biases in prisoner treatment. When Hastings, writing in her own name, accused the WSPU of regarding prison reform as a 'side issue' (25 May 1911: 93), Lytton conceded that the WSPU felt it was 'harmful to attempt legal readjustment of great social problems, amongst them prison reform,' before women were enfranchised (8 June 1911: 140). After enumerating the ways that prison and the judicial system were failing, Hastings retorted, 'But still, it can all wait until we get the vote? Pah! One gets to hate the very word "vote"' (15 June 1911: 165). Thus Hastings came to regard the *vote* as a side issue among other, to her more pressing, social and political reforms. Second, as Lucy Delap has shown, Hastings increasingly embraced a radical individualism that made her eschew collective movements (2007: 102–38); we have seen that this individualism, which can be traced to her earliest writings, becomes more pronounced in her Triformis writings. Third, Hastings was clearly exasperated that most of the movement's leaders ignored her, as she resorted at last to arguing with herself. Finally, Hastings became increasingly 'skeptical of the influence of women in public life' (Delap 2005: 397). A turning point was her opposition to the White Slavery Bill, which legalised the flogging of pimps and procurers and was widely supported by suffragettes. Decrying the practice of flogging as barbaric and white slavery (forced prostitution) as a fiction, Hastings cited the 'white slave agitation' as 'proof' of women's 'unrestrained mania for brutal and dangerous purification by punishment' (17 Apr 1913: 592). As this remark suggests, Hastings's wariness of the women's movement blurred into misogyny, as if she were disavowing her own female identity.[14] Admittedly, this vitriol against women, from one who had pseudonymously defended suffrage militancy and radical feminism, remains somewhat puzzling. Although Hastings's relationship to feminism ultimately became very vexed, she remained committed to provoking argument in the (counter)public sphere: as she reflected in her memoir, 'I still love the social rebel, and challenge mere man-made laws and hate the Pankursts and Christabel who sold the feminist movement. I am the same crusading, anti-philistine woman that I ever was' (1936: 9).

As Benjamin Johnson recently observed, Hastings 'would be easier to promote if she were simply a forgotten modernist innovator or a lost feminist heroine, but she was neither' (2016: 23). Hastings's exceptional mutability also makes her difficult to promote. She lacks a single signature style – or even a unified signature. Moreover, she thrived on the intricate exchanges modern periodical networks enabled, and her writings are hard to disentangle from the web of those exchanges. In other words, the very facets of her work which make her most interesting help to obscure her contribution. Hastings's adeptness at deploying pseudonyms and Correspondence to engineer debate highlighted the fault lines within the women's suffrage movement, while calling attention to her striking capacity to rethink and revise prior opinions. A provocateur par excellence, Hastings promoted discord as an essential element of healthy public debate. With her many voices, she attacked problems from multiple angles – at times, even arguing with herself.

Notes

1. On the anti-feminism of Hastings and the *New Age*, see Delap 2005, Snyder 2016, and Villis 2006.
2. First used in the *Daily Mail* as a term of derision (10 Jan 1906, according to the *OED*), the 'suffragette' label was embraced by many militants. Despite tactical differences between the militant and constitutional societies, individual women not only changed affiliations over time, but also sometimes held overlapping memberships.
3. See Mercer 2004 for discussion of the relationship between *Votes for Women* and the mainstream press.
4. Flora Drummond and Teresa Billington-Greig both led demonstrations with Annie Kenney to 10 Downing Street in 1906, and were refused audience with the prime minister. On 20 March 1907, not long before C. Pankhurst wrote into the *New Age*, the second 'Women's Parliament' was held at Caxton Hall, symbolising the exclusion of women from political forums; the demonstration led to the arrest of seventy-five women and one man: *New Age* editor A. R. Orage. See Pankhurst 1931: 256.
5. For leaders that are sympathetic to women's enfranchisement, see 'Notes of the Week' 4 Nov 1909 and those of 30 June and 7 July 1910, and for mockery, see Lavina King's *The Suffragette: A Farce* in the 30 May 1908 *New Age* (91–2). See also the 13 June 1908 issue that juxtaposes an anti-suffrage article by Bax with two pro-suffrage sonnets by James H. Cousins, reprinted from *Votes for Women* (March and April 1908 issues).
6. Of the fifty-nine respondents, only nine were women, but these included such prominent figures as Mona Caird, Elizabeth C. Wolstenholme Elmy, Beatrice Harraden, and Frances Swiney. By my count, forty-four are clearly in favour of women's suffrage; five clearly against it; and ten present arguments both for *and* against.
7. In 'Feminist and anti-feminist encounters,' Lucy Delap defines a 'periodical community' as that comprised of journals that 'identify each other as important players, promote debate and controversy between each other, exchange material, share contributors, and generally inhabit the same intellectual milieu' (2005: 388, note 48).
8. First division prisoners were allowed to wear their own clothes, eat their own food, and receive mail and visitors with few restrictions, while 'second division' prisoners wore uncomfortable prison garb, and were subject to solitary confinement, labour, and other harsh restrictions and regulations.
9. Text from the *New Age* advertisement for *Woman's Worst Enemy, Woman*, which ran weekly 15 July–28 October 1909.
10. She makes the latter point in another article, in which she continues her criticism of Robins's series: Triformis [Hastings], 'Feminism and the Franchise,' *New Age* 3 Mar 1910: 415.
11. Triformis [Hastings], ibid.; Pethick-Lawrence, 11 Mar 1910: 373.
12. Review of Billington-Greig's *The Militant Suffrage Movement, Common Cause* 6 Apr 1911: 852. The remark was made in response to Billington-Greig's criticism that suffrage organs were unwilling to criticise the WSPU.
13. See Henry Mead's essay on the *Freewoman* in Chapter 15 of this volume.
14. Hastings wrote in *Woman's Worst Enemy, Woman*, 'I so hated at one time being female that I could have denied the fact' (1909: 8).

Works Cited

Ardis, Ann. 2007. 'Debating Feminism, Modernism, and Socialism.' *Gender in Modernism*. Ed. Bonnie Kime Scott. Urbana and Chicago: University of Illinois Press. 160–8.

Carswell, John. 1978. *Life and Letters: A. R. Orage, Beatrice Hastings, Katherine Mansfield, John Middleton Murry, S. S. Koteliansky: 1906–1957*. London: New Directions.

Delap, Lucy. 2005. 'Feminist and Anti-Feminist Encounters in Edwardian Britain.' *Historical Research* 78.201: 377–99.
—. 2007. *The Feminist Avant-Garde: Transatlantic Encounters of the Early Twentieth Century.* Cambridge: Cambridge University Press.
DiCenzo, Maria. 2011. 'Unity and Dissent: Official Organs of the Suffrage Campaign.' *Feminist Media History: Suffrage, Periodicals and the Public Sphere.* Ed. Maria DiCenzo, Lucy Delap, and Leila Ryan. New York: Palgrave. 73–119.
Green, Barbara. 1997. *Spectacular Confessions: Autobiography, Performative Activism, and the Sites of Suffrage, 1905–1938.* New York: St Martin's Press.
—. 2012. 'Complaints of Everyday Life: Feminist Periodical Culture and Correspondence Columns in *The Woman Worker*, *Women Folk*, and *The Freewoman*.' *Modernism/modernity* 19.3: 464.
Grey, Stephen. 2004. *Beatrice Hastings: A Literary Life.* Johannesburg: Penguin Books.
Hastings, Beatrice. 1936. *The Old 'New Age,' Orage and Others.* London: Blue Moon Press.
[Hastings, Beatrice] Beatrice Tina. 1909. *Woman's Worst Enemy, Woman.* London: New Age Press.
Johnson, Benjamin. 2016. *Beatrice Hastings: On the Life & Work of a Lost Modern Master.* Warrensburg, MO: Pleiades Press.
Kelly, Katherine E. 2004. 'Seeing Through Spectacles: The Woman Suffrage Movement and London Newspapers, 1906–13.' *European Journal of Women's Studies* 11.3: 327–53.
Marek, Jayne E. 1995. *Women Editing Modernism: 'Little' Magazines and Literary History.* Lexington: University Press of Kentucky.
Mercer, John. 2004. 'Making the News: *Votes for Women* and the Mainstream Press.' *Media History* 10.3: 187–99.
Nielsen, Rasmus Kleis. 2010. 'Participation Through Letters to the Editor: Circulation, Considerations, and Genres in the Letters Institution.' *Journalism: Theory, Practice, and Criticism* 11.1: 21–35.
Pankhurst, E. Sylvia. 1931. *The Suffragette Movement: An Intimate Account of Persons and Ideals.* London: Longmans, Green and Co.
Robins, Elizabeth. [1907] 1980. *The Convert.* Ed. Jane Marcus. New York: The Feminist Press.
Rosen, Andrew. 1974. *Rise Up, Women! The Militant Campaign of the Women's Social and Political Union 1903–1914.* London and Boston: Routledge & Kegan Paul.
Snyder, Carey. 2016. 'Beatrice Hastings's Sparring Pseudonyms, Feminism, and *The New Age*.' *Beatrice Hastings: On the Life & Work of a Lost Modern Master.* Ed. Benjamin Johnson. Warrensburg, MO: Pleiades Press & Gulf Coast. 170–87.
Tickner, Lisa. 1988. *The Spectacle of Women: Imagery of the Suffrage Campaign 1907–14.* Chicago: University of Chicago Press.
Tusan, Michelle Elizabeth. 2005. *Women Making News: Gender and Journalism in Modern Britain.* Urbana and Chicago: University of Illinois Press.
Villis, Tom. 2006. *Reaction and the Avant-Garde: The Revolt Against Liberal Democracy in Early Twentieth-Century Britain.* London: Tauris Academic Studies. 174–91.

17

'A KIND OF *MINUTE NOTE-BOOK*, TO BE PUBLISHED SOME DAY': KATHERINE MANSFIELD IN THE *ADELPHI*, 1923–1924

Faith Binckes

IN MAY 1922, while in Paris undergoing treatment for tuberculosis, Katherine Mansfield sent a note to Violet Schiff, accepting an invitation to lunch and promising to bring with her the latest number of the *Dial*. The *Dial*, a signal publication of international modernism, was showing increasing interest in Mansfield's work. The magazine had accepted both 'The Doll's House' in January 1922 (Mansfield 2002: 2.315), and 'The Fly' (Kirkpatrick 1989: 160), although it would back out upon discovering that the stories had already appeared in the *Nation and Athenaeum*. However, what Mansfield wanted to show the Schiffs concerned not her, but her husband John Middleton Murry. 'I shall bring *The Dial* on Sunday, with the "slashing" attack on Murry – queer world!' she wrote (Mansfield 2008: 175). Mansfield might have been surprised because this attack was on an article that the *Dial* itself had published. In December 1921, Murry had contributed a critical appraisal of Flaubert, marking the author's centenary. It was a provocative, iconoclastic piece, which asserted that 'to be critical of Flaubert is to prejudice a vested interest, so large an edifice has been built upon the insecure foundation' (Dec 1921: 636). Murry argued, contrasting Flaubert with Baudelaire, that his 'doctrine of the sovereign autonomy of art,' and his love of 'the ivory tower' had been misguided and limiting (Dec 1921: 628). The '"slashing" attack' – which was also a form of self-defence – came from just such a 'vested interest': Ezra Pound. In his reply, Pound pointed to Flaubert's influence on writers such as Laforgue and Joyce, before mocking the reading for its 'flim-flam of wobbling from work to personality' and for Murry's suggestion that Flaubert should have concentrated on the '"expansion of his sensibility"' (Apr 1922: 402). He connected Murry's article with a dying breed of British periodical criticism, which he memorably characterised by the 'insular dunderness' of its Edwardian practitioners (Apr 1922: 401). This was in sharp contrast to Pound's position at the end of 1920, when he had praised Murry's editorship of the *Athenaeum* to the *Dial*'s co-editor Scofield Thayer. Pound observed that Murry 'publishes some of the best work in the Ath,' including Mansfield on his list (Sutton 1994: 20).

This snapshot of Murry and Mansfield's interactions with the *Dial*, the two of them poised on seemingly opposing trajectories in modernism's headline year, is all the more resonant for what happened next. Only a month or so after her note to Schiff, Mansfield's symptoms returned with ferocity, and on 9 January 1923 she died at the Gurdjieff Institute, Fontainebleau. Her death precipitated a crisis for Murry. He emerged from it to edit the *Adelphi*, which made its first appearance in June 1923. In a development of the position he had taken in 'Gustave Flaubert,' the magazine deliberately took aim at modernism's affiliation with the 'ivory tower.' Its prospectus assured readers that it would promote 'literature' over the cliquishly 'literary' (Lea 1959: 106–7). Sydney Janet Kaplan quotes Murry's own unpublished assessment of this move: 'I crossed the Rubicon, and burned my boats, with a vengeance' (2010: 205). It was in this boat-burning publication that Murry crafted his earliest posthumous image of Mansfield. His role was threefold: editor of the periodical in which her works appeared, literary executor, and textual editor of her papers. On all counts, he has received further 'slashing' reviews, from interested contemporaries but also from later critics. One of Murry's most astute readers, David Goldie, observed of the *Adelphi*: 'the spiritual egotism of which Katherine Mansfield had always been suspicious in Murry's character was now given full rein' (1988: 94). For Gerri Kimber, the *Adelphi*'s presentation of Mansfield was marred by the 'sycophantic tone' that would characterise Murry's subsequent marketing of Mansfield's writing (2007: 74). Mansfield scholarship has committed itself to correcting these distortions, and recent readings of her position in periodical culture has continued this tradition. This work has revealed a magazine modernist par excellence, thoroughly embedded in its dialogic networks, playing with identity and bubbling with irreverent humour, shaping traditions as a female, colonial author writing both with and against the grain of her literary inheritances.[1] Surely, then, the *Adelphi*'s 'Katherine Mansfield' was yet another sanitised and sanctified version, marginal to the modernist agenda she had helped to construct?

The aim of this chapter is to reconsider this question. In particular, I am interested in Murry's presentation of the first iterations of Mansfield's 'journal' in the *Adelphi* in 1923 and 1924, when her work was most prominent. The editorial decisions Murry made when constructing the first volume of the *Journal of Katherine Mansfield* (published by Constable in 1927) were contentious from the start, and have been radically reshaped on various occasions. These have included revisions of Murry's own, Margaret Scott's groundbreaking two-volume transcription *The Katherine Mansfield Notebooks* ([1997] 2002), and most recently Gerri Kimber and Claire Davison's 2016 edition *The Diaries of Katherine Mansfield: Including Miscellaneous Works*. The latter has particularly strong words for Murry's editorial efforts on the *Journal*: 'it is to JMM's credit as an editor that he was able to create such a seamless text from so many bits and scraps, but this should not detract from the essentially duplicitous nature of his endeavours, which allowed for a false impression of the legacy of KM's personal writing that lasted for over three-quarters of a century' (Kimber and Davison 2016: 3). Within the limits of this article, I would like to test whether a closer attention to the specifics of this very first, 'magazine edition' alters existing perceptions: of Murry's work as editor, of Mansfield in the *Adelphi*, and how we read both in relation to a modernism shaped by both print and manuscript culture.

Pound's accusation – that Murry had betrayed the aesthetic values of modernism in favour of a middlebrow, retrograde journalistic tradition – anticipates many of the criticisms levelled at the *Adelphi*.[2] Murry himself clearly felt that some sort of boundary had been crossed. But if periodical scholarship has shown us anything, it is that this sort of territory-marking statement has to be treated with caution. As a species of text, periodicals lend themselves to critical paradoxes – rather like modernism itself, as Robert Scholes has suggested (Beetham 1989: 96–100; Scholes 2006). They are both 'closed' and 'open,' collaborative and competitive. The *Adelphi* was a long-running publication, and Michael Whitworth is correct in contrasting its wider position with that of its more identifiably 'modernist' predecessor the *Athenaeum* (2009: 387). But Murry had imported two of the *Athenaeum*'s key figures into the original group behind the *Adelphi*: the mathematically gifted popular science writer J. W. N. Sullivan and the pacifist travel-writer H. M. Tomlinson. As Kaplan has shown, the *Adelphi* also continued the longstanding co-circulation of Murry, Mansfield, and D. H. Lawrence that had started in *Rhythm* and the *Blue Review* (Kaplan 2010). S. S. Koteliansky, who had worked on the 1916 anti-war magazine the *Signature* with them, was also heavily involved before a terminal falling-out with Murry. Koteliansky was central to the magazine's engagement with Russian authors, which also continued a commitment established in the *Athenaeum*. According to Galya Diment, he also played a pivotal role in the founding of the magazine, in suggesting its format, and in the 'understanding' that the *Adelphi* could act as a venue for Lawrence when he was ready to come on board (2011: 142–6). Several of Mansfield's collaborative translations with Koteliansky appeared during the period under consideration – Maxim Gorky's 'Reminiscences of Leonid Andreyev,' which ran between February and April 1924, and another from Chekhov's letters in June (June 1924: 38–45).[3] The *Adelphi* was dominated by male writers, and it certainly featured several of Pound's scions of 'dunderness': H. G. Wells, Arnold Bennett, and Frank Swinnerton. Swinnerton criticised the experimental novels of Joyce and Richardson in the opening number (June 1923: 61–2). Yet from April of the following year the *Adelphi* published Richardson fairly regularly, beginning with her article 'About Punctuation.' Given his work on Mansfield's papers, Richardson's comments on the different reading experiences provided by 'mechanical' print texts, as opposed to manuscripts, might well have resonated with Murry at this point (Apr 1924: 990–1). The *Adelphi* also included figures happy on either side of the vexed modernist/non-modernist divide: Iris Barry, for instance, who reviewed films such as *The Cabinet of Dr Caligari* (Mar 1924: 926–9) and Chaplin's *A Woman of Paris* (Apr 1924: 1009–111).[4] Noëlle Cuny argues that Barry's arrival, especially so close to Richardson's, ushered a welcome modern female component into the magazine (2016: 22). Chaplin himself – viewed by some as master of a modernist medium and by others as a vulgar clown – contributed to the magazine later in its run (Jan 1924: 702–10). This was a publication that, in its early years at least, took a range of approaches to modernist authors, subjects, and forms, rather than jettisoning a singular, Pound-approved modernism in favour of 'insular dunderness.' For instance, Barry and Richardson appeared alongside H.D. in December 1924, an issue that also featured Mansfield (Dec 1924: 618, 581–7).

The *Adelphi* had a form tailored to this more inclusive and eclectic approach. It was modelled on the miscellaneous or 'compendious' magazine (Lea 1959: 105). Murry emphasised the importance of this format in his opening editorial, 'The Cause of it All.' The element he presented as truly distinctive – a 'feature unique in English journalism' (June 1923: 11) – was the magazine's collection of short pieces written by a 'Contributor's Club' who were left free to choose their own subject. At the end of every number the *Adelphi* would print a series of shorter extracts still, headed 'Multum in Parvo.' Murry invited readers (gendered male) to participate, with either 'an article of 1,500–3,000 words or a note of 50–500 words': 'If some imbecility in a newspaper exasperates him, if some casual sight in the street excites him, if some reading in a forgotten or unknown book encourages and stimulates him, if he finds some interesting and valuable fact, then let him write a note' (ibid.).

'Multum in Parvo' – 'much in little' – captured several functions of the 'extract' within this modern miscellaneous periodical. First, a succession of short notes enabled a wide range of material to be covered in a small amount of space. This imitated the format of more popular publications, such as *Tit-Bits*, while the 'Club' connected the *Adelphi* with a periodical tradition as old as Addison and Steele's the *Spectator*. The fleeting everydayness that Murry sought from such pieces was not purely defined by a collective approach, however. It also linked them to modernism's interest in the aesthetics of daily life, one of the principal subjects of periodical publication that could traverse the 'high' and 'middle' brows (Green 2017: 280). Such pieces could also function as a mode of correspondence, and Murry certainly deployed them – in the time-honoured fashion of the 'letters' page – to generate debate. When a male reader sent in a bizarre and misogynistic 'note' about original sin and 'The Ugliness of Women' (Apr 1924: 1025–6), Murry invited a response.[5] Finally, such short reflections also echoed the sort of writing you would find in a diary or a journal, genres which share the time-specific nature of a magazine. Murry announced that from 'next month we shall begin to publish Katherine Mansfield's "Journal"' (June 1923: 11), but his wasn't the only example that the *Adelphi* circulated. It was joined by 'Roger Dataller''s 'From A Miner's Journal' in January 1924 (711–18), and included Koteliansky's translation of parts of Maxim Gorky's diary in October 1923 (383–8).

This emphasis on eclectic individualism was accompanied by Murry's stated ambivalence toward his editorial role. When he received complaints about the lack of a clear direction to his publication, he responded in his second editorial 'A Month After': 'it is not to be expected that the "editorial" and the rest of the magazine should be in unison. We are not singing the same tune: each is singing his own tune. But they are all people in whom I believe, or in whose work I believe' (July 1923: 99). This statement is crucial, less for what it says, but for how Murry chose to say it. In a characteristic manoeuvre, he naturalised an effect that was deliberate and constructed, making 'belief' stand in for editorial power. In 'The Cause of It All' Murry had stated: '*The Adelphi* is nothing if it is not an act' (June 1923: 8), and it is tempting to see this phrase as an illustration of his position more generally. In its intended sense, 'act' means pure 'action' – a 'risk,' an uncalculated gesture of commitment and 'faith' (ibid.). This uses the quasi-religious language that Murry's critics found particularly infuriating, but the phrase also conjures up 'act' in its additional meaning, as conscious performance. A miscellaneous format, with contributions from a wide range of sources, does create a more open and heterogeneous periodical text, but that does not indicate a lack of editorial authority or control.

A similar doubleness was in operation in the second editorial role Murry was performing: his work on Mansfield's papers. Peter Shillingsburg has noted that textual editors, particularly those editing the writing of the deceased, are expected to function as both 'Restorer and Preserver' (1997: 22). This is another uncomfortable, if not impossible position, since 'to restore, a change must take place, to preserve, a change must not take place' (ibid.). Furthermore, not only is such 'change' inevitable as archival material is sifted and prepared for publication, it is mediated by a publishing milieu and marketplace with its own priorities and demands (Tanselle 2013: 333–5). Murry's early presentation of Mansfield in the *Adelphi* must, then, be seen in the light of the materiality of Mansfield's archive, and also the materiality and trajectory of the magazine. As the *Adelphi* had come into existence in part to promote Mansfield, we can imagine a sort of two-way traffic between these points. Nowhere were the pressures and opportunities of this curious position more obvious than in Murry's treatment of Mansfield's previously unpublished material. Here, the greatest number of editorial decisions had to be made, the tension between 'restoration' and 'preservation' was most stark, and the dual implications of Murry's editorial 'act' were most apparent.

In its raw state, Mansfield's 'journal' was a large collection of bound notebooks, exercise books, and the loose sheets that Margaret Scott refers to as 'unbound papers.' Scott (whose transcriptions I have used throughout) described these as a 'huge, amorphous, nearly illegible mass' (Scott qtd in Mansfield 2002: 1.xiii). For obvious reasons, editors of the book volumes have struggled to find a single designation for these variegated textual objects: Murry used both 'Journal' and 'Scrapbook'; Scott tried 'Notebooks'; Kimber and Davison, 'Diaries' with the addition of 'miscellaneous works.' As Mansfield was frequently on the move, she didn't necessarily finish one notebook before starting another, or write in a linear order. She also used the notebooks in a semi-editorial capacity herself, copying out selected sections from the 'unbound papers' in some cases, annotating her writing in others. By the time Constable published the 1927 *Journal of Katherine Mansfield*, Murry had agreed on a consistent format, regularising Mansfield's manuscript forms within a coherently designed volume. This format, and the chronological ordering of the texts by year, was maintained in the 1954 'Definitive' edition. The alternative opportunities presented by the *Adelphi's* periodicity and eclecticism are clear. Just as Mansfield's writing had been heterodox, so the *Adelphi*'s 'magazine edition' of Mansfield could be heterodox. In addition to the unpublished 'Extracts from a Journal' and the co-translations, Murry also reproduced Mansfield's poetry (some previously published in magazines such as *Rhythm*), and short fiction including 'The Samuel Josephs,' 'The Little Girl,' 'A Suburban Fairy Tale,' and 'Something Childish But Very Natural.' Equally important for Murry's first attempts to present Mansfield's 'journal,' the *Adelphi*'s composite format, and its periodicity, allowed different approaches to that writing to be taken. Murry was an experienced editor of periodicals, but this was his first attempt at textual editorship. It is also important to note that in the early 1920s no guidelines existed on how such work should be undertaken, particularly in the case of modern manuscript collections.

To assess what this meant in practice, we should start at the beginning. Mansfield had been represented in the inaugural number of the *Adelphi* in June 1923. This was essentially a memorial issue, including her photograph (previously unpublished), and her story 'The Samuel Josephs' (June 1923: 12–19). Murry had promised material from 'Katherine Mansfield's "Journal"' in the first number, but when it came to it opted for a more accurate designation. The 'Extracts from a Journal' series started in the second number, in July 1923 (137–46), and was preceded by Mansfield's poem 'To L. H. B. (1894–1915)' (136). Murry supplied a preface, explaining that 'L. H. B.' was Mansfield's younger brother Leslie, giving an account of Leslie's death, and providing a description of where the 'majority' of the extracts had originated. As Murry was obviously aware, these are extraordinary pieces of work, produced at a turning point in Mansfield's personal and professional life. Some of the most important and best-known statements concerning her writing about New Zealand appear here, particularly in the section dated 'January 22nd 1916' (July 1923: 140–1). Mansfield's self-examination – 'Now, really, what is it that I do want to write?' (July 1923: 140) – conflates her emotional state with stylistic experiment, refracting both through the lens of memory. Throughout, she addresses her absent brother:

> Now – now I want to write recollections of my own country. Yes, I want to write about my own country until I simply exhaust my store [. . .] Oh, I want for one moment to make our undiscovered country leap into the eyes of the Old World. It must be mysterious, as though floating. It must take the breath [. . .]
>
> Then I want to write poetry. I feel always trembling on the brink of poetry. The almond tree, the birds, the little wood where you are, the flowers you do not see, the open window out of which I lean and dream that you are against my shoulder, and the times when your photograph 'looks sad.' But especially I want to write a kind of long elegy to you . . . perhaps not in poetry. Not perhaps in prose. Almost certainly in a kind of *special* prose.
>
> And lastly, I want to keep a kind of *minute note-book*, to be published some day. That's all. No novels, no problem stories, nothing that is not simple, open. K.M. (July 1923: 141)

The extracts appeared in the same number as Murry's editorial 'A Month After' where, in addition to its response to readers' letters and his defence of the *Adelphi*'s eclectic form, he drew Mansfield's absence back into the foreground: 'Not many months ago I lost someone whom it was impossible for me to lose [. . .] This impossible thing happened. Katherine Mansfield died' (July 1923: 94). Readers could not have missed the connection between Mansfield's description of her bereavement and his own, nor between Murry's description of how this loss connected with his decision to start the *Adelphi*, and Mansfield's own connections between her brother's death and the development of her own writing. These entries came from 1915 and 1916, the period in which (as Murry informed readers) Mansfield was writing *The Aloe*, later to become 'Prelude.' This established a sort of starting point for her mature career, and encouraged readers to view the *Adelphi* in a similar light.

Thus, Mansfield's framing within the *Adelphi* stitched her into the pattern of its concerns, and forged thematic connections not only between her writing and Murry's editorship, but between her work and that of other contributors. The priority given the New Zealand in the first 'Extracts from a Journal' of July 1923 was reflected in pieces that dealt with aspects of colonial experience. The *Adelphi* published a number of stories by South African-born writer Pauline Smith. An important figure in South African women's literature of this period, Smith wrote about the rural Afrikaaner communities of Oudsthoorn, in the 'little Karoo,' an area that she had lived in until the age of twelve. Her fiction explored the religious and gender politics of a largely patriarchal culture. These pieces could be connected to Murry's interest in writing with a religious theme, or to the fact that Smith was promoted by Arnold Bennett, one of the *Adelphi*'s contributors. J. M. Coetzee's influential analysis of Smith's role in the construction of a 'white writing' in pre-apartheid South Africa focused on the nostalgic elements of her depiction of rural life, a reading that encourages us to see her work as part of the *Adelphi*'s indulgence in what D. H. Lawrence called 'introspective sentiment' (Coetzee 1988: 63–81, 115–26; Whitworth 2009: 387). Other critics, however, have drawn attention back to Smith's narrative practices – including her extensive use of free indirect discourse and an English inflected by Afrikaans – and her exploration of gendered subjectivity (Gorak 2007–8). Smith's stories also recalled Mansfield's depiction of marginalised, rural communities, and their sexual politics, in 'The Woman at the Store,' 'Millie,' and 'Ole Underwood,' that had appeared in 1912 and 1913, when Murry and Mansfield were working together on *Rhythm*. Sue Kossew's analysis of the 'farm novel' genre makes a direct comparison between Smith's fiction and 'the drover's wife stories in Australian literary and cultural tradition,' a tradition which undoubtedly influenced Mansfield (2004: 121).

Another thematic connection was made in the number for December 1923. Here, H. M. Tomlinson's essay 'Barbarism' appeared with Mansfield's satirical 1919 story 'A Suburban Fairy Tale.' Tomlinson's piece records a journey 'home' to wartime Britain. The article combined a Conradian perspective on the 'barbarism' of the imperial centre with a very un-Conradian idealisation of Malaysian culture:

> I had become used to the Malays. I had learned to understand fairly well, their ways of living and of looking at things. After a while I had no doubt that they had rightly solved the problem of accommodating themselves to their circumstances. They are a happy folk. You hardly ever see an anxious face among them, and never a hungry child. (Dec 1923: 579)

'A Suburban Fairy Tale' – one of the many writings about childhood Murry published in the *Adelphi* – featured a flock of just such hungry children in post-war London. 'Little B.,' the empathetic son of smug, overfed parents, deserts them as he transforms into a sparrow along with these other little boys, and flies away 'out of sight – out of call' (Dec 1923: 574). Mansfield's satire is obvious, but at other times the more socially aware comment offered in the *Adelphi* drew out the less conspicuous politics of her work. In the fourth number, for September 1923, two long extracts from her journal were published: the first 'A Recollection of Childhood' (316–19); the second 'A Recollection of College' (319–22). In the latter, Mansfield initially expressed frustration at her ability to remember her 'wonderful' teachers but not what they taught her – 'I was thinking yesterday of my *wasted, wasted* early girlhood' (Sep 1923: 319) – before launching into a comic but pointed description of her 'old Principal':

> They told us he was a very learned man, but I could not help seeing him in a double-breasted frock-coat, a large pseudo-clerical pith helmet, a white handkerchief falling over the back of his neck, standing and pointing out with an umbrella a probable site of a probable encampment of some wandering tribe, to his wife, an elderly lady with a threatening [indecipherable] who had to go everywhere in a basket-chair arranged on the back of a donkey. (Sep 1923: 321)

This elaborately constructed figure of late Victorian imperialism was the one who notoriously dismissed Mansfield as 'a little savage from New Zealand' (ibid.). What began as a criticism of her 'idleness,' and continued as a testament to her powers of description and recall, takes on a different resonance after this section (319). Her failure to absorb 'English Literature' and 'English History,' or to properly learn French could be viewed both as the consequence of her distracting, writerly impulses, and as a consequence of her cultural displacement (Sep 1923: 320). The piece was followed by a series of contributions on the current condition of English schools, criticising in particular the quality of state education (Sep 1923: 323–30). This was not a context that encouraged readers to blame children for their *'wasted'* schooldays.

These pieces were retrospective, written in the past and about the past, a past concerned with youth, childhood, and family life. But, as 'A Suburban Fairy Tale' shows, their cosy titles were deceptive. 'A Recollection of Childhood' also invited the reader in, before pulling the rug from under their feet. It opened with the line: 'Things happened so simply then, without preparation and without any shock' (Sep 1923: 316). Far from providing a nostalgic account of simpler times, the 'recollection' was of Mansfield's sister, Gwen, who had died in infancy while Mansfield was a young child. The text tied the three stages of birth, death, and commemoration to three thwarted kisses. The first is a kiss Mansfield's mother refuses her: 'mother did not want to kiss me. Very languid, leaning against pillows, she was eating some sago' (Sep 1923: 317). Second is the kiss Mansfield tries to give Gwen, which only touches the 'goldy tuft' of Gwen's hair (ibid.). Finally comes the kiss Mansfield is instructed to give her 'little sister' – actually a memorial photograph that has been hung in the nursery (319). The *Adelphi* had its own equivalent of this image, in the photograph of Mansfield that Murry had published in the opening pages of the first number. But if anything, 'A Recollection of Childhood' was about the distance between the living and the dead – and sometimes the living and the living – that neither art nor memory can bridge, with 'introspective sentiment' barred by Mansfield's narration.

The material composition of the *Adelphi*, and its ambitions to be an eclectic magazine committed to modern writing beyond the supposed 'ivory tower,' facilitated the two-way contact between Mansfield's work and those of other contributors. But we have been reading these texts as a reflection of Murry's editorial 'acts' principally on the level of content. Equally important were Murry's experiments with form. In the first, July 1923 suite of extracts, Murry chose a piece in which Mansfield linked thematic and stylistic priorities to a specific object: a *'minute note-book*, to be published some day' that would contain 'nothing that is not simple, open.' The '*note-book*' became an object of real significance in the *Adelphi*'s presentation of Mansfield, one with several implications and applications. Like the miscellaneous magazine, its form allowed Murry to record Mansfield's differing methods of presenting her works-in-progress. In a periodical interested in loss and recollection, it represented a form of archive. Like all diaristic writing, preserved yet not explicitly written for publication, a notebook promised the sort of communicative openness that Murry prized. A good, if unusual, example of its use occurs in an extract from 'Multum in Parvo' of September 1923, 'Katherine Mansfield, Stendhal, and Style.' Murry opened thus:

> Lately while turning over the pages of an old notebook – how bitterly one regrets that these old notebooks are always so scattered and so fragmentary! – I lighted on the scraps of conversations with Katherine Mansfield on the ever-new question of style . . .
> She first described the essential of style in a simple and striking metaphor; it was 'to speak to the back of the room.' (342–3)

Mansfield's mastery of rhythm and implication was captured well. Murry quoted her reasons for adding the phrase 'Laura leaned over and gently, very gently, bit her mother's ear,' to her story 'The Garden Party,' in order to avoid a sentence that was too 'naked' or 'too vague' (343). He was even more interested in her 'intuitive' choice of the 'simple and striking metaphor . . . "to speak to the back of the room"' to describe her intended literary effect. Mansfield's imagined audience was, he quoted again, a '"dearly beloved but *simple* person, whose sympathies and desire to comprehend go with you, but who needs to be given a *lead*"' (Sep 1923: 343). Both Mansfield's idiomatic expression and her implied reader suggested similarities to, but also differences from, modernist modes of expression. They combined verbal economy and intellectual ambition, but added intimacy and accessibility. But Murry's drive to construct authenticity by emphasising the 'intuitive' aspect of Mansfield's process both elevated and diminished her. He drew from the critical canon, while she, although 'precise' and 'cogent,' was instinctive (343). He described her statements on how to write as only 'almost authoritative,' despite asserting the uniqueness of her technique. This tension weighs in the textual material too. His invocation of the 'scraps of conversation' and the 'fragmentary' old notebook, witnesses to the unpolished immediacy of that moment, were in contrast to the thorough account of the conversation that he went on to provide. In other words, 'Katherine Mansfield, Stendhal, and Style' drew attention to Murry's Boswellian interventions as 'Restorer and Preserver.'

'Katherine Mansfield, Stendahl, and Style' supports what we have been led to expect from Murry's later editorial constructions of Mansfield. But Murry's more substantial engagements with the 'notebooks' in the *Adelphi* show a similar level of editorial construction to a different end. His introduction to the first 'Extracts from a Journal' claimed that the 'majority' of these entries had been drawn from 'one of the little exercise-books in which she did most of her writing' (July 1923: 137). He favoured diminutives in this introduction – the word 'little' appears several times – but this phrase also invoked the '*minute note-book*' already mentioned, with its suggestion of an incipient work the publication of which Mansfield would have approved. In fact, according to Margaret Scott's transcriptions, while the extracts were written during the same period, only some of this material came from the notebook he described.[6] A large portion of it – including much of the material addressed to Leslie – derived from unbound papers. The mention of the '*minute note-book*' was part of a long passage from another notebook, which, on the evidence of Scott's transcripts, Murry also included on the basis of its date.[7] But Murry's decision to treat these texts as a form of book (albeit only one book of several) did not homogenise or sanitise Mansfield. If anything, this collation of texts makes the differing textures in her writing more, not less, visible. For instance, as we saw in the first long quotation, the majority of the July 1923 'Extracts from a Journal' were deeply serious, concerned with the death of Mansfield's brother, her memories of New Zealand, and her thoughts on the direction her writing should take. But in the middle of these, an encounter while walking by the seaside at Bandol was recorded:

> When I came to the end the sun was going down. So, feeling extremely solitary and romantic, I sat me down on a stone and watched the red sun, which looked horribly like a morsel of tinned apricot, sink into a sea like a huge junket. I began, feebly but certainly perceptibly, to harp 'Alone between sea and sky, &c.' But suddenly

I saw a minute speck on the bar coming towards me. It grew. It turned into a young officer in dark blue, slim, with an olive skin, fine eyebrows, long black eyes, a fine silky moustache.
   You are alone, Madame?
   Alone, Monsieur.
   You are living at the hotel, Madame?
   At the hotel, Monsieur.
   Ah, I have noticed you walking alone several times, Madame.
   It is possible, Monsieur.
   He blushed and put his hand to his cap.
   I am very indiscreet, Madame.
   Very indiscreet, Monsieur. (July 1923: 140; Mansfield 2002: 2.18)

Murry added 'Madame' and 'Monsieur' where Mansfield had written simply 'M.,' but otherwise the section follows Scott's transcription exactly, allowing a sharp shift in content and in tone to stand. Far from promoting 'sentiment,' the extract shows Mansfield ruthlessly and wittily mocking it. The extract is also shot through with an eroticism that figured in her recollections of her brother earlier in the suite of extracts, and in the familial ear-biting scene in 'The Garden-Party.' Although Murry had used his editorial introduction to minimise the appearance of his own input, he had taken very few liberties with the extracts reproduced. He had created the illusion of coherence in one sense (invoking one notebook rather than a combination of notebooks and papers) yet he had loosened it in another, giving the reader access to differing writing voices. He also noted the absence of a page.[8]

A more powerful example of this strategy can be found in Murry's treatment of extracts drawn from 'Notebook 42.' The 1927 edition organises these into the '1919' chapter, adding headings, and noting when Mansfield had selected sections and rewritten them (Mansfield 1927: 102–36). In the *Adelphi*, extracts appeared in the numbers for January 1924 (Jan 1924: 675–80; Mansfield 2002: 2.158–61) and May 1924 (May 1924: 1068–73; Mansfield 2002: 2.161–4). In the May number, Murry published the material he had collected from the later pages of the notebook. He supplemented this with extra passages from Notebook 24 (Mansfield 2002: 2.92–9), and throughout followed the convention of titling each section that Mansfield had adopted in the latter. Unlike Murry's book versions of the *Journal*, and Kimber and Davison's 2016 edition, this approach does not produce a chronological sequence. All the same, the titles do provide a series of frames – a trace, perhaps, of the fact that parts of two of these pieces had already appeared in the *New Age* on 19 April 1917 (595).[9] Mansfield noted this, although Murry followed his usual editorial policy and did not indicate where, or if, a text had been previously published unless copyright required it.

The January 1924 *Adelphi* 'Extracts' included even lighter editorial intervention, with no titling aside from Mansfield's own, and no annotations.[10] On the page this arrangement looks particularly striking (Figure 17.1). No dates or place names were provided, and the only indications of any kind of time were the words 'Saturday,' 'breakfast,' and the striking of midday bells. The extracts contained sections intended for the story 'Second Violin' and direct quotations that might have been fictional, or overheard. There are thirty sections altogether, ranging from a single line to a fairly

THE ADELPHI

As I opened the door I saw her sitting in the middle of the room hunched, hunched, still... She got up, obedient, like a prisoner when you enter a cell. And her eyes said, like a prisoner's eyes say, "Knowing the life I've had, I'm the last to be surprised at finding myself here."

It's raining, but the air is soft, smoky, warm. Big drops patter on the languid leaves, the tobacco flowers lean over. Now there is a rustle in the ivy. Wingley has appeared from the garden next door; he bounds from the wall. And delicately, lifting his paws, pointing his ears, very afraid that big wave will overtake him, he wades over the lake of green grass.

X. loves the louse for its own sake. He has pedigree lice and keeps them in tiny bottles. They feed from his arm. And he spends his life dissecting them and finding their glands and so on.

As S. stood at the door he said quietly, "Nothing is incurable. What seems so useless to-day may be the link that will make all plain to-morrow." We had been discussing hydatids, the Egyptian parasite that begins its cycle of existence in a water-snail, and the effects of hydrophobia. He smiled gently. There was nothing to be alarmed or surprised at. It was all a question of knowing these things as they should be known and not otherwise. But he said none of this and went off to his next case....

At breakfast time a mosquito and a wasp came to the edge of the honey dish to drink. The mosquito was a lovely little high-stepping gazelle, but the wasp was a fierce roaring tiger. Drink, my darlings!

When the coffee is cold L. M. says: "These things have to happen sometimes." And she looks mysterious and important, as if, as a matter of fact, she had known all along that this was a cold coffee day.

What I felt was, he said, that I wasn't in the whole of myself at all. I'd got locked in, somehow, in some little... top room in my mind, and strangers had got in—people I'd never seen before were making free of the rest of it. There was a dreadful feeling of confusion, chiefly that, and... vague noises—like things being moved—changed about—in my head. I lit the candle and sat up and in the mirror I saw a dark, brooding, strangely lengthened face.

"The feeling roused by the cause is more important than the cause itself."... That is the kind of thing I like to say to myself as I get into the train. And then, as one settles into the corner, "For example"—or "Take—for instance"... It's a good game for *one*.

She fastens on a white veil and hardly knows herself. Is it becoming or is it not becoming? Ah, who is there to say? There is a lace butterfly on her left cheek and a spray of flowers on her right. Two dark bold eyes stare through the mesh. Surely not hers. Her lips tremble; faint, she sinks on her bed. And now she doesn't want to go. Must she? She is being driven out of the flat by those bold eyes. Out you go! Ah, how cruel! (*Second Violin.*)

But her hand is large and cold with big knuckles and short square nails. It is not a little velvet hand that sighs, that yields—faints dead away and has to be revived again only to faint once more. (*S. V.*)

What do I want? she thought. What do I really

Figure 17.1 Page spread from 'More Extracts from a Journal' by Katherine Mansfield. The *Adelphi*, January 1924.

long paragraph. They address a range of scenes. The speaker – or speakers, as the status of these texts as fact or fiction is often uncertain – is alone in the house, or garden, which is uninhabited yet animated by objects, plants, and animals. B. ('Jack' in the original) 'digs the garden as though he were exhuming a hated body or making a hole for a loved one' (675). The speaker opens a door to find a woman 'hunched' in the centre of the room 'like a prisoner when you enter a cell' (676). The speaker encounters 'X' who collects lice, who feed 'from his arm' before he kills and dissects them (ibid.). 'S' discusses parasites, water-snails, and the effects of 'hydrophobia' with the speaker, who imagines the reassuring diagnosis 'there was nothing to be alarmed or shocked or surprised at' that is never actually delivered (ibid.). A mosquito and a wasp drink from a bowl, like a gazelle and a tiger (ibid.). A man discusses the feeling of being 'locked in, somehow, in some little . . . top room in my mind' that is invaded by strangers (677). The proposed character from 'Second Violin' sees herself – a stranger – through a veil; another character from 'Second Violin' asks herself (as Mansfield had done) 'What do I want?' (677). The extracts are often located in domestic settings, but they switch unpredictably from the cultivated to the wild, the familiar to the weird, foregrounding the sense of the uncanny and the fantastic that Clare Hanson and Gina Wisker have viewed as a central destabilising effect in Mansfield's fiction (Hanson 2011; Wisker 2012). They certainly invite the reader to see shifting patterns within and across the texts. 'Is it becoming or is it not becoming? Ah, who is there to say?' wonders the unnamed character of her veiled self, the word 'becoming' seeming to transform in its own right, as it hovers between the ordinary meaning ('does the veil suit me?') and the less ordinary ('is something coming into being?') (677).

These collections of 'extracts' call to mind Viktor Shklovsky's comment on the effect created when manuscript fragments are 'printed so to speak naked' in a form of 'original montage': 'This is a writer's notebook, but one presented – and legitimately so – as a finished work of art' (Davison-Pégon 2011: 341). Here, editorial and publishing practice participates not only in the tradition of the 'miscellany,' but in the modernist aesthetic of 'original montage,' legitimising the eclecticism and seeming disorder of the texts. Shklovsky's remarks have an even more definite relationship to Mansfield's writing and to Murry's presentation of it, as they referred to the publication of Chekhov's notebooks. Claire Davison-Pégon uses them in her illuminating discussions of the 1921 Hogarth Press translation of these notebooks by Koteliansky and Leonard Woolf. As a counter-example, Davison-Pégon quotes none other than Murry, in his 4 June 1921 review in the *Nation and Athenaeum*. In another piece of Bloomsbury boat-burning, Murry praised the prose but asserted that it was 'almost a crime to make public fragments of an author's manuscripts which he obviously did not mean to show the world' (Davison-Pégon 2011: 341). The 'Extracts from a Journal' were not absolutely identical in form to this publication – the percentage of single line entries in Chekhov's notebooks is far higher – and yet it begs an obvious question (Chekhov 1921). Did Murry change his mind about the Hogarth Press edition? His fraught construction of Mansfield as the 'English Tchekhov' is well known. This has tended to be viewed as a self-interested, saccharine misrepresentation of both authors (Polonsky 2012: 211–13). But if Davison-Pégon's observation is born in mind then the 'original montage' in the *Adelphi* could be read as a form of modernist publishing practice, which serves not to separate Mansfield from an emerging canon, but to position her within it.

The possibility that Murry was experimenting with not only a modern, but a modernist, form is increased when we consider another posthumous notebook edition that crossed his path around this time. 'The Note-Books of T. E. Hulme,' edited by Herbert Read, appeared in the *New Age* from 19 January 1922 (148–9) and were eventually published in volume form as *Speculations* in early 1924. Murry wrote on *Speculations* in the *Adelphi* in March 1925. Here, he expressed his doubts about Hulme's essays, but not his aphoristic writing, collected under the heading 'Cinders.' He found these 'smaller pieces' admirable, regretting that 'the critical aphorism is a genre which receives very little encouragement in England. Otherwise Hulme might have left behind him a remarkable book' (Mar 1925: 851). However, as Goldie notes, Murry had reviewed *Speculations* elsewhere a year earlier, and the *Adelphi* reprinted two sections from 'Cinders' in the April 1924 'Multum in Parvo' (Goldie 1988: 113; Apr 1924: 982, 1027). Was Murry aware of Read's 1922 'magazine edition' prior to 1924, or to his publication of Mansfield's 'Extracts from a Journal'? No form of direct influence can yet be established, but Murry knew of Read by 1920, when he corresponded with him.[11] Both Murry and Mansfield were extremely well acquainted with the *New Age*. Scott revealed that Mansfield had the 26 January number of the *New Age*, which contained the second instalment of Hulme's 'Cinders,' sent to her in Switzerland (Mansfield 2002: 321; 26 Jan 1922: 167–8). She noted reading it on 28 January, when Murry was visiting. Read's treatment of Hulme's note-form writing and Murry's construction of Mansfield's '*minute note-book*' shared formal parallels, as well as representing similar experiments in the posthumous 'magazine edition.' While their introductions to their respective subjects were very different – Read described Hulme as 'a man of intense masculine force' and 'a military genius' – the divide between this arch-modernist and Murry's supposedly sentimentalised 'Mansfield' is far less clear if we accept that the form in which texts are produced is part of their meaning and effect (19 Jan 1922: 148). It also generates another question concerning the materiality of periodical texts – by nature eclectic and agonistic – and the 'original montage' of the manuscript notebook. To what extent was the privileged, 'original' site of the latter already affected by the more aphoristic, vignette forms of the former, rather than the other way around?

So, where does this lead us? Shillingsburg reminds us: 'editorial work is authoritative; it is an act of power and appropriation. This is just a fact, not a criticism' (1997: 17). To this reader at least, it is clear that this power should be critiqued (and often criticised) along gendered lines, as has certainly been the case for Murry's editorial interventions in Mansfield's work. However, this doesn't mean the *Adelphi*'s 'Katherine Mansfield' is identical to the Mansfield constructed in later, book volumes. The way Murry selected and framed Mansfield's work in the magazine – the focus on childhood, on memory, on social questions, on the colony, on the 'simple, open' – pulled both toward and away from other participants in its modernist matrix, whether they were associated with Bloomsbury, or with publications like the *New Age* and the *Dial*. Equally important, the print forms evoked or constructed – the notebook, the journal, the editorial, the miscellany – carried implications that moved fluently from one literary tradition to another. As such, they were powerful tools that could be used to engage, as well as to subvert, the modernist conventions under construction in 1923 and 1924. The *Adelphi*'s commitment to the eclectic miscellany was, like Murry's criticism of Flaubert, another element of this deliberate challenge, facilitating a treatment of Mansfield's manuscript materials that allowed them to be read alongside other notebook editions produced by precisely these 'competing' groups. There is still a lot of work to be done on actual editorial practice in magazines, and theorists and historians of editorship have much to teach those interested in periodical culture. This is not least due to their sense of texts as generally complex, and frequently compromised, as likely to generate paradox as they are to resolve it. Far from offering a straightforward route into Mansfield's legacy and Murry's curation of it, the 'kind of *minute note-book*' of the *Adelphi* points us to a richer, more provocative territory, in which modes of modernism are everywhere marked by the variousness of manuscript, print, and periodical culture.

Notes

1. We can think here of works by Faith Binckes, Lee Garver, Sydney Janet Kaplan, Jenny McDonnell, Chris Mourant, Angela Smith, and Carey Snyder.
2. The best introduction to the *Adelphi* is Whitworth 2009. For a sustained reading, see Goldie 1988. For a perspective centered on the *Criterion*, Harding 2002. Galya Diment's excellent 2011 monograph on Koteliansky draws extensively on archival material to produce a new perspective on the magazine.
3. Feb 1924: 806–20; Mar 1924: 892–905; Apr 1924: 983–9. For the complex history of Mansfield's work as a translator, and Murry's mediation of it, see Davison 2014.
4. See Dunham-Hickman (Chapter 8 in this volume).
5. Apparently, Lawrence took up the challenge, blasting the writer on his view of woman as 'a piece of lurid meat.' Murry chose not to publish (Harrison 2013: 15; Cuny 2016: 15–16). Harrison attributed this to concerns about libel. Cuny posited some sort of personal offence on Murry's part.
6. Murry's description makes it clear that one notebook is 'Notebook 34' [qMS-1252], which he annotated with dates. Scott recorded one insertion – not included in the *Adelphi* text – and two removed pages (Mansfield 2002: 2.57). The 'Unbound Papers' are taken from MS–Papers-4006-03. Murry edited out references to himself, including a very intimate sentence addressed to Leslie – 'You know I can never be Jack's lover again' (Mansfield 2002: 2.16).
7. This is Notebook 45 [qMS–1253] (Mansfield 2002: 2.32–3). This was the same notebook in which Mansfield had included 'To L. H. B.,' and the passage that Murry included as 'A Recollection of College' (Mansfield 2002: 2.30–2).
8. Probably rather more than a page, judging by Scott (Mansfield 2002: 2.17). Murry either found, or reinstated, these, dated them using Mansfield's letters, and subsequently published them in the *Journal*.
9. Mourant (2016) discusses these pieces as part of Mansfield's experiments in discontinuous narrative – following the 'tradition of Colette' – and to other debates about French literature in the *New Age* (121). It is unlikely that these 'fragments' originated in the notebook Murry was transcribing.
10. There was some alteration of identifying initials, some additional punctuation, and the very occasional cut. Murry's most substantial changes were in order.
11. See the date-list for Herbert Read's Papers, held at the University of Victoria, British Columbia (Read SC100).

Works Cited

Beetham, Margaret. 1989. 'Open and Closed.' *Victorian Periodicals Review* 22.3: 96–100.
Chekhov, Anton. 1921. *The Note-books of Anton Tchekhov*. Trans. S. S. Koteliansky and Leonard Woolf. London: Hogarth Press.
Coetzee, J. M. 1988. *White Writing: On the Culture of Letters in South Africa*. New Haven, CT: Yale University Press.
Cuny, Noëlle. 2016. 'Gender, the Demotic and the Cinema in the Early *Adelphi* (1923–1924): The Iris Barry Moment.' *Études britanniques contemporaines* 50: 1–22. <http://journals.openedition.org/ebc/3080> (last accessed 6 August 2018).
Davison, Claire. 2014. *Translation as Collaboration: Virginia Woolf, Katherine Mansfield, and S. S. Koteliansky*. Edinburgh: Edinburgh University Press.
Davison-Pégon, Claire. 2011. 'Samuel Solomonovich Koteliansky and British Modernism.' *Translation and Literature* 20.3: 334–47.
Diment, Galya. 2011. *A Russian Jew of Bloomsbury: The Life and Times of Samuel Koteliansky*. Montreal: McGill-Queens University Press.
Goldie, David. 1988. *A Critical Difference: T. S. Eliot and John Middleton Murry in English Literary Criticism, 1919–1928*. Oxford: Oxford University Press.
Gorak, Irene. 2007-8. 'A Response to Myrtle Hooper's "Textual Surprise in Pauline Smith's 'The Sinner.'"' *Connotations* 17.1: 68–79.
Green, Barbara. 2017. *Feminist Periodicals and Daily Life: Women and Modernity in British Culture*. Basingstoke: Palgrave Macmillan.
Hanson, Clare. 2011. 'Katherine Mansfield's Uncanniness.' *Celebrating Katherine Mansfield*. Ed. Gerri Kimber and Janet Wilson. Basingstoke: Palgrave Macmillan. 115–30.
Harding, Jason. 2002. *The Criterion: Cultural Politics and Periodical Networks in Inter-War Britain*. Oxford: Oxford University Press.
Harrison, Andrew. 2013. 'Meat-Lust: An Unpublished Manuscript by D. H. Lawrence.' *Times Literary Supplement*, 29 Mar 2013: 15.
Hulme, T. E. 1924. *Speculations: Essays on Humanism and the Philosophy of Art*. London: Kegan Paul.
Kaplan, Sydney Janet. 2010. *Circulating Genius: John Middleton Murry, Katherine Mansfield, and D. H. Lawrence*. Edinburgh: Edinburgh University Press.
Kimber, Gerri. 2007. 'From Flagrant to Fragrant: Reinventing Katherine Mansfield.' *Moveable Type* 3: 71–102.
Kimber, Gerri and Claire Davison, eds. 2016. *The Diaries of Katherine Mansfield: Including Miscellaneous Works*. Edinburgh: Edinburgh University Press.
Kirkpatrick, B. J. 1989. *A Bibliography of Katherine Mansfield*. Oxford: Clarendon Press.
Kossew, Sue. 2004. *Writing Woman, Writing Place: Contemporary Australian and South African Fiction*. London: Routledge.
Lea, Frank. 1959. *The Life of John Middleton Murry*. London: Methuen.
Mansfield, Katherine. 1927. *Journal of Katherine Mansfield*. Ed. John Middleton Murry. London: Constable.
—. 1954. *Journal of Katherine Mansfield: The Definitive Edition*. Ed. John Middleton Murry. London: Constable.
—. [1997] 2002. *The Katherine Mansfield Notebooks*. Ed. Margaret Scott. Complete edition. Originally published in two volumes. Minneapolis: University of Minnesota Press.
—. 2008. *The Collected Letters of Katherine Mansfield: Volume 5, 1922–1923*. Ed. Margaret Scott and Vincent O'Sullivan. Oxford: Oxford University Press.
Mourant, Chris. 2016. '"Alors, Je Pars": Katherine Mansfield and the *New Age*, 1915–17.' *Katherine Mansfield's French Lives*. Ed. Claire Davison and Gerri Kimber. Amsterdam: Rodopi/Brill. 108–24.

Murry, John Middleton. Correspondence with Herbert Read. Herbert Read Fonds (Read SC100). Special Collections, Library of the University of Victoria.
Polonsky, Rachel. 2012. 'Chekhov and the Buried Life of Katherine Mansfield.' *A People Passing Rude*. Ed. Anthony Cross. Cambridge: Open Book Publishers. 201–14.
Scholes, Robert. 2006. *The Paradoxy of Modernism*. New Haven, CT: Yale University Press.
Shillingsburg, Peter. 1997. *Resisting Texts: Authority and Submission in Constructions of Meaning*. Ann Arbor: University of Michigan Press.
Sutton, Walter, ed. 1994. *Pound, Thayer, Watson and* The Dial: *A Story in Letters*. Gainesville: University of Florida Press.
Tanselle, Thomas. 2013. 'Varieties of Scholarly Editing.' *Essays in Bibliographical History*. Ed. Thomas Tanselle. Charlottesville: University of Virginia Press. 331–52.
Whitworth, Michael. 2009. 'Enemies of Cant: *The Athenaeum* (1919–1921) and *The Adelphi* (1923–1948).' *The Oxford Critical and Cultural History of Modernist Magazines: Volume 1, Great Britain and Ireland*. Ed. Peter Brooker and Andrew Thacker. Oxford: Oxford University Press. 364–88.
Wisker, Gina. 2012. 'Katherine Mansfield's Suburban Fairy Tale Gothic.' *Katherine Mansfield Studies* 4.1: 20–32.

18

May Sinclair, Magazine Writer: Exploring Modernisms through Diverse Journals

Laurel Forster

May Sinclair was a working woman writer: she wrote to earn an income and to forge a career and was successful at both, despite 'persistent cultural misogyny' (Marek 2010: 64). Sinclair's background boasted no family connections, established literary traditions, or financial sponsorship; she had to pursue her professional path through her own efforts and industry, with limited help from her friend, Anthony Deane, in placing her poems and in offering professional advice (Raitt 2000: 62–3). Sinclair had a professional writing career that spanned from the late nineteenth century when she translated German, to the late 1920s, with her last collection of short stories, *The Intercessor and Other Stories*, published by Macmillan in 1932. Sinclair had built a reputation for being a writer who tackled difficult issues concerning women's lives, and at times was more popular in Europe and America than Britain.[1] Long known for only three of her novels, *Mary Olivier: A Life* (1919), *Life and Death of Harriett Frean* (1922), and *The Three Sisters* (1914), originally published by Macmillan and others but importantly reprinted by Virago in the early 1980s, Sinclair's extensive *oeuvre* in fact includes over twenty novels, nearly forty stories, two full-length works of philosophy, numerous reviews, editorial work on the Brontës, and various war and feminist writings. Gradually, she is becoming better known and appreciated.[2] Alison Pease has argued that May Sinclair's 'increasing narrative experiment [. . .] align[s] her with other modernists experimenting with narrative, perspective, time compressions and ruptures of sequence, elisions, ironies of climax and epiphanic moments' (Pease 2012: 57). She started out modestly with German translation work that she found arduous and tedious, needing an income to support herself and her dependent mother. However, by contrast, at the high point of her career Sinclair competed with much better-remembered writers such as Thomas Hardy, and was feted on an American book tour.[3] Moreover, Sinclair's success and position enabled her to use her influence to support younger writers, notably Ezra Pound (Raitt 2000: 4). From obscurity to celebrity, Sinclair had known the vagaries of the life of a writer, the struggles common to the profession, both internal and external. She took her writing career seriously, eliminating and redacting biographical material, determined that no personal records would remain and that her work would stand for itself. The subject matter of the struggling writer is often to be discerned, in one way or another, in much of her fiction, and non-fiction too. Indeed, the novel that made her name, *The Divine Fire* (1904) focuses upon the professional booksellers' marketplace and the ethical choices of writers, agents, and publishers. Sinclair's knowledge of 'the book trade' made fine and relevant subject matter for her fiction, but undoubtedly, given her growing reputation as a novelist, was also put to good use in using periodical publications to expand her readership and develop her career.

Although Sinclair's fiction was published by significant publishers on both sides of the Atlantic such as Hutchinson, Cassell, Collins, Constable, Holt, and Blackwood as well as Macmillan, much of her work first made its appearance elsewhere, in magazines and periodicals. This less well-known portion of Sinclair's writing output, such as the appearance, and sometimes duplicate publication, of her short stories in magazines before issuing them in collections, the serialisation of her novels in periodicals before full publication, and the printing of her reviews and commentary in a vast array of journals, periodicals, and magazines, is brought into greater focus here. Like other writers of the time, publication in a variety of magazines of the modernist period was a crucial part of the process of getting Sinclair's name known. Equally important, these publications allowed her to access and to address different readerships for her work. In the past, Sinclair has been criticised for failing to find a home for her writing, for adopting different modes of modernism, and even of being a 'literary copycat.'[4] Indeed, the range of periodicals she published in was exceptionally broad, accommodating her particularly wide range of interests. Moreover, diverse periodical publication enabled Sinclair to present her work to various publics and the situatedness of her stories and articles in magazines offers insight into the numerous modern arenas and periodical cultures with which she engaged. This chapter will consider some of the ways in which these venues contributed to May Sinclair's career, by initially offering a summary of the range of Sinclair's inclusion in periodical publications, and then by discussing three distinct scenarios in which she benefited from different aspects of distinctive periodical fields. The first of these is through her affiliation to the Society of Authors and her 'professional' interventions in the *Author*, which reveal Sinclair's understanding of her position as a writer. Second, is through the work of other reviewers whose writing had a marked impact on her career and status, indicating a dependency upon the work of unknown others for her success. Third, is the appearance in women's magazines of Sinclair's First World War writings in the early part of the war, and the ways Sinclair, as a well-known woman writer by this time, adapted her war experiences into different offerings and was simultaneously adopted by a range of publications targeted at female audiences.

Modernism, Modernity, and Diverse Magazines

In their 2010 study *Modernism in the Magazines*, Scholes and Wulfman drew upon Ezra Pound's taxonomy of the magazine field. This included his classification of experimental magazines as 'free,' 'impractical,' or 'fugitive,' and his recognition that these publications existed in tandem with 'commercial' venues that kept their ideas in circulation. Scholes and Wulfman argued, therefore, that 'to understand modernism we must follow its workings in both the "free" magazines and those that are bound to the marketplace' (Scholes and Wulfman 2010: 24–5). Sinclair's work spans both kinds of magazines and it is possible to understand career advancements and risks associated with both types of venture.

George Bornstein's emphasis upon the politics of the page in *Material Modernism*, draws attention to the significance of multiple editions or versions of a text and a text's 'bibliographic code' of 'cover design, page layout, or spacing, among other factors' (5–7). Because Sinclair sold a number of her novels as serialisations, and because of the wide variety of publication placement of her work, the implications of this 'bibliographic code' are important to the present discussion. Sean Latham, in discussing the recovery of magazine archives, has drawn attention to the complexity of magazines, following McGann's notion of the 'radiant' text, to include interactions between magazines and advertisements and illustrations (2011: 412). Latham calls for the reading of 'more than just the things we already recognise' and for the consideration of the 'intertextual connections' potentially made by the reader (412). Magazines and journals – from highbrow to popular, whether they were free, select by subscription-membership, or reliant upon advertisements – were, through their specific focus, in a position to reflect the developing dynamics of literary, cultural, and social movements. The placing of Sinclair's writing across a range of magazines, I argue, demonstrates her engagement with diverse modernisms and modernities. I have discussed elsewhere Sinclair's interest in and commitment to the Imagist style of writing and the ways she supported this nascent modernist movement through her writing, reviews, and essays (Forster 2006: 99–122). In the present discussion, I will argue further that through Sinclair's engagement with a whole host of periodical cultures, we can discern an engagement with a broad range of cultural modernities. However, at the same time this cultural diversity can also be understood in more commercial terms. Rosenquist and Wood identify the problem of trying to understand modernism's complex relationship to the public, arguing that: '"the public" itself is either historically or regionally contingent, bound by a specific event or locale or entirely defined by the discourse that addresses it' (2016: 303). If different periodicals serve different publics, we can understand the attractions associated with multiple publication. For instance, Sinclair, despite her personal reticence and shyness at times, was clearly aware that she needed an American audience to advance her career, but also for pragmatic purposes. I discuss the rare interview in which she addresses this issue later in this chapter.

The Range of Sinclair's Work Across Periodical Publications

May Sinclair has been described as 'a transitional writer who repeatedly remade herself, testing the limits of acceptable content and then form' (Kunka and Troy 2006: 5). In this way her writings are, Andrew Kunka and Michelle Troy argue, 'a genealogy of literary modernism's development from its roots in traditional realism to the experiments with narrative point-of-view and stream-of-consciousness phrasing that became its hallmarks' (5). Sinclair's writings, then, may be understood against the 'spectrum of emerging modernism' (5). However, this has been seen as an awkward fit, with Sinclair problematically existing 'inside' and 'outside' modernism, and pushing back against stable definitions of both modernism and feminism (Kunka and Troy: 7; Pykett: 103). Furthermore, Sinclair's own need to earn money from her writing, her eventual fame with her third novel, *The Divine Fire* (1904), and her support of emerging modernist writers, raises the often-asked question of the high cultural position of some modernist writing versus the appeal to a mass audience in order to procure sales and income. It has been noted by Sinclair's second biographer, Suzanne Raitt, that Sinclair was 'simultaneously excited and uneasy at the idea of herself as a novelist' and that the 'many advantages of being a writer [. . .] were made more fraught by Sinclair's realisation that now part of her intellectual and creative life was for sale in a market that was much more savage and pervasive than that in which her early poems and stories had appeared' (2000: 78).

Sinclair published in various magazines. This included periodicals devoted to feminism, to the developing fields of philosophy and psychology, and to more experimental fields such as psychical research. The appearance of her work, or discussions of her work, across so many journals is testament to her intellectual engagement with not just differing modes of modernism, but with a range of intellectual fields of study. May Sinclair's early consciousness of herself as a writer was clear from her philosophical studies and poetry contributions to the *Cheltenham Ladies' College Magazine* made at the end of the nineteenth century. She attended the College for a year while Dorothea Beale, campaigner for women's education, was principal. Sinclair's interest in Freud and psychology, as well as philosophy, led her to publish articles in the *Medical Press*, *Proceedings of the Aristotelian Society*, and other learned journals. In a different context, and despite the dislike of suffragette violence and rallies evident in her novel *Tree of Heaven*, Sinclair offered brief messages of support for the pro-suffrage *Votes for Women*. Furthermore, in 1912 she wrote very publicly to the *Times* to argue against the work of prominent anti-suffragist Sir Almroth Wright (Gough 2009: 1–17).[5]

Her review work was published in the British and US presses such as the *New York Times*, the *Bookman*, the *English Review* and the *Literary Digest International Book Review*, as well as in specialist modernist magazines. Some of her early poetry was published in the *Pall Mall Magazine*, but later her work appeared in the *Egoist* and the *Criterion*. Her short stories appeared in large-circulation literary magazines such as *Century Illustrated Monthly Magazine*, *Macmillan's*, and *Harper's Magazine*. However, Sinclair's understanding of the support that could be offered through the networks of magazine publishing extended to the 'free' or highbrow modernist magazines. When T. S. Eliot's the *Criterion: A Quarterly Review* (1922–39) made its debut, Sinclair lent her support to this intellectual literary magazine with her new short story 'The Victim' (*Criterion* Oct 1922: 65–88). The situatedness of this story is significant. It keeps high literary modernist company, being faced on the opposite page by T. S. Eliot's famous ending to *The Waste Land*, 'Shantih, shantih, shantih' (64). Also in this volume is Virginia Woolf and S. S. Koteliansky's translation of F. M. Dostoevsky's 'Plan of the Novel, "The Life of a Great Sinner"' (16–33) and Valery Larbaud's 'The "Ulysses" of James Joyce' (94–103). Woolf, Eliot, E. M. Forster, W. B. Yeats, Ezra Pound, Wyndham Lewis, and Ford Madox Ford all published in Eliot's magazine, and Sinclair published another short story and a poem here. Sinclair, keen to assist younger writers, 'lent her popularity and reputation to this venture' (Kunka and Troy 2006: 8). In a similarly supportive vein, Sinclair argued for the Imagist poets in the *Dial* and special edition of the *Egoist* in 1915. But Sinclair also published in more commercial women's magazines too, such as the American edition of *Good Housekeeping*, the *Queen*, and *Woman at Home*. In short, a range of publication destinations may be discerned, ranging from the specific professional journal to the general interest magazine, from the daily press to the annuals, from the commercial women's magazines, serving as a marketplace for advertisers of all descriptions, to the rarefied, elite literary journal destined to be read by smaller, dedicated followers of modernist fashions. Sinclair serialised her novels in *Ainslee's Magazine*, *Atlantic Monthly*, *Century Illustrated*, *Little Review*, and *North American Review*. Such a broad spread of outlets for her work illustrates ways in which magazine publishing potentially opened up new markets, that is new reading publics, for Sinclair. Sinclair was fully aware of the ways a magazine could enhance a writer's reputation, enabling that writer to earn a living. However, she was writing at a time of flux in the publishing world, with writers and others vulnerable to the power of the publishers and the vagaries of the commercial market. Despite professing 'a wanton ignorance of economics' (*Author*, Feb 1905: 147–8) she was acutely aware of the role that writers played in the business side of the literary world.

Building a Writing Career

Sinclair's consciousness of writers' responsibilities in their professional lives may be glimpsed from her contributions to the *Author* (1890–1926). This periodical was set up and edited by Walter Besant as the organ of his Society of Authors (1885), a professional organisation intended to establish the protection of literary property, instruct writers in copyright law and to protect them in their dealings with publishers. Besant (1836–1901) was a successful writer of novels, biographies, and histories, whose work brings to life a social consciousness about London slums. The *Author*, founded in 1890 and published on the first of each month, was known for its debates about developments in the writing profession and matters concerning authors and their work, such as income tax, and, importantly, instructed authors how best to use the society. In addition, it offered notes and commentary on members' publications, while also regularly overviewing the contents of other magazines. Although not specifically a 'modernist' magazine, this periodical offered access to writing cultures of the time, supporting its writers and making their professional views known. Latham and Scholes, amongst others, have discussed the importance of periodicals as conduits for unfolding conversations, particularly with other magazines (Latham and Scholes 2006: 517–31). The *Author* participated in this through its reports of the contents of other magazines certainly, but also in a particularly industry-intensive way, through articles that offered specific warnings to its members about the actions and behaviours of certain publishers and outlets. Anthony Deane, Sinclair's curate friend, sponsored her membership of the society in 1897 (Raitt 2000: 79, note10). For a writer like Sinclair, this societal affiliation offered much-needed industry-related knowledge and professional information. As Morag Shiach has shown, between 1899 and 1905 the *Author* engaged in a protracted discussion of typewriting, and of fees payable to typists, as it became increasingly common for publishers to request typewritten manuscripts (Shiach 2004: 67). In an article titled 'Type-writing: A Protest' published in February 1905, Sinclair contributed to this debate. She wrote to protest about 'the increasing tendency of typists to lower their prices, which were low enough before in all conscience,' and in this article was trying to protect the payment of workers adjunctive to the writing profession, taking into account aspects such as the quality of the work and the seasonal employment variations of the local town

(147–8). Such matters concerning the writing industry frequently took place through the correspondence pages of this journal for writing professionals; of note were the discussions about the honesty of agents and the tactics of magazines in their dealings with authors. We might speculate that Sinclair was influenced by cautionary letters to the *Author* about *Smart Set: A Magazine of Cleverness* (1900–30), because in 1908 she declined the serialisation of her early novel *Kitty Tailleur* (1908) in the *Smart Set*, despite realising that the one thousand pounds offered would have made her 'independent at one stroke' (Raitt 2000: 77, note 1).

Sinclair was a generous supporter of the work of the Society of Authors and in 1909, records show in the *Author* that she donated a substantial fifteen pounds to the cause, far in excess of many donations which were one or two pounds at most (1 Oct 1909: 2). Sinclair's name appears as one of the members who undertook not to publish very cheap editions of her work (1 June 1909: 240–2). And, on the death of George Meredith (1828–1909), it was May Sinclair who had attended both the private, family funeral and the memorial service, and who wrote the review of his work. The editorial obituary, complete with illustration of Meredith, praises him as the 'father of the profession' and points to Sinclair's appreciation of his work (1 June 1909: 248–50). Sinclair's long review, 'George Meredith,' refers to him as 'king to the kings and great lords of literature,' but she also questions, at some length, the fall in his popularity (*Author* 1 Jun 1909: 250–4). The article also demonstrates an awareness of the growing interest and concern over copyright, expressed in the journal. Sinclair's obituary article has a footnote claiming copyright in the United States, and this very matter was brought to attention in the previous month's edition in an article, 'The United States Copyright Act' (1 May 1909: 207–9). In this long review of Meredith's work, Sinclair models the new mode of authors protecting their own work, perhaps in the full knowledge of her developing American profile.

Another professional writing matter that vexed Sinclair, and others, was the rising power of the literary agent. Sinclair had experienced difficulties with literary agents. In 1897, risking her relationship with Blackwoods, she appointed the literary agent A. P. Watt, but 'soon regretted it' and by 1904 had dismissed him (Raitt 2000: 79–81, 86). Yet in 1911, she wrote to the *Author* again, this time in favour of literary agents (1 Dec 1911: 80–1). Sinclair entered the debate, acknowledging that although some perhaps did 'play into the hands of the publishers against the interests of the author' (81), she claimed that her own 'has actually disregarded his own immediate interests in the interests of his clients' (81). Sinclair's sense of responsibility to those connected with the writing profession and to her fellow writers was evident through her engagement with this profession-oriented periodical, the *Author*. However, this was not the only way in which a periodical had influenced the professional career of May Sinclair.

The Significance of Review Work

From early in her career, Sinclair wrote reviews of writers' work, and in a rare interview she was clear about her reasons: 'I wrote a great deal of poetry at first, and then, as I was compelled to make writing a profession, I did a good deal of reviewing. I translated a good many books, too' (*New York Times* 12 Nov 1905: 6). Sinclair started her reviewing career with a review of a teacher's textbook in the *Cheltenham*

Ladies' College Magazine in 1896, moving on to reviews in the *Bookman* at the *fin de siècle*, then in the *Atlantic Monthly*, the *North American Review*, the *Little Review*, the *Egoist*, the *English Review*, the *Dial*, and more. Her subjects included the work of T. S. Eliot, Dorothy Richardson, Ezra Pound, Richard Aldington, H.D., Rabindranath Tagore, and Violet Hunt, amongst others, to say nothing of her extensive work on the Brontë sisters. She had been invited by Ezra Pound to write on T. S Eliot's *Prufrock And Other Observations* for the *Little Review*, and this was an important review for Eliot's career (Kunka and Troy 2006: 8). Sinclair wrote reviews to earn a living, but clearly understood the significance of a favourable review in an influential periodical.

Indeed, Raitt has discussed how Sinclair's big break in America was largely due to the favourable reviews she received in US periodicals. While *The Divine Fire* initially received lukewarm reviews in Britain, it was appreciated by the wider American market. Writing in November 1905, by which point *The Divine Fire* was into an astonishing fifteenth US edition, 'Pendennis' observed that the *New York Times* 'foresaw its literary importance and hailed it as one of the unusual Autumn books of 1904' (*New York Times* 12 Nov 1905: 6). Once the *Nation* (1865–) and the New York edition of the *Bookman* had conferred great praise, so other magazine offers of publication ensued. Sales in Britain improved after a positive review by Owen Seaman in *Punch*, which praised the American reading public for their '"keener *flair* for genius"' (*Punch* 1 Feb 1905: 90; Raitt: 95). As Raitt has noted, following this the *New York Times* responded with two further, related pieces, and sales hiked even further.[6] This transatlantic parrying over American and British reading publics, led by reviewers, brought Sinclair's third novel to international attention and endowed her with the literary and financial success she needed. This had been achieved by addressing a range of audiences and succeeding with the American reading public, a larger market than the British one. Furthermore, after *The Divine Fire* had received favourable reviews in America, Sinclair was approached by *Ainslee's Magazine* (New York), *Lippincott's Magazine*, and *McClure's Magazine*, all of whom wanted to publish her stories or serialise her novels (Raitt 2000: 93). This branching out to the American literary and magazine market was seen by Sinclair as a way of securing an income, with sales improved by an endorsement from the manager of Wanamaker's department store in New York, and perhaps because the US market erroneously believed it to be her first novel (Raitt 2000: 94). Raitt has argued that Sinclair was financially dependent upon the success of *The Divine Fire*, and acutely aware of the difference that positive reviews would make to sales in America and hence her own income (2000: 93). Following this magazine-based attention, Sinclair went on a 'triumphal tour of the East Coast to meet her readers and prominent American literati' (Raitt 2000: 96). This included an invitation to meet the president, and Mark Twain's seventieth-birthday dinner party, where she sat next to Twain himself (Raitt 2000: 96–7).

Sinclair, despite her aversion to this format, was described in detail in the *New York Times* 'Pendennis' interview. Her American tour and her novel, *The Divine Fire*, were all introduced and explored for a New York audience, along with a profile illustration of the young May Sinclair. Much is made in the interview of both the anticipated worldliness of Sinclair – revealing an underlying assumption that fiction is fundamentally autobiographical – and the surprise when she told the interviewer that she had never participated in boarding house life, or met the poet who forms the central character of her book. Sinclair reveals that until she came to New York she had never met a poet, but swiftly praises Richard Guilder and his poems, and expresses 'her delight' in her first visit to America. 'Pendennis' is therefore astonished at the strength of Sinclair's imagination, arriving at glowing praise for the realism of the novel. Sinclair is described as 'intellectually toned,' and much is made of the 'added interest' of her English accent (ibid). The diverse audiences for this novel are made apparent: 'the authoress had been surprised she said, to find that it was read in the slums of London a great deal, where the only divine fire is usually an inspiration of stale beer or maddening gin' (ibid). And in this relentlessly positive review, the ultimate praise is showered upon Sinclair: 'May Sinclair is herself a poet, consumed with an ardent divine fire of her own, that she trims and pokes, and keeps clear of ashes and dust with her intellectual sense of rational truths. She is the modern Charlotte Brontë' (ibid). Little wonder, then, that Sinclair afforded this interviewer another ten minutes of her time, and related a story of an unhappy, furtive interview experience beforehand. This review works hard to reveal both Sinclair and her book, expounding her qualities as an intriguing and intellectual English writer, dealing with complex issues of the day in a realistic fashion. The important work of magazines and the periodical press in reaching an American market, and thus securing an income for Sinclair, is evident in such glowing reviews.

Sinclair's book tour was a year after *The Divine Fire*'s publication, and in this light Sinclair was advised by McClure to serialise her next novel before its publication in book form, in order to receive more immediate attention: she duly accepted a handsome fee for the serialisation of *The Helpmate* (1907) in the *Atlantic Monthly* Jan–Sep 1907 (Raitt 2000: 96). The *Atlantic Monthly: A Magazine of Literature, Science, Art and Politics* was published in Boston and New York and printed by the Riverside Press, Cambridge, MA. The first instalment of Sinclair's 'The Helpmate' appears immediately after the editorial section written by 'B.P.' which addresses the readers and writers directly, highlighting the feelings that a New Year brings, mentioning that this is the *Atlantic's* jubilee year and as toastmaster, thanks the writers and subscribers (Jan 1907: 1–4). This coded placement within the periodical indicates the privileged position given to Sinclair's work. Sinclair's serialised novel comes with a footnote that declares 'Copyright, 1906, by May Sinclair' (again, perhaps, professional practice learnt from the *Author*, as works were not always protected without a declaration). Following the nineteen-and-a-half-page section of Sinclair's novel, set out in two newspaper-like columns (5–24), is a discussion of 'Japan and the Philippine Islands' by James S. Le Roy (24–34), then a poem, 'To One Impatient of Form in Art' (35) by Richard Watson Gilder, and then a short story set in the American 'wilderness,' 'The Tall Man,' by S. Carleton (36–44). Following this are discussions of the 'Criminaloid' (prominent quasi-criminals), life insurance, autobiography, and of a country newspaper editor's work (44–96). Then the second part of Edith Wharton's 'A Motor-Flight Through France' (98–105), reviews of 'The New Novels' by Mary Moss (113–26), and 'The Contributors' Club' – a section of shorter pieces (137–44). This latter was a regular feature specifically designed to be 'briskly controversial' and an opportunity for emerging writers (Sedgewick 1994: 153). In this way fiction is juxtaposed with travel and general-interest writing. There is variety and quality, drawing in, it might be assumed, a range of readership groups. Such a mixed bag of contents would appeal to men and women of a literate, class-conscious readership, perhaps with money or leisure to travel, a conservative interest in culture, and some position in society. Sinclair's novel, the first article of the *Atlantic Monthly*'s year, sits amongst other short fiction, non-fiction, travel writing, accounts of social and cultural issues, and reviews. And although the *Atlantic Monthly* insisted on deleting a suggestive sentence (Raitt 2000: 100), the inclusion of Sinclair's serialised novel about marital fidelity and female sexuality in such a wide-ranging journal, appealing to a literate audience of the cultural elite, but also presenting itself as a commentator on contemporary life, exposed Sinclair's work to a more general audience than other purely literary journals.[7]

Writing the War in Women's Magazines

Sinclair may have declined the *Smart Set* in 1908, a journal that published Vernon Lee and Djuna Barnes in the same period, but by 1917 Sinclair had published short stories in *Good Housekeeping* (US), *Harper's Magazine* (US), *Woman at Home*, and *Queen: The Lady's Newspaper*. Sinclair's support for women, and her writerly inclination to expose and explore the limitations of women's lives is a strong theme throughout her fiction, and in many ways Sinclair's feminism runs through her work. However, the cause of women beyond fiction continued to be important to Sinclair to the extent that in 1915 she placed 'Women's Sacrifices for the War' in the widely read *Woman at Home* (1893–1920) magazine. This magazine, started as a sixpenny monthly, was concerned with aspects of middle-class domestic life for women, supporting their class distinctions in opposition to aristocratic values. It often led with a biographical article and photo-portrait (Beetham 1996: 161). Sinclair's reputation as a writer, her status within the literary landscape, and her knowledge of publishing with magazines and periodicals in England and in the United States, served her well at the outbreak of war.

Sinclair entered the physical space of the First World War when she accepted the challenge of travelling with an ambulance corps to the Belgian front line in 1915. This had come about because of her association with Dr Hector Munro of the Medico-Psychological Clinic, (which later became the Tavistock) and her financial contribution toward the trip. Her role was that of secretary, publicity officer, and reporter, and her record of that time was promptly published as *A Journal of Impressions in Belgium* (1915). Although Sinclair's trip was curtailed (perhaps as a consequence of her own behaviour), she was conscious of traversing established war zones, both in terms of physical front-line locations and in terms of adopting an unusual mode of war reporting. Her journal focuses less on the factual aspects of war, and more on her emotional, psychological, and impressionistic responses (Forster 2008: 231). In this 'emotional honesty' she defied convention, and in the employment of modernist techniques of fragmentation and unreliability she subverted the usual masculinised mode of war reporting (232–4).[8] Sinclair reworked her short time in Belgium and her emotionally charged responses and connection with 'Reality' into her fictions, moulding her experiences and impressions into material for a number of her postwar novels (Forster 2008: 243–6). It has been remarked that Sinclair's war writing represented a 'backtracking in her development as a novelist' (Zegger 1976: 82). However, her impressions, although controversial at the time, offered a radically different view of war. Written from the restricted point of view of a middle-class, middle-aged woman's ability to participate, she pursues comprehension by searching for a sense of reality. Her impressions struck a chord with women's view of war as presented by women's magazines.

Many of Sinclair's war writings appeared in periodicals. An early serialisation of her *Journal of Impressions* appeared as 'From a Journal' in the *English Review* (May–July 1915). Even earlier than this, in November 1914, Sinclair had published 'Red Tape' in *Queen: The Lady's Newspaper and Court Chronicle* (14 Nov 1914: 802–3), and in December she published a commentary, 'Chauffeurs at the Front' in the *New Statesman* (26 Dec 1914: 295–7). In a more conventional mode, Sinclair reported the work of women in the war in her reportage for the press such as the *Daily Chronicle* about the women of Pervyse.

Sinclair's short story, 'Red Tape,' about a comfortable pair who consider participation in the war, but miss their chance because they are over forty and therefore too old, draws attention to the age-related limitations of usefulness in war. It also pointedly criticises a middle-class complacency. As if further to rouse the readers of *Queen*, the story is accompanied by an illustration of a lady of leisure, reading on her chaise longue, in long Edwardian dress. The story of the couple, and the interaction with the illustration, provocatively questions class codes regarding wartime participation. It appears in the 'Christmas Number' of *Queen*, complete with its full-page colour illustration of a children's Christmas Eve 'fete' at the Savoy, Father Christmas and a Christmas Tree in the background. The paper itself carried a number of items that related to the dress and social codes of the upper classes, and in this issue a number of Christmas items and advertisements were skewed to relate to the war. This large-size paper, launched by Beeton in 1861, is among those described by Margaret Beetham as '"ladies' illustrated newspapers" because they brought the concept of the lady, the techniques of illustration and the category of news into dynamic relationship with each other' (Beetham 1996: 89).

Sinclair's writing about the War appeared in other women's magazines too. In her article 'Women's Sacrifices for the War,' Sinclair examines the term 'sacrifice,' not one, she claims, of her own choosing. She is not to discuss the sacrifices of women in terms of the deaths of their husbands and sons, nor in their displacement and loss of their homes, but she interprets sacrifice to mean the work that women are doing for the war and the things they have given up to accomplish that work. 'Women's Sacrifices for the War' appeared in the British *Woman at Home* (Feb 1915: 7–11). Targeted at the middle-class woman, this magazine carried many advertisements as well as a prominent interest in women's consumption practices, but was aimed at a less wealthy readership than the *Queen* (Beetham 1996: 158–9).[9] Sinclair had already published an early short story, 'A Servant of the Earth' in 1899, and would, two years later, publish another story, 'The Frewin Affair' (1917) with this magazine. Sinclair's article is given top billing and advertised on the contents insert on the front page above an article by Lady Baden-Powell on 'Woman's Work in the War,' even through Baden-Powell's article appears first inside the issue. This is strong bibliographic coding for the reader. *Woman at Home*, February 1915, with its scarlet background and cover image of a well-to-do woman, fashionably and wealthily attired in feathered hat and fur stole and wraps, straight-skirted dress of the period, neatly wrapped parcels in hand and small, chic, beribboned white dog in tow, could not give an image of a magazine's readership further from that of the 'little' modernist magazines. These two war-focused articles drawing attention to women's part in the war, are followed by other stories and articles with a more feminine tone. For example: a short story, 'The Pink Silk Dress' by Sophie Kerr Underwood; and a duologue about shopping for 'A Spring Hat,' which is an at-home rehearsal of a shopping experience (Figure 18.1). The advertisement pages include half- and quarter-page illustrated advertisements for toffee, cocoa, buttons, and so on, with many advertisements using images of soldiers

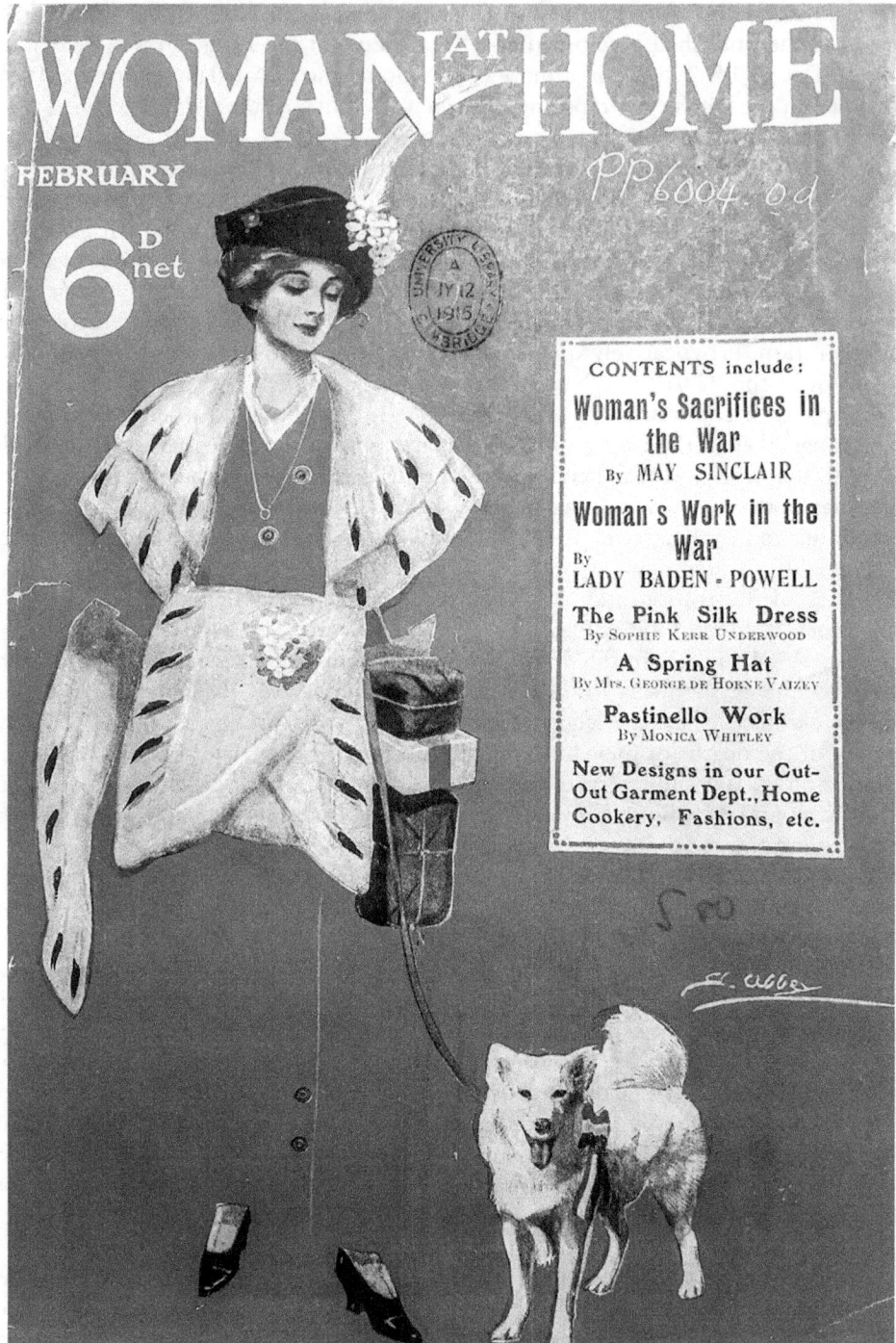

Figure 18.1 Front cover of *Woman At Home*, showing May Sinclair's 'Woman's Sacrifices in the War.' February 1915.

and references to the war to enhance the patriotism implied in the purchase and use of the product. Sinclair's article is accompanied by a press shot of her attributed to Elliot and Fry, reproduced as a circular cameo-style, typical of other articles in the magazine, and an introduction to her as 'Miss May Sinclair, One of the Most Distinguished of Women Writers.' In this context, then, Sinclair's writing is to be understood as part of the women's magazine-led wartime education and rallying call for women's participation on the home front.

Less well known is that this same article, 'Women's Sacrifices for the War' was first published in November of the previous year, 1914, in the American magazine, *Collier's: The National Weekly* (21 Nov 1914: 13, 24, 25). In this edition, Sinclair's article does not just top the billing, but is the only item mentioned on the front cover and has a large-size, full-page illustration by Alice Barber Stephens, a professional American illustrator who had produced a number of *Collier's* (and other) magazine front covers (Figure 18.2). Stephens's illustrations have been regarded as pioneering, and this one, depicting a mother and child overlooking a front line of soldiers firing rifles, evokes a strong sense of anxiety. The text of the article itself has an illustration by Ernest Fuhr, specifically quoting Sinclair and depicting the moment when she agreed that she should stand up on the bus and give up the last seat to a soldier. This text, drawing on both the everyday realities of women's lives and the philosophical and epiphanic experiences of reality Sinclair recounted from her short time in Belgium, serves to inform two distinct markets: one in the United Kingdom, with women already experiencing the war and its implications of war zones and home front; and one in the US, perhaps keen for news of the war, but not yet a country at war. For both readerships, the article is meant to be inspirational, perhaps propagandist, but with distinct intended outcomes. In this way, the same message serves different reading publics, regionally contingent but bound by the specific event of war. In all these varied war writings, Sinclair is ahead of her time. Fundamentally, she attempts to bring the war to women, making accessible some kind of comprehension.

Conclusion

May Sinclair's publication of her work across a wide range of journals, periodicals, little magazines, and commercial magazines for women, was important both to her livelihood and her career as a writer. The appearance of her name as writer of different kinds of material and as the subject of reviews was an important aspect of building a name in an environment of celebrity writers, and crucial to the sales of her novels to different markets. The huge diversity of modernism and modernity, its literary and artistic movements, its new ways of thinking about the human mind and human condition, its reflections upon the social role of women, the emerging professionalisation of a writing industry, and the medical developments regarding the impact of modern warfare, all formed part of May Sinclair's interest and engagement with her cultural moment. The breadth of her own intellectual engagement can be seen in the range of magazines which publish her work. She appealed to diverse markets, and she used this diversity of periodical publication to exhibit her writing talents and capacities. She used the different modes of reviews, letters, articles, fiction (both long and short forms), and war reportage and so appeared in different sections of a magazine or journal as an important writer and profound commentator of her day.

Figure 18.2 Front cover of *Collier's: The National Weekly*, showing May Sinclair's 'Women's War Sacrifices.' November 1914.

Notes

1. See Michele K. Troy 'A Very "Un-English" Writer: May Sinclair's Early Reception in Europe' in Kunka and Troy 2006: 23–48.
2. Single studies and edited collections have brought Sinclair's work to greater attention. In addition to Kunka and Troy 2006, Raitt 2000, and Zegger 1976, see T. E. Boll, *Miss May Sinclair: Novelist* (1973); and Rebecca Bowler and Claire Drewery, *May Sinclair: Re-Thinking Bodies and Minds* (2016). At the time of publication, Edinburgh University Press is planning a series of critical editions of the works of May Sinclair.
3. This American tour was, however, marred by the news of her brother's death (Raitt 2000: 97).
4. Kunka and Troy quote Raymond Mortimer's 1922 *Dial* review of the *Life and Death of Harriett Frean* on this point (5).
5. Sir Almroth Wright (1861–1947) was a bacteriologist and Professor of Experimental Pathology at the University of London.
6. These were 'Topics of the Week,' *New York Times* 18 Feb 1905: 97; H. I. Brock 'Fire and Smoke,' *New York Times* 11 Mar 1905: 150. Raitt 2000: 95, note 78.
7. Raitt remarks upon the impact on American magazine publishing of the serialisation of this novel in the 'prudish' *Atlantic Monthly* (2000: 100).
8. For a reading of Sinclair's *Journal* that focuses on sexual fantasy and disavowal, see Thurston 2014. Suzanne Raitt highlights the shame and anxiety Sinclair felt in '"Contagious Ecstasy": May Sinclair's War Journals.' *Women's Fiction and the Great War* (Raitt and Tate 1997). Clare Tylee argues that Sinclair was voyeuristic and sentimental in *The Great War and Women's Consciousness* (1990).
9. Beetham has also discussed Annie Swan's (Mrs Burnett Smith) fiction and her role as the first magazine agony aunt (1996: 65–6).

Works Cited

Beetham, Margaret. 1996. *A Magazine of her Own?: Domesticity and desire in the woman's Magazine 1800–1914*. London: Routledge.
Boll, T. E. 1973. *Miss May Sinclair: Novelist*. Madison, NJ: Farleigh Dickinson University Press.
Bornstein, George. 2001. *Material Modernism: The Politics of the Page*. Cambridge: Cambridge University Press.
Bowler, Rebecca and Claire Drewery, 2016. *May Sinclair: Re-Thinking Bodies and Minds*. Edinburgh: Edinburgh University Press.
Forster, Laurel. 2006. '"Imagism . . . Is a State of Soul": May Sinclair's Imagist Writing and *Life and Death of Harriett Frean*.' *May Sinclair: Moving Towards the Modern*. Ed. Andrew J. Kunka and Michele K. Troy. Aldershot: Ashgate. 99–122.
—. 2008. 'Women and War Zones: May Sinclair's Personal Negotiation with the First World War.' *Inside Out: Women negotiating, subverting, appropriating public and private space*. Ed. Teresa Gomez Reus and Aranzazu Usandizaga. New York: Rodopi. 229–48.
Gough, Jim. 2009. 'May Sinclair: Idealism-Feminism and the Suffragist Movement.' *Rhetor* 3: 1–17. <www.cssr-scer.ca> (last accessed 10 August 2018).
Kunka, Andrew J. and Michele K. Troy, eds. 2006. *May Sinclair: Moving Towards the Modern*. Aldershot: Ashgate.
Latham, Sean. 2011. 'The Mess and the Muddle of Modernism: The Modernist Journals Project and Modern Periodical Studies.' *Tulsa Studies in Women's Literature* 30.2 (Fall): 402–28.
Latham, Sean and Robert Scholes. 2006. 'The Rise of Periodical Studies.' *Modern Languages Association* 121.2: 517–31.

Marek, Jayne. 2010. 'Magazines, presses and salons in women's modernism.' *The Cambridge Companion to Modernist Women Writers.* Ed. Maren Tova Linett. Cambridge: Cambridge University Press. 62–77.

Pease, Allison. 2012. *Modernism, Feminism and the Culture of Boredom.* Cambridge: Cambridge University Press.

Pykett, Lyn. 2013. 'Writing Around Modernism: May Sinclair and Rebecca West.' *Outside Modernism, In Pursuit of the English Novel, 1900–30.* Ed. Lynne Hapgood and Nancy L. Paxton. Basingstoke: Macmillan Press.

Raitt, Suzanne. 2000. *May Sinclair: A Modern Victorian.* Oxford: Oxford University Press.

Raitt, Suzanne and Trudi Tate, eds. 1997. '"Contagious Ecstasy": May Sinclair's War Journals.' *Women's Fiction and the Great War.* Oxford: Clarendon Press. 65–84.

Rosenquist, Rod and Alice Wood. 2016. 'Introduction: Modernism in Public.' *Modernist Cultures* 11.3: 299–311.

Scholes, Robert and Clifford Wulfman. 2010. *Modernism in the Magazines: An Introduction.* New Haven: Yale University Press.

Sedgewick, Ellery. 1994. *A History of The Atlantic Monthly 1857–1909: Yankee Humanism at High Tide and Ebb.* Amhurst: University of Massachusetts Press.

Shiach, Morag. 2004. *Modernism, Labour and Selfhood in British Literature and Culture, 1890–1930.* Cambridge: Cambridge University Press.

Thurston, Luke. 2014. 'Clouds and Power: May Sinclair's War' in *Journal of Modern Literature* 37.3: 18–35.

Tylee, Clare. 1990. *The Great War and Women's Consciousness: Images of Militarism and Womanhood in Women's Writings, 1914–64.* Basingstoke: Macmillan.

Zegger, Hrisey D. 1976. *May Sinclair.* Boston: Twayne.

Part IV

Networks, Circles, and Margins

NETWORKS, CIRCLES, AND MARGINS: INTRODUCTION

Carey Snyder

THE ESSAYS IN THIS section work to recover women writers whom scholars have frequently marginalised, but who once figured prominently in periodicals across the cultural spectrum, from pulps to classic little magazines. They bring into focus figures seldom glimpsed on syllabi or conference programmes, such as poets Charlotte Mew and Anna Wickham, editor and writer Edith Sitwell, drama critic and actress Florence Farr, and Fabian Socialist Edith Nesbit, best known as a children's book author, but recovered here in two contexts – as a science fiction writer for the popular *Strand* magazine and as poet and short-fiction writer for the radical weekly the *New Age*. The essays position individual authors within what Lawrence Rainey calls the 'social reality' of modernism – 'a configuration of agents and practices' including publishing networks formed by literary circles and periodical communities (1998: 5). They consider the impact of such networks on the production and reception of modernist-era women's writing in diverse genres, from poetry and journalism to genre fiction. By employing novel methodologies from the digital humanities, as well as those adapted from media studies, feminist theory, and literary history, these essays assess the relationship between individual authors' reputations and the social and publishing networks in which they circulated.

This section builds on scholarship that highlights the social formations that gave rise to modernism, including the physical spaces – salons, cafes, and bookshops – where writers met and exchanged ideas. Michael Levenson underscores the social dimension of the movement: 'the circles forming around Stein, Woolf, Pound, and DuBois [. . .] were as much the condition of Modernism as any set of formal gestures' (2011: 5). Although the writers discussed in this section are neither canonical nor necessarily 'modernist' in a narrow aesthetic sense, they similarly benefited from the social networks in which they participated, and their writings and reputations were shaped by those associations. Helen Southworth and Alina Oboza highlight the importance of Harold Monro's Poetry Bookshop, a meeting ground for both Georgian and modernist poets, in the linked careers of Mew and Wickham. However, they suggest that Monro's association with what was increasingly perceived as retrograde Georgian verse (cemented by his publishing of Edward Marsh's *Georgian Poetry* anthologies) may in fact have been a drag on these poets' reputations. Like Monro, *New Age* editor A. R. Orage cultivated literary talent, creating a hub for a circle of writers that included Edwardian fixtures like H. G. Wells and George Bernard Shaw as well as emerging modernists, Katherine Mansfield and Ezra Pound. Contributors had an opportunity to mix and mingle at the informal editorial meetings Orage held in the basement of the ABC Teashop in Chancery Lane. In his chapter here, Lee Garver pushes back against the impression that the *New Age* was primarily a masculine forum, stressing how the circle included many prominent, though now obscure, female contributors, including Farr and Nesbit (as well as Mansfield and Beatrice Hastings, discussed in the Key Literary Figures section). Edith Sitwell's anthology, *Wheels*, which Melissa Bradshaw discusses in another chapter here, was also associated with a literary circle rooted in a physical place: the Eiffel Tower restaurant on the border of Bloomsbury and Soho (Cotsell). The members of this bohemian coterie included Nancy Cunard and Iris Tree, along with the Sitwell siblings Edith, Osbert, and Sacheverell, all of whom became contributors to *Wheels*. According to Bradshaw, Sitwell plays an important role promoting WWI poetry, including that of Wilfred Owen. The literary circles that formed around Monro, Orage, and, to a more limited extent, Edith Sitwell, provided writers with opportunities for inspiration, collaboration, and, critically, publication.

Our contributors position the women writers they study within interlocking publishing, as well as social, networks. Clearly, the viability of any author's reputation relies upon access to such networks, which link together constellations of authors, editors, and reviewers. Modernist-era writers relied on periodicals not only to publish their creative work, but also, as scholars like Rainey (1998) and Jaffe (2005) have made clear, to promote that work through reviews and critical essays. In a recent essay, Mark Gaipa and James Murphy draw the creative analogy between the digital landscape of today and the similarly proliferating print culture of the early twentieth century, arguing that periodicals functioned as tastemakers, helping readers make informed choices from a glut of print materials: like the algorithms used by media giants like Netflix or Amazon, modern periodicals helped readers navigate a bewildering density of print choices by grouping together authors and titles likely to appeal to them (Murphy and Gaipa: 2014). Authors that successfully linked into multiple periodical networks ensured their greater visibility and professional viability.

Periodical publishing could also be a gateway to less transient forms of publication. The Poetry Bookshop doubled as a printing press, and the *New Age* also published books and pamphlets, sometimes drawing on content published in the magazine, and conversely promoting these publications within the magazine's pages. Thus individual periodicals were part of larger print networks that included book publishers as well as other periodicals aimed at similar readerships, members of what Lucy Delap terms the same 'periodical community' (2000). Dora Marsden's *Freewoman*, for example, shared contributors and at times entered into dialogue with the *New Age*, as well as with suffrage periodicals, like *Votes for Women* (see essays by Mead and Snyder, respectively, in Key Literary Figures). Canonical authors emerge as well-connected nodes within such publishing networks. However, Bart Brinkman's essay uses digital methods to locate lesser-known authors that might otherwise escape our notice, highlighting dim nodes within modernist networks. Anthony Camara's essay moves in another direction, pointing out networks of consumer society that link communities of readers, including mass transportation (the *Strand* magazine was a mainstay of railway commuters) and mass attractions like wax museums, which drew similar audiences as popular periodicals like the *Strand*.

Like the essays in the next section, the essays here are also concerned with periodicals' coverage of social and political concerns. Camara traces the feminist dimensions of Nesbit's gothic fiction, while Garver argues that Farr's and Nesbit's *New Age* writings were central to the political and cultural upheavals of the day. Brinkman considers poetry published in a cross-section of modernist-era periodicals as a means of criticising gender and class constraints. And finally Bradshaw argues that *Wheels* was an important vehicle for anti-war sentiment, conceived as a response to the jingoistic verse of the Georgian poets published by Monro's press. The contributors thus trace the relationship between social and publishing networks and social and political change, anticipating the main focus of Part V: Social Movements. These frequently marginalised figures address central issues of modern society, complicating the centre-periphery model of understanding the period's print culture.

Works Cited

Cotsell, Michael. 'Wheels: An Introduction.' Modernist Journals Project, <http://modjourn.org/render.php?id=mjp.2005.00.112&view=mjp_object> (last accessed 9 August 2018).

Delap, Lucy. 2000. 'The Freewoman, Periodical Communities, and the Feminist Reading Public.' *Princeton University Library Chronicle* 61.2: 233–76.

Jaffe, Aaron. 2005. *Modernism and the Culture of Celebrity*. New York: Cambridge University Press.

Levenson, Michael. 2011. *Cambridge Companion to Modernism*. Cambridge: Cambridge University Press.

Murphy, James and Mark Gaipa. 2014. 'You Might Also Like . . . : Magazine Networks and Modernist Tastemaking in the Dora Marsden Magazines.' *Journal of Modern Periodical Studies* 5.1: 27–68.

Rainey, Lawrence. 1998. *Institutions of Modernism: Literary Elites and Public Culture*. New Haven: Yale University Press.

19

On Poets and Publishing Networks: Charting the Careers of Charlotte Mew and Anna Wickham

Helen Southworth and Alina Oboza

In a 1921 *Literary Review* (*New York Evening Post*) essay, entitled 'The Poems of Charlotte Mew,' American poet, anthologist, and reviewer Louis Untermeyer notes the 'remarkable' synchronicity of '[t]he simultaneous appearance of Anna Wickham's "The Contemplative Quarry" (Harcourt, Brace & Co.) and Charlotte Mew's "Saturday Market" [The MacMillan Company],' which, to him, is 'something more than a string of coincidences' (23 July 1921: 2). Both are English and, despite long careers, have only just made it to America. Furthermore:

> Neither of them is a member of any group or movement; they are no longer fiercely experimental or (*pace* the paper-jacket) 'young'. Both are passionate to a pitch unattained in the poetry of most women, yet the intellect of both controls the sense with a force even greater than their emotions. Both write in the natural speech of the day concentrated to an intense degree. Both, discarding mere prettiness and sugar wafer conceits, deal with elemental concerns; they blaze psychological paths without ever losing themselves in the dark forests of the unconscious. (ibid.)

But Untermeyer also finds in the work of the two poets 'differences as striking as these similarities':

> Where Anna Wickham, 'hot for certainties,' is so intent upon discovering a method of adjustment for the nervous analytic woman of the day that she rarely sees with any eyes but her own, Charlotte Mew projects herself continually, displaying often (and in the same poem) two transparent personalities, supplementing each other's dramas. Where the younger woman is rebellious the older, not unnaturally, is resigned. Anna Wickham, moved by fresh angers, hot ironies, clashing hates, is still engaged in her bitter and bewildering conflict—Charlotte Mew has weathered (not without scars) the storm of passions; her soul, quiet and reflectively calm is above the battle. (ibid.)

This chapter uses Untermeyer's observations, and the coming together of Mew (1869–1928) and Wickham (1883–1947) in America in 1921, on the eve of high modernism's apex, as a starting point for an analysis of the publishing careers of these two writers. We propose that these 'unaffiliated' poets (as Untermeyer calls them in his introduction to his 1925 *Modern British Poetry* anthology) and their stand against, or indifference to, radical formal experimentation in favour of a plainly expressed intensity, meaningfully shaped their exploitation of periodical culture. Tracing the dialogue between these two eccentric women in the pages of the periodicals in which they appeared illustrates the importance of networks and affiliation to the reputation of women poets during the modernist period. At the same time, it highlights the barriers such structures presented for two women whose work is characterised by its simultaneous defiance both of convention and avant-garde experimentation.

Untermeyer was important to both Mew and Wickham in the United States. He was particularly crucial to Wickham, helping to find a US publisher, as well as contributing an introduction and organising for reviews and appearances in US magazines (Jones 2003: 156). In this regard, Untermeyer continued the support afforded by Harold Monro, whose Bloomsbury-based Poetry Bookshop (1913–26) – part salon, part publishing house, part performance space – was essential to the careers of both women. Monro published chapbook editions of Mew's and Wickham's poetry, and regularly printed their poems in his periodicals *Poetry and Drama* (1913–14), and the *Chapbook* (1919–25). The Bookshop's twice-weekly poetry readings featured both poets. In its capacity as a place to which American editors like Harriet Monroe and Alfred Kreymborg went in search of new authors, the Poetry Bookshop also served as a launching pad to the US.

At the same time, the coterie quality of Monro's, and literary assistant and wife Alida Klementaski Monro's operations, may in fact have hampered Mew's and Wickham's rise to notoriety. Publishing Georgian and modernist poetry cheek by jowl, the Bookshop quickly came to be associated with Georgian, rather than modernist, poetry. The homespun quality of the Bookshop's chapbooks with small circulations, and Monro's dislike of 'popularisation' (Grant 1967: 43), further limited the scale of Monro's hoped-for 'poetic revolution' (Morrisson 2001: 72). While it seems that Monro's tactics initially suited the unassuming Mew, Wickham found his publication of her work too 'innocent,' and ultimately resented him for not selling more copies of her poetry (Jones 2003: 116).

As Mark S. Morrisson argues, whereas Monro (like Ford Madox Ford) 'embraced a vision of the public sphere in decline in order to promote modernist literature as a means to rejuvenate it,' magazines like the *Freewoman* and the *Egoist* 'instead engag[ed] much more directly with the world of commercial advertising and mass market publication to . . . bring modernism to bear upon public culture' (2001: 84). Does a look beyond Monro show Mew as well as Wickham investing in more commercial strategies? To what extent were transatlantic publishing networks essential to the securing of a broader audience in the rapidly changing literary market of the teens and twenties of the twentieth century? How does an account of the publishing trajectories of Mew and Wickham overturn or support what even in terms of new modernist studies continues to be, for both women, a marginalisation?

Existing readings of Mew and Wickham together are mostly limited to scholarship on the Poetry Bookshop (where the two women appear largely separately), but there has been a continuous interest in re-affiliating the two poets. Thus, Celeste Schenck places Mew and Wickham alongside Sylvia Townsend Warner, Francis Meynell, and Edith Sitwell, as representative of 'the dispersive underside of the "Modernist" monolith' (1990: 317); Diana Collecott makes Mew one of her 'Women of 1916' alongside H.D., May Sinclair, and Klementaski (but also mentioning Wickham) (2004: 68); Jane Dowson and Alice Entwistle suggest that if modern anthologisation sets canons and contemporary anthologisation cements them, Mew and Wickham belong with Meynell, Sackville-West, Raine, Riddler, Stevie Smith, Pitter, Cornford, Sitwell, Wellesley, Bowes Lyon, and Townsend Warner as the canonical early twentieth-century women poets (2005: 8); Nelljean Rice's cultural biography of Mew and Wickham links the two women through their shared status as 'angels in the house,' daughters 'trying to keep faith with outmoded obligations but also attuned to a modern vision of women's place in the twentieth century' (2003: 8); and, most recently, Laura Severin, focusing on performance, ties Wickham and Mew to Stevie Smith and later Jackie Kay and Liz Lochhead. This chapter builds on and extends efforts to reaffiliate these two poets. In reading their work and reception back into periodicals, it shows how publishing networks influenced their careers, and conversely, how Mew and Wickham navigated and shaped the shifting contemporary periodical culture. Considering buried periodical publications vis-à-vis the competing, yet overlapping, categories of 'Georgian,' 'modern,' and 'modernist,' this chapter shows that the fact that neither woman ultimately found success in terms of securing long-term reputation attests to their innovation beyond the established categories.

Beginnings

Mew's literary career started promisingly, with the publication in 1894 of her short fiction 'Passed' in the *Yellow Book*, Britain's leading avant-garde periodical of the 1890s. 'Passed' appeared alongside short fiction by Henry James; the *Yellow Book*'s New Women – Ella D'Arcy, editor Henry Harland's secretary and lover; and the quarterly's most frequent contributor, fiction writer Netta Syrett. However, Mew's career at the *Yellow Book* was short-lived. Harland rejected a second story, 'The China Bowl,' due to its length, even though he had published longer texts. Harland offered to include it in another collection of stories, but when the Oscar Wilde scandal broke in April, the lesbian Mew withdrew from the *Yellow Book* altogether, fearing exposure and loss of reputation due to the scandal's connection to the magazine. Mew's biographer Penelope Fitzgerald views this as a pattern in Mew's life: divided between her passionate, socially, and sexually dissident self on the one hand, and a deeply ingrained morality on the other, she 'clung ... desperately ... to dear respectability' (1984: 45). However, as we show in the essay, her subsequent career reveals a more tenacious poet actively trying to find her voice, as well as new venues for her work.

Mew's next appearances in the more mainstream middlebrow magazines *Temple Bar* (1861–1906), the *Academy* (1869–1916), and the *Pall Mall Magazine* (1893–1914) represent a step backward in terms of artistic value. After *Temple Bar* published 'The China Bowl' in 1899, Mew made regular contributions until it was discontinued in 1906. Kyriaki Hadjiafxendi and John Plunkett count *Temple Bar* among 'shilling monthly journals' which serialised the fiction of the major novelists of the period and which opened to great success in the 1860s. These titles dwindled toward the end of the century, when newspapers became the main arena for serial fiction (2015: 44–5). The bulk of Mew's contributions to *Temple Bar* are still prose (six short stories and five essays), but, perhaps marking a transition point in Mew's career from prose writer to poet, the monthly also published four early poems. Among them are reflections on death and afterlife, such as 'To a Little Child in Death' (Sep 1901), which expresses Mew's grief for her brother Richard who died when she was seven, and 'At the Convent Gate' (Jan 1902).

Mew's one-time appearances in the *Academy* and the *Pall Mall Magazine* at the turn of the century testify to her search for fitting publication venues in the early stages of her career. By the time Mew appeared in the *Academy* in 1899, its reputation as a serious scholarly journal had started to decline. Laurel Brake and Marysa Demoor note that after Charles Lewis Hind became the editor in 1896, the *Academy* became 'Britain's liveliest literary journal,' publishing bestseller lists and snappy reviews (2009: 2). After her essay 'The Governess in Fiction' was edited too heavily, she opted to have it published under 'M.' (12 Aug 1899), and never contributed to the weekly again. When *Pall Mall* published Mew's short story 'Some Ways of Love' in September 1901, it was still a popular magazine publishing prominent authors, such as Sir Conan Doyle and Thomas Hardy, alongside unknown writers. But *Pall Mall* would soon start to decline as well.

The turning point in Mew's poetic career, her move out of middlebrow venues, came with her 1912 appearance in the *Nation*, Henry William Massingham's leading British radical weekly (1907–23). Mew had appeared previously in the *Nation* in 1909, but it was the publication of 'The Farmer's Bride' in 1912 that earned her a reputation as a poet. However, it is in the context of the female-led *Englishwoman*, to which Mew contributed between 1912 and 1914, that we find an emerging poet finding her own voice.[1] The *Englishwoman* (1909–21), founded and edited by Elisina Grant Richards (first wife to publisher Grant Richards) was, for Leila Ryan and Maria DiCenzo, one of the most significant journals concerned with women's issues in the time (2011: 121, 125). Poetry was printed in every issue, scattered among political and editorial sections of the magazine. The better-known poets who appeared around the time Mew arrived in the *Englishwoman* included the Cambridge poet Frances Cornford, children's and war poet Lady Margaret Sackville, and the then emerging Richard Aldington (Bristow 2006: 7). However, most of Mew's poems in the *Englishwoman* appeared alongside now largely forgotten writers and poets. In March 1912 'The Voice' was published alongside work by Grace James, the Tokyo-born children's writer and Japanese folklorist. 'The Changeling,' one of her most personal poems, appeared in the February 1913 issue alongside Irish poet Helen Lanyon and the forgotten Thomas O'Meara. The range of poets in whose company Mew found herself in the pages of these periodicals suggests the indecision on the part of editors as to where to place her.

It was Mew's *Nation* appearance (rather than her work in the *Englishwoman*) that brought her to the attention of two female 'literary networkers': writer and founder of International PEN, Catherine Dawson Scott, and the Poetry Bookshop's literary assistant, Alida Klementaski. Both became instrumental in promoting Mew's work. In 1913, Dawson Scott introduced Mew to May Sinclair. Although Sinclair did not understand Mew's experiments in free verse, 'fe[eling] that they needed tidying up,' she appreciated their 'profound vitality' and showed them to Ezra Pound (Fitzgerald 1984: 125, 124).[2]

Poetry, Pound's suggested publication venue for Mew, rejected her poems. Like Harold Monro, Harriet Monroe, kept an 'open door' policy at *Poetry*, which she founded in 1912, 'hop[ing] to keep free of entangling alliances with any single class or school' (qtd in Carr 2015: 55–6). Helen Carr notes that while *Poetry* 'played an important role in establishing the new [modernist] movement,' it also 'nourished other forms of modernism besides that associated with the Men of 1914' (2015: 43). This relative inclusivity is reflected in the range of British poets who appeared before 1920, among them Walter de la Mare, Rupert Brooke, Padraic Colum, F. S. Flint, Ford Madox Ford, James Joyce, D. H. Lawrence, and Anna Wickham. It is possible that Monroe failed to appreciate what was new about Mew. In an editorial comment, entitled 'The New Beauty,' April 1913, Monroe complained that many *Poetry* contributors were 'as unaware of the twentieth century as if they had spent these recent years in an Elizabethan manor-house or a vine-clad Victorian cottage' (Apr 1913: 22).

Despite *Poetry*'s rejection, Pound did publish Mew's 'The Fête' in the *Egoist* on 1 May 1914 (9, 1), alongside part two of Joyce's *A Portrait of the Artist as a Young Man*, and poems by Aldington.[3] Morrisson describes the *Egoist* as being 'in broad opposition to bourgeois social norms, liberal and statist politics and, above all . . . bourgeois literary tastes' (2001: 86).[4] An important venue for the Imagist movement, the *Egoist* gave prominent space to H.D., Amy Lowell, and Marianne Moore. Looking beyond Imagism further highlights the magazine's strong transatlantic connections; between 1914 and 1916 (around the time Mew appeared there) the magazine favoured American women poets, among them Frances Gregg and *Poetry*'s associate editor, Helen Hoyt. Among the British women included in the publication at that time were May Sinclair (again, through her connection to the Imagist movement), the now largely forgotten Margaret Maitland Radford, as well as Mew and Wickham. *Poetry*'s rejection and the *Egoist*'s acceptance of Mew's work highlights the diversity of responses to her poetry; she was embraced in certain progressive venues, but rejected in others. The range of publication venues Mew explored in the early stages of her career – from avant-garde publications, through Victorian periodicals, to suffrage press – shows a writer determined to find new networks, and new audiences for her work. This certainly challenges the impression given by Fitzgerald.

Suggesting some overlap, Wickham's 'Spoken to Adonis' appeared in the *Egoist* a year after Mew's alongside Hoyt, Gregg, Aldington, and Joyce. However, whereas Mew's *Egoist* appearance had preceded a monograph, Wickham's followed the Poetry Bookshop's publication of her second collection *The Contemplative Quarry* (1915). Thus, while the *Egoist* represented a stepping stone to Monro for Mew, Wickham came to the *Egoist* via Monro. In contrast to Mew, an established short fiction and essayist first and poet second, Wickham went straight to poetry. Indicating tenacity and privilege, Wickham self-published her first volume, *Songs* (1911), using the pseudonym 'John Oland.' Highlighting the importance of female networks for Wickham's career, the volume was printed by the Women's Printing Society, an important player in the suffrage movement. For Wickham's biographer, Jennifer Vaughan Jones, '[t]he appearance of Anna's experimental little book . . . before the First World War places it in the vanguard of early modernist poetry' (2003: 84). Just like Mew's appearances in the *Englishwoman*, Wickham's debut shows particularly well the significance of suffrage networks to the emergence of women's modernism.

Alongside Wickham's poem, Aldington reviewed *The Contemplative Quarry* in the *Egoist* with three other Poetry Bookshop publications, James Elroy Flecker's *The Old Ship*, Cornford's *Spring Morning*, and Edward Shanks's *Songs*. Dismissive of Cornford and Shanks, Aldington treats Flecker and Wickham at length. Wickham's book is, for Aldington, 'a chunk of life.' Wickham 'makes [Aldington] think of those punching machines on Folkstone pier; you hit a leather projection and a dial registers the force of the blow' (1 June 1915: 90). Wickham is egotistical, but Aldington sees her as representative of modern women: 'She wants to know what the devil women are to do with their lives . . . Her misfortune is to be clear-sighted among the blind, vital among the insipid, natural among the affected, sane among the stupid . . .' (1 June 1915: 90). For Aldington, Wickham's volume is the most worth printing of the four books reviewed. This attests to the significance of Wickham's collection and confirms the *Egoist* as a venue in which women's poetry could be promoted as distinctive and 'modern.'

Mew and Wickham at the Poetry Bookshop

Wickham's 1911 *Songs* served as her entrée to the Poetry Bookshop. After seeing the volume, Monro published an unprecedented fifteen of Wickham's poems in his quarterly *Poetry and Drama*, her periodical debut, in June 1914. Pound was printed in the preceding issue and Wickham's work appeared alongside historical novelist and poet, Maurice Hewlett, American Imagist poet, John Gould Fletcher, and Irish poet, Francis Macnamara.

Monro, Poetry Bookshop's founder and manager, was already a fixture in London's literary circles. Forced out as editor of the Poetry Society's *Poetry Review*, he had launched *Poetry and Drama* (1913–14) aiming to popularise poetry: '[*Poetry and Drama*] strongly opposed the modernist tendency to move poetry "into the study"' (Hibberd 2015: 191). Monro wanted to include a broad spectrum of contemporary poetry, seeing all of the 'strands of pre-war poetry' as 'participating in a single poetic renaissance' (Morrisson 2015: 405). This eclectic strategy is most clearly reflected in the crossover between 'Georgian' and 'modern' poetry typical of the Bookshop's publications. In 1912, alongside *Poetry and Drama*, Monro brought out the first volume of *Georgian Poetry*, Edward Marsh's popular anthology. Marsh's success established the Poetry Bookshop's reputation as 'some kind of Georgian headquarters,' ultimately undermining Monro's contribution to popularising modernist verse: Monro published Pound's *Des Imagistes* anthology and brought to the British readership what would become foundational modernist texts (Hibberd 2015: 189). Neither Mew nor Wickham made it into *Georgian Poetry* despite efforts, in Wickham's case, by D. H. Lawrence (Wickham's neighbour in late 1915) who lobbied Marsh in 1915; and in Mew's, Monro himself. In 1917, Monro recommended Mew's 'The Farmer's Bride' and urged Marsh to include her work again in 1919 and 1922. The only women Marsh published were Fredegond Shove and Vita Sackville-West (Fitzgerald 1984: 169–70). Arguably to Mew's detriment, even though Marsh excluded her, Mew's poetry came to be associated with Georgian verse in part because Monro published her alongside poets featured in the anthology. *Poetry and Drama* proved a more positive arena for Wickham. On 25 June, London's the *Morning Post* praised

Wickham for 'seeking after new truth and beauty' in her 'strangely enhancing poems' (qtd in Jones 2003: 103). Perhaps as a result of this early appearance, Wyndham Lewis included Wickham (as 'Mrs. Hepburn') among the blessed in the first volume of *BLAST* (20 June 1914: 28).[5] In this way, Monro quickly became an active promoter of Wickham's work, publishing *The Contemplative Quarry* in 1915.

In contrast to Wickham's, Mew's route to the Poetry Bookshop was mediated by Klementaski and periodical publication. Logically, periodicals were an important vehicle on the front end for the less connected Mew. Echoing Dawson Scott, Klementaski was 'electrified to find' 'The Farmer's Bride' in the *Nation*, and in Autumn 1915, she invited Mew to a Poetry Bookshop reading (Monro 1953: vii). In 1916, a year after Wickham, the Poetry Bookshop brought out the only collection published in Mew's lifetime, *The Farmer's Bride*. Sales were poor, perhaps due to the ongoing war: according to Alida (Klementaski) Monro, the 500 copies initially printed 'took years to sell out' (1953: xx). Expressing her disappointment, Mew wrote to Monro that she did hope 'the 1 or 2 more or less influential people who have used all sorts of adjectives about *The Farmer's Bride* would have put same into print' (qtd in Grant 1967: 124).

Although it sold poorly, Mew's book got notable attention in September 1916 in the *Egoist*, as had Wickham's. H.D., assistant editor from mid-1916 to mid-1917, praised Mew's reinterpretation of the dramatic lyric: 'She alone of our generation, with the exception of Mr. Hueffer [Ford Madox Ford] and Mr. Frost, has succeeded in this form, has grown a new blossom from the seed of Browning's sowing, has followed a master without imitating him, has given us a transmutation of his spirit, not a parody of his flesh' (Sep 1916: 135). H.D.'s response shows the degree to which an appreciation of Mew's unconventionality hinged on an awareness of her revisions of traditional forms. As Collecott notes, H.D. published only three reviews while at the *Egoist*: Moore, Mew, and John Gould Fletcher, 'a conscious attempt [on H.D.'s part],' Collecott believes, 'to present the magazine's readers with a body of writing by modernist women to compare with that of modernist men' (2004: 65). H.D.'s inclusion of Mew in this group (and perhaps also Monro's rejection of Mew's poems) uncovers the extent to which the reception of Mew's work was contingent on critics' assessment (their appreciation or rejection) of the interpenetration of Georgian and modernist spheres; a context made visible via buried publishing networks.

Despite good exposure, in terms of poem placement and H.D.'s praise, Mew's collection was mostly poorly received. In the *Athenaeum* Mew's 'pretty musical effects' are attributed to 'random experiment' (June 1916: 284; qtd in Kircher 1990: 24). For the reviewer in the *Englishwoman*, which had provided Mew with the room to develop her style as a poet, her poems are only partly comprehensible, and 'unable to rise into the serene region beyond anger and despair' (Aug 1916: 184–5; qtd in Kircher 1990: 24–5). The reviewer of the *Times Literary Supplement* similarly predicts that the poems will often seem unintelligible to the reader, as many of them bear 'all the grotesque inconsequence of a dream' (21 Sep 1916: 455). Yet, he or she recognises Mew's unique 'gift of expression': 'when [Mew] is at her strangest there is something before you that is true and human, that there is a meaning, a unifying thread, running through it all . . .' (ibid.). In the *Nation*, a venue which had served to launch Mew in pre-war 1909, Henry Wood Nevinson praises Mew for translating deeply personal emotions into 'concrete forms, appealing to wider sympathies' (8 July 1916: 444).

'The Farmer's Bride' (along with 'The Fête' and 'The Changeling') is among poems he singles out as excellent, ('clearly realised, full of hard and definitive vision!'), although he thinks the farmer is rendered too sympathetic and sensitive for any bride to run away from him (ibid.). May Sinclair recommended Mew's collection to every editor she knew, but, perhaps explaining Mew's change of fortune, she acknowledged the difficulty '[of getting] poetry reviewed at present – unless it is written from the trenches' (qtd in Fitzgerald 1984: 165).

At about the same time, apart from Aldington's praise in the *Egoist*, Wickham's monograph was also poorly reviewed. In August of 1915, a parodic review of *The Contemplative Quarry* appeared in A. R. Orage's literary magazine *New Age*. The anonymous reviewer mocks Wickham's feminist voice: 'Man prefers to kiss her than talk philosophy, so she asks Oblivion to steep her senses in forgetfulness that she may forget her loneliness' (19 Aug 1915: 387). The same month, the unnamed *The New Statesman* reviewer is more ambivalent. Wickham is viewed as a poet 'in revolt against conventional morality, sluggishness, artistic rules, outworn subjects, and accepted conceptions of Beauty' (14 Aug 1915: 452). Her poems are not 'completely satisfactory' to the reviewer, and he notes her curious interest in 'anything freakish in form,' but he appreciates the fact that she frankly 'confronts her own impulses' (ibid.).

In the US, an ambivalent review appeared in *Poetry* in August 1915 from the pen of Irish poet and playwright Padraic Colum: 'Here is woman claiming experiences for herself, songs for herself. The intention of the writer has put her emotions awry, and her songs are hard and twisted' (Aug 1915: 255). American critic, poet, and editor Max Eastman, who picked up Wickham's *The Contemplative Quarry* at the Poetry Bookshop, responded more positively. In his January 1916 *Masses* review, Eastman called Wickham 'mighty wise and sassy': 'She has about the same attitude to rhyme and meter that she has to "male and proper man." Use him, and—well, love him (you can't help it), but don't be fooled' (Jan 1916: 11). In the second 'Status Rerum' of *Poetry* in April 1916, Pound admits they have been remiss in *not* publishing Wickham or Monro (Apr 1916: 39). He sets that right with five poems by Wickham in 1917, apparently again at D. H. Lawrence's behest (Jones 2003: 126).

Despite the mixed reception of her work in British periodicals, in 1916 Grant Richards, publisher of Shaw, A. E. Housman, and Joyce's *Dubliners*, brought out Wickham's second British collection, *The Man With a Hammer* (Jones 2003: 132). Richards wanted to include a preface by controversial sex expert, Havelock Ellis, and to have the book appear at Christmas. Although these plans fell through, his efforts testify to his awareness of modern marketing. Echoing the *New Statesman* review of *The Contemplative Quarry*, Richards advertised the book as 'very notable . . . a poet in revolt . . . against the stupider bonds of convention, of domesticity, or ordinary urban and suburban life' (qtd in Jones 2003: 134). Possibly due to the wartime date of the publication of the volume, few reviews appeared.

Mew in the US (1921–3)

Perhaps liberated in terms of topic as the traumas of the First World War fell away, an initially unwilling Macmillan New York did bring out an edition of Mew's poetry, at Monro's prompting, containing eleven additional poems under the title *Saturday*

Market (1921) (Fitzgerald 1984: 170). The Poetry Bookshop published the extended edition of *The Farmer's Bride* the same year, keeping the original title. Untermeyer finally got hold of Mew's poetry, more prominent in its second appearance, having been fascinated with her 'Madeleine' since another admirer, Siegfried Sassoon read it to him a year earlier (Fitzgerald 1984: 187).[6] *Saturday Market* did well in America. In the remainder of the review quoted in the introduction to this chapter, Untermeyer highlights the Hardyesque quality of her 'tragic episodes' and the Lawrence-like looseness of form, extolling above all 'Madeleine in Church' (23 July 1921: 2). He considers her one of the best living poets: 'Hers is the distillation, the essence of emotion, rather than the stirring up of passions' (ibid.).

Despite an already long career, much of the US response saw Mew as an emerging voice. *Boston Evening Transcript* reviewer, poet William Stanley Braithwaite, praised *Saturday Market* as 'precious with the freight of a promise that is going to make the arrival of a genius'; he applauded the loose form of the poems, their intellectual quality, and (echoing the 1916 *TLS* review) the 'thrilling confusion of wonder' which arises as her poems oscillate between dream and reality (18 May 1921: 4; qtd in Kircher 1990: 26). Another American promoter, poet Marguerite Wilkinson, considered Mew an exception among contemporary English women poets, whose work she calls 'staid,' 'poky,' and 'ultra-conventional' (19 June 1921: 10).[7] Wilkinson finds Mew's poems difficult to classify, calling them 'lyrical ballads' while acknowledging that 'the term suggests something quite alien to them in structure and atmosphere . . . they are narratives in which moods of men, women and children are dramatised in a strongly subjective way that makes them lyrical' (ibid.). The Imagist poet John Gould Fletcher compared Mew's work to Emily Dickinson's and to Japanese and Chinese poetry. He concludes that 'with more concentration Mew could be a great poet' (*New York Freeman* 15 Mar 1922: 20; qtd in Kircher 1990: 29–30).

On its American appearance, Mew's volume was also reviewed in *Poetry*. Wickham's poems appeared in the same issue, marking the two poets' first 'meeting' in the pages of periodicals. Unlike most of her American colleagues, however, in 1922 associate editor, poet Marion Strobel, criticised the intellectual quality of Mew's poetry as 'laden with so much observation, knowledge, passion, sentiment, that it is like an apple-tree burdened by the excess of its own beauty' (June 1922: 152).

Despite Mew's growing popularity,[8] even in the United Kingdom the poet was still often seen as a discovery, and reviews were mixed. British women reviewers responded positively. Edith Sitwell dubbed Mew a poet's poet in the London *Daily Herald* (4 Apr 1922): 'The book [. . .] came, indeed, with the shock of a *discovery*; for here was none of the self-consciousness or the self-protective weakness to which we had become accustomed in emotional poems by women' (qtd in Kircher 1990: 28). In the British conservative weekly the *Spectator*, Lady Amabel Williams-Ellis praised Mew's economy of language, seeing in her work 'a wonderful degree of craftsmanship; there is not a word out of place or weak' (26 Mar 1921: 403–4; qtd in Kircher 1990: 28–9). The *Sphere* reviewer praises *The Farmer's Bride* as 'full of that thrill and charm only the very best poetry can give,' and counts himself/herself among 'those who give a very hearty *welcome*' to Mew's poetry (16 Apr 1921: 74). In contrast, in the *Nation* (27 July 1921: 104), Mew's poems are deemed 'narrow and not quite "powerful" enough to be successful' (qtd in Kircher 1990: 27). In the *New*

Statesman (2 Apr 1921: 759), English poet Edgell Rickword criticised Mew's lack of clarity, as well as the juxtaposition of dialect and sophisticated syntax: 'one feels that one has come to a good poem, then it wavers, becomes argumentative, or conventional with some undefined "you," and loses itself finally in the morasses of the confessional' (qtd in Kircher 1990: 27).

Wickham in the US (1917–22)

While Mew's US presence mainly took the form of reviews, Wickham pursued an active publication agenda. Her mobilisation of transatlantic networks brought her a degree of celebrity in the US. Subsequent to *The Contemplative Quarry*, Wickham's 'Host' appeared in the September 1917 issue of San Francisco-based Theodore F. Bonnet and Edward F. O'Day's *Lantern: A Periodical of Lucid Intervals*. Others published in this Anglophile magazine include Lawrence and Sassoon, indicating Wickham's possible route to this remote publication. This, and a simultaneous *Poetry* appearance, brought Wickham to the attention of American readers, including, importantly, Untermeyer. In his 1920 anthology *Modern British Poetry*, he introduced Wickham as 'one of the most individual of the younger women-poets' (Untermeyer 1925: 186). He then persuaded Harcourt Brace to publish a combined US edition of *The Contemplative Quarry* and *The Man With a Hammer*. The volume appeared in 1921 introduced by Untermeyer's article for the *New Republic* (27 Apr 1921: 269–72). In this prefatory statement, Untermeyer groups Wickham with an impressive group of established female prose writers:

> [A]lready a small and widely-scattered group of women are taking stock of themselves—appraising their limitations, inventions and energies without a thought of man's contempt or condescension . . . May Sinclair, Virginia Woolf, Rebecca West, Willa Cather and Dorothy Richardson are working in prose that illuminates their experiments. In poetry, a regiment of young women are recording an even more rigorous self-examination. The most typical and, in many ways, the best of these singers and seekers is Anna Wickham. (1921: viii–ix)

Ironically echoing some of the negative UK reviews, but finding power where British critics found weakness, Untermeyer calls Wickham's book 'a vivid, fully-developed confessional of modernity,' her second 'more restrained but even richer' (1921: ix). He praises 'the strength of her candor,' 'the intense singleness of her purpose' (ibid.). He concedes that her poems are not pleasant; rather, they are 'astringent and sometimes harsh; gnarled frequently in their own perturbations' (1921: x). However, they remain lyrical. Significantly, for Untermeyer, Wickham is a liminal figure; she 'typifies the woman of today who has repudiated the old order and and is, as yet, pitifully unadjusted to a new one . . . Her very mercurial temperament is representative of the nervous spirit of her age . . .' (1921: xi–xii).

The Harcourt Brace edition of Wickham's poetry raised her profile in America where reviews indicate greater tolerance for her outspoken verse. Perhaps due to Untermeyer's mainstream network, Wickham entered a commercial market. Ten poems appeared ahead of the volume in July 1921 in *Vanity Fair*, for Faye Hammill and Karen Leick a quality magazine located 'in a middle space between the author-centred production model of the avant-garde magazines and the market-driven arena of the daily papers and mass-circulation weeklies' (2015: 176).[9] Here Wickham joined a group of women poets that included Edna St. Vincent Millay (whom Wickham would later meet in Paris). It is possible that Untermeyer, who published a review in this issue and was nominated for the *Vanity Fair* 'Hall of Fame,' wrote the short unsigned blurb accompanying the poems in which he explains that although Wickham is known in England, she has not made it to the US because she is not part of the Sitwells' *Wheels* crowd,[10] nor is she a 'conservative Georgian' (*Vanity Fair*, July 1921: 53). Wickham is 'an authentic and original poet'; 'her verse is quite unmannered'; 'she is always the woman, and she would seem to have set down a number of feminine reactions which had not before found their way into English poetry' (ibid.).

The response of critics to Wickham's work in the US was generally positive (although, as was the case with Mew in the United Kingdom, she was better received by female critics than male). In December 1921, Wilkinson (who had reviewed Mew's collection only a few months earlier) described Wickham's *The Contemplative Quarry* as 'a veritable poetic thunderstorm': '[i]t shows the lightning of a swift, vivid, uncertain modern intellect zigzagging from wrath to love and from scorn to faith' (*Bookman*, Dec 1921: 383). Wilkinson extols Wickham for making room for contradictions in her volume: 'To acclaim love and to doubt it, to defy man, as a feminist, and then to offer him the specious homage of precedence, to inveigh against the church and then to pray reverently to the Mater Dolorosa in one and the same book, surely this is to offer a series of unusual contrasts in thought and emotion' (ibid.).

In *Poetry* 1922 (Vol. 20, No. 2), echoing a negative response to the British edition of *Contemplative Quarry* in 1915, Wickham's American collection is, just as Mew's was, poorly reviewed. In a review titled 'Woman with a Hammer,' US poet Yvor Winters finds only 'platitudes,' 'stale[ness],' and the 'barrenness of trodden ground' (May 1922: 94, 95). Untermeyer responded in the subsequent issue of *Poetry*, calling Winters's review a 'scornful . . . attack on feminist poetry' (June 1922: 168). Wickham also received a negative review in Scofield Thayer and then Marianne Moore's Chicago-based *Dial* (Dec 1921); at the time a significant venue 'for the more experimental women's writing,' publishing mainly American writers (Taylor 2001: 73). The *Dial*'s anonymous reviewer suggested that Wickham's poetry 'would resolve itself into entertainingly argumentative essays on feminism if it were not chopped up into rather bad verse' (Dec 1921: 716).

In January 1922, at home in the radical US press, Wickham published a new poem 'The Singing Wives,' in Eastman's *Liberator*, alongside a piece by Jewish American communist novelist Michael Gold. The *Liberator* was a Communist Party organ founded by Eastman and his sister in 1918, a less radical successor to Eastman's *Masses*; Untermeyer was a contributing editor. Appearing in the same issue were poets ranging from Claude McKay, the Jamaica-born Harlem Renaissance poet and at this point an executive editor of the journal, and 'Chicago' poet, Carl Sandburg to, among others, the now unknown Daytie Randle, whose poem 'Lament' begins 'I am a Negro Woman.'

Subsequent to the *Liberator*, the liberal, New York-based weekly *New Republic* published Wickham's poetry three times in January 1922. In the 4 January issue, six poems sit alongside work by W. H. Davies and Bertrand Russell. The six Wickham poems (all new) included 'The Winds' and 'The Muddle,' and mostly feature violent, powerful language. Wickham's 'To a Crucifix,' which laments that the Christ who is remembered is the Christ of 'wounds and grief,' rather than that of 'cure and relief,' is then published apart from a later group of more conservative poems on 18 January (18 Jan 1922: 203). In the 25 January issue, Wickham's 'Code' is published with an article by Bloomsbury's Clive Bell and Elinor Wylie's poem 'Beware!'

In April 1922, Wylie, perhaps alerted to Wickham due to their simultaneous appearance in *The New Republic*, singled out Wickham's 'The Winds' from the *New Republic* cluster in 'The Poems of the Month' feature in US *The Bookman*, praising it for its 'quality of courage' and 'defiance' (Apr 1922: 189). In one of the few US periodical encounters of Mew and Wickham, Mew's poem 'To A Child in Death' was published in this same issue. This appears to have been the only instance of a Mew poem appearing in the US which was not a reprint from a British publication. Two more of Wickham's poems appeared in *Poetry* in July 1922 (Vol. 20, No. 4) alongside Monroe, Kreymborg, Lola Ridge, John Hall Wheelock, Louis Golding, and Morris Gilbert. Here Wickham again meets Mew: the same issue includes Marion Strobel's review of Mew's *Saturday Market*. This is Wickham's last *Poetry* appearance. In her 1923 article 'The Editor in England' Monroe recalled Wickham's reading of her 'brief, peppery, searching household-feminist poems: a woman of large build physically and spiritually, with a head and frame like Juno's, to be sculptured in simple lines' (Oct 1923: 34–5). But it is the Scottish Muriel Stuart (who had already appeared in *Poetry* a few times), not Wickham, who she singles out as 'the most interesting of the younger English poets' (Oct 1923: 38).

In August 1922, Kreymborg published one of Wickham's poems in the *Measure: A Journal of Poetry*, a magazine Andrew Thacker characterises as a reaction against the chaos of Imagism, despite Kreymborg's earlier support of the Imagists (2015: 322–3). At that time (already in Paris) Wickham met St Vincent Millay who also published in the *Chapbook*. St Vincent Millay was heavily featured in *The Measure* suggesting she was the person who took Wickham there. In 1923, Wickham returned to the *Liberator*. In April, her new poem 'Ascetics' appeared and in July, 'Eugenics' (from *The Contemplative Quarry*), a poem about class, appeared along with Herbert Jones's 'Song of Brotherhood' as the first contributions, directly following the editorials page.

Wickham's somewhat miscellaneous appearances in the US demonstrate the degree to which her work eludes classification. Thus, despite her appearances in *Poetry*, the fact that Wickham was never embraced by Monroe meant that her feminist poetry was instead mostly relegated to radical left-wing publications, mainstream magazines, and small anti-establishment venues. Suggesting a similar failure for the work to find its place, Mew's equally unusual poetry, although praised and supported by critics like Untermeyer and Wilkinson, made only very few appearances in US periodicals.

Mew and Wickham back in England

Reflecting an ongoing relationship, between 1919 and 1923, in the years leading up to modernism's *annus mirabilis* 1922, Mew's work appeared regularly in the *Monthly Chapbook*, later called the *Chapbook* (1919–25), the last of Monro's periodicals: 'Sea

Love' in July 1919; 'I Have Been Through the Gates' in July 1920; 'The Rambling Sailor' in February 1922; and finally, 'The Trees are Down' in January 1923. Suggesting the eclectic nature of Monro's project, in the *Chapbook*, Mew found herself in the company of Georgian poets, among them Walter de la Mare, Wilfred Wilson Gibson, W. H. Davies, T. Sturge Moore, as well as the (pre-war) avant-garde F. S. Flint and Aldington. Women included H.D., St Vincent Millay, Edith Sitwell, and the now largely obscure Narcisse Wood, Rose Macaulay, Ethel Talbot, Camilla Doyle, and Theodora Bosanquet.[11]

Overlapping very briefly with Mew, although the two never appeared in the same volume, in January 1920 Wickham's 'Due for Hospitality' and 'The Little Old House' were published in the *Chapbook*. Both poems were reprinted in *The Little Old House* which Monro published in 1921 alongside the American collection (*The Contemplative Quarry* is listed as 'out of print' here). Wickham's third volume was deemed 'more conventional' than her earlier work by reviewers and by Wickham herself, but some still saw 'signs of a rebellious temperament' (qtd in Jones 2003: 154). In March 1923, shortly after the last of Mew's appearances, Wickham's 'Three Love Songs' were published alongside, among others, Aldington and Thomas Hardy. 'Mare Bred from Pegasus' appeared in June 1923, and finally, a few of Wickham's poems were published in the penultimate issue of the magazine in 1924, alongside Monro, T. S. Eliot, and the *Chapbook* 'regulars' like Camilla Doyle, the Sitwell brothers, and Eleanor Farjeon.

In addition to the *Chapbook*, Mew also made a couple of appearances in other UK venues, and, with the exception of two publications in a US reprint magazine, *Living Age*, her poetry appeared in the United States for the first time. The liberal London-based newspaper *Westminster Gazette* (well known for its short stories, including Katherine Mansfield's 'The Garden Party') printed 'The Cenotaph' on 27 September 1919. 'Song: Love, Love To-day' appeared in the *Athenaeum* on 24 October 1919, and was reprinted in the popular US weekly *Literary Digest* (a rival to *Current Opinion*, which it absorbed in 1925) on 17 January 1920. Possibly suggested by Wilkinson (who published poems and reviews there), 'To a Child in Death' appeared in US *The Bookman* (Apr 1922: 117), in front of a piece by Theodore Dreiser and alongside poetry by Witter Bynner and Milton Raison. 'The Rambling Sailor' was reprinted both in *Literary Digest* in April 1922 and (prominently, with an illustration) in US *The Bookman* in June 1923. The publication of 'Fin de Fête' on 17 February 1923 in the *Sphere* was Mew's last appearance in her lifetime. After Mew's death in 1928 the Poetry Bookshop brought out *The Rambling Sailor* (with an introduction by Alida Monro) in 1929. Edith Sitwell paid tribute to Mew in *Time and Tide* (21 June 1929) and in *Criterion* (Oct 1929). Also in the feminist and socially progressive magazine the *Bermondsey Book* Mew was called 'one of the greatest poets of her time' (qtd in Dowson 2015: 546).

While Mew had been reluctant in terms of anthologisation, perhaps due to the mainstreaming it implied, Wickham embraced it. Anthologies of the period promoted a range of approaches to 'modern' verse, which was often but not always 'modernist.' Although she did appear in Untermeyer's anthologies *Modern American and British Poetry* (1922) and *Modern British Poetry* (1925), and *Bookman Anthology* (1922), Mew refused to have her poetry included in Macmillan's *Golden Treasury of Modern Lyrics* (1924)

(Fitzgerald 1984: 207). The year 1923 saw Wickham's poems in Monroe and Alice Corbin Henderson's *The New Poetry: An Anthology of the Twentieth-Century Verse in English* (1923), Jessie B. Rittenhouse's *The Little Book of Modern British Verse: One Hundred Poets Since Henley* (1924), Robert Haven Schauffler's *The Poetry Cure: A Pocket Medicine Chest of Verse* (1925); and in Britain in Monro's *Twentieth Century Poetry: An Anthology* (1929). Testifying to ongoing celebrity in England, two of Wickham's poems were parodied in *Punch* on 16 February 1927 (other poets featured include T. S. Eliot and Mew).

In several last appearances, in 1928, Wickham's 'Salut d'Amour' was published in the *London Aphrodite*, a bimonthly founded by Jack Lindsay and P. R. Stevenson, and, in 1928 and 1929, in London-based the *Sackbut*. The *London Aphrodite* was a direct 'retort' to J. C. Squire's 'non- or anti-modernist' magazine the *London Mercury*, and an attempt 'to blast both modernist and anti-modernist positions' (Brooker and Thacker 2015: 15–16). Wickham's poem appeared alongside Lindsay's partner Elza de Locre and Sacheverell Sitwell. The *Sackbut*, which published Robert Nichols and Arthur Symons among others, is praised by John Rodker in the *Little Review* for the 'asperity of its opinions and the violence of it correspondence' (July–Aug 1920: 68). Wickham's final collection, *Thirty-Six New Poems* (1936), was brought out by her last promoter, poet and anthologist, John Gawsworth. Announced as part of a series called 'Shilling Selections from Edwardian Poets,' in the end only two more collections appeared.[12] Reviews were favourable but limited to obscure magazines and newspapers (Jones 2003: 241).

Conclusion

But could I spare
In the blind Earth's great silences and spaces,
The din, the scuffle, the long stare
If I went back and it was not there?
'Fame' by Charlotte Mew (1913)

I am sending you a few fragments that I have written during the last weeks—I am the vulgarian who must have a public.
    Anna Wickham, Letter to Untermeyer, 21 September 1921 (qtd in Jones 2003: 237)

A study of the periodical networks deployed by Mew and Wickham makes visible the agency available to the early twentieth-century woman poet in terms of publication, as well as the barriers. While networks of female contemporaries provided access to progressive venues, at the same time they hampered mainstream celebrity and long-term reputation. Supporters like Monro both helped and hindered Mew's and Wickham's affiliation with emerging modernist publications, such as *Poetry* and the *Egoist*. There is at once a pattern and an unpredictable range to the venues Mew and Wickham chose, not necessarily feminist, not necessarily modernist, often commercial, often ephemeral. Their relationship to the publishing establishment might thus be described as unsettled, restless, peripatetic, unsatisfactory; interestingly many of the same adjectives that appear in reviews of their poetry. As Joseph Bristow has argued of Mew: 'Attempts to categorize Mew as a Victorian, *fin-de-siècle*, or modernist writer cannot account for the defiant manner in which her best writings, with their unrestrained rhythms and overextended rhymes, reconfigure as far as they can the formalities of the literary past in the name of renewing her longstanding protest against modernity' (2009: 275–6).

But maybe the margin was exactly where Mew and Wickham had to be; both were uncompromisingly individualist and notoriously difficult to classify, albeit in somewhat different ways. As our analysis demonstrates, both had an ambivalent relationship with mainstream publication as well as with avant-garde modernist movements which resonates in terms of contemporary marginalisation. On the one hand, both poets actively sought different audiences and understood the value of networks, both domestic and transatlantic. On the other, to 'fit in,' or affiliate to return to Untermeyer's comments with which we open the chapter, would have represented compromise.

Irish poet Eavan Boland calls Mew 'dissident, . . . lost, . . . out on a margin of voice, craft and canon,' and goes on to assert that only someone 'so estranged from the society that made the [limiting] category [of poetess] could begin to dismantle it' (2001: 114). In her defiant, astringent way, bohemian Wickham also pulls apart any efforts at categorisation. In her 'Note on Method,' prefacing her 1921 US collection, she subversively asserts 'I give you "Woman." / Let it be known for our old world's relief, / I give you woman – and my method's brief!' Whereas Wickham, who fashions herself as 'the vulgarian in need of a public' for Untermeyer, fearlessly entered the fray in the 1920s and made a name for herself in the US, Mew never shed her ambivalent attitude to 'the din, the scuffle, the long stare.' But, toward the end of her life, in an autobiographical fragment, a world-weary Wickham acknowledged her likeness to Mew, uniting with her in not belonging and in adversity:

> In spite of my long endurance and impotent courage, I have made some profound mistakes. I feel that I am myself a profound mistake and that I was doomed from my conception by being myself: I feel that women of my kind are a profound mistake. There have been few women poets of distinction, and if we count only the suicides of Sappho, Lawrence Hope [Adela Florence Nicolson (1865–1904)] and Charlotte Mew, their despair rate has been very high. (1984: 52–3)

Notes

1. At that time Mew published her last essays. 'Mary Stuart in Fiction' (Apr 1912) and her environmentalist tract in two parts, 'Men and Trees' (Feb and Mar 1913), appeared in the *Englishwoman*. The newly founded radical weekly the *New Statesman* published 'An Old Servant' (18 Oct 1913), a portrait of Elizabeth Goodman who was a servant in Mew's childhood home, and 'The Hay-Market' (14 Feb 1914), a portrait of London neighbourhood of that name.
2. For more on Mew's relationship with Sinclair see Raitt 1995.
3. In 1914 Mew also placed two poems, 'Fame' and 'Pêcheresse,' in the newly established *New Weekly*, which only survived until the outbreak of the war.
4. For further discussion, see Rabaté 2015 and Mead (Chapter 15 in this volume).
5. Thanks to Helen Carr for this information.

Table 19.1 Timeline for UK and US publications by Charlotte Mew and Anna Wickham

Charlotte Mew (1869–1928)			Anna Wickham (1883–1947)	
US	UK		UK	US
	The Yellow Book (1894) 1 story	1890		
	Temple Bar (1899–1905) 5 poems, 5 essays, 6 stories			
Living Age (1899) 1 story	*The Academy* (1899) 1 essay			
	Pall Mall Magazine (1901) 1 story			
	The Nation (1909)	1910		
	The Nation (1912)		*Songs* (as John Oland; 1911) The Women's Printing Society	
	The Englishwoman (1912–14) 5 poems, 3 essays			
Living Age (1913)	*New Statesman* (1913, 1914) 2 essays			
	The Egoist (1914) *The New Weekly* (1914) 2 poems *Theosophist* (1914) 1 story		*Poetry and Drama* (1914) 15 poems	
		1915	*The Contemplative Quarry* (1915) The Poetry Bookshop	
			Egoist (1915)	
	The Farmer's Bride (1916) The Poetry Bookshop		*The Man with a Hammer* (1916) G. Richards	
				Poetry (1917) 2 poems *The Lantern* (1917)
	The Chapbook (1919) *Westminster Gazette* (1919) *The Athenaeum* (1919)		*The Disorderly Shepherdess* (drama; 1919) The Salamander Press	
Literary Digest (1920)	*The Chapbook* (1920)	1920	*The Chapbook* (1920) 2 poems	
Saturday Market (1921)	*The Farmer's Bride* (1921, extended edition) The Poetry Bookshop		*The Little Old House* (1921) The Poetry Bookshop	*The Contemplative Quarry, and The Man With a Hammer* (1921) Harcourt, Brace
				Current Opinion (1921) 2 issues; 6 poems *Vanity Fair* (1921) 10 poems
The Bookman (1922, 1923) *Literary Digest* (1922)	*The Chapbook* (1922, 1923)			*The Bookman* (1922) *The New Republic* (1922) 3 issues; 8 poems *Poetry* (1922) 2 poems *The Measure* (1922)
	The Sphere (1923)		*The Chapbook* (1923) 2 issues, 4 poems *The Chapbook* (1924) 4 poems	*The Liberator* (1922) *The Liberator* (1923) 2 issues
	The Bookman (1928, posthumous appearance)		*The London Aphrodite* (1928)	
	The Rambling Sailor (1929, posthumous) The Poetry Bookshop		*The Sackbut* (1928, 1929)	
		1930	*Thirty-six New Poems* (1936) Richards Press	

6. Virginia Woolf also seems to have read Mew only in 1921, praising her in letters to Vita Sackville-West in November 1924 and R. C. Trevelyan in January 1925. Although she judged her 'the greatest living poetess,' Mew did not become a Hogarth Press author; however, that Woolf considered publishing Mew is suggested by the appearance of her name on a list of other poets published at the press, written on the verso of a page of a draft of *To the Lighthouse*.
7. From Wilkinson's 1921 *New York Times Book Review and Magazine* review of *Saturday Market*: 'Lyrics That Are Not for Polyanna.'
8. In 1921 *Punch* included Mew in its series of parodies on well-known poets. The *Sphere* asked for a photo of Mew, but Mew refused to send one; she told Klementaski she did not have one (Fitzgerald 1984: 187).
9. 'The Cherry Blossom Wand,' 'All Men to Women,' 'The Stormy Moon,' 'Song to a Young John,' 'A Girl in Summer,' 'The Meeting,' 'Contemplative Quarry,' 'Sehnsucht,' 'The Faithful Amorist,' 'Soul's Liberty.'
10. Aldous Huxley, Iris Tree, Wilfred Owen, Helen Rootham, and Sherard Vines.
11. Some of the other women in the *Chapbook* include: Frances Cornford, Fredegond Shove, Mary Morison Webster, Ethel Talbot, Eleanor Farjeon, Iris Barry, Babette Deutsch, and Marianne Moore. See Catherine Clay's work on Theodora Bosanquet.
12. One by poet E. H. Visiak and the other one by the popular fiction writer M. P. Shiel. Gawsworth anthologised Wickham's poetry four times in the 1930s and 1940s.

Works Cited

Boland, Eavan. 2001. 'Charlotte Mew.' *Brick* 67: 113–14.
Brake, Laurel and Marysa Demoor, eds. 2009. 'The Academy.' *DNCJ: Dictionary of Nineteenth-Century Journalism in Great Britain and Ireland*. Gent and London: Academia Press and The British Library. 1–2.
Bristow, Gemma. 2006. 'Brief Encounter: Richard Aldington and the *Englishwoman*.' *English Literature in Transition, 1880–1920* 49.1: 3–13.
Bristow, Joseph. 2009. 'Charlotte Mew's Aftereffects.' *Modernism/modernity* 16.2: 255–80.
Brooker, Peter, and Andrew Thacker, eds. [2009] 2015. 'General Introduction.' *The Oxford Critical and Cultural History of Modernist Magazines: Volume I: Britain and Ireland 1880–1955*. Oxford: Oxford University Press. Oxford Scholarship Online. 1–26.
Carr, Helen. [2012] 2015. '*Poetry*: a Magazine of Verse (1912–36), "Biggest of Little Magazines."' *The Oxford Critical and Cultural History of Modernist Magazines: Volume II: North America 1894–1960*. Ed. Peter Brooker and Andrew Thacker. Oxford: Oxford University Press. Oxford Scholarship Online. 40–60.
Clay, Catherine. 2018. *Time and Tide: The Feminist and Cultural Politics of a Modern Magazine*. Edinburgh: Edinburgh University Press.
Collecott, Diana. 2004. 'Another Bloomsbury.' *Networking Women: Subjects, Place, Links Europe-America*. Ed. Marina Camboni. Roma: Edizioni di Storia e Letteratura. 59–80.
Dowson, Jane. [2009] 2015. 'Interventions in the Public Sphere: *Time and Tide* (1920–30) and *The Bermondsey Book* (1923–30).' *The Oxford Critical and Cultural History of Modernist Magazines: Volume I: Britain and Ireland 1880–1955*. Ed. Peter Brooker and Andrew Thacker. Oxford: Oxford University Press. Oxford Scholarship Online. 530–51.
Dowson, Jane and Alice Entwistle. 2005. *A History of Twentieth-Century British Women's Poetry*. Cambridge: Cambridge University Press.
Fitzgerald, Penelope. 1984. *Charlotte Mew and Her Friends*. London: Collins.
Grant, Joy. 1967. *Harold Monro and The Poetry Bookshop*. London: Routledge and Kegan Paul.

Hadjiafxendi, Kyriaki and John Plunkett. [2009] 2015. 'The Pre-History of the "Little Magazine."' *The Oxford Critical and Cultural History of Modernist Magazines: Volume I: Britain and Ireland 1880–1955*. Ed. Peter Brooker and Andrew Thacker. Oxford: Oxford University Press. Oxford Scholarship Online. 33–50.

Hammill, Faye and Karen Leick. [2012] 2015. 'Modernism and the Quality Magazines: *Vanity Fair* (1914–36); *American Mercury* (1924–81); *New Yorker* (1925–); *Esquire* (1933–).' *The Oxford Critical and Cultural History of Modernist Magazines: Volume II: North America 1894–1960*. Ed. Peter Brooker and Andrew Thacker. Oxford: Oxford University Press. Oxford Scholarship Online. 176–96.

Hibberd, Dominic. [2009] 2015. 'The New Poetry, Georgians and Others: *The Open Window* (1910–11), *The Poetry Review* (1912–15), *Poetry and Drama* (1913–14), and *New Numbers* (1914).' *The Oxford Critical and Cultural History of Modernist Magazines: Volume I: Britain and Ireland 1880–1955*. Ed. Peter Brooker and Andrew Thacker. Oxford: Oxford University Press. Oxford Scholarship Online. 176–96.

Jones, Jennifer Vaughan. 2003. *Anna Wickham: A Poet's Daring Life*. Lanham, MD: First Madison Books.

Kircher, Pamela. 1990. 'Appraisals of Charlotte Mew's Poetry 1916–1989: An Annotated Bibliography and Critical Essay.' M.L.S. Research Paper, Kent State University.

Mew, Charlotte. 1981. *Charlotte Mew: Collected Poems and Prose*. Ed. Val Warner. London: Virago Press.

Monro, Alida. 1953. 'Charlotte Mew – A Memoir.' *Collected Poems of Charlotte Mew*. London: Gerald Duckworth & Co. Ltd. vii–xx.

Monro, Harold. 1920. *Some Contemporary Poets*. London: Leonard Parsons.

Morrisson, Mark S. 2001. *The Public Face of Modernism: Little Magazines, Audiences, and Reception, 1905–1920*. Madison: University of Wisconsin Press.

—. [2009] 2015. 'The Cause of Poetry: Thomas Moult and *Voices* (1919–21), Harold Monro and *The Monthly Chapbook* (1919–25).' *The Oxford Critical and Cultural History of Modernist Magazines: Volume I: Britain and Ireland 1880–1955*. Ed. Peter Brooker and Andrew Thacker. Oxford: Oxford University Press. Oxford Scholarship Online. 405–27.

Rabaté, Jean-Michel. [2009] 2015. 'Gender and Modernism: *The Freewoman* (1911–12), *The New Freewoman* (1913), and *The Egoist* (1914–19).' *The Oxford Critical and Cultural History of Modernist Magazines: Volume I: Britain and Ireland 1880–1955*. Ed. Peter Brooker and Andrew Thacker. Oxford: Oxford University Press. Oxford Scholarship Online. 269–89.

Raitt, Suzanne. 1995. 'Charlotte Mew and May Sinclair: A Love Song.' *Critical Quarterly* 37.3: 3–17.

Rice, Nelljean McConeghey. 2003. *A New Matrix for Modernism: A Study of the Lives and Works of Charlotte Mew and Anna Wickham*. New York: Routledge.

Ryan, Leila and Maria DiCenzo. 2011. '*The Englishwoman*: "Twelve Years of Brilliant Life."' *Feminist Media History: Suffrage, Periodicals and the Public Sphere*. Ed. Maria DiCenzo, Lucy Delap, and Leila Ryan. Basingstoke: Palgrave Macmillan. 120–58.

Schenck, Celeste M. 1990. 'Anna Wickham.' *The Gender of Modernism*. Ed. Bonnie Kime Scott. Bloomington and Indianapolis: Indiana University Press. 613–17.

—. 1990. 'Charlotte Mew.' *The Gender of Modernism*. Ed. Bonnie Kime Scott. Bloomington and Indianapolis: Indiana University Press. 316–21.

Severin, Laura. 2004. *Poetry Off the Page: Twentieth-Century British Women Poets in Performance*. Burlington, VT: Ashgate.

Taylor, Georgina. 2001. *H.D. and the Public Sphere of Modernist Women Writers 1913–1946: Talking Women*. Oxford: Oxford University Press.

Thacker, Andrew. [2012] 2015. 'Poetry in Perspective: The Melange of the 1920s: *The Measure* (1921–6); *Rhythmus* (1923–4); and *Palms* (1923–30).' *The Oxford Critical and*

Cultural History of Modernist Magazines: Volume II: North America 1894–1960. Ed. Peter Brooker and Andrew Thacker. Oxford: Oxford University Press. Oxford Scholarship Online. 320–46.

Untermeyer, Louis. [1920] 1925. *Modern British Poetry*. New York: Harcourt Brace.

—. 1921. 'Introduction.' *The Contemplative Quarry and The Man With the Hammer.* New York: Harcourt Brace and Co. Inc. vii–xv.

Wickham, Anna. 1984. *The Writings of Anna Wickham: Free Woman and Poet.* Ed. R. D. Smith. London: Virago Press.

Wilkinson, Marguerite. [1919] 1924. *New Voices: An Introduction to Contemporary Poetry.* New York: Macmillan.

20

Women's Poetry in the Modern British Magazines: A Case for Medium Reading

Bartholomew Brinkman

In his *ABC of Reading*, Ezra Pound – the modernist poet who Robert Scholes and Clifford Wulfman dubbed the founder of modern periodical studies in their influential book, *Modernism in the Magazines* – quipped that '"Literature is news that STAYS News"' (1934: 29). In making such a claim, Pound suggests that literature (particularly poetry) is simultaneously and paradoxically that which is both permanent and ephemeral. It stays and it stays new. Aside from providing a provocative means of understanding how literature can both maintain its historicity and be rearticulated to new contexts, framing literature in such a way highlights the relationship between imaginative writing and news media that informs both modernist literary study and modern periodical studies, productively complicating those shared areas of inquiry. When literature, and poetry in particular, is read into its periodical context alongside other constitutive texts – a practice facilitated through digital tools and methods – its political edge often becomes more obvious than when it is encountered in a collected works or an anthology. This is certainly the case with a great deal of women's poetry (much of which has not made its way into either of these critical constructions) that served to voice and help shape evolving understandings of feminism, women's rights, and gender dynamics more broadly.

To suggest that modern poetry can and should be read into its political context is nothing new. Modern periodicals have often been seen as key vehicles for placing poems in the public (or counterpublic) sphere, where they can have both immediate and more lasting effects. As Paige Reynolds has argued:

> The radical diversity and tenuous cultural status of the modernist periodical allowed it to play a crucial role in the development of modernist poetry. A liminal material object situated between the sturdy book and the ephemeral performance, these publications offered poets a laboratory in which they could indulge a style of performativity enabling the advancement of modernist aesthetics. (2015: 121)

Such performativity extends to the performance of gender identity and gender roles within a sanctioned public space, as well as to social and political advancement. It is important to note that this gender performativity was to a certain extent a transnational and trans-lingual phenomenon. As Rachel Mesch argues, for example,

Belle Epoque French magazines, including *Femina* and *La Vie Heureuse*, actively promoted the idea of the *femme moderne*. As part of these efforts, such magazines would champion the woman poet and through a series of poetry contests would attract a wide variety of contributors in order to emphasise the everyday presence of poetry.

The *femme moderne* would find her counterpart in the notion of the (often class-privileged) New Woman, lauded in the modern British and American contexts at the end of the nineteenth century, and to the chorus of suffrage movements in the late nineteenth and early twentieth centuries. Such organisations as the National Society for Women's Suffrage, formed in 1867, and the National Union of Women's Suffrage Societies, formed in 1897, drove the suffragist movement that culminated in the Representation of the People Act of 1918 and finally the Representation of the People (Equal Franchise) Act a decade later. Taken as a whole, these movements emphasised a shared gender identity that cut across traditional class standings and that were evident in a 'suffrage' discourse emphasising political action and votes. This discourse, a dominant one in modern magazines, was complemented and complicated by two other pervasive discourses: one surrounding 'sex' and one surrounding 'domesticity.'

In order to attain a specific and concrete understanding of these discourses, we might think of them as systems of words and, as such, attempt to quantify the system: which words are most prominent? Which words most frequently occur alongside other words of interest? Does the frequency of particular words change over time? While it is certainly possible to begin to answer these questions using traditional methods of extensive close reading and printed concordances, the rise of the digital humanities has made other approaches more efficient and effective for the increasingly large amount of textual data that many humanists now confront. As Matthew L. Jockers has asserted in *Macroanalysis: Digital Methods and Literary History*, 'we have reached a tipping point, an event horizon where enough texts and literature have been encoded to both allow and, indeed, force us to ask an entirely new set of questions about literature and the literary record' (2013: 4). These questions are often concerned with the deep structural make-up of texts and of uncovering patterns within and across texts, both synchronically and diachronically, in ways that have previously been impractical.

While Jockers is primarily concerned with the nineteenth-century novel, his observations also hold true for other genres. Natalie M. Houston has turned her attention to Victorian poems, including those published in periodicals, to argue for what she refers to as a 'sociological poetics that takes into account the newly expanded digital archive' (2014: 499). Such a poetics acknowledges that the cadre of poets central for most critical analysis make up a very small fraction of the period's actual poetic output and in order to have a fuller sense of the age we need to be on the lookout for figures that we may have previously missed. In doing so, we can better understand poetic genre as a whole, including its structural relationship to social and cultural forces expressed through other literary and non-literary texts. Scholars of modernism can practice such a sociological poetics through a variety of 'distant reading' computational approaches, including topic modelling, data mining, network analysis, and semantic analysis.

As powerful and persuasive as such approaches are, they might cause us to miss the trees for the forest. Reading at a distance necessarily flattens genre and form, while obscuring deeper dimensions of meaning lingering beneath a text's surface, as it turns highly structured texts into big bags of words. In order to deepen our computational analyses, it is necessary to preserve this textual structure and one of the most straightforward ways of doing so is to encode such structure into textual data and metadata themselves. The Text Encoding Initiative (TEI), which has evolved the standard in humanities textual encoding, provides guidelines for the encoding of XML files at any level of granularity, from the corpus (such as a periodical run) to the individual text, poetic line, or even individual character. This provides an important supplement to distant-reading approaches, and is akin to traditional close-reading.

But like traditional close-reading, it is slow, labour intensive, and does not scale well. Adam Hammond notes: 'The mind boggles at the research opportunities of a universal library that is universally encoded in TEI. Yet the creation of such a resource will be immensely difficult, if not impossible. The greatest barrier is that text encoding is premised on the notion that we, humans, understand things about texts that it, the computer, cannot understand without our help. As such, most text encoding is done by humans' (2016: 125). As a result, digital humanities approaches often function at two vastly different scales – one that might involve thousands or millions of unstructured texts across nations and epochs, and one that is centred on an individual text or relatively small corpus of texts by an author or small set of authors deemed worthy of the cost and effort to consider more closely. The perceived opposition between distant-reading quantitative approaches and close-reading textual encoding approaches is as much a practical one as a principled one.

It is possible and often necessary to bridge these two approaches, however, through a strategic employment of what Allison Booth has referred to as 'mid-range reading' and what I call 'medium' reading that not only tries to claim a (shifting) middle ground between big- and close-reading strategies, but which acknowledges that an effort to do so often necessarily draws attention to the textual medium itself (Booth 2017). Such medium reading foregrounds a disciplinary-specific approach to studies of modernism, heeding Shawna Ross and James O'Sullivan's call to 'devise tailor-made DH processes appropriate to a specific field. Devising these will in turn require returning to questions of style, to aesthetics and revisiting the period's or field's non-fiction, manifestos, artist statements and contemporaneous reviews and criticism – particularly with an eye toward book history, media and technology' (2016: 5). Moreover, medium reading has important implications for studying modern periodicals in particular. Jeffrey Drouin, current director of the Modernist Journals Project (which has scanned and encoded the digital files I am working with here),[1] points to the importance of such an approach for modern periodical studies in noting that research often involves a blend of approaches that attempts to make sense of big unstructured data through things like graphs and trees, while at the same time relying upon human mark-up of such attributes as author and genre in order to better locate and understand individual texts. This combination can often best reveal both the nuanced meanings of texts and their places within wider contextual terrains.

Embracing a medium-reading approach, in this essay I examine women's poems in several modern little magazines: the *Freewoman* (1911–12), the *New Freewoman* (1913), the *Egoist* (1914–19), the *English Review* (1908–10), and the *New Age* (1907–22). The *Freewoman* in particular (and to a lesser extent, its successors, the *New Freewoman* and the *Egoist*) has become an important touchstone for understanding the intersection of feminism and modern literary expression in the modern magazines. Magazines like the *English Review* and the *New Age* offer a more general sense of how women's concerns were explored within the wider periodical field of literary and cultural modernism. To distinguish poems in these magazines from other texts and to better understand them collectively, I have marked up XML files of magazine issues at the level of genre (or have relied on mark-up available through the MJP).

Rather than imposing from the outset a set of women-centred topics and terms that may or may not be frequently represented in these magazines, I used statistical topic modelling to uncover hypothetical 'topics' across these magazines as a whole through an algorithm that determines which terms most frequently occur together in a given set of documents. I found 'suffrage,' 'domestic,' and 'sex' topics to be the most common and relevant to my line of inquiry.[2] As Ted Underwood has suggested, we might think of these topics themselves as the discourses from which a given text has derived. For example, a text might be built up of a combination of words that occur in a 'domestic' topic (drawing on the discourse traditionally surrounding domesticity, such as references to marriage and children) and a 'sex' topic (drawing on a sex discourse emphasising sexual activity or its abstention).

Having determined which topics/ discourses are generally dominant in these magazines, I then consider the extent to which these general topics are present in periodical poetry by women (it should be noted that there are also several poems by men that address these topics, but these poems are beyond the scope of this essay). Focusing on the *Egoist* as a test case for the intersection of feminism and modernism, I also consider some of the most canonical modernist women poets in light of these topics. Finally, I use the most common terms in each topic to perform a KWIC (keyword in context) search as a means of locating poems by lesser-known poets, making them available for traditional close readings.

The *Freewoman* is an obvious starting point for exploring women's topics in the modern British magazines. Started in 1911 by Dora Marsden as a weekly feminist review, the *Freewoman* served as an important bridge between suffrage journals and an embryonic modernism. As Mark S. Morrisson has argued of the magazine's intentions:

> The *Freewoman* was not simply part of the discursive space of the suffrage/feminist counterpublic sphere. A large measure of its importance to modernist authors came from its attempt to form a broader and more generally antibourgeois oppositional public sphere that would involve not just public discussion of suffrage but would include topics that the bourgeois suffrage magazines would consider 'improper,' like homosexuality, radical monetary reforms, experimental or radical art and literature, and antistatist politics. (2001: 92)

Lucy Delap and Maria DiCenzo complicate the reception of the magazine, tracing how the *Freewoman* transformed from a little magazine to a kind of suffrage pamphlet as it crossed the pond from Britain to the US – foregrounding a mutability of media across transatlantic reading communities and social formations. It is clear, though, that from the standpoint of both production and reception, the *Freewoman* had one foot in the suffragist political sphere and one in the sphere of an emerging literary modernism.

The stance would eventually shift to the latter and aesthetic concerns would slowly eclipse the original firebrand rhetoric as the magazine evolved into the *New Freewoman* in 1913 and finally into the *Egoist* for the half decade, 1914–19. Taking the three magazines together therefore offers an opportunity to both spotlight particular issues and to follow the ups and downs of women-centred discourse in the modern little magazines.

As I have suggested, the magazines and their constitutive texts (including poetic and non-poetic texts) reveal over the decade 1911–19 three clear topics related to women. First, there is what we might call a 'suffrage' topic, whose top words (in order of prominence) include 'Mr,' 'women,' 'suffrage,' 'political,' 'government,' 'Mrs,' 'vote,' 'suffragists,' 'movement,' and 'public.' In addition to including terms that directly invoke women's suffrage, closely associated terms in this topic highlight the political dimension of the movement. Second, there is a 'domestic' topic, whose top words include 'children,' 'marriage,' 'women,' 'mother,' 'child,' 'woman,' 'state,' 'husband,' 'wife,' and 'married.' These terms underscore women's dual domestic roles as wife and mother. Finally, the third topic is a 'sex' topic, including in its top words 'sex,' 'love,' 'sexual,' 'passion,' 'man,' 'women,' 'men,' 'desire,' 'woman,' and 'prostitution.' The relative prominence of these terms in each topic is represented by the word clouds in Figure 20.1.

Some of these terms are likely to produce a fair amount of noise in the data. While it is helpful to identify the pronouns 'Mr' and 'Mrs,' these terms occur frequently in a wide variety of contexts (as in the formal naming of authors) and are not necessarily tied to gender concerns. Similarly, while the terms 'political,' 'government,' 'movement,' 'public,' and 'state' emphasise the political nature of the 'suffrage' topic, they are often tied to other causes as well – a term like 'movement,' for example, may refer to a political, cultural, or aesthetic transformation (as in the Imagist movement). This suggests an intriguing overlap of discourses that would be worth studying further (though it muddies up attention to women-centred discourse that is my particular interest here) as it simultaneously serves as an important reminder that terms uncovered through quantitative approaches often require closer inspection and human interpretation in order to fully make sense.

Figure 20.1 Word clouds for 'suffrage,' 'sex,' and 'domestic' topics for the *Freewoman*, the *New Freewoman*, and the *Egoist*.

Eliminating such terms from analysis allows for tighter focus on those terms that most clearly point to women's topics even as it interrogates processes of categorisation.[3] The frequency of these terms is in flux over the run of the three magazines. To gain a better understanding of how the magazines may have shifted thematic and generic focus over time, the three magazines can be examined together and the results graphed (issues 1–47 are from the *Freewoman*, issues 48–60 are from the *New Freewoman* and issues 61–134 are from the *Egoist*). Since 'woman' and 'women' are commonly present in all three topics, and offer an overarching meta-topic in themselves, plotting these terms together in chronological order gives a rough sense of how present women and women's issues are at any given moment as well as over time. It is not surprising to find that 'woman/women' appear frequently in issues of the *Freewoman*. These terms would appear up to 300 times in a single issue, with an approximate mean of 0.506 per cent of the total word count (including editorial apparatus and advertisements), and peaking at more than 1 per cent of the text count per issue.[4] One appearance out of every two hundred words or so may not seem like much, but it is actually a rather high number, considering that all words (including articles and pronouns) have been included in the analysis.

A steady decline in the use of 'woman/women' is evident throughout the run of the *Freewoman* and the *New Freewoman*, so that by the time the magazine had morphed into the *Egoist* the mean term count is approximately 0.064 per cent of each issue's text count – about 10 per cent of what it had been in the *Freewoman*. Plotting this trend against the use of the terms 'man/men' also reveals that while these terms are less frequently used than 'woman/women' throughout the run of the *Freewoman*, they had become more frequent in the *New Freewoman* and the *Egoist* (Figure 20.2). This trend suggests that attention to women and women's issues declined over time, a conjecture

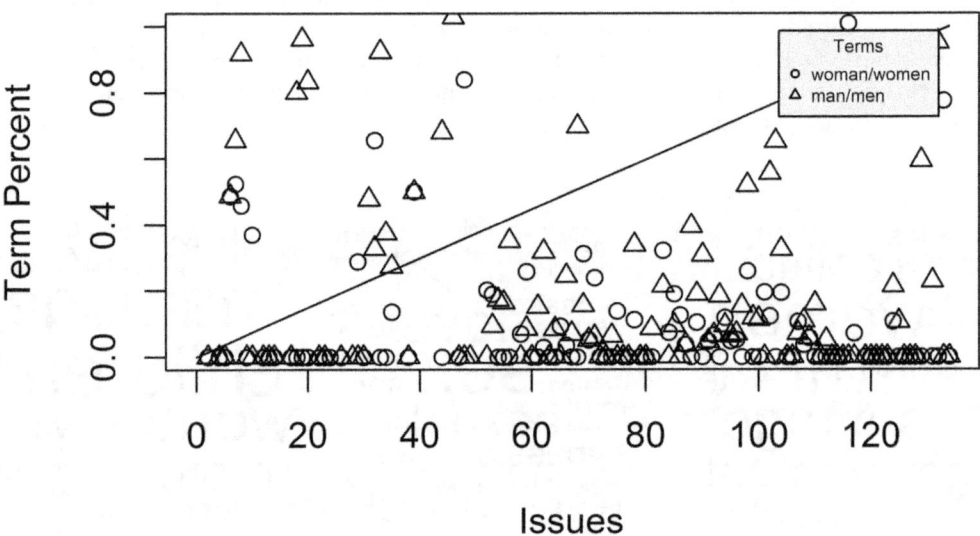

Figure 20.2 Distribution of 'women' and 'men' in the *Freewoman*, the *New Freewoman*, and the *Egoist*.

that is in line with the general critical assumption that the magazine became increasingly less socially and politically minded as it grew into a key vehicle for modernist literary experimentation. In its showcasing of such quintessential modernist movements as Imagism – which often celebrated the cold, hard, masculinised depiction of the image (even when practiced by women poets), one might even go so far as to say that this experimentation was gendered masculine by default. Such an assumed masculinity aligns with what Andreas Huyssen has pointed to as a masculinised high modernism against a more feminised mass culture.

The veracity of Huyssen's claim has often been challenged by scholars of modernism who point to women poets, editors, and publishers foregrounding feminised textual production and distribution. As Huyssen's point is fundamentally about the gendering of the discourse of modernism, though, we might test his conjecture through the evolution of these three major topics over the run of these magazines. For the 'suffrage' topic, I have focused on the key terms 'suffrage,' 'vote,' and 'suffragists' for reasons indicated above.[5] These appear relatively frequently in the *Freewoman* but decline in the magazine's later incarnations. This downward trend is generally the same for the terms in the 'domestic' and 'sex' topics as illustrated in Figure 20.3 and Table 20.1. Both the 'domestic' and 'sex' topics slide from a peak of about 0.4 per cent to under 0.2 per cent; the 'suffrage' topic slides from up to 0.2 per cent to being almost non-existent. Through each of these three women-centred topics, an overall trend can be detected in which most terms are significantly more prominent in the *Freewoman* issues and less so in the later magazines.

A focus on these terms also allows for concrete comparison of the *Freewoman/ New Freewoman/ Egoist* with other magazines, so that they can be better understood within the larger field of modern British periodicals. The *English Review*, for example,

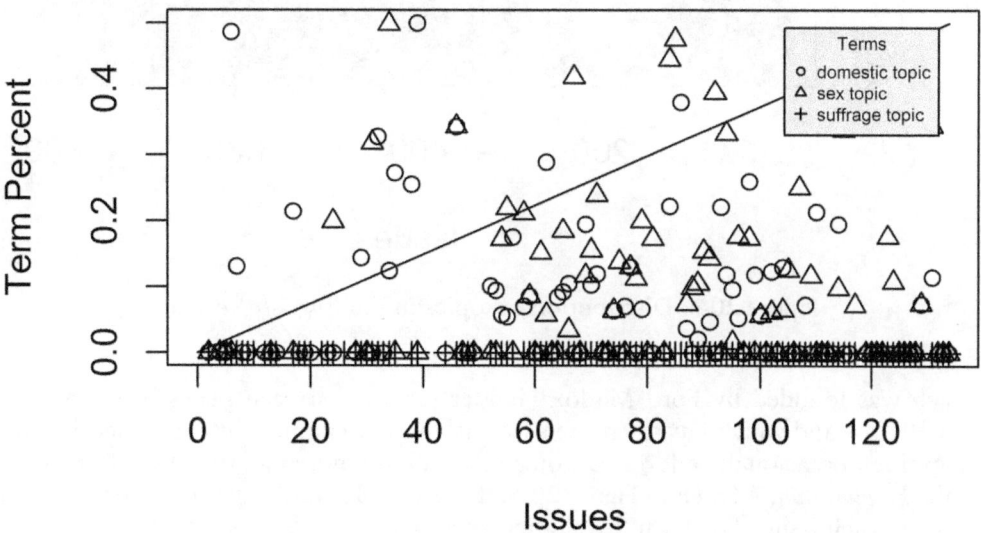

Figure 20.3 Distribution of topics in the *Freewoman*, the *New Freewoman*, and the *Egoist*.

Table 20.1 Term Frequencies in the *Freewoman*, the *New Freewoman*, and the *Egoist*.

Term(s)	*Freewoman*	*New Freewoman*	*Egoist*
suffrage/suffragists	0.033%	0.007%	0.002%
vote	0.032%	0.015%	0.015%
child/children	0.130%	0.044%	0.028%
marriage/married	0.045%	0.014%	0.008%
mother	0.071%	0.019%	0.014%
wife	0.037%	0.014%	0.009%
love	0.078%	0.094%	0.051%
passion	0.040%	0.024%	0.015%
sex	0.104%	0.056%	0.014%

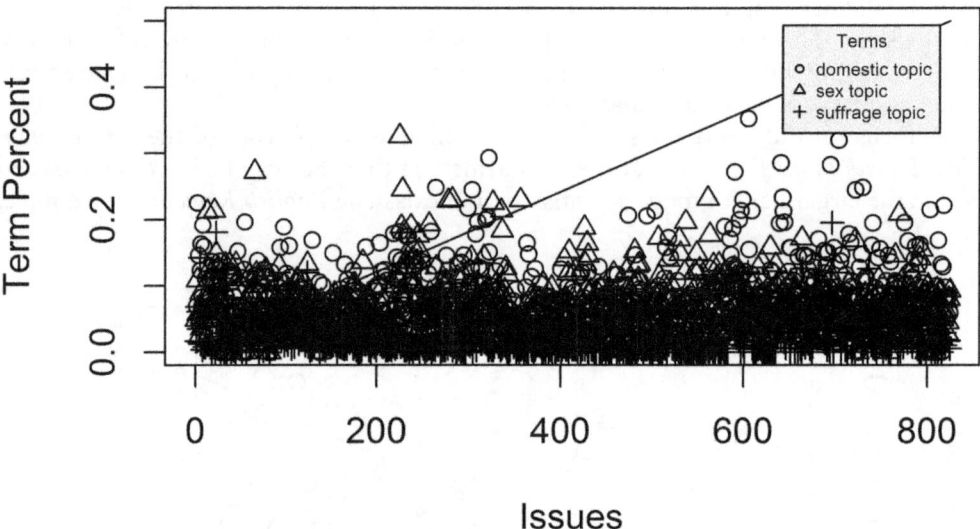

Figure 20.4 Distribution of topics in the *English Review*.

which was founded by Ford Madox Hueffer (printing sixteen issues between 1908 and 1910) – and which has often been seen as an early example of the modernist little magazine – occasionally addresses women's topics, but not at all to the same degree as in the *Freewoman*. As seen in Figure 20.4, there are relatively few occurrences of these terms in each issue. The term 'love' appears about 5 per cent as frequently as in the *Freewoman*; 'woman/women,' child/children,' 'mother,' and 'wife' each appear about 1 per cent as frequently.[6]

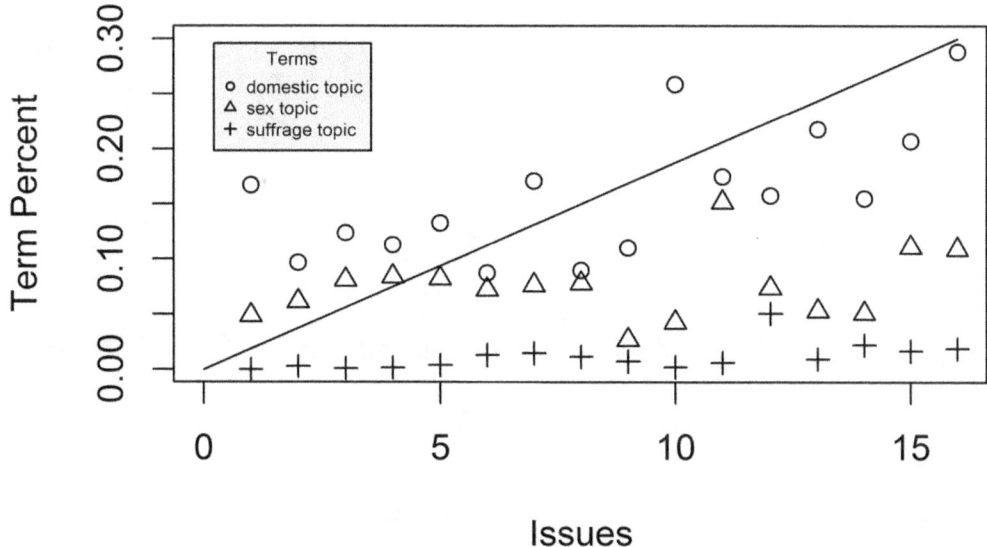

Figure 20.5 Distribution of topics in the *New Age*.

The *New Age*, a radical weekly edited by A. R. Orage that produced 825 issues between 1907 and 1922 is closer in frequency to that of the *Freewoman*. As indicated in Figure 20.5, the 'domestic' and 'sex' topics appear somewhat frequently; the 'suffrage' topic appears hardly at all.[7] The terms 'woman/women' and 'sex' appear about one-sixth as often as in the *Freewoman*, 'passion' about one-third as much, 'love' about half as frequently, 'suffrage' three-quarters as frequently, and 'vote' about the same. In general, these less women-oriented journals do address gender concerns, but do so alongside a host of other matters so that the overall attention is diminished.

To what extent, though, did poems by women draw on these particular topics? To return to the run of the *Freewoman*, *New Freewoman*, and *Egoist*, we see that the use of the terms 'woman/women' in poems in these magazines roughly parallels its appearance elsewhere in the magazine. As indicated in Figure 20.6, 'domestic' and 'sex' topics also follow this general trend, though they appear less consistently. Terms specific to the suffrage movement, such as 'suffrage' and 'vote' are non-existent, a notable absence suggesting that the political discourse at work elsewhere in the magazine is not present in the poetry – at least not in such an overt form. Distant reading suggests key terms that constitute the topics of modern women's magazine poetry, how these terms correlate to the topics and discourses that construct these magazines as a whole, and how these change over time – even as we are careful to recognise potential slippages of meaning.

While such comparisons can be fruitful for viewing at a glance the extent to which poetic discourse aligns with other discourses available in these magazines, this surface-level attention is ultimately insufficient for understanding *how* these discourses are being used. As I have already noted, polyvalent words like 'movement' and 'love' demand critical interpretation beyond a basic quantification. Modern poetry – an

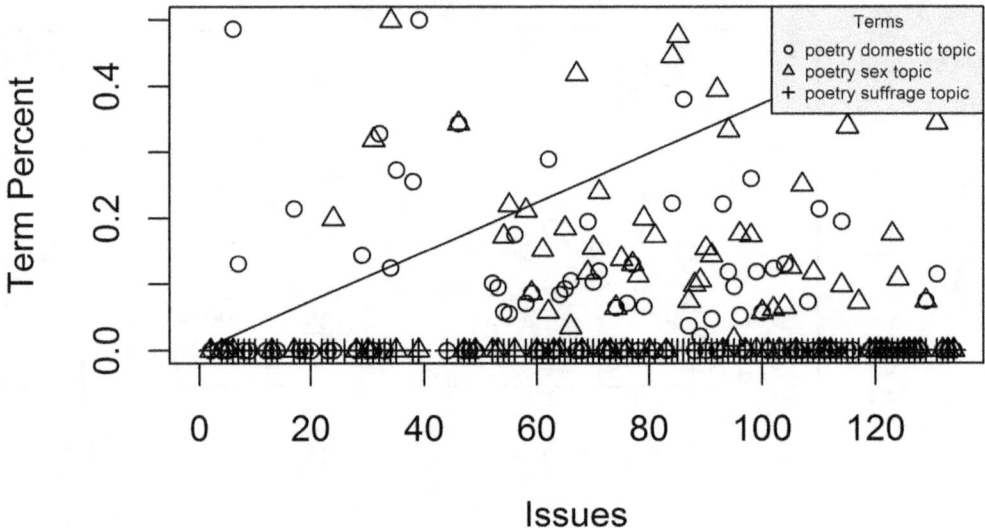

Figure 20.6 Distribution of poetry topics in the *Freewoman*, the *New Freewoman*, and the *Egoist*.

imaginative genre that frequently foregrounds the instability of linguistic meaning through figurative language and irregular syntax – makes distant reading approaches even more of a challenge. While it is certainly worthwhile to develop ways of accounting for these special conditions in distantly reading poems, it also often makes sense to shift scales and focus more closely on particular poets and poems of interest, using computational approaches to facilitate, test, and complicate more traditional literary approaches.

For example, through an author-centred approach we might determine the degree to which certain canonical poets drew upon the topics outlined above and, by extension, the degree to which their poems were or were not typical of others published in the magazines. That is, were these poems and poets exemplars of women-centred discourse or exceptions to the rule? We can begin to answer this question by examining the three women poets who most frequently appeared over the run of the *Egoist* (the magazine, of the ones I am examining, with the highest representation of canonical women poets): Amy Lowell with twenty poems, Marianne Moore with ten poems, and H.D. (Hilda Doolittle) with twenty-one poems. The frequent appearance of this small coterie of poets (along with their male counterparts, such as Ezra Pound, F. S. Flint, William Carlos Williams, and Richard Aldington) exemplifies what J. Stephen Murphy and Mark Gaipa have identified through digital network analysis as a tight network of linked authors that would become more exclusive in the transition from the *Freewoman* to the *Egoist*.

An examination of terms confirms a critical consensus that Marianne Moore does not typically participate much in these gendered discourses, with only the term 'love' making an appearance, in ironically quoted form in 'Pedantic Literalist': '"Irritating things in the midst of love and / Tears," you invite destruction' (*Egoist* 1 June

1916: 95, lines 4–5). Amy Lowell employs 'children,' 'desire,' and 'woman' once each, though the last term is used to great effect in her poem 'Vintage' (*Egoist* 9 Aug 1914: 288). The speaker mixes a drink 'And I will pour the cold scorn of my Beloved into it,' concluding, 'And I shall be hot, and laugh, / Forgetting that I have ever known a woman' (ibid.). 'Woman' takes on important meaning as the last word in the poem, 'known' to the speaker in the intimate, and possibly sexual, sense.

H.D. draws on several of the terms in her poetry to a relatively high degree (at least within this small sample size). The terms 'woman/women' make up a total of 0.5 per cent of her poetry in the magazine (about the same as the general appearance in the *Freewoman*), and the term is prominent in the title of 'Chorus of the Women of Chalkis' (*Egoist* 1 Nov 1915: 171–2). The terms, 'desire' (0.1 per cent) and 'passion' (0.1 per cent) are couched within mythological rendering, as is 'love,' which constitutes 0.25 per cent of the poetry. Likewise, 'child' and 'children' make up 0.6 per cent of the poetry, appearing three times in 'The Last Gift' (in second, first, and third person): 'You are like the children / who haunt your own steps / for chance bits,' 'I who have snatched at you / as the street-child clutched / at the seed-pearls you spilt,' 'as a child, a flower, any flower / tore my breast' (*Egoist* 1 Mar 1916: 35). As Georgina Taylor notes, the poem 'argues for the possibility of individuality against great constraining forces' (2001: 48). The repeated invocation of the child, however, places this individuality squarely within the domestic discourse that has long permeated the magazine, suggesting that this assertion is also necessarily a qualification of prescribed gender roles.

As H.D.'s *oeuvre* is heavily inspired by ancient Greek poetry (especially the work of the poet Sappho) and includes several translations and adaptations from the Greek, it is tempting to place her negotiation of gender identity within a long Western tradition as it was framed and articulated by literary modernism. While H.D.'s translations of Sappho do not appear in the *Egoist*, Sapphic poems and fragments, translated by Edward Storer, do appear in the magazine (1 Oct 1915: 153–5). These translations helped to popularise Sappho's poetry and were later reprinted in book form alongside 'The Poems of Anyte of Tegea,' by H.D.'s husband, Richard Aldington, which also had been originally printed in the *Egoist* (1 Sep 1915: 139–40). These are both male translators, but if we keep in mind Walter Benjamin's observation that in translations 'the life of the originals attains its latest, continually renewed, and most complete unfolding' (2002: 255), we might consider the ways in which Sappho and Anyte function as modern poets in their own right and as inspiration to H.D. and other modernist women poets.

Through a brief examination of these three canonical figures, it would appear that Lowell and H.D. both draw significantly on women-centred topics in interesting and somewhat unexpected ways, while Moore largely does not. This is hardly surprising, but it does serve to confirm the general critical understanding of these poets while at the same time validating the usefulness of a computational process for locating individual poems and reading them against the periodical discourses in which they are embedded. Such a process is potentially more valuable, though, as a means of drawing attention to poets and poems with less of a critical history behind them. One way of finding these often-ignored poets and poems without knowing who to look for beforehand is to perform a KWIC (keyword in context) search, locating key terms and placing them within their surrounding textual context. This process allows for the isolation of particular poems of interest in a much quicker and more efficient manner than exhaustively turning yellowing pages or even scrolling through PDFs of digitised texts.

Looping a KWIC search through the ten most frequent terms in the 'suffrage,' 'sex,' and 'domestic,' topics reveals several poems that can be made available for traditional close readings within poems and for cross-readings among poems. One thing that becomes clear through these poems is that gender is often tied to – and splintered by – economic and social class. Gladys Jones's quatrain, 'A Common Woman,' published in the *Freewoman*, succinctly reminds readers of the anonymity and untapped potential of women who are not able to transcend the expectations of their class:

> She lived and toiled for many weary days,
> Renounced the joys her soul had dreamed;
> Followed harsh Duty without praise:
> She died, the world was not redeemed. (11 Jan 1912: 159)

This unnamed woman is 'common' both in the sense of being a commoner and of being quite typical – both of which might be understood pejoratively by someone in the upper classes.

Similarly, 'Their Wrongs are Mine' by M. J. (Mary Jennette) Marshall, published in the *Freewoman*, underscores the tensions between gender and class identity that many women were facing at the time (28 Dec 1911: 117). The speaker, a 'Daughter of luxury,' recognises that her position is not like that of less fortunate women and girls 'unsexed by toil,' 'Careworn, depraved, and weakly stained with tears,' those 'Whom the selfish realm of man despises' (ibid.). She is financially better off than many women and does not share in their hardships, but still stands as their advocate, lamenting in a refrain that 'I ask not for mine own' (ibid.). By the end of the poem, however, the speaker questions: 'What of my baby girl, if aught befall me?' and recognises that 'shamed, I confess myself their partisan. / I ask now for mine own' (ibid.). The speaker is shamed because, although she had been willing to voice the concerns of other women, she had not seen those being applicable to herself. She thought that her economic privilege allowed her to be above such things. Now she recognises that class status is fleeting and that by virtue of her gender other women's problems are also her own. In stressing the importance of a shared gender identity and sense of community, where the speaker is necessarily a 'partisan,' even in the face of other inequalities and possible oppositions, this poem participates in the general suffrage discourse of the magazine, while also exposing some of the obstacles standing in the way of women binding together into a political and social movement.

More representative of the topic of domesticity is Claire de Sèvres's 'A Psalm of Motherhood,' published in the *New Age*, in which the speaker celebrates the child that came about after she left her abusive husband for another lover (18 July 1918: 192). Although 'Soft mother-crooning never was my part. . . .' she had 'paid my rebel's toll in woman's tears,' and now 'Joy – fiercest joy is mine' (ibid.). She has succumbed to 'A miracle of spirit-winged desire!' (ibid.). This is not a cliché depiction of childhood, but a difficult reckoning between two seemingly contradictory impulses that characterise the domesticity and suffrage discourses common in the magazine and in many women's daily lives.

Children are a blessing for the mother, but also could be a burden for other women who have been pressed into maternal roles as governesses, as is the case with the central figure in Margaret Sanders's 'A Modern Brontë,' published in the *New Age* (30 June 1921: 108). The body of the poem depicts a chaotic domestic scene, in which a governess is trapped in an existence of thanklessly caring for other people's rowdy children (without any end in sight) so that even the 'city gardens were a prison place' (ibid.). Like those pitied women in 'Their Wrongs are Mine,' this woman has – through a structural inequality that is beyond her control – been preordained by gender and class to fulfil the role of hired caretaker. As disheartening as her circumstances can be, it is the title of the poem that lends a tinge of tragic irony. This woman is depicted as a modern Brontë (both Charlotte and Anne Brontë served as governesses), and she may still one day reach her fullest potential. But as the years tick on this seems increasingly unlikely – and perhaps because she is modern she is more deeply imbricated into a class system that denies her the creative outlet that the Brontës were able to pursue.

In the face of such individual and societal inequalities, the fight for suffrage and women's equality more generally not only meant a reconsideration of relationships among women, but between men and women as well. A positive portrayal of this relationship is depicted in 'A Vindication' by Muriel Nelson d'Auvergne, published in the *Freewoman* (4 Jan 1912: 139), the title of which recalls Mary Wollstonecraft's influential *A Vindication of the Rights of Women*. The 74-line narrative poem opens with the speaker cursing a 'Grim tragedy, beneath a painted smile; / Heaven and earth's great mystery – Sex – / Bartered for gold' (ibid.). In addition to these blatant acts of prostitution, the speaker finds everywhere 'marriage itself a cankering fetter of steel' (ibid.). After falling asleep, however, the speaker is visited by a god who chastises her for cursing sex and beauty, but acknowledges that these have been corrupted by money and that 'Your women have been held for centuries / With wings close sheared of the mind and the soul, / Taught cringing submission as servants, not masters of sex' (ibid.). Sex in itself is beautiful and natural, not evil, but it must come from a place of equality. If woman is given back her freedom, though, 'the clash of brain upon brain shall mark her the equal of man' and 'As comrades and large-hearted friends they shall work out the race's salvation' (ibid.). The poem paints an optimistic portrait of women's equality – one rooted in a deep, lost past and the possibility of cooperation over conflict.

These poems are relatively unknown and are unlikely to be looked for based on the reputations of their makers. Still, they are poems worth closely reading for how they address topics of suffrage, sex, and domesticity – both individually and collectively – in important ways that are fundamentally different from how they are explored elsewhere in these magazines. A KWIC search makes these poems readily available for this kind of close-reading interpretation, even as it supplements and challenges traditional author-centred approaches.

My readings of poems by both canonical and lesser-known poets, found through modelled topics and keyword searches, is one example of what I have been calling medium reading: a pragmatic approach to the rich middle ground between big unstructured data and highly structured individual texts that strategically toggles between distant-reading and close-reading approaches. This middle ground is perhaps best exemplified by the modern periodical itself, which, on the one hand, stretches the ability of any individual critic to read and understand it in a general sense without the aid of computational approaches and, on the other hand, requires critical intervention at every level to make sense of the data and to devise new critical questions.

In my medium reading of women's poetry in the modern magazines, I have not tried to do everything and there are still many productive avenues to explore.[8] What I have tried to do is to demonstrate how well-known and lesser-known modern women's poetry in several key little magazines participated in discourses of suffrage, sex, and domesticity at the individual textual level and the broader level of genre that added to and complicated those available (in varying degrees) across the magazines as a whole. In doing so, I have also outlined benefits and acknowledged limitations of computational approaches for investigating texts and topics within and across the modern British magazines.

Notes

1. I am grateful to the Modernist Journals Project, available at <http://modjourn.org/> for digitising and making available the XML files for several modernist magazines that has enabled this exploration, and especially to Drouin and Mark Gaipa for providing some additional files that have not yet been made publicly available.
2. A Latent Dirichlet allocation (LDA) topic model was trained at fifty topics for 20,000 iterations, using the Mallet package for R. For more on topic analysis, see Jockers 2013.
3. It should be stressed that these are by no means the only terms that could be explored, and that other terms could become available if topics were initially derived from another run of magazines. This analysis is therefore not exhaustive; rather it is suggestive of gendered discourses at work in the magazines. Also, noting the appearance of a term or overall topic does not reveal whether this is portrayed in a positive, negative or neutral light. Such a determination demands that these terms be read into context. For example, the relative frequency of the 'domestic' terms that highlights women's traditional roles as wife and mother suggests that discussion of women's issues – whether progressive or not – are often framed in relation to these traditional activities. One must dig deeper into texts to see if these activities are criticised or affirmed.
4. Since magazine issues are of different lengths and appear with different degrees of frequency, comparing textual percentages gives the most accurate sense of relative frequency of terms and topics.
5. Through a process of stemming, in which words are trimmed to their roots to facilitate text mining, 'suffrage' and 'suffragists' have been combined into a single term 'suffr*.' This is also true for other terms, such as 'child/children' and 'married/marriage' that share root words with different suffixes. A term like 'love' likewise includes the terms 'lovely' and 'beloved.'
6. The term 'love,' a long-time literary staple, is a broad term that might invoke romantic, familial, and other feelings, and is another good example of how a blanket quantitative approach is often insufficient for studying poetic discourse. Given a large enough sample size and a line of inquiry that is beyond my focus here, one might locate which terms cluster around the term 'love,' or determine if there are multiple coherent topics that include 'love' as a frequent term, but such analyses serve to emphasise the importance of the human critic in directing computational approaches.

7. It should be noted that representing topics in 825 issues, this figure contains thousands of data points and becomes impossible to read completely at this scale. It is therefore worth focusing on examples of topics that appear more frequently than 0.2 per cent.
8. I have restricted my focus to a relatively few well-known little magazines in large part because these are the ones that have been digitised and textually encoded, but a more comprehensive understanding would require an exploration of lesser-known literary magazines, suffrage journals, and bigger magazines – most of which are not yet available in sufficient digital form. While I have compared poems against periodicals as a whole, I have not attempted to generically distinguish other periodical texts, so that a poem could be directly compared to, say, a short story. I have not been particularly attentive to poetic form and have not attempted to quantify formal features, such as line length or the use of simile. There are other distant-reading approaches, including network analysis and semantic analysis, I have not employed here. These are all worthwhile pursuits and would contribute to a more robust middle-reading framework.

Works Cited

Benjamin, Walter. 2002. 'The Task of the Translator.' *Walter Benjamin Selected Writings, Volume 1: 1913–1926*. Ed. Marcus Bullock and Michael W. Jennings. Cambridge, MA: The Belknap Press of Harvard University Press. 253–63.

Booth, Alison. 2017. 'Mid-Range Reading: Not a Manifesto.' *PMLA: Publications of the Modern Language Association of America* 132.3: 620–7.

D'Auvergne, Muriel Nelson, ed. 1912. *An Anthology of Babyhood*. London: Hutchinson.

Delap, Lucy and Maria DiCenzo. 2008. 'Transatlantic Print Culture: The Anglo-American Feminist Press and Emerging "Modernities."' *Transatlantic Print Culture, 1880–1940: Emerging Media, Emerging Modernisms*. Ed. Ann Ardis and Patrick Collier. Houndsmills: Palgrave Macmillan. 48–65.

DiCenzo, Maria. 2015. 'Remediating the Past: Doing 'Periodical Studies' in the Digital Era.' *English Studies in Canada* 41.1: 19–39.

Drouin, Jeffrey. 2014. 'Close- and Distant-Reading Modernism: Network Analysis, Text Mining, and Teaching the *Little Review*.' *Journal of Modern Periodical Studies* 5.1: 110–35.

Hammond, Adam. 2016. *Literature in the Digital Age, An Introduction*. Cambridge: Cambridge University Press.

Houston, Natalie M. 2014. 'Toward a Computational Analysis of Victorian Poetics.' *Victorian Studies* 56.3: 498–510.

Huyssen, Andreas. 1987. *After the Great Divide: Modernism, Mass Culture, Postmodernism*. Bloomington: Indiana University Press.

Jockers, Matthew L. 2013. *Macroanalysis: Digital Methods and Literary History*, Urbana: University Illinois Press.

Mesch, Rachel. 2013. *Having it All in the Belle Epoque: How French Women's Magazines Invented the Modern Woman*. Stanford: Stanford University Press.

Morrisson, Mark S. 2001. *The Public Face of Modernism: Little Magazines, Audiences, and Reception: 1905–1920*. Madison: University of Wisconsin Press.

Murphy, J. Stephen and Mark Gaipa. 2014. 'You Might Also Like . . . : Magazine Networks and Modernist Tastemaking in the Dora Marsden Magazines.' *Journal of Modern Periodical Studies* 5.1: 27–68.

Pound, Ezra. 1934. *ABC of Reading*. London: Faber & Faber.

Reynolds, Paige. 2015. 'Modernist Periodicals.' *A History of Modernist Poetry*. Ed. Alex Davis and Lee M. Jenkins. Cambridge: Cambridge University Press.

Ross, Shawna, and James O'Sullivan, eds. 2016. *Reading Machines: Digital Humanities and Modernist Literature*. Basingstoke: Palgrave Macmillan.

Scholes, Robert and Clifford Wulfman. 2010. *Modernism in the Magazines: An Introduction*. New Haven: Yale University Press.

Taylor, Georgina. 2001. *H.D. and the Public Sphere of Modernist Women Writers 1913–1946: Talking Women*. Oxford: Oxford University Press.

TEI: Text Encoding Initiative. TEI Consortium, <http://www.tei-c.org/index.xml> (last accessed 11 June 2018).

Underwood, Ted. 'Topic Modeling Made Just Simple Enough.' *The Stone and the Shell: Using Large Digital Libraries to Advance Literary History*, 7 April 2012, <https://tedunderwood.com/2012/04/07/topic-modeling-made-just-simple-enough/> (last accessed 26 September 2016).

21

WHEELPOLITIK: THE MORAL AND AESTHETIC PROJECT OF EDITH SITWELL'S *WHEELS*, 1916–1921

Melissa Bradshaw

Wheels: An Anthology of Verse (1916–21) occupies an anecdotal place in modernist literary history. That is, while modernist critics might know of it as a vanguard in Britain's modernist movement, what was in it, or why it matters remains a difficult question to answer.[1] This might be, in part, because *Wheels* does not feature poets we associate with canonical modernism. Its editor, Edith Sitwell, is recognised as an important modernist figure, but F. R. Leavis's infamous pronouncement in *New Bearings in English Poetry* (1932) that Sitwell and her brothers, Osbert and Sacheverell, 'belong to the history of publicity rather than of poetry' has been unfortunately pervasive, and her work has not received the sustained critical attention it deserves (qtd in Jaffe 2005: 159).[2] Sitwell is not the only *Wheels* poet to suffer critical neglect; with the exception of Wilfred Owen, Nancy Cunard, and Aldous Huxley (whom we remember as a novelist, not a poet), none of the contributors to *Wheels* are major, or even minor, figures in modern literary history, their work long out of print, their names forgotten.

The obscurity of *Wheels* might also reflect the difficulty of the poems themselves: ornate, suffused with arcadian imagery and references and symbols from the *Commedia dell'Arte*, their aesthetic owes more to nineteenth-century French symbolism than to early modernist poetic experimentation (contributor Helen Rootham translates three poems of Arthur Rimbaud for the first cycle, for example). Despite a common ideological goal of reshaping and reimagining poetry, the work in *Wheels* bears little resemblance to modernist poetry as we understand it today. Meandering stanzas describe merry-go-rounds and barrel organs, follow fauns and Pans through city parks, and mourn lonely, aged Pierrots who cannot die, an aesthetic Deborah Longworth describes as 'Ornamental Modernism,' or 'decorative avant-gardism' (2017: 53). The colourful, vivacious, often dizzying poetics of *Wheels* – comparable more to Diaghilev's Ballets Russes, or the music of Stravinsky than to Ezra Pound's *Cantos* – challenge the imperative toward sparseness governing prevailing definitions of modernism.

Of course, *Wheels* was not always obscure. As the reviews and critical notices Sitwell reprinted as appendices to each volume testify, its noisy debut attracted critical attention from all sides, with some critics calling it a failure 'despite a good deal of dark and sinister language,' whose 'foetidness ... clings to the nostrils,' while others lauded it as exemplary in its 'willingness to experiment, [its] tolerance of various emotions, and [its] complete indifference to simplicity' (1919: 94; 1917: 107). Appreciative reviews celebrated *Wheels* as heralding a new school of British poetry that offered relief from the patriotic propaganda of Edward Marsh's popular *Georgian Poetry* anthologies. While Marsh's five-volume anthology, published between 1911 and 1922, began as a vehicle for drawing the public's attention to the best of new British poetry and the work of younger poets, within a few years critics dismissed it as retrograde, focused as it was on the pleasures of sporting and country life.[3] The *Athenaeum*'s review of *Wheels*'s third cycle (1918) explicitly contrasts *Wheels* with *Georgian Poetry*, arguing that where the latter makes a fetish of simplicity, *Wheels* succeeds by 'show[ing] a willingness to experiment, a tolerance of various emotions, and a complete indifference to simplicity. . . . [It] has stood on the side of intelligence. It recognize[s] that there are some pretty complicated feelings in life which are worth a little pains to express' (1919: 94).

Wheels's Woman Problem

Though she would not appear on the masthead as editor until the third cycle, *Wheels* was Edith Sitwell's project and passion, and she served as its primary editor and impresario for all six cycles. The three Sitwell siblings appear in every volume, with a rotating cast of contributors including Huxley, Arnold James, Iris Tree, and most notably, Wilfred Owen, who was first posthumously published in the fourth cycle (1919).

I approached this project assuming the primary significance of *Wheels* to be Sitwell's editorship, as a woman steering a major, multi-authored modernist project. Notably, she does not take credit for her editorial work until the third volume, when she moves her name from one of the spokes of the illustrated wheel at the front of the volume to the centre of the wheel (Figures 21.1 and 21.2). This editorship marks an important stage in her career, and an important identity for her – Alvaro de Guevara's portrait 'Edith Sitwell, Editor of *Wheels*,' (1916) which hangs in the Tate, attests to its significance – as with it she first claims the role of tastemaker that will inform her long career. But that she is a woman does not alone make her editorship of *Wheels* exceptional. Several seminal annuals and little magazines had female editors: the *Little Review*, edited by Margaret Anderson and Jane Heap; the *Egoist*, edited by Harriet Weaver; *Poetry: A Magazine of Verse*, edited by Harriet Monroe; and *Some Imagist Poets*, edited by Amy Lowell, come quickly to mind. And like these other female editors, while Sitwell was in a position to publish and promote the work of female authors, she did not use her editorial powers to this end: only five of the twenty contributors to *Wheels*'s six volumes, including Sitwell, are women, their representation dwindling over the life of the series so that by the sixth and final cycle, she is the lone female poet in the collection.[4]

Jane Dowson has argued that despite the paucity of women published in *Wheels*, the women that do appear are significant enough as to constitute an avant-garde. These 'women of *Wheels*,' as she calls Cunard, Sitwell, Iris Tree, and to a lesser extent, Helen Rootham, 'indicate a new aesthetic freedom and confidence in women poets' (2002: 90).[5] Tree and Cunard, in particular, strike Dowson as critical to the cultural capital of *Wheels*, as women 'holding their own among the intellectual elite' (ibid.). Fixtures in London's society set, they famously rebelled against their parents (Tree was the daughter of Sir Herbert Beerbohm Tree, actor and manager of the Haymarket

Figure 21.1 Image from the first (1916) cycle of *Wheels*.

Figure 21.2 Image from the third (1918) cycle of *Wheels*.

Theatre, and later founder of the Royal Academy of the Dramatic Art; Cunard, heiress to the Cunard Shipping Line) to participate in the bohemian artistic scenes centred around Paris's Left Bank and London's Eiffel Tower restaurant.

Tree is well represented in *Wheels*, with thirty-three poems in the first four volumes, offering as complete a look at her as a poet as it is possible to get in one place, outside two slim volumes, *Poems* (1920) and *The Traveller and Other Poems* (1927), since her occasional poems, published in magazines and newspapers have never been collected. She is best remembered as one of London's 'bright young things,' a sometime actress (she made a cameo appearance as herself in *La Dolce Vita*) known for her trademark blunt blonde bob and memorialised in paintings by Augustus John, Duncan Grant, Roger Fry, and Vanessa Bell, among others. Poetry was one of Tree's many artistic expressions, but it makes up a relatively small part of the art for which she is known.[6]

Poetry similarly accounts for only a slim fraction of Cunard's output.[7] Her four collections of poems are overshadowed by her work as a publisher with the Hours Press, her editorial work on the anthology *Negro* (1934), her activism on behalf of racial and social justice, and her flamboyant dress and jewellery, memorialised in iconic portraits by artists like Cecil Beaton and Man Ray. She appears only in *Wheels* 1916, with six poems, including 'Wheels,' from which the series takes its name. While Cunard apparently had an editorial role in the first cycle, the extent of her involvement and the reasons for her departure from the project are unclear.[8] Sitwell biographer Victoria Glendinning claims that Sitwell and Cunard fell out when the painter Alvaro de Guevara, who designed the end papers for the first cycle and contributed Spanish translations to the third and fourth cycles, became romantically involved with Cunard instead of Sitwell, who had an unrequited crush on him (1981: 60–1). The gossipy drama of Glendinning's unsupported claim has been unfortunately pervasive – Richard Greene repeats it in his *Selected Letters of Edith Sitwell*, for example – undermining these women as professionals in favour of caricaturing them as bickering rivals (Sitwell 1997: 454).

Even as Tree and Cunard broke with their parents' gendered habits, they drew on their resources to live loudly, performing in their dress, in the company they kept, in the art they made, and in the art of which they were the subject an avant-garde aesthetic and a counter-culture politic. Dowson rightly notes their importance in lending *Wheels* avant-garde credibility. Very little of Cunard's poetry actually appears in *Wheels*, however, and the difference between being one of 'the Women of *Wheels*' and actually *being* in *Wheels* is an important one. Very little of Tree's art translates into a written record at all, leaving her without the kind of legacy that allows for recuperation as a literary artist. To make an argument for the significance of *Wheels* based in part on these female contributors, as Dowson does, is a bit of a stretch, although it does suggest a richer understanding of the anthologies as more than a literary objects, but, rather, as multimodal nodes where various modernisms – written, visual, and performed – intersect.

So, if Sitwell's editorship of *Wheels* is not notable for the degree to which she used it to foster and support other women's careers, why include a chapter on it in a volume on women's print culture in Britain? Certainly *Wheels* frustrates feminist recuperation efforts, but the argument Aaron Jaffe makes in *Modernism and the Culture of Celebrity* that Sitwell's endgame is 'the return of a closed, undifferentiated, authoritarian literary system for throwing out geniuses,' namely Sitwell and her brothers, and that her editorship of *Wheels* 'does nothing to alter, undermine, or open up the male authority of which she makes use' misses the degree to which *Wheels* operates at a remove from navel-gazing modernist arms races (2005: 159). *Wheels*'s avant-garde is designed to be in direct contact and immediate conversation with the mainstream culture it mocks. Sitwell's editorship of *Wheels* merits revisiting because with it she oversees a sustained critique of the anti-intellectual, masculinist war rhetoric gripping Britain during and in the years following the Great War. Each of its six cycles savages a culture that has doubled down on an idealised understanding of a homogenised homeland, a Britain that is safe, simple, and proud. As Huxley puts it, the poets of *Wheels* take a 'toreador attitude toward the bloody-bloodies of this world' (qtd in Glendinning 1981: 59).

Wheels's Anti-War Avant-Garde

The *Lancet*'s review of the first cycle understands the anti-war politics of *Wheels* and its modernism as inseparable, connecting *Wheels*'s embrace of imagistic technique to strategies used in a new wave of war poetry. 'Though little of its contents may have been written in the circumstances of war,' the review explains, it 'has an origin similar to that of the rapidly increasing war anthology,' in that it refuses narrative in favour of impressions (1917: 109). 'The idea of these young poets is that the role of poetry is rather to crystalise fleeting views and aspects, to catch and fix vague and half-formed ideas, than to do any of the brave things associated in popular literature with the title of poet – to lead, to uplift, to amaze' (ibid.). The aesthetic of impressions influences the kind of anti-war poetry *Wheels* publishes, war poems that stand out from their predecessors in their commitment to conveying the terrifying minutiae of a soldier's daily experience, and in their refusal to comfort readers through stories of patriotic valour.

As has often been noted, the *Georgian Poetry* anthologies are the immediate target of *Wheels*'s poetic protest against the war and the dumbing-down of British culture. But too much emphasis on *Wheels* as the anti-*Georgian Poetry* elides the degree to which it registers a larger protest against anti-intellectualism and nationalistic smugness. *Wheels*'s protest, an organised, sustained, highly publicised effort that stretches from the middle of the war to the years immediately following it, reshapes the narrative of the solitary soldier poet and puts him at the centre of a culture of vigorous anti-war protest.

However, because *Wheels* opens enigmatically, its politics are not immediately evident. No epigraph or preface announces its aesthetic vision or indicates its targeted audience.[9] The *Little Review*, by contrast, declares its guiding principle, 'Making No Compromise With The Public Taste,' in its masthead, as does *Poetry Magazine*, which quotes Walt Whitman: 'To have great poets there must be great audiences.' *Some Imagist Poets* (1915, 1916, 1917), the American anthology series most closely matching the *Wheels* project, begins with a preface describing its editorial process ('We thought it wise to tell the public what our aims are, and why we banded together between one set of covers') and offering an introduction to Imagist poetry (1916: vi). In fact, the Imagists are so determined to make their aims clear that the preface to the second volume corrects popular misunderstandings of Imagism by reasserting the poetic principles drawing these poets together. Even Robert Grave's short-lived and insistently apolitical quarterly the *Owl* opens with a disclaimer announcing that the journal 'has no politics, leads no new movement and is not even the organ of any particular generation' (1919: 1).

The closest *Wheels* comes to an introductory statement of principle and scope are two poems by Osbert Sitwell, both titled 'In Bad Taste,' which appear before the table of contents in the first two volumes. The first appears belatedly as a preface to the second printing of the first cycle (1917), as if to reinforce a message lost in the initial reception of the anthology. The poem's title, set in quotation marks, parrots the volume's reception in the popular press, turning the criticism on itself. Those guilty of acting 'in bad taste' are not the *Wheels* poets, but an older generation 'singing and gamboling through a joyous day . . . displaying with pride, their childish ignorance,' while a generation dies in a badly planned war led by inept leaders, sacrificial offerings to 'Moloch, God of Blood,' who rides 'on a triumphal car . . . in his hand a fingered treatise on Simplicity' (1916: v, vi). Equally guilty are 'the platitudinous multitude' who mimic them, who crave 'sweet simplicity,' and who 'read . . . "Country Life" and worship "Punch" . . . Full of clean humour and of simple fun' (ibid.). As a preface, 'In Bad Taste' frames *Wheels* as a rebellion against facile patriotism, jingoism, and the prettification of battle.

Osbert served as an officer in the General Guard during the war, having trained at the Army College to be a cavalry officer (Zeigler 1999: 34–44). In the decade following the war he emerged as a prominent anti-establishment voice, writing op-ed pieces for the Labour newspaper, the *Daily Herald*, and poetic satires of conservative cultural figures. He begins the second cycle of *Wheels* (1917) with another brutal satire, 'Armchair (In Bad Taste, 2),' this time narrowing in for a close-up of the patrician class parodied in the first 'In Bad Taste' poem. His gentleman speaker, a would-be politician, dreams of power. Caught in the liminal stage between 'handsome middle age' and 'only seventy,' he feels helpless to aid the war effort, since he is too old to have sons young enough to send to France, but not yet old enough to have grandsons ready to send (1917: v). He dreams of being 'seventy . . . a great man in his prime,' positioned to 'rule army-corps: at [his] command / Men would rise up, salute [him], and attack / – And die –' (ibid.). He fantasises making 'a noble toothless speech,' cheered on by parliament and the Church, promising to

> . . . never end this war
> Till all the younger men with martial mien
> Have entered capitals; never make peace
> Till they are cripples, on one leg, or dead!
> Then would the Bishops all go mad with joy
> . . .
> In every pulpit they would preach and prance;
> And our great Church would work, as heretofore
> To bring this poor old Nation to its knees. (1917: vi)

Countering the truism that one becomes wiser with age, Osbert's angry narrative shows an out of touch ruling class becoming more foolish with age, even as they bask in power, 'these grand old men who . . . sacrifice each other's sons each day' (ibid.). He returns to the hypocrisy of an older generation demanding respect while making careless decisions that jeopardise the lives of those who serve them again in the third cycle's 'Youth and Age,'[10] complaining that while youth are expected to mourn 'the short appearance on this stage' of the elderly when they die, their elders can only drivel platitudes at the death of young soldiers (1918: 16). '"They knew not sorrow, cast their lives away / In all their powerful promise of the spring. / They saw not autumn, thus were doubly blest"' (ibid.).

Regular *Wheels* contributor Sherard Vines, who served in the British Army until he was invalided out in 1917, similarly mourns the cheapness of servicemen's lives in 'The Soldiers.' Feted 'at first with fruit and flowers and drink' by 'maniac mobs' as they make their way to war, the soldiers soon find themselves neglected, or worse, disparaged – 'who wants / To fuss about a common clod, / A stupid sensual soldier' – because 'two years of war have taught / The people it's the soldiers' job / To stop a bullet' (1917: 65). Where Osbert uses sarcasm, Vines uses plain language to tenderly describe his soldiers, men who 'will not forget,' who witness and mourn the death of the common soldier.

> No Cuchulain whose hero-light
> Enaureoles him, but a dour man
> Brother to hunger, cold, and fear,
> Content to dirty work; content
> To dirty death among the rats
> If that is in his days' schedule. (1917: 67)

'The Mad Soldier,' written by E. Wyndham (Bim) Tennant three months before his death in battle at nineteen, gives the common soldier his own voice. His soldier may be mad or he may be dead.[11] The poem's horrific ambiguity – the mad soldier has spent three weeks in a trench trapped under bodies, listening to rats eat corpses, maybe those of prisoners, maybe those of his comrades, maybe his own – conveys the terror of trench warfare. The soldier, wondering if he would 'know the bloke [on top of him] if [he] woke,' wondering, even, if he himself is asleep or dead, knows for certain only that he is in Hell either way (1917: 92).

> – It's a sin
> To say that Hell is hot – 'cause it's not:
> Mind you, I know very well we're in hell. –
> In a twisted hump we lie – heaping high
> Yes! an' higher every day. – Oh, I say,
> This chap's heavy on my thighs – damn his eyes. (ibid.)

Tennant's graphic description of trench warfare is his only poem in the second cycle. His representative selections in the first cycle stand out from the other poets' in their earnestness and their lack of cynicism. 'Home Thoughts in Laventie,' for example, while technically a war poem – it tells of the homesickness of soldiers searching for patches of grass among the ruins of a bombed French town – lingers on flowers, 'some yellow daffodils and jasmine hanging high,' and has its narrator daydream of England's 'meadows with their glittering streams, and silver scurrying dace' (1916: 69). 'Home,' it ends, 'what a perfect place' (ibid.). 'The Mad Soldier,' with its low diction and its lurid details contrasts with Tennant's previously published poems. A footnote explains that it was not included in Tennant's posthumously published volume, *Worple Flit and other poems* (1916) 'since it was not intended for publication' (1917: 91). Sitwell does not disclose how she got permission to publish a poem that was 'not intended for publication,' but she justifies the act by explaining 'the editor deems this example of his versatility too valuable to be lost' (ibid.). Note that Edith publishes this poem in 1917, just before the best known poetry of Siegfried Sassoon, Wilfred Owen, Robert Graves, and other war poets exposed the devastation and brutality of modern warfare.

In fact, 'The Mad Soldier' may have played a role in encouraging Owen to continue documenting his own experiences in poetry. Owen, who met his friend and poetic mentor Sassoon while convalescing at Craiglockhart War Hospital, had been writing poetry since adolescence. Sassoon, whose friendship with the Sitwells began when Edith congratulated him on the occasion of his infamous letter protesting the continuance of the war being read out in the House of Commons, pushed Owen to write about what he had seen in the war, and most likely introduced him to *Wheels* (Sitwell 1997: 23). Owen bought the second cycle as he contemplated accepting an invitation to publish in the annual (Bradford et al. 1994: 60); he wrote and revised many of his war poems while on home-duty in Scarborough from autumn of 1917 through the summer of 1918, sending some of them in manuscript to Osbert, who gave them to Edith after Owen's death.

Edith, who never met Owen, requested permission from his mother, Susan Owen, to publish what she believed to be 'among the very finest poems of the war,' explaining that this would be a 'great privilege and [a] sacred honour' (Sitwell 1970: 13, 16). Edith's role in preparing the poems for publication involved transcribing them from Owen's written drafts and making editorial decisions, since many of the poems had several drafts. 'I can't tell you what it has been like – copying out these poems of his for *Wheels*,' she writes Susan Owen. 'They get home so hard that one finds oneself crying . . . It has been sometimes impossible to go on' (Sitwell 1970: 16).[12] Seven of Owen's poems, including 'Strange Meeting,' appear in the fourth cycle of *Wheels* (1919), the first time his war poems appear in print. Edith's promise to his mother that this 'will awaken all those who care for poetry to the fact that he is by far our greatest war poet,' proving, of course, true (Sitwell 1970: 19).

War and the Women of *Wheels*

Significantly, *Wheels* also published women's perspectives on the war. Some, such as Helen Rootham's 'Etat 19,' proffer conventional wartime sentiments, mourning the loss of young life ('Good it was to live, oh Lord, / Good it was to be young') while not necessarily condemning the war (1917: 96). The persona of Edith Sitwell's 'A Histrion' struggles to perform normalcy in the face of grief, as the title, an antiquated term for theatrical performer, suggests. Her grief overwhelms her: 'O the scream that tears my body into tatters, / Beats my brain to pulp' (1917: 78). When forced to go out she hides behind feigned smiles and make-up. 'To the crowd, as to a mirror / I posture, and I practice smiles that crack my face apart, / And I paint my cheeks blood-red' (1917: 79). Sitwell's overwrought description of grieving becomes more interesting when the persona returns home and watches herself grieve in the mirror and, from a remove, wonders if it, too, is a performance:

> Posture once more at my mirror; watch with interest my face alter
> From the cracking smile, the mirth that wrapp'd my body like a shroud.
> Yes, I watch the dreadful tears that bleed and sizzle from my eyelids:
> And God knows if I'm acting to myself or to the crowd. (ibid.)

'Histrion' gets at the unreality of life in wartime, when both grief and happiness begin to feel like rote expectations that must be met. Iris Tree's 'Return' similarly describes disconnectedness in the ordinary, as a woman returns home from a night out and feels judged by the seriousness and stillness of her room: 'Garish a little in the room's sedateness, you / Returning dressed so frivolously in all your coloured clothes!' (1918: 66). But she cautions of the danger of looking too far inward in 'The Complex Life,' noting that 'Our lives are spoilt by introspective guile, / We vivisect our souls with elaborate tools' (1919: 43). She challenges the ethics of making art out of this terror:

> Subconscious visions hold us and we fashion
> Delirious verses, tortured statues, spasm of paint,
> Make cryptic perorations of complaint,
> Inverted religion, and perverted passion. (ibid.)

This very poem, Tree suggests, walks a fine line between creative resilience and cold-hearted exploitation. 'Our patriotism is piracy,' Tree warns, 'But since we are children of this age, / and must in curious ways discover salvation / I will not quit my muddled generation, / But ever plead for Beauty in this rage' (1919: 44).

A number of poems by female contributors to *Wheels* express liminality as an experience of modernity – 'I am the day before disaster,' Tree writes in 'Analysis,' 'The morning after feasting,' – and use subjunctive verbs to express the impotence of being silent bystanders to chaos, an impotence that cannot be resolved through art, the only weapon they have access to (1918: 61). 'Had I a clearer brain, imagination, / A flowing pen and better ending rhymes' Cunard writes in 'The Carnivals of Peace,' 'I'd write a song to conquer all our tears' (1916: 29). Tree's poem 'Rebellion' begins forcefully: 'If I were what I would be, and could break / The buttressed fortress of stupidity' (1918: 57). But her thought trails off into meandering description and she never picks it up again, as though powerless to articulate what she would do or even whom she rebels against (ibid.). In 'Confessional' she insists she

> ... could explain
> The complicated lore that drags the soul
> From what shall profit him
> To gild damnation with his choicest gold.
> But you
> Are pouring over precious books and do not hear
> Our plaintive, frivolous songs. (1918: 58)

The speaker, at first a solitary confessional 'I' until she becomes part of a 'we' (the singers of plaintive, frivolous songs), addresses her opponent, the 'you' who is turned toward a past (pouring over precious books) and away from life with the promise of knowledge. Tree draws on Shakespearean figures and stage metaphors to convey impermanence and vulnerability. There is something Prospero-like to the person pouring over their books, and the unlistened to 'we' suggests an actor playing Romeo:

> For we in stubborn vanity ascend
> On ladders insecure,
> Toward the tottering balconies
> To serenade our painted paramours. (ibid.)

Meanwhile, Desdemona and a deracialised Othello lurk in the background,

> Caught by the lure of dangerous pale hands,
> Oblivion's heavy lure on sleepless eyes
> That cheat between unrest and false repose.
> And we are haunted
> By spectral Joy once murdered in a rage,
> Now taking shape of Pleasure,
> Disguised in many clothes and skillful masks. (ibid.)

The poem meditates on agency and power, its blurry metaphors vacillating between acting and the everyday performativity of being a woman. The speaker has no agency as she pleads with the Prospero figure; she has all the agency as she ascends toward a painted paramour on a tottering balcony; she has no agency as a Desdemona 'caught by the lure of dangerous pale hands.' Only when she acts the male part can she access agency, but even then, she climbs toward the liminal space of a balcony, and a vulnerable, tottering one at that. Women, like actors, traffic in representation, not reality; the safety of a gendered role – clothes and skilful masks – allows the pleasures of familiarity, but not joy. The 'truth' this poem confesses is that women

> are not happy,
> And you make us dumb with loving hands
> Reproachful on our lips,
> Nor can we sob our sorrows on your breast,
> For we have bartered diamonds for glass. (1918: 59)

Tree juxtaposes two points of view, one, that seems to be male, turned toward a past (Britain's military past? a chivalric past where gender roles made sense?), the other, seemingly female, haunted by that past but living with the shame of a reality that is frivolous, unstable, and ultimately without value (they have traded diamonds for glass). This pseudo-reality, perhaps the pretence of normality during wartime, keeps the 'we' somewhat distracted from the truth of their unhappiness, but not enough to avoid recognising their complicity in the farce.

Conclusion

Even as *Wheels* gives voice to the experiences and emotions of women, its burlesques hold them equally accountable for the cultural excesses that foment and sustain the war. Osbert Sitwell, in particular, contributes several satirical poems to the last two volumes that critique bourgeois frivolity and complacency. Unfortunately, the poems direct that critique so ferociously toward women that their misogyny threatens to overshadow their politics. During high tea 'At the House of Mrs. Kinfoot,' guests are treated to 'the gospel of Mrs. Kinfoot,' – a vulgar caricature of the sort of society matron Virginia Woolf will so tenderly and sympathetically interpret in *Mrs Dalloway* (1920: 23). '"The world was made for the British bourgeoisie,"' Mrs Kinfoot helpfully explains, who, as '"its Swiss Family Robinson"' draw on their courage and self-reliance to make order out of the wreckage of a '"world [that] is not what it was"' (ibid.). As if her complicity in the culture that produced the war is not clear enough, Osbert has his bourgeois matron murmur 'The War was splendid, wasn't it? / O yes, splendid, splendid,' as the poem ends (1920: 24).

However malevolent Osbert's jibes at the women of Britain's bourgeoisie, he places blame above all on a culture that renders them silly, bored, and desperate to be relevant, even if only through dinner parties. So when Mrs Kinfoot returns in 'Malgré Lui,' arriving in heaven on Judgement Day to the disappointing realisation that because she has been 'a worthy mother and a good wife,' she has landed far from all the interesting people down in hell, it is difficult not to feel sympathy for her (1920: 26). Unable to imagine a selfhood outside her domesticity, she balks at the blandness of a heaven where she will never again throw a successful dinner party. Even the indefatigable sexual seductress Messalina, the subject of Edith's satiric 'Messalina at Margate,' succumbs to the stultification of appropriate, upright church-going British womanhood, turning 'old and fat, – / The church's parrot now, and dull at that' (1917: 88).

Edith's poem 'The County Calls,' following immediately after the decorative flourishes of 'Messalina at Margate,' startles with its simplicity, offering a nuanced glimpse of the expectation that women participate in this segregated culture. The poem, at once arch and vulnerable, reads autobiographically: it is difficult not to imagine Edith as the speaker, a woman receiving a county's worth of Mrs Kinfoots who 'advance' on her like an army, or like 'a train; / A rush, a scream, – then gone again' (1917: 90, 89). They chatter at her, 'each face, a plaster monument / Of some beloved aliment . . . Each tongue, a noisy clockwork bell' (1917: 89). The poem's ostensible argument, that these women 'with bodies like a continent / Encased in silken seas,' earn the speaker's scorn with their shallowness, their officiousness, and their false piety, wobbles when the speaker notices her visitors looking 'askance / At [her] thin insignificance' (1917: 89, 90). Seeing 'little thoughts like fishes glide / Beneath their eyes' pale glassy tide,' even as they try to make small talk about her father, she knows that their talk masks their judgement of her, and seems to fault them for their insincerity (1917: 90). But since the narrator, who characterises herself as silent during the visit, does the same thing, her poem a more aggressive, because public, version of her guests' unspoken thoughts, her critique of them falters. Seen, as well as seeing, the speaker and her guests are left in a kind of detente.

'The County Calls' reminds us how much *Wheels*, at its most serious and at its most satiric, reflects its contributors' need to rebel, whether against war, or gender roles, or aesthetics. Early critics seize on *Wheels*'s all-purpose anti-establishmentarianism as its weakness, accusing the Sitwells of being provocateurs for the sake of provocation. 'What we can do to be original?' a sarcastic review in *The Literary World* imagines 'Mr. Osbert and Miss Edith Sitwell . . . anxiously asking themselves' (1917: 104). I've thought a lot about why Edith Sitwell chose to republish that review in the back of the second cycle of *Wheels*. Obviously, she reprints it because she finds it funny. I imagine she does it, as well, because highlighting the criticism deflates it. But I imagine, mostly, she reprints it because it gets the anthologies' aesthetic and moral aim exactly right: to shock, and in shocking, challenge, question, and disrupt a brutal, masculinist, greedy, anti-intellectual culture.

Notes

1. *Wheels* is routinely discussed in biographies of Edith Sitwell, and is allotted a few paragraphs in histories of modern poetry, but Ledbetter 1995 is the only journal article or book chapter to focus exclusively on the anthologies. Dowson 2002 includes a chapter on female contributors to *Wheels*.
2. The first collection of critical essays on Edith Sitwell, *The Many Facades of Edith Sitwell*, edited by Gyllian Phillips and Allan Pero, was published by the University Press of Florida in Spring 2017.
3. David Perkins notes that this sort of poetry (he calls it 'insipid, slack and escapist verse') only describes about half the content in the *Georgian Anthologies*, and points out that the significance of the anthologies in pioneering the modern poetry anthology should not be underestimated (1976: 206).
4. Aaron Jaffe points out that the near gender parity represented in *Wheels* 1916 (four women to five men) makes the anthology notably more gender inclusive than predecessors such as *Georgian Poetry* and *Des Imagistes*. As the number of women contributors drops in subsequent volumes, the total number of women comes to less than a fifth of the contributors (Jaffe 2005: 154).
5. Rootham fits uneasily into this grouping, participating in London avant-garde circles only loosely, through her connection to Edith Sitwell. She was Sitwell's companion from 1903 until her death in 1938, first as her governess, then her chaperone when Sitwell moved from her parents' home, and finally as her dependent. Sitwell biographies characterise her as a boon – she introduced her young charge to Swinburne, Christina Rossetti, and French symbolist poets – who eventually became an emotional and financial burden. She published two books of poetry translations, *Kossovo: Heroic Songs of the Serbs* (Houghton Mifflin, 1920), a collection of epic poems from Serbia, and *Prose Poems from the Illuminations of Arthur Rimbaud* (Faber & Faber, 1932), but virtually no critical work has been done on her.
6. Tree appears frequently in memoirs and correspondences from this period, but the only biography of her is Fielding's (1974), which is more a sentimental memoir by a friend than a biography.
7. Cunard's long poem *Parallax*, published by Hogarth Press in 1925 has received critical attention in the last decade, after being unfavourably compared to *The Waste Land* by F. R. Leavis in *New Bearings in English Poetry*. See Harding 2007.
8. Artist Nina Hamnett's memoir, *Laughing Torso*, is the reference Sitwell biographers cite for this claim. She writes, 'Nancy Cunard, who was often at the Eiffel Tower (restaurant in London), started a poetry magazine called *Wheels*. Three young poets called Sitwell wrote for it' (qtd in Pearson 1978: 106).
9. The wheel disappears with volume five, perhaps at the suggestion of the new publisher, Duckworth, who takes over from Blackwell, publisher of all previous volumes. C. W. Daniel publishes the sixth and final volume.
10. While no 'In Bad Taste' poems act as a preface to *Wheels* after the second cycle, Osbert Sitwell continues satirising and savaging Britain's [ruling class] in at least one poem per subsequent volume.
11. E. Wyndham Tennant died in the Battle of the Somme in September 1916. He was a brother of Stephen Tennant, eccentric aesthete and one-time lover of Seigfried Sassoon, and David

Tennant founder of the Gargoyle Club, was a school friend of Osbert Sitwell, and ran in the same social circles as the Sitwell siblings. He submitted his selections for the first cycle.
12. With Susan Owen's permission, Edith Sitwell secured a publisher for a volume of Owen's poems and had almost completed an edition when she unfortunately asked Sassoon for help deciding which of several versions of a poem was correct. At that point, she writes to Susan Owen, Sassoon took over the project. '[He] told me it would have been your son's wish that he (Captain Sassoon) should see to the publication of the poems, because they were such friends. In those circumstances I could do nothing but offer to hand them over to him; though it has cost me more to relinquish them than I can tell you' (Sitwell 1970: 23–4). Sassoon does not finish the volume, however, before leaving for a trip to America. Sitwell completes the volume and submits it to the publisher, though Sassoon is listed as the editor and her work is uncredited (Glendinning 1981: 62).

Works Cited

Bradford, Sarah, Honor Clerk, Jonathan Fryer, Robin Gibson, and John Pearson. 1994. *The Sitwells and the Arts of the 1920s and 1930s*. Austin: University of Texas Press.
Dowson, Jane. 2002. *Women, Modernism and British Poetry, 1910–1939*. Burlington, VT: Ashgate.
Fielding, Daphne. 1974. *The Rainbow Picnic: A Portrait of Iris Tree*. London: Eyre Methuen.
Glendinning, Victoria. 1981. *Edith Sitwell: A Unicorn Among Lions*. New York: Knopf.
Harding, Jason. 2007. 'Modernist Poetry and the Canon.' *The Cambridge Companion to Modernist Poetry*. Ed. Alex Davis and Lee M. Jenkins. Cambridge: Cambridge University Press. 225–43.
Jaffe, Aaron. 2005. *Modernism and the Culture of Celebrity*. Cambridge: Cambridge University Press.
Ledbetter, Kathryn. 1995. *Journal of Modern Literature* 19.2: 322–8.
Longworth, Deborah. 2017. 'The Sitwells and Sitwellism: An Ornamental Modernism.' *The Many Facades of Edith Sitwell*. Ed. Gyllian Phillips and Allan Pero. Gainesville: University Press of Florida. 31, 33.
Pearson, John. 1978. *The Sitwells: A Family's Biography*. New York: Harcourt, Brace, Jovanovich.
Perkins, David. 1976. *A History of Modern Poetry: From the 1890s to the High Modernist Mode*. Cambridge, MA: Harvard University Press. 206.
Sitwell, Edith. 1970. *Edith Sitwell: Selected Letters, 1919–1964*. Ed. John Lehmann and Derek Parker. New York: Vanguard Press.
—. 1997. *Selected Letters of Edith Sitwell*. Ed. Richard Greene. London: Virago.
Ziegler, Philip. 1999. *Osbert Sitwell*. New York: Knopf.

22

NEW AGE WOMEN'S WRITING: EDITH NESBIT, FLORENCE FARR, AND NIETZSCHEAN SOCIALIST MODERNISM

Lee Garver

WHEN MODERNIST SCHOLARS discuss the British radical political-cultural weekly the *New Age* (1907–22), they typically focus on its best-known male contributors – Ezra Pound, T. E. Hulme, Wyndham Lewis, George Bernard Shaw, H. G. Wells, Arnold Bennett, G. K. Chesterton, and Hilaire Belloc.[1] Although it is generally well known that Katherine Mansfield published her first significant short stories in this publication[2] and interest has grown in recent years in the enormously varied contributions of South African expatriate Beatrice Hastings,[3] few, if any, critics have bothered to examine any of the other women writers who wrote for the magazine, and as a consequence scholars tend to be unaware that, during its first years of publication, from 1907–10, the *New Age* was a place that welcomed a variety of different female contributors, including many prominent socialists, feminists, and members of the artistic avant-garde. In the pages that follow, I would like to examine two of the most interesting and unjustly neglected women writers who made the *New Age* one of the most exciting and important Edwardian-era publications: Fabian Socialist, poet, and children's author Edith Nesbit and actress, playwright, and theosophist Florence Farr. While Nesbit's children's novels remain popular and continue to be read today and Virginia Woolf scholar and biographer Julia Briggs has argued for the importance of Nesbit's children's writing, especially to later children's authors,[4] modernist scholars have generally had little or nothing to say about Nesbit.[5] Although Farr has fared better and makes regular appearances in biographical studies of George Bernard Shaw, William Butler Yeats, and Ezra Pound, she has been regarded more as mistress, mouthpiece, and muse than fellow modernist.[6] However, when the writings of these once-prominent female artists are examined in the context of the *New Age*, they reveal a strain of early modernist women's writing that drew power and purpose from its engagement with issues of childhood poverty, legal and educational reform, middle-class feminist revolt, and the Nietzschean transvaluation of all values. Expressing in their work the belief that women, children, and artists possessed a capacity for visionary, dreamlike perception that, if unshackled from legal and cultural restraint, might shatter capitalist, middle-class norms and laws and usher in a new socialist dawn, Nesbit and Farr make it possible to see that modernist women's writing was more central to the *New Age* and radical political-cultural upheaval of the era than heretofore realised. They also reveal that our definitions of modernism need to be more flexible if we are to appreciate the full range of contributions women made to modernist culture during the pre-war period.

While it is impossible to convey in any detail in an essay of this brevity the extraordinarily diverse range of content and opinion found in the *New Age* during its first four years of existence, it is important to note that the magazine had strong ties to the socialist and women's suffrage movements and a deep and abiding interest in advanced art and philosophy. Founded in 1907 with the assistance and support of the Fabian Society, the *New Age* included among its early contributors some of the most prominent socialist intellectuals of the period: playwright George Bernard Shaw, novelist H. G. Wells, Nesbit's Tory socialist husband Hubert Bland, Labour Party agitator Victor Grayson, and future guild socialist S. G. Hobson. Although the magazine also published work by a number of conservative and unapologetically reactionary intellectuals, including Christian critics of socialism G. K. Chesterton and Hilaire Belloc and Nietzsche translators Oscar Levy, J. M. Kennedy, and Anthony Ludovici, it remained a vital place of debate for left-leaning intellectuals and artists throughout the pre-war era. In addition to the aforementioned Shaw and Wells, the *New Age* published work by social prophet, gay rights activist, and simple life advocate Edward Carpenter; sexologist Havelock Ellis; pan-African nationalist Duse Mohamed Ali, and Russian novelist Maxim Gorky. Even more importantly, the magazine made itself a friendly home to a surprisingly large number of progressive women writers and activists. Scottish novelist and suffragist Mona Caird; suffragette and future *Freewoman* co-editor Mary Gawthorpe; Women's Freedom League founder Teresa Billington-Greig; Irish poet, illustrator, and Yeats collaborator Althea Gyles; social scientist and women's rights activist Beatrice L. Hutchins; and dance critic Marcelle Azra Hincks are just a few of the women who shaped political-cultural debate in the periodical. What is more, during this same period, the New Age Press published and advertised in the back of the magazine a number of books by prominent female contributors. These included Fabian socialist, actress, and future Bergson translator Millicent Murby's *The Common-Sense of the Woman Question* (1908), playwright Erica Cotterill's *A Professional Socialist: A Play in Five Acts* (1908), and suffragist and artist Constance Smedley's *Woman: Her Position Today* (1908).

In addition to being a place where radical women writers could share their work with a community of like-minded readers and contributors, the *New Age* was a magazine that held Nesbit and Farr in the highest possible esteem. In the very first issue of the publication, Nesbit was one of only a small number of individuals, including anarchist Prince Peter Kropotkin and Fabian Society leader Sidney Webb, whose congratulatory greetings, under the title 'Letters from the Front,' were published in the periodical (2 May 1907: 3). Later, in an 'Important Announcement,' she would be the fourth person named (after Shaw, Wells, and Chesterton) in a long list of 'distinguished and brilliant writers' who had contributed to the second volume of the magazine (2 May 1908: 20), and in a review of two of her children's novels, *The Phoenix and the Carpet* (1904) and *The House of Arden* (1908), reviewer W. R. Titterton declared her a better author than Joseph Conrad, George Meredith, and Arnold Bennett. In addition, he went on to claim that these two works had 'more driving power for Socialism than many Fabian pamphlets' (14 Jan 1909: 247). While not similarly lionised, Farr was no less central to the magazine's identity. Several of her contributions received front-page, banner promotion during the weekly's first six months of publication, and two of her book-length works – the novel *A Dancing Faun* (1894) and the play *The Mystery of Time* (1905) – were published by the New Age Press and heavily promoted in the back pages of the periodical. In addition to these honours, she was entrusted with the task of reviewing *New Age* editor A. R. Orage's *Consciousness: Animal, Human, and Superman* (1907), a book that collected together lectures originally presented by Orage to the Theosophical Lodges of Manchester and Leeds (6 June 1907: 92). As former Chief Adept of the Hermetic Order of the Golden Dawn, an occult organisation that once included Nesbit as a member,[7] and an eminent figure in British theosophical circles, Farr shared many of Orage's literary-philosophical enthusiasms, including his interests in Nietzsche, Shaw, and Ibsen, and was among the most qualified people in Great Britain to reflect on the book's significance.[8]

Finally, it is crucial to emphasise that the editor of the *New Age* shared many of Nesbit's and Farr's views on the importance of imaginative vision, women, and children to any proposed socialist revolution. As a dedicated Nietzschean who had published three different books about the German philosopher between 1906 and 1907, Orage believed strongly in the principles of individual self-realisation and self-overcoming, and he regarded the revolutionary political-cultural ferment of the early twentieth century as heralding a Nietzschean transvaluation of all values and the development of new forms of consciousness.[9] He also argued that 'the world as we behold it is through and through an imaginative creation' and that the artist is 'the standard-bearer, the inspiring pioneer, the creator of new worlds, new values, new meanings' (Orage 1910: 124–5). In his very first editorial for the magazine, titled 'The Future of the "New Age,"' for example, he claimed that the best utopias drew upon 'the nobler spiritual and imaginative faculties of men' and boldly declared that the primary purpose of his magazine was to 'co-operate with the purposes of life, and to enlist in that noble service the help of serious students of the new contemplative and imaginative order' (2 May 1907: 8). Furthermore, in positioning his magazine as a site where art and philosophy would provide inspiration and direction to an as-yet-to-be-determined course of political action, Orage made a clear point of including, at least initially, women, children, and other social outsiders amongst those who might contribute to such a project. Although he occasionally published inflammatory attacks on the women's rights movement by Marxist philosopher and notorious anti-feminist Ernest Belfort Bax and would later himself become a fierce critic of the women's suffrage movement and pen a number of overtly misogynist stories for the *New Age*, Orage was among the magazine's staunchest supporters of the women's suffrage movement during the years 1907–10, and he regarded feminist revolt as entirely integral to the brand of Nietzschean socialism he advocated. In one of his 'Unedited Opinions' columns on the topic of 'Votes for Women,' he warmly praised the militant suffragette protests that were taking place during this period and expressed frustration that many socialists, including some of his own contributors and readers, perceived them as having little to do with socialism. Claiming that 'the cursed fate of everything vigorous in England is to become bowdlerised – that is to have its references to women deleted,' Orage lamented that nineteenth-century utopian socialist Robert Owens's ideas about 'free marriage, free women, and free love' had been 'hushed up' by contemporary socialists and declared that, if socialists were 'more wide-awake,' they would recognise that the socialist movement could only succeed if it acknowledged that the fight for economic justice was indivisible from battles being fought on behalf of women's liberty, artistic freedom, children's rights, and penal reform (4 Feb 1909: 309). 'Suppose,' he continued, 'the Socialist movement boldly declared war on behalf of the five outcasts of civilisation, and refused to put one before the other, don't you think we should gather strength?' (ibid.). Answering his own question in the affirmative and casting his reflections in a larger religious framework, he brazenly asserted, 'Only when women, the poor, artists, children, and criminals unite will the world be redeemed' (ibid.).

It is against the backdrop of statements such as these, I wish to argue, that Nesbit's and Farr's contributions to the *New Age* accrue deeper meaning and purpose. In 'Utopia,' only the second work of literature ever published in the magazine, Nesbit foregrounds the central role that she believes imagination and visionary perception must play in any socialist revolution in a manner that echoes the poetry of William Blake, the English writer who Orage believed most 'closely resembled' Nietzsche.[10]

> There is a garden, made for our delight,
>   Where all the dreams we dare not dream come true.
>   I know it, but I do not know the way.
> We slip and stumble in the doubtful night,
>   Where everything is difficult and new,
>   And clouds our breath has made obscure the day.
>
> The blank, unhappy towns, where sick men strive,
>   Still doing work that yet is never done,
>   The hymns to Gold that drown their desperate voice;
> The weeds that grow where once corn stood, alive,
>   The black injustice that puts out the sun,
>   These are our portion, since they are our choice.
>
> Yet there the garden blows, with rose on rose,
>   The sunny shadow-dappled lawns are there,
>   There the immortal lilies, heavenly-sweet.
> Oh roses that for us shall not unclose!
>   Oh lilies that we shall not pluck or wear!
> Oh dewy lawns untrodden by our feet! (9 May 1907: 22)

In offering an alternative to the industrial misery that leaves workers in factory towns across Great Britain 'blank,' 'sick,' and 'desperate,' Nesbit does not present practical proposals for reform or even call for greater class unity. Instead, she asserts her belief in the existence of an immortal and 'heavenly-sweet' garden 'where all the dreams we dare not dream come true.' Such a declaration of faith in a better and more beautiful reality makes it clear from the outset that Nesbit's poem is unapologetically visionary and utopian and that she is far more focused on dreams, or what Orage refers to as the 'nobler spiritual and imaginative faculties of men,' than she is with current material conditions and their transformation (2 May 1907: 8). Indeed, while she laments that she and her readers lack the courage and daring to discover this garden, whose location is shrouded by doubt ('We slip and stumble in the doubtful night'), human frailty ('clouds our breath has made obscure the day'), and moral corruption ('These are our portion, since they are our choice'), she nevertheless holds out the possibility that, if some brave soul or set of souls were bold enough to embrace in modernist fashion the 'difficult and new,' they might become, in Orage's words, 'the creator of new worlds, new values, new meanings'(Orage 1910 : 124–5). In other words, Nesbit's poem dares readers of the *New Age* to dream fearlessly and to assist in the building of 'the new contemplative and imaginative order' that the magazine declared to be its primary aim and purpose.

In other poems, Nesbit locates visionary hope for the future more specifically among the children of the poor, who were for her God's unacknowledged emissaries on earth. In 'These Little Ones,' for example, Nesbit writes about respectable, middle-class callousness toward child poverty in a manner that communicates not only anger at the selfishness of the ruling class but also bitter sadness at all of the youthful imaginative potential brought to ruin by capitalist injustice. The poem, which is written in dialogue form, is framed by two questions posed by God to the speaker of the poem. In the first half of 'These Little Ones,' God asks the speaker, '"What of the garden I gave?"' (18 July 1907: 183). In the lines that follow, the speaker responds that she has taken extraordinary care of this magnificent natural inheritance and has 'not lost a flower of all the flowers / That blessed my hours' (ibid.). In the second half of the poem, however, the speaker gives a much less satisfactory response to a much more important question, one that asks if she has taken similar care of a much more precious gift and inheritance.

> 'What of the child I gave?'
>   God said to me,
> 'The little, little thing I died to save,
>   And gave in trust to thee?
> How have the flowers grown
> That in its soul were sown,
> The lovely, living miracles of youth
> And hope, and joy, and truth?'
>
> 'The child's face is all white,'
>   I said to God.
> 'It cries for cold and hunger in the night;
>   Its feet have trod
> The pavement muddy and cold;
> It has no flowers to hold,
> And in its soul the flowers you set are dead.'
> 'Thou fool!' God said. (ibid.)

The key lines in these stanzas are not, as one might at first assume, those that refer to cold, hunger, sickness, and muddy streets, though they are certainly the most topical and socially engaged insofar as they catalogue the mistreatment and neglect suffered by the children of the poor. They are instead the lines that refer to the beautiful 'flowers' that are said to grow in the soul of the child, flowers described as 'lovely, living miracles of youth / And hope, and joy, and truth' (ibid.). These lines depict the interior subjective life, or soul, of a child as a place of sacred, utopian potential that might, under the right social conditions, develop into something genuinely extraordinary but instead, under current social conditions, too often becomes a barren wasteland of stunted development. In other words, these lines damn, with wickedly Blakean indignation, the speaker, and early twentieth-century Britain more generally, not just for strangling and blighting the lives of innocent children but for killing in a deeper sense the very possibility of 'hope, and joy, and truth' in British society (ibid.).

Although Farr was a very different writer than Nesbit, she shared many of her fellow contributor's views on the importance of children and imagination to the reform of Great Britain. In a letter to the editor of the *New Age* that appeared under the title 'Clever Women and the State,' Farr made it abundantly clear that she regarded childhood poverty as one of the central issues of her time. Coming to the defence of women who refused to bear children under current social conditions, she argued that it was women's duty to think critically about what role they were playing in propping up a broken social system.

> The one cry of the State to women is: give us sons; give us food for powder; give us such millions of men that they may come to us and make themselves into slaves in exchange for a minimum wage. But women are learning to see for themselves, and we reply to the State: Until the great questions of hygiene and prevention of disease, and the feeding of starving children are dealt with to some purpose, we refuse to put children into a world that is little better than Hell . . . Intelligence has benignly made it possible for all women but a small percentage, to stand firm under the curse of Eve, and now that men are beginning to feel the danger of this attitude to the continuance of the species they may soon learn to set a value upon human life. They may think it worth while this very year to see that the little children of the poor do not become imbecile from starvation; for that is what is happening every moment in this great over-crowded city of tortured lives. (7 Dec 1907: 119)

For Farr, like so many other progressive women of her era, Britain had an obligation to protect the most innocent and vulnerable members of society, and she believed that women had a leading role to play in making sure that children were not regarded as future wage slaves but instead as unique individuals with untapped and heretofore unappreciated potential. If this meant abstaining from procreating or barring men from their marriage beds, these were necessary steps women needed to take in order to teach men 'to set a value upon human life' (ibid.).

In addition to sharing Nesbit's anger at childhood poverty, Farr had many of the same views regarding dreams, imagination, and young adulthood. This is particularly evident in an essay titled 'The Silence of Adolescence.' Although Farr's focus is more on the limitations of a British educational system that silences the young, herds them into schools, and imposes on them a series of dreary and rote lessons than on the sacredness of childhood per se, she shares the view that youth, particularly adolescence, is 'the great blossoming time of subjective life' and the period of life when the 'extraordinary power of the mind called faith or imagination is in its full power' (6 June 1907: 89). 'Many philosophers,' comments Farr, 'have said that life is a dream, but nobody believes it; not even the young, whose dreams make them a strange, silent race walking among us like reproachful angels' (ibid.). While she admits that adolescents can be 'aggressive and a little demonic' and more often than not 'can express nothing but the most foolish platitudes,' she insists that they possess visionary powers that, if properly cultivated by a Socratic educator, could prove revolutionary and transformative (ibid.). If instead of bristling at their criticisms of our 'conversations and manners,' banishing them, like 'outcasts,' from our presence, and sending them off to school 'to do [their] lessons and get on with [their] arithmetic,' we encouraged the growth of their imagination, we might produce, she claims, a 'real aristocracy' (ibid.). Unfortunately, she argues, we do everything in our power to ensure that 'the subjective life sickens and dies' (ibid.). At exactly the moment when young people would 'desire above all things to listen to the discourses of Socrates on the nature of the soul or dream over the passionate poetry which makes reality so dim by comparison,' we teach them that they must get on with the task of 'propagating and nourishing, nourishing and propagating' (ibid.). The only exceptions to this unfortunate narrative, she argues, are women and artists. 'Most successful women,' she contends, 'keep the charm of adolescence all through their lives' (ibid.). What is more, she asserts, 'The wonderful richness of the adolescent life is used by artists and poets who have common sense enough to remember the visions they saw when they were young' (ibid.). In sum, Farr shared with Orage the view that women, artists, and above all children were those most likely to possess the visionary power necessary to reform and reconstruct a corrupt and damaged society.[11] As Orage would eloquently put it in an 'Unedited Opinions' column titled 'On Education,' 'Every child carries a demi-god's caduceus in his mind. There is no telling what marvellous changes the world might have enjoyed had each rising generation been allowed to experiment on its own account, instead of being driven to follow the mistakes of its predecessors' (4 Feb 1909: 260).

If Farr, like Orage and Nesbit, tended to regard British society's treatment of children with extraordinary pessimism, she was more optimistic about the role women might play in bringing radical change. This optimism was most visibly on display in a series of articles that Farr wrote about Norwegian playwright Henrik Ibsen's most famous female protagonists, one of whom, Rebecca West, Farr had played to great acclaim during the London premiere of *Rosmerholm* in 1891. In this series, which took advantage of the electric excitement that Ibsen still generated among progressive women, Farr turned to Ibsen's plays to make sense of the feminist unrest unsettling Great Britain during the first decade of the twentieth century, and she made the argument that middle-class British women, like their tragic counterparts in Ibsen's dramas, were acquiring a Nietzschean sense of the hollowness of all man-made norms, values, and conventions.[12]

For Farr, perhaps the most important aspect of the women's movement was that it was making it possible, as she argued in an essay titled 'The Sword of Laughter,' for middle-class women to confront 'the reality that lies behind human delusions' (18 July 1907: 182). It was also allowing them to perceive that they were in no way slaves to natural law or the social expectations of their sex. 'Man is a cunning fox,' she commented in an article titled 'Man' (19 Sep 1907: 326). 'He ingeniously frames moral codes to his own advantage and pretends they are inspired by the divine being who shines alike on the evil and the good' (ibid.). However, as women were becoming more aware that 'the general run of the sex appear to wear a paper-maché mask all day in order that they may conceal until dark the horrid truth they know to be quite unfit for exhibition,' many women were incapable of coming to terms with this truth or breaking free from the suburban ideals amidst which they had been raised (ibid.).

In writing about Ibsen's *Hedda Gabler* (1891), a play whose English premiere provided her with 'one of the best remembered sensations of [her] life' and had struck and continued to strike a powerful chord among feminists in Britain,[13] Farr argued that the drama presents the 'never-to-be forgotten' tragedy of a woman who can see through the illusions of so much about middle-class life but lacks the courage and will to push past these illusions and 'seek the heart of the mystery' (17 Oct 1907: 389). For Farr, this iconic character was the very archetype of a kind of transitional figure now increasingly to be found in middle-class home across Great Britain.

> The physiology of the sexes appears to be undergoing extraordinary modifications. Co-incident in time with the overpopulation question there have arisen amidst us women who hate motherhood. These beings are filled with emotional ideals. They are eloquent and clever; they are often the most conspicuous members of their families; they go through life exciting strong enthusiasms and strong antipathies; they look upon average men and women as indecent swine. Hedda Gabler is the great type of this transitional womanhood. (ibid.)

On one hand, Hedda is something of a pioneer feminist. Eloquent, clever, filled with 'emotional ideals,' and repulsed by sex and motherhood, she finds her nerves, as we are elsewhere informed, 'set on edge by the very facts of middle-class life' (ibid.). In particular, she discovers herself continually irritated by a family 'content to shed tears and laugh and accept death and birth and marriage in the regular course of things without thought of [the] impossible wonders which the rich imagination can enjoy and the poor imagination can only crave' (ibid.). On the other hand, like so many talented and restless women in early twentieth-century Britain whose rebellions would never fully take flight, Hedda's imagination remains tragically 'bounded by suburban ideas' (ibid.). While Hedda understands that women should aspire to be more than simply mothers and has a dawning awareness that relations between men and women could be nobler, more intellectual, and more emotionally honest, a 'quaint touch of poetry,' Farr interjects, 'that justifies her beautiful name,' she nevertheless still 'dreams of men in livery and riding horses' and wants to 'put a stately retinue between herself and natural necessities' (ibid.). By indulging in the most trivial and conventional fantasies of social escape and flinching before the animal nature of so much of human existence, Hedda lacks the courage to do anything more than play at revolt, and when she finds herself caught in scandal and confronted with the 'hideous dissipation' of a man she believed to be above such things, she takes her own life (17 Oct 1907: 390). The lesson to be drawn from this tragedy, Farr suggests, is that the 'thousands and thousands of girls in every part of the world' who share Hedda's restless feelings and imagination, whose journey toward self-realisation is transitional and not yet fully achieved, must break more decisively with convention and learn 'to stand up to life' (ibid.). Otherwise, they will remain trapped in the same 'purposeless grooves of thought' as Hedda (ibid.).

In writing about Rebecca West, the protagonist of Ibsen's *Rosmerholm* (1886), and Nora Helmer, the protagonist of *A Doll's House* (1879), Farr found examples of women who more boldly went down the path of self-realisation and offered more hopeful evidence that the woman's movement in Great Britain might indeed herald a revolutionary change in human relations. While Rebecca West's life ends in suicide and the play traces for Farr the 'gradual deadening of the living woman' as she is ground down by forces opposed to revolution and change, Rebecca embodied for Farr a latent power found in all women who recognised the social limitations placed on their self-development (31 Oct 1907: 9). After spending much of her young adult life self-sacrificially nursing her paralytic adoptive father, Rebecca's 'womanhood,' we are told, 'overtook her' (31 Oct 1907: 8). 'She was at the dangerous age,' comments Farr, 'when women suddenly awake: when the old easy life of acceptance ceases, when they desire to choose for themselves instead of submitting eternally to being chosen' (ibid.). If this awakening ultimately ended tragically, it nevertheless opened possibilities for a new generation of women who desired something better for themselves. The same thing, she suggests, could be said about Nora Helmer, who personified for Farr the difficult journey all human beings faced in coming to a deeper and more authentic understanding of themselves and their place in the universe. Although Farr claims that a certain amount of illusion is a human necessity and strongly insinuates that Nora's decision at the end of the play to leave her husband and children is not likely to help her find the 'master-key' to all of human existence, she praises Ibsen's famous heroine for perceiving that 'laws are man-made, morals are man-made, convention – good taste, is man-made; and that the prestige which all of them have borrowed from religion and divine right is vanities of vanities' (14 Nov 1907: 48). She also honours Nora for her belief that she 'must go outside the ready-made ideas of her husband and father – outside the region of unjust law – outside the region where abstract principles, such as justice and order, are called in to justify the majority, and put the thoughtless, or rather, those who have trained themselves to think for their own advantage, in an unassailable position of authority and trust' (ibid.). In Farr's view, then, Nora's individualistic journey sets a template for how we might all lead a 'braver life' and clears a path for a 'new kind of family' to emerge from the ruins of a decadent civilisation (14 Nov 1907: 49).

However, as important as Nora is to Farr in delineating a potentially productive path of resistance for the women's movement, it is Ellida Wangel, the protagonist of Ibsen's *The Lady from the Sea* (1888), who probably elicits Farr's greatest admiration. If, as is her wont, Farr cannot help but ask whether Ellida's decision at the end of the play to remain with her husband instead of running away with a romantic stranger from her past might condemn her to a life of darning socks and raising children, she otherwise celebrates Ellida for undergoing a 'mental transformation from servitude to responsibility that is good for the development of human intelligence' (30 Nov 1907: 87). In Farr's view, Ellida becomes more and more 'leonine,' a crucial stage in the Nietzschean overcoming of the self,[14] over the course of the play (ibid.). At first, as someone who feels trapped by her middle-class marriage and existence, she is merely 'oppressed by social convention' (ibid.). But when a mysterious lover from her past returns and beckons her to a 'more elemental life,' a Dionysian freedom that is both dangerous and potentially self-destructive, Ellida develops an intense yearning to abandon and destroy nearly everything that has defined and shaped her up until this point (ibid.). In reflecting on the significance of this yearning, Farr claims that Ibsen's heroine becomes 'not so much the type of a wife longing for emancipation as of the human will longing to free itself both from civilisation and from Life itself' (ibid.). As this comment makes clear, Farr sees in Ellida not simply an advocate for women's rights but a champion of the human will who longs to shake herself free from the chains of law, morality, and social convention and discover, no matter how recklessly, new forms of human community, association, and meaning. Although Ellida ultimately chooses to stay with her husband after he releases her from any obligation to him and encourages her to 'follow [her] own will,' her decision to stay, Farr takes pains to emphasise, is only meaningful and worthy of respect because it is an act of genuinely free choice, a radical Nietzschean exercise of responsibility that gets at the heart, in Farr's view, of what feminists like herself were fighting for in Great Britain (ibid.). Echoing Nietzsche's call for a transvaluation of all values, Farr declares, 'We who are crying for a re-valuation of all values want, after all, only what Ellida wanted, – freedom to choose for ourselves. We want more scope for the responsibility of human beings; we want it to be possible for a greater variety of social standards to exist in the little stagnant corners of the world' (ibid.). In short, feminist rebellion, for Farr, is not dissimilar to Nesbit's championing of children and Orage's advocacy of 'the five outcasts of civilisation'; it is part of a larger socialist critique of middle-class, capitalist values that has as its aim the unleashing of untapped human potential and the modernist destruction and remaking of a broken civilisation.

As I hope is now evident, the *New Age* is a magazine with a very different relationship to modernist women's writing than has hitherto been appreciated. Contrary to what most scholars of the periodical would have us believe, Katherine Mansfield and Beatrice Hastings were not the only women writers to make a significant contribution to the publication. During the periodical's first four years of existence, from 1907 to 1910, *New Age* editor A. R. Orage encouraged an astonishingly varied range of radical female artists and cultural activists to contribute to his magazine. More significantly, he promoted a brand of Nietzschean socialism that assigned women, children, and other social outsiders a privileged role in overturning a corrupt capitalist political order. Although Orage would later, in summer 1911, turn viciously against the women's suffrage movement and begin composing under the pen name R. H. Congreve a set of disturbingly misogynist stories titled 'Tales for Men Only,'[15] it is important not to let this abrupt shift in political outlook colour how we perceive the early history of the *New Age*. Prior to this shift, the magazine provided a supportive home to a vital and influential strain of modernist women's writing that drew strength and purpose from its engagement with issues of childhood poverty, legal and educational reform, middle-class feminist revolt, and the Nietzschean transvaluation of all values. Led by Fabian socialist, poet, and children's author Edith Nesbit and actress, playwright, and theosophist Florence Farr, both of whom are hiding in plain sight in the early volumes of the magazine, this strain of modernism was much more central to the mission and identity of the *New Age* than scholars of the magazine have heretofore realised.

Indeed, when examined closely, Nesbit's and Farr's contributions to the *New Age* make it clear that our definitions of modernism need to be more elastic if we are to understand the full range of contributions women made to modernist culture during the pre-war period. Although Nesbit's poetry is not formally experimental and her identity as a children's author probably predisposes many scholars to regard her writing as peripheral to modernism, her contributions to the *New Age* are undeniably visionary, iconoclastic, and marked by a pronounced break with tradition. They also reveal that a concern for child welfare, which might be thought of as too sentimental or traditionally feminine to qualify as modernist, can be every bit as revolutionary, every bit as concerned with making things new, as a concern with the male world of work and labour. The same kinds of things might be said about Farr's writings. While her contributions do not break new ground in terms of form and cannot be said to occupy an obvious genre, they display a person of keen intelligence reflecting on the power of dreams and imagination, especially those of children and women, to challenge and expose the hollowness of man-made norms, values, and conventions. They also disclose the deep Nietzschean affinities, in particular the shared concerns with self-realisation and self-overcoming, that linked advanced feminists such as herself with the revolutionary cultural politics of the *New Age* and the modernist movement more generally.

Notes

1. See, for example, Martin 1967, Ferrall 2001, and Villis 2006.
2. For instance, see Garver 2001 and Snyder 2010.
3. See, for example, Ardis 2007 and Snyder 2016.
4. See Briggs 1987.
5. One exception is Magree 2014. While Magree does not specifically focus on modernism, she argues that Nesbit expresses a feminist orientation in her gothic writing.
6. See, for example, Johnson 1975, Laity 1985, and DuPlessis 2002. One notable exception is Litz 1997. While Litz shares the view that Farr is a marginal figure, he praises her work for the *New Age* and claims that in her essays about playwright Henrik Ibsen she offered independent reflection on what it meant to be a woman living through a 'transitional' period in cultural history.
7. See Owen 2006: 61.
8. In a review of Orage's *Consciousness: Animal, Human, and Superman* in *The New Age*, Farr writes, 'England has been trembling on the verge of the Socialism that levels down for half a century; and the shade of Nietzsche, more powerful in death than ever in life, overshadows the great reforming movement and informs it with the aristocratic spirit. Mr. A. R. Orage, who rides on the wings of many storms, has made clear this great mission of the dead master in his little book on Nietzsche; and now in this book on "Consciousness: Animal, Human, and Superman," we realise that Mr. Orage's mind is equipped by nature and subtle Eastern practices to give us a far clearer idea of Superman or Aristocratic Consciousness than we gather from the songs of Nietzsche or from Shaw's great classic, "Man and Superman," with its prefaces, notes, and appendices' (6 June 1907: 92). See also Owen 2006: 132–5.
9. For more on Orage and Nietzsche, see Thatcher 1970.
10. 'William Blake alone among English writers seems to have closely resembled Nietzsche, and he who has read the Marriage of Heaven and Hell, and grasped its significance, will have little to learn from the apostle of Zarathustra' (Orage 1906: 12).
11. See also Farr's review of Orage's *Consciousness: Animal, Human, and Superman*, where she argues that 'the state of consciousness, now identified by leading modern thinkers as the state called superman, is mystically feminine' (6 June 1907: 92).
12. For more on the relationship between Ibsen and turn-of-the-century feminism, see Ledger 2001.
13. For more on the extraordinary influence of Ibsen on progressive women and feminists in Great Britain, see Barstow 2001.
14. In *Thus Spoke Zarathustra* (1891), Nietzsche speaks of 'the three metamorphoses' the spirit undergoes on its journey to self-overcoming. See Nietzsche and Kaufmann 1982: 'In the loneliest desert, however, the second metamorphosis occurs: here the spirit becomes a lion who would conquer his freedom and be master in his own desert' (138).
15. See *New Age* 10 Aug 1911: 349–50; *New Age* 14 Sep 1911: 469–70.

Works Cited

Ardis, Ann L. 2007. 'The Dialogics of Modernism(s) in *The New Age*.' *Modernism/modernity* 14.3: 407–34.
Barstow, Torrey. 2001. '"Hedda is All of Us": Late-Victorian Women at the Matinee.' *Victorian Studies* 43.3: 387–411.
Briggs, Julia. 1987. *A Woman of Passion: The Life of E. Nesbit, 1858–1924*. New York: New Amsterdam.
DuPlessis, R. B. 2002. 'Propounding Modernist Maleness: How Pound Managed a Muse.' *Modernism/modernity* 9.3: 389–405.
Ferrall, Charles. 2001. *Modernist Writing and Reactionary Politics*. Cambridge: Cambridge University Press.
Garver, Lee. 2001. 'The Political Katherine Mansfield.' *Modernism/modernity* 8.2: 225–43.
Johnson, Josephine. 1975. *Florence Farr: Bernard Shaw's 'New Woman.'* Totowa, NJ: Rowman and Littlefield.
Laity, Cassandra. 1985. 'W. B. Yeats and Florence Farr: The Influence of the "New Woman" Actress on Yeats's Changing Images of Women.' *Modern Drama* 28.4: 620–37.
Ledger, Sally. 2001. 'Ibsen, the New Woman, and the Actress.' *The New Woman in Fiction and Fact: Fin-de-Siècle Feminisms*. Ed. Angelique Richardson and Chris Willis. New York: Palgrave. 79–93.
Litz, A. Walton. 1997. 'Florence Farr: A "Transitional" Woman.' *High and Low Moderns: Literature and Culture, 1889–1939*. Ed. Maria DiBattista and Lucy McDiarmid. Oxford: Oxford University Press. 85–90.
Magree, Victoria. 2014. 'The Feminist Orientation in Edith Nesbit's Gothic Fiction.' *Women's Writing* 21.4: 425–43.
Martin, Wallace. 1967. *'The New Age' under Orage: Chapters in English Cultural History*. Manchester: Manchester University Press.
Nietzsche, Friedrich and Walter Kaufmann. [1954] 1982. *The Portable Nietzsche*. New York: Penguin.
Orage, A. R. 1906. *Friedrich Nietzsche: The Dionysian Spirit of the Age*. London: T. N. Foulis.
—. [1907] 1910. *Nietzsche in Outline and Aphorism*. Chicago: A. C. McClurg.
Owen, Alex. 2006. *The Place of Enchantment: British Occultism and the Culture of the Modern*. Chicago: University of Chicago Press.
Snyder, Carey. 2010. 'Katherine Mansfield and the *New Age* School of Satire.' *Journal of Modern Periodical Studies* 1.2: 125–58.
—. 2016. 'Beatrice Hastings's Sparring Pseudonyms, Feminism, and the *New Age*.' *Beatrice Hastings: On the Life and Work of a Lost Modern Master*. Ed. Benjamin Johnson and Erika Jo Brown. Warrensburg, MO: Pleiades. 170–87.
Thatcher, David. 1970. *Nietzsche in England, 1890–1914*. Toronto: University of Toronto Press.
Villis, Tom. 2006. *Reaction and the Avant-Garde: The Revolt Against Liberal Democracy in Early Twentieth-Century Britain*. London and New York: Tauris.

23

Horror in the Wax Museum: Edith Nesbit's 'The Power of Darkness' and the *Strand Magazine*

Anthony Camara

Today, critics primarily recognise Edith Nesbit as a writer of children's literature, if not the first modern author of that genre (Park 2010: 501–17).[1] Although Nesbit's contribution to children's literature must stand foremost in any holistic appraisal of her work, critics have recently been focusing more attention on her horror stories. Nick Freeman argues that these tales constitute a distinct form of writing that he terms 'New Woman Gothic,' in which the frequently misogynistic conventions of the aforementioned genre are reconfigured in order to comment on the plight of politically dissident women at the *fin de siècle* and in the early twentieth century (2008: 454–69). In response to Freeman's study, which is centred on the much-anthologised 'Man-Size in Marble' (1893), Victoria Margree examines a wider selection of tales that evince the feminist orientation of Nesbit's gothic fictions while nevertheless addressing the author's ambivalence toward New Woman politics (2014: 425–43).

Margree's article increases the scholarship on Nesbit's masterful gothic tales, but many of these works have yet to receive any thorough analysis. Moreover, although it is often noted that these supernatural short stories debuted in popular magazines, to date no critic has undertaken a sustained discussion of the importance of their publication in the context of British periodical culture during the modernist period. In this chapter, I examine one of Nesbit's understudied gothic tales that appeared in the famous *Strand* magazine, a title that was absolutely integral to the construction of English middle-class identity in the late nineteenth and early twentieth century (Hoberman 2004: 1). So popular and influential was the *Strand* that David Jasen remarks, '[j]ust as *Punch* was the ultimate goal of every writer of humorous articles, so the *Strand* was that of every short-story writer' (Chan 2008: 62). While remaining attentive to the heterogeneous content of the periodical, I analyse 'The Power of Darkness' (April 1905), a gothic thriller that is all the more striking for transpiring in a wax museum. In the first part of this paper, I show how wax figures bring anxious philosophical questions into relief that pertain to the relationship between organic life and inanimate matter, thereby expanding on Margree's feminist analysis of abjection in Nesbit's gothic fictions. In the second part of the chapter, I argue that the setting of this story shows how a market-driven, popular periodical such as the *Strand* capitalised on modern, mass-cultural forms of urban entertainment. By setting these gothic stories in waxworks filled with human forms ambiguously poised between life and death, Nesbit offers her readers the thrill of experiencing the uncanny, a sensation that itself had become commercialised by wax museums such as Madame Tussaud's in London and the Musée Grévin in Paris. Thus, these tales show the economic synergy between magazines and forms of mass entertainment, as well as the interrelations between the literary space of the popular periodical and the physical space of the modern metropolis, with its infrastructure of commercial attractions. This argument demonstrates the under-recognised importance of notions of modernity and modernism to studies of the *Strand* and popular 'middle-brow' periodicals like it, even in spite of the 'naturally conservative tendencies of the *Strand*'s editorial team and their deep antipathy towards artistic and literary modernism,' as J. L. Cranfield puts it (2013: 25).

The Abject

Drawing on conventions from gothic and sensation fiction, 'The Power of Darkness' tells of a scheming lover, Vincent, who connives to make use of the wax figures in Paris's Musée Grévin in order to eliminate his romantic rival and former schoolfellow, Edward. Vincent knows that a shock received in childhood has left Edward with an overactive imagination and an intense fear of the dark.[2] Discovering that his beloved, Rose, has fallen for Edward, Vincent decides to torment his squeamish rival by taking him to the Musée Grévin. After witnessing gruesome tableaux depicting scenes from the French Revolution, the Reign of Terror, and the martyrdom of Christians fed to lions in the Coliseum, Edward is in bad need of a vermouth, and so the two men visit a café where tempers flare and bets are made, each man wagering that his rival lacks the courage to spend a night in the Musée Grévin. While Vincent bets five pounds, Edward ups the stakes, stipulating that should he win, Vincent must never speak to Rose again. After Edward departs, Vincent schemes to outfit a wax figure with strings in order to create an illusion of movement that will literally scare Edward out of his wits, if not to his death. Vincent then returns to the Musée Grévin in order to promptly win his five pounds and scout some exhibits suitable for rigging when Edward revisits the museum. Little does Vincent know that Edward has delayed his trip home so that he can return to the museum that night to win the bet. Unbeknownst to each other, the men hide themselves among the wax replicas, waiting for the Musée Grévin to close and the lights to go off, leaving them in an oppressive darkness from which only one man will emerge sane.

Throughout the story, Nesbit writes of encounters with the wax figure that do not describe its ghastly form as much as the abject and uncanny experiences that it induces. For example, as he coaxes Edward into the Musée Grévin, Vincent describes the figure as 'Wax-modelled and retouched till it seems as near life as death is' (*Strand* Apr 1905: 443). Vincent's simile implies that in the wax figure, inanimate matter approaches life just as closely as the aura of life clings to the cadaver. And yet, if wax figures and corpses present the spectacle of death's proximity to life, then it would appear that the distinction between living and dead bodies, be they flesh or wax, is essentially a vanishing point, a limit upon which these material entities threaten to converge. It is as if the vitality of the living body itself announces the coming of death and stillness, while the deathly inertia of the wax figure and the cadaver presage an imminent coming-to-life, an un-dead outburst into animated movement. Thus the wax replica abolishes distinctions between life and death, doing so by not only adumbrating the spectacle of life-in-death, of inanimate matter becoming vitalised, but also depicting a state of death-in-life that makes the viewer's own living body visible as a dead thing – and not merely the waxen mass of flesh that it is to become, but the utterly material corpse that it already is. Edward explicitly links the wax forms to corpses when he declares that 'They're like life – but much more like death' (Apr 1905: 445), an observation that prompts Vincent to recall a vigil that he kept over the body of a dead friend. The conflation of the wax replica and the cadaver becomes more apparent considering that many of the figures in the Musée Grévin depict corpses: severed heads from the French Revolution; torsos mutilated by wild animals in the Coliseum; and the bodies of Christians receiving their final blessings.

Throughout history, the wax replica has been intimately associated with the corpse. Marina Warner notes that 'The word "mummy," applied to bodies embalmed according to Egyptian burial rites, derives from "moum," the word for wax or tallow; since those remote times, wax has been the principal material used in preserving the dead so as to make them look as if they are still alive' (2006: 23). In his 'History of Portraiture in Wax' (1911), Julius Von Schlosser writes of the *cerae*, or wax death masks of the Roman patricians, which were displayed in the atrium of the house and occasionally removed for public sacrifices so that the living could gaze upon the faces of their virtuous ancestors and be moved to great deeds (2008: 181–3). And in the eighteenth century, Pope Benedict XIV, a famous patron of the arts and sciences, commissioned the wax sculptor Ercole Lelli to create full-sized anatomical figures for use by the Medical Faculty of Bologna University. Lelli not only used corpses to cast the waxen body parts, but he also assembled them around the bones of real skeletons (Warner 2006: 31). Most pertinent to 'The Power of Darkness' – which contains many references to Madame Tussaud's Wax Museum – Tussaud herself allegedly modelled the wax heads of the victims of the Great Terror from their originals while they still dripped blood from the guillotine (Melman 2006: 29). Maximilien Robespierre, Jean-Paul Marat, and the Princess de Lamballe were also among Madame Tussaud's 'unfortunate models,' as Billie Melman puts it (2006: 37).

I emphasise the connection between the wax figure and the corpse because it touches on a central concern of Nesbit's gothic tales. Alongside romantic rivalry and thwarted love, Margree argues that the fear of death and horror of corpses is a keynote theme in Nesbit's work (2014: 428). Margree contends that Nesbit's corpses embody the developmental psychoanalytic of abjection as theorised by Julia Kristeva. In her concept of the abject, the inchoate ego that will become the 'I' must first separate itself off from the pre-symbolic flow of primordial experience so as to constitute itself as a subject distinct from the world of objects (Margree 2014: 429). Kristeva refers to this act as the 'primal repression' (1982: 10), the first exclusionary ejection of materiality that enables the child to define him or herself as a subject, over and against objects. What is deemed 'abject,' then, forces the subject to confront his or her own corporeal materiality, thereby threatening to undo the work of the primal repression and plunge the 'I' back into the nausea of being a thing that is neither subject nor object. Hence, for Kristeva, 'Abjection preserves what existed in the archaism of pre-objectile relationships' (ibid.). Excreta, blood, and mucus invoke the affective force of the abject, and yet, as Margree writes, for Kristeva, nothing embodies the abject as fully as the corpse, 'the waste that has not been ejected but that has ejected me. The cadaver reveals to me the corpse that I am always on the brink of becoming. It "show[s] me" the death (my death) that I continually repress in order to live' (2014: 428).

As opposed to Nesbit's other gothic tales that approach abjection through the figure of the revivified – and often female – corpse, I argue that in 'The Power of Darkness' it is the wax replica that serves as the avatar of the abject. It is at once a material thing that seemingly lives, and a graphic demonstration of the cadaverous thingness of life itself, the emblem of the mutual contamination of subjectivity and objectivity. Accordingly, the wax figure raises anxious philosophical questions about the relationship between organic life and matter. Vincent projects these very concerns when he speculates on the possibility of waxes waking up: 'Suppose ... when all the lights were out, these things did move. A corpse was a thing that had moved – given a certain condition – Life. What if there were such a condition, given which these things could move? What if such conditions were present now?' (Apr 1905: 447). As Kelly Hurley shows, late nineteenth- and early twentieth-century scientific discourses – among them Darwinism, degeneration theory, and vivisection – posed such philosophical questions pertaining to life, but their articulation in literature that hybridised the gothic and science fiction bestowed them with speculative horizons to be explored (1996: 16).

Such problems are not only enunciated in genre fictions like 'The Power of Darkness,' but they also register a high level of cultural visibility within the non-fictional essays that appeared in popular magazines such as the *Strand*, which had a massive circulation of nearly 400,000 in 1896 (Hoberman 2004: 2). The April 1905 *Strand* containing 'The Power of Darkness' also features a scientific essay titled 'Things That Get in Our Eyes,' by Fred W. Saxby. The article, which positions reader as scientist by incorporating circular microscopy photographs, states that 'Few people are aware of the fact that we are all constantly collecting curious things without looking for them. There are wide-awake collectors who go about with their eyes open, and they are the very people who make the largest collection of specimens which they neither see nor want' (Apr 1905: 381). Invoking collections and cabinets of curiosities[3] in its discussion of the geological and biological sediments in our eyes, the article describes a succession of airborne particles with exquisitely patterned microscopic configurations that render them virtual tomes of natural history and precious collector's objects in their own right: meteoric residues, volcanic dust, diatom shells, pollen grains, and scales from butterfly wings. In this procession of artefacts invisible to the naked eye, inorganic matter imperceptibly merges with species of organic material, as the series follows a trend of increasing complexity and vitality that elides the difference between inanimate and animate matter. The last sentence makes this elision evident: 'In the mighty laboratory of Nature the giant forces are ever at work upon the material particles of a boundless universe – elaborating, disintegrating, reconstructing in one glorious cycle of unending change' (Apr 1905: 384). The passage adopts the tone of wonder and grandeur at the end of Charles Darwin's *On the Origin of Species* (1859), proposing that everything, from geological formations to animal life, consists of 'material particles' worked on by evolutionary forces that give rise to the marvellously fine-tuned intricacies curated by the article. And yet, underneath the passage's pomp, if the universe is a series of random permutations in matter, then it also resembles Hurley's gothic cosmos of metamorphic matter and abject things 'in which no fixity remains, only an endless series of monstrous becomings' (1996: 28).

Using abjection to interpret 'The Power of Darkness,' as well as the various textual materials of the *Strand* in which it was published, registers urgent concerns about the materiality of life that preoccupied the mainstream cultural imagination. Additionally, following Margree's assertion that women 'appear in Nesbit's gothic fiction in the place of the abject' (2014: 429), I contend that the story's engagement with wax figures suggests a feminist reading, notwithstanding Nesbit's reticence toward New Woman politics. Returning to the story, as he passes the night in the Musée Grévin, Vincent is ever the more unnerved by his own imagination, which drives him deeper into the catacombs, where he takes refuge among a set of waxes portraying a Christian burial. Shaken by the thought of the figures coming to life and hunting him down, the waxen corpse in his midst soon recalls to Vincent the watch that he kept over his dead friend, and his conviction that night that if the corpse had moved, he would have gone mad (Apr 1905: 445). When he hears noises from a nearby funeral scene, Vincent lights a match and investigates. Finding himself encircled by a group of hooded forms, he exclaims that the figures are just wax, and delivers a kick to a seated martyr, which responds by lifting its head and meeting Vincent's horrified gaze with a pair of living eyes. As he reels backward, Vincent's match goes out, and he is engulfed by darkness and insanity. The setting shifts to the sunny Mediterranean, where Edward and Rose are honeymooning. Rose asks Edward what drove Vincent mad that night, to which Edward responds that Vincent mistook him for a wax figure, adding that his old friend now 'thinks everyone in the asylum is made out of wax, and he screams if they come near him' (Apr 1905: 449). Explaining to Rose how he was not frightened that night, Edward relates that he imagined himself to be one of the Christian martyrs, whose bonds of friendship and exemplary calmness in the face of death soothed him to sleep.

There seems to be little here to suggest a feminist reading, yet Nesbit's description of Rose as she departs from Paris by train invites closer scrutiny. Nesbit writes that 'She was one of those agitating blondes, with the naturally rippled hair, the rounded rose-leaf cheeks, the large violet blue eyes . . . She held her court like a queen, leaning out of the carriage window' (Apr 1905: 441). Rose's blonde hair, flushed cheeks, and royal mien create disconcerting parallels with the bloodied wax replica of the severed head of the Princess de Lamballe, which Vincent shows to Edward. Nesbit writes: 'There was a window to the room. Outside was sunshine – the sunshine of 1792 – and, gleaming in it, blonde hair flowing, red mouth half open, what seemed the just-severed head of a beautiful woman. It was raised on a pike, so that it seemed to be looking in at the window' (Apr 1905: 443). In addition to their golden hair and aristocratic auras, Nesbit frames both Rose's and the princess's heads in windows, a detail that renders the men's viewing of the wax head as a fatal doubling of the scene of Rose's departure. As an aperture liable to close suddenly and forcefully, the carriage window hints at the guillotine and potential violence directed at Rose, not only as the shared object of the rivals' affections, but also as a muse for the ateliers of Paris, and therefore as the subject (or is it object?) of artistic representations that fetishise her body and reduce it into pieces. Such fetishism is evident in the disconcerting sexualisation of Rose's uncanny double, the wax head, an aesthetic object which is 'beautiful' despite being 'just-severed.' More distressingly, the 'red mouth half open' implies that the male gaze perversely transforms the princess's slack-jawed expression of death into a sign of necrophilic sexual availability, the bloodstained mouth becoming a pair of crimson, sensually parted lips, which gesture to Rose's name. Lastly, by depicting (parts of) these women within windows, Nesbit suggests the liminal position of woman in patriarchal society, which underwrites the physical and aesthetic violence aimed at them.

Christopher Hibbert stresses the singular brutality to which the Princess de Lamballe, a favourite – and perhaps sexual intimate – of Marie Antoinette, was subjected. He notes that she 'had been stripped and raped; her breasts had been cut off; the rest of her body mutilated,' before citing an official report that declares, 'I must not venture to describe the excesses of barbarity and lustful indecency with which this corpse was defiled' (1981: 175). Thus the wax head is not just a marker of the history of the French Revolution, but also a (dis-figured) figuration of the trans-historical violence perpetrated against women. As a symbol of aesthetic exquisiteness and shocking cruelty, the head insinuates that this objectifying violence is physical and representational in nature, a notion borne out of the men's specular delectation of the decapitated head, in which gruesome marks of wounding stimulate sexual arousal and aesthetic appreciation. Following Margree, I argue that the correspondences between Rose and the wax head of the princess convey to the reader 'an awareness of how certain forms of femininity are rendered abject by a patriarchal society that requires their repression to reproduce itself' (2014: 430). Thus the slippages between the head and Rose reflect their shared status as abject entities, as material beings that pose a threatening liminality to the men of the tale. Just as the wax figure hovers between inert objectivity and animated subjectivity, Rose is at once the tale's exalted beloved and an object to be won in a competition. Like the abject substances that Kristeva describes, which are ejected from the body but also essential to its vitality, women are violently expelled from the social body but nevertheless central to it, providing the material preconditions for its very existence.

Given that femininity and abjection are so closely associated in 'The Power of Darkness,' I contend that the different comportment shown toward the wax figures by Vincent and Edward designate opposed masculine attitudes toward material femininity. In the case of Vincent, who repeatedly degrades the feminine by using it as an insult against Edward ('He oughtn't to be such a schoolgirl,' [Apr 1905: 446] thinks Vincent), he can only imagine the wax statues existing in violent opposition to himself, as potential torturers and murderers brought to life when darkness falls: 'What if all of them – Napoleon, yellow-white from his death-sleep; the beasts from the Amphitheatre, gore dribbling from their jaws; that soldier with the legs – all were drawing near to him in this full silence?' (Apr 1905: 447). Note that the waxes symbolise war, savagery, and death, revealing Vincent's aggression toward material femininity and, by extension, the substance of his own body. To the contrary, Edward controls his imagination by using it to resurrect the peaceful Christian martyrs, and while Vincent's imagination animates horrors inimical to his life, Edward's creates a community of which he is a part.

At the limit, however, both men's fantasies fixate on death and becoming a corpse. Vincent's death wish is to join history's corpses by being murdered by them, while Edward's solidarity with the martyrs is predicated on his acceptance of a death sentence. The crucial distinction to be made here is that Vincent manifests a fearful resistance to his death and becoming-corpse – that is, he disavows abjection – while Edward seeks, through martyrdom, to calmly and wilfully embrace the sufferings, humiliations, and mutilations that strip him of subjectivity and leave him an abject thing. Accordingly, as Vincent becomes more frightened, the more animated and panicked his body becomes, as if his frantic movements about the museum were a subconscious, defiant assertion of his own lively subjectivity in the face of death. Conversely, Edward's imaginings induce a state of bodily relaxation and immobility that culminates in sleep. As an indicator of his willingness to relinquish subjectivity and invite the stillness of death into his body, Edward's sleep signals communion with the martyrs. More immediately, however, this sleep literally turns Edward into an unconscious, subject-less thing bearing a human shape – namely, a wax statue. He therefore joins the figures in abjection not just through imagined martyrdom, but also through becoming a wax replica. Edward says that 'Those wax people, they sort of seemed as if they were alive, and were telling me there wasn't anything to be frightened about. *I felt as if I were one of them* . . . So I just went to sleep' (Apr 1905: 449; my emphasis). In a Capuchin cloak and rendered motionless by sleep, Edward disappears into the group of hooded figures, his in-distinguishability suggesting a total identification with these waxen figures of abjection. And so, when Vincent awakens Edward with a kick, it is as if a wax statue really did come to life.

Recalling the interrelatedness of abjection and femininity, Vincent's denigration of women[4] resonates with his violent revulsion toward the statues, which remind him that he too is a finite, material creature, and therefore a cadaver-to-be, not unlike the wax corpses that he imagines are stalking him. His horror of vitalised waxes and conviction that they are coming to get him suggest his denial of abjection and existential anxiety over the physical composition of his own body. Hence, after going mad, Vincent sees all human flesh as wax, the substance out of which his tormentors are composed. Edward's imaginings, on the other hand, attempt to achieve comfort with the material nature of his body in and through its fragile vulnerability and susceptibility to pain. His abandonment of subjectivity acknowledges its transitory, material constitution, thus undermining the subject-object binary. In other words, Edward's becoming-wax is not just a limit experience of death, but also an imaginative endeavour to approach abjection and the material feminine, which the text validates by ending with Edward's marriage to Rose. This interpretation adds an extra dimension to feminist readings of 'The Power of Darkness,' as the tale would not only explore how femininity is rendered abject, but it would also call for a re-envisioning of masculine courage. Branded an over-imaginative coward, Edward hardly fits the role of gothic hero. What he learns in the Musée Grévin is not the conventional male courage to conquer fear by curbing the imagination; instead, he learns to have the courage to use his imagination, and to do so in order to come to terms with death and his physical existence, which the text suggests as an alternative to the repressions, disavowals, and binaries that produce violence against women and the material world.

One might argue that the feminist potential of this reading is curtailed by the fact that Edward's becoming-wax takes place within the patriarchal imaginary of Christian martyrdom, and that furthermore, Edward chooses martyrdom because of the promise of glorious resurrection that represents the spirit's ultimate revenge on matter – the masculine, transcendental subject's triumph over the object as well as the feminine abject.

Edward, however, never even so much as mentions the resurrection, and his identification with the statues is less as a martyr than a waxen corpse. Put flatly, Edward does not want to be a spirit; he wants to know what it is to be a cadaver, and so he is pursuing an existential and psychosexual curiosity that has its wellspring in matter. Indeed, Kristeva asserts that 'abjection accompanies all religious structurings and reappears, to be worked out in a new guise, at the time of their collapse' (1982: 17). What Nesbit finds in martyrdom, then, is Christianity's own abject, its perverse materialism, and so this 'heretical' feminist interpretation proposes itself under the cover of conventional moralism and reassuring religious dogma that flatters the ideologies of the readership. Indeed, in his collection of anecdotal reminiscences of the *Strand* magazine, former editor Reginald Pound writes that '[c]ertainly the middle-classes of England never cast a clearer image of themselves in print than they did in the *Strand Magazine*. Confirming their preference for mental as well as physical comfort, for more than half a century it faithfully mirrored their tastes, prejudices, and intellectual limitations' (1966: 7). This reading enables us to appreciate how Nesbit used the widely circulating, politically conservative *Strand* – which Newnes marketed as a source of 'cheap, healthful literature' (Pittard 2007: 2), and touted as 'the Leading and most Popular Magazine of the day' (Hoberman 2004: 6) – in order to propagate her feminist ideas.

There is one final complexity here to acknowledge. A literal interpretation of the text would stress that Edward's identification with the martyrs is actually on the side of life, and that he becomes one of these waxen figures because they are eternally frozen (read: 'life everlasting') in the moment before their doom, enabling him to keep death and abjection at a safe distance rather than fall headlong into them. That fate would belong to Vincent, whose imagination, in fulfilment of a death wish, creates zombies and killers of the waxes. Thus this literal reading of the tale makes it into a parable about the necessity of disciplining the imagination: not shutting it off, but sublimating it to produce life-affirming visions and affects. To make this parable legible, it features a simple binary with a 'good,' successful character and his failed, 'evil' rival. These interpretations map to the imaginative impressions that the wax figure invokes in its viewer: Edward sees its living side, while Vincent fixates on its deadness. Yet there is a third impression that the wax replica imparts: that of abjection, and it is to this that my readings have attended. Abjection runs between life and death, collapses binaries, and disrupts the parable by rendering the wax statue a figuration of ambiguity, as well as an allegory for the uncertainties of reading. Accordingly, I suggest that no one reading be prioritised, but instead taken together to recognise gothic horror fictions as complex, contradictory fields of identifications and repulsions in which Nesbit could imaginatively explore death and abjection while also disciplining and regulating these impulses.

As well as uncovering intersections with her children's fiction, wherein mastering magic is a metaphor for learning how to govern the imagination, this analysis suggests a more nuanced appreciation of the significance of the publication of the gothic tales in the *Strand*. In addition to providing a vehicle for feminist ideas under a cover of middle-class propriety, the appearance of the tales in the conservative *Strand* required Nesbit to produce fictions palatable to an audience with an appetite for sensation but also bland optimism, at least where religious and political matters were involved. For instance, Cranfield identifies 'the immutability of heterosexual love; a Judeo-Christian belief in the immortality of the soul; the correctness and desirability of empire as a historical certainty; and . . . the transcendent nature of heroism and chivalry' as the four fundamental tropes that were intermixed and recombined in order to generate the *Strand*'s 'grand narratives of choice' (2012: 551). Moreover, Kate Jackson demonstrates that the formation of reading communities – that is, 'categories of readers linked together by a common experience or expectation of reading, and by common social, political, ideological or cultural objectives or bonds rather than by physical proximity' – constituted the explicit objective of Newnes's publishing enterprises (Pittard 2007: 1). On account of her audience, then, Nesbit had to check the dark bent of her gothic imagination. Far from simply encouraging self-censorship, the horror tales that ran in the *Strand* enabled Nesbit to explore the sensationalistic, shadowy terrain of sexual jealousy, murder, insanity, abjection, and death, while at the same time controlling a luxurious imagination that could very easily run wild. Hence her gothic tales might sound the depths of destructive forces – indeed, as Maria Cairney points out, *Strand* texts often show a 'prurient fixation' (2007: 65) with 'the violence of urban life, criminality, and even drug use' (2007: 70), despite the magazine's reputation as 'healthful' reading material – but the constraints imposed by her respectable, middle-class *Strand* readers always reminded Nesbit to resurface when faced with the intolerable. Doing so reassured her that she had self-control. In other words, publishing gothic horror in the *Strand* was a way of disciplining her power of darkness by chastening it in the light of the public.

The Uncanny

In this final section, I argue that Nesbit's wax museum fictions replicate the sensation of the uncanny in her readership, thereby demonstrating how popular fictions in the *Strand* capitalised on modern, mass-cultural forms of entertainment in order to entice a purchasing readership. This argument first requires clarifying the definition of the 'uncanny.' The etymological, first section of Sigmund Freud's 1919 essay by that title reveals how laden the term is with heterogeneous meanings. When I use the term, I do so with resonance to the Freudian classification of the uncanny as that which is both familiar and strange; however, I predominantly use the term in the way that Ernst Jentsch does in his 1908 essay, 'On the Psychology of the Uncanny,' which Freud cites at the outset of his own study. Jentsch's uncanny refers to 'doubt as to whether an apparently animate object really is alive and, conversely, whether a lifeless object might not perhaps be animate' (Freud 2003: 135). Three years prior to the publication of Jentsch's essay, Nesbit uses the term in the 'The Power of Darkness' to describe the wax figures. While there is more than a hint of the Freudian uncanny about these statues, the waxes are indiscernible as alive or dead, thus strongly suggesting Jentsch's formulation. The tale's drawings, done by Arthur Watts, use chiaroscuro to render the human and wax figures indistinguishable, thereby visually registering and enhancing the uncanny sensation that Nesbit's text strives to capture.

According to Jentsch, as a 'lifeless object' that might be animate, the wax figure undoubtedly qualifies as uncanny. Yet his definition also accounts for the reverse case, wherein the sensation of the uncanny is generated by an animate object that appears to be lifeless. Immediately following 'The Power of Darkness' in the April 1905 *Strand* is an interview titled 'The Automaton Girl,' by M. Dinorben Griffith.

This article profiles an American woman, Doris Chertney, who could so convincingly impersonate a machine that she gained fame in Europe and America as the star of a successful travelling attraction. Chertney donned a metal corset, metallic tubing, copper-soled slippers, and a back-mounted wind-up clockwork mechanism in order to become 'The Motogirl,' a mechanised, Steampunk doll. Chertney's stage manager, Mr Frederic Melville, began the show by asking an audience member to wind up the Motogirl, who then 'makes spasmodic doll-like movements across the stage, and is finally carried about among the audience, who are allowed to touch and lift her; and who, one and all, agree that it is a wonderfully-constructed automaton' (Apr 1905: 451). The attraction featured various contortionist stunts and feats of balance showcasing the Motogirl's ability to assume postures no human body could sustain. Photographs in the *Strand* show her folded up inside a basket for ease of transportation, and the interview alleges that the Motogirl was once shipped from St Petersburg to Paris inside a small box. So perfect was Chertney's illusion of total mechanisation that she fooled Russian customs officials; Emperor Francis Josef and the Austrian Court; a panel of judges from the *Kammergericht*, or German Supreme Court; and Émile François Loubet, France's President from 1899 to 1906. That 'The Power of Darkness' and 'The Automaton Girl' ran in sequence in the April 1905 *Strand* is no coincidence. Recalling Jentsch's two-part definition, one might say that the features, placed together for the reader's enjoyment, articulate the dual pleasure of the uncanny across the inorganic-organic spectrum traced out in Saxby's article, which preceded this uncanny row of sensational literary entertainments in the same instalment of the *Strand*.

Griffith's piece attempts to capture the sensation of the uncanny through its vivid depictions of the Motogirl, which the interview emphasises as consummate illusions by relating that judicial officials and eminent politicians – men whose professional lives were staked on the capability to make fine discernments – were hoodwinked by Chertney's act. But it is arguably the technology of the photograph rather than the written word that the interview relies on the most, as the essential indexical supplement to language that provides the means to capture the phenomenological signature of the uncanny by arresting its singular visual texture. The feature contains ten photographs of the Motogirl performing feats described in the interview. Whether she is folded up in her basket, frozen in impossible contortions, or locked into rigid poses, she stares vacantly off the page and into space, often meeting the reader's gaze with glassy eyes and a made-up face like a painted piece of ceramic. The most eerily evocative photographs include referent objects that convey a sense of her size, such as the one that depicts the Motogirl leaning sideways against a chair, straight as a plank, or being lifted from her basket by Melville, her limp body troublingly suggesting a dance partner, a lover, and a corpse. With their referent objects, these photographs essentially contaminate the others, as they turn what could just be pictures of a child's little, ordinary doll into photographs of a life-sized automaton.

And yet, while the feature marshals text and image to replicate the uncanny, it also seeks a critical distance so that this sensation can be documented as a psychological artefact and commodity rather than a supernatural event. Early in the interview, Griffith writes that, 'From her earliest girlhood little Doris delighted in amusing and startling her child friends with her marvellous impersonation of mechanical toys. She had phenomenal facial control, and could assume at will the immobility or the peculiarity of movement of an automaton' (Apr 1905: 451). The essence of this knowledge – that all along, Chertney has been a 'natural,' so to speak – is visually transmitted through a large photograph that depicts her in 'real life,' attired in typical period dress instead of her Motogirl costume, and smiling knowingly at the reader, who is now in on the joke: if an automaton can imitate life, then vice-versa. Thus the interview reveals that the true marvel here is not the uncanny phenomenon in itself, but that which produces the uncanny as a spectacular effect. In other words, the true wonder of the article is not the Motogirl automaton, which the informed reader of the *Strand* knows is just a phenomenal appearance, but rather the fantastically fine-controlled, living machine that is Chertney's own body, which becomes machinic in and through its production of the spectacle of the uncanny as a marketable good. Hence the feature configures her body as a profitable technology that functions by imitating technology: a process of uncanny duplication that allows the whole revenue-generating apparatus of the travelling show, and the trappings of print-media celebrity, to spring up around her. This notion accords with J. L. Cranfield's argument that the *Strand* used bodies as 'vehicles for ideas and, in a wider sense, for narratives' (2012: 550). In retrospect, the photographs illustrate much of this; on the side of the Motogirl's basket there is a label that reads: 'STRAND MAGAZINE [,] FRAGILE [,] WITH CARE' (Apr 1905: 452). This sign boasts the exclusivity of the interview to the readership, yet it also announces that the uncanny spectacle of the Motogirl and her secrets were a valuable consumer product that had been packaged, sold, and delivered to readers by the *Strand*.

The Motogirl interview emphases how features in the *Strand* produced and commodified the uncanny by drawing on popular, mass-cultural entertainments that did likewise. Yet this dynamic is hardly restricted to just the non-fictional pieces published in the magazine. Via its prominent references to the Musée Grévin and Madame Tussaud's, 'The Power of Darkness,' like the Motogirl feature, was capitalising on these spectacular mass entertainments. By adopting the Musée Grévin as a fictional setting – as well as likening it to Madame Tussaud's – Nesbit's gothic tale articulates these famous waxworks as public sites for the production of uncanny sensations and spectacles that could be profitably translated into the consumer goods of sensation fiction. In an especially memorable passage, the voice of the third-person narrator states that 'The Musée Grévin is a waxworks show. Your mind, at the word, flies instantly to the excellent exhibition founded by the worthy Mme Tussaud. And you think you know what waxworks mean. But you are wrong. The Musée Grévin contains the work of artists for a nation of artists' (Apr 1905: 443). The passage can be read as free indirect discourse relating Vincent's thoughts as he baits Edward, but the second-person pronouns in the passage make it a direct address to the reader, whose imagination is invoked as a precondition for the fiction's accomplishment of its own objectives and effects. The story thus taps the reader's memories, experiences, and expectations of Madame Tussaud's as a way of invoking the sensation of the uncanny. And to further captivate the reader, the passage sets up the Musée Grévin as an exotic, 'other' French waxworks boasting more powerful uncanny effects than its British counterpart. Thus the passage alludes to the reputation of the Musée Grévin as an exceptional museum where, as the *Moniteur universel* newspaper reported in 1881, 'the resemblance is perfect, striking, [and] extraordinary. You begin to ask yourself whether you are in the presence of the real person' (Schwartz 1998: 119). The story's use of the Musée Grévin and Madame Tussaud's, then, demonstrates how the urban space of the metropolis and its mass attractions were intimately connected to the imaginative, literary spaces of popular periodicals such as the *Strand*. John T. Tussaud once claimed that the macabre wax figures in the Chamber of Horrors were so shockingly effective that he had to 'write to the army requesting that they dissuade soldiers from trying to prove their courage by attempting to spend the night there' (McEvoy 2016: 68). According to an urban legend, Madame Tussaud's financially rewarded anyone with the courage to spend a night in the Chamber of Horrors – a myth that apparently originated in 1909 with the debut of the play *The Whip* on Drury Lane (McEvoy 2016: 218). Therefore, gothic horror stories such as 'The Power of Darkness' played to the fantasies of readers who imagined what it would be like to spend a night inside the waxworks.

'The Power of Darkness' also registers the economic synergy between popular periodicals such as the *Strand* and urban mass attractions. In an article considering the periodical as an environmental form, Cranfield specifies the readership of the *Strand* as a middle-class commuting market that consumed the magazine during railway travels, such that 'the *Strand*'s appearance, huge success, and subsequent domination of the periodical marketplace were based upon it responding to the emergence of a whole new space for reading (the train carriage)' (2014: 223). This observation suggests that the Musée Grévin would not have been out of reach, geographically or financially, for the employed, mobile readership of the *Strand*. Moreover, as Schwartz notes, the Musée Grévin 'constantly cultivated different sources for, and sites of, publicity' (1998: 117), efforts that specifically included attracting British bourgeois tourists. The museum 'worked with the British Thomas Cook tours, placed large albums containing photographs of the dioramas in major hotel lobbies in Paris such as the Grand Hôtel and the Continental, and in hotels at the thermal stations and seaside resorts' (ibid.). Thus the *Strand* profited by bringing this well-advertised attraction to their readers, just as the Musée Grévin profited from the publicity of being featured in 'The Power of Darkness.' The tale also promoted economic synergy with domestic institutions, especially Madame Tussaud's. Although the story is set in the Musée Grévin, after exploring its interior and wax groups, Edward declares that the museum is just like Madame Tussaud's (Apr 1905: 443). Moreover, Nesbit makes the inside of the Musée Grévin resemble its British counterpart, as the gory depictions of the Christian martyrs and the severed heads suggest the Chamber of Horrors at Madame Tussaud's far more so than the relatively conservative and artistic Musée Grévin. These settings, and the sensational events of the tale, would have piqued the interest of readers who had not yet seen Madame Tussaud's, and perhaps inspired return visits for those who had. Hoberman points out that the *Strand*'s copious advertisements 'often borrowed format and even characters from the magazine: Sherlock Holmes, who made his first appearance in the *Strand* in 1891, appears in two 1903 advertisements, one for a constipation cure, another for a cigar' (2004: 7). Considering how *Strand* advertisements turned to fiction for material, one might recognise how 'The Power of Darkness' presents the inverse case: fictional material functioning as advertisement, which resounds with Ellen Garvey's argument that ads and stories 'each helped naturalize one another for their viewers or reader' (ibid.). Interestingly enough, later versions of 'The Power of Darkness' published in books include an addition to Vincent's description of the Musée Grévin. Comparing that institution to its British rival, the narrator declares that the 'exhibition of Madame Tussaud – in these days, at any rate – is the work of bourgeois for a bourgeois class' (Nesbit 2006: 181). While this line might represent a late addition lamenting the fall of the museum to a vulgar tabloid entertainment, it is just as easy to imagine it being killed by *Strand* editors, who would have not only seen it as insulting to readers, but also destructive of the economic mutualism outlined above; one could not, after all, have one British national institution disparaging another.

Notes

1. For a discussion of Nesbit's work in the *New Age*, see Lee Garver's chapter in this volume.
2. Edward received his scare when he mistook a statue for a ghost, highlighting the threat the wax figures pose. Edward's fright recalls an incident from Nesbit's youth, in which she woke in the middle of the night to a 'corpse laid out under white draperies, and at its foot a skeleton with luminous skull and outstretched bony arm' (Briggs 1987: 20). The corpse turned out to be a white dress draped over an ottoman, and the glowing skull nothing more than the globe of a lit gas lamp. Apropos to 'The Power of Darkness' and its exploration of the imagination as a source of terror – as that which imbues inanimate objects like wax figures with malicious life – Nesbit rationalises her fearful hallucination by claiming 'that [it] was not reason's hour. Imagination held sway' (ibid.).
3. Notably, at this time, editions of the *Strand* ended with a 'Curiosities' section boasting wonders from around the world, bespeaking its readership's appetite for the sensational.
4. Discussing Edward's boyhood scare, Vincent tells him, 'Oh, it's nothing to be ashamed of; some women are afraid of mice or spiders. I say, does Rose know you're a coward?' (Apr 1905: 445). This insult feminises Edward, recalling Vincent's use of 'schoolgirl' as a slur, while implicitly associating femininity with cowardice.

Works Cited

Briggs, Julia. 1987. *A Woman of Passion*. London: Hutchinson.
Cairney, Maria. 2007. '"The Healing Art of Detection" Sherlock Holmes and the Disease of Crime in the *Strand Magazine*.' *Clues: A Journal of Detection* 26.1: 62–74.
Chan, Winnie. 2008. 'The Linked Excitements of L. T. Meade and . . . in the *Strand* Magazine.' *Scribbling Women and the Short Story Form: Approaches by American and British Women Writers*. Ed. Ellen Burton Harrington. New York: Peter Lang. 60–73.
Cranfield, J. L. 2012. 'Chivalric Machines: the Boer War, the Male Body, and the Grand Narrative in *The Strand Magazine*.' *Victorian Literature and Culture* 40: 549–73.
—. 2013. 'Arthur Conan Doyle, H. G. Wells and *The Strand Magazine*'s Long 1901: From Baskerville to the Moon.' *English Literature in Transition, 1880–1920* 56.1: 3–32.
—. 2014. 'Sherlock's Slums: The Periodical as an Environmental Form.' *Textual Practice* 28.2: 215–41.
Freeman, Nick. 2008. 'E. Nesbit's New Woman Gothic.' *Women's Writing* 15.3: 454–69.
Freud, Sigmund. 2003. *The Uncanny*. New York: Penguin Books.
Hibbert, Christopher. 1981. *The Days of the French Revolution*. New York: Morrow Quill Paperbacks.
Hoberman, Ruth. 2004. 'Constructing the Turn-of-the-Century Shopper: Narratives about Purchased Objects in the *Strand* Magazine, 1891–1910.' *Victorian Periodicals Review* 37.1: 1–17.
Hurley, Kelly. 1996. *The Gothic Body*. Cambridge: Cambridge University Press.
Kristeva, Julia. 1982. *The Powers of Horror*. New York: Columbia University Press.

McEvoy, Emma. 2016. *Gothic Tourism*. New York: Palgrave MacMillan.
Margree, Victoria. 2014. 'The Feminist Orientation in Edith Nesbit's Gothic Short Fiction.' *Women's Writing* 21.4: 425–43.
Melman, Billie. 2006. *The Culture of History*. Oxford: Oxford University Press.
Nesbit, Edith. 2006. 'The Power of Darkness.' *The Power of Darkness: Tales of Terror*. Ed. David Stuart Davies. Ware: Wordsworth Editions.
Park, Sojin. 2010. '"Magic Imperialism": The Logic of Magic in Edith Nesbit's Fantasy Novels.' *English Language and Literature* 56.10: 501–17.
Pittard, Christopher. 2007. '"Cheap, Healthful Literature": *The Strand Magazine*, Fictions of Crime, and Purified Reading Communities.' *Victorian Periodicals Review* 40.1: 1–23.
Pound, Reginald. 1966. *The Strand Magazine 1891–1950*. London: Heinemann.
Schwartz, Vanessa R. 1998. *Spectacular Realities*. Berkeley: University of California Press.
Von Schlosser, Julius. 2008. 'History of Portraiture in Wax.' Trans. James Michael Loughridge. *Ephemeral Bodies*. Ed. Roberta Panzanelli. Los Angeles: Getty Research Institute. 171–314.
Warner, Marina. 2006. *Phantasmagoria*. Oxford: Oxford University Press.

Part V
Social Movements

Social Movements: Introduction

Carey Snyder

THE PERIODICALS THAT proliferated in Britain from the 1890s to the 1920s played a central role in propelling a wide range of movements, which significantly reshaped women's political, economic, and social realities. As the authors of *Feminist Media History* have documented, 'women's movements used print media to organize, mobilize, disseminate ideas, and engage with the social and political groups and structures around them' (DiCenzo et al. 2011: 29). This section contributes to scholarship on feminist print culture by exploring a largely neglected archive of periodicals associated with the intertwined movements for women's suffrage, socialism, birth control, and esotericism.

Among the movements that most radically reshaped women's experience in the twentieth century was that for women's suffrage, inaugurated by the first parliamentary petition for the cause in 1867. As periodicals of the day record, suffrage agitation reached its zenith in the decade leading up to the First World War, with headline-generating mass demonstrations and rising acts of militancy, including window-breaking and arson, as well as the hunger-striking of imprisoned suffragettes and their consequent subjugation to government-sanctioned force-feeding. (The WSPU declared a hiatus on militant activism during the war, and the vote was granted to women over thirty who met certain property qualifications in 1918; and to women twenty-one and over – that is, on an equal basis with men – in 1928.) As scholars have documented, the militants were adept at harnessing the power of modern publicity in forwarding their political aims (e.g. Green 1997; Lysack 2008). To that end, militants and constitutional suffragists alike founded their own periodicals, with the twin aims of compensating for the distortions and negligence of the mainstream press and distinguishing the differing suffrage organisations' approaches and viewpoints from one another. In this section, Krista Lysack examines the reciprocal religious and political objectives of the little-known periodical, the *Church League for Women's Suffrage Monthly Paper*, which Lysack argues emulates but also repurposes the 'template' of leading suffrage journals such as *Votes for Women* (discussed in Snyder's chapter on Hastings in Part III: Key Literary Figures). Lysack shows that the *Monthly Paper* borrows the rhetoric of militancy from the secular suffrage movement – rhetoric already infused with religious metaphors of martyrdom and conversion – to express its pacifist methods of suffrage advocacy.

Like the suffrage movement, the socialist movement in Britain generated – and was sustained by – a robust periodical network in which women took an active part. According to the authors of *Socialist Women*, June Hannam and Karen Hunt, 'the woman question was debated extensively from the 1880s on' in British socialist organisations, including the Social Democratic Federation (SDF) and the Fabian Society (both founded in 1884), and the Independent Labour Party (ILP), founded in 1893 (2002: 56). Many women held dual memberships in socialist and suffrage organisations; indeed, the leaders of the WSPU, Emmeline and Christabel Pankhurst, had close ties with the ILP until 1906 and patterned the organisation's early activism on that of labour organisations. As Hannam and Hunt document, a wide range of socialist women negotiated overlapping commitments to issues of class and gender oppression, often within the pages of an expanding socialist press. Elizabeth Carolyn Miller deepens our understanding of this dynamic in her essay, arguing that such columns articulated a collective identity for socialist-feminists that was oppositional within the largely masculinist socialist counterpublic. Such columns, Miller argues, express links between patriarchy and capitalism, but do so within a conventionally feminine idiom, using domestic metaphors and tropes of intimacy.

Another print-driven counterpublic in which women worked to gain a foothold was the birth control movement, which began to take shape in Britain in 1877 with the formation of the Malthusian League and its paper, the *Malthusian*. It was Annie Besant who proposed forming the league, after she and Charles Bradlaugh were acquitted for obscenity charges for distributing information about contraception. A socialist, suffragist, and theosophist, as well as a birth control advocate, Besant epitomises the intertwining of social movements and the periodicals that propelled them. As the Besant-Bradlaugh trial suggests, the *Malthusian* first propagandised for population control at a time when distributing contraception or information about it was socially and legally condemned; these strictures began to relax in the postwar period, as indicated by birth control pioneer Marie Stopes's 1918 publication of her influential and bestselling book *Married Love*, and by her establishment in 1921 of the first birth control clinic in the UK. As Layne Parish Craig details in her contribution to this volume, the *Malthusian* was dominated by masculine voices that curiously effaced women's bodies from the discussion of a proposed wartime birth strike; yet female contributors and correspondents created 'fissures' in the periodical's masculinist ideology by inserting representations of women's embodied experience into this debate. Craig's essay contributes to modern periodical scholarship that explores how (women) readers can push back against editorial platforms and agendas (e.g. Fraser et al. 2003: 73–80; Beetham 1996: 3–14).

Finally, Mark S. Morrisson's essay focuses on women writers' contributions to what he describes as 'a vast network' of periodicals concerned with the esoteric and the occult. Explaining the appeal of these unorthodox belief systems to women in particular, Joy Dixon notes that 'the conservative churchmen who dominated both Anglicanism and Nonconformity proved slow to endorse women's rights,' whereas occult alternatives enabled resourceful women to negotiate a feminist version of spirituality and to assume positions of power and authority in affiliated organisations (2003: 3). (Lysack's study of the *Church League for Women's Suffrage Monthly Paper* demonstrates that there were also some women who managed to reconcile traditional religious faith with women's rights advocacy.) Morrisson traces how a set of women writers, editors, and publishers capitalised on the growing network of occult periodicals to disseminate their views and to 'build [their] own authority,' helping to spread a 'distinctly modern fascination' with the occult in Britain.

These movement-based periodicals not only documented social change, but helped to engineer it by positing sexuality, religion, and the occult as potential, if problematic, means of modern women's agency. This section helps expand the borders of modernist studies beyond the literary, while at the same time suggesting provocative intersections between the modernist women writers discussed elsewhere in this collection and those who navigated and helped create the networks of social-movement media.

Works Cited

Beetham, Margaret. 1996. *A Magazine of Her Own? Domesticity and Desire in the Woman's Magazine, 1800–1914*. London: Routledge.

DiCenzo, Maria, Lucy Delap and Leila Ryan. 2011. *Feminist Media History: Suffrage, Periodicals, and the Public Sphere*. Basingstoke: Palgrave Macmillan.

Dixon, Joy. 2003. *Divine Feminine: Theosophy and Feminism in England*. Baltimore: Johns Hopkins University Press.

Fraser, Hilary, Stephanie Green and Judith Johnston. 2003. *Gender and the Victorian Periodical*. Cambridge: Cambridge University Press.

Green, Barbara. 1997. *Spectacular Confessions: Autobiography, Performative Activism, and the Sites of Suffrage 1905–1938*. New York: St Martin's Press.

Hannam, June and Karen Hunt. 2002. *Socialist Women: Britain, 1880s to 1920s*. London: Routledge.

Lysack, Krista. 2008. *Come Buy, Come Buy: Shopping and the Culture of Consumption in Victorian Women's Writing*. Athens: Ohio University Press.

24

WOMEN, PERIODICALS, AND ESOTERICISM IN MODERNIST-ERA PRINT CULTURE

Mark S. Morrisson

THE PERIOD FROM THE last few decades of the nineteenth century through the late 1920s witnessed a widespread and distinctly modern fascination with things 'occult' or 'esoteric' in Britain, the United States, and much of Western Europe. The mid-Victorian Spiritualist movement, noted for its efforts to communicate with the dead, was later joined by a rapidly growing interest in such subjects as alchemy, witchcraft, and ritual magic, along with wide-ranging investigations of esoteric threads of Christianity, Judaism, and Eastern religions such as Buddhism or Hinduism. Scholars have attempted to define the features common to the disparate practices and ideas that were drawn together in this new esotericism. Antoine Faivre, for instance, identifies several commonalities: a belief in 'symbolic and real correspondences . . . among all parts of the universe, both seen and unseen'; a sense of a 'Living Nature' animated by a life energy or divinity; an understanding that the imagination is capable of exploring unknown realms between the material and divine; a belief in the spiritual transmutation of humans to realise their connection to the divine; a belief in the fundamental connections among spiritual traditions as evidence of a 'primordial Tradition'; and finally an understanding that 'an esoteric teaching can or must be transmitted from master to disciple following a preestablished channel, respecting a previously marked path' (1994: 14). Such beliefs were manifest in the Theosophical Society (founded in 1875) and several secret or well-known initiatory orders devoted to Hermetic or Rosicrucian wisdom, ritual magic, and even alchemy, such as the Hermetic Order of the Golden Dawn (1888), Aleister Crowley's A. A. (1907) and his Abbey of Thelema in Sicily (1920), and Dion Fortune's Fraternity (later Society) of the Inner Light (1922).

Rather than viewing this occultism or esotericism as an anti-modern backlash against a scientific age, some historians have emphasised the modernity, and even modernism, of these beliefs. Noting that those espousing the 'new occultism' thought of themselves as boldly modern, historian Alex Owen argues that they found it 'attractive partly because it offered a spiritual alternative to religious orthodoxy, but one that ostensibly operated without the requirement of faith' (2004: 12). Occultism was thus, she continues, 'intrinsic to a contemporary shift in ideas about what might constitute belief and unbelief or mark the limits of the sacred and the profane' (ibid.). The emphasis upon initiation, ritual magic, and connections of the mind and soul to an unseen world, Owen observes, contributed to 'a newly conceptualized subjectivity, that innovative sense of self that so often characterized those self-identified "we moderns" of the *fin de siècle*' (2004: 7).

A remarkable feature of this new esotericism was the high degree of participation by women. Unlike many of the masonic orders upon which it based its initiation system, the Golden Dawn initiated women, as did its successor orders. The Theosophical Society not only admitted women but was founded by and for many years presided over by women. Joy Dixon argues that 'theosophy held a special appeal for women, especially those in the feminist movement. Late-Victorian and Edwardian feminists were substantially over-represented within the TS and within esoteric religions more broadly; almost 10 per cent of prominent women active in the feminist movement were involved in the Theosophical Society or similar movements' (2010: 219).[1]

A key feature of the new esotericism that also marked its modernity – and was a significant aspect of its access to women – is the astonishing proliferation of periodicals that publicised its aspirations and concerns, shaped its very nature in the public sphere, and made it a widespread phenomenon rather than something practised in isolation and secrecy. As I have argued elsewhere, a major difference between modern esotericism and the ancient and medieval sources from which it often drew inspiration was this public dimension and the periodical culture that created and sustained it. If the occult revival emphasised esoteric wisdom and initiation, it did so by building exoteric institutions outside of the traditional framework of group worship and belief organised by established churches (Morrisson 2008: 1–22).

A vast network of periodicals supported various esoteric movements, helping legitimise esoteric knowledge, support its truth claims in the public sphere, and expand its reach. These periodicals ranged from the *Spiritual Magazine*, *Spiritualist Newspaper*, and *Light*, which reached middle-class, educated, metropolitan spiritualist readers, to *Two Worlds*, designed for provincial readers (Oppenheim 1985: 46); they also included Theosophical papers, such as the *Theosophist, Lucifer* (edited by Blavatsky and Mabel Collins and then Annie Besant, later becoming the *Theosophical Review*), the *Irish Theosophist*, and G. R. S. Mead's *Quest*. Still other esoteric periodicals were *Inner Light Magazine*, edited by Dion Fortune; Aleister Crowley's *Equinox*; and the *Journal of the Alchemical Society*. Some periodicals, such as *Unknown World* and the *Occult Review*, covered esoteric and hermetic subjects but were not connected to any specific movement or order. As this chapter will argue, women's increasing access to careers in journalism, periodical literature, and magazine editing helped them become major voices in esotericism.

Women and Spiritual Authority

The proliferation of women as authors of occult texts raises many issues for feminist historiography. Miriam Wallraven has shown that the imaginative literature of occultism can reveal much about women's efforts to grapple with the 'gendered restrictions in religious traditions, in new spiritual movements, and in society as a whole' (2015: 3). We can augment this analysis of modern occultism by exploring (if briefly) the professional roles open to women in modern Britain.

While women were making modest gains in education and professional career paths in the later nineteenth century – the UK Medical Act of 1876 opened the door to women's receiving medical training, for example, and two years later, the University of London became the first UK university to award degrees to women – they were still excluded from many positions of influence. Established Christian churches, for the most part, were far behind the medical profession in allowing women to hold positions of authority. In the nineteenth century, as Hugh McLeod and others have shown, women were more involved in the religious life of their families and communities than men, yet 'the clergy, ministers and priests of the five largest denominations (the Anglicans, Wesleyan Methodists, Independents, Baptists and Roman Catholics) were all exclusively male' (1996: 160). Noting the disjunction between an explosion of women's participation in religious life in the second half of the nineteenth century (women were leading Sunday schools and were highly involved in missionary work, and up to two-thirds of congregants were women) and their lack of formal clerical authority, Pamela J. Walker argues that 'debates about women's place and role can be found in every aspect of British religious life throughout the period. Women's preaching was both a contentious theological question, as well as a practical concern which remained unresolved throughout the twentieth century' (2010: 94).

The occult revival offered spiritual alternatives to churches and traditional religion that also afforded women new roles and allowed newly modern syntheses of science and spiritual traditions. Indeed, the mid-nineteenth century had seen an unusual role emerge for women: as spirit mediums. In 1848, Kate and Margaret Fox, two young daughters of a poor family in Hydesville, New York, attracted widespread attention for their claims to be able to communicate with a spirit haunting their house through an alphabetical code that the spirit knocked out for them. A frenzy of seances and other such activities quickly spread across the United States and to Britain, launching a movement that came to be known as 'spiritualism,' which waxed and waned for the next eighty years. (Margaret Fox admitted in the late 1880s that the knockings had been a hoax, and the Society for Psychical Research in late Victorian Britain debunked many spirit mediums' claims, but the practices and beliefs endured.) In Britain, what had originally been a phenomenon of the working- and lower-middle classes spread to middle- and upper-class believers and dabblers and even caught the fancy of the aristocracy. The spirit mediums themselves tended to be from working-class backgrounds, but they were brought into the private homes of wealthier families for private seances (Oppenheim 1985: 28–9; McLeod 1996: 53).

But the power of those (mostly female) spirit mediums rested, seemingly paradoxically, upon their passivity. They claimed to act only as a 'medium' through which the dead communicated with the living. Alex Owen notes that the conformity of that role to Victorian notions of femininity (that is, moral and spiritual superiority and passivity) granted women a form of spiritual authority that allowed them freedom to transgress gender and sexuality norms of the day:

> the Victorian séance room became a battle ground across which the tensions implicit in the acquisition of gendered subjectivity and the assumption of female spiritual power were played out. Renunciation of the conscious personality was the price paid for the authoritative voice. The ultimate irony of spirit mediumship, and the measure of its adherence to prescriptive norms, lay in the fact that it operated around a fundamental power/powerlessness duality. (1989: 11)

By the late nineteenth and early twentieth centuries, some of the mediums used their claims of spirit channelling differently: the spirits (or hidden mahatmas) no longer communicated to others in the room but, instead, directly to the medium, and they communicated occult wisdom and, above all, texts. The authority of texts revealed through this new kind of medium – such as Helena Petrovna Blavatsky, founder of Theosophy; Mabel Collins, a major Theosophical author; or Dion Fortune, founder of the Society of the Inner Light – could be immense. Notably, it took the strategic use of periodical culture to bring those 'revealed' texts into the broader public sphere and position the female 'scribes' as major spiritual authorities. Blavatsky died in 1891, and most of her enigmatic career falls far outside the boundaries of this volume; therefore, I turn to Mabel Collins and Dion Fortune to explore the spiritual authority of the 'woman writer' created and contested within the occult periodical culture of the late Victorian and Edwardian eras.

Mabel Collins

Collins (1851–1927) is best known to Theosophists today as the author, or 'scribe,' of major spiritual treatises and the founding co-editor (with Blavatsky) of *Lucifer*, the most significant anglophone Theosophical magazine published in Britain. Much of Collins's authority originated, however, in her career as a successful popular romance novelist in late Victorian periodicals. The daughter of Mortimer Collins, a poet, mathematician, journalist, and newspaper editor (as well as an alcoholic and hopeless debtor), Collins had been publishing romance novels regularly in serial and book form since 1875. While many female authors of romance novels published under their married names, Collins did not, even though she was widely known in reviews and articles by her married name, Mrs Keningale Cook.[2] Her early works, with such titles as *An Innocent Sinner* (1877), *In the Flower of Her Youth* (1883), and *The Prettiest Woman in Warsaw* (1885), were reviewed favourably in mainstream journals of the period but were clearly understood in terms of popular romance fiction; noting Collins's relationship to a famous father with almost gossipy interest, reviewers praised the 'clever' novels of a Bohemian's daughter.[3] That affirmation was sometimes tempered by reproach. For instance, a reviewer in the 'Novels of the Week' section of the *Athenaeum* complained that *In the Flower of Her Youth* contained 'diatribe against our modern marriage law': 'Miss Collins' ably written story is likely to be well received, though its polemical side will not commend itself to common sense' (14 Apr 1883: 473–4). The romance novel and critical social commentary were deemed incompatible, and Collins's publisher at the time, F. V. White, clearly signalled the genre by which it wanted her novels to be recognised, advertising *In the Flower of Her Youth* among other new novels that would entertain rather than mobilise readers: *Facing the Footlights*, by Florence Marryat (daughter of Captain Frederick Marryat, a magazine editor and author of popular novels of naval combat); *A Peeress of 1882*, by Mrs Fraser; and *Out of the Pale*, by Mrs Eiloart (*Athenaeum* 20 Jan 1883: 73). While the other authors advertised were popular romance novelists of the late Victorian period, they had other distinctly modern commonalities with Mabel Collins. Florence Marryat was a divorcee who would become involved in the world of spiritualist seances, act on the stage, support herself as a writer, and use her authority as a popular novelist and daughter of a famous author to challenge the constraints of her gender as she founded and managed a school of journalism (Neisius). Mrs Fraser, wife of General Alexander Fraser, launched her successful writing career during the collapse of her marriage.

Elizabeth Eiloart, who published as Mrs C. J. Eiloart, was a writer of romance and children's fiction but also a suffragist and feminist; she became the editor of the feminist *English Woman's Journal* in 1864.

Collins's career as a romance novelist was well established by the time she began to write novels and spiritual treatises that emerged from her interest in mysticism, spiritualism (she served as a medium from time to time), and Theosophy in the 1870s and 1880s. This brought her work into occult-revival periodicals. Her novel *The Idyll of the White Lotus* had been serialised in the New York spiritualist magazine *Banner of Light* before being published in 1884 in book form by Reeves and Turner, a small London publisher and bookshop on the Strand (Peterson 1991: 187–8). That novel and the two major Theosophical treatises that followed it, *Light on the Path* (1885) and *Through the Gates of Gold* (1887), both 'written down by M. C.,' show the quick rise of Collins's reputation in the publishing world of Theosophy through an interesting hybrid publication strategy. *Light on the Path*, subtitled 'A Treatise Written for the Personal Use of Those Who Are Ignorant of the Eastern Wisdom, and Desire to Enter within Its Influence,' was published in book form by Reeves and Turner. But *Through the Gates of Gold* was first published by Ward and Downey, the British publisher of some of Collins's romance novels. Both books were then amplified in their influence by key Theosophical periodicals; *Lucifer* published further 'comments' on *Light on the Path* in its first volume in 1887–8. William Quan Judge, a founding member and General Secretary of the American section of the Theosophical Society, then catapulted Collins to greater heights of authority by publishing a commentary on *Through the Gates of Gold* in the March 1887 issue of *The Path*, his recently founded independent Theosophical magazine. Not just the book publication of Collins's treatises but also the game of 'open secrets' involving the identity of the author – M. C. – and the support of key figures in other Theosophical periodicals would be crucial in augmenting Collins's authority. In *The Path*, Quan wrote:

> The most notable book for guidance in Mysticism which has appeared since *Light on the Path* was written has just been published under the significant title of *Through the Gates of Gold*. Though the author's name is withheld, the occult student will quickly discern that it must proceed from a very high source. In certain respects the book may be regarded as a commentary on *Light on the Path*. . . . *Through the Gates of Gold* is a work to be kept constantly at hand for reference and study. It will surely take rank as one of the standard books of Theosophy. (Mar 1887: 372)

Such publicity – pronouncing Collins (and her mahatma) a 'very high source' and elevating two of her books to the status of 'standard books' of the movement – in one of the most important Theosophical periodicals in America led, in turn, to several new editions of *Through the Gates of Gold*. The book appeared in Boston, New York, and Chicago with different publishers, and then was brought out in England by George Redway, a significant commercial publishing house with extensive interest in esoteric subjects. The new Theosophical Publishing Society in London would soon be publishing all of Collins's Theosophical works.

The growing network of Theosophical periodicals was intricately connected and key to Theosophy's expansion. As Peter Washington notes:

Throughout the 1880s the Theosophical Society steadily recruited members. By 1885, 121 lodges had been chartered – 106 of them in India, Burma and Ceylon, where the Society had the bulk of its membership. Within a decade of Theosophy's foundation that membership was running into thousands, and distinguished converts included the poet Ella Wheeler Wilcox, Darwin's collaborator Alfred Russel Wallace and the inventor Thomas Edison. (1995: 68)

Growth in Britain, America, and Russia quickly followed. As I have argued elsewhere, the movement engaged early with periodical culture. Theosophical periodicals often included high production values, numerous illustrations, and offerings in virtually every periodical category – quarterly, monthly, and weekly – aimed at virtually every class of reader and at significantly lower purchase prices than most strictly commercial periodicals of each type (Morrisson 2008: 8).

The women in the Theosophical movement who created spiritual authority for themselves all brought significant experience as journalists to their Theosophical work. Blavatsky herself had written extensively for papers before moving the headquarters of the Theosophical Society to India and founding the first Theosophical journal, *The Theosophist*, in 1879. Anna Kingsford acquired and edited a commercial women's paper, *Lady's Own Paper*, in 1872, turning it to her spiritual and reformist causes before becoming one of the first British women to become a medical doctor in 1880, an opponent of vivisection, an advocate of vegetarianism, and the president of the British Theosophical Society in 1883. Annie Besant had significant experience with radical political papers before her move into Theosophy, and her ascendancy to the presidency of the Society in 1907 and to the editorship of the *Theosophical Review* cemented her position as a spiritual leader of the new esotericism.

Collins herself presented perhaps the clearest example of the esoteric version of the 'New Woman' who could mobilise her skills as a journalist and popular writer to propel herself to occult power. Her career as a popular novelist and a Theosophical writer was established before she hosted Madame Blavatsky at her suburban London cottage in 1887 and launched *Lucifer* as Blavatsky's co-editor. For its launch, *Lucifer* needed Collins's reputation as a novelist – indeed, it needed a new novel by her to serialise – as much as she needed the esoteric credentials it conferred upon her. The ads for the 15 September 1887 first issue of *Lucifer*, such as the one placed in the *Athenaeum* (24 Sep 1887: 416), simply listed the new monthly's contents but gave Collins's novel, *The Blossom and the Fruit*, a subtitle that would resonate with her career as a romance novelist veering into increasingly occult paths: 'A Tale of Love and Magic.' Within the magazine itself, which was meant to reach Theosophists as well as a broader readership, the first page of the novel marked this dual appeal, reading: 'The Blossom and the Fruit: A Tale of Love and Magic by Mabel Collins, Author of "The Prettiest Woman in Warsaw" *etc.*, *etc*... And Scribe of "The Idyll of the White Lotus" and "Through the Gates of Gold"' (*Lucifer* 15 Sep 1887: 23).

The Idyll of the White Lotus (1884) was the first of several works Collins claimed to have written by channelling Egyptian priests who passed through her room as she worked – hence the distinction between 'author' and 'scribe' in *Lucifer*. Moreover, in both the serialisation and the book form of *The Blossom and the Fruit*, Collins included this preface: 'THIS strange story has come to me from a far country and was brought to me in a mysterious manner; I claim only to be the scribe and the editor. In this capacity, however, it is I who am answerable to the public and the critics. I therefore ask in advance one favour only of the reader; that he will accept (while reading this story) the theory of the reincarnation of souls as a living fact. M. C.' (1888: [ii]). The book edition of the novel replaced the periodical's subtitle, 'A Tale of Love and Magic,' with a new subtitle that left behind all genre cues for her romance work. The new title was *The Blossom and the Fruit; A True Story of a Black Magician*. Authorship was ascribed not simply to 'M. C.' but to 'Mabel Collins . . . And— —.' Many Theosophists believed that the mysterious anonymous co-author was none other than Blavatsky herself (Farnell 5).

Because of her reputation as a successful novelist and the growing popularity of Theosophy in Britain in the 1880s and 1890s, Collins's Theosophical and esoteric writings were received well even in the mainstream press. Even as respectable a journal as the *Athenaeum* announced in its 'Literary Gossip' section for 13 August 1887 that Redway's upcoming 'books, more or less concerned with the black arts' included, along with works by Golden Dawn luminaries A. E. Waite and MacGregor Mathers as well as Theosophy co-founder H. S. Olcott, 'the first number of *Lucifer: a Theosophical Monthly,* edited by Madame Blavatsky and Miss Mabel Collins (Mrs. Keningale Cook)' (214–15). A *Saturday Review* piece on 'Occultism,' reviewing Collins's *Light on the Path* and Franz Hartmann's *Magic*, notes that 'occultism and theosophy now enjoy no inconsiderable vogue, and have a very respectable literature of their own' (23 June 1888: 772). The reviewer mentions the new '"theosophical monthly" entitled *Lucifer,* "designed to bring light to the hidden things of darkness," under the editorship of H. P. Blavatsky and Mabel Collins' and praises Collins's treatise for being, 'so far as we can gather from the mystic language in which it is couched . . . intended to guide the footsteps of those who have discarded the forms of religion while retaining the moral principle to its fullest extent' (ibid.). Indeed, the mainstream press displayed significant interest in occult publications, including the large number of occult periodicals. In the Edwardian period and beyond, W. T. Stead's popular *Review of Reviews* regularly included sections such as 'The Occult Magazines' (Dec 1912: 689) and 'Theosophical and Psychic Magazines' (Mar 1913: 318).

Having set herself up through her periodical and book publications first as a successful writer of popular romances and then as a writer of channelled occult fiction and co-editor of Theosophy's flagship British journal, Collins could make the turn that Blavatsky herself had made, from a spirit medium offering her personal authority as a purveyor of spiritual truths to a spiritual authority in the public sphere. With the profile she had gained as co-editor of *Lucifer,* her occult work was now published under the same name she used for her romance novels, Mabel Collins. (She continued to earn income under pseudonyms; for instance, she wrote a weekly 'Tea Table Talk' column on such non-Theosophical topics as clothing, make-up, and dog spas for the *World* under the name 'Flower o'the May' (Farnell 4).)

Though mediums, astral travel, and automatic writing were a major part of the occult revival, that form of authorship was often not mentioned in reviews published in the mainstream press. For instance, the *Saturday Review*'s positive discussion of Collins's *The Light on the Path* does not mention its mode of dictation. In the occult world, however, the authority of the writer (as well as her channelled sources) was a paramount issue. An argument about whether *The Light on the Path* had been dictated by one of Blavatsky's Theosophical mahatmas, as Collins had originally claimed (at Blavatsky's prompting), or simply arose from a vision (as Collins privately asserted in a letter a few years later) created a rift in the Theosophical world in 1889 that eventually played out in the Chicago-based progressive spiritualist weekly *Religio-Philosophical Journal*; the English spiritualist journal, *Light*; various Theosophical journals; and eventually in the *New York Sun*. (The veracity of Blavatsky's letters from her mahatmas had already been called into question by the famous Hodgson Report of the Society for Psychical Research in 1885, and in the early years of Theosophy in England, the existence and authority of those masters were crucial to the acceptance of Blavatsky's writings as foundational texts of a spiritual movement.) Yet in spite of her falling out with Blavatsky, Collins had been established as an occult author of interest to a broader public as well as an authority within the periodical networks of the occult revival. She would be referenced regularly and positively in occult periodicals until her death in 1929.

Dion Fortune

Like Collins, Kingsford, Blavatsky, Besant, and other leading women in modernist-era esotericism, Dion Fortune (1890–1946) used the period's wide range of periodicals and book publishers astutely to build her own authority, disseminate her esoteric vision publicly, and enter disputes on a wide range of scientific and social issues of the day. Some of these exchanges with other occultists amounted to contests over authority, and the periodicals were clearly the place to make such claims public.

From early in her career, Fortune saw the value of using esoteric fiction to promote and illustrate the concepts laid out in her treatises and essays. As Fortune would later explain, 'The "Mystical Qabalah" [her chief non-fiction work] gives the theory, but the novels give the practice.... [T]hose who study the "Mystical Qabalah" with the help of the novels get the keys of the Temple put into their hands' (2003: v). Her first publication as 'Dion Fortune' (rather than under her maiden name, Violet Firth) comprised stories from her first published fiction, *The Secrets of Dr Taverner* (now an occult classic). Fortune had already been significantly involved in esoteric orders for some years. As a woman, she could not be admitted into the Freemasonry of her mentor in psychology, Theodore Moriarty, the inspiration for Dr Taverner (Richardson 1991: 82–3), but she had been involved in Theosophy and been initiated into the Alpha et Omega and then the Stella Matutina, both Golden Dawn successor orders. Yet rather than publish her occult-themed detective stories in an occult periodical, she placed them in 1922 in a widely circulating literary monthly, the *Royal Magazine*, published by the newspaper magnate Sir Arthur Pearson. The *Royal Magazine* published popular fiction, including 'Miss Marple' detective stories by Agatha Christie. Fortune's choice to publish in the *Royal Magazine* thus flagged the Taverner stories as recognisable genre fiction, even though these medical/psychological mysteries with occult dimensions diverged significantly from typical detective stories. Though she had turned to occult publisher Rider to bring out her 1924 book, *The Esoteric Philosophy of Love and Marriage* (a treatise she prepared after beginning her experiments as a trance medium), Fortune chose commercial London publisher Noel Douglas to bring out the first book edition of *The Secrets of Dr Taverner* in 1926.

Gareth Knight notes that 'During this period Dion Fortune wrote several esoteric novels to illustrate the possible practical application of the content of her textbooks and articles in her house journal, the *Inner Light Magazine*' (Knight, 'About Dion Fortune'). The Society of the Inner Light, which possesses an archive of this rare magazine, explains that she first published much of her non-fiction work there, including *The Mystical Qabalah* ('Dion Fortune'). Moreover, Fortune often published articles on her esoteric novels in the magazine and hoped that identification with the characters in her novels would allow a broader range of readers safe access to the positive psychological effects of ritual magic (Knight, 'Magical Novels'). By the 1930s, when she had assumed a significant authority in the world of esotericism, she followed a strategy to consolidate and expand it. She published the esoteric works that needed new audiences – works such as *The Mystical Qabalah* – as well as the novels that were to make their teachings psychologically available to readers with the well-established and reputable publisher Williams & Norgate. Williams & Norgate's list included scientific works by T. H. Huxley and others as well as periodicals such as *Natural History Review* and the *Hibbert Journal*. The house must have viewed Fortune's esoteric writings as appealing; Williams & Norgate published several of her books, including the esoteric novels *The Winged Bull: A Romance of Modern Magic* and *The Goat-Foot God*.

But Fortune still had work to do to consolidate her gains, and again, periodicals other than her house magazine played a necessary role. Ralph Shirley's *Occult Review* (published by Rider) was perhaps the best known of the esoteric periodicals not aligned with any particular order or society, and it opened its pages to debate among its readers and contributors on a monthly basis. Fortune used it to establish her reputation outside the readers of *Inner Light Magazine*, and between 1925 and 1935, she published thirty articles in the *Occult Review*. Many of these pieces were later collected or developed into books, and several explored what Fortune saw as the scientific basis of occultism and its relationship to psychology.[4]

Perhaps because it was not aligned with a specific movement or order, the *Occult Review* was an important venue. Mabel Collins published fifteen articles in the journal from its founding in 1905 to her death in the late 1920s, but she also published ten letters to the editor (often in response to other content published in the journal, including discussions of esotericism, vegetarianism, and vivisection). Moreover, Collins reviewed works in its pages, and seven of her books were reviewed in it during this late stage of her career. Fortune used the journal in the same way, both reviewing work and seeing her own books reviewed in it, and she used the regular Correspondence section to participate in a significant skirmish over her esoteric authority.

In the November 1928 issue of the *Occult Review*, Fortune's article 'The Left-Hand Path, Part One' used her signature synthesis of psychoanalytic and esoteric concepts to make an argument about the occult sublimation of sex force. In the next issue, Winnifred Leisenring, a Theosophist of some standing in London circles, took her to task for suggesting that sex force can be sublimated, arguing that 'The persistence of such old and erroneous theories gives support to the contention of men of science that "education" should include a knowledge of the elementary principles of physics and biology' (*Occult Review* Dec 1928: 408). Fortune then sent in her own letter to the editor, responding directly to Leisenring's rejection of her theory by invoking her own scientific authorities: 'My theory of the sublimation of sex forces is based firstly on the work of Dr Freud of Vienna, and secondly on the researches of Professor Spearman, head of the University College Psychology Laboratory, into the nature of General Energy. The work of both of these authorities has found general acceptance and has passed beyond the region of speculation. I think, therefore, that I may claim that I was not without adequate scientific grounds in making the statement to which Mrs. Leisenring takes exception' (*Occult Review* Jan 1929: 51). She then recommends her own volume, *The Problem of Purity*, and suggests that Leisenring 'apparently has not realized that in discussing sex energy we are in the realm of psychology, not of physics' (ibid.). Finally, she accuses Leisenring of lacking proper scientific training: 'Common sense, in the absence of technical knowledge, is an insufficient criterion of judgment in any science, and no dogmatic statement, however strongly worded, carries any weight of itself; it needs to be supported by argument, data, and the citation of authorities' (ibid.).

This exchange of letters (which continued into February 1929) had become a contest over occult authority – one played out many times in the pages of esoteric periodicals. Like Collins, Fortune, and many of the women who took their often controversial agendas into various periodical networks, Leisenring was a presence in multiple types of journals. She had been a subscriber and active voice in the discussion circles of Dora Marsden's 'Weekly Feminist Review,' the *Freewoman*, during that journal's short life in 1911–12, and had been the General Secretary of the Blavatsky Institute and the Theosophical summer school at Peebles, Scotland, which Marsden twice attended.[5] Moreover, Leisenring was involved in fundraising to relaunch the *Freewoman* when finances forced it to cease publication in 1912, and the Blavatsky Institute headquarters had provided Marsden with office space for the *Freewoman* (Dixon 2003: 195). Leisenring had also been involved in productive dialogue with Marsden within the pages of Marsden's successor journal, the *New Freewoman*, known to most scholars of modernism for its bringing philosophical and political Egoism into contact with a significant set of literary figures, including Rebecca West, Ezra Pound, and Richard Aldington. In what Bruce Clarke calls the *New Freewoman*'s 'wild dialogism,' Marsden would often engage responses to her own articles in the journal, including, for instance, remarks on race alongside Leisenring's 'A Race of Individuals' (1996: 104). Such debates within the pages of a single journal were a heady feature of the periodicals of the day.

Leisenring's February 1929 letter in the *Occult Review* used every form of authority available to a woman who had mastered self-promotion in the esoteric public sphere. Defending herself against Fortune's claim that her arguments 'serve no useful purpose,' Leisenring asserted her hard-earned authority: 'twenty-five years' experience of "things occult" and otherwise may be useful to some few who are bewildered in the mazes of modern "occultism" and by the multiplicity of teachers and diverse authorities' (*Occult Review* Feb 1929: 119). Dion Fortune, Leisenring implied, had not yet earned her position in modern occultism. Much of the rest of the rebuttal focused on a distinction between the two women's understanding of the mind. Fortune, with her training in psychology and reading in psychoanalysis, had based her arguments essentially upon Freudian psychoanalytic views of mind and drive. Leisenring dismissed her as a materialist, noting that the mind is not part of nature at all (Feb 1929: 120). And in response to Fortune's comment about 'argument, data and the citation of authorities' (Feb 1929: 119), Leisenring proceeded to cite scientists published in the *Times* and *Nature*, but then fell back on the authority of Blavatsky on the subject of divine consciousness and spirit versus animal mind in sublimation. Refusing even to mention Fortune by name, Leisenring concluded that

> the psychologists on whose authority the 'sublimation' of physiological energy is declared possible, make no pretensions to occult knowledge. The greatest authority on Occultism in modern times in Europe, H. P. Blavatsky, made a fundamental distinction between real occultism (true wisdom) and the various occult sciences based on knowledge of the essence of things in the realm of *material* Nature. (Feb 1929: 121)

In short, Leisenring invokes the weight of her own authority, derived from Blavatsky, to dismiss the upstart Fortune. But she also invokes published scientific research and suggests that her own 'year among post-graduates in the psychological laboratory of Toronto University under Dr. August Kirschman of Leipsig, entitles [her] to speak from experience' (*Occult Review* Feb 1929: 119). Academic credentials and authority, often invoked in esoteric magazines by including degrees along with names, might seem beside the point given the ultimate recourse to the cult of Blavatsky. Nevertheless, Leisenring, who proudly included 'BA' by her name in some publications, could lord that authority over Fortune, who had no university degree or medical licence, though she had attended courses in psychology and psychoanalysis with a Professor Flugel (a member of the Society for Psychical Research) at the University of London and worked as a lay Freudian psychotherapist at the Medico-Psychological Clinic in London's Brunswick Square. She practised as a lay analyst before the war, but the British Medical Association refused to accord full recognition to the profession (Richardson 1991: 52). By 1914, while she was turning her attentions to her magical encounters, she – like many of her fellow occultists – continued to bring a psychotherapist's sensibility to her occult practice.

I have elsewhere turned to Roy Wallis's term 'sanitization' and Thomas Gieryn's notion of 'boundary-work' to describe public efforts to demarcate the scientific from the pseudoscientific and to conceptualise the insistent claims to scientific legitimacy by occult authors (from Blavatsky to Crowley) and the journals that supported them (Morrisson 2007 and 2008; Wallis 1985; Gieryn 1983). But skirmishes *within* the periodical communities of esoteric Britain suggest the degree to which this boundary work was structured along the same fault lines in struggles over authority between women who only recently, and partially, could claim scientific training and access.

New Occult Uses of Periodicals

While periodicals such as Crowley's *Equinox* or the various Theosophical magazines reflect the consolidation of power by various feuding factions within the offshoots of the original Golden Dawn or within the Theosophical Society in the early twentieth century, they continued to serve as organs to disseminate occult knowledge beyond the small base of initiates of a particular order. As Dion Fortune launched the Inner Light, first as an offshoot of Theosophy and then as an order more like the Golden Dawn, with its own apparatus of initiation (and even a correspondence course for potential initiates), the status of the monthly *Inner Light Magazine* evolved. While the order later claimed that the magazine was confidential and meant for members, its advertisements in widely circulated periodicals, such as the *Occult Review*, clearly show that the magazine was to be circulated publicly and sold either by individual copy or subscription. The organisation was faced with the very material issues of periodical publication early on. As Alan Richardson explains:

> Initially they had printed 500 copies of their magazine and stacked them up high on the altar in their Sanctuary, whereupon they said a prayer of consecration over them and sent them out into the world. They sold out within a fortnight, and had to put the tattered stencils back into the duplicator to try and coax out a few more impressions. (1991: 165)

The magazine, which published articles but also poetry and communications from Fortune herself, remained part of the Inner Light's publishing operations until 1940.

But Fortune also launched a more exclusive periodical initiative as a response to the horrors of the Second World War. In 1939, she began a series of weekly letters to a smaller subset of Inner Light initiates and occultists that disseminated a ritual and magical working aimed at defending Britain against the Nazis. These weekly letters would be sent out on Wednesdays; members would have them in advance of a simultaneous meditative magical working every Sunday at noon. By 1940, paper shortages forced Fortune to choose between the weekly letter and the monthly review. She chose the letter (Richardson 1991: 229), though by 1942, as the crisis seemed to be easing, she briefly returned to the monthly.

Though the monthly had published the key ritual bases of the Inner Light, the weekly letter was a distinctly different use of a periodical. The letter was invested with magical energy and then became a material part of the ritual meditative working. In the first letter, at the beginning of October 1939, Fortune instructed participants in how to arrange their meditation space, facing toward London, where the Inner Light's sanctuary was located. But what followed made the letter itself indispensable in the ritual: 'sit in such an attitude that your feet are together and your hands clasped, thus making a closed circuit of yourself. Your hands should rest on the weekly letter lying in your lap, for these letters will be consecrated before they are sent out in order that they may form a link' (Fortune 2012: 2). The participants were then instructed each week on a set of symbols and visual cues upon which to focus their meditations as they built a cave, library, and watchtower on the astral plane. From here, they would focus the energies of the group soul of the race and construct a channel to the secret Masters of Wisdom (Fortune 2012: 3). (The first image was the all-important hermetic symbol, the Rose on the Cross.) Ultimately, the astral cave was to be built upon the cavern beneath Mount Abiegnus, the Hill of Vision, at Glastonbury Tor.

Coda: From Modernist Era to New Age

The roots of post-Second World War New Age spiritual culture can easily be found in these modernist-era periodicals and authors of the occult revival. Dion Fortune's novels and prose writings influenced neopaganism as well as Christian esotericism; almost all of her major works are still in print and sold in New Age bookstores. The genesis and shaping of later twentieth-century New Religious Movements such as Wicca and other neopagan Goddess religions can be tracked across the publishing careers of other significant women authors of the modernist era. One deserves particular mention here: Ithell Colquhoun. Like Collins and Fortune, she also used periodical publications to consolidate her authority within an evolving occult context.

Ithell Colquhoun (1906–88) is known to scholars of modernism as a British surrealist painter and writer, but her esoteric commitments were always a significant aspect of her work. Drawn to esotericism at the age of seventeen through an article in the *Sunday Express* about Crowley's Abbey of Thelema, she attended lectures at prominent Theosophist G. R. S. Mead's Quest Society in the 1920s while an art student at the Slade. Her first publication was an article in Mead's journal, *The Quest*, in 1930. She was a member of several esoteric and neopagan orders across her lifetime (including Kenneth Grant's Nu Isis Lodge of the OTO, Bernard Crow's Order of the Keltic Cross, Tamara Bourkoun's Order of the Pyramid and Sphinx, and British and French druidical orders), and she was ordained a Priestess of Isis by the Fellowship of Isis in Ireland. Her career unfolded in surrealist journals, such as the *London Bulletin* in the 1930s, but under the male authority structure of the British surrealist circle under E. L. T. Mesens, Colquhoun and other women were marginalised – and, in her case, she was driven out of the group because of her occult activities. Colquhoun then turned to a wider set of independent periodicals, such as *New Road*, the *Bell*, and *Enquiry*, a journal exploring psychic research (with Jung and several British doctors on its advisory board). Later in her life, she published in surrealist revival periodicals, such as *Fantasmagie*, *Melmoth*, and *TRANSFORMAcTION*; in occult periodicals such as the *Hermetic Journal*; periodicals of Celtic/Druid-oriented New Age Britain, such as *Wood and Water*, *Ore*, *Sangrael*, and *New Celtic Review*; and even in the mass-market paranormal magazine *Prediction*. Colquhoun used these periodicals to sustain an occult surrealism that resonated more clearly in post-Second World War Britain than it had in the modernist era.

As we have seen, at the turn of the century, women turned to new forms of spirituality and leveraged the professional authority open to them as authors and journalists, skilfully manipulating the conventions and affordances of periodical culture to forge greater spiritual authority in the public sphere. Colquhoun used similar strategies across the twentieth century to achieve a position of autonomy and authority in the art world, defying the male authorities who had rejected the synthesis of surrealism and esoteric spirituality that defined her art.

Notes

1. Dixon notes that women had come to make up a majority of members of the Theosophical Society by 1907, when Annie Besant became president (2010: 218).
2. When she began publishing as 'Mabel Collins,' Collins was already married to Robert Keningale Cook, son of the Canon of Manchester, and a minor poet, lawyer, stockbroker, owner of the *Dublin University Magazine*, and spiritualist. When that marriage failed some decades later, no change of name nor comment on her marital status was required by simply continuing to publish as 'Mabel Collins.'
3. In his 1883 review in *The Academy*, Richard Littledale praises *In the Flower of her Youth*, the story of love, marriage, infidelity, and a self-sacrificing heroine who starts over as an

actress, as 'a very clever one, despite all faults,' and notes the source of the father in the story as Collins's own, describing the heroine as a young, clever, and beautiful only daughter of a Bohemian man of letters, in whom the reader will not fail to recognise an idealised portrait drawn by filial affection (14 Apr 1883: 253). Littledale reviewed her novel along with such fare as *What Hast Thou Done?*, *The New Mistress*, and *He Died for the Love of Woman*.
4. Such as significant essays she published in the *Occult Review* in the year leading up to her launch of the *Inner Light Magazine*, including 'The Use and Power of Ritual' in the March 1926 issue, 'Sane Occultism' in July 1926, or 'Evidence and Proof in Occult Science' in September 1926.
5. Dora Marsden attended it in the teens to argue with the Theosophists who made up a substantial portion of her readership. Marsden noted that, 'before I spoke at Peables [sic] they were indifferent. They made no effort to understand that "Freewoman" is just the rooting out of "Theosophia"! It was ridiculous to imagine that I could have anything acceptable to say to theosophists.' Yet she was delighted to have sold out the stock of the *New Freewoman* at Peebles (qtd in Morrisson 2001: 235).

Works Cited

Clarke, Bruce. 1996. *Dora Marsden and Early Modernism: Gender, Individualism, Science*. Ann Arbor: University of Michigan.
Collins, Mabel, and ——. 1888. *The Blossom and the Fruit: A True Story of a Black Magician*. London: Published by the Authors.
'Dion Fortune.' *The Society of the Inner Light*, <http://www.innerlight.org.uk/dionfortune2.html> (last accessed 30 August 2016).
Dixon, Joy. 2003. *Divine Feminine: Theosophy and Feminism in England*. Baltimore: Johns Hopkins University Press.
——. 2010. 'Modernity, Heterodoxy and the Transformation of Religious Cultures.' *Women, Gender and Religious Cultures in Britain, 1800–1940*. Ed. Sue Morgan and Jacquelie deVries. London: Routledge. 211–30.
Faivre, Antoine. 1994. *Access to Western Esotericism*. Albany: SUNY Press.
Farnell, Kim. 'Theosophy.' *The Many Lives of Mabel Collins*, <http://www.katinkahesselink.net/his/farnell3.html> (last accessed 27 August 2016).
Fortune, Dion. 2003. *Moon Magic*. York Beach, ME: Red Wheel/Weiser.
——. 2012. *The Magical Battle of Britain: The War Letters of Dion Fortune*. Ed. Gareth Knight. Cheltenham: Skylight Press.
Gieryn, Thomas F. 1983. 'Boundary-Work and the Demarcation of Science from Non-Science: Strains and Interests in Professional Ideologies of Scientists.' *American Sociological Review* 48.6: 781–95.
Knight, Gareth. 'About Dion Fortune.' <http://www.angelfire.com/az/garethknight/aboutdf.html> (last accessed 30 August 2016).
——. 'Magical Novels and Magical Rites.' *Gareth Knight News & Ideas*, 30 October 2013. <http://garethknight.blogspot.com/2013/10/magical-novels-and-magical-rites.html> (last accessed 1 September 2016).
McLeod, Hugh. 1996. *Religion and Society in England, 1850–1914*. New York: St. Martin's.
Morrisson, Mark S. 2001. *The Public Face of Modernism: Little Magazines, Audiences, and Reception, 1905–1920*. Madison: University of Wisconsin Press.
——. 2007. *Modern Alchemy: Occultism and the Emergence of Atomic Theory*. Oxford: Oxford University Press.
——. 2008. 'The Periodical Culture of the Occult Revival: Esoteric Wisdom, Modernity and Counter-Public Spheres.' *Journal of Modern Literature* 31.2: 1–22.

Neisius, Jean G. 'Marryat, Florence.' *Oxford Dictionary of National Biography*. Oxford: Oxford University Press, 2004–16. Online. (Last accessed 1 September 2016.)

Oppenheim, Janet. 1985. *The Other World: Spiritualism and Psychical Research In England, 1850–1914*. Cambridge: Cambridge University Press.

Owen, Alex. 1989. *The Darkened Room: Women, Power, and Spiritualism in Late Nineteenth Century England*. London: Virago.

—. 2004. *The Place of Enchantment: British Occultism and the Culture of the Modern*. Chicago: University of Chicago Press.

Peterson, William S. 1991. *The Kelmscott Press: A History of William Morris's Typographical Adventure*. Berkeley: University of California Press.

Richardson, Alan. 1991. *The Magical Life of Dion Fortune: Priestess of the 20th Century*. London: Aquarian Press.

Walker, Pamela J. 2010. '"With Fear and Trembling," Women, Preaching and Spiritual Authority.' *Women, Gender and Religious Cultures in Britain, 1800–1940*. Ed. Sue Morgan and Jacquelie deVries. London: Routledge. 94–116.

Wallis, Roy. 1985. 'Science and Pseudo-Science.' *Social Science Information* 24.3: 585–601.

Wallraven, Miriam. 2015. *Women Writers and the Occult in Literature and Culture*. London: Routledge.

Washington, Peter. 1995. *Madame Blavatsky's Baboon: A History of the Mystics, Mediums, and Misfits Who Brought Spiritualism to America*. New York: Shocken.

25

Lysistrata on the Home Front: Locating Women's Reproductive Bodies in the Birth Strike Rhetoric of the *Malthusian* during the First World War

Layne Parish Craig

JUST WEEKS BEFORE the outbreak of the First World War, the editors of the *Malthusian*, the official publication of the pro-contraception Malthusian League, reprinted a piece of doggerel from the populist magazine *John Bull*, which reads in part:

> A dreadfully wicked thing is Sex –
>   So some would have us think.
> To mention it in company
>   All proper people shrink . . .
> Young people should not know, you know,
>   About such things at all;
> Although such holy ignorance
>   Results in many a fall.
> They should not know what marriage is,
>   Or how the babies come:
> These things are fearful mysteries
>   On which the *good* are dumb. (15 June 1914: 48)

The poem's author satirises the serious issue of sexual ignorance among young people that preoccupied pro-contraception and sexual freedom activists in the 1910s – an issue surrounding which the stakes grew with the advent of conflict in Europe. While the years of the First World War have popularly been viewed as an era in which restrictions on sexuality were loosened in Britain, public discourse about sex and reproduction retained the un-embodied, 'mysterious' aspects described in the poem. At the same time, Britons' reproductive choices had to be newly reconciled both with the circumstances of war and with increasingly nationalistic public narratives surrounding women, sex, and family planning. Those public narratives can be traced in the propaganda, literature, and popular culture of the First World War, but they are perhaps most visible in newspapers and journals, whose pages reveal ideological and practical anxieties about women's power to effect social change through their reproductive choices. This essay examines this conversation as it occurred in the pages of the *Malthusian*, the journal of the pro-contraception society the Malthusian League, whose writers were among the few to factor the practical realities of family planning into their calculations of the relationships among war, sex, and reproduction in the late 1910s.

In her 2015 book *The New Death*, Pearl James articulates a paradigm for textual scholarship on the First World War that focuses on the bodily realities underlying the rhetoric of war narratives, in particular on war wounds and representations of death. James makes an observation about wartime writing that resonates with the *Malthusian*'s satire of public silence on sex: 'many writers and witnesses insist on the fundamental inadequacy of language. What matters here is not whether war really is unspeakable but that unspeakability itself becomes a trope for talking about war' (2013: 5). The trope of 'unspeakability' in war narratives creates blank spaces at the most crucial geographic locations of the war: the places where each nation's military personnel accomplishes war's central goal of killing and maiming other nation's military personnel. At the same time, as Elaine Scarry has shown, it creates blank spaces at the location of the wounded body itself (Scarry 1985: 8–9; Bourke 2013: 45). However, scholars of wartime writing could profitably extend our understanding of the 'unspeakability' of the physical body at war to encompass another unarticulated 'blank space' in war literature: the womb, whose contents are vested with the fate of nations but whose corporeality, the 'center and periphery' (Scarry 1985: 3) of reproductive action, is consistently ignored, avoided, and metaphorised in the public arena.

During the war era, women's reproductive decision-making emerged within a unique and shifting set of pressures arising from public discourse about genetics, personal freedom, and nationalism. These pressures, rather than their consequences for individuals and families, were foregrounded in representations of sex, fertility, and mothering, resulting in the depiction of these concrete forces in women's lives in abstract, circumspect, and aggregated terms. Evidence of women's encouragement or prevention of conception, sense of control over their reproductive lives, and experiences with pregnancy and childbirth during the First World War is most often found, as James describes representations of death, in 'tropes of omission, implication, and inference; gendered metaphors; unreliable narrators; and disjointed, jarring, narrative structures in order to evoke without naming the obscene realities and fantasies' (2013: 25). Like death, the reproductive body is both everywhere and nowhere in wartime public discourse. The ephemeral, politically reactive pages of wartime periodicals mark a unique site of its potential excavation, a site where the outlines of individual women's subjectivity can emerge through the anxious crosstalk surrounding reproduction's aggregate impact.

Birth Rates and War Babies: The Womb and Wartime Statistical Anxiety

War broke out in Europe at the peak of official concern in Britain over the nation's falling birth rate. Several factors – economic, cultural, and technological – combined to lead to a decrease in the British birth rate beginning in the 1870s (Soloway 1982: 4; Hall 2000: 66). The formation of a National Birth-Rate Commission by the National Council on Public Morals in 1913 demonstrates the anxiety caused by this trend (Hall 2000: 28–9, 90). This anxiety was heightened by the war: in 1916, the Birth-Rate

Commission's report, citing low birth statistics in 1914 and 1915, suggested 'measures to encourage early marriage, the birth of more children, and improvements in their chances of survival . . . tax inducements, educational bonuses, better housing, expanded medical facilities, and improved prenatal and postnatal care' (Soloway 1982: 160). Lesley Hall has argued that as the war began, awareness of the low birth rate contributed to a shift in attitudes toward premarital sex, at least within heterosexual partnerships: she states, 'Concerns over "war babies" were more ambivalent in an atmosphere of intense pronatalism seeing reproduction as an essential national resource' (2000: 94).

This theory is amply supported by mainstream periodicals of the day: 1915 saw the release in British newspapers of dozens of editorials and letters to the editor on the topic of 'war babies,' with titles ranging from 'The Unmarried Mother: Work of the War Babies' League' (*Manchester Guardian* 23 Feb 1915) to 'A New Social Problem' (*Times* 19 Apr 1915) to 'The Myth of War Babies' (*Independent* 11 Oct 1915). The way this conversation played out across periodicals highlights the conflicts illegitimacy in wartime posed for moral traditionalists, while also revealing the romanticised, hegemonising lens through which mothers of soldiers' children were seen. In a 1915 *Review of Reviews* article, Presbyterian minister and social purity activist James Marchant, secretary of the National Birth-Rate Commission (Soloway 1995: 9, 139), admits, 'owing to our falling birth rate, and no doubt because of the intense admiration we have for our brave men who have flocked to the Colours, the nation, or some considerable section of it, desires to make the best of . . . "war babies"' (June 1915: 467). 'Making the best,' for Marchant, doesn't include relaxing illegitimacy statutes to remove the stigma attached to children of unwed mothers, but his article cites others who do advocate for such changes to accommodate the special circumstances of war. In fact, Marchant refers by name to Liberal editor Austin Harrison, who waxed poetic in his call in the *English Review* for mercy toward unwed mothers in wartime:

> the man who would denounce them, who for the sake of principle or traditional theory would judge them according to the canons of law obtaining in the land in the blithe times of peace, passes sentence perforce on himself. It is he, the condemner, who stands outside the pale of humanity, not they; not those young mothers who knew their soldier lovers in the ardour and beauty of their hearts. (May 1915: 232)

While Marchant and Harrison disagree about the nation's ideal reaction to war babies, they share a sentimental perception of 'brave men' and 'soldier lovers' that obscures individuals' reproductive decision-making in a fog of 'ardour' created by the war.

Moves toward the relaxation of illegitimacy statutes evoke one assumption about the war era: that it represented a time of relaxed restrictions on young people's sexuality, which corresponded with an increased public presence for women aiding the war effort. Certainly, progressive intellectuals of the era, like sex researcher Havelock Ellis, advocated for a universal lifting of restrictions on women's opportunities and behaviour: in 1919 Ellis stated, 'Never before has it been so urgent to enlarge and requicken our sexual morality and social customs in such a way that women may be enabled to allow free play to their best impulses and ideals' (qtd in Robb 2015: 78). Some feminist activists, like Stella Browne, who gave a lecture in 1915 entitled 'The Sexual Variety and Variability of Women and their Bearing on Social Reconstruction' (Hall 2011: 47), also supported greater sexual freedom for women. However, such 'free play' was by no means the experience of most young Britons, and especially not the experience of most women. Laura Doan's research suggests that women's increased sexual freedom in the 1910s was contingent on social class, age, geography, and other situational characteristics (2013: 167). Indeed, as Angela Woollacott and others have demonstrated, a strong backlash against women's sexual freedom became apparent during the war years, with terms like 'khaki fever,' denoting young women's supposed obsession with men in uniform, and 'amateurs,' denoting female non-prostitutes who engaged in sex for social or economic favours, entering media and political discourse (1994: 325, 342–3).[1] The 1918 revival of the Contagious Diseases Act as part of the Defence of the Realm Act (Section 40D) indeed 'provided for the forcible removal for treatment of any woman known to be a source of infection' (Hall 2000: 95), literally encoding sexually active women as enemy combatants.

Thus, simultaneously, young women's sexuality was pathologised and criminalised, and, as potential mothers, those same women were lauded as romantic patriots and producers of a potentially scarce national resource, British babies. All embodiments of this resource were not valued equally, however. Dovetailing with concerns about the *quantity* of new British citizens produced was rhetoric concerning its *quality*. Eugenics, or the science of producing a 'better race,' provided a lens through which academic, scientific, and political communities viewed women's reproductive agency, and calls to 'breed' a more 'fit' population were common in newspapers, textbooks, and magazines. Discourse on eugenics across the political spectrum suggests a bright line between abstractions of 'good' and 'bad' wartime mothering, prescribing patriotic procreation for the former (so-called 'positive eugenics') and family limitation for the latter ('negative eugenics').

In his analysis of British proto-fascist discourse, Dan Stone suggests that before the 1920s, versions of eugenics ideology promoted by right- and left-wing thinkers were indistinguishable from each other (2002: 6). Stone particularly argues for an important confluence of Nietzschean thought and eugenics in the work of A. R. Orage, who from 1907–22 edited the *New Age*, a journal most well known for its socialist leanings (2002: 74–6). One wartime nationalist application of eugenics discourse can be found in a 1916 article in the *New Age* by Margaret MacGregor, which employs a classic eugenic argument against procreation among the lower classes:

> Not to the overburdened mother in the over-crowded tenement in the slums should we look for the recruiting of the race, but to the women of the upper and middle classes, who, with a rich inheritance to pass on to another generation, are wilfully [sic] restricting its endowment to one or two individuals. The babies who are never born are England's greatest loss, the children who would have come into the world with every advantage, both of heredity and environment, and whom the women of England refuse to bear. Why? (19 Oct 1916: 585)

While MacGregor's suggestion draws on language long associated with eugenic ideology, her use of the term 'recruiting' suggests the special responsibility the war placed on women to bear healthy offspring as future soldiers. MacGregor's article reflects the official view of the National Birth-Rate Commission, whose 1916 report Richard Soloway summarises thus: 'In their opinion the war had conclusively shown that the selfishness of the better classes in leading the flight from maternity was every bit as reprehensible and far more dangerous than the fabled recklessness of the poor' (1982: 160–1). Contemporary responses to the Commission's Report noted that its experts specifically condemned contraception, a practice that the report associated with the upper classes (*Fortnightly Review* July 1917: 93, 100). To choose or advocate for the prevention of pregnancy in this context, particularly among the 'eugenic' middle classes, was to act in opposition to one's culture's understanding of nation, religion, and human decency.

The Malthusian League and 'Family Limitation'

For those officials who touted the evils of contraception at the turn of the twentieth century, as well as for the increasing numbers of individuals who made use of contraceptive techniques and technologies, advocacy for family limitation was synonymous with the work of the Malthusian League. The Malthusian League was founded in 1877 by the members of the defence team of Annie Besant and Charles Bradlaugh in their obscenity trial for distributing information about contraception (D'Arcy 1977: 429–30). The League's name reflects its emergence from the population control doctrines of Thomas Malthus; in calling themselves 'Neo-Malthusians,' however, its members indicated an important difference in methodology. Soloway puts it thus: 'Malthus had identified the cause, overpopulation, at the opening of the [nineteenth] century; the new, or Neo-Malthusians, by promoting early marriage and normal sexual relations without the risk of pregnancy, offered the solution' (1982: 55). The possibility of contraception allowed an entirely different approach to population control within 'normal' sexual relations that ultimately proved very attractive to the British public, even as the League itself remained controversial.

The League began publishing its journal, the *Malthusian*, in 1879, and this periodical continued as the mouthpiece of the Malthusian League until 1952, changing its name to *New Generation* in 1921, then back to the *Malthusian* in 1949 (Ledbetter 1976: xviii). Published from 1879 to 1891 through the Freethought Publishing Company, then by George Standring after Freethought closed, the journal was the brainchild of Charles Robert (C. R.) Drysdale, the League's first president and the journal's first editor. In 1907, editorship of the *Malthusian* passed to Charles Vickery (C. V.) Drysdale, his son, who ceded the position briefly to Binnie Dunlop in 1916, returned in 1918, was succeeded by Robert B. Kerr from 1923 to 1951, then briefly returned to editing upon Kerr's death in 1951. Though he took a hiatus from his editorship, C. V. Drysdale's voice and vision are central to the *Malthusian*'s content throughout the 1910s. The eight-page publication was subtitled 'A Crusade Against Poverty,' and beginning in 1909, was published in a cover with a floral design, though the cover page was left off during the war. In the 1910s it sold for one penny, but many copies were given away in an attempt to attract supporters to the cause (Ledbetter 1976: 63, 78–9). Its structure varied considerably in the 1910s, but most issues contained these elements: a several-column article on a topic related to Malthus's writings or their application by C. V. Drysdale, whose byline appears in almost every issue; shorter articles on issues related to population control, contraception, or eugenics by Malthusian League members, including Binnie Dunlop, Bessie Drysdale, and Stella Browne; 'Notes' covering current events from a population control perspective (often excerpted from other periodicals); and signed and unsigned letters supporting the cause. More propagandistic elements were also incorporated, including calls for donations, descriptions of new pamphlets available for distribution, and, as I discuss below, the publication of letters from working parents seeking the League's 'Practical Leaflet' on contraception.

Despite its significance to their agenda, for several decades the League resisted disseminating practical information about contraception, in part to mitigate the notoriety that arose from their association with the Besant/Bradlaugh trial. Following pressure from members, however, in 1913 the League published *Hygienic Methods of Family Limitation*, a pamphlet on birth control methods that was studied and adapted by Margaret Sanger during her sojourn in England in 1915 (Soloway 1982: 58; Engelman 2011: 48). This pamphlet, called the 'Practical Leaflet,' was circulated separately from the *Malthusian*, and was only available to those who signed a declaration of their status as married; Malthusian League historian Rosanna Ledbetter has argued that this requirement probably suppressed the leaflet's distribution numbers, but she notes that around 200 leaflets were distributed each month in 1913 and 1914 despite a lack of advertisers and the strict limitation to married readers (1976: 211).

Despite this important shift in policy and focus, the perception of the Malthusian League among the British public remained unchanged through the Victorian and Edwardian eras: it was consistently seen as a radical organisation advocating for free love and the destruction of the nuclear family (Soloway 1982: 57). At the same time, its historical legacy among scholars of birth control has emphasised its conservatism on issues such as social class, eugenics, and sexual morality,[2] sometimes with the consequence of obscuring the diversity of thought among Malthusian League members and contributors to the *Malthusian*. In her biography of Stella Browne, whose work appeared frequently in the *Malthusian* beginning in the 1910s, Lesley Hall states, 'as did a number of her contemporaries, [Browne] distinguished the valuable work she felt the League was doing in raising the issue of birth control from [its leaders'] antisocialist and eugenicist views' (2011: 35). Due to the contributions of members like Browne, the pages of the *Malthusian* during the First World War reflect not a monovocal expression of Malthus's population theories (though those do feature prominently in each issue), but a more nuanced conversation about the ideology and methodology of reproductive control in the late nineteenth and early twentieth centuries.

The Malthusian Birth Strike

The overall thrust of the Malthusian League's published response to the war was twofold: to reiterate its members' opinion that the war was caused by overpopulation and to praise the 'fitness' of British society over the barbarity of Germany's unchecked reproduction (Figures 25.1 and 25.2). The August 1914 issue of the *Malthusian* was largely dedicated to the theme of the war, leading off with an editorial on 'The European Conflict and Its Cause,' which insists 'every item of the Neo-Malthusian doctrine and propaganda is being justified by events, and it cannot be long before its importance as a factor in the attainment of the world's peace is recognized' (15 Aug 1914: 58). Even prior to the outbreak of the war, Neo-Malthusians had expressed concern about Germany's high birth rate, referring in 1908 to Germany and the Balkans as 'semi-civilized nations who have not learned how to restrain their population to their

Figure 25.1 Front cover of the *Malthusian*, produced during wartime. December 1916.

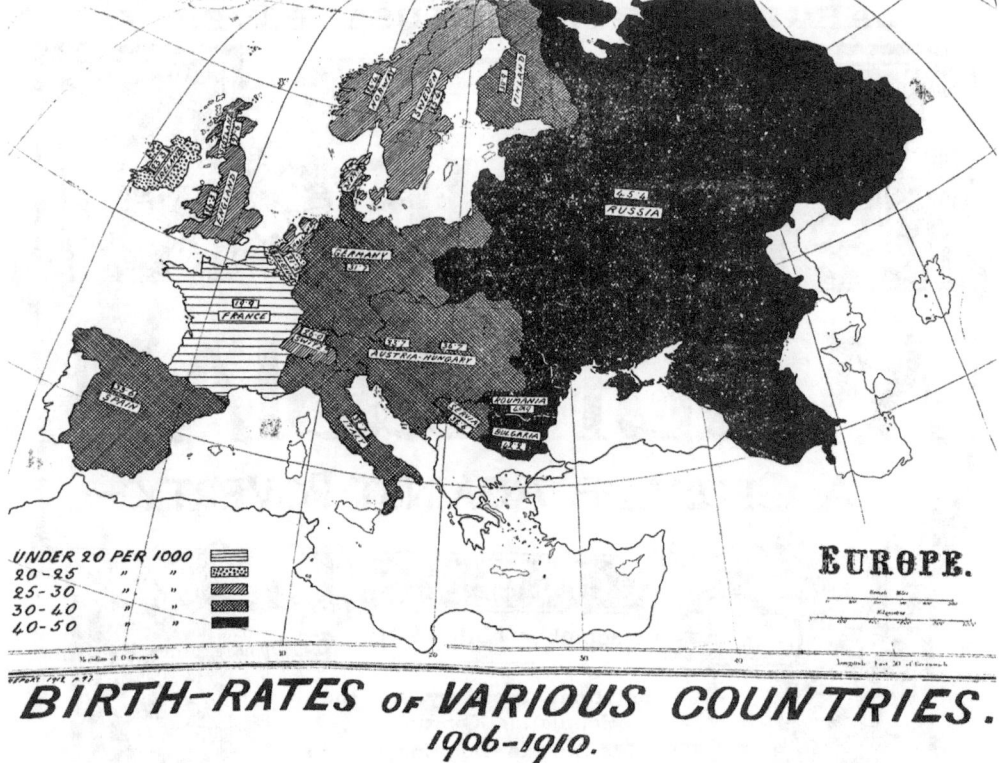

Figure 25.2 The 'Malthusian War Map' illustrating 'birth-rates of various countries.' November 1915.

resources' (Soloway 1982: 163). A 'Malthusian War Map' published in November 1915 illustrates the perspective of the editors of the *Malthusian* on the differences between these nations and 'civilized' Western Europe: Russia, with the highest birth rate, is filled in an ominous black, while Eastern Europe is shaded in dark grey, and France, the only nation of the lightest shade representing 'Under 20 Per 1000' stands as a white beacon crowded in by its over-reproducing neighbours (15 Nov 1915: 84). The colour symbolism of the map was not the only place where the Malthusian reflected a preoccupation with Western European whiteness. While articles in the journal often cited (and condemned) British pronatalism, Drysdale also engaged with arguments by eugenicists about the 'racial' causes and effects of the war on their own terms, holding up, for example, the high rates of volunteerism for military service from among smaller middle- and upper-class families as proof that such families produced superior citizens (Soloway 1982: 177).

Drysdale's conviction that overpopulation caused the war led him to a more radical conclusion that came to be the League's most strongly held position on wartime reproduction; in a controversial break with mainline eugenicists, he called in 1914 for a complete suspension of British reproduction for the duration of the war, in order to focus the nation's resources on feeding and mobilising its existing population. Drysdale's first statement about wartime reproduction appears in a short article framed as a letter he attempted to have published in the *Daily News*: 'Last, but not least, no more children should be engendered until the war is over. We want all the energies of our men and women, and no more mouths to feed than we can help' (15 Aug 1914: 64). Drysdale's statement evokes Malthusian themes of scarcity: war, to the League, is associated with the fear of famine that is prominent in Malthus's work, and here the conservation of food is paralleled with the conservation of both male and female time and effort for war work.[3] The *Malthusian*'s birth strike was also steeped in eugenics rhetoric. Ledbetter quotes from a 1916 article titled 'Why the Malthusian League Has Advised Against Having Children in War Time': '"From the eugenic standpoint this is the worst of all possible times for engendering children. The young, strong, and virile men of our country have been taken away, leaving the physically and mentally unfit, the immature, and the aged behind"' (1976: 211–12; 15 Mar 1916: 31). However, Drysdale's main position is notably distinct from that of mainline eugenicists: for example, in his articles he uses terms such as 'no more children' without the expected qualifiers 'no more poor children,' or 'no more children in labouring class families.' In addition, his references to the strike incorporate the pronoun 'we,' identifying himself and *Malthusian* readers with the group to forego reproduction, rejecting the separation between 'eugenic' and 'dysgenic' reproduction that would make this call palatable to an audience accustomed to reproductive distinctions between the upper and lower classes.

In the months following August 1914, the theme of a birth strike for the duration of the war appears frequently in the pages of the *Malthusian*: by March 1915, Drysdale is able to claim in the issue's 'Notes,' 'From the moment of the outbreak of war we have consistently advocated that no more children should be begotten while the war lasts, in complete opposition to the cry for more children to replace the men killed in war' (15 Mar 1915: 24). For a group that had previously blunted its positions to appeal to moderate Britons, this definite stance was a departure with visible consequences. Soloway has traced the conflict between the Neo-Malthusians and groups on the left and the right over the correct reproductive response to war. Soloway states, 'Once it was apparent that the Malthusian League not only intended to press on with its campaign, but actually viewed the war as an opportunity to reduce the birthrate further, the reaction was swift and predictably acrimonious,' evidenced, for example, by the response of neurologist Sir James Crichton-Browne, a collaborator of Charles Darwin, who called in a speech for the censorship of the Malthusian League's publications and decried their attempts to circumvent the 'copious reinforcements of infant life ... so vitally important to the economical future of the country' (Soloway 1982: 175–6). Even progressive institutions that had supported the aims of the league before the war, like the *New Statesman*, publicly renounced the Neo-Malthusians' wartime rhetoric (Soloway 1982: 177), drawing a furious response from socialist Malthusian League member Stella Browne (15 Nov 1915: 92).[4] In the pages of the *Malthusian*, however, support for the birth strike was unwavering – though as we will see, those contributors brought differing perspectives to their articulations of anti-natalist sentiment.

Despite their animosity to one another, both the resistance to and the defence of the Malthusian League's position were marked by abstract, statistically driven understandings of reproduction: specifically, the question of whether the production of British infants augmented or detracted from the success of the British Empire. The responses to the *Malthusian*'s anti-reproduction stance often arise from male speakers and writers, reflecting men's dominance in public discourse, but also the ways in which male pundits, medical professionals, and even clergy drove representations of political questions surrounding reproductive choice. Such questions – and prominent men's responses to them – were not entirely new with the war. The concept of a 'birth strike' had entered public discourse a year before the war in connection with a nation and political agenda generally at odds with that of Drysdale and the Neo-Malthusians. German socialists famously called in 1913 for a 'Gebärstreik' led by male doctors, which leading female socialists, notably Clara Zetkin and Rosa Luxemburg, decried as likely to weaken the political influence of the working classes (Weindling 1989: 251). The British *Review of Reviews* took note of the German birth strike, stating in a summary of a debate between German socialists, 'it would be no exaggeration to say that the spectre of Socialism has been driven into the background by the spectre of the birth-strike' (Dec 1913: 464). In January 1914, a short note in the *Malthusian*, apparently excerpted from the *Daily News*, suggests that the concept of a class-based birth strike was under discussion in England as well. Under the headline 'Race Suicide Strike,' the note states:

> A strike against bringing children into the world was discussed by the Rev. W. R. Harvey, pastor of the Primrose Hill Congregational Church, Northampton.... Mr. Harvey said that ... when he watched the children at play and remembered that most of them would go into factories ... he had wondered if the best strike we could organise would be a strike against bringing little boys and girls into the world until we had made our towns and cities a little better to receive them. (15 Jan 1914: 5)

The methods by which a birth strike would be enacted are vague in these references; however, the idea seems to have been perceived as a concrete possibility, suggesting some public acceptance of family limitation as a potential political tool as well as a lack of definition of the role of women in supporting or carrying out such a strike.[5]

Drysdale's call for a birth strike is similarly male-initiated and similarly vague in its use of passive voice and emphasis on national security and economic interests to the elision of individual women's bodies and choices. In the *Malthusian*'s November 1914 issue, Drysdale reported responses from three military officers to the question, 'Do you think the advice of the League to the poorest classes not to engender any more children[6] until the war is over is in any way objectionable from the patriotic standpoint?' (15 Nov 1914: 82). Their negative responses prompt him to claim, 'The views of some of the military members of our League ... will at least serve to show any doubters that our propaganda can be defended from the purely military point of view' (15 Nov 1914: 83). The legitimacy the journal derives from 'the purely military point of view' suggests that the League's call for a birth strike was promoted by Drysdale not as a pacifist or populist, but as a patriotic gesture, the flipside of the wartime pronatalist motherhood narrative: reproduce/do not reproduce for king and country.

Populism leaked through, however, in the League's pro-contraception activities. The different audiences for the journal and the 'Practical Leaflet' and its associated materials resulted in a rhetorical dichotomy that highlighted the journal's dual position as part of elitist academic and political discourse and as a purveyor of contraceptives to working-class families. The 'Practical Leaflet' was tied to the birth strike through an advertising tract distributed along with the *Malthusian* in August 1914 (Ledbetter 1976:

211); it also was printed as part of the journal in December 1914. The tract begins in a patriotic vein: 'You will all be thinking how you can best help the country, and there are already plenty of people in authority to tell you what to do. BUT THERE IS ONE VERY IMPORTANT MATTER YOU WILL NOT BE TOLD ABOUT' (15 Dec 1914: 89). The ominousness of the all-caps line leads into a paragraph about the economic burden children create for families during war, providing evidence for Soloway's contention that Drysdale's call for a birth strike was a somewhat opportunistic move to bring the stress of the circumstances to bear on arguments the League had been making for decades (Soloway 1982: 175). In its closing paragraphs, however, the tract moves from rhetoric to practicality: 'The parental prudence which this leaflet is advocating is not any unnatural and hard self-denial. It is merely a question of using the simple and harmless methods of family limitation whereby couples can live their natural married lives, and yet avoid having any more children than they want' (15 Dec 1914: 89–90).

The connection of the *War Leaflet* and the *Practical Leaflet* marks this iteration of birth strike rhetoric as significant for its acknowledgement of the intimate and somewhat labour-intensive involvement of the physical body in preventing the birth of children in adverse circumstances: the leaflet contains instructions for washing condoms, recipes for douche solutions and soluble pessaries, and recommendations for the best methods of removing cervical caps (Haire 1922: 10–15).[7] Indirectly and perhaps unknowingly evoking Aristophanes' representation of the difficulties posed by a similar strike in *Lysistrata*, the pamphlet references the possibility of 'hard self denial' as a necessity of the solution it advocates. This possibility is mitigated, however, not only by an acknowledgement of contraception's existence, but also by the evocation of the 'holy grail' of birth control propaganda: instructions on how to use contraception. If wartime discourse on reproduction prioritised the ideological over the physical, the *Malthusian's* call reinserted the practicalities of heterosexual intercourse into that landscape.

Subverting Strike Ideology: Women Contributors to the *Malthusian*

The Malthusian League was dominated by the Drysdale family – C. R. Drysdale, one of its founders and its first president, his wife, Alice Vickery Drysdale, who became president upon his death, and C. V. Drysdale, his son and her successor – for most of its existence (Soloway 1982: 55). Charles Vickery's wife, Bessie, did not serve as president of the League, but assisted her husband with the editorship of the *Malthusian* and served as its secretary in the 1910s (Ledbetter 1976: 63, 78). While Bessie Drysdale's writings reflect her own and the League's commitment to eugenic philosophies, they also cast a new light on the journal's birth strike rhetoric, one that prioritises individual women's reproductive rights over the aggregate and abstract benefits of the strike.

Bessie Drysdale's critique of wartime rhetoric's erasure of women can be read in her response to the illegitimacy controversy, published in the *Malthusian* in May 1915:

> Every daily paper in the kingdom must by now have given utterance to its views on this human drama . . . But, so far as I know, the one person who has not given us her views is the mother, actual or potential, of the 'war baby.' One would have liked to hear what she had to say for her case. (15 May 1915: 36)

Similarly, in a scathing article titled 'Varied Counsels,' Drysdale analyses the perspectives of several men advocating for some form of increased reproduction during war, including that of a representative of the Eugenics Society. She states:

> I indignantly resent the inhumane slight on women which is contained in the following sentence: 'It is desirable that all who distinguish themselves in war should be able on their return to marry and become fathers of large families. For this purpose their pensions might be increased with each additional child.' The woman, upon whom the pain, danger, and cares of maternity fall, the more responsible in many ways of the two parents, is to be passed over as though she did not exist! (15 Sep 1915: 69)

Drysdale's point that women's bodily investment in childbirth is often ignored in the conversations to which she alludes directly impugns the misogynistic erasure of women's agency in national discourse about reproduction during wartime, but also more subtly directs attention to eugenicists' blind spot surrounding women's reproductive preferences. While according to the philosophies shared by Bessie Drysdale, her husband, and many Neo-Malthusians, reproduction should be curtailed according to the needs of the nation and the 'race,' her articles suggest a more active role for women in managing and directing that curtailment.

Moreover, Bessie Drysdale's articles permit a reading that connects the Malthusian League with more radical women-led political movements. In 'Varied Counsels,' Drysdale goes on to hint at the power of a women's peace movement focused specifically on reproduction: summarising an article in the *Daily Mirror*, she writes:

> He [the author] evidently thinks . . . that women might refuse *en masse* to give up any of their male children for the purposes of war, and to refuse motherhood altogether if the men would not listen to them. Of course the difficulty would be to organise all women and make them share this point of view and act fearlessly on it, though I am far from thinking it could not be done. (15 Sep 1915: 70)

While the *Malthusian*'s birth strike rhetoric is generally not pacifist, Drysdale seems to hint here at rhetoric of the movement dubbed 'maternal pacifism' by Sharon Ouditt and espoused by British feminists such as Olive Schreiner, Helena Swanwick, and Frances Hallowes. 'Maternal pacifists,' according to Ouditt, are characterised by their belief in women's biologically predestined opposition to war, arising out of their natural maternal instincts (1994: 131–68). In 1915, Hallowes argued 'women realise deeply the worth and preciousness of life,' suggesting a fundamental, pacifist unity among mothers (qtd in Grayzel 1999: 160). Drysdale's gesture toward a similar notion of unity, but directed toward action in the form of a birth strike, opens up surprising connections between Neo-Malthusian rhetoric surrounding reproduction and pro-peace movements.

Despite Bessie Drysdale's prominence, few women were significant contributors to the *Malthusian*. When they do appear, women's perspectives most often serve to underscore the journal's proletarian elements. 'Letters from Struggling Parents,' a feature that sometimes ran on the front page of the journal, contained pleas for information about contraception from presumably working-class parents, often women, signed with initials: in the December 1916 issue, these included 'Mrs. W.,' 'Mrs. G.,' Mrs. S.,' and 'Mrs. B.' (15 Dec 1916: 101). Though their voices are mediated by the journal's editors, the women's narratives are deeply personal and dominated by an awareness of their bodies: 'I am 39 years of age and there is plenty time [sic] to have more children which we do not want'. . . . 'I have very poor health as suffer [sic] from ulcers in the Leg'. . . . 'I am dreading having any more as my sufferings are dreadful when pregnant, and also when giving birth . . . I would do anything reasonable if I could prevent bringing any more delicate children into the home' (ibid.).[8] Presented as they are with very little context, these letters, like Bessie Drysdale's articles, open space in the journal for the concerns of individual mothers, who are most often the objects rather than the subjects in nationalist discourse about reproductive decision-making.

Perhaps the most historically prominent female *Malthusian* writer, and certainly the most interesting connection between the *Malthusian* and the pacifist and feminist communities, was the famed socialist and women's reproductive rights advocate Stella Browne, who joined the Malthusian League in 1914. As a member of the British Society for the Study of Sex Psychology, a contributor to the *Freewoman*, and a researcher in women's sexual expression and reproductive rights, Browne's consistent presence in the pages of the *Malthusian* throughout the 1910s cast the publication in a much more radical light than the Drysdales may have intended. Moreover, despite her early support for the Allies, following the advent of conscription in 1916 Browne became a vocal pacifist (Hall 2011: 54). Her radicalism was on full display in March 1915, when the *Malthusian* published, '"Baby Killers," and Others,' a letter in which Browne protested 'the present savage penalties' imposed against doctors who performed abortions, arguing that inadequate contraception and sex education, as well as societal failures to grant women 'full opportunities of expressing their wishes' mitigate against the criminality of abortion (15 Mar 1915: 22; Hall 2011: 48). Of note is the postscript to this article, which specifically calls for the decriminalisation of abortion in the cases of rape perpetrated by German soldiers against French and Belgian women: 'Here, surely, is a case in which abortion is imperatively indicated, unless the woman herself prefers to have the child. That this obvious remedy should be refused . . . is surely the limit of the absurdity and cruelty involved in denying a woman's right over her own body' (15 Mar 1915: 22). References to Belgian women as the victims of German cruelty mark Browne's article as connected to British pro-war rhetoric; at the same time, however, her invocation of 'a woman's right over her own body' indicates a universal value for womanhood that challenges the premises of every position in mainstream debates over the social value of wartime reproduction.

Browne further lends her feminist credentials to the *Malthusian*'s birth strike proposal in a December 1914 article titled 'Women in War,' in which she states, 'it *is* possible for women to refuse to bring new lives into the world unless they have a reasonable hope of a tolerable environment for their children. To diffuse the knowledge of our League's principles and the methods it recommends . . . is to render a service to humanity' (15 Dec 1914: 91). Browne's anti-war stance also found its way into the *Malthusian*; her 1916 letter, 'Reflections from a (Female) Briton,' states 'apology is owed' to the women of Britain from their leaders 'for this climax of their management of national and international affairs' (15 Jan 1916: 10–11). The inclusion of Browne's work alongside the population tables and dry economic analysis of C. V. Drysdale, not to mention the journal's references to a top-down eugenics model of reproduction, creates fissures in the well-defined ideology of the *Malthusian*, allowing for interpretations of its position on the war and on women's roles in public life that are much broader than its editors may have intended. Indeed, the context suggests that while Drysdale himself did not intend his 'birth strike' as an anti-war or a pro-woman move, it was possible for readers of the journal to ascribe these sentiments to the journal's positions, construing the *Malthusian* as a radical organ that offered a path of practical resistance to the narrow path of pronatalist patriotism laid out for '(female) Britons' during the war years.

The legacy of the *Malthusian*'s participation in wartime rhetoric surrounding women's reproductive decision-making, ultimately, is striking for its implied imbrication of ideological affiliation and practical action, two elements rarely united prior to Marie Stopes's postwar birth control advocacy. The League's 1913 publication of its family limitation tract and its association with contraception made its positions on wartime reproduction threatening to the pro-war mainstream precisely because they were usable on an individual and family level. After all, if public opinion seemed to reject the argument that it was not economically sustainable to produce offspring during wartime, that argument might still be, and probably was, compelling to private citizens: despite well-publicised handwringing, British birth rates continued to drop over the course of the war and afterward (Hall 2000: 140–3). Women's reproductive bodies are consistently missing from national rhetoric about the benefits and drawbacks of a changing birth rate, about the duty of families to reproduce the state, and about the economic and social value of children. In the case of the *Malthusian*, space for those bodies is created by an imperfect and in some ways unexpected vehicle, whose rhetorical and contraceptive 'devices' overlapped to broaden the concept of wartime reproductive choice. The interplay of men's and women's voices as this journal's intervention in wartime discourse surrounding reproduction unfolded suggests the complexity of the relationships between wartime narratives of motherhood and the options and pressures experienced by individual women.

Notes

1. Carol Acton looks at this disciplining specifically in the context of girls' magazines of the war era (2008).
2. See, for example, the chapters 'Before "Birth Control"' in Engelman 2011; 'Shifting Ideologies: Birth Controllers, Feminists, the Malthusian League and Eugenics Society,' in Debenham 2014. Soloway 1982 is an in-depth analysis of the League; Soloway's sense of its failures to adapt to the changes brought by the twentieth century are apparent in Part II: 'War, Reconstruction, and Birth Control, 1914–1930.'
3. An unsigned editorial from February 1915 titled 'The War and the Cost of Living' ends with a sentence that lays out this connection: 'However Socialists may decry the laws of supply and demand, they are the only safe guide; and the Neo-Malthusian injunction to restrain reproduction during the war, and leave the regulation of prices alone, is by far the best and most humane in the long run' (15 Feb 1915: 13).
4. This letter, which, as Lesley Hall has noted (2011: 52), also expresses disappointment for the *New Statesman*'s failure to support Margaret Sanger, reads in part: 'And now Dr. Saleeby denounces neo-Malthusianism with his usual wealth of hyperbole and simile, and there are signs that the capitalist press ... are starting a campaign for unlimited families. I hope, Sir, that you are proud of your allies.

I can assure you that if the birth-control propaganda would ever be penalised, there are some of us who would feel we had lost all right to self-respect if we did not "go among the people," like the Russian revolutionaries, to bring the women of the poor the knowledge they need' (15 Nov 1915: 92).
5. Literature also participated in this anxiety. Two plays produced during the war portray opposite, but equally unconventional approaches, Marie Stopes's *The Race* (1918), in which a British woman makes the decision to have premarital sex with her fiancé before he leaves for war in the hopes that he will impregnate her (Grayzel 1999: 101), and American playwright Marion Craig Wentworth's *War Brides* (1915), about a German woman who chooses suicide rather than bear a son to fight in the Kaiser's army. Edwin Pugh's socialist utopian novel *The Great Unborn: A Dream of Tomorrow* (1918) imagines a future in which the potential of the 'Gebärstreik' is fulfilled, and the working class achieves its goals through birth control (Soloway 1982: 178–9).
6. This reference to 'the poorer classes' is an interesting backtrack, since poverty, while an important reference for Neo-Malthusians, isn't listed as a particular reason for the birth strike in most of its mentions in the journal.
7. The version of the pamphlet consulted for this information is likely postwar, because it contains an advertisement for *The New Generation*, the later title of the *Malthusian*; however, Ledbetter indicates that the contents of the 'Practical Leaflet' remained the same during those years (1976: 210–11).
8. See Craig 2013, Chapter 3, for a discussion of a similar column in Margaret Sanger's *Birth Control Review*.

Works Cited

Acton, Carol. 2008. 'Best Boys and Aching Hearts: The Rhetoric of Social Control in Wartime Magazines for Young Women.' *The First World War and Popular Culture*. Ed. Jessica Meyer. Boston: Brill Press. 173–93.
Bourke, Joanna. 2013. 'Bodily Pain, Combat, and the Politics of Memoirs Between the American Civil War and the War in Vietnam.' *Histoire Sociale/Social History* 24.91: 43–61.
Craig, Layne Parish. 2013. *When Sex Changed: Birth Control Politics and Literature between the World Wars*. New Brunswick, NJ: Rutgers University Press.
D'Arcy, F. 1977. 'The Malthusian League and the Resistance to Birth Control Propaganda in Late Victorian Britain.' *Population Studies* 31.32: 429–48.
Debenham, Claire. 2014. *Birth Control and the Rights of Women: Post-Suffrage Feminism in the Early Twentieth Century*. London: I. B. Tauris.
Doan, Laura L. 2013. *Disturbing Practices: History, Sexuality, and Women's Experience of Modern War*. Chicago: University of Chicago Press.
Engelman, Peter C. 2011. *A History of the Birth Control Movement in America*. Westport, CT: Praeger.
Grayzel, Susan R. 1999. *Women's Identities at War: Gender, Motherhood, and Politics in Britain and France during the First World War*. Chapel Hill: University of North Carolina Press.
Haire, Norman. [1922]. *Hygienic Methods of Family Limitation*. London: Malthusian League. Nineteenth Century Collections Online. <http://tinyurl.galegroup.com/tinyurl/8Z2bm0/> (last accessed 12 December 2018).
Hall, Lesley A. 2000. *Sex, Gender and Social Change in Britain since 1880*. New York: St Martin's Press.
—. 2011. *The Life and Times of Stella Browne, Feminist and Free Spirit*. London: I. B. Tauris.
James, Pearl. 2013. *The New Death: American Modernism and World War I*. Charlottesville: University of Virginia Press.
Ledbetter, Rosanna. 1976. *A History of the Malthusian League, 1877–1927*. Columbus: Ohio State University Press.

Ouditt, Sharon. 1994. *Fighting Forces, Writing Women: Identity and Ideology in the First World War*. New York: Routledge.
Robb, George. 2015. *British Culture and the First World War*. 2nd edn. London: Palgrave.
Scarry, Elaine. 1985. 'Injury and the Structure of War.' *Representations* 10.1: 1–51.
Soloway, Richard Allen. 1982. *Birth Control and the Population Question in England, 1877–1930*. Charlottesville: University of North Carolina Press.
—. 1995. *Demography and Degeneration: Eugenics and the Declining Birthrate in Twentieth-Century Britain*. 2nd edn. Charlottesville: University of North Carolina Press.
Stone, Dan. 2002. *Breeding Superman: Nietzsche, Race, and Eugenics in Edwardian and Interwar Britain*. Liverpool: Liverpool University Press.
Weindling, Paul. 1989. *Health, Race, and German Politics between National Unification and Nazism, 1870–1945*. Cambridge: Cambridge University Press.
Woolacott, Angela. 1994. '"Khaki Fever" and Its Control: Gender, Class, Age and Sexual Morality on the British Homefront in the First World War.' *Journal of Contemporary History* 29.2: 325–47.

26

A Column of Our Own: Women's Columns in Socialist Newspapers

Elizabeth Carolyn Miller

RECENT WORK IN MODERN periodical studies has been increasingly attentive to the marginal corners of print culture where modernism's aesthetic and material forms took root. Women's contributions to modernist writing were particularly reliant on little magazines, small presses, the private theatrical sphere, alternative periodicals, and other small-scale venues that enabled women's participation in the broader currents of modernist experimentation. This chapter will take up the theme of women and marginal media in the modernist period – a theme previously explored by such critics as Lucy Delap and Maria DiCenzo, Ann Ardis, and Barbara Green – and connect it to debates about socialism and capitalism within literary culture.[1] At the intersection of these two fields of inquiry one finds a print archive that has been largely ignored by literary scholars: women's columns in socialist newspapers.

While the women's column as a feature of the journalistic landscape was not invented by the modernist-era socialist press, socialist newspapers adopted this form in the late nineteenth and early twentieth centuries as a means of drawing women readers, bringing women into the movement, and articulating a socialist account of working-class feminism. Examining women's columns in the *Clarion* (1891–1934), the *Labour Leader* (1894–1987), *Forward* (1906–60), and *Justice* (1884–1925), I will consider how such columns articulate a class-conscious, anti-capitalist version of Virginia Woolf's feminist call for a 'room of one's own.'[2] They claimed space for what I am calling 'a column of *our* own' rather than '*one's* own' – for a community of women readers and writers rather than for the independent woman writer. They staked this claim in two different senses. On the one hand, the columns aimed at interpellating working-class women who had precious little time for reading, leisure, or (more to the point) participation in socialist politics. Many of these women worked full-time outside the home, and if they were married, as the columnists were quick to point out, they were typically burdened with the primary childcare and household responsibilities, too, in what feminists now call the 'second shift.' The columns' authors call on women readers to carve out some time and space for themselves – to read the column, to participate in its discourse community, and to participate in the movement more broadly – yet their tone is ever conscious of the constrained lives of women readers and their lack of free time and space. On the other hand, the columnists are also mindful of their *own* marginal space within the broader newspapers they inhabit, and they openly discuss debates with editors about how much print space their women's columns might occupy as well as the degree of editorial control or editorial freedom they experience.

This chapter will examine columns authored by Eleanor Keeling and Julia Dawson in the *Clarion*, Lily Bell in the *Labour Leader*, Mary Phillips in *Forward*, and Dora Montefiore and Margaretta Hicks in *Justice*. In no case did any of these women play a prominent role in the general editing of the paper in which their column ran. Julia Dawson, who wrote the popular 'Our Woman's Letter' in the *Clarion* – which, having run from 1895 to 1911, was the most successful and long-running women's column in the era's socialist press – considered her marginal position within the context of the socialist newspaper as allowing her certain freedoms: '*I* have no influence with the Board whatever, nor with any other member of the staff. . . . So long as I keep within this little three-column space, they let me alone, and that is all that I can say of them' (11 Apr 1896: 120). A few months later, however, she complained to readers, 'my third column is going to be taken away from me,' making for new constraints on what she would be able to accomplish within her little corner of the paper (*Clarion* 8 Aug 1896: 256). Indeed, while the authors who conducted these columns liked to emphasise the freedom that came with their marginal, separate role within the larger publications that hosted their columns, it was always an uneasy freedom. This chapter shows how Dawson, Keeling, Bell, Phillips, Montefiore, and Hicks, as conductors of women's columns in the socialist press, inhabited new authorial subject positions and made new demands on their audience in service of articulating a socialist-feminist vision from within the marginal columns of the radical press.

To invite readers to imagine and conceptualise the space of the women's column within each of these papers was, in itself, to claim a space for female discourse within a larger socialist conversation that was not always attentive to the situation of women. Friedrich Engels's *The Origin of the Family, Private Property, and the State* (1884) was one of the first works of socialist theory to recognise how fundamental patriarchy and the submission of women were to the capitalist economy, but within the broader socialist movement, recognition of this key tenet of socialist feminism was uneven. The authors of socialist women's columns all attempted, in various ways, to articulate the connections between patriarchy and capitalism, but they also sought to reach readers in terms that were inviting and familiar. Consequently, they often conceptualised women's space within the socialist movement, and, by extension, the space of the column within the socialist newspaper, in conventionally feminine terms.

In 'Matrons and Maidens,' which ran in the *Labour Leader* from 1894 to 1898, making it the earliest socialist women's column discussed in this chapter, Lily Bell encouraged readers to write to her, to interact with the column, and to think of the column as the drawing room or salon within the broader architecture of the paper: 'I want you all to have a feeling of proprietorship in this column, and not to look upon it as simply a place for airing my own particular views on matters in general. I should like to make it a sort of meeting place, where I should be playing the part of hostess' (28 Apr 1894: 7). Such language was quite obviously gendered in the terms of female domestic space, but it was also a plea for interaction, female community, and dialogue:

> What I want is that you should join in the conversation, and give expression to your thoughts and ideas on any subject that may come up, not confining yourselves to such matters as are most particularly associated with women, but remembering that there is really nothing that can come under discussion anywhere, in which, directly or indirectly, women are not in some way interested. (ibid.)

This passage suggests, importantly, not that the women's column is marginal to the paper but that it is, rather, an alternative sphere *within* the paper; far from limiting its proper field of inquiry by virtue of the audience it seeks to reach, the column insists instead that *all* fields of inquiry belong, properly, to women.[3] Bell rejects the notion that women constitute a special faction within the socialist movement, but suggests instead the centrality of women's political interests to the entirety of socialist thought.

This model of the socialist women's column as interactive and community-based would persist in later columns that ran after the turn of the century, following the example of Bell and other early conductors. Mary Phillips, for example, in her column 'Woman's Point of View' for the Glasgow socialist paper *Forward*, barely found it necessary to encourage her readers to write, so established was this discursive format already: 'Will readers please remember – I have never said it before, because I thought it went without saying – that I am always glad to receive comments on anything I write in this column or suggestions for any subject to be dealt with?' (5 Oct 1907: 4).

Among all the columnists I will discuss, Julia Dawson is especially notable for her efforts to draw her readers into a column of their own, to invite them into a space of intimacy and companionship that would attract them to political discourse and the socialist movement. She often expressed a desire to transcend the distance of print and interact physically with the readers of her column. Her column ran for the first time on 5 October 1895, and just over a month later she was already expressing herself in terms of great intimacy and warmth to her readers:

> I should love to split myself up into a thousand Julias, and take a peep at you all by your own firesides, but alas I cannot, and this cold sheet of *Clarion* paper is of necessity my only means of communication with you. When you read it, therefore, will you try to believe that I am there in the flesh and blood, talking to you, and that I shall feel horribly repulsed and left out in the cold if you never have a word to say to me? (16 Nov 1895: 368)

Dawson actually used a pen name in her column – her real name is variously identified as Mrs D. J. Myddleton-Worral (Barrow and Bullock 1996: 157) or Mrs D. Middleton Worrall (Hunt and Hannam 1999: 171) – so her expressed desire for warm, intimate exchange with readers, apart from the 'cold' world of print, is itself the affectation of a print persona. Likewise, when a reader requested that she include a photograph of herself at the head of her column, Dawson balked at the request, ostensibly out of modesty; but given her use of a pen name, it is clear that maintenance of pseudonymity was also at stake: 'I do not think many people would feel that my Column would be improved if my photograph appeared at the head of it! I should dearly love to see you in your little study, and to give your hand a right good grip' (21 Dec 1895: 408).

Dawson's effort at developing an intimate rapport with readers was, despite such artifice, crucial to her mission. She included an 'Answers to Correspondents' section in nearly all of her columns, allowing her readers to follow ostensibly private conversations between Dawson and individual readers. Readers wrote to her for advice on everything from marriage to underwear and to voice their opinions on all manner of subjects. Dawson replied to one reader, E. B., with suggestions on 'a nice pattern for knickers' that are 'comfortable' as well as 'hygienic' (23 Nov 1895: 376). Another reader, F. H., appears to have revealed an injustice at the factory where she worked, to which Dawson replied, 'You will not get into any trouble, as I treat all such letters in strict confidence. The factory inspector has already been put on the track' (20 Mar 1897: 96). Some readers would write for material help, which Dawson would try to provide, as in the case of a poor young mother's request for a new perambulator (1 Aug 1896: 248). In many cases, Dawson would also reprint letters from readers, as in the 27 February 1897 issue of the column, which includes a letter from a reader named Isa Nicholson on the subject of municipal crèches, or daycare (72). The public nature of Dawson's replies to her readers, whether their missives were printed or not, meant that her communications had a dual audience: the individual reader who is being addressed and answered as well as the wider community of readers who are following such exchanges in the column. The effect of this dual audience was to help readers understand themselves as an intimate community, despite the mediation of print, and to give Dawson an opportunity to articulate a collective identity for the group. Sometimes she did this through a gentle form of group pressure, replying to one woman reader, L. H., that '*Clarion* women in all stations of life are thoroughly up to date, so you really must change your opinions' (23 Nov 1895: 376).

Dawson also sought to translate the collective feeling of the column into political actions outside the domain of the paper. The Clarion Van is the most famous example of this, although the effort was apparent in many aspects of her column. The Clarion Van was the brainchild of Dawson: a horse-drawn soup caravan repurposed for socialist agitation and staffed by Clarionettes (the paper's term for its community of readers) who would travel around various English districts in the summer months holding speeches, rallies, and lectures and distributing literature to advocate for socialism. Dawson first proposed the idea of the Van in her 29 February 1896 'Our Woman's Letter' (72), and within her column she gave regular updates on its progress. From the perspective of modernist literary history, one of her most interesting updates describes how Charlotte Perkins Gilman (here called Mrs Charlotte Perkins Stetson) accompanied the Clarion Van on a summer 1896 propaganda campaign. Dawson described Gilman to her readers as 'a thorough, out-and-out Socialist, with an amount of energy and determination which is truly refreshing to see. The fire of enthusiasm flashes from her eyes. She is here, there, and everywhere, all in a minute' (1 Aug 1896: 248).[4] A few weeks later, Dawson describes how Gilman addressed a crowd of 2,000 at South Shields, a coastal town on the Tyne, east of Newcastle, as part of the 'Clarion Women's Van Meeting': 'Not a single person moved away till the last speaker had said her last word, and the last question had been answered. Mrs. Stetson answered the questions in rapid succession, and the recitation of her poem, "The Cart Before the Horse," was warmly appreciated' (19 Sep 1896: 304).[5]

Dawson called on her readers to participate in the Van if they could: 'It would be lovely if some of our ablest women would kindly consent to occupy this Van, two or three at a time, during the sunny months of the year . . . and from it distribute *Clarions*, "Merrie Englands," and other explanatory and convincing Socialistic literature' (29 Feb 1896: 72). A political commitment of this scope would not, however, have been possible for most of the busy women readers of socialist newspapers. Nevertheless, the conductors of these columns continually encouraged their women readers to claim some space and time to exercise political and social agency in whatever manner they could, and the question of free time emerged, in itself, as a major issue of socialist feminism from the perspective of the columns. In 'Maids and Maidens,' Lily Bell urged her readers, 'It is an absurdity for men to make such a fuss about overtime work, so long as women are kept on the grind from morning to night without cessation, and without question as to the justice of it. Surely we, too, have a right to call some time our own' (*Labour Leader* 15 Dec 1894: 7). She predicted that, 'the time is coming when women, too, will see the need for some rearrangement which will add to their freedom' (ibid.). In another column, Bell again raised the question of women's unpaid and thoroughly unregulated labour in the domestic sphere: 'the working man who now clamours for his "eight hours day," [*sic*] will have to face the problem of reducing his wife's hours of labour also' (5 May 1894: 3). That women – more specifically, working-class women – constituted the proletariat of the sexual order was a point beginning to be expressed by socialist feminists like Bell.

Reproduction was likewise an area of life where women's unpaid labour contributed, in a way rarely acknowledged at this time, to the supply of workers for capitalism. As I discuss elsewhere, Julia Dawson addressed this issue through the campaign for birth control that she launched in her *Clarion* column in December 1895.[6] But even beyond her advocacy of birth control as a means to improve the lives of working-class women, Dawson also demanded attention to and respect for the difficult labour of bringing a child into the world, and rearing it once it is here. Such social labour weighed most heavily on working-class women, who, unlike wealthier women, had little resources for domestic help:

> the heaviest curse which the competitive system has brought about rests upon women – I mean working women, of course. After a confinement the woman who does not work (and therefore feeds and clothes herself at the expense of those who do) can take the period of rest which is absolutely necessary in order to regain full strength. But the working woman must be up and doing as soon as ever she can crawl out of bed. (*Clarion* 27 Mar 1897: 104)

Recognising the limited opportunities many of their readers had to claim time for political action, given their responsibilities to their children and others, Bell and the other columnists worked to provide readers with a number of possible on-ramps and entry points by which they might translate reading the women's column into political action. Often they encouraged readers to effect political change from within the bounds of traditional feminine roles. Dawson's column, for example, compares the great struggle of socialism to an epic cleaning project: 'This grand tidal wave of loving sympathy for the poor and oppressed which is surging through our land will leave its mark behind it. It will not cleanse every foul spot at the first wash, but each succeeding wave will help to finish the work of its predecessor, till all is bright and clean!' (*Clarion* 21 Dec 1895: 408). Because women were often the primary shoppers in their families, many writers of socialist women's columns were especially prone to encourage their women readers toward socialistic habits of consumption. While production, rather than consumption, generally dominated socialist discussions of political economy at this time, we find a countervailing emphasis on consumption in socialist women's columns. In the 7 December 1895 issue of the *Clarion*, for example, Dawson asked her readers to pledge themselves to the 'Clarion Early Shopping League,' even including a pledge form for readers to submit. Readers who signed the pledge promised 'not to do any shopping after the hour of 7 p.m. (unless compelled by urgent necessity)' (392). Late closure was a major issue for the National Union of Shop Assistants, and in asking her readers to finish their shopping early, Dawson was calling on them to be more responsible toward workers in the retail sector. Clearly, however, such a promise would be easier to keep for women who were not compelled to work outside the home.

In *Justice*, England's first socialist newspaper and the official paper of its first socialist organisation, the Social Democratic Federation, Margaretta Hicks's women's column paid particularly close attention to the matter of consumption. Of all the columnists discussed here, Hicks was the most invested in the issue and did the most to recruit her readers into socialist habits of consumption. In the 10 May 1913 instalment of her column 'Women's Work in the Movement,' Hicks made her appeal by way of traditional feminine roles and encouraged her readers toward socialist action in the political and domestic spheres. Describing a May Day rally, she notes, 'the Women's Council was there, too, with its motto, "The Children of Earth Need Our Protection," that expresses perhaps the strongest appeal that can be made to any woman' (*Justice* 10 May 1913: 3). She went on to describe how women socialists are 'trying to use their power of buying for the spread of Socialism' (ibid.). This was a major interest of Hicks's, who was Secretary of the Women's Council of the British Socialist Party and who was, unlike other authors of socialist women's columns discussed in this chapter, a working woman: she was employed as a tailoress, and was the daughter of Amie Hicks, a ropemaker and midwife (Hunt and Hannam 1999: 169). Perhaps because her financial situation was more straitened than the other authors discussed here, a great many of her columns address the rise in cost of living as a socialist issue. She believed that women consumers clubbing together could actually exert a control on prices. As part of this large effort, she spearheaded cooperative purchasing schemes among women socialists, including the purchase of a coal supply in March 1913: 'The practical work of our co-operative clubs is also being taken up. Don't forget that we have taken over our own coal supply. All Socialists in the four-mile radius should order their coal through the Women's Council. . . . Send your orders at once. It will speed up our movement' (29 Mar 1913: 2).

Dora Montefiore, who wrote an earlier column called 'Our Women's Circle' for *Justice* from 1909 to 1910, also made her appeal to women readers through accessible identity formations. She argued that socialist women were crucial to the movement because they were uniquely situated to counter widespread 'misrepresentations' about socialism: 'the two principal outspoken lies used against us Socialists are that our teaching is anti-Christian and anti-marriage' (*Justice* 9 Apr 1910: 5). Religion and marriage were, of course, two topics that were thought to be squarely within women's proper realm of action. But instead of simply presenting women as defenders of religion and marriage, all of these columns instead ask women to think critically about such institutions as part of being a woman socialist. Lily Bell addressed the marriage service of the Church of England, for example, and especially the ritual portion in which women vow to 'obey' their husbands, concluding that the ceremony 'is just a proof of the fact that woman owes to so-called "religions" much of the burden of her slavery. . . . The religions of the past have been religions *of* man and *for* man' (*Labour Leader* 14 July 1894: 7). Julia Dawson, for her part, often presented socialism as the obligatory political adjunct to true Christianity, replying to one reader, 'a good Christian *must* be a good Socialist, although it does not necessarily follow that a Socialist must be a Christian. Christ was the greatest social reformer the world has ever seen. But many of the orthodox clergy and Christian teachers of to-day conveniently ignore His Socialistic teachings' (*Clarion* 14 Dec 1895: 400).

Montefiore was a veteran of Julia Dawson's Clarion Van, and thus her column could be said to have evolved in part out of the community of socialist women that was created and nurtured by Dawson's successful 'Our Woman's Column.' Like Dawson and other socialist women's columnists, part of Montefiore's goal as a columnist was to direct more socialist education toward children, and such advocacy for children was, again, an accessible identity formation for women socialist readers. In the 10 April 1909 issue of 'Our Women's Circle' in *Justice*, Montefiore reported on one women speaker who pointed out that:

> In our Socialist propaganda attention seemed chiefly directed to adults, and in many cases this was labour lost, as old prejudices and customs were so ingrained as to be almost impossible of removal. With children it was different; with them nothing was impossible, but our organisation seemed to overlook the possibilities in that direction. (5)

Montefiore went on to encourage her readers, 'This capturing of the children for Socialism was great work for . . . Socialist women' (ibid.). Montefiore was a member of the Women's Social and Political Union (WSPU) – the militant wing of the suffrage movement – in addition to the Social Democratic Federation (SDF). Her radical bona fides are established. And yet, here, she is redefining what it means to be radical by drawing children's education and children's activities into the domain of the socialist press.[7]

In another column, Montefiore called her women readers' attention to the waste of food that happens under capitalism, referring to an article about fresh fish being sent to manure works due to oversupply. This is another instance of appealing to women readers' domestic roles as a means of reaching them politically: 'I hope this fact will appeal to the imagination of some good housewives, who are not Socialists yet, but will, through this object lesson in wilful [sic] capitalist waste, see the force of our argument' (*Justice* 17 July 1909: 7). Fish wasted through an alleged 'glut' in the supply chain is, Montefiore argues, a perfect encapsulation of how 'the essence of capitalism is waste' (ibid.). There was no more visceral evidence of the evils of capitalism than a market-driven surplus of food while poor people remain hungry, and Montefiore appealed to women, so often responsible for cooking and feeding, at the level of their 'hearts': 'These facts,' she says, 'should specially be taken to heart by women, who are the purchasers of food, and who know that whatever "glut" of fish or other good food there may be, it does not help the wife of the working man in laying out her few shillings in necessary food for the family' (ibid.).

If writers of socialist women's columns appealed to women readers through socialist arguments that revolved around women's domestic and caretaking duties, however, they also encouraged women to reinvent the domestic sphere so as to free women from its round-the-clock demands, to allow them time to pursue other work and other interests. Montefiore, for example, took up the issue of municipal laundries in the 20 June 1909 issue of 'Our Women's Circle' for the London socialist paper *Justice*: 'Every London borough should have its municipal laundry, and the larger industrial boroughs should have one in every ward' (5). Laundry was one of the most loathsome and detested of chores for nineteenth-century women, but municipal facilities could make it easier by means of better equipment and economies of scale. Montefiore recognised that socialist backing for municipal laundries could have a major effect in bringing more women to the cause, since it was an issue that bore so directly on women's working lives. She recommended that socialist women comrades speaking to non-socialist women 'should talk to them about municipal milk-supply for the children, coal supply for the long, dreary winter, and municipal laundries for relieving working-class mothers from some of their drudgery' (*Justice* 20 June 1909: 7).

Similarly, Eleanor Keeling of Liverpool, who launched the first, short-lived version of 'Our Woman's Column' for the *Clarion* from February to April 1895, wrote in favour of collectivising domestic labours to reduce their burden on individual women. In the 2 March 1895 issue of her column, Keeling reports that one correspondent complained of her proposal for communal cooking since he enjoys eating meals together with his family at home. Keeling responds, 'it is not at all necessary to *eat* in public. It is the *cooking* which should be carried out on co-operative lines' (*Clarion* 2 Mar 1895: 72). Again, the central issue of women's unpaid labour in the domestic sphere emerges as a flash point within women's socialist columns: this male reader defends his domestic arrangements as they are, but Keeling wants to free up his wife's time while still preserving the tradition of family meals at home. Ironically, Keeling gave up writing 'Our Woman's Column' around the time of her own marriage, a possible indication of the gap between the ideal and the practical even for socialist women of this era.[8]

Keeling wrote one of the earlier women's columns discussed in this article, since hers began appearing in the *Clarion* less than a year after Lily Bell's in the *Labour Leader*, and she was as deeply concerned with clearing a space for women within the socialist press as she was with clearing their burdensome schedules at home. When she began writing 'Our Woman's Column' in the 9 February 1895 issue of the *Clarion*, Keeling defined the column's space as a separate corner independent of Robert Blatchford, the paper's editor, and the rest of his male staff: 'This is not a woman's article; it is not even a woman's letter; it is a woman's column. Herein we women may settle down to a cosy gossip about our own affairs and what we say will be no business of the other sex' (43). Her somewhat secessionary tone reflects the context of the paper more broadly: Blatchford and many of his fellow writers in the *Clarion* had had their start in journalism by way of the sporting press, so they tended toward a certain style of male camaraderie defined by nicknames, slang, and jokiness.[9] Keeling's task was to carve out a space for female community within the atmosphere of male homosociality that dominated this popular socialist paper: 'Now we women have got a column all to ourselves in the *Clarion* and I hope we shall make good use of it. Therefore sistren – why not sistren as well as brethren? – I hope you'll write to poor me, lest the candid one blow me out, like a dim candle, because of my insufficient light' (*Clarion* 9 Feb 1895: 43). Keeling acknowledges, at the very beginning of her column's run, that Blatchford and the other male members of the staff have the power to 'snuff out' the women's column, but so long as it appears to be popular among readers, Keeling has hope of being left alone.

Keeling's column didn't last long – it ended but a few months later in April 1895 – but Julia Dawson, one of the most important figures in the *Clarion* movement, picked up where it left off and began publishing her successful and influential women's column 'Our Woman's Letter' in the 5 October 1895 issue of the *Clarion*.[10] Her first instalment likewise presents the column's space as oppositional within the paper: 'I am told that few women read the *Clarion*, and that, therefore, it will be very uphill work to make a Woman's Column popular' (5 Oct 1895: 320). A few weeks later, Dawson reprinted a letter from a reader who pessimistically predicts that though 'it is nice to think that we women are to have a little corner of our own, there is not much chance of our making ourselves heard amidst Nunquam's Clarion note, clear and penetrating' (19 Oct 1895: 336). (Nunquam was the nickname of Blatchford, the paper's editor, for 'Nunquam Dormio' or 'I Never Sleep.') But Dawson's vision for the column remained steady from the beginning: 'I want to swell the ranks of the women readers of the *Clarion*. Most of us have aspirations, many of us have grievances. Can we not mutually help each other to realise the one, and to remove the other? Let us use this column to this end' (12 Oct 1895: 328).

Almost across the board, the most significant means by which women's socialist columns defined themselves spatially within their newspapers was through illustrations and headings. Not all columns enjoyed such visual distinction – Margaretta Hicks's column, 'The Women's Council B.S.P.,' did not – but most were set off in some way to provide visual difference from the rest of the paper. Mary Phillips's column in *Forward*, 'A Woman's Point of View,' was not illustrated but had an ample heading with enough white space to set it clearly apart. Dora Montefiore's column in *Justice*, 'Our Women's Circle,' featured a prominent illustration and heading that extended beyond the width of the actual column in some instances. A number of different illustrations were rotated through to accompany Julia Dawson's column in the *Clarion*, yet it bears mentioning that all of them failed to negotiate the complex class dynamics at work in the column. In one frequently occurring image, a middle-class woman with upswept hair and a low-cut evening gown looks away from the reader, with her face in partial profile. The woman is elegant, but removed, in a way that hardly seems to speak to the working-class women readers to whom Dawson frequently appealed (Figure 26.1). In the next image to appear, the column makes an attempt to present itself, visually, to working-class women readers, but the exhausted

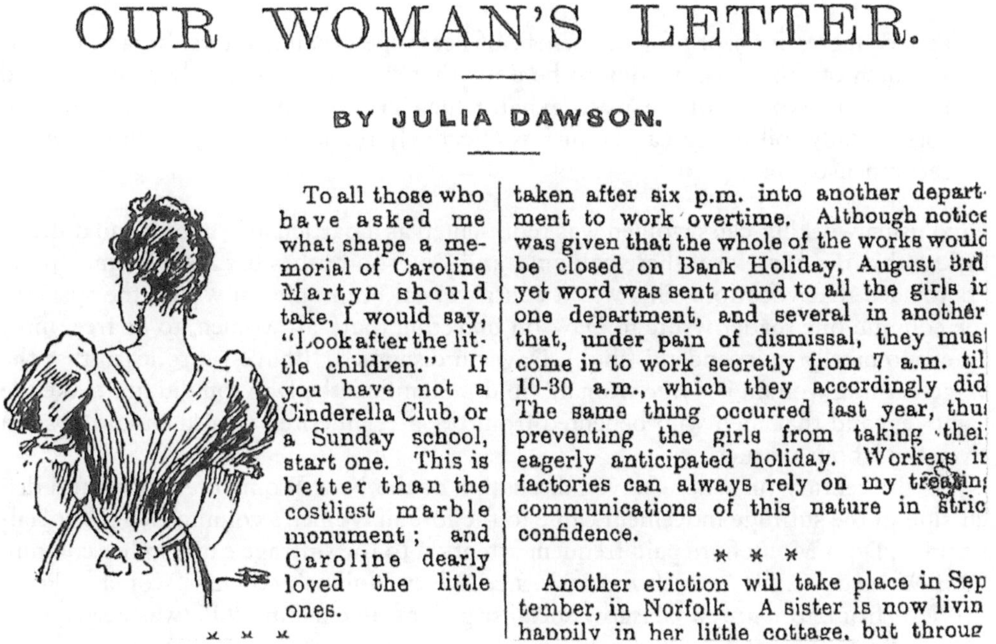

OUR WOMAN'S LETTER.

BY JULIA DAWSON.

To all those who have asked me what shape a memorial of Caroline Martyn should take, I would say, "Look after the little children." If you have not a Cinderella Club, or a Sunday school, start one. This is better than the costliest marble monument; and Caroline dearly loved the little ones.

* * *

taken after six p.m. into another department to work overtime. Although notice was given that the whole of the works would be closed on Bank Holiday, August 3rd yet word was sent round to all the girls in one department, and several in another that, under pain of dismissal, they must come in to work secretly from 7 a.m. til 10-30 a.m., which they accordingly did The same thing occurred last year, thus preventing the girls from taking their eagerly anticipated holiday. Workers in factories can always rely on my treating communications of this nature in stric confidence.

* * *

Another eviction will take place in September, in Norfolk. A sister is now living happily in her little cottage, but throug

Figure 26.1 Julia Dawson's column in the *Clarion* (August 1896).

and unhappy-looking drudge who looks up from her tub of laundry – one of the most hated chores for women of this era – fails to offer a model of working-class womanhood that readers would have wanted to emulate (Figure 26.2). Lily Bell's 'Matrons and Maidens' in the *Labour Leader* likewise used more than one illustration, but the one that accompanied the column most frequently depicted a serious-looking New Woman writer, musing over her work with a pen at her mouth (Figure 26.3).

On the subject of the New Woman, the authors of socialist women's columns were ambivalent. They admired, on the one hand, the possibilities for female autonomy and agency that this figure embodied; Eleanor Keeling wrote that, 'A New Woman is one who has high ideals of what life should be, and (this is the point) who is determined *to think for herself*, to use her newly-discovered reasoning powers' (*Clarion* 23 Mar 1895: 90). But the distinctly bourgeois class status of the prototypical New Woman also made her a figure of capitalist privilege. That the New Woman would *choose* to work as a means of self-actualisation or fulfilment alienated her as a subject of identification for working-class women, whose labour was often low paid and exploited. In one column, Julia Dawson addressed the issue of the New Woman's labour outside the home by arguing 'that girls who have private means, or whose parents can afford to keep them at home, should not go out into the world as wage-earners, thereby taking the bread out of the mouths of those whose own hard work is their only means of support' (30 Nov 1895: 384). Presenting paid labour as a zero-sum game within the capitalist economy, Dawson suggests that middle-class socialist women, despite their desire for financial independence or for fulfilling work outside the home, have a duty to leave paid work for their working-class brothers and sisters. Should the socialistically inclined daughter of the bourgeoisie, then, amuse herself at home? Dawson suggests rather that she should engage in unpaid labour on behalf of the socialist movement, especially

> active, aggressive work for the benefit of her wage-earning sisters. In fact, there is so much of this work waiting to be done that the world positively cannot afford to allow its women of means to exhaust their energies and their strength in that sort of daily toil which can be just as effectively rendered by those who *need* the recompense. (ibid.)

Unionising working-class women was represented as a particularly urgent and difficult task within the context of these columns, and Dawson pushes her New Women readers toward that vocation. This was a controversial opinion even within the space of the column: one reader wrote to Dawson objecting that, 'all women, to be free, must be economically independent' (ibid.). Dawson disagreed, 'I have yet to learn that the wage-earning woman is a *free* woman' (ibid.). Significantly, Dawson did not make the same demand that men who benefited from private, inherited wealth should abstain from the labour market.

As the century turned, however, discussion of the New Woman fell away and discussion of the suffrage movement came to the fore in women's columns for the socialist press. Dora Montefiore paid frequent attention to the suffrage cause in her column, 'Our Women's Circle,' which ran in *Justice*. Mary Phillips's column 'Woman's Point of View' from *Forward*, a Glasgow socialist paper launched in 1906, was perhaps, of

OUR WOMAN'S LETTER.

BY JULIA DAWSON.

In Glasgow a Cinderella Club is to be started in memory of Caroline, and their first effort will be to take some children to Helensburgh at the autumn holiday. One of the sisters there says: "I used to tell Miss Martyn I could do nothing. I am too nervous to speak or to second motions; but I can help to prepare food for the little ones." This truly is work the least of us women can do. We all know how to cut bread and butter, and little beginnings may have great endings.

Figure 26.2 Julia Dawson's column in the *Clarion* (September 1896).

Figure 26.3 Lily Bell's column in the *Labour Leader* (August 1894).

all the columns under consideration here, the most explicitly aligned with the suffrage cause. Phillips was a supporter of the Women's Social and Political Union and their more activist approach to the suffrage cause; the WSPU favoured civil disobedience and other militant tactics in contrast to the 'constitutional' approach of the more moderate groups. In her column, Phillips regularly referred to the WSPU's paper, *Votes for Women*, acting as a link and a channel between the socialist and feminist presses. In the 12 October 1907 issue of her column, she announced this new publication in terms that suggest her dual allegiance to both spheres of discourse:

> 'VOTES FOR WOMEN,' the slogan of the new Suffrage movement, is the title of our own new monthly paper, the official organ of the National W.S.P.U. . . . I hope if you have not already seen it you will have done so before the next *Forward* reaches you. I have promised myself the pleasure of making some extracts . . . [but] I must defer the pleasure until next week. (5)

A few weeks later, she provided some justification for this early version of cross-posting: 'As it is my duty to comment on all that concerns the welfare of my sex, I naturally wrote a review of the first number of "Votes for Women" – a paper that cannot fail to be appreciated by everyone gifted with a literary taste, and zealous for the emancipation of women' (*Forward* 2 Nov 1907: 8).[11]

As such serious-minded examples may suggest, all of these writers appear to have taken pride in the extent to which their socialist women's columns steered clear of the sorts of topics that dominated women's columns in mainstream papers. Indeed, the extent to which they sought to avoid discussion of women's dress, for example, was a frequent topic in and of itself. One reader, Ethel Edwards, wrote to Lily Bell in the *Labour Leader*, '*Re* your recent strictures upon the "Ladies' Column" of the *Graphic*, permit me to say that I heartily endorse your sentiments, and consider your condemnation to apply with equal force to nearly, if not all, the "columns" and periodicals published expressly for women' (15 Dec 1894: 7). Even rational dress – presumably the socialist-feminist women's answer to the fashion magazines – was a subject of little interest for these columnists. Mary Phillips, in 'Woman's Point of View,' wrote that 'Rational dress is a matter to which, I must confess, I have not given so much thought as it deserves since my early days, when finding skirts a serious impediment to my numerous tree-climbing and ladder-scaling exploits, I rebelled against them accordingly' (*Forward* 15 June 1907: 5). She considers dress a topic, like others, that must be approached through 'reason' rather than 'convention,' but feels that agitation on the subject 'is a little belated' (ibid.). On the one hand, she said, such matters will be of little import in the context of widespread social change after the dawn of socialism: 'with the dawn of the day that is coming, when womanhood will, for the first time, have freedom to develop its natural powers, we shall have less time to waste on fashions and frivolities' (ibid.). In the meantime, she says, a fixation on rational dress could be detrimental to the socialist cause: 'The radical changes proposed by the advocates of dress reform are on the whole improvements, but if we suddenly adopted them, we should have to face a storm of Ridicule and Opposition that would tend to draw off our energies from more vital conflicts' (ibid.). Phillips discourages the socialist 'faddism' in matters of dress, food, and lifestyle that had, so often, been a cause for ridicule in the mainstream press (ibid.).

Phillips was not the only columnist, however, to speculate about what socialism would mean for women's fashion. Only a few months into her column, Lily Bell wrote to her readers, 'If I come across anything really pretty in the way of dresses, hats, or materials, I shall be glad to tell you about them, but I should be sorry to let this column degenerate into a mere description of the "latest fashions," which are often the most hideous things possible' (*Labour Leader* 28 Apr 1894: 7). But Bell, while attempting to appeal to readers' interest in fashion, cannot resist the socialist tendency to think of dress commodities in terms of labour and production. In the future, she imagines, socialist production might introduce a new aesthetics of dress utterly distinct from contemporary conceptions of fashion: 'I wonder whether, when we get the length of nationalising industries, and the state runs the milliners' and dressmakers' shops, we shall get rid of the ugly, inartistic arrangements which are so often brought forward as "the latest thing out!"' (ibid.).

Socialist discourse was prone toward such musings on future possibilities – it was, indeed, one of its greatest pleasures. The challenge that women's columns in the socialist press had was to navigate the gap between the imagined future and the possibilities of the present. What might be achievable in the way of women's rights now? What might be achievable for workers? What aspects of women's oppression would fall away under a more just distribution of social goods? And what aspects of capitalist oppression would fall away under more equitable social conditions for women? Negotiating the fault lines between socialism and feminism, and articulating a unified ideology of socialist-feminism, were the significant challenges these authors faced. Writing a new discourse of political possibility, their response was to claim space for women as a collective group. Whether that space was in the paper itself, which must provide room for these women's columns, or whether that space involved freeing some time for political agency in the busy lives of women workers, all of these columnists were unified in their demand for such space as a condition of possibility for women's collective political agency. In that sense, the scope of their advocacy overlaps with the work of modernist women writers across all kinds of print platforms in the late nineteenth and early twentieth centuries, but most especially with those women writers who made use of under-commercialised corners in marginal media, spaces that allowed for a uniquely feminist form of expression.

Notes

1. For more on this topic, see Delap and DiCenzo 2008; Ardis 2007; or Green 2009.
2. For more background on these journals, see Hunt and Hannam 1999, and Brake and Demoor 2009. See also Miller 2013, which includes material on many of these papers, as well as a section on the representation of birth control and biopolitics in socialist women's columns in Chapter 6.
3. Over the years, many critics have assumed that Lily Bell was actually a pseudonym for Keir Hardie, owner and editor of the *Labour Leader*, but more recent research has shown her to be a pseudonym for Isabella Bream Pearce, president of the Glasgow Women's Labour Party (see Hunt and Hannam 1999: 171, and Hannam 1992: 209). When Hardie introduced Bell to the papers' readers in the 31 March 1894 issue, he called her 'a Scotch lassie, with a warm heart and a clear, strong brain' (2). Despite this description, rumours that the column was really written by a man were widespread, as is indicated by a letter from a

reader printed in the paper on 1 September 1894. The fact that this early socialist women's column was thought, for many years, to be the work of a male editor in disguise demonstrates that women columnists in these papers had their work cut out for them in terms of establishing a column of their own.

4. This was not Charlotte Perkins Gilman's first appearance in the *Clarion*'s columns for women. Keeling referred to Gilman a few times, including in her 30 March 1895 column. In a discussion of the importance of married socialist women taking on public roles and becoming involved with and elected to boards of guardians and school boards, Keeling quotes Stetson's poetry in support: 'Have you no dream of life in fuller store? / Of growing to be more than that you are? / Doing the things you now do better far? / Yet doing others – more? // Losing no love but finding as you grow / That as you enter upon nobler life, / You so become a richer, sweeter wife, / A wiser mother, too' (30 Mar 1895: 98).

5. The poem, not reprinted in the journal, is a poem about labour, and while it conceptualises the abstract figure of the worker as male rather than female, it also acknowledges the labour of motherhood and child rearing as an integral part of the capitalist economy: 'A baby! with an appetite to fit! / You have to feed him years and years, / And train him up with toil and tears, / Before he works a bit!' (Charlotte Perkins Gilman, 'The Cart Before the Horse,' *Commonwealth* Oct 1902: 25).

6. See Chapter 6 of Miller 2013.

7. For more on Montefiore, see Hannam and Hunt 2002 and Hunt 1996.

8. Keeling was married to Joseph Edwards, editor of the *Labour Annual*, and both were deeply involved in the socialist movement. For more on this Liverpool couple, see Fidler 1979.

9. In the 10 March 1894 issue, for example, Blatchford made a mild criticism of a Margaret McMillan article on music that had run the week before, and though writing in a jovial tone, he portrayed the woman author as an interloper on the all-male staff's print domain: 'Is a lady to come into our columns and calmly tell us that our birds and brooks and winds are not musical? This comes of the higher education of women. Did I not warn the delegates at the Labour Conference that the emancipation of women would lead to trouble?' (8).

10. Dawson's prominence in the movement is due not only to her work on the *Clarion*'s women's column, but more especially because of her idea to start the Clarion Van, discussed previously. Dawson also served as honorary secretary of the Clarion Guild of Handicraft, which worked to promote Arts and Crafts principles among the Clarionette community (*Reformers' Year Book*, 1908: 208).

11. There was also occasional cross-referencing among women columnists in socialist papers, as when Lily Bell wrote a letter to *Forward* praising a position taken in Mary Phillips's 'Woman's Point of View Column.' The editors printed Bell's letter just after the column in the 7 December 1907 issue (6).

Works Cited

Ardis, Ann L. 2007. 'The Dialogics of Modernism(s) in the *New Age*.' *Modernism/modernity* 14.3: 407–34.

Barrow, Logie and Ian Bullock. 1996. *Democratic Ideas and the British Labour Movement, 1880–1914*. Cambridge: Cambridge University Press.

Brake, Laurel and Marysa Demoor, eds. 2009. *Dictionary of Nineteenth Century Journalism*. London: British Library.

Delap, Lucy and Maria DiCenzo. 2008. 'Transatlantic Print Culture: The Anglo-American Feminist Press and Emerging "Modernities."' *Transatlantic Print Culture, 1880–1940*. Ed. Ann Ardis and Patrick Collier. Houndmills: Palgrave. 48–65.

Fidler, Geoffrey. 1979. 'The Work of Joseph and Eleanor Edwards.' *International Review of Social History* 24.3: 293–319.

Green, Barbara. 2009. 'The Feminist Periodical Press: Women, Periodical Studies, and Modernity.' *Literature Compass* 6.1: 191–205.

Hannam, June. 1992. 'Women and the ILP, 1890–1914.' *The Centennial History of the Independent Labour Party*. Ed. David James, Tony Jowitt, and Keith Laybourn. Halifax: Ryburn Publishing. 209.

Hannam, June and Karen Hunt. 2002. *Socialist Women: Britain, 1880s to 1920s*. London: Routledge.

Hunt, Karen. 1996. *Equivocal Feminists: The Social Democratic Federation and the Woman Question, 1884–1911*. Cambridge: Cambridge University Press.

Hunt, Karen and June Hannam. 1999. 'Propagandising as Socialist Women: The Case of the Women Columns in British Socialist Newspapers, 1884–1914.' *Propaganda: Political Rhetoric and Identity, 1300–2000*. Ed. Bertrand Taithe and Tim Thornton. Stroud: Sutton. 167–82.

Miller, Elizabeth Carolyn. 2013. *Slow Print: Literary Radicalism in Late Victorian Print Culture*. Stanford: Stanford University Press.

27

Prayer Warriors: Denominational Feminism, the Vote, and the *Church League for Women's Suffrage Monthly Paper*

Krista Lysack

Cultural historians of British suffrage have for some time now encouraged us to view the campaign for women's votes in Britain as a heterogeneous movement rather than as a monoculture, one not limited to the efforts and concerns of a particular class of women.[1] The WSPU, for instance, was formed out of the Manchester labour movement and struggles for workers' rights. It was also the case that religion, and in particular the rise of denominational feminism,[2] provided compelling arguments for others to join the cause for women's votes. The fact that even the ostensibly secular quarters of the suffrage movement regularly 'adopt[ed] . . . religious languages and motifs' of conversion, revival, and martyrdom attests to the role religion played in the cause (deVries 1998b: 323).[3] But there were also several groups who organised their aspirations for the vote around a particular religious or denominational identity. Sophia A. van Wingerden explains that '[e]ach major religion in Britain had its group of suffragists, for each of whom suffragism seemed to flow naturally from their religious principles' (1999: 110).[4] The largest of these and the first to be founded was the Church League for Women's Suffrage (hereafter the Church League or the CLWS), established in 1909 in order to unite Church of England suffragists (ibid.). This essay seeks to uncover more about the intersections of religious fervour and non-militant political activism in the suffrage movement by examining the CLWS's official organ, the *Church League for Women's Suffrage Monthly Paper* (1912–17).

Still not as well documented by historians and literary critics as other suffrage newspapers – such as the Women's Social and Political Union's *Votes for Women* (1907–18),[5] the National Union of Women's Suffrage Societies' *Common Cause* (1909–20), or the Women Freedom League's the *Vote* (1909–33)[6] – the *Monthly Paper* affords us the opportunity to consider how, by attending to the malleable and transposable potential of the periodical form, we might discover something about the range of women's relationships to modernity where religion and politics are concerned. The *Monthly Paper* regularly cast religious practice and civic reform as overlapping domains that Church League members were seen to negotiate successfully throughout the pages of this newspaper. Engaging simultaneously in devotional and political endeavours with equal aplomb, the *Monthly Paper* is testament to the richly diverse work of first-wave feminism.

The accommodating and capacious nature of the periodical form is one that has become well acknowledged in periodical studies, especially where feminist scholarship is concerned. Such scholarship has considered how the study of periodicals may usefully disturb and expand the notion of the woman writer and, in so doing, begin to address the ways in which authorship can also be a matter of collective and communal effort. Barbara Green, for instance, has observed that with periodicals the 'author' becomes a usefully 'unstable' category in keeping with what 'feminist theory has taught us it should be' and surmises that 'periodical culture encourages us to recover not the single woman writer, but the network, the dialogue, the conversation' (2013: 56, 58).[7] Sean Latham and Robert Scholes also point to the inherently collaborative nature of periodicals; comprised of multiple issues, periodicals 'are frequently in dialogue with one another' (2006: 529). Periodicals 'thus create and occupy typically complex and often unstable positions in sometimes collaborative and sometimes competitive cultural networks' (ibid.). In terms of their contents, periodicals are also uneven and miscellaneous; they are often a mix of genres, of high- and low-art, of text and paratext (Latham and Scholes 2006: 519–20). Moreover, the manner in which they are read is not necessarily uniform; while they are produced in regular increments – temporalities that were typically enshrined by the nineteenth century as daily, weekly, monthly, biannual, and annual formats – they could be read less predictably, browsed, or read out of order.[8] In short, periodicals challenge much of what we assume about stable authorship, of the fixed boundaries of the text, and how readers of periodicals go about reading.

Produced by a lively, collaborative community of Church of England suffragists, the *Church League for Women's Suffrage Monthly Paper* is a periodical that we can consider in light of these kinds of observations about authorial, textual, and temporal non-fixity and blend. Indeed, the fact that it was an official organ made the *Monthly Paper* that much more available for revision and adaptation. Instead of dismissing the official organ genre as formulaic and programmatic, we might, as Maria DiCenzo has demonstrated, see how '[s]uffrage periodicals played an increasingly strategic role in how rival organisations communicated and managed their differences in terms of both their memberships and the wider public alike. The proliferation of official organs after 1907 indicated not just a growing movement, but also a changing and diversified movement' (2011: 77). '[O]fficial organs,' she continues, 'negotiated the tension between the need for a coherent movement and the reality of its fractionalism' (ibid.), revealing that while there may have been disagreement between those who expressed different approaches to waging the suffrage campaign, this conflict is also indicative of a whole host of reasons why people were drawn to the movement (DiCenzo 2011: 119). For all of their typical and seemingly prescriptive contents (statements of league objectives, reports of chapters from around the country, news of public processions and protests, appeals for support, advertisement, some of which I will go on to consider later), suffrage official organs nevertheless were texts through which the movement could express the variety of its many adherences and alliances. In the case of the *Monthly Paper*, this diversity expresses itself through the convergence of suffrage politics and Church of England affiliation. Far from indicating the fringe interests of a suffrage offshoot, the *Monthly Paper* is therefore indicative of how the official organ periodical – as template that lends itself to reinvention rather than mere replication and to miscellany rather than script – was a shifting discursive space that could arrange and rearrange the often overlapping, even competing aims.

In the case of the Church League, the intersections of suffrage activism and religious devotion produced a potential impasse that the *Monthly Paper* ameliorated: the question of whether the Church League was a political or a religious organisation. In asserting that it could be and was both, the *Monthly Paper* furthermore articulated a nuanced stance on the use of militant tactics; indeed, the *Monthly Paper* managed to telegraph the Church League's seriousness about and commitment to the suffrage cause by revising what was meant by militancy. Like other constitutional suffragists, notably the NUWSS, and in contrast to the suffragette WSPU which became notorious for often violent and spectacular tactics (window-smashing, arson, and other spectacular acts of public vandalism and protest), the CLWS declared itself neutral. But even as the CLWS cleaved to its non-militant stance, the *Monthly Paper*, as I will go on to show, underscored the commitment of its members to the suffrage cause by casting them collectively as the 'Church Militant' whose religious fervour substituted for militant tactics. The paper deployed the discourse of militancy, often through its appeals to communal prayer and other organised devotional practices, without having to resort to acts of violence.

The Church League for Women's Suffrage: Formation and Object

The emergence of the CLWS can be linked to the turn-of-the century movement within the Church of England to permit women to vote in church councils (Smith 2010: 31). But two of its founding members, Margaret Wynne Nevinson and the Reverend Claude Hinscliff, both recount a more immediate impetus for the Church League: prayer vigils for women's votes that were being held at Parliament in 1909. As part of these regular vigils, some members of the constitutional Women's Freedom League were meeting to pray. Nevinson remembers 'the evening of July 5, 1909, [when] the Women's Freedom League held simultaneous meetings in the vicinity of Westminster, from which delegates were sent, carrying the resolutions passed by huge crowds, to the Prime Minister' (May 1913: 217). The desire to continue the practice of intercessory prayer for the cause of women's suffrage then lead to a preliminary meeting on 25 October 'to consider the question of forming a Church League for Women's Suffrage' (Oct 1913: 299). Hinscliff became 'daily more convinced that only a great cause could bind together women of all classes and all shades of religious and political opinion to endure so much for an idea' (May 1913: 217). The new League's inaugural meeting was held on 2 December at St Mark's in Regent's Park ('The Church League and Women's Suffrage' 1909: n.p.).

Prominent Church League members included its founder, Hinscliff (who also acted as its first secretary),[9] Nevinson, Maude Royden, Maud Bell, Emily Wilding Davison, Constance Lytton, parliamentary advocate George Lansbury, and half a dozen bishops of the Church of England (Inkpin n.d.). The Church League was governed by a general council (chosen by the branches) that met once a year in order to select its executive and twice-yearly to conduct business (Oct 1913: 300). Charging a minimum annual subscription of one shilling, the CLWS went on to establish branches across Great Britain, and at least one branch in Dublin. At one point in 1913, it had ninety-one branches and over 500 members (ibid.). Membership was open to men as well as women who were members of the Church of England (or of any church in communion with it), who 'approve of the Rules of the League,' and 'pay the annual subscription' as determined by their local branch ('Objects and Methods,' Jan 1912: 1).

In many ways, the work of the CLWS resembled that of the larger and secular suffrage groups which was already underway. 'Like other suffrage societies,' writes van Wingerden, 'the League held public meetings, drawing-room and garden meetings, and took part in processions' (1999: 111). Indeed, many of its members held simultaneous membership in other societies.[10] But its religious programme rendered it distinctive. Hinscliff describes the major religious observances of the Church League as 'the use of special prayers during times of crisis; attendance at the Holy Communion on Corporate Communion Day once a month; or at Special Celebrations arranged from time to time; the Observance of Quiet Days; and participation in various types of Devotional meetings' (Oct 1913: 300). In a 1909 pamphlet,[11] the CLWS laid out its 'Object' in this way: 'To secure for women the Parliamentary Vote as it is or may be granted to men; to use the power thus obtained to establish the equality of rights and opportunities between the sexes, and to promote the social and industrial well-being of the community'('The Church League and Women's Suffrage' 1909: n.p.). The pamphlet goes on to discuss the group's aims and to qualify its non-partisan and non-violent stance:

> The C.L.W.S. has been formed to band together Churchpeople who are Suffragists for devotional purposes and to further the cause of Women's Franchise in the Name of God. Its aim is simply to proclaim the why and wherefore of the Vote, and is therefore of an educational character. The League, as such, knows no 'party.' Tactics concern the secular societies. The CLWS must be catholic in its sympathies by providing a rallying ground on essentials for Suffragists of every shade of opinion. (ibid.)

Along with its commitment to 'Corporate Devotions, both public and private' (Oct 1913: 300), 'the Distribution of Literature' was one of the Church League's stated aims. Although the Church League did produce pamphlets,[12] *The Church League for Women's Suffrage Monthly Paper*, begun almost three years after the CLWS was established and to which I now turn, was its most significant and sustained print endeavour.[13]

The *Monthly Paper*: Workaday Suffragism and the Suffrage Official Organ

While circulation numbers for the *Church League for Women's Suffrage Monthly Paper* are difficult to ascertain, the paper does state in its June 1912 issue that in order to remain financially viable the paper must maintain a monthly circulation of 8,000 copies ('Circulation,' June 1912: 35).[14] Selling for one penny, the paper ran each month, beginning in January 1912 and ending with its final and seventy-second issue in December 1917, just as the Representation of the People Bill was at the report stage. Over the course of its six-year run, the *Monthly Paper*, as we shall see, maintained its religious programme but did so in response to the current and pressing issues that informed the fight for women's votes over the crucial years that lead up to electoral reform in 1918. The first issue of the *Monthly Paper* included, at the outset, the Church League's 'Charter':

> Christianity is the proclamation of the Divine entry into History; of the Divine submission to the historical conditions of human experience; of the Divine sanction given to the things of time and the affairs of earth, to the body, the home, the city, the nation. A kingdom of God come down here, visibly, audibly, tangibly, evidently, manifested on earth – this is its first and last message. (Jan 1912: 1)

This Charter, which is attributed to Henry Scott Holland, would appear almost regularly over the course of the paper's run. So too would the Church League's 'Objects and Methods,' which elaborated on the 'Object' (above) that the CLWS had outlined in its first pamphlet three years earlier by stipulating the methods by which it would now accomplish its goals: 'The methods used are (a) Corporate Devotions, both public and private (b) Conferences, Meetings, and the distribution of Literature' (Jan 1912: 1).

From its first issue, the paper not only telegraphs its role as one of the Church League's key 'methods' but also gives the impression of an already well-underway organisation. This inaugural issue includes, for instance, a treasury report for the preceding month, a list of clergy who are members of the CLWS (around 100), an article on the nursing profession, and a calendar of events for the month ahead which includes details for special services and branch meetings. At this stage only a short, four-page leaflet, the paper would grow to a longer length by the end of its first year; the December 1912 issue was sixteen pages long. The typeface and layout, too, show that the paper, even from its first issue, was a going concern, and these graphical characteristics changed very little over the course of the paper's run. Printed by Francis and Co. in Chancery Lane, London, it was not an amateur product. And while not as visually resplendent as *Votes for Women*, whose pages regularly included illustrations and photographs, the *Monthly Paper*, from the outset, did feature a distinctive visual signature in the form of an illustration that decorates the top of the paper and that was used in every issue to follow. It was designed by Dorothy Grey, who had already established her artistic credentials with the League by designing for it a calendar and Christmas cards (Jan 1912: 1). Grey's illustration for the paper includes the CLWS's badge in the middle, an image of a kneeling woman at the Cross on the left, and a sailboat on the right. The paper explains these emblems' significance:

> Woman yet bows her head beside the Tree, knowing full well that 'suffering is not foreign to the experience of God himself.' Still over the waters of life must God's Ship, the Church, with sail full set and on a path of light, make the Dawn. Ever remains the mystery of Redemptive Love. The Sovereign Cross touching the whole Circle of Life is the Christian's message to the World. (ibid.)

The image neatly summed up in visual form both the struggle in which women were engaged and the hope that could await them should their cause finally succeed.

If the visual arrangements of the paper aroused a sense of Church League aspirations, the contents of the *Monthly Paper* attest to the variety of ways in which it maintained an active presence in the suffrage campaign through many activities and related causes, on which the paper regularly reported. It is a newspaper that reveals both the everyday textures of the life of the CLWS and the larger goal to which it attached itself. Alongside seemingly grander events like the progress of the electoral reform bill or of multi-society suffrage demonstrations, reported as 'United Demonstration' (June 1912: 35), news of the smaller-scale and more quotidian details of the CLWS also received column space. The paper includes, for example, reports on the Church League's coffee stall, which was set up both to generate funds for the League and in hope that it might act as an extension of the CLWS's rescue work (Feb 1912: 5). In a short November 1912 item, co-founder Gertrude M. Hinscliff announces 'that a beautiful new banner has been presented to the League' which featured an image of St Margaret of Antioch,[15] and also requests orders for home-made sweets – 'chocolates, marzipan, peppermint creams, &c. – ' in order to pay for the banner and to contribute to the League's general fund (Nov 1912: 116). In an even shorter item and just above in the layout, the paper announces that the Church League once again will be 'issuing Christmas cards' on which its banner will appear, priced at one shilling each (or nine shillings for a dozen), and appeals for members to get in their orders early (Nov 1912: 116).

These kinds of activities (CLWS rummage sales being another) were not unique to the League. Jill Rappoport has explored how suffragettes, following in the tradition of women's charitable bazaars, produced home-made goods for sale: contributions that underscored a gift economy of selflessness that recall some of the more spectacular sacrifices of the campaigns like imprisonment and force-feeding. Elsewhere I have explored how, by selling suffrage-themed merchandise in their own shops, groups like the WSPU adapted the trappings of commercial culture in order to signal women's participation as profitable players and viable citizens in the public sphere.[16] While the CLWS's ideas for fundraising schemes and commercial enterprises may not have originated with them, they are nevertheless indicative of the inventive ways by which it sought to realise its religious mission beyond mere proselytising.

The *Monthly Paper* also documents the kinds of internal conversations that the Church League was having within its own quarters, including how best to get out the word of the League through more successful sales of the paper. From time to time, the *Monthly Paper* would underscore the need to sell copies, and recommended ways to do this. An article titled 'Selling the Paper' stated that:

> All we want is publicity to ensure the continued success of our Monthly Paper. There are these great opportunities: (1) Outside all Suffrage Meetings . . . (2) outside religious meetings . . . (3) On the streets . . . [where] [a] regular 'pitch' should be taken at a definite time and on a certain day of the week. (May 1912: 26)

In 'Circulation of Monthly Paper,' it was recommended that branch members ask their local newsagents to stock the paper: 'go to any newsagent in your vicinity and ask him if he will take in the paper "on sale or return" at trade terms (thirteen for 9*d.*), and display a contents bill' (Nov 1912: 116). A later issue provides tips for paper sellers, such as 'Always dress as well as possible,' and 'Don't get depressed if you do not sell any papers for the first half-hour or so' (Feb 1913: 167).

The Church League did not count these sorts of fundraising activities or internal matters as frivolous. Indeed, the paper includes appeals to support the paper during several periods of financial precarity. But it is worth pointing out that along with reporting on these kinds of endeavours, the *Monthly Paper* just as regularly engaged in discussions about social reform issues that were strongly linked or allied to the suffrage cause and women's advancement. In addition to rescue work, to which their coffee stall was linked, the Church League endorsed many other causes as well, such as child welfare, temperance, rights for industrial workers, and the fight against sex trafficking. For instance, the November 1912 issue includes an article by Gladys Tatham, 'Women's Suffrage in Connexion with Public Health,' which begins by linking the so-called White Slave Trade to the need for women's political representation: 'If any fresh proof were needed of the urgent necessity for woman's intervention and influence in politics, the disgraceful whittling down of the Bill known as the Criminal Law Amendment Bill, which has been passed through Committee in such an emasculated form, affords yet another argument for Women's representation' (Nov 1912: 116). The paper also frequently advocated for women's work, doing so with an article on the nursing profession in its very first issue, which concludes on this rhetorical high note: 'Whether Political Enfranchisement for Women, or Professional Enfranchisement for Nurses, will come first, I cannot say, but an undeniable fact is – that both reforms are urgently needed. The Reform Movement among nurses is all part of the great Women's Movement' (Jan 1912: 4). In ways like this, the *Monthly Paper* made clear the alignment between women's professions and votes for women.

The *Monthly Paper* moreover inserted itself into conversations about the CLWS's relevance vis-à-vis national and international events.[17] In the case of the former, the *Monthly Paper* made occasional but pointed reference to the tendency of the non-suffrage press to boycott coverage of the women's suffrage movement, except when it served its own interests to sensationalise or propagandise. Late in the run, the *Monthly Paper* observes in 'Notes of the Times,' 'We, suffragists have long been familiar with the fact that one of the chief difficulties the Women's Cause has had to encounter was misrepresentation and boycott by the press. This, we must believe, was not due mainly to the journalists, but to those in whose hands lies the control' (Nov 1916: 190). The paper also shows its interest in current events when it cites the Cat and Mouse Act, 'too well known to need repetition' in a March 1914 piece with the title 'Meddlesome Bishops' (Mar 1914: 50).[18] Moreover, it was quick to signal the Church League's patriotism upon the outbreak of the Great War, connecting the work of suffrage with national unity: 'Who, since the expectant, breathless night when war was declared, has not felt with a proud humility that it was good to be one with this nation?' and commending 'the whole body of Suffrage workers [that] has come forward so adequately for patriotic work' (Oct 1914: 176). The paper soon began publishing 'Names of C.L.W.S. Members on Active Service' (Feb 1915: 29), both men as well as women, and, eventually, a 'C.L.W.S. Roll of Honour' containing the names of those members of the Church League who perished while in service (Feb 1917: 21). Most of all, the paper kept tabs on the progress of electoral reform in Parliament through the various stages of reading until, in 'Suffrage Notes' that appeared in the final issue in December 1917, it can report that 'the Representation of the People Bill is going through its Report Stage, and, barring unforeseen accidents, its position most hopeful' (Dec 1917: 290). The bill did indeed pass in February 1918, extending the franchise to certain women over thirty.

Together, the contents of the *Monthly Paper* begin to assemble a picture of the CLWS that shows how it was engaged in a variety of practices that positioned the League as an active player in the suffrage campaign, but they do more than just this. For what is also notable is the extent to which the paper shows an awareness of, a citational familiarity with, the format of other and more prominent suffrage newspapers like *Votes for Women*, the *Common Cause*, and *Vote*. As DiCenzo suggests (and as I mentioned at the outset), the genre of the official organ provides a ready-made template that users can simply replicate but, equally, reformulate to their own ends. There was, not surprisingly, a sense of formal affinity between the various suffrage newspapers, even when there were ideological differences between the different leagues. Most papers brandished their league name and badge on the front page, included the aims of their organisation, carried news stories of the most current suffrage protests and processions (sometimes with photographs), ran special series on issues that related closely to votes for women (such as fair pay and hours for shop workers), and reported regularly on the activities of branches from across the nation. The ways in which the various suffrage papers resembled one another in contents and layout is perhaps best illustrated in their nearly universal use of advertisements. As Lisa Tickner (1988), Barbara Green (1997), and others have shown, a number of suffrage societies found ways to represent suffrage through highly choreographed public performances and visual spectacles, including print advertising. Many suffrage papers courted advertisers who would support the cause, sometimes even featuring ads from the same or similar kinds of retailers (Kaplan and Stowell 1994: 172–6; Lysack 2008: 145–50). The *Monthly Paper* was no exception; it began to introduce advertisements at the end of its June 1912 issue. The CLWS's first accounts are from businesses like drapers, milliners, and florists, but these later extend to include booksellers and beauticians, and also to the promotion of other suffrage societies and their respective newspapers. And like the other suffrage papers, the *Monthly Paper* urged its 'readers that by giving their patronage to those who advertise in our paper they will render the C.L.W.S. invaluable assistance. The utmost care is taken to ensure that only firms of high standing and reliability advertise in these papers' (June 1912: 35).[19] The *Monthly Paper* therefore cites a familiar vocabulary in its use of advertisements, and in doing so establishes its affiliation with the visual and print culture of the suffrage campaign.

Periodical studies have for some time now encouraged us to pay attention to paratextual features like advertisements.[20] In the case of the *Monthly Paper*, the advertisements indeed have significance, suggesting the paper's formal (though not political) affiliations with other suffrage papers, especially to those major ones, *Votes for Women*, *Common Cause*, and *Vote* that were already up and running by 1907 or 1909. By the time the *Monthly Paper* was established in 1912, the formula of a suffrage paper is already well established by such precursors. The resemblance between the various papers is but one instance of what Barbara Green has described as the 'cross-referencing, cross-pollinations, and critical commentary on other journals' that characterised early twentieth-century feminist print culture (2009: 196–7). In its layout, contents, and use of advertisements, there are few ways in which the *Monthly Paper* doesn't resemble its peers.[21]

And yet in one other important way, the *Monthly Paper* exceeds the status of mere imitator of the larger suffrage newspapers that preceded it. The *Monthly Paper* cannot be so easily dismissed as a lesser knock-off of the official suffrage organs that came a few years before, nor is it merely a transcript or record of the Church League's activities and aims. The *Monthly Paper* was rather an active space of reformulation of an already a familiar format. Through its pages it generated a simultaneously political and religious discourse of suffrage activism, and provided an effective and affecting re-framing of militancy.

'Political or Religious:' Militancy for the Non-Militant

'The process of reading a magazine,' Faye Hammill, Paul Hjartarson, and Hannah McGregor remind us, 'involves actively assembling the different components – articles, advertisements, illustrations, letters to the editor – into an unpredictable, idiosyncratic, and ultimately unstable whole. With its capacity for reading across large quantities of text in non-linear ways and discovering unlikely patterns, distant reading is a promising method for capturing this quality of emergence . . .' (2015: 3). This is a compelling recommendation. What impressions are left by the repetitions and iterations of the *Monthly Paper*'s content over its five-year run? James Mussell observes that '[n]o single issue [of a periodical] exists in isolation, but instead is haunted by the larger serial of which it is a part. This larger serial structure is invoked through the repetition of certain formal features, issue after issue' (2015: 343). What lingers is a sense of urgency on the part of the Church League to realise its jointly religious and political goals. One might say that the *Monthly Paper* transposed the ideological fervour associated with the suffrage cause, adapting it to a religious register that at once maintained a political credibility. In other words, *Monthly Paper* is indicative of how periodicals may organise affective relationships for their reading communities.[22]

The question of whether the CLWS was a political or a religious group was one that the Church League was apparently asked regularly, and it was therefore a question the *Monthly Paper* felt compelled to address directly in its pages:

> We have been asked whether our League is political or religious. We answer that it is both. It seeks to reform in the political sphere, viz., the enfranchisement of women. To this extent, therefore, it is political. It seeks to that reform on religious grounds and by methods, educative and devotional, which religion employs . . . Moreover, we insistently teach that it is impossible for a religious man to divorce religion from his political action. ('Political or Religious?' Nov 1912: 115)

This article continues, qualifying that 'our League is absolutely non-political in the party acceptation of that term,' and noting the diverse political views of the C.LW.S.'s membership (Nov 1912: 116). The *Monthly Paper* thus helped to construct the Church League's reciprocal goals, and it frequently commented on the felicity and compatibility of these goals: 'women's demand for enfranchisement is in harmony with the teaching of our Masters, the granting of which is essential to the perfecting of his kingdom. In our view the subjection of one sex to another . . . is in contradiction to the whole ethic of Christianity' ('Why the Church League Exists,' June 1913: 228). Nevinson's account, 'How the Church League was Founded,' recollects not just the terms but the sentiments under with the League came into being: 'Why not a religious league for what was clearly a religion to many? Why should not the prayers of the faithful strengthen the hands of those who worked and suffered? Why not a Church League?' (May 1913: 217). Religious enthusiasm here spills into the political arena; the feeling, the ardour, underscored by Nevinson's soaring, anaphoric rhetoric, is an endorsement for both domains, for both endeavours. The zeal for women's votes was like a religion, and this is something that the CLWS both understood and institutionalised.

One of the reasons that the CLWS may have felt some pressure to justify its political seriousness is because of its neutral stance on militant tactics. Like the much larger NUWSS, it was an organisation of constitutional suffragists, not suffragettes.[23] In April 1912 'Our Difficulty' addressed the fact that whereas other groups, especially the WSPU, could publicise the cause through spectacular and galvanising displays such as vandalism and arson, the neutral CLWS discouraged violence, seeing it as inconsistent with its religious stance: 'our attitude as a League is a neutral one' (17). The paper goes on to recommend the need for neutrality over militancy: 'Those who accuse us of cowardice might also remember two things. It is not just a question of the Church's continual timidity, but rather the sense of the holiness of our religion' (ibid.). The League's 'stable vantage-group,' after all, was 'our devotions' (ibid.). In place of militant tactics, the League's affective appeals came through its advocating for prayer, the very practice through which it first came into being:

> While other Suffrage Societies are calling their members to 'militant action,' . . . it is for us . . . to enforce the need of prayer [. . .] Prayer is our weapon – the prayer of brave, unselfish, loving hearts. Others have their own armoury. We do not affect to despise them. But this we say, that if in the past we had used our weapons as selflessly, as persistently, as fearlessly, as other weapons have been used by other hands, the victory had been won ere now. Let us pray. (Sep 1912: 88)

The CLWS returned to the issue of militancy again in April 1914 in a piece called 'The Weapons of Our Warfare,' citing a desire for unity across the suffrage societies and suggesting that those who employed militant tactics created a barrier to the united front that the cause would require if it was to succeed (Apr 1914: 68).

Interestingly, then, the CLWS found a way to deploy the discourse of militancy without having to resort to militant tactics. Adapting the scriptural metaphor of spiritual warfare, the paper regularly touted prayer as the Church League's chief and best weapon. Moreover, from time to time, the *Monthly Paper* found a way to visualise and even to coordinate and standardise this 'weapon' through the use of prayer charts. Titled, 'Plan of Continuous Intercession,' the charts organised a week of corporate prayer for Monday through Saturday, scheduling blocks of time, both daytime and evening, for which members were to sign up. By the time such charts made it to press, some of the slots were already booked by members and were shaded in to indicate that they were no longer available. The blank spots on the chart were an invitation for other members to commit their time. 'Each represents an hour and each hour is divided into quarters,' the text below this chart explains (May 1915: 85). 'It will be a great help if Members able to find a definite time, will, before writing to

Headquarters, consult this Chart, and, if possible choose a time which is still free' (ibid.). With a kind of military precision, the CLWS prayer charts timetabled the weapon of prayers to the cause.[24]

In addition to its charts, the *Monthly Paper* also encodes its rousing calls to non-militant action in still other ways through its repurposing of the conventions of hymns and catechisms. It printed ardent suffrage hymns which transposed the prosody of that genre to the Church League's political aims, as in 'A Suffrage Hymn,' published in the April 1912 issue: 'In our further fight for freedom / Help the women of to-day; / Give us greater power for service, / Great strength our part to play' (lines 9–12) (Apr 1912: 18). The paper also ran a series called 'A Suffrage Catechism' that appropriated the catechism form and began, 'Q. What are the main reasons for which women desire the Vote? A. Women desire the Vote (1) as a recognition and symbolism of their citizenship; (2) as a means whereby to procure the remedy of certain glaring injustices under which women suffer; (3) as an effective instrument of social service' (June 1913: 228). This series went on to run for several months, but then had to be postponed when the editors found that it was taking up too much space. Even as it found ways to reinvent well-known formats as these, the *Monthly Paper* still relied upon another tried and true genre to generate religious fervour, the sermon, frequently reprinting the sermons and addresses of clergyman who held a pro-suffrage stance. Staunchly both political *and* religious, the paper encoded in these various ways the CLWS's sense of righteous urgency.

Soon after the passing of the Representation of the People Act in 1918,[25] the CLWS took on a new and perhaps even more suitable name: the League of the Church Militant. It also adopted a new name for the newspaper, the *Church Militant*. In this new instantiation, which lasted until 1928, the Church League began to shift its priorities. Having accomplished its main goal of the vote, it turned all the more to matters of reforming women's governance roles in the Church of England and to the ordination of women.[26] But it was during its pre-1918 years that the *Monthly Paper* first reveals the manner in which politics and religion were intertwined for the CLWS.[27] The *Monthly Paper* defended the worth of fighting a struggle in which the legitimate concerns of both were inextricably bound, in which expressions of both attracted many to the cause. Among the many sermons the paper printed over the course of its run was an address by the Rev. Mered J. Rush, 'The Place of Religion in the Women's Movement,' which underscores this claim: 'There never has been a Woman's Movement and never will be a Woman Movement which is progressive and vital unaccompanied by religion' (June 1914: 109). The *Monthly Paper* arranged in close proximity the aims of religion, progress, and women's votes. Through its confluence of faith and activism, of fervour and resolve, this official suffrage organ negotiated the complexities and possibilities of denominational feminism's alliance with broader first-wave British feminism.

Notes

1. Delap et al.'s wide-ranging anthology, *Feminism and the Periodical Press, 1900–1918* (2006), attests to the diversity and the transatlantic remit of the suffrage movement and its periodicals. Purvis (2000) has explored how the suffrage movement was by no means monolithic in its leadership, organisation, and class make-up.
2. I first came across this term in DiCenzo 2011: 201.

3. See also deVries's brief but judicious account of the CLWS in 'Challenging Traditions: Denominational Feminism in Britain, 1910–1920' (1998a), and in 'More than Paradoxes to Offer: Feminism, History and Religious Cultures' (2010).
4. Among these organisations were the Free Church League for Women Suffrage (a Nonconformist organisation), the Friends' League for Women's Suffrage (a Quaker group), the Catholic Women's Suffrage Society, and the Jewish League for Woman Suffrage (van Wingerden 1999: 110–13).
5. From 1907–12, *Votes for Women* was the organ of the WSPU. After they were expelled from the WSPU because of disagreements over militant tactics, *VFW* editors Emmeline and Frederick Pethick-Lawrence took the paper with them, running it under the aegis of their Votes for Women Alliance until 1914. In 1914, they gave the paper over to the United Suffragists, who published it until 1918.
6. *Votes for Women* remains the most studied of these suffrage newspapers. For further reading on the suffrage press, see, for instance, Murray 2000 and DiCenzo 2003.
7. Green cites Laurel Brake, who argues that periodicals more generally explode the notion of single authorship: 'periodicals . . . subvert the dominance of the notion of the author as individual genius, a notion which is a construct of ideologies interested primarily in the romantic individual' (1991: 167).
8. See, for instance Turner 2002 on periodical time.
9. Varying accounts also cite Hinscliff's wife, Gertrude Hinscliff and/or Dr (Agnes) Maude Royden as co-founders. The secretary role was later taken up by Maude Royden who also acted at one point as chairman. See Roydon 1938.
10. Some members of the CLWS were also and simultaneously members of other suffrage societies. Claude Hinscliff was a member of the Men's League for Women's Suffrage and Gertrude Hinscliff belonged to the Women's Freedom League.
11. The pamphlet is designated 'No. 1' and appears to be the League's first published pamphlet.
12. I have mentioned this first pamphlet in the note above. Some of the CLWS's other pamphlet titles include 'The Church and Women's Suffrage,' by Rev. Maurice F. Bell, 'From East to West – Women's Suffrage in relation to Foreign Missions,' by Dr Helen B. Hanson, 'The Woman Wage Earner,' by George H. Wood, and 'The Cause of Purity and Women's Suffrage,' by Ursula Roberts. These are listed in the May 1912 issue of the *Monthly Paper* ('C.L.W.S. Literature,' May 1912: 32). The titles indicate many of the issues that intersected with the League's goal of suffrage for women. Most of the pamphlets sold for either one or two shillings.
13. Not all of the religion suffrage societies had newspapers, but the Catholic Suffrage Society published *The Catholic Suffragist* (1915–18) and the Free Church League for Women Suffrage published the *Free Church Suffrage Times* (1913–15) (later renamed *Coming Day* (1916–20)).
14. For comparison, we might note that *Votes for Women*'s circulation 'rose from 5000 per month in April 1908 to 22000 per week in May 1909, to over 30000 a week in early 1910' (Crawford 1999: 459).
15. An image of this banner can be found at <www.stgite.org.uk/media/clws.html> (last accessed 31 May 2016). Elizabeth Crawford notes that the League's main banner 'was a depiction of St. Margaret of Antioch from a design by Oswald Fleuss and worked by the Audrey School of Needlework,' and that several of the branches had their own banners as well (1999: 111).
16. On the home-made fundraising and retail enterprise of suffrage societies, see Rappoport 2011 and Lysack 2008.
17. This interest was usually political, but in at least one case it was aesthetic. One of the more unusual articles of the paper's run (at least on the face of it) that indicates its direct engagement with the aesthetically avante-garde of the day is a review by member (and

frequent contributor) Maud Bell of an exhibit of Italian Futurist painters – unusual only because while the paper shows its debt to a theologically informed intellectual tradition, it seems rarely (apart from some occasional book reviews) to venture much into cultural matters (June 1914: 105). And yet this art review (which states that '[t]here is nothing in common between Christianity and Futurism') seems less anomalous when it goes on to urge the reader 'not . . . to scoff' at the new (ibid.). The radical and revolutionary spirit of the Futurists holds some lesson, Bell suggests, to the cause of suffragists.

18. The Cat and Mouse Bill referred colloquially to a 1913 Parliamentary Act of the then-Liberal government. Imprisoned suffragettes who became ill (often as the result of hunger strikes to resist force-feeding) were released in order to recover, and then re-imprisoned on the same charges once they were well again.
19. *Votes for Women* regularly included similar injunctions to its readers to patronise the businesses of its advertisers. See Lysack 2008: 148.
20. See, for example, Beetham 1996: 142–53.
21. One difference between the *Monthly Paper* and the premier suffrage paper, *Votes for Women* (apart from the latter's impressive visual content) is the *Monthly Paper*'s dearth of fiction, something that *Votes For Women* includes on a semi-regular basis.
22. The prompt to think through the affective work of periodicals arises in part from recent work in media studies that concerns the affective relationships users/readers strike up through their use of different media forms. See Madianou and Miller 2012.
23. Although the NUWSS declared a principled and confident commitment to its policy of non-militancy, and while it avoided criticising those suffrage organisations that advocated militancy, it was dealt from time to time with the criticism from some suffragettes that it was 'timid' (Pugh 2008: 251). But for the most part, there was amongst the various suffrage organisations 'a tacit agreement to avoid attacking one another in the interests of the cause' (DiCenzo 2011: 95).
24. On the uses of timetabling in Victorian devotional books, periodicals, and reading, see Lysack 2013.
25. The bill, which passed on 6 February of that year, extended the franchise to new parts of the population, including women over the age of thirty who had the right to vote in local elections (i.e. university graduates, those who held or were married to someone who held property, and those who paid or were married to someone who paid at least 5 pounds annually in rent).
26. When the League for the Church Militant eventually dissolved in 1928, members did so with the aim of moving on to pursuing a new goal, that of the ordination of women (Heeney 1988: 113). On the LCM, see also deVries 1998b.
27. This is not to suggest that the CLWS was somehow less political in its post-1918 years. Jacqueline deVries writes compellingly that we must not '[assume] that in the twentieth century women's activism within religious contexts, which engages religious ideas and employs religious languages, is a less potent form of radicalism than the demand for secular legal and political change' (1998b: 319).

Work Cited

Beetham, Margaret. 1996. *A Magazine of Her Own?: Domesticity and Desire in the Woman's Magazine, 1800–1914*. London and New York: Routledge.

Brake, Laurel. 1991. 'Production of Meaning in Periodical Studies: Versions of the *English Review*.' *Victorian Periodicals Review* 24.4: 163–70.

'The Church League and Women's Suffrage. Sermon before the Inaugural Meeting of the Church League for Women's Suffrage, at St. Mark's, Regent's Park, Thursday, Dec 2, 1909. By the Vicar, the Rev. Maurice F. Bell' (1909), *C.L.W. S. Pamphlets*, No. 1, Piccadilly, London: Printed by the Women's Printing Society.

Crawford, Elizabeth. [1999] 2001, 2002. *The Women's Suffrage Movement: A Reference Guide 1866–1928*. London and New York: Routledge.
Delap, Lucy, Maria DiCenzo, and Leila Ryan, eds. 2006. *Feminism and the Periodical Press, 1900–1918, Volume I*. London and New York: Routledge.
deVries, Jacqueline R. 1998a. 'Challenging Traditions: Denominational Feminism in Britain, 1910–1920. *Borderlines: Genders and Identities in War and Peace, 1870–1930*. Ed. Billie Melman. New York and London: Routledge. 265–83.
—. 1998b. 'Transforming the Pulpit: Preaching and Prophecy in the British Women's Suffrage Movement.' *Women Preachers and Prophets through Two Millennia of Christianity*. Ed. Beverly Mayne Kienzle and Pamela J. Walker. Berkeley: University of California Press. 318–33.
—. 2010. 'More than Paradoxes to Offer: Feminism, History and Religious Cultures.' *Women, Gender and Religious Cultures in Britain, 1800–1940*. Ed. Sue Morgan and Jacqueline deVries. London and New York: Routledge. 188–210.
DiCenzo, Maria. 2003. 'Gutter Politics: Women Newsies and the Suffrage Press.' *Women's History Review* 12.1: 15–33.
—. 2011. 'Unity and Dissent: Official Organs of the Suffrage Campaign.' *Feminist Media History: Suffrage, Periodicals and the Public Sphere*. Ed. Maria DiCenzo, Lucy Delap, and Leila Ryan. Houndmills: Palgrave Macmillan. 76–119.
Green, Barbara. 1997. *Spectacular Confessions: Autobiography, Performative Activism, and the Sites of Suffrage, 1905–1938*. New York: St Martin's Press.
—. 2009. 'The Feminist Periodical Press: Women, Periodical Studies, and Modernity.' *Literature Compass* 6.1: 191–205.
—. 2013. 'Recovering Feminist Criticism: Modern Women Writers and Feminist Periodical Studies.' *Literature Compass* 10.1: 53–60.
Hammill, Faye, Paul Hjartarson, and Hannah McGregor. 2015. 'Introducing Magazines and/ as Media: The Aesthetics and Politics of Serial Form.' *ESC: English Studies in Canada* 41.1: 1–18.
Heeney, Brian. 1988. *The Women's Movement in the Church of England 1850–1930*. Oxford: Clarendon.
Inkpin, Jo. *Making a Track: A Selection of First Christian Feminists*. <http://www.makingatrack.wordpress.com> (last accessed 31 May 2016).
Kaplan, Joel H. and Sheila Stowell. 1994. *Theatre and Fashion: Oscar Wilde to the Suffragettes*. Cambridge: Cambridge University Press.
Latham, Sean and Robert Scholes. 2006. 'The Rise of Periodical Studies.' *PMLA* 121.2: 517–31.
Lysack, Krista. 2008. *Come Buy, Come Buy: Shopping and the Culture of Consumption in Victorian Women's Writing*. Athens: Ohio University Press.
—. 2013. 'The Productions of Time: Keble, Rossetti, and Victorian Devotional Reading.' *Victorian Studies* 55.3: 451–70.
Madianou, Mirca and Daniel Miller. 2012. 'Polymedia: Towards a New Theory of Digital Media in Interpersonal Communication.' *International Journal of Cultural Studies* 16.2: 169–87.
Murray, Simone. 2000. '"Deeds *and* Words": The Woman's Press and the Politics of Print.' *Women: A Cultural Review* 11.3: 192–222.
Mussell, James. 2015. 'Repetition: Or, "In Our Last."' *Victorian Periodicals Review* 48: 343–58.
Pugh, Martin. 2008. *The Pankhursts: The History of One Radical Family*. London: Vintage.
Purvis, June. 2000. '"Deeds, Not Words": Daily Life in the Women's Social and Political Union in Edwardian Britain.' *Votes for Women*. Ed. June Purvis and Sandra Stanley Holton. London: Routledge: 135–58.

Rappoport, Jill. 2011. *Giving Women: Alliance and Exchange in Victorian Culture.* New York and Oxford: Oxford University Press.

Royden, Maude. 1938. *Myself When Young.* London: Muller.

Smith, Harold L. 2010. *The British Women's Suffrage Campaign, 1866–1928.* Rev. 2nd edn. London: Pearson.

Tickner, Lisa. 1988. *The Spectacle of Women: Imagery of the Suffrage Campaign 1907–14.* Chicago: University of Chicago Press.

Turner, Mark W. 2002. 'Periodical Time in the Nineteenth Century.' *Media History* 8.2: 183–96.

Van Wingerden, Sophia A. 1999. *The Women's Suffrage Movement in Britain, 1866–1928.* Houndmills and London: Macmillan Press.

Appendix

Locations

BL   British Library, London
MJP   Modernist Journals Project, an online archive currently hosted by Brown University, available at <http://modjourn.org/about.html>
Each journal included on the MJP is a searchable facsimile, and is accompanied by a critical introduction.
HTDL   Hathi Trust Digital Library. Digital resource that reproduces bound volumes of periodicals, usually from US university collections, once they are in the public domain. Runs vary in completeness, and in levels of access.

The Acorn
A Quarterly Magazine of Literature and Art, illustrated and described as 'deluxe.' The two volumes have continuous pagination.

Dates: 1905–6
Periodicity: Two volumes only; one in 1905, one in 1906
Price: 2s 6d
Place of publication: 47 Great Russell Street, London
Publisher: The Caradoc Press (George Webb and Co. Ltd), 1 Priory Gardens, Bedford Park, Chiswick, London; also Philadelphia: J. B. Lippincott Co.
Editor: Gertrude Hudson
Location: HTDL; New York Public Library; BL, available at <http://arts-search.com/>

The Adelphi (also *The New Adelphi*, Sep 1927–Aug 1930)
Magazine founded and edited by John Middleton Murry, with input initially from S. S. Koteliansky and figures from Murry's previous periodical, the *Athenaeum*. The first issue is said to have sold more than 18,000 copies; but after this the number of readers fell to the range of 7,000 (Whitworth 2009: 375–87). Circulation was an average of 4,200 during the period 1923–7 (see Q. D. Leavis, *Fiction and the Reading Public*). Initially, during his editorship of the early to mid-1920s, the journal emphasised the work of Murry's late spouse Katherine Mansfield and the ideas of D. H. Lawrence. The *Adelphi* attempted to position itself against competing elements in British modernism, and to seek a broader reading public than any of Murry's previous periodical ventures.

Dates: 1923–55; here we only address 1923–30
Periodicity: Initially monthly, June 1923–June 1927; then quarterly (at that point called *The New Adelphi*), Sep 1927–Aug 1930
Price: Vols 1–4, 1923–1925, 1s; then 1s 6d from June 1925–June 1927; then 2s 6d Sep 1927–Aug 1930
Place of publication: London
Publisher: British Periodicals Ltd
Editor: John Middleton Murry (June 1923–August 1930); for vols 1–4 and the new series (*The New Adelphi*), vols 1–3. Directly after this Max Plowman took over as editor, assisted by Sir Richard Rees.
Location: BL; Bodleian Library, University of Oxford; accessed at McGill University Library, Rare Books and Special Collections

Atalanta's Garland

Special Issue magazine to celebrate the twenty-first anniversary of the opening of Edinburgh University Women's Union, and to raise funds for the development of the Union. This miscellany of short stories, poems, articles, and reproductions of artworks gives evidence of the achievement of women in various areas of public life.

Date: 1926
Periodicity: One 'Special Issue' only
Price: Currently unknown
Place of publication: Edinburgh
Publisher: Edinburgh University Women's Union
Editor: Editorial Committee, Edinburgh University Women's Union
Location: Centre for Research Collections, University of Edinburgh

BLAST: Review of the Great English Vortex

Only two issues of this iconic modernist little magazine, edited by Wyndham Lewis, were ever published, No. 1 in 1914 and the July 1915 'War Number.' Launch pad of Lewis's Vorticist movement, *Blast* 'was a manifesto (or, . . . a set of manifestos with supporting art and literature) intended to promote a nascent avant-garde group comprising painters, writers and a sculptor' ('*BLAST*: An Introduction,' Mark S. Morrisson, MJP). Contributors included Lewis himself, Ezra Pound, Ford Madox Hueffer (Ford), T. S. Eliot, Jacob Epstein, Henri Gaudier-Brzeska, and a limited number of women; Rebecca West, and artists Jessica Dismorr, Dorothy Shakespear (Pound), and Helen Saunders.

Dates: Two issues: 1914–15
Periodicity: Quarterly (only two volumes published)
Price: 2s 6d
Place of publication: London
Publisher: John Lane
Editor: Wyndham Lewis
Location: Bodleian Library, University of Oxford; BL; MJP

The Calendar of Modern Letters
Influential but short-lived monthly (later quarterly) literary review that published creative work and literary criticism. It had an initial circulation of around 7,000–8,000. This dropped to 2,000–3,000 after its first year, and fell to 1,000 after it became a quarterly (Bradbury 1966: x)

Dates: Mar 1925–July 1927
Periodicity: Initially monthly (twelve editions); quarterly from April 1926
Price: Unknown
Place of publication: London
Publisher: Wishart
Editor: Edgell Rickword
Location: BL

The Chapbook (initially named *The Monthly Chapbook*)
A little magazine devoted to showcasing contemporary poetry in an accessible, entertaining, and affordable format. Like *Poetry and Drama*, *The Chapbook* set out to present a miscellany of contemporary British poetry – both Georgian and experimental verse – as well as critical articles on contemporary poetry and drama. A number of special issues appeared, among them chapbooks on French poetry (Oct 1919 and Nov 1920), an issue on American poetry (May 1920), and a chapbook carrying Edna St Vincent Millay's one-act play *Aria Da Capo* (Aug 1920). Keeping his promise of providing a lightweight magazine, Monro also published illustrated issues containing songs with sheet music, 'Rhymes for Children' (Nov 1919) as well as 'Old Broadside Ballads' (Sep 1920). Its circulation figures are not recorded (Hibberd 2009: 190).

Dates: July 1919–Oct 1925
Periodicity: Monthly until June 1923 (with two hiatuses: July 1921–Jan 1922 and Mar–June 1922); the two final issues appeared annually, in October 1924 and 1925
Price: 1s–1s 6d
Place of publication: London
Publisher: The Poetry Bookshop
Editor: Harold Monro
Location: BL; also available at HTDL

The Chord: A Quarterly Devoted to Music
Brown paper cover. Bound in book form with paper boards. Foolscap quarto. Illustrated with full page engraved plates.

Dates: May 1899–Sep 1900
Periodicity: Quarterly
Price: 1s
Place of publication: Cecil Court, London
Publisher: The Unicorn Press
Editor: John F. Runciman
Location: British Periodicals online (ProQuest)

The Church League for Women's Suffrage Monthly Paper

Established in 1909, the Church League for Women's Suffrage sought to unite Church of England suffragists. In addition to holding public and house meetings, undertaking special communion services, and participating in processions, the Church League adopted a lively print campaign, most notably through its *Monthly Paper*. Its circulation was around 8,000 in 1912. The *Monthly Paper* inscribed the CLWS's goal of securing the enfranchisement of women on religious grounds.

Dates: 1912–17
Periodicity: Monthly
Price: 1d for subscribers or 1½d for single copies
Place of publication: London
Publisher: Francis & Co.
Editor: The paper does not list a regular editor(s), although it initially lists Miss Lillian A. Cowell as Honorary Editor
Location: Women's Library Archives; BL; British Newspaper Archive; Harvester Microforms

The Church Militant

Soon after the passing of the Representation of the People Act in 1918, the Church League for Women's Suffrage adopted a new name, the League of the Church Militant. It also changed the name of its newspaper from the *Monthly Paper* to *The Church Militant*. This instantiation of the paper reflected the League's new focus on reforming women's governance roles in the Church of England and on the ordination of women.

Dates: 1918–28
Periodicity: Monthly
Price: 2d
Place of publication: London
Location: Women's Library Archives; BL; British Newspaper Archive; Harvester Microforms

Clarion

Socialist newspaper aimed at a wide, working-class audience and written in the New Journalism mode. Its circulation was around 34,000, with a peak of 83,000 in 1910. It included a broad range of materials to engage a large audience, including news, politics, arts, and sports, as well as columns for women and for children. Associated with the journal were a variety of social clubs that readers could join, the most popular of which was the Clarion Cycling Club, which took on a life of its own and sparked a spin-off journal.

Dates: 1891–1934
Periodicity: Weekly
Price: 1d
Place of publication: Manchester originally; moved to London in 1895
Publisher: Clarion Newspaper Co.
Editor: Robert Blatchford ('Nunquam')
Location: Gale Nineteenth-Century Collections Online; Cornell University Library; microfilm

Coterie: A Quarterly: Art, Prose, and Poetry
Short-lived modernist little magazine, influenced by Wyndham Lewis's *BLAST*, featured literature and the visual arts. Certain issues had a circulation of around 1,000 copies (Tollers 1986: 112). Editor Chaman Lall, an Oxford student, 'fostered acceptance of artists and writers of various nationalities and schools of thought.' (MJP) Numerous female artists and writers also contributed, including Edith Sitwell, Helen Rootham, Iris Tree, and Nina Hamnett.

Dates: No. 1 (May Day 1919)–Nos. 6 & 7 (Winter 1920/21)
Periodicity: Quarterly
Price: 2s 8d
Place of publication: London
Publisher: Hendersons, 66 Charing Cross Road, London
Editor: Chaman Lall (first five issues) and Russell Green (final double issue published Winter 1921)
Location: Bodleian Library, University of Oxford; BL; University of North Carolina, Chapel Hill; Stanford University; Harvard University; Columbia University; Cornell University; Brown University; University of Virginia; McGill University; MJP

The Crank (and *Open Road*)
A little monthly periodical aimed at Tolstoyans, pacifists, vegetarians, and anarchists, *The Crank* began as *The Tolystoyan* (1902–3) before becoming *The Crank* and later *Ye Crank* (1904–7). The magazine was finally renamed *The Open Road* (1907–13). Mary Everett Boole chose the name, *The Crank*, to reflect the progressive and countercultural ethos of the publication and its editors. 'A crank is a little thing that makes revolutions' was the slogan suggested by mathematician and frequent contributor, Mary Everest Boole, and it was printed on the front cover of the *Crank*'s first issue.

Dates: 1904–7
Periodicity: Monthly
Price: 3d/month
Place of publication: London
Publisher: C.W. Daniel Company Ltd
Editor: Florence E. Worland
Location: BL

The Dental Record: a monthly journal of dental science, art, and literature
Professional journal largely aimed at an audience familiar with dentistry but also included articles of more general interest regarding the impact of science, diet, and lifestyle on oral health. The magazine also included reviews of books (fiction and nonfiction) featuring topics of interest to those working in the profession. A note under the journal's full title on its cover page states: 'Dental Politics rigidly excluded.'

Dates: 1881–1955
Periodicity: Monthly
Price: 6d/month
Place of publication: London
Publisher: The Dental Manufacturing Company, Limited
Editor: Thomas Gaddes
Location: BL

The Dome

As the subtitle of the first series (Mar 1897–Apr 1898) indicates, 'An Illustrated Magazine and Review of Literature, Music, Architecture, and the Graphic Arts.' The subtitle was dropped from May 1898. A Foolscap Quarto on antique laid paper with plates separately printed. American and Collector's editions were also published.

Dates: Mar 1897–July 1900, ending vol. 7, no. 19; two series
Periodicity: First series – quarterly (Lady Day 1897 to May Day 1898), thereafter monthly
Price: Quarterly 1s; quarterly (in bound volumes) 3s 6d.
Place of publication: London
Publisher: The Unicorn Press
Editor: Ernest J. Oldmeadow (assisted by Laurence Binyon)
Location: British Periodicals online (ProQuest), The Modernist Journals Project (Series 1), 1897–1900, available at <http://www.arts-search.com/>

The Egoist: An Individualist Review

Following *The Freewoman* and *The New Freewoman* to become one of the most significant of the little magazines, publishing key works by many of the most prominent modernist figures. Harriet Shaw Weaver was the publication's main benefactor and editor, after Marsden (Jan–June 1914). Issues ran approx. 20–30 pages and featured poetry, short fictions, serialised novels, reviews of books, and theatre criticism. Little magazine published poetry, illustrations, literature reviews, and criticisms, as well as evaluations of modern thought and philosophy, philosophic editorials, and essays on the 'New Woman.' Some advertisements in the back pages, mostly for other little magazines or modernist works.

Dates: Jan 1914 (1.1)–Dec 1919 (6.5)
Periodicity: Biweekly: Jan 1914–Dec 1914; monthly: Jan 1915–Oct 1918; bimonthly: Nov/Dec 1918–Mar/Apr 1919; irregular: July, Sep, Dec 1919
Place of publication: London
Publisher: The New Freewoman, Ltd, Oakley House, Bloomsbury St, London, W. C. (Jan 1914–Jan 1918); The Egoist, Limited, 23 Adelphi Terrace House, Robert St, Adelphi, London; W. C. 2 (Feb 1918–Dec 1919)
Editor(s): Dora Marsden (Jan–June 1914); Harriet Shaw Weaver (July 1914–Dec 1919)
Associate Editor(s): Richard Aldington (Jan 1914–May 1916); Leonard A. Compton-Rickett (Jan–June 1914); H.D. (June 1914–May 1916)
Location: Harvard University; Columbia University; US Library of Congress; Yale University; Bodleian Library; British Museum; Edinburgh Public Library; Reprint Editions: Millwood, NY: Kraus Reprint, 1967; Datamics, Inc., New York (Microform)

The English Illustrated Magazine

A monthly popular illustrated magazine that ran between 1883 and 1913. At its peak, its circulation was around 100,000, but this declined over its lifetime. Originally published by Macmillan & Co. from Covent Garden, London, the magazine published fiction and poetry by writers including Margaret Oliphant, Wilkie Collins, Henry James, Thomas Hardy, Max Pemberton, and William Morris. Non-fiction articles on travel, natural history, popular science, history, political economy, sport, and celebrity profiles were geared to appeal to a wide, family-oriented audience. It also published illustrations and reproductions of artwork by a wide range of artists belonging to different temporal periods, including Lucas Cranach, Kate Greenaway, Walter Crane, Carlo Perugini, Hugh Thomson, H. Fitzner Davie, and J. D. Cooper. When it began, it was the only competitor to *Cassell's Weekly*, but better-known illustrated magazines like *The Strand* and *Pearson's Magazine* soon eclipsed its circulation.

Dates: 1883–1913
Periodicity: Monthly
Price: 6d (from 1893)
Place of publication: Covent Garden, London
Publisher: Macmillan (1883–92); Edward Arnold (1892–92); *Illustrated London News* (1893–8); William Ingram (1898–1901); T. Fisher Unwin (1901–3); Hutchinson's (1903–5); Central Publishing (1905–13)
Editor: J. Comyns Carr (Oct 1883–Sep 1889); Clement Kinloch-Cooke (Oct 1889–Sep 1893); Clement King Shorter (Oct 1893–Aug 1899); Bruce Ingram (Sep 1899–Sep 1901); Hannaford Bennett (Oct 1901–Mar 1903); Oscar Parker (Mar 1905–Aug 1913)
Location: BL; HTDL have a complete run (vols 1–49)

The English Review

The English Review was a British monthly literary magazine that ran between 1908 and 1937, with a circulation of around 1,000. Featuring a mix of poetry, short stories, political comment, and reviews, the *Review*'s most famous 'golden age' was under the editorship of Ford Madox Ford (then Hueffer).

Dates: 1908–37
Periodicity: Monthly
Price: 2s 6d
Place of publication: London
Publisher: Duckworth & Co.
Editor: Ford Madox Hueffer (Dec 1908–Feb 1910)
Location: MJP

The Englishwoman

A magazine devoted to promoting constitutional suffrage among the middle and upper classes. Seeking to appeal to a broad, cultured readership, the *Englishwoman* placed articles relating to the suffrage cause and women's issues alongside literary contributions, and literary and art criticism. The *Englishwoman* had close ties to the NUWSS (The National Union of Women's Suffrage Societies). It has long been seen as an unofficial journal of the NUWSS, but as DiCenzo, Ryan and Delap point out, this connection was never confirmed in the pages of the magazine or its reviews (2011: 122–3). A few members of its all-female editorial committee were active members of the LSWS (London Society for Women's Suffrage).

Dates: 1909–21
Periodicity: Monthly
Price: 1s

Place of publication: London
Publisher: Grant Richards; Sidgwick and Jackson (since 1910); The Englishwoman Ltd (since 1916)
Editor: Mrs (Elisina) Grant Richards (other members of the editorial committee included Lady Frances Balfour, Lady Strachey, Cicely Hamilton, and Mary Lowndes)
Location: BL; available digitally through ProQuest

The Evergreen
This magazine reflects editor Patrick Geddes's interests in the Arts and Crafts movement and his belief in a Scottish renaissance. Women were well represented in poetry and prose contributions, although female illustrators were limited to head-and tailpiece decorations while male artists still made the full-page illustrations.

Dates: 1895–7
Periodicity: Quarterly
Price: Currently unknown
Place of publication: Edinburgh
Publisher: P. Geddes
Editor: Patrick Geddes
Location: National Library of Scotland

Forward
Scottish socialist newspaper associated with the Fabian Society of Glasgow and later with the Independent Labour Party in Scotland, as well as the temperance movement. An important aid in the publicising and discussion of women's suffrage affairs in Scotland, including a 'Women's Points of View' column to which suffrage campaigners were regular contributors. Published a range of materials including news and features as well as literature. In 1914 it had a circulation of around 10,000.

Dates: 1906–31 under editorship of Tom Johnstone; continuing until 1953 under other editors
Periodicity: Weekly
Price: 2d
Place of publication: Glasgow
Publisher: Forward Printing and Publishing Company
Editor: Tom Johnston
Location: National Library of Scotland; Mitchell Library, Glasgow; University of Cambridge; microfilm, University of Chicago

The Freewoman: a weekly feminist review
A radical feminist magazine launched and edited by militant feminist and anarchist, Dora Marsden, and initially co-edited (1911–12) by socialist and suffragist, Mary Gawthorpe. From its inception, the *Freewoman* boasted 'exceptional success of a militant feminist turned anarchist review with publishing innovative and experimental literature' and 'served as a unique forum for suffragists, feminists, anarchists, and socialists' (Rabaté 2009: 269–70). 'Probably only around 2000–2500 copies were printed of each issue. A surviving undated subscription list reveals fewer than 300 names, of which roughly 63 are male' (Delap 2000: 235). The challenging

subject matter of this magazine resulted in battles with its publisher, a distributor boycott, and thus financial struggles. It was relaunched eight months later as *The New Freewoman*.

Dates: 1911–12
Periodicity: Weekly
Price: 3d/week
Place of publication: London
Publisher: Stephen Swift & Co. Ltd, 1911–12
Editors: Dora Marsden and Mary Gawthorpe (23 Nov 1911–7 Mar 1912); Dora Marsden (14 Mar 1912–10 Oct 1912)
Location: Bodleian Library, University of Oxford; BL; Princeton University; MJP

Good Housekeeping (British Edition)
Good Housekeeping was launched as the UK edition of the American magazine (founded 1885) in March 1922, its first editorial declaring: 'we believe that the time is ripe for a great new magazine which shall worthily meet the needs of the housekeeping woman of today' (qtd in White 1970: 103). This woman was understood to be firmly middle class and a figure who needed guidance in matters of housekeeping as servants began to become harder to find. It was successful, with a circulation of 150,000 recorded in 1922. Its content ranged from recipes, instruction, and guidance on homemaking to information about household goods and services (in 1924 the Good Housekeeping Institute was created and served to test products which would be given the magazine's seal of approval). That the housekeeping woman of today also required a knowledge of current affairs and culture is evident in the fact that, especially under the editorship of Alice Head, the magazine also published articles by contributors including Rebecca West, Ellen Wilkinson, and Lady Rhondda, as well as short fiction.

Dates: 1922–present
Periodicity: Monthly
Price: 1s (1922)
Place of publication: London
Publisher: William Randolph Hearst; National Magazine Company
Editor: J. Y. McPeake (1922–4); Alice Maud Head (1924–39)
Location: BL

Home Notes
One of the cheap penny domestic magazines that were aimed at women and emerged in the 1890s. Margaret Beetham suggests that such magazines were a significant journalistic development for women writers and readers (1996: 190). In 1938 its circulation was 151,000.

Dates: 1894–1958 (when the magazine merged with *Woman's Own*)
Periodicity: Weekly
Price: 1d at its inception

Place of publication: London
Publisher: Pearson, then Newnes & Pearson from 1914
Editor: The first editor was K. Maud Bennett aka 'Isobel'
Location: BL

Justice
Newspaper of the Social Democratic Federation, a revolutionary socialist group based in London. Often considered the first socialist newspaper in England, it had a circulation of around 4,000 in 1889. Marxist in orientation, the paper in its earliest days printed work by such socialist luminaries as William Morris, George Bernard Shaw, and Eleanor Marx Aveling; however, its tenure was also marked by controversy surrounding its founder and editor, H. M. Hyndman.

Dates: 1884–1925
Periodicity: Weekly
Price: 1d
Place of publication: London
Publisher: Social Democratic Federation
Editor: H. M. Hyndman
Location: Cambridge University Library; Manchester University Library; The Bodleian Library, University of Oxford. Some articles reproduced online in various resources.

Labour Leader
Organ of the Independent Labour Party, which brought together various threads of the socialist movement and the trades union movement into a united front, which eventually contributed to the establishing of Britain's Labour Party. The paper sought to appeal to a wide working-class audience using features of New Journalism and including a broad range of material such as news, politics, trades union columns, literature, and columns for women and child readers.

Dates: 1894–1987
Periodicity: Weekly
Price: 1d
Place of publication: London
Publisher: Keir Hardie
Editor: Keir Hardie (founding editor)
Circulation: Approx. 50,000 (1895)
Location: Gale Nineteenth-Century Collections Online; University of California Berkeley Libraries; microform

Ladies' Field
Kate Jackson notes the magazine's appeal to the metropolitan, independent, professionalised, modern woman while being sympathetic to women with domestic concerns. Its readership was 'clearly middle class and upper middle class' (Jackson 2001: 210). Jackson notes that the magazine was essentially a 'society' magazine and had high production values.

Dates: 1898–Mar 1922, when it became *Ladies Field Fashions* and was then incorporated into *Home Magazine* in 1928
Periodicity: Weekly
Price: 6d at its inception
Place of publication: London
Publisher: Newnes
Editor: Mrs Macdonald was the first editor
Circulation: It was claimed that the magazine was in every country house in Britain, a figure which Jackson suggests would put its circulation in the hundreds of thousands, although she notes this would put its circulation substantially above other ladies' magazines (2001: 214). It was circulated outside Britain in Paris, the US, Canada Cape Town, and India.
Location: BL

The Lady of the House and Domestic Economist (1890–1); then: ***The Irish Sketch and the Lady of the House*** (1891–1924)
Originally an advertising circular for Findlater's Grocers in Dublin, the magazine catered for urban Irish women with articles on women in society, homemaking, fashion, but also women's access to work and the progress of suffrage. Its circulation was in the region of 20,000.

Dates: 1890–1924
Periodicity: Quarterly, then monthly
Price: Free, then 1d (1894)
Place of publication: Dublin
Publisher: Hartnell & Co.
Editor: Henry Crawford Hartnell
Location: BL; National Library of Ireland

The Lady's Realm
A magazine for the upper-class and aspiring middle-class woman, marketed as an 'illustrated monthly magazine.' *The Lady's Realm* included fiction, discussion of high society and prominent figures of interest, and editorials regarding wider sociopolitical issues, such as votes for women. While no circulation figures are known, the magazine includes a hefty sum of advertisements (over twenty pages for the January 1911 issue), which suggests a fairly wide readership.

Dates: 1896–1914 (possibly 1915, though no copies of the 1915 issues seem to exist)
Periodicity: Monthly
Price: 6d
Place of publication: London
Publisher: Nov 1896–Oct 1909 Hutchinson; Nov 1909–Oct 1910 Stanley Paul & Co.; Nov 1910–Oct 1914 Amalgamated Magazine Co.
Editor: W. H. Wilkins until 1902
Location: The following have substantial holdings: Chicago Public Library; Harvard University Library; University of Minnesota Libraries; BL; Bradford City Library;

University of Cambridge Library; Manchester Public Library; University of Queensland Library. Many issues of the journal have been digitised without advertisements by HTDL. The MJP has digitised the January 1911 issue of the magazine, with advertisements.

The Lantern: A Periodical of Lucid Intervals

Anglophile magazine, the motto of which was: 'It is better to hunt for the truth of what concerns us than to search for an honest man.' *The Lantern* had 400 regular subscribers and news-stand purchasers. In an article in the final issue, editor Theodore F. Bonnet says that the magazine began as a diversion for himself and co-editor Edward F. O'Day, its purpose 'to interest the few and please themselves' and to offer a break from the 'drudgery' of their professional pursuit, 'journalism' (282). Both publish work in almost every issue. Authors published include D. H. Lawrence (a short story, 'Samson and Delilah' in 1917, the year in which it was written) and Siegfried Sassoon, Ernest Dowson, R. B. Cunninghame Graham, Anglo-Irish writers Lord Dunsany and Robert Lynd, British poet Brenda Murray Draper, and French writer Paul Marguerit[t]e. Anna Wickham's 'Host' appeared in the September 1917 issue. The magazine contained advertisements for the railroads, lodging, and storage, among other things. When the magazine ceased publication in March 1918, the editors blamed US Treasury Secretary, Williams Gibbs McAdoo. 'When the Government took over the railroads, the railroads ceased to advertise,' an event that *The Lantern* could not weather financially (Edward O'Day, 'Au Revoir': 384–6).

Dates: Mar 1915–Mar 1918
Periodicity: Monthly
Price: 15 cents/copy or $1.50/annum
Place of publication: 88 First Street, San Francisco
Publisher: San Francisco News Company
Editors: Theodore F. Bonnet and Edward F. O'Day
Location: HTDL (incomplete)

Liberty

A seminal anarchist publication, the main conduit of Stirnerite egoism and of radical Spencerian thought from Europe to America. Known for its high editorial standards and production values, contributors included Lysander Spooner, Auberon Herbert, Joshua K. Ingalls, John Henry Mackay, Victor Yarros, and Wordsworth Donisthorpe. Articles dealt with a range of subjects from heterodox economic theory to radical civil liberties to children's rights. Other notable contents included George Bernard Shaw's first original article to appear in the United States, the first American translated excerpts of Friedrich Nietzsche, and discussions of the work of Max Stirner.

Dates: Aug 1881–Apr 1908
Periodicity: During its run, *Liberty* varied from a weekly to a fortnightly and, then finally to a monthly schedule (Feb 1906–Apr 1908)
Place(s) of Publication: Boston (1881–92); New York (1892–1908)
Publisher: Benjamin Tucker

Location: Representative excerpts from *Liberty* are available in Benjamin R. Tucker's *Instead of a Book by a Man too Busy to Write One* (1893) and *Individual Liberty*, ed. Clarence Lee Swartz (1926). Some parts are also available online.

Lucifer
Theosophical magazine edited by H. P. Blavatsky, a founder of the Theosophical Society, publishing 80–90 pages of articles on theosophical concerns, philosophy, science and religion, and esoteric topics, as well as some poetry.

Dates: 1887–97 (succeeded by the *Theosophical Review*)
Periodicity: Monthly
Price: 1s 6d
Place of publication: London
Publisher: George Redway and then the Theosophical Publishing Company
Editor: H. P. Blavatsky and Mabel Collins; Annie Besant; G. R. S. Mead
Location: Online from The International Association for the Preservation of Spiritualist and Occult Periodicals, available at <http://www.iapsop.com/archive/materials/lucifer/>

The Magazine
A magazine that speaks strongly of women's aspirations in a changing modern world, with its 'editress' and most contributors being female students at Glasgow School of Art during the Directorship of Francis (Fra) Newbery, who were also part of the 'Immortals' group which included the Macdonald sisters and architect and designer Charles Rennie Mackintosh. A lively, often ironic, magazine that displays the camaraderie and aspirations of its young female contributors and editress. Circulation figures are unknown, although it was probably distributed among students and associates of GSA.

Dates: Nov 1983–Spring 1896; no issue in 1895
Periodicity: Spring and Autumn
Price: Currently unknown
Place of publication: Glasgow
Publisher: Glasgow School of Art
Editor: Lucy Raeburn, who styled herself 'editress'
Location: Glasgow School of Art archives, available at <www.gsathemagazine.net>

The Malthusian
Newsletter published by the Malthusian League. Its circulation was approximately 400, although distribution was uneven and many copies were given away without charge.

Dates: 1879–1921, 1949–52 (published as *The New Generation*, 1922–49)
Periodicity: Monthly
Price: 1d
Place of publication: London
Publisher: The Malthusian League

Editor: C. R. Drysdale (1879–1907); C. V. Drysdale (1907–16, 1916–22, 1922–3, 1951–2); Binnie Dunlop (1916); Arthur J. S. Preece (1922); and Robert Kerr (1923–51)
Location: Perry-Castañeda Library, The University of Texas at Austin; excerpts available in Nineteenth Century Collections Online

The Mask
Journal, and briefly a leaflet, dedicated to international theatre history and the theatre arts. It included essays and reviews of books about theatre; it also included reproductions of costume and set designs from archives as well as new work by contemporary artists and designers. The style of the periodical was based on art nouveau publications and dependent upon the typefaces and paper available in and around Florence. Almost exclusively written by British theatre theorist Edward Gordon Craig with the assistance of Dorothy Neville Lees under a wide variety of pseudonyms.

Dates: 1908–29
Periodicity: Initially monthly, then quarterly (irregular). Publication suspended August 1914 to April 1915; May 1915 to March 1918; May 1919 to August 1923. Vols 8 and 9 exist as leaflets due to financial issues.
Price: 1s rising to 2s 6d; also sold in volumes
Place of publication: Florence
Publisher: The Mask Press
Editor: Edward Gordon Craig (writing as 'The Editor' John Semar)
Location: The Blue Mountain Project hosted by Princeton University (digital); BL

Mother Earth
An anarchist journal, advocating radical feminism, labour agitation, free love, and opposition to the US government in a number of issues. Contributors include Goldman, M. Bodenheim, M. Gorky, C. L. R. James, E. O'Neil, M. Sanger, L. Tolstoy. Founded and edited by Emma Goldman; co-edited from May 1908 with Alexander Berkman, who joined the magazine after release from prison in May 1908. Known as the main venue for Goldman's anarchist writings. Her revenue from the public lecture circuit provided funds for 136 issues before the US government banned the journal's delivery through the postal service.

Dates: Mar 1906–Aug 1917
Periodicity: Monthly
Place(s) of Publication: New York
Editor(s): Emma Goldman (Mar 1906–Oct 1908; Apr 1915–Apr 1918); Alexander Berkman (Nov 1908–Mar 1915)
Location: Complete Original Issues: Cornell University, Columbia University, Ohio State University; Reprint Editions: New York: Greenwood Reprint Co., 1968
Fully searchable PDF of April 1911 issue available online at MJP. Full images of February 1915 issue available online at PBS's *American Experience*.

The Musical Standard: a newspaper for musicians, professional and amateur
Brief descripton: One of the leading mainstream national general music magazines, also available to subscribers from abroad.

Dates: 1862–1933 (to series 4, vol. 38)
Periodicity: Weekly, July 1862; semi-monthly, Aug 1862–Dec 1863; biweekly, Jan 1864–June 1871; weekly 1871–93.
Price: Annual subscription 6s 6d, half yearly 3s 3d
Place of publication: London
Publisher: Reeves and Turner
Editor: Edward A. Baughan (1892–1902); J. H. G Baughan (1902–13)
Location: BL; Bodleian Library, University of Oxford; British Periodicals Collection II (ProQuest) covers 1862–1912 inclusive

The New Age
Radical political-cultural weekly that promoted debate and discussion among advanced writers and intellectuals. Its peak circulation was around 22,000 in 1908, with 4,500 recorded in 1913. Helped usher in an emerging modernism, publishing debates over modern social and political issues, and including several of the leading literary figures of the day. Printed in double columns, folio-sized, and composed mostly of small type and few illustrations or images, the *New Age* offered political commentary and cultural reflection from a wide variety of ideological perspectives. In addition, it published new works of poetry and fiction.

Dates: 1907–22
Periodicity: Weekly
Price: 1d (1907–9); 3d (1909–13); 6d (1913–18); 7d (1918–22)
Place of publication: London
Publisher: The New Age Press
Editor: Alfred R. Orage (1907–22)
Location: MJP

New Freewoman: An Individualist Review
Even more short-lived than its predecessor, the *Freewoman*, the relaunched magazine took a more literary and, following its editor Dora Marsden's interests, individualist turn. 'In June [1913] the New Freewoman Company had . . . less than 200 subscribers' (Garner 1990: 99). 'In August 1913 its guaranteed circulation was a meagre 266 with 26 going to the USA and one (presumably Tucker's) going to France . . . Open sales amounted to around 120 per issue, making a grand total of around 400' (Garner 1990: 116). Harriet Shaw Weaver and Rebecca West played major roles in the establishment of the *New Freewoman*, West providing editorial assistance and introducing a more literary focus. In 1914 the magazine changed its name again, this time to the *Egoist: An Individualist Review* (1914–19).

Dates: 15 June 1915–15 Dec 1915
Periodicity: Semi-monthly
Price: 6d

Place of publication: Oxford
Publisher: New Freewoman Ltd Printer (Robert Johnson & Co.)
Editor: Dora Marsden
Location: BL; Manchester University Library; Sheffield University; York University; Princeton University Library; US Library of Congress; available digitally via MJP

New Stories
Established by H. E. Bates with Arthur Calder-Marshall, Hamish Miles, Edward J. O'Brien, L. A. Pavey, and Geoffrey West, to provide a platform for the work of short-story writers (Jones 1968: 35). Published the work of several Welsh writers including Glyn Jones and S. Beryl Jones.

Dates: 1934–6
Periodicity: Bimonthly, six times a year
Price: 1s 6d
Place of publication: Oxford
Publisher: Basil Blackwell
Editor: H. E. Bates
Location: BL

The Occult Review
Most successful occult magazine of the first quarter of the twentieth century. Issues of around fifty pages of articles on a wide range of occult topics, including telepathy, hauntings, spiritualism, hypnotism, satanism, alchemy, astrology, Hermeticism, Gnosticism, and the conflict between scientific and religious thought.

Dates: 1905–33 (became the *London Forum*)
Periodicity: Monthly
Price: 6d initially
Place of publication: London
Publisher: William Rider & Son
Editor: Ralph Shirley (1905–26)
Location: Online from The International Association for the Preservation of Spiritualist and Occult Periodicals, available at <http://www.iapsop.com/archive/materials/occult_review/>

The Outlook
A weekly review of 'Politics, Life, Letters, and the Arts.'

Dates: Feb 1898–30 June 1928 (vol. 61, no. 1587)
Periodicity: Weekly
Price: 3d
Place of publication: London
Publisher: 'The Outlook' Publishing Company
Editor: Percy Hurd (1898–1904); James Louis Garvin (1904–8)
Location: British Periodicals (ProQuest): 5 Feb 1898 (vol. 1, no. 1)–26 Jan 1901 (vol. 6, no. 156); Cambridge University Library

The Playgoer and Society Illustrated

Theatre, fashion, and society journal amalgamated with *Theatre* in 1909. Contained news and reviews of plays and interviews with playwrights, actors, and actresses of the time; also included fashion and society news. Fully illustrated with photographs and drawings, mostly black and white some colour images.

Dates: 1909–13
Periodicity: Monthly
Price: 6d; 12 months prepaid 6s
Place of publication: London
Publisher: The Kingshurst Publishing Company Ltd
Editor: Clilverd Young
Location: BL and ProQuest (digital)

Poetry: a Magazine of Verse

Founded by Harriet Monroe in 1912, the Chicago-based magazine published work by influential poets from around the globe, including H. D., Pound (who also served as the magazine's foreign correspondent), William Carlos Williams, Yeats, Tagore, Noguchi, Eliot, Lowell, Flint, and Aldington. The magazine formed the platform for the Imagist movement, and had a circulation of around 10,000 in the late 1910s.

Dates: Oct 1912–Present
Periodicity: Monthly
Price: 15 cents (1912)
Place of publication: 543 Cass Street, Chicago
Publisher: Ralph F. Seymour
Editor: Harriet Monroe (1912–36); Morton Dauwen Zabel (1936–7); George Dillon (1937–42); (group) (1942–9); Hayden Carruth (1949–50); Karl Shapiro (1950–5); Henry Rago (1955–69); Daryl Hine (1969–77); John Frederick Nims (1978–83); Joseph Parisi (1983–2003); Christian Wiman (2003–13); Don Share (2013–)
Location: MJP; University of Wisconsin-Milwaukee; University College London Library, London; National Library of Scotland, Edinburgh.

Poetry and Drama

A magazine aiming at disseminating contemporary verse. Poet and proprietor of the Poetry Bookshop, Harold Monro launched and edited *Poetry and Drama* as part of his mission to popularise poetry. Eclectic and 'non-partisan' (as Monro described it), the magazine published a wide range of verse and criticism (June 1913: 136). While its main focus was on British poetry, 'chronicles' of European and American poetry appeared (F. S. Flint's 'French Chronicle' was included in every issue). The special September 1913 issue devoted to Futurism even featured Monro's own translations of poems by Italian Futurists, among them Filippo Tommaso Marinetti.

Dates: Mar 1913–Dec 1914
Periodicity: Quarterly
Price: 2s 6d
Place of publication: London

Publisher: The Poetry Bookshop
Editor: Harold Monro
Location: BL; available digitally at archive.org

The Queen
A significant and long-running women's magazine, founded by Samuel Beeton in 1861 and sold to William Cox in 1862 (Brake and Demoor 2009: 523–4). In 1863, its 'formula' was fixed (Beetham 1996: 89). Initially conservative in tone, and directed principally toward domestic interests, White records that 'as a newspaper it provided women with more topical and factual information than the orthodox magazines' alongside its articles on fashion and society life (White 1970: 50). It is analysed in detail in Beetham (1996), who particularly notes its eclectic constructions of femininity and of the home as 'domestic theatre' (90). *Queen*'s success made it a favoured venue for advertisers, and while it retained its status as a publication for women of the upper- and upper-middle classes, its content also reflected changes in the country's economic fortunes and social fabric. Its production values remained high, and it took advantage of new printing and paper-making technologies throughout its run. In 1970 it merged with *Harper's Bazaar* (Beetham 1996: 217).

Dates: Sep 1861–late Oct 1970
Periodicity: Biweekly (also available in monthly parts)
Price: 1s (during the 1920s)
Place of publication: London
Editor: Nora Shackleton-Heald (ending 1930)
Location: BL; Bodleian Library, University of Oxford

Rhythm
A modernist review of the arts and literature, a classic 'little magazine,' launched by John Middleton Murry and Michael T. H. Sadler in 1911. Its circulation was around 250. It was inspired in part by Fauvist painter J. D. Fergusson (the review's art editor) and joined by Katherine Mansfield as assistant editor and core contributor in the fifth issue. Underpinned by the philosophy of Henri Bergson, 'rhythm' was a watchword for the magazine's modern artistic endeavour. It included artworks by Picasso, Gaudier-Brzeska, J. Dismorr; writing dominated by Murry and Mansfield; and rivalled *New Age* with contributions focusing on visual arts, poetry, dance, and the short story. During its short run of fourteen issues it became increasingly internationalist in scope. It was briefly succeeded by *The Blue Review* May–July 1913.

Dates: June 1911–March 1913
Periodicity: Initially a quarterly, monthly from June 1912
Price: 1s
Place of publication: London
Publisher: St Catherine's Press; Stephen Swift and Company (from June 1912); Martin Secker (from November 1912)
Editor: John Middleton Murry
Location: Bodleian Library; MJP

The Saturday review of politics, literature, science and art
The Saturday Review was a weekly journal about politics and culture for the educated and politically engaged classes. Published in black and white, featuring no pictures, and with lengthy articles, the *Saturday* established itself as a reliable, if conservative-leaning, source of information and editorial opinion on contemporary political, cultural, and economic issues and trends.

Dates: 1855–1938
Periodicity: Weekly
Price: 6d
Place of publication: London
Publisher: J. W. Parker and Son
Location: BL on paper and microfilm; issues are also available digitally on Proquest

The Strand Magazine
Regarded as a British national institution, the *Strand* was a massively popular illustrated monthly magazine featuring general interest articles, interviews, and fiction from the likes of Arthur Conan Doyle, Arthur Morrison, P. G. Wodehouse, and Edith Nesbit. Its circulation was 400,000 in 1896 (Jackson 2001: 95).

Dates: 1891–1950
Periodicity: Monthly
Price: Initially 6d
Place of publication: United Kingdom
Publisher: George Newnes Ltd
Editor: George Newnes (general); Reginald Pound (general); H. Greenhough Smith (literary)
Location: University of Michigan; Princeton University

Time and Tide
General magazine of news and opinion with book reviews and reviews of cultural events such as dance, theatre, music, film, etc., along with profiles of prominent people and some serialised fiction – notably, E. M. Delafield's *The Diary of a Provincial Lady*. Its circulation was 14,000 at its peak, and its political orientation, especially during its early years of existence, was feminist and leftist-progressive. Although it aimed to appeal to both women and men, its advertising in its first decade leaned heavily toward women's fashion, and its contributors were often women, especially those who had been allied with the suffrage movement and/or friends of its founder, Margaret, Lady Rhondda.

Dates: 1920–58 (as a feminist weekly under the control of its founder); later it was a weekly and then a monthly with a different mission until 1979, under a series of different publishers/editors
Periodicity: weekly (monthly after 1970)
Price: 4d (original price)
Place of publication: Fleet Street, London
Publisher: Margaret, Lady Rhondda

Editor: Helen Archdale (1920–6); then Lady Rhondda (1926–58)
Location: BL; widely available on microform

To-day's Woman; a weekly, literary, artistic and industrial paper to further woman's pursuits
A miscellany intended for the 'new woman,' with specific attention to opportunities for women in the professions. Included articles on suffrage, Irish women's employment and entrepreneurship, but also fashion, society, Irish sport.

Dates: 1894–6
Periodicity: weekly
Price: 1d
Place of publication: Dublin
Publisher: Bryers and Walker Sealy
Location: BL

The Tramp
Published for just a year from March 1910–February 1911, *The Tramp* was a monthly publication that acted as a hybrid literary commercial journal. Estimates suggest around 500 peak circulation. Pieces by Wyndham Lewis jostled for space with reproductions of Marinetti's Futurist manifesto, advertisements for expensive motor cars, and outdoor 'tramping' gear. The title harks back to the Victorian fondness for 'tramping' – the act of rambling and camping in the European countryside with minimal equipment.

Dates: 1910–11
Periodicity: Monthly
Price: 6d
Place of publication: Adelphi Press, 11 Adam Street, Adelphi (now The Strand), London, WC
Publisher: Adelphi Press
Editor: Douglas Goldring
Location: Bodleian Library, University of Oxford; Yale University Library

The Unknown World
A magazine that proclaimed itself 'devoted to the occult sciences, magic, mystical philosophy, alchemy, hermetic archaeology, and the hidden problems of science, literature, speculation and history.'

Dates: 1894–5
Periodicity: monthly
Price: 6d
Place of publication: London
Publisher: James Elliott & Co.
Editor: Arthur Edward Waite
Location: online from The International Association for the Preservation of Spiritualist and Occult Periodicals, available at <http://www.iapsop.com/archive/materials/unknown_world/>

Vogue (British Edition)
Glossy-paged fashion and society journal, started in the US in 1892; UK edition launched in 1916. Under Dorothy Todd's editorship (1922–6), extensively covered modernist art and literature. Its circulation in 1925 was 137,000.

Dates: 1916–present
Periodicity: Initially monthly; fortnightly from 1927
Price: 1s 6d
Place of publication: London
Publisher: Condé Nast
Editor: Elspeth Champcommunal (1916–22); Dorothy Todd (1922–6); Alison Settle (1926–34)
Location: BL

Votes for Women
Founded by Emmeline and Frederick Pethick-Lawrence in 1907, the newspaper was the organ for the Women's Social and Political Union until 1912, when the Pethick-Lawrences were expelled from the organisation. They continued to run the paper independently until 1914 when they transferred control to the United Suffragists and Eveline Sharp became editor. From 1907 to 1912, the paper was a tool for fundraising and recruitment to the WSPU; it was aggressively marketed by street-sellers, a suffragette bus, and permanent pitches in central London.

Dates: 1907–18
Periodicity: Monthly (until April 1908); then weekly
Price: 3d/month; 1p/week
Place of publication: London
Publisher: Clement's Inn
Editor: Emmeline and Frederick Pethick-Lawrence (1907–14); Eveline Sharp (1914–18)
Location: BL

Wales
Established with the intention of providing a progressive voice for the new English-medium writers of Wales, this was a literary and political magazine that also gave a general view of Welsh affairs. Like *The Welsh Review*, *Wales* played a key role in discovering new Welsh writers.

Dates: Summer 1937–Winter 1939/40 (11 nos); July 1943–Oct 1949 (18 nos.); Sep 1958–Jan 1960 (13 nos.) (Stephens 1998: 763)
Periodicity: Quarterly; six-monthly; monthly.
Price: 1s–2s 6d
Place of publication: Carmarthen; London
Publisher: The Druid Press, Carmarthen; Tudor Press, London
Editor: Keidrych Rhys
Location: National Library of Wales

The Welsh Review
Intended for an English-speaking Welsh audience, *The Welsh Review* published short stories and poetry in the medium of English as well as translations of Welsh-medium pieces, notably from Kate Roberts. It was a key platform for the Welsh short story,

which flourished in the 1930s. It also featured items on history, education, politics, and health, alongside some artwork. Its strapline was 'A monthly journal about Wales, its people, and their activities.'

Dates: Feb–Nov 1939; Mar 1944–Dec 1948
Periodicity: Monthly; quarterly
Price: 1s
Place of publication: Cardiff
Publisher: Penmark Press
Editor: Gwyn Jones
Location: National Library of Wales

Wheels: An Anthology of Verse
Avant-garde annual poetry anthology, primarily featuring work by Edith, Osbert, and Sacheverell Sitwell, as well as Iris Tree, Sherard Vines, and Arnold James. Nancy Cunard published several poems in the first volume, including the eponymous poem 'Wheels.' The fourth volume included seven posthumously published poems by Wilfred Owen. Cover art and endpapers by modernist artists such as Alvaro de Guevara, Gino Severini, and William Roberts reinforced the anthologies' commitment to an aesthetic of difficult, abstract, often shocking modernity.

Dates: 1916–21
Periodicity: Annual
Price: 2s 6d
Place of publication: Oxford
Publisher: B. H. Blackwell (1916–19); Leonard Parsons Ltd (1920); C. W. Daniel Ltd (1921)
Editor: Edith Sitwell
Location: Simon Fraser University; Northwestern University; University of Tulsa; Brown University; University of Iowa; available digitally through MJP

Woman's Life
One of the cheap penny domestic magazines that were aimed at women and emerged in the 1890s, with a circulation of 200,000 in 1896. Margaret Beetham suggests that such magazines were a significant journalistic development for women writers and readers (Beetham 1996: 190). Kate Jackson describes the magazine as having 'cross-class' appeal (Jackson 2001: 214).

Dates: 1895–1934 (when the magazine merged with *Woman's Own*)
Periodicity: weekly
Price: 1p at its inception
Place of publication: London
Publisher: Newnes, then Newnes & Pearson from 1914
Editor: No named editor
Location: BL

Works Cited and Helpful Sources

Beetham, Margaret. 1996. *A Magazine of Her Own?: Domesticity and Desire in the Woman's Magazine, 1800–1914*. London: Routledge.
Bradbury, Malcolm. 1966. 'A Review in Retrospect,' in *The Calendar of Modern Letters March 1925–July 1927, Volume I March 1925–August 1925*. Ed. Edgell Rickword and Douglas Garman. London: Frank Cass. vii–xix.
—.1968. '*Rhythm* and *The Blue Review*.' Special feature on 'The Little Magazines,' *Times Literary Supplement* 25 April 1968: 423–4.
Brake, Laurel and Marysa Demoor (eds). 2009. *Dictionary of Nineteenth Century Journalism in Great Britain and Ireland*. Ghent: Academia Press.
Delap, Lucy. 2000. 'The *Freewoman*, Periodical Communities and the Feminist Reading Public,' *Princeton University Library Chronicle* vol. 61 no. 2: 233–76.
Garner, Les. 1990. *A Brave and Beautiful Spirit: Dora Marsden, 1882–1960*. Aldershot: Avebury/Gower.
Hibberd, Dominic. 2009. 'The New Poetry, Georgians and Others: *The Open Window* (1910–11), *The Poetry Review* (1912–15), *Poetry and Drama* (1913–14), and *New Numbers* (1914).' *The Oxford Critical and Cultural History of Modernist Magazines: Volume 1, Great Britain and Ireland*. Ed. Peter Brooker and Andrew Thacker. Oxford: Oxford University Press. 176–96.
Hoffman, Frederick, Charles Allen, and Carolyn F. Ulrich. 1946. *The Little Magazine: A History and Bibliography*. Princeton: Princeton University Press.
Jackson. 2001. *George Newnes and the New Journalism in Britain, 1880–1910*. Aldershot: Ashgate.
Jones, Glyn. 1968. *The Dragon Has Two Tongues: Essays on Anglo-Welsh Writers and Writing*. London: Dent.
Leavis, Q. D. 1932. *Fiction and the Reading Public*. London: Chatto & Windus.
The Modernist Magazines Project: <http://modmags.dmu.ac.uk/home.html> (last accessed 21 December 2018).
Rabaté, Jean-Paul. 2009. 'Gender and Modernism: *The Freewoman* (1911–12), *The New Freewoman* (1913), and *The Egoist* (1914–19).' *The Oxford Critical and Cultural History of Modernist Magazines: Volume 1, Great Britain and Ireland*. Ed. Peter Brooker and Andrew Thacker. Oxford: Oxford University Press. 269–89.
Ryan, Leila and Maria DiCenzo. 2011. '*The Englishwoman*: "Twelve Years of Brilliant Life."' *Feminist Media History: Suffrage, Periodicals and the Public Sphere*. Ed. Maria DiCenzo, Lucy Delap, and Leila Ryan. Basingstoke: Palgrave Macmillan.

Stephens, Meic. 1998. *The New Companion to the Literature of Wales*. Cardiff: University of Wales Press.
Swartz, Clarence Lee, ed. 1926. '*Individual Liberty*: selections from the writings of B. R. Tucker.' New York: Vanguard Press.
Tollers, Vincent. 1986. '*Coterie.*' *British Literary Magazines: The Modern Age (1914–1984)*. Ed. Alvin Sullivan. London and Westport CT: Greenwood Press. 110–12.
Tucker, Benjamin R. 1893. *Instead of a Book by a Man too Busy to Write One*. New York: B. R. Tucker.
White, Cynthia. 1970. *Women's Magazines, 1693–1968*. Ann Arbor: University of Michigan Press.
Whitworth, Michael. 2009. 'Enemies of Cant: *The Athenaeum* (1919–21) and *The Adelphi* (1923–48).' *The Oxford Critical and Cultural History of Modernist Magazines: Volume 1, Great Britain and Ireland*. Ed. Peter Brooker and Andrew Thacker. Oxford: Oxford University Press. 364–88.

Notes on Contributors

Faith Binckes is Senior Lecturer in Modern and Contemporary Literature at Bath Spa University. She publishes on periodical culture, women's writing, modernist literature, and the visual arts. Her monograph *Modernism, Magazines, and the British avant-garde: reading Rhythm* was published by Oxford University Press in 2010. She has co-authored *Hannah Lynch (1859–1904): Irish Writer, Cosmopolitan, New Woman* with Dr Kathryn Laing (Cork University Press, 2019). In addition to co-editing the current volume, she is working on an edition of the later art writings of Wyndham Lewis for Oxford University Press.

Melissa Bradshaw teaches in the English department at Loyola University Chicago. Her research focuses on publicity, personality, and fandom in twentieth-century American literature and popular culture. She has published extensively on the poet Amy Lowell, co-editing a volume of her poems as well as a volume of scholarly essays about her. Her book *Amy Lowell, Diva Poet* (Ashgate, 2011) won the 2011 MLA Book Prize for Independent Scholars. She has also published on Edith Sitwell, Edna St Vincent Millay, and divas more generally. She is currently working on an edition of Amy Lowell's collected letters and a book on early twentieth-century female poets and material culture, titled *Collectable Women: Ephemera and the Poetry Archive*.

Bartholomew Brinkman is an Associate Professor of English at Framingham State University. He has published on modern poetry, print culture, and periodical studies in such journals and collections as *Journal of Modern Literature*, *Modernism/modernity*, *Journal of Modern Periodical Studies*, and the *Cambridge Companion to Modern American Poetry*. His first book, *Poetic Modernism in the Culture of Mass Print* was published in 2016 by the Hopkins Studies in Modernism Series at Johns Hopkins University Press. He co-edits the Modern American Poetry Site (MAPS), available at <www.modernamericanpoetry.org>.

Anthony Camara is Assistant Professor of English at the University of Calgary. He is a literature and science specialist whose critical work focuses on the popular genres of horror and science fiction. Camara obtained his doctorate in 2013 from the University of California, Los Angeles. His current book project investigates early modernist practitioners of the Weird tale, a unique kind of narrative that produces and explores philosophical questions by combining the supernatural and the techno-scientific. His scholarship is informed by his background in ecology, biology, and evolutionary theory, in which he holds a degree.

Layne Parish Craig is the author of *When Sex Changed: Birth Control and Literature between the World Wars* (Rutgers, 2013). She teaches modernist literature, gender studies, and digital and expository writing in the English Department at TCU (Texas Christian University). She has published on topics ranging from interwar romance fiction to digital narratives of in vitro fertilisation to James Joyce, and she is currently working on a manuscript titled *Distraction and Amusement: World War One-Era Women Writing Sex and Sexuality*.

Elizabeth Darling is Reader in Architectural History at Oxford Brookes University. She works on twentieth-century British architectural history with a particular interest in modernism, social housing, and gender. Her book on British architectural modernism, *Re-forming Britain: Narratives of Modernity before Reconstruction*, was published by Routledge in early 2007 while an edited volume (with Lesley Whitworth), *Women and the Making of Built Space in England, 1870–1950* was published by Ashgate in autumn 2007. Her most recent publication is *Wells Coates* (RIBA Publishing, 2012). Forthcoming work includes a discussion of modernism and the neo-Georgian in 1930s England, and the introduction to a new edition of Elizabeth Denby's 1938 book *Europe Rehoused*.

Miranda Dunham-Hickman is Associate Professor of English at McGill University in Montreal. *The Classics in Modernist Translation*, co-edited with Lynn Kozak, appeared through Bloomsbury in 2019; Kozak's and Hickman's work on H.D.'s translations appear both in this collection and in the *Classical Receptions Journal* 10.4 (2018). Recent publications also include work on Wyndham Lewis's Self Condemned (2015), an essay on painters Jessie Dismorr and Helen Saunders in *Vorticism: New Perspectives* (Oxford University Press, 2013), and the collection *Rereading the New Criticism*, co-edited with John McIntyre (Ohio State University Press, 2012). She is editor of *One Must Not Go Altogether with the Tide: The Letters of Ezra Pound and Stanley Nott* (McGill-Queen's University Press, 2011) and author of *The Geometry of Modernism* (University of Texas Press, 2005). Her work appears in *The Blackwell Companion to Modernist Poetry* (2014), *A History of Modernist Poetry* (Cambridge, 2015), the *Cambridge Companion to H.D.* (2012), and the *Cambridge Companion to Modernist Women Poets*. Her book in progress addresses women in cultural criticism between the world wars.

Claire Flay-Petty is a member of the *New Welsh Review* editorial board and has taught Welsh writing in English and Women's Writing at the University of South Wales. Her monograph of the modernist short-story writer Dorothy Edwards, was published by University of Wales Press in 2011. She is currently working, with Michelle Deininger, on *Scholarship and Sisterhood: Women, Writing, and Higher Education* (forthcoming with University of Wales Press)

Laurel Forster is Senior Lecturer in Media Studies at the University of Portsmouth and her research interests are in women's writing and women's cultures. She has published on representations of femininity and feminism on television and film, on domesticity, on modernism, especially the writings of May Sinclair, and on women's magazines and their cultural significance. Her latest book is *Magazine Movements: Women's Culture, Feminisms and Media Form* (Bloomsbury, 2015).

Lee Garver is Associate Professor of English at Butler University, Indianapolis. His research focuses on the politics and culture of early British modernism, especially the work of authors who wrote for the British radical political-cultural magazine the *New Age*. In addition to writing introductions to volumes 8 and 19 of The Modernist Journals Project edition of this magazine, he has published articles on such figures as Katherine Mansfield, Ezra Pound, and T. E. Hulme. He is currently working on a book project titled *Modernism, Magazines, and Radical Politics: The New Age and British Cultural Conflict 1907–1914*.

Susan Jones is Professor of English Literature at St Hilda's College, University of Oxford. She has published extensively on literary modernism and the cultures of modern dance. Her monograph *Literature, Modernism, and Dance* was published by Oxford University Press in 2013. Two future research projects will come out of this work: one which extensively explores the reception of the Ballets Russes in Britain and its impact on British literary aesthetics in the later twentieth century; the second is an extended project on Samuel Beckett and choreography, which explores Beckett's relationship to innovations in European modern dance and dramaturgy. She is contributing, with Allan Simmons, to the Cambridge Edition of Joseph Conrad's *Chance*.

Louise Kane is Assistant Professor of Global Modernisms at the University of Central Florida. She has published widely on early twentieth-century periodical cultures and is currently working on a monograph about modern periodicals, transnationalism, and the Digital Humanities. She also edits the *Journal of Wyndham Lewis Studies*.

Kathryn Laing lectures in the Department of English Language and Literature, Mary Immaculate College, University of Limerick. She discovered, edited, and published Rebecca West's unfinished suffrage novel, *The Sentinel* (Legenda, 2002). Her essay '"Am I a Vorticist?": Re-Reading Rebecca West's "Indissoluble Matrimony"' appeared in Philip Coleman et al., eds, *Blast at 100: Centenary Essays* (Brill, 2016). Her research interests are principally in late nineteenth-century Irish writing, suffrage fiction, and modernist women writers. She has published widely on Rebecca West, Virginia Woolf, George Moore, and F. Mabel Robinson. She has co-authored *Hannah Lynch (1859–1904): Irish Writer, Cosmopolitan, New Woman* with Dr Faith Binckes (Cork University Press, 2019).

Krista Lysack is Associate Professor of English at King's University College at The University of Western Ontario. She is the author of *Come Buy, Come Buy: Shopping and the Culture of Consumption in Victorian Women's Writing* (Ohio University Press, 2008) and *Chronometres: Devotional Literature, Duration, and Victorian Reading* (forthcoming Oxford University Press).

Scott McCracken is Professor of Twentieth-Century Literature at Queen Mary, University of London. He is General Editor of *Dorothy Richardson Scholarly Editions Project*, which is preparing ten volumes of Dorothy Richardson's letters and fiction for publication with Oxford University Press. His most recent book was *Masculinities, Modernist Fiction, and the Urban Public Sphere* (Manchester University Press, 2007). He is co-author of *Benjamin's Arcades: An Unguided Tour* (Manchester University Press, 2016) and co-editor with David Glover of *The Cambridge Companion to Popular Fiction* (2012). He is currently working on a new monograph, *Thinking Through Defeat: Literary Responses to Political Failure from the Paris Commune to the Berlin Wall*.

Margery Palmer McCulloch is Senior Research Fellow in Scottish Literature at the University of Glasgow. She is co-editor of *Scottish Literary Review*. Her recent books include *Modernism and Nationalism: Source Documents for the Scottish Renaissance*, and *Scottish Modernism and its Contexts 1918–1959: Literature, National Identity and Cultural Exchange*, published by Edinburgh University Press in 2009.

Henry Mead is a Research Fellow at Tallinn University, working on the ERC 'Between the Times' project. He also teaches for Worcester College, Oxford, where he completed his DPhil in 2013. He co-edited the 2014 collection *Broadcasting in the Modernist Era*, and published his first monograph, *T. E. Hulme and the Ideological Politics of Early Modernism* in 2015. He has written articles and book chapters on various aspects of modernist ideology and radical periodical writing, and is working on a study of the 'fall' motif in modern literature.

Elizabeth Carolyn Miller is Professor of English at the University of California, Davis. Her book *Slow Print: Literary Radicalism and Late Victorian Print Culture* (Stanford University Press, 2013) received the Best Book of the Year award from the North American Victorian Studies Association as well as Honorable Mention for the Modernist Studies Association Book Prize. She has also published *Framed: The New Woman Criminal in British Culture at the Fin de Siècle* (Michigan University Press, 2008) and her articles have appeared in *Feminist Studies, Modernism/modernity, Victorian Literature and Culture, Victorian Studies* and other venues. Her current book project is titled 'Extraction Ecologies and the Literature of the Long Exhaustion, 1830s–1930s'.

Mark S. Morrisson is Professor and Head of English at Penn State University. He teaches courses in British, Irish, and American modernism, periodical studies, and science studies. Morrisson is the author of *The Public Face of Modernism: Little Magazines, Audiences, and Reception, 1905–1920* (2001); *Modern Alchemy: Occultism and the Emergence of Atomic Theory* (2007), and *Modernism, Science, and Technology* (2016). He was a founding co-editor of the *Journal of Modern Periodical Studies*, and he co-edited with Jack Selzer a facsimile edition of Harold J. Salemson's Parisian little magazine *Tambour* (1929–1930), and co-edited with Richard Shillitoe an edition of Ithell Colquhoun's occult surrealist novel, *I Saw Water*.

Chris Mourant is a Lecturer in Early Twentieth-Century English Literature and Co-Director of the Centre for Modernist Cultures at the University of Birmingham. He is the author of *Katherine Mansfield and Periodical Culture* (Edinburgh University Press, 2019).

Alina Oboza is a Lecturer in English Literature at the University of Tromsø – The Arctic University of Norway. She is currently completing a PhD in English Literature at the same university. Her thesis explores the conjunction of liminality, space, and gender in Virginia Woolf's novels, interrogating the ways Woolf reworks the traditional pattern of rites of passage.

Annie Paige is a PhD candidate at the University of Tulsa. She has served as a research assistant for the Modernist Journals Project and as an editorial intern for *Tulsa Studies in Women's Literature*. She is currently writing her doctoral dissertation on women's social performance and the modernist party.

Natasha Periyan is a Research Associate at the University of Kent on the AHRC funded project 'Literary Culture, Meritocracy and the Assessment of Intelligence in Britain and America, 1880–1920.' She has previously taught at Goldsmiths, Falmouth and Royal Holloway. Her book, *The Politics of 1930s British Literature: Education, Class, Gender,* was published in Bloomsbury's 'Historicizing Modernism' series in 2018 and she has also published book chapters and articles on Virginia Woolf, D. H. Lawrence, George Orwell and the politics of interwar women writers.

Elizabeth Pritchett teaches English at St John's School of Leatherhead and is a Teaching Fellow at Queen Mary University of London. Her doctoral thesis was on intertextuality in Dorothy Richardson's *Pilgrimage*. Research interests include Victorian modernisms, modernist gender and sexuality, music in the stream-of-consciousness novel, and the relationship between democracy and aesthetics.

Charlotte Purkis is Principal Lecturer in Drama in the department of Performing Arts, University of Winchester. She is also a musician. She specialises in connections between the performing arts and modernisms, has published on European dance and opera history, and is particularly interested in critical writing practices and in the roles played by women in the early twentieth-century cultural avant-garde. Other research interests include autoethnographic practices in contemporary performance studies, building on her involvement in the British critical musicology movement. She is an associate member of The Gate Theatre Research Network writing on mid-twentieth-century theatre clubs. and is completing a monograph on the Anglo-American writer and theatre director Velona Pilcher.

Carey Snyder is an Associate Professor of English at Ohio University, the author *of British Fiction and Cross-Cultural Encounters: Ethnographic Modernism from Wells to Woolf* (Palgrave, 2008), and the editor of the Broadview Press edition of H. G. Wells's *Ann Veronica* (2015). Her work in modernist periodical studies has been published in such venues as the *Journal of Modern Periodical Studies*; the collection, *Brave New World: Texts and Contexts* (Palgrave, 2016); and the volume *Beatrice Hastings: On the Life and Work of a 20th Century Master* (Pleiades Press, 2016).

Helen Southworth is Professor of Literature at the Robert D. Clark Honors College at the University of Oregon. She is the author of *The Intersecting Realities and Fictions of Virginia Woolf and Colette* (Ohio State University Press, 2004) and the editor of *Leonard and Virginia Woolf, the Hogarth Press and the Networks of Modernism*

(Edinburgh University Press, 2010) and, with Elisa Sparks, *Virginia Woolf and the Art of Exploration* (Clemson University Press, 2006). Southworth has also published on gender and space, modernist magazines, and book art, among other things. She is a founding editor with five colleagues of the Digital Humanities Project MAPP or Modernist Archives Publishing Project. In 2017, Southworth published *Fresca: A Life in the Making: A Biographer's Quest for a Forgotten Bloomsbury Polymath* (Sussex Academic Press) and, with Battershill, Staveley, Willson Gordon, Widner and Wilson, *Scholarly Adventure in Digital Humanities: Making the Modernist Archives Publishing Project* (Palgrave).

Margaret D. Stetz is the Mae and Robert Carter Professor of Women's Studies and Professor of Humanities in the Department of Women and Gender Studies at the University of Delaware. In March 2015, she was named by the magazine *Diverse: Issues in Higher Education* to its list of the 'Top 25 Women in Higher Education.' As well as being the author of volumes such as *British Women's Comic Fiction, 1890–1990* and *Gender and the London Theatre, 1880–1920*, she has published more than 100 scholarly essays on subjects ranging from fashion studies to publishing history. She has been curator or co-curator of thirteen exhibitions on turn-of-the-century gender, art, literature, and print culture, including 'Everything Is Going on Brilliantly: Oscar Wilde and Philadelphia,' for The Rosenbach of the Free Library of Philadelphia in spring 2015, and she was co-curator in 2016, with Mark Samuels Lasner, of an exhibition at the Central Library in Liverpool (UK) commemorating the 150th anniversary of the birth of the late Victorian writer Richard Le Gallienne.

Elizabeth Tilley is Senior Lecturer in Victorian Literature at the National University of Ireland, Galway. She has published extensively on nineteenth century Irish book culture and periodical history, and was one of the Associate Editors of the *Dictionary of Nineteenth-Century Journalism* (2009). Her new edition of J.S. LeFanu's *In a Glass Darkly* (2018) recovered the periodical versions of Le Fanu's fiction, and her monograph, *The Periodical Press in Nineteenth-Century Ireland*, is forthcoming from Palgrave in 2019.

Elizabeth Wright is a playwright and senior lecturer in English and European Literature at Bath Spa University. Her play *Vanessa and Virginia* has been nominated for five Off West End Awards including Best New Play and Most Promising Playwright and has been published by Play Dead Press. Her academic publications include a biography of Virginia Woolf (Hesperus 2011), as well as an edited collection of essays on the Bloomsbury Group and various articles covering the Bloomsbury theatricals, Joseph Conrad, Henrik Ibsen and Maggie Gee. She is currently researching a monograph on Bloomsbury and drama and is writing an article on interwar pacifist women playwrights.

INDEX

Abercrombie, Lascelles, 95, 103
Academy, 102, 296–7
Academy of Dramatic Art, 188–9
Acorn, 75, 79, 81, 87, 436
Actresses' Franchise League, 97
Adelphi, 7, 48, 50, 76, 121, 124, 124, 126, 129, 167, 197, 259–73, 436–7
advertising/advertisement, 4, 20–5, 29–30, 67, 77, 101, 129–30, 146–64, 175–9, 276, 278, 283–6, 295, 365, 428–9
    advertorial, 64, 67–8, 157
aesthetes, female, 83, 84, 87
Ainslee's Magazine, 278, 280
Aldington, Richard, 92, 95, 179, 181, 280, 297, 322, 323, 383, 441
Ali, Duse Mohamed, 343
Allan, Maud, 107–8
anarchism/anarchist, 196, 199, 201, 226–40, 343, 440, 443, 447
Anderson, Margaret, 167, 178, 181, 214, 216, 244, 330
Anglo-American Magazine, 223
Angus, Marion, 42
anthologies/anthologisation, 7, 295, 296, 299, 306–7, 310n, 329–41, 457
architecture, 78, 134–44, 441;
    see also criticism, women as critics of: architecture
Arnold, Matthew (Arnoldian), 3, 76
    ideas of culture, 121–2, 127, 130
Arts and Crafts Movement, 34, 47

Atalanta's Garland, 33, 43–6, 437
Athenaeum, 7, 81, 106, 260, 300, 306, 309, 330, 377, 379, 380, 436
Atlantic Monthly, 278–88
Augustus, John, 332
Author, 275, 278–9, 281
Ayrton, Hertha, 232, 238

Baines, Alice, 135, 143
Ballets Russes/Russian Ballet, 106–19, 191–2, 329
Banks, Dorothy 'Georges', 76, 107, 115, 118
Barry, Iris, 4, 10, 18, 50, 76, 120–34, 260, 310
Baudelaire, Charles, 177, 258
Bax, Belfort, 242–5, 344
Beale, Dorothea, 277
Beardsley, Aubrey, 91, 100, 186
Belgravia, 215–16
Bell, Lily, 406–19
Belloc, Hilaire, 228, 342n, 343
Bennett, K. Maud ('Isobel'), 62, 66–7
Bergson, Henri, 109, 453
Besant, Annie, 372, 375, 379, 381, 386, 393–4, 448
Besant, Walter, 278
Billington-Greig, Teresa, 4, 6, 39, 214, 234, 243–4, 252, 254, 256, 343
birth control/contraception, 5, 235, 248, 372, 389–404, 409, 418
Birth-Rate Commission, 390–2
birth strike, 389–404

Black and White, 217
Blake, William, 345, 352
Bland, Hubert, 343
BLAST: Review of the Great English Vortex, 95, 170, 174–6, 179, 180n, 192, 216, 220, 300, 437, 440
Blatchford, Robert, 412, 439
Blavatsky, Helena Petrovna, 375, 377, 379, 380–4, 448
Bloomsbury Group (Clive Bell, Vanessa Bell, Roger Fry, Duncan Grant, Lytton Strachey), 50, 106, 110, 115, 136–7, 140, 195, 269–70, 291, 305, 332; *see also* Woolf, Virginia
Boole, Mary Everest, 199, 440
Bosanquet, Theodora, 306
Bourdieu, Pierre, 123
Boyle, Kay, 50
Bradlaugh, Charles, 372, 393
British Musician, 89
Brontë sisters, 274, 280–1, 325
Brooke, Rupert, 298
Browne, Stella, 391–4, 401
Bryher (Ellerman, Annie Winifred), 195, 197
Butts, Mary, 18, 50

Caird, Mona, 249, 256, 343
Calendar of Modern Letters, 18, 48, 50–3, 438
Campbell, Mrs Patrick, 100, 101
Cannan, Gilbert, 95
canon/canonicity, 2, 8, 10, 123–31, 146, 167, 170, 202–3, 266, 270, 291–2, 296, 308, 322–3, 326, 329
Carpenter, Edward, 199, 230, 343
Carswell, Catherine, 17, 43
Carter, Huntly, 107–8, 233
Cather, Willa, 303
Century Illustrated Monthly Magazine, 277–8
Chamber's Journal, 215, 216
Chapbook (initially named *The Monthly Chapbook*), 295, 305–11, 438
Chaplin, Charlie, 124, 126, 130–1, 260
Chekhov, Anton, 102, 260, 269

Cheltenham Ladies' College Magazine, 277, 279
Chertney, Doris 'Motogirl', 363, 364
Chesterton, G. K., 50, 342, 343
Chord: A Quarterly Devoted to Music, 79–87, 438
Church League for Women's Suffrage (CLWS), 423–4, 430–1
Church League for Women's Suffrage Monthly Paper, 424–31
Church Militant, 431, 433, 439
Clarion, 5–6, 171, 178, 407–19, 439
class/socio-economic status, 21–2, 27–9, 39, 64–5, 93, 96, 103, 121–31, 134–5, 139, 143, 147–9, 151, 154–8, 190, 200–7, 282–3, 324–5, 342, 345–52, 361–2, 365–6, 375–6, 392–4, 396–8, 400–1, 405, 409, 412–14, 439, 442, 444, 445, 446, 453, 457
  middle-class, 21–2, 29, 53, 93, 96, 127, 143, 146–58, 190, 193, 202, 203, 248, 282–3, 339, 342, 346, 348–51, 345, 361–2, 365–6, 375–6, 393, 396, 422, 444, 445, 446, 453
  upper-class, 64–5, 124, 129, 140, 146–58, 218, 334, 346, 376, 393, 396, 442, 446, 453
  working-class, 39, 49, 51, 139, 201, 204, 228, 233, 324, 376, 397–400, 405–15, 439
classical (Greek)
  education in, 43, 45
  influence on art, dance and criticism, 35, 95, 108–9, 110–14
  literature/mythology, 51, 54, 108, 215–16, 232, 323
clubs/groups for women, 5–6, 35, 43, 64, 66, 81, 89, 239, 410; *see also* Freewoman Discussion Group
Coates, Wells, 136–7
Collier's, 285–6
Collins, Mabel (Mrs. Keningale Cook), 375–86
Colquhoun, Ithell, 386
Common Cause, 38–9, 231, 245, 254, 256, 421, 428

Conrad, Joseph, 209n, 217, 343
consumer/consumerism/consumption, 21–31, 67–8, 138, 140–2, 151–60, 177–8, 283, 409–10
Contagious Diseases Act (1918), 392
Contemporary Review, 89
copyright law
  and digitisation projects, 7
  and the professional author, 278–81
Corbusier, Le, 77, 134–43
Cornford, Francis, 296, 297, 299, 310n
Cornhill, 97, 223
Correspondence columns/ letters, 2, 4, 25–9, 44–5, 60, 70, 166, 171, 199–202, 209, 242–57, 261, 279, 307, 382–3, 401, 408, 429
Cosmopolis, 217
Coterie: A Quarterly: Art, Prose, and Poetry, 179, 440
Cotterill, Erica, 343
Coward, No l, 191
Craig, Edith, 94, 95, 101–3
Craig, Edward Gordon, 76, 88, 101, 105, 115, 449
Crank (and *Open Road*), 199–205, 440
Criterion, 48, 50, 271n, 277, 306
criticism, women as critics of
  architecture, 134–45
  dance, 106–19
  drama/ theatre, 92–105, 188–93
  film, 120–33
  music, 78–91, 188, 193
Crowley, Aleister, 374, 375, 384, 386
culture, stratification of ('highbrow', 'middlebrow', etc.), 5, 10, 60, 120–31, 140, 165, 170–1, 181n, 192, 218, 259, 261, 277, 296, 297, 355; *see also* Arnold/'Arnoldian'
Cunard, Nancy, 292, 330–2, 337, 340, 457

Daily Herald, 334
Daily Mail, 120–1, 124, 132n, 256n
Daily News, 177
dance, 52, 106–19, 191–2, 329; *see also* criticism, women as critics of: dance
Dancing Times, 107

Daniel, Charles, 196–203, 210, 340, 440, 457
D'Arcy, Ella, 81, 296
Davies, W. H., 220, 305, 206
Davison, Emily Wilding, 423
Dawson, Julia, 406–15
Deane, Anthony, 274, 278
Defence of the Realm Act (DORA), 392
democracy/democratic, 4, 6, 195–210, 226, 231, 234–5
Dental Record: a monthly journal of dental science, art, and literature, 10, 197, 203–9, 440
design
  interior design, 134–8, 141, 143–4
  page layout in magazines, 30–1, 130, 154–7, 174–5, 267–9, 283, 406, 413, 418
  theatrical design, 100, 116–18
Diaghilev, Sergei, 106, 109, 115, 119, 191
Dial, 258, 270, 277, 280, 287, 304
dialogism, 146–64, 166, 196–7, 201–4, 209, 259; *see also* periodicals as heterogeneous media
digital humanities, 214, 291, 313–28
Dome, 78–88, 95, 441
domestic/domesticity, 233, 245, 314, 321–7, 406–49
domestic magazines, 1, 3–7, 18–19, 20–32, 60–74, 99, 131, 134, 164, 186–7
Doolittle, Hilda *see* H.D.
Doyle, Camilla, 306
Doyle, Sir Arthur Conan, 217, 297, 454
drama/theatrical performance, 30, 92–105, 188–93; *see also* criticism, women as critics of: dance; drama
Drinkwater, John, 95, 103n
Drysdale family (Alice Vickery, Bessie, Charles Robert, Charles Vickery), 393, 396–400, 449
Duncan, Isadora, 107–10
Dunlop, Binnie, 393, 449

Eagle and the Serpent, 230, 236
East London Federation of Suffragettes (ELF), 243

Eastman, Max, 178, 301
Edinburgh University Women's Union, 45–6
editorship
　editorials and editorial personae, 42, 49, 56, 62–3, 65–8, 120, 130, 138, 146–60, 173, 204, 214, 232–8, 247, 251, 254, 261–3, 355
　textual editing, 261–71, 336, 341n
　women as editors, 34–5, 45, 78, 89, 107, 115, 130, 135, 140, 172, 183, 226, 243, 298, 300, 302, 329–41, 377–80, 399, 418n
education (higher education of women), 17–18, 22–3, 26, 27, 28, 40–6, 51, 53, 56, 66, 88, 94, 139, 277, 375, 419
Edwards, Dorothy, 48–58
Egoist: An Individualist Review, 124, 167, 179, 221–2, 227, 234, 236–9, 295, 298–9, 307, 316–26, 441
Eiffel Tower Restaurant, 292, 332, 340n
Eiloart, Elizabeth, 377, 378
Eliot, T. S., 57n, 81, 108, 110, 117, 122, 179, 239, 277, 280, 306–7, 437, 452
Ellis, Havelock, 301, 343, 391
Empire/imperialism, 2, 17, 18, 52, 60–74, 85, 209, 264, 361, 397
English Illustrated Magazine, 92, 217, 441–2
English Review, 9, 89, 95, 104, 213, 215, 219–22, 277, 280, 282, 315, 316, 319, 320, 442
Englishwoman, 96, 97, 297–8, 300, 308n, 442–3
ephemera, printed (pamphlets, leaflets, posters, cards), 6, 38–40, 42, 171–6, 292, 394, 424–6, 432n
Equinox, 375, 384
esoteric, 5, 140, 371–2, 374–88
　occult, 231, 344, 374–88, 448, 451, 455
　　Theosophical Society, 374–5, 378–9, 384, 386, 448
　　Theosophy, 231–2, 309, 342, 344, 374–88

ethnography/anthropology, 26, 63–4, 66–8, 109, 111–15, 124, 281, 297, 302
eugenics, 305, 392–4, 397–9, 401–2
Evening Standard, London [and St. James Gazette], 188, 228
Evergreen, 33, 38, 443
Ewer, Monica, 188, 193
Ezra Pound ('William Atheling', 'B.H. Dias'), 121, 160, 166, 179, 203, 258, 274, 275, 277, 280, 297, 322, 329, 342, 383, 437

Fabian Society, 39, 177, 196, 199; 201, 204, 243, 291, 342–3, 371
　Fabian Arts Group, 239
　Fabianism and feminism, 245
Farjeon, Eleanor, 306, 310
Farr, Florence, 234, 244, 291–2, 342–53
fashion, 3–5, 11n, 21, 29, 100, 132n, 135, 137, 417–18
Fawcett, Millicent Garrett, 38
Felix the Cat, 126, 127
feminist activism *see* birth control, socialist feminism, women's suffrage
feminist and suffrage press, 1–9, 11n, 38–40, 95–7, 101–3, 146–7, 153–4, 166–7, 169–82, 184, 202–4, 214–19, 232–5, 242–57, 296, 316, 371–2; *see also Church League for Women's Suffrage Monthly Paper*; *Church Militant*; *Common Cause*; *Englishwoman*; *Forward*; *Freewoman/New Freewoman*; *Hour and the Woman*; *Time and Tide*; *To-day's Woman*; *Votes for Women*; women's columns
Feuerbach, Ludwig, 229
film/cinema *see* criticism, women as critics of: film
fin de siecle, 78–91
First World War/Great War, 17, 46, 63, 100, 103, 208, 275, 282–6, 333–40, 371, 389–404, 427
Flaubert, Gustave, 258–9, 271
Fletcher, John Gould, 299, 300, 302
Flint, F. S., 298, 306, 322, 452

Fokine, Michael, 111, 115
Ford, Madox, Ford, 213–14, 219, 224n, 277, 295, 298, 300, 320, 437, 442
Fortune, Dion, 374, 375, 377, 381–5
Forward (Fabian Society of Glasgow), 443
Fox, Kate and Margaret, 376
Frazer, Sir James, 112, 114
Freewoman: a weekly feminist review, 235–9, 244, 254, 292, 295, 315–25, 343, 383, 387, 401, 441, 443
Freewoman Discussion Group, 239
Freud, Sigmund, 277, 362, 366, 383, 384
Futurism, 192, 443n, 452

Gawthorpe, Mary, 5, 6, 171–2, 203, 232–4, 238, 254, 343, 443–4
Georgian Poetry, 291, 295, 299–300, 304, 306, 333
Gibson, Wilfred Wilson, 95, 103n, 306
Gilman, Charlotte Perkins, 196, 202, 408, 419
Glasgow School of Art/Glasgow Style, 34–7, 448
Goldman, Emma, 227, 234–5, 449
Goldring, Douglas, 179, 219–21, 455
Good Housekeeping (British Edition), 139, 142–3, 277, 282, 444
Gorky, Maxim, 188, 260–1, 343
gothic, 292, 254–370
Graves, Robert, 18, 182, 338
Green Sheaf, 96
Grévin, Musée, 355–6
Grew, Eva Mary, 89
Guest, L. Haden, 107–8

Habermas, Jurgen, 6
Hallowes, Frances, 400
Hamilton, Cicely, 94–7, 443
Hamilton, Helen, 96
Hardy, Thomas, 216, 274, 297, 306, 441
Harmsworth, Alfred (Lord Northcliffe), 3, 4, 61
Harraden, Beatrice, 94, 96, 256
Harrison, Austin, 391

Harrison, Jane, 113
Harrison, Marie, 89
Hastings, Beatrice [Beatrice Tina, D. Triformis], 165–6, 242–55, 256n, 257n, 342, 351
Haweis, Mrs. M. E., 141
H.D. (Hilda Doolittle), 260, 280, 296, 298, 300, 306, 322–3, 441, 452
Heald, Nora Shackleton, 134, 140–3, 153, 453
Heap, Jane, 167, 244, 300
Hearst, William Randolph, 444
Hegel, 229–30, 239
Henderson, Alice Corbin, 307
Hermetic Order of the Golden Dawn, 344, 374–5
Hibbert Journal, 382
Hicks, Margaretta, 406, 410, 413
Highbrow culture *see* culture, stratification of
Hincks, Marcelle Azra (Countess Morphy), 76, 106–19
Hinscliff, Gertrude M., 423n, 426
Hinscliff, Reverend Claude, 423–4, 423n
Hogarth Press, 43, 44, 213, 269, 310n, 340n
Holland, Emily Frances, 89
Holloway Gaol, 247
'Holloway Jingles', 40
Holms, Beatrix, 50
Home Chat, 3, 19, 60–74
Home Notes, 18, 20, 60–74, 444
Horniman, Annie, 101
Hour and the Woman, 214
Hours Press, 332
Hudson, Gertrude ('Israfel'), 75, 78–91, 436
Hulme, T. E., 236, 238, 270, 342
Hutchins, Beatrice L., 177, 343
Huxley, Aldous, 50, 57n, 310, 329, 300
Hyndman, Henry Mayers, 201, 445

Illustrated London News, 102, 442
Illustrated Sunday Herald, 171, 178

Imagism/Imagist, 276, 298–9, 302, 305, 319, 333
'Immortals, The', 34, 36, 46; *see also* Glasgow School of Art
Independent Labour Party, 39, 371, 443, 445
India, 63, 65, 68–9, 379, 446
Inner Light Magazine, 375, 382, 384–5, 387n
International PEN *see* Catherine Dawson Scott
Interviews, 25, 39, 64, 89, 99–100, 228, 280, 281, 362–4, 452, 454
Ireland, 20–31, 249
Irish Sketch and the Lady of the House, 446
Irish Theosophist, 375

Jackson, Holbrook, 82, 106, 232
James, Arnold, 330, 457
James, Henry, 176, 178, 209n, 216, 296, 441
Jameson, Storm, 97
Japan/Japanese culture, 64, 68–9, 107–9, 281, 297, 302
Japan-British Exhibition, 17, 107
Jaques-Dalcroze, Émile, 108
Jerome, Jerome K., 178, 224n
John Bull, 389
Jones, Sarah Beryl, 18, 53–6
Joyce, James, 146, 183, 277, 298
Justice, 405, 406, 410–14, 445

Keaton, Buster, 126–7
Keeling, Eleanor, 406, 412, 414
Kennedy, J. M., 233, 343
Kennedy-Fraser, Marjorie, 89
Kingsford, Anna, 379
Klementaski, Alida, 295, 296, 297, 300, 310
Koteliansky, S. S., 260, 261, 269, 277, 436
Kreymborg, Alfred, 295, 305
Kropotkin, Prince Peter, 230, 235, 236, 343
KWIC (keyword in context), 316, 323–5

Labour Leader, 405, 406, 409–10, 412, 414, 416–18, 445
Labour movement, 17, 26–7, 30, 103, 154, 177, 190, 195, 204, 219, 234–7, 343, 372, 397, 405–20, 421, 443, 445, 449
Ladies' Field, 64–5, 445–6
Lady of the House and Domestic Economist (1890–1) then *The Irish Sketch and the Lady of the House* (1891–1924), 21–31, 446
Lady's Own Paper, 379
Lady's Realm, 146–60, 218, 446–7
Lantern: A Periodical of Lucid Intervals, 303, 309, 447
Lawrence, D. H., 43, 57n, 113, 210n, 260, 263, 271n, 298–9, 301, 302, 303, 436, 447
Leavis, F. R., 18, 121–2, 127, 329, 340n, 436
Leavis, Q. D., 121–2, 127
Lee, Vernon (Violet Paget), 50, 89, 282
Leeds Art Club, 232, 239, 240, 241
Lees, Dorothy Neville, 97, 104, 449
Leisenring, Winnifred, 381–4
Lewis, Wyndham, 95, 121, 136, 137, 170, 174, 181, 216, 220, 221, 277, 300, 342, 437, 440, 455
Liberty, 236, 447–8
Life and Letters To-day, 46, 58n
Light, 375, 381
Light on the Path, 380
Literary Digest International Book Review, 277, 306
Little Review, 124, 165, 178, 181n, 197–8, 214, 216, 244, 278, 307, 333
London Aphrodite, 307
London Film Society, 124
Lowell, Amy, 221, 322–3, 330, 452
Lucifer, 375, 377–80, 448
Ludovici, Anthony, 343
Luxembourg, Rosa, 398
Lyceum Club, 81, 89
Lytton, Lady Constance, 175, 255, 423

Macaulay, Rose, 183, 184, 185, 193, 306
MacDiarmid, Hugh ('Isobel Guthrie'), 42
Macdonald, Frances and Margaret, 33–8, 392, 448
McKay, Claude, 304
Mackay, John Henry, 229, 447
Mackintosh, Charles Rennie, 33–4
Madame Tussaud's Wax Museum, 355, 356, 364–5
Magazine, 33–8, 46, 448
Mallarmé, Stéphane, 109
Malthusian, 372, 389–90, 393–402, 448
Malthusian League, 372, 389, 393–4
Mansfield, Katherine, 46, 108, 115, 167, 214, 219, 258–71, 306, 342, 436, 453
Marinetti, Filippo, 192, 220, 452, 455
marriage, 51–3, 60, 66–8, 70–1, 187, 207, 219, 248, 316–17, 320, 325–6, 344, 347, 349–50, 377, 389, 391, 393, 410
Marriage Laws, 154, 178, 377
Marryat, Florence, 377
Marsden, Dora, 6, 43–4, 92, 101, 166–7, 170–2, 176, 179, 181n, 204, 216, 227–40, 254, 292, 383, 387n, 441, 443–4, 450–1
Marshall, Mary Jennette, 324
Marx, Karl/Marxism/Marxian, 196–7, 229, 230, 235, 344, 445
Mask, 76, 97–101, 104, 108, 449
Massingham, Henry William, 297
Mead, G. R. S., 386, 448
Meade, L. T., 29
medium reading, 313–26
Meredith, George, 279, 343
Mew, Charlotte, 46, 291, 294–310
Mew, Egan, 102
Meynell, Alice, 81
Meynell, Francis, 295–6
Middlebrow *see* culture, stratification of
Millay, Edna St. Vincent, 304, 305, 306, 438, 460
modern periodical studies, 2, 7–11, 153, 170, 214–15, 222–4, 226–7, 295, 315, 405

modernism/modernist studies, 2–3, 8–10, 214–15, 222–3
Monro, Alida Klementaski, 295–7, 300, 310
Monro, Harold, 95, 103, 291, 295, 298, 438, 452, 453
Monroe, Harriet, 214, 221, 295, 298, 330, 452
Montefiore, Dora, 406, 410–14, 419
Monthly Musical Record, 86
Moore, Marianne, 128, 298, 300, 304, 322, 323
Mordkin, Mikhail, 107, 110, 118
Morris, Margaret, 107
Morris, William, 201, 230, 236, 441, 445
Morrow, George, 99, 101
Mother Earth, 167, 234–5, 449
motherhood/maternity, 43–5, 62–3, 67–8, 173–4, 186–7, 201–2, 242, 245–8, 285, 317, 320, 324–6, 349, 390–3, 399–402, 408, 412, 419
Muir, Edwin, 43, 45
Muir, Willa, 33, 43, 45, 46
Murby, Millicent, 343, 345
Murray, Eunice, 39–40
Murry, John Middleton, 7, 46
  Adelphi, 121, 167, 197, 258–71, 436–7
  Rhythm, 108, 115, 214, 453
Musical Standard: a newspaper for musicians, professional and amateur, 81, 89, 450

nation/nationalism, 21–4, 26, 33–47, 48–56, 60–71, 85, 92, 101, 104n, 121, 124, 128, 131n, 156–7, 236, 334, 389–402, 427, 454
Nation and Athenaeum, 97, 213, 222, 258, 269
National Society for Women's Suffrage, 314
National Union of Women's Suffrage Societies (NUWSS), 5, 38, 39, 314, 421, 423, 430, 433n, 442
Nesbit, Edith, 10, 245, 291–2, 342–53, 354–70

networks, 5, 6, 17, 18, 51, 78, 81–2, 165–7, 170–1, 176, 180, 214–24, 226–39, 255, 259, 291–3, 314, 322, 327, 371–2, 375, 378, 380–4, 422
Nevinson, Henry Wood, 80, 88, 300
Nevinson, Margaret Wynne, 423, 430
New Age, 6, 43, 76, 106–15, 118, 166–7, 199, 214, 219, 227, 230–8, 240, 242–57, 313–28, 342, 353, 450, 453
'New Age' magazines, 386
New Freewoman: An Individualist Review, 316–25, 383, 387, 443, 451
New Generation (title of *Malthusian*, 1922–49), 393, 403, 448
New Journalism, 3–4, 25, 28, 439, 445
New Statesman, 89, 97, 102, 104n, 106, 183, 301, 302–3, 308n, 309, 397, 402n
New Stories, 50, 53, 54–7
New Woman, 3–4, 18, 22–5, 30, 36, 43, 84, 123, 128–30, 147, 213, 217–18, 224n, 414
New Woman critic, 84, 123, 128–30; *see also* criticism, women as critics
Newbery, Jessie, 38
Newmarch, Rosa, 89
Newnes, George, 3, 18, 60–74, 361–2, 445–6, 454, 457
Nicholson, Adela Florence ['Lawrence Hope'], 308
Nietzsche, Friedrich, 109, 229–36, 240, 342–53, 392, 447
Nijinsky, Vaslav, 110, 116, 118
Nordau, Max, 82, 83
Norman, C. H., 233, 244
Northcliffe Revolution, 3–4

Occult Review, 382, 385, 451
O'Day, Edward, 303, 447
Oldmeadow, Ernest J., 80–2, 88, 441
Oliphant, Margaret, 216, 441
Open Window, 95
Orage, A. R., 43, 106, 167, 199, 227, 230–40, 242–5, 251, 254, 256, 291, 292, 301, 321, 344, 348, 351, 352, 450

Outlook, 220–2, 251, 451
Owen, Wilfred, 292, 310, 328, 330, 336, 341
Owens, Robert, 344
Owl, 333

pacifism/peace movement, 2, 180, 199, 201, 210, 260, 293, 333–8, 371, 394, 398, 400–2, 440
Pageant, 95, 104
Pall Mall Gazette, 81, 89, 120, 218
Pall Mall Magazine, 277, 296–7, 309
Pankhursts, 38, 39, 231–2, 252
  Christabel, 244–5, 247, 249–50, 256
  Emmeline, 39, 252, 257, 371
  Sylvia, 243
Pater, Walter, 75, 78, 87
Patterson, Annie, 89
Pavlova, Anna, 107–11, 117, 118
Pearson, Arthur, 18, 60–74, 224, 340, 381, 442, 445, 457
Pearson's Magazine, 62, 69, 71, 224, 442
'Pepita', 111, 119n
periodical communities, 28, 166–7, 214, 221, 238–9, 245, 256, 291–2; *see also* networks
periodicals and/as heterogeneous media, 9–11, 20, 24, 31, 43–6, 48, 50, 66–7, 75, 77, 150, 153, 165–6, 184, 196, 208, 220, 222–3, 237, 260–71, 306, 354, 423, 437, 438, 452, 453, 455; *see also* dialogism
Pethick-Lawrence, Emmeline, 243, 244, 247, 250–2, 432, 456
Pethick-Lawrence, Fredrick, 243, 432, 456
Phillips, Mary, 407, 413–14, 417, 419
Pilcher, Velona, 89, 188, 193
Pioneer Players, 97, 101, 102, 104
Plato, 109, 117, 231
Playgoer and Society Illustrated, 94, 100, 452
Poetry: a Magazine of Verse, 121, 197, 214, 221–3, 298, 301–5, 307, 330, 333, 452
Poetry and Drama, 93, 95, 96, 295, 299, 309, 438, 452

Poetry Bookshop, 291–2, 295–301, 438, 452
Pound, Ezra, 108, 110, 115, 121, 160, 166, 179, 203, 219–21, 239, 258–60, 274–5, 277, 280, 291, 297–9, 301, 313, 322, 329, 342, 383, 437, 452
Pre-Raphaelite, 35–6, 213–14, 222
professions/professionalism, 22, 24, 27–8, 30, 40, 46, 93–4, 99, 103, 142, 143, 190, 207, 218–19, 233, 274–81, 332, 363, 375–6, 384, 398, 425, 427; see also criticism, women as critics of
Proudhon, Pierre-Joseph, 235–9
pseudonyms, 42, 62, 75, 81–9, 166–7, 242, 249, 252, 255, 351, 407, 418
public sphere/counter-public sphere, 6, 22, 62, 125, 139, 146, 153, 170–1, 223, 239, 243, 255, 295, 313, 316, 332, 372, 375, 380
Punch, 100–1, 307, 310, 334, 354

Queen, 77, 134, 139–43, 156, 277, 282–3, 453
Quest, 386
Quest Society, 386

race, discourses, 62–71, 383, 392, 396, 400, 112–14
Raeburn, Lucy, 34–6, 448
Randle, Daytie, 304
Read, Herbert, 179, 270, 271
Representation of the People Bill and Act, 228, 314, 425, 428, 431, 439
Rhythm, 76, 115–17, 214, 223, 260, 262, 264, 453
Rice, Anne Estelle, 76, 107, 115–18
Richards, I. A., 76, 121–2
Richardson, Dorothy, x, 10, 51, 165–6, 195–212, 216, 260, 280, 303, 381
Rickword, Edgell, 18, 50, 303, 438
Rimbaud, Arthur, 329
Roberts, William, 137, 457
Rootham, Helen, 329–30, 336, 340, 440
Rothermere, Lord, 124; see also Northcliffe Revolution

Royal Academy of Dance (RAD), 106–7
Royal Academy of the Dramatic Art, 332
Royal Institute of British Architects, 142
Royal Magazine, 381
Royden, Maude, 423, 432

Sackbut, 89, 307
Sackville, Lady Margaret, 297
Sackville-West, Vita, 111, 296, 299, 310
Sadler, Michael, 115–16, 453
St John, Christopher (Christabel Marshall), 89, 94, 96, 104, 183, 188
Sanger, Margaret, 235, 394, 402, 403, 449
Sassoon, Siegfried, 302, 303, 336, 340, 341, 447
Saturday review of politics, literature, science and art, 197, 204–9, 454
Schiff, Violet, 258
Schreiner, Olive, 180, 196, 400
Scotland, 24, 28, 29, 30, 33–47, 407, 414, 417, 443
Scott, Catherine Dawson, 297
Scott, Marion, 89
Scottish Literary Revival, 42
Scottish Women and the Vote Scrapbook, 40–1
Scribner's Monthly, 213, 215
Semar, John, 98, 101, 449
sexual violence, 248, 358–9, 401
sexuality, female, 99, 101, 111–12, 171–5, 218, 248, 266–7, 316–17, 325, 382–3, 389–94, 401
  Free love, 235, 344, 394
  'khaki fever', 391–2
  sexual orientation/gender fluidity, 24, 53–4, 82–4, 88, 172, 180n, 205, 210n, 296
  see also birth control/contraception; birth strike
Shove, Fredegond, 299, 310
Sinclair, May, 4, 53, 163, 165, 179, 195, 203, 209, 216, 219, 274–90, 296–8, 301, 303, 308
Sitwells, the
  Edith, 167, 291–2, 295, 302, 304, 306, 329–43, 440, 457

Osbert, 137–8, 292, 329, 334–5, 338–40
Sacheverell, 137–8, 292, 329
Smart Set, 223, 279, 282
Smedley, Constance, 89, 343
Smith, Pamela Colman, 96
Smith, Pauline, 440
Smith, Stevie, 18, 60, 69–71, 296
Smyth, Ethel, 89
Social Democratic Federation, 371, 410, 411, 445
socialism, 174, 196–210n, 230, 232–4, 236, 342–52, 371, 398, 405–19, 439, 443, 445
socialist feminism, 342–53, 405–20; see also Dora Marsden; Edith Nesbit; Rebecca West
Society for Psychical Research, 376, 381, 384
Society of Authors, 275, 278–9
South Lodge, 213, 220
Sowerby, Katherine Githa, 94
Spectator, 76, 120, 121, 123–4, 132n, 218, 302
Spectator (Addison and Steele), 261
Spiritual Magazine, 375
Spiritualist Newspaper, 375
Stirner, Max, 227–39, 447
Stopes, Marie, 372, 402–3
Storer, Edward, 95, 323
Strachey, John St Loe, 120
Strachey, Lytton, 106, 110
Strachey, Marjorie, 97
Strand Magazine, 291, 292, 354–66
Strauss, Richard, 84, 108
Strobel, Marion, 302, 305
Struthers, Christina, 89
Stuart, Muriel, 305
Surrealist revival journals, 386, 279
Sutton, Emma, 89
Swanwick, Helena, 6, 400
Swinburne, A. C., 87, 340
Symons, Arthur, 81, 107, 109, 307
Syrett, Nettta, 296

Tagore, Rabindranath, 280, 452
Temple Bar, 296

temporality, 2, 220, 261, 422
Terry, Ellen, 100–1
Thayer, Scofield, 258, 304
theatre managers, women as, 101
Theosophist, 309, 375, 379
Thrush, 223
Time and Tide, 5, 89, 166, 171, 179, 180, 183–94, 214, 306, 454–5
Tit-Bits, 3, 61, 66, 261
Titterton, W. R. (William Richard), 108, 183, 343
To-Day's Woman, 20–31, 445
Todd, Dorothy (editor of British *Vogue*), 76–7, 89, 121–32, 134–44, 456
Tolstoy, Leo/ Tolstoyan, 196, 199, 203, 235, 440
Tomlinson, H. M., 260, 264
Trade unions, 27, 409–10, 445
Tramp, 220–3, 455
travel/mobility, 62–71, 78–82, 84–7, 126, 190–2, 281–2, 363–5, 408, 441
Tree, Iris, 292, 310, 330, 332, 337–8, 340, 440, 457
Tucker, Benjamin, 227, 234–8, 447, 450

Unknown World, 375, 455
university magazines and print culture, 17–18, 42–3, 45–6, 50
Untermeyer, Louis, 294–5, 302–4, 306

Valentine de Saint-Point, 117
Vanity Fair, 303–4
Visiak, E. H., 233, 310
Vogue (British edition), 76–7, 89, 121–32, 134–44, 456
Votes for Women, 5, 39, 95, 96, 166, 171, 172, 175, 231, 242–54, 256n, 277, 292, 371, 417, 421, 425, 428, 432n, 433n, 456

Wagner, Richard, 79, 83, 89
Wales, 49, 456
Warner, Sylvia Townsend, 295–6
Watt, A. P., 279
Watts, Arthur, 100, 362

Weaver, Harriet Shaw, 6, 121, 197, 239, 330, 441, 450
Weissenhof Siedlung exhibition, 139–40, 143
Welfare State, 135, 226
Welsh fiction (English language), 18, 48–57
Welsh Review, 456–7
West, Rebecca, 4, 7, 19, 76, 97, 107, 110, 117, 118, 156–65, 170, 174–6, 180, 203, 216, 228, 383, 437, 444, 450
Westminster Gazette, 9, 99, 100, 306, 309
Weston, Annie T., 89
Wheels: An Anthology of Verse, 167, 292–3, 304, 329–41, 457
White Slavery Bill, 255, 427
Wickham, Anna ('John Oland'), 7, 291, 294–310, 447
Wide World Magazine, 68
Wilde, Oscar, 78, 81–3, 87, 191, 210, 213, 215, 218, 224, 236, 251, 296
Wilkinson, Marguerite, 302, 304–6, 310
Williams, William Carlos, 203, 322, 452
Williams-Ellis, Lady Amabel, 302
Wollstonecraft, Mary, 123, 325
Woman at Home, 61, 65–6, 165, 218, 277, 282, 284
Woman Worker, 5, 11
Woman's Life, 18, 61–71, 457
Woman's Own, 61, 444, 457
Woman's World, 218
Women Writers' Suffrage League, 219

women's columns, 34, 21–2, 60–3, 65–7, 70, 140–1, 186–7, 218, 287, 405–20
Women's Council of British Socialist Party, 410, 413
Women's Freedom League (WFL), 5, 39–40, 228, 243, 252, 343, 423, 432
women's magazines *see* domestic magazines
women's suffrage, 1, 7, 17, 20, 24, 29, 31, 33, 38, 43–4, 46, 48, 76, 92–8, 102–4, 153–4, 158, 166, 169–80, 184, 203, 214–15, 219, 223, 226–9, 231–5, 238–9, 277, 314, 316, 321, 324–6, 343–4, 351, 371, 411, 414, 417; *see also* feminist and suffrage press; women's suffrage societies
women's suffrage societies *see* National Union for Women's Suffrage Society (NUWSS); Women's Freedom League (WFL)
Woolf, Virginia, 40, 46, 89, 97, 213, 277, 303, 310, 339, 342, 405
Worland, Florence, 196, 199, 440
Wornum, Miriam, 134, 143–4

Yeats, W. B., 81, 107, 109, 116, 197, 210, 277, 342–3, 452
Yellow Book, 7, 81, 95, 100, 104n, 296, 309

Zangwill, Israel, 87
Zetkin, Clara, 398

EU representative:
Easy Access System Europe
Mustamäe tee 50, 10621 Tallinn, Estonia
Gpsr.requests@easproject.com